The Complete Plays of
Christopher Marlowe

The Complete Plays
of
Christopher Marlowe

Edited, with an Introduction and Notes by

IRVING RIBNER

THE ODYSSEY PRESS, INC.

A Division of Bobbs-Merrill Educational Publishing
Indianapolis

FOR

HARDIN CRAIG

Contents

Preface

The aim of this edition has been to make the plays of Marlowe available to the modern student and the general reader in a form which preserves what the author wrote as closely as modern scholarship can determine, but which does not preserve the vagaries of the Elizabethan printing house, of orthography or pointing. Each of the plays has been freshly edited from the early text which is demonstrably most authoritative. Spelling has been brought into conformity with modern American usage, although archaic forms of words generally have been retained when such forms are not mere examples of variant spelling. In instances such as *murther / murder* or *renowmed / renowned,* where both forms occur in the copy texts, I have used the modern form throughout, indicating my departures from the copy text in the textual notes. I have repunctuated, following the copy texts only where they do not conflict with modern usage, and striving always to preserve Marlowe's sense. In general I have tried to avoid the overpunctuation of nineteenth-century editors, retaining only what is essential to clarity.

The stage directions of the copy texts have been preserved as fully as possible. Necessary substitutions are indicated in the textual notes, and all additions are enclosed within brackets. I have silently relocated those directions which seem out of place. Speech headings have been expanded and regularized. In place of the elisions of the copy texts, I have used the *ed* endings throughout and have indicated by an accent mark (*èd*) where stress upon a final syllable is made necessary by the meter. Mislineation has been corrected, and where poetry has been found printed as prose, or vice versa, I have made the necessary rearrangements. Otherwise the copy texts have been departed from

only in cases of obvious error, and all such departures are indicated in the textual notes. I have accepted the emendations of
earlier editors where they seem to rest upon reasonable assump-
tions and where the copy texts are clearly in need of emendation.

Only the two parts of *Tamburlaine* are divided into acts and
scenes in the earliest versions, and even here there is some confusion in the scene division. *The Jew of Malta* and *Dido Queen
of Carthage* are divided into acts only, while *The Massacre at
Paris, Edward II,* and *Doctor Faustus* reveal no act or scene division of any kind. Where the plays are divided, we cannot be sure
that this division is the work of the author. I have accordingly
retained in the margins the conjectural act and scene divisions
established in the nineteenth-century editions of Alexander Dyce,
although in some instances I have varied from these. *The Massacre at Paris* is divided into scenes only, for what we have of this
play has proved too fragmentary for satisfactory act division.
Printer's ornaments have been used to designate those places
where a bare stage seems to indicate a change of scene. The lines
of each play have been freshly numbered, and the suppositions
about place designations which are the work of earlier editors
have been avoided. Much of the action on the Elizabethan stage
was vague in locale, and when a dramatist wished to make clear
the location of a specific scene, he usually indicated it in the
dialogue.

Of all the plays, only *Dido Queen of Carthage,* the two parts
of *Tamburlaine,* and *Edward II* survive in substantive texts
which are at all reliable, and of these only *Tamburlaine* was
printed during the author's lifetime. Since we are forced to work
with texts of varying degrees of reliability, each of the plays
presents a separate problem, and I have indicated in the textual
notes the procedure I have followed in each instance. For the
1604 and 1616 quartos of *Doctor Faustus* and for the 1594 octavo
of *Edward II,* I have been forced to rely upon photostatic copies;
for all of the other texts I have fortunately had access to the
originals.

I am very grateful to Dr. John Pomfret and the staff of the
Huntington Library, Miss Mary Isabel Fry and Miss Constance
Lodge in particular, for assistance, kindness, and the most con-
genial kind of atmosphere in which one could work. To the

Huntington Library I am grateful also for permission to reproduce the title pages of *Tamburlaine, Dido Queen of Carthage, The Massacre at Paris,* and *The Jew of Malta.* The *Doctor Faustus* title page is reproduced by permission of the British Museum, and that of *Edward II* by permission of the Zentralbibliothek in Zurich, Switzerland. I am grateful to Dr. Louis B. Wright for permission to use the 'Collier Leaf' of *The Massacre at Paris,* now in the Folger Library. Dr. James G. McManaway has been a constant source of assistance and advice. Professor Richard M. Hosley and the directors of the University of Missouri Press have kindly granted me permission to reproduce in the Introduction some passages already published in *Essays on Shakespeare and Elizabethan Drama in Honor of Hardin Craig.* To Professor Craig, my teacher and my friend, this edition also is fondly dedicated.

Needless to say, this edition could not have been completed without the efforts of those earlier editors—Dyce, Bullen, Tucker Brooke, F. S. Boas, W. W. Greg, U. M. Ellis-Fermor, H. S. Bennett, and others—upon whose work I have so freely drawn.

Introduction

The year 1564 is a momentous one in English literary history, for some two months before William Shakespeare was born in Stratford-on-Avon there was born in the cathedral city of Canterbury Christopher Marlowe, the parish register of St. George's church in that city recording his baptism on the twenty-sixth day of February. Both poets came of middle-class merchant origins. Marlowe's family appears to have been firmly established in Canterbury, for we can trace the name of Marlowe, Marley or Marlin, as it was variously spelled, back to the beginning of the fifteenth century. A William Morle became a freeman of the city as early as 1414, and the poet's great-great-grandfather, John Marley, was the first of several generations of tanners who were to rise to prominence in Canterbury. The poet's father, another John Marley, was an important member of the Shoemakers' guild, maintaining in his household at least four apprentices who were sons of other Canterbury tradesmen. Although the poet's family was long considered to have been a socially prominent and prosperous one, recent discoveries in the Canterbury archives suggest that John Marley was frequently involved in lawsuits, in many of which he was forced to answer charges of debt. Two of the poet's sisters, moreover, seem to have acquired somewhat unsavory reputations among their neighbors.

We know nothing of Marlowe's earliest schooling, but sometime before he reached the age of fifteen he was admitted to the King's School at Canterbury, as one of the "fifty poor boys, both destitute of the help of friends and endowed with minds apt for learning," whose education was provided for by the new charter issued to the cathedral establishment by King Henry VIII when the ancient monastic control was replaced. The requirement of poverty, however, was never enforced, and Archbishop Cranmer, it seems, had to make special efforts to see that the scholarships were not restricted to the sons of gentlemen entirely.

From the King's School Marlowe moved at the age of seventeen to Corpus Christi College, Cambridge, having been awarded one of the three new scholarships established by the will of Archbishop Matthew Parker, one of which had to be filled by a native of Canterbury. The Parker scholars were expected to prepare for the clergy, being entitled to their stipends for six years if they chose to do so, but obliged to give them up after three years should they decline to enter holy orders. Marlowe held his scholarship for the full six-year period, taking his B.A. degree at the age of twenty in 1584 and his M.A. degree in 1587, being regarded by the college authorities apparently as a proper candidate for the ministry.

After completing the requirements for his M.A. degree in March of 1587, Marlowe left Cambridge, for there was no reason for him to remain there, although he was obliged to return for the actual conferring of the degree at the July commencement. On the 20th of June the Queen's Privy Council addressed a letter to the university authorities denying a report that Marlowe had gone across the channel to Reims—at that time a center for exiled English Catholics, many of whom had been converted at Cambridge—holding that "in all his actions he had behaved himself orderly and discreetly, whereby he had done her majesty good service and deserved to be rewarded for his faithful dealings," and requesting that he be granted his degree, "because it was not her Majesty's pleasure that any one employed as he had been in matters touching the benefit of his country should be defamed by those who are ignorant in th' affairs he went about."

The letter would indicate that sometime soon after his departure from Cambridge Marlowe had come under suspicion of conversion to Catholicism, something easy for the authorities to assume if he had renounced his intention of entering the Anglican clergy and if he had gone abroad, as so many Catholic converts were doing. The letter makes clear that such suspicions were without foundation and that if Marlowe went abroad it was in the service of his country. He appears to have been employed in some secret mission, the exact nature of which probably we shall never know, but which may have had some connection with the elaborate espionage system which Elizabeth's government maintained abroad, largely as a check upon Catholic exiles.

After taking his Cambridge degree Marlowe came down to London, where he appears to have associated with such literary men as his Cambridge fellows, Robert Greene and Thomas Nashe, with George Peele, who had come down from Oxford, and with such notables as Sir Walter Ralegh and Thomas Walsingham. In the slightly less than six years that remained to him, all of his plays were written, as well as the long narrative poem, *Hero and Leander,* which he left unfinished and which was completed after his death by George Chapman, who probably also had been one of his associates. Of his connection with the dramatic companies we know very little, and it probably was not a very active one, for compared with that of his contemporary playwrights Marlowe's output was very small. He appears to have begun in association with the Lord Admiral's Men who produced his *Tamburlaine* with Edward Alleyn in the starring role. He must then have moved to Lord Strange's Men who produced *The Jew of Malta* and *The Massacre at Paris* and then to Lord Pembroke's Men who produced *Edward II* and who might have been responsible for the first performance of *Doctor Faustus* in the winter of 1592/3. The title page of the 1604 quarto, however, shows only that it was acted by the Earl of Nottingham's Men, the name assumed by the Lord Admiral's Men after 1596, and we know from Henslowe's diary that this company had acted the play as early as September 30, 1594. For a time Marlowe shared a room with the dramatist, Thomas Kyd, who later was to accuse him of atheism.

His London life appears to have been very turbulent, and we know that he spent somewhat more than a week in Newgate prison before he was acquitted of charges stemming from a murder in which he and the poet, Thomas Watson, were involved. We have the evidence of a bond dated October 1, 1589, in which two friends of Marlowe pledge his appearance at the next New-gate sessions to answer charges. It appears that while Marlowe was engaged in a struggle with one William Bradley, the son of a London innkeeper, Watson chanced along and came to Marlowe's assistance, at which point Marlowe left the fight, leaving his friend Watson to stab Bradley fatally. Both men were acquitted, Watson being judged to have acted in self-defense, although he was obliged to spend almost five months in prison awaiting the Queen's pardon. During his own short stay in Newgate, Marlowe seems to have made the acquaintance of one John Poole, imprisoned for coining, and from this may stem Marlowe's later boast that he knew how to coin money and had as much right to do so as the Queen of England. We also learn from the records of this affair—discovered by Professor Mark Eccles—that Marlowe and Watson were living close together in Norton Folgate, a district close to the theaters in Shoreditch and inhabited by many theatrical personalities.

This was not the last of Marlowe's difficulties with the law, for we find that on May 9, 1592, he was forced under penalty of a £20 bond to keep peace toward the constable of Holywell Street and his sub-constable, and to appear at the next General Sessions of the Peace to answer charges against him. The charges do not appear to have been serious ones, and nothing further is heard of them. Marlowe soon began to encounter real difficulties, however, for against him were levelled the charges of atheism which were still unresolved at the time of his tragic death and which were to blacken his reputation after it.

Atheism in Marlowe's time was a general term applied to almost any departure from orthodox belief, and it came to be used to describe any of the varieties of skeptical or naturalistic thought common in the sixteenth century. Cambridge was a center of intellectual ferment, but there is no evidence that Marlowe was ever accused of atheism during his university days. The earliest such charge seems to come from his fellow dramatist, Robert Greene, who, evidently jealous of Marlowe's success in *Tamburlaine*, in the preface to *Perimedes the Blacksmith*, published in 1588, referred to Marlowe as "daring God out of heaven with that atheist Tamburlan or blaspheming with the mad priest of the sun." Shortly before his own death in 1592, Greene again accused Marlowe of atheism in the preface to his *Groatsworth of Wit.*

It was not until May of 1593, however, that the charges against Marlowe began to come to a head. On May 12 Thomas Kyd was arrested on suspicion of atheism. He was tortured on the rack, and when his chambers were searched, among his papers was found a heretical religious tract. Kyd, perhaps to save himself, declared that the document had belonged to Marlowe, with whom he had shared a room in 1591. He must have accused Marlowe of atheism with a particular vehemence at the time of his examination, for in two extant letters written to the Lord Keeper, Sir John Puckering, after Marlowe's death, Kyd reports Marlowe's supposedly blasphemous statements in considerable detail, and it is likely that he is here repeating statements he had made orally at the time of his arrest.

Kyd's letters connect Marlowe, moreover, with Thomas Harriott, a mathematician in the service of Sir Walter Ralegh, and thus by implication with Ralegh himself and a group of men associated with him, including the poets Matthew Royden and William Warner and probably George Chapman. The extent to which this group constituted a "school of atheism" or "school of night," as it has been called, is uncertain and has been much debated, but that Marlowe knew these men is more than likely. A direct association between Ralegh and Marlowe was later made by a government agent named Richard Cholmley.

Some days after Kyd's accusation, the Queen's Privy Council on May 18 issued a warrant for Marlowe's arrest. He was apprehended at the estate of Thomas Walsingham at Scadbury in Kent, where he had been staying, possibly to escape the plague then raging in London, but instead of being imprisoned and tortured like Kyd, he was ordered merely to be in daily attendance upon the Council until the disposition of his case. As it happened, he was dead before this disposition could occur.

Ten days after his appearance before the Council Christopher Marlowe lay murdered at Deptford, but probably at some time during these ten days (the exact date of the document is uncertain) the case against him was strengthened by a lengthy account of his supposed blasphemies delivered to the Council by a professional informer named Richard Baines. We do not know of

any connection between Baines and Marlowe, and the accusations read like random gossip which Baines may have gathered in
Bohemian circles where both men had common associates. Much
of the matter Baines reports is very scurrilous, and since he was
a professional informer his word cannot be accepted without
question. His accusations do, however, corroborate many of the
points made by Kyd. Many of the questionings of scripture he
attributes to Marlowe sound like the clever witticisms of a young
man, probably half-drunk, trying to shock an audience. It is
Baines who reports the association of Marlowe with the coiner,
John Poole whom he had met at Newgate, and Baines, like Kyd,
connects Marlowe with Harriott, and thus with the circle of Sir
Walter Ralegh. Scholars have long debated the significance of
these various accusations, and it is likely that we shall never
know the truth, but it is clear that in his own day Marlowe was
known as a skeptic and a heretic, not above uttering what more
sober Elizabethans might consider blasphemous. His plays give
evidence that he did not accept without question the ordinary
Tudor notions of man's relation to society and to God. Among the
Elizabethan dramatists, Shakespeare included, Marlowe was certainly the most daring in his philosophical speculation and the
most unorthodox, but that he was an atheist in any modern sense
remains to be demonstrated.

The discoveries of Leslie Hotson have done much to clear up
the mystery surrounding the poet's untimely death, but there is
still much that we do not know and much in what we do know
that is extremely puzzling. Marlowe probably did not return to
Walsingham's estate at Scadbury, for on the morning of May 30,
1593, just ten days after his session with the Privy Council, we
find him at Deptford, where he had been invited to dinner by
one Ingram Frizer, a Kentish gentleman who had been involved
in some unsavory financial schemes, who we know had been in
the service of Walsingham, and who was to remain in his service
for many years after Marlowe's death. Present at the dinner also
were Robert Poley, a professional espionage agent of rather shady
character who had been employed in various secret missions, and
Nicholas Skeres, who seems also to have been an unscrupulous
character, frequently in trouble with the law, and sometimes
employed by the government in secret missions. Why Marlowe

should have journeyed to Deptford to dine with these men is not clear. According to the records of the coroner's inquest following Marlowe's death, the three men met at 10:00 o'clock in the morning, later had dinner and then spent the afternoon walking in the garden of Eleanor Bull's tavern, probably in close conversation with one another. Toward evening they retired to their room for supper, after which a quarrel between Frizer and Marlowe arose over the reckoning. Frizer was sitting so tightly between Skeres and Poley that he could not move to defend himself adequately when Marlowe, who had been reclining on a bed behind the other three, seized Frizer's dagger from behind and inflicted two superficial wounds upon his head. Frizer then seized the dagger and in self-defense stabbed Marlowe above the right eye, inflicting a two-inch-deep wound from which Marlowe died instantly.

Frizer was judged by the court to have acted in self-defense and was accordingly acquitted. But the story told by Marlowe's three companions raises many questions. One wonders why Skeres and Poley did nothing to restrain the actions of the man sitting between them so closely that he could not move, or why Marlowe from a reclining position should have attacked a man sitting upright with his own dagger. Medical men have further argued that a two-inch wound above the right eye is not likely to have caused death very quickly. We are left with the possibility that the entire story may have been a fabrication and that Marlowe may have been the victim of a planned assassination. We wonder why Frizer should have returned to the service of Marlowe's friend and host, Walsingham, and what, in fact, Marlowe's relation may have been to this younger relative (later to be knighted after entertaining the Queen at Scadbury) of Elizabeth's great secretary, Sir Francis Walsingham. Probably we shall never know the answers to these questions which continue to tease our imaginations and cause us to speculate about the secret life of Shakespeare's most gifted contemporary.

There is considerable irony in the fact that this tragic end of one of England's most promising literary geniuses should have appeared in contemporary accounts not in such terms, but rather as a striking example of God's punishment visited upon a blaspheming atheist. Thus a distorted version of the death was told by one Thomas Beard in his *Theatre of Gods Judgements* (1597): "But herein did the justice of God most notably appear, in that he compelled his own hand which had written those blasphemies to be the instrument to punish him, and that in his brain, which had devised the same." And William Vaughan, telling another distorted account in his *Golden Grove* (1600) concluded that "Thus did God, the true executioner of divine justice, invoke the end of impious atheists." In this way Marlowe's memory was used to his discredit by the theologians of his day, and among the actors he did not fare much better, for the great popularity of his plays upon the stage seems to have ended with his death, and some of his greatest lines were subjected to burlesque and derision. Among the poets, however, he was honored. Peele, Chapman, and Drayton wrote of him with reverence and affection, and it is likely that Shakespeare alluded to him in *As You Like It*. Gradually he came to be recognized as one who might have equalled the achievement of Shakespeare, had he not been cut off in his prime.

2. THE MARLOWE CANON

Marlowe seems to have turned to literature while still at Cambridge, for as a student he translated the *Amores* of Ovid and the first book of Lucan's *Pharsalia,* and it is possible that *Dido Queen of Carthage,* the earliest of the seven plays which constitute his dramatic canon, may date also from his university days. We know nothing about the composition of this play other than that the title page of the 1594 quarto bears the names of Christopher Marlowe and Thomas Nashe as authors and records that it was performed by the children of the Chapel Royal. Since there is no record of any performances by the children in London between 1584 and 1601, but we do know that in 1586/7 they performed at Ipswich and Norwich, it has been conjectured that Nashe and Marlowe, who were then at Cambridge, prepared the play together for performance by the troupe acting close by. Most scholars would agree that the version preserved in the 1594 quarto is a later recension, for the blank verse seems to illustrate two separate stages of artistic maturity. There is nothing in this final version which we have any reason to attribute to Nashe, and it is possible that his share was excised entirely in the revision. It has been suggested also that his only connection with the play may have been that he prepared it for publication after Marlowe's death. *Dido* is based closely upon Virgil's *Æneid,* and although some elements, such as the opening scene for instance, represent Marlowe's quite un-Virgilian elaboration of his source, many whole passages are based so closely upon the Latin as to be mere translation.

It is possible that the first part of *Tamburlaine* may have been sketched out also while Marlowe was still at Cambridge, for the play—in its act and scene divisions, for instance—bears signs of the rarified academic drama written at the universities, although the final product must have been completed after Marlowe's arrival in London. When the two parts of *Tamburlaine* were printed together in 1590, Marlowe's name did not appear upon the title page, but there can be no serious doubt of his authorship. Not only is this testified to by contemporary allusions, but the style of the plays is such as we can attribute to no other writer. Both parts appear to have been written in the summer and autumn of 1587, and when acted upon the public stages by the Lord Admiral's Men were so popular that they have often been regarded as ushering in a whole new era in English drama.

The career of Tamburlaine, or Timur Khan (1336–1405), the Mongolian conqueror who had defeated the Turks at Ankara in 1402 and thus unwittingly become the savior of Christian Europe, was a favorite Renaissance subject, and Marlowe might have read of him in many places. In the library at Corpus Christi College was the Latin *Magni Tamerlanis Scythiarum Imperatoris Vita* (1553) of Petrus Perondinus, which he certainly consulted. He probably read also Thomas Fortescue's *The Forest, or Collection of Histories* (1571), itself translated from the Spanish of Pedro Mexia's *Silva de Varia Lection* (1542). Many other versions were available to him in Latin and Italian, and the chances are that Marlowe studied the history of Tamburlaine in many places, although he may have relied chiefly upon an English account, *The English Mirror* (1586) by George Whetstone, whose recent publications may, in fact, have aroused Marlowe's interest in the subject.

The second part of *Tamburlaine* appears to have been an afterthought occasioned by the great popularity of the first part.

When Marlowe came to write it, he seems to have pretty well exhausted his sources. Most of the play is of his own invention, although the Olympia-Theridamas episode is borrowed from Ariosto's *Orlando Furioso,* and the perfidy of King Sigismund of Hungary is based upon actual historical events which led up to the battle of Varna in 1444. Marlowe probably read of these in the *Rerum Ungaricarum decades quator* (1543) of Antonius Bonfinius and the *Chronicorum Turcicorum tomi duo* (1578) of Philippus Lonicerus. For much of his military detail Marlowe seems to have used *The Practice of Fortification* by Paul Ive, which was not published until 1589, but which there is good reason to believe that Marlowe was able to consult in manuscript. For the geography of both parts of *Tamburlaine,* on which Marlowe dwells in great detail, he consulted a great new atlas of the world, published first in Antwerp in 1570, the *Theatrum Orbis Terrarum* of Abraham Ortelius. With Ortelius' maps before us, it is possible to follow the movements of the armies moving across the world in Marlowe's play.

We can date *The Jew of Malta* with some confidence between December 23, 1588, when the Duke of Guise, whose death is referred to in the prologue, was assassinated, and February 26, 1592, when a performance of the play by Lord Strange's Men is recorded in Philip Henslowe's diary. The play, however, was not printed until 1633, and we cannot doubt that the version in which it has come down to us is much altered from what Marlowe originally wrote. There is no known source, although Marlowe seems to have been influenced by the careers of two Jews involved historically in Turkish affairs. In the work of Lonicerus, which he consulted for the second part of *Tamburlaine,* he might have read of a Portuguese Jew, Juan Miques, who was a favorite of the Turkish Sultan Selim II and was raised by him to great power. Miques is said to have urged the Sultan in 1569 to break faith with Venice and to take the island of Cyprus. Marlowe might have read of him also in François de Belleforest's *Cosmographie Universelle.* He may also have drawn some details from the career of one David Passi, a powerful Jew living in Constantinople, who was involved in the Turkish campaign against Malta. Although we do not know where Marlowe might have read of Passi, he was sufficiently involved in English affairs in the Mediterranean for his doings to have been well known in Marlowe's London.

Marlowe's next play probably was *The Massacre at Paris,* although this is not certain, for the play was never entered in the Stationers' Register, and even the single corrupt octavo in which it has come down to us bears no date. It must, of course, have been written after the death of King Henry III of France on August 2, 1589, but there is little else we can say with certainty, other than that Henslowe referred to the play as "new" in his diary entry for January 26, 1592/3.

The play deals with contemporary events very close to Marlowe's own time. The scenes prior to the accession of Henry III are based upon the tenth book of Thomas Timme's *Commentaries on the Civil Wars in France* (1576), translated from *De Furoribus Gallicus* of the Huguenot François Hotman (although the rest of Timme's work is translated from the French historian, Jean de Serres, long assumed erroneously to have been Marlowe's ultimate source). For the later scenes of the play, there is no specific source. The events were well-known recent history, and Marlowe probably supplemented his general knowledge by reference to the many anti-Catholic pamphlets circulated in London by the Huguenots.

Edward II was written probably in 1591 or 1592, and based primarily upon the 1587 edition of Raphael Holinshed's *Chronicles of England, Scotland, and Ireland,* that massive compilation used also by Shakespeare for his plays on English history. Marlowe seems also to have consulted Robert Fabyan's *New Chronicles of England and France* and John Stow's *Summary of English Chronicles,* both of which were available to him in many editions. He may also have read Thomas Churchyard's "The Two Mortimers" in the 1578 edition of *A Mirror for Magistrates,* his age's great verse compilation of tragic stories of the falls of kings from high place. He dealt with a period of English history from the accession of Edward II in 1307 to the execution of Roger Mortimer in 1330, condensing the events of 23 years into what seems to be about one year, and altering his sources radically as dramatic necessity required.

Whether *Doctor Faustus* preceded or followed *Edward II* has been much debated, but most authorities are inclined today to regard it as the later play, written probably late in 1592 or early in 1593. The source of the play is a German *Historia von D. Johann Fausten,* first published in 1587 at Frankfurt-am-Main and reissued with additional chapters in that same year and again in 1589, 1590, 1592, and 1599, attesting to its wide popularity. We are fairly certain, however, that Marlowe did not use the German, but relied instead upon an English translation, *The Historie of the damnable life and deserued death of Doctor Iohn Faustus,* printed in 1592. The translator was a "P. F. Gent," who has never been identified.

The problems of *Doctor Faustus* are multiplied by the textual history of the play, discussed more fully in the Textual Notes (see pp. 429–432), but we may be fairly certain that only part of what is preserved in the quartos of 1604 and 1616 can have come from the pen of Marlowe. The play seems to have been written in collaboration, probably with one of the literary hacks who worked for Philip Henslowe. Henslowe's diary records payment on November 22, 1602, of £4 to William Birde and Samuel Rowley "for their adicyones in doctor Fostes." Most commentators would attribute the bulk of the non-Marlovian matter in the play to Samuel Rowley.

Various other plays have at times been attributed to Marlowe, most notably *The First Part of the Contention* and *The True Tragedy of Richard, Duke of York,* but these plays have been shown to be merely corrupt versions (bad quartos) of the second and third parts of Shakespeare's *Henry VI,* and not sources for Shakespeare as was for a long time supposed. There is no reason to include in the Marlowe canon any others than the seven plays discussed above.

3. MARLOWE AND ENGLISH TRAGEDY

Marlowe's great contribution to English drama springs from the fact that he was the first genuine poet to write for the public stage. In his hands blank verse, which had been used by the authors of *Gorboduc* some twenty-five years before him, became a great and flexible instrument. Marlowe had also the introspection and vision of the poet, and thus he became the first great writer of tragedy in English, for no one before him had been capable of forging upon the stage a comprehensive vision of man's relation to the forces of evil in the world, and among his immediate successors he is surpassed in this achievement only by Shakespeare. But Marlowe came to the writing of tragedy very slowly, attaining a fully tragic vision only in his two final plays.

Perhaps more surely than any of his contemporaries, Marlowe reflected in his plays his own changing and developing vision of man's place in the universe, and at some point in his intellectual progression tragedy became possible. Certainly it could never have sprung from the view of the world reflected in his earliest work. *Dido Queen of Carthage* falls far short of tragedy in spite of the death of its heroine, and if *Tamburlaine* is to be viewed in a "tragic glass," as the prologue invites us, this glass reveals only pathos in the deaths of those lesser figures who must be destroyed to prepare the path of the conquering superman with whom Marlowe is concerned. Only when he came to recognize the fraility and limitation of humanity did tragedy become possible for Marlowe.

If the first part of *Tamburlaine* was indeed planned while Marlowe was still at Cambridge, his turning to the drama may have coincided with a turning away from the theological studies to which his scholarship committed him. This departure from theology seems to have accompanied an absorption with classical poetry, for the translations of Ovid and Lucan were done also at Cambridge, indicating a concern for the two themes to which he was constantly to return, love and war. The first stage of Marlowe's development seems to have been one of change from Christian contemplation of the divine to pagan concern with the sensual aspect of man and with his involvement in great political and military affairs. It is easy to see *Dido* and *Tamburlaine* as each reflecting one of these concerns; in *Dido* we can see their relation to one another.

In the first part of *Tamburlaine,* Marlowe took a historical figure—praised in a long series of humanistic histories as a successful ruler whose own cruelty had been a visitation of punishment upon sinners—and he framed a play which might exalt such a figure by revealing his steady movement toward conquest of the world. The play became an episodic sequence of scenes, each one designed to make clearer the greatness of the hero. If in the second part of *Tamburlaine* some elements intrude to diminish the hero's brightness, we must remember that the sequel was a later addition which represents a further stage in Marlowe's growth, and that the first part was conceived entirely independently of it.

Marlowe approached his subject not with the Christian view of history as the working out of God's purposes on earth, but rather with the premises of the classical historians he had read at Cambridge. He seems to have been influenced in particular by Polybius, who in his history of Rome had exalted individual prowess, who had seen historical event as the product of human ability and will in a world ruled by a blind fortune. The hero of such a view of history could assert his will in opposition to fortune and master it for a brief time. Finally he must be cut off by death, and this being so, he must accept his end with stoical resignation and fortitude. Of this human ability to master fortune, the first part of *Tamburlaine* provides a supreme example, while the second part depicts the inevitable triumph of death in spite of human prowess. In Marlowe's hero is also reflected the Machiavellian ideal of the lawgiver, the superman who by his own *virtù*, his power of mind and will, can arrest the processes of decay to which all civilizations are subject and create new nations. While doing so he stands outside of all morality. That Marlowe, like many of his Cambridge fellow students, had read the *Prince* and *Discourses* of Machiavelli is very likely.

In the first part of *Tamburlaine*, a fully drawn man of destiny passes from one static scene to the next as he goes about his conquests, the dramatist never displaying change or development in his hero's character. From his first appearance Tamburlaine is destined to conquer the world, and from this end nothing can deter him, not even the tears of the Zenocrate he loves. He must destroy her native city because it is in his unalterable nature to do so. The virgins of Damascus must be destroyed because the principle for which he stands demands it. The play is concerned not with development of character, but with revelation of it.

The subject of the second part of *Tamburlaine* is the death of the hero, and in George Whetstone's *English Mirror* Marlowe might have read that "this great personage, without disgrace of fortune, after sundry great victories, by the course of nature died."

This view is in accord with a general treatment of Tamburlaine's end by humanist historians who had seen him as one who had mastered fortune as long as it was possible for any man to do so, until death finally had triumphed. His death need not be viewed in moralistic terms as punishment for sin, but rather as the necessary culmination of his greatness, for he was cut off, as classical historians held that great men should be, at the very peak of his glory.

Marlowe's hero dies because all who live must die. His conquests are undiminished; his one weak son has been destroyed, and his two remaining sons are ready to complete their father's domination of the world. (That historically they did not do so, but instead brought about the dissolution of their father's empire is a consideration outside the scope of the play.) But since the death of Tamburlaine was not sufficient matter for a play, Marlowe had to fill in his historical matter with other elements from various sources. The treachery of the Christian King Sigismund of Hungary has been taken as Marlowe's indictment of the moral pretensions of Christianity, but it could just as easily be taken as a defense of true Christianity against the doctrine of equivocation being preached in some papal quarters. It is related to the play's central theme, the death of Tamburlaine, in its emphasis upon the existence of some superior power, for it is important to remember that this power beyond man—whatever it may be—is what decrees the death of the hero. The story of Olympia, which Marlowe borrowed from Ariosto, draws attention, as in *Dido,* to the cost in simple human terms of the superman's march toward fulfillment of great destiny.

These elements contribute to a change of tone in the second part of *Tamburlaine* which tends to detract from the theme of the triumphant conqueror. They convey a sense of futility and death which supports the sombre return to reality in the very fact that Tamburlaine must die. There is a reminder of human mortality and human loss, a note sounded in the death of Zenocrate, the decay of beauty. The basic conception of Tamburlaine's death is still that of the humanist historians, but in the futile preservation of Zenocrate's enbalmed body, in the burning of the Koran, and in the mockery which answers Tamburlaine's ineffectual challenge of the gods, there is a sense of futility, frustration, and waste which in another context might be tragic. That Tamburlaine's sickness follows immediately upon his burning of the Koran does not mean that we are to take his death as divine punishment for blasphemy or regard the scene as Marlowe's defense of religion, with Christianity and Islam strangely identified. Coming at the moment when it does, the sickness of the hero is Marlowe's ironic manner of showing the futility of Tamburlaine's attempt to master the powers of the universe which no man, no matter how great, can finally master. Death finally must triumph, and it does so when the hero is loudest in his defiance. The "daring God" who torments his body is that inscrutable force in the universe which decrees death even to the most powerful of men. The madness of Tamburlaine's defiance is succeeded by the calm of the deathbed scene in which the hero, in true stoic manner, accepts the inevitable and dies the superman he has always been. Fortune wins the final triumph, and in our awareness that this inevitably must be so, although there is no real sense of tragedy, we do have a sense of human limitation which when considered more deeply and developed in other contexts may at last give rise to genuine tragedy.

In its classical features *Tamburlaine* is related to *Dido Queen of Carthage* which was probably conceived in the same period of Marlowe's development. There is a tendency to dismiss this play as evidence only of a young scholar fascinated with classical myth and giving range to his most sensuous verse in exploitation of one of the world's great love stories. But there are elements in Marlowe's *Dido* other than its love story, and not only do these relate to *Tamburlaine,* but the love story itself looks forward to things to come in later plays.

Although Marlowe dwells on the emotional aspects of Dido's plight, and he captures the poignancy of frustrated love in a manner new to the English stage, the general conception of this earliest of his plays remains very close to that of its source, Virgil's *Æneid,* and Virgil's theme is always the destiny of Rome. While Marlowe shows us the suffering of Dido, paralleled by that of Anna and Iarbas, and he dwells upon the temptation of Æneas to linger in Carthage and his remorse when finally he departs, the whole love affair is still but an episode in the career of a superman who, like Tamburlaine, is destined to create an empire.

That Æneas is the chosen instrument of the gods allows Marlowe to linger for a moment on the possible opposition between divine will and human desire, and this creates in the play all that is intensely personal and human. Æneas shows a brief suscepti- bility to human passion which for a moment deters him from his purpose, but this is quickly pushed aside and destiny is allowed to resume its course. In *Dido* Marlowe dealt with a legendary superman who, as an instrument in a conflict among pagan gods, was to create the greatest empire the world had ever known. From this subject he turned probably to history and found in Tambur- laine a man of similar destiny, but one whom he could treat without reference to the affairs of a mythical Olympus.

Dido is as static a play as *Tamburlaine.* It opens with a still pageant, the curtain parting to reveal Jupiter and his Ganymede; Venus interrupts to plead for assistance for her son; Jupiter ex- plains the heroic destiny which awaits him, and then we pass to a succession of scenes which reveal Æneas obeying the impulses of destiny. The lover is a passive figure for most of the play. Not until the beginning of the third act does Dido fall in love with Æneas, and when he declares his love for her in the cave scene it is merely an acceptance of Dido's offer of marriage agreed on beforehand by Juno and Venus. Immediately afterwards he is ready to obey the call of destiny, to leave Carthage without regard to the vow he has made to Dido. He pays a token respect to the demands of courtesy and the courtly obligations of the lover, but there is no real conflict in his mind. When briefly at the end of the fourth act he succumbs to Dido's blandishments and agrees to remain as king of Carthage, this is but a momentary weakness which stays him. No sooner does Hermes appear to remind him of his duty, than all question of his remaining dis- appears, and for the rest of the play he is concerned only with how to escape. Marlowe's momentary concentration upon the human side of the story does not impede the forward march of the superman to his destined goal.

Æneas is as changeless as Tamburlaine, as impervious at last to the tears of Dido as Tamburlaine is to those of Zenocrate. Æneas permits Dido to give him her aid, her treasure, and her- self, for which he promises himself in return, but when fate calls he leaves her. The love for which Dido kills herself, all consuming though it may be, is still the human result of a stratagem by which the goddess Venus seeks to forward the destiny of her son; it is all part of the larger plan. The death of a heroine for love must be seen within the larger context of the story of a hero who will not permit love to deter him from a triumphant destiny. There are tragic implications in the human cost which Æneas' obedience involves, and this element is foreign to the first part of *Tamburlaine*. It is not so foreign to the second part where the suicide of Olympia accents also the human cost of power, a motif to which Marlowe is to return and which is to give birth at last to real tragedy.

The intellectual position implicit in these early plays allies Marlowe to the currents of Renaissance skepticism which were challenging the medieval notion of a harmonious creation ruled over by the providence of God. Marlowe stands at the beginning of his career in opposition to the Christian humanism of Richard Hooker; he is in the company of Bruno, Montaigne, and Machiavelli. In its simplest terms the conflict between these opposing attitudes may be narrowed to an opposition between rival views of nature and the power of human reason in relation to it. Nature for the Christian humanist is the creation of God, controlled only by God, and human reason is an acceptance of divine will in recognition of the law of God which operates in all of nature, and thus a willingness to live by those moral laws —the altruistic feelings, love, kindness, loyalty, etc.—which all men intuitively recognize and which are enshrined in Christian belief as reflections in normal human intercourse of the love of God by which the whole creation moves. The skeptics, on the other hand, exalt the power of man to control the universe by his own strength and reason, without regard to divine influence. They see nature not so much as the reflection of divine will, but as something governed by immutable laws which may be studied; nature can be controlled once these laws are understood. They envision man as the potential master of his environment.

Tamburlaine and *Dido*, each in its own way, stand opposed to the Christian humanist position, *Tamburlaine* in its exaltation of *virtù*, and *Dido* in its implicit denial of love as a legitimate concern in the execution of the purpose of the gods, and in its very view of the universe as governed by the capricious quarrelsome deities of classical myth. Human *virtù* could manifest itself in two forms, as Machiavelli explained, the strength of the lion and the cunning of the fox, and Machiavelli held that each was necessary to the successful ruler. The strength of the lion is obvious in *Tamburlaine*. That cunning is the weapon by which the ends of the gods are assured in *Dido* is not always so obvious, but the entire Ascanius-Cupid sub-plot is, after all, little more than a cunning device by which Dido is outwitted so that the destiny of Æneas may be forwarded. Venus uses Ascanius first to trick Dido into loving Æneas so that his fleet may be repaired, and then her use of Ascanius as the false hostage creates the sense of security on Dido's part which permits Æneas to escape.

This kind of cunning, the manipulation of worldly affairs and of other men by one's own powers of mind came to be known as policy. Marlowe, in three plays, *The Jew of Malta, The Massacre at Paris,* and *Edward II,* went on to explore the implications of policy in human affairs, and we must note that in doing so he was exploring the implications of a system of values he had postulated in *Dido* and the two parts of *Tamburlaine.*

The first two acts of *The Jew of Malta* are so different from the final three that it is difficult to conceive of the same mind as responsible for the entire play. The aspiring superman of the play's beginning has been converted by its end into the caricature of a villain upon whom retribution is visited in conventional terms of poetic justice. That the end does not give us what we may have been led to expect at the beginning, however, should not obscure the fact that the focus of the play in its original conception must still have been upon the failure of its central character, whereas that of Marlowe's earlier plays had been upon the hero's triumph. Barabas at the beginning of the play is, like Tamburlaine, a man of boundless power and imagination. He rules the world by his wealth as Tamburlaine rules it by his strength. Like Marlowe's earlier heroes, Barabas stands deliberately in opposition to Christianity; Tamburlaine is a Scythian and Æneas a pagan Trojan; all stand for essentially non-Christian ideals, and Barabas by his name is specifically marked as the antithesis of Christ.

The play as we have it is blatantly anti-Semitic, castigating the Jew as a remorseless villain, holding him up to ridicule, and showing him finally as the victim of a punishment as ludicrous as it is merited. But, at least in those parts which are certainly Marlowe's, it is at least as anti-Christian as it is anti-Semitic, and on moral grounds Barabas certainly gets the better of his quarrel with Ferneze in the first act. It has been suggested that Marlowe uses Barabas as an instrument for an attack upon Christianity, not out of affection for Jews, but out of scorn for Christians.

Barabas is not a comic or a craven figure at the beginning of the play. He is the aspiring pagan, drawing his wealth from all corners of the world, wielding global power, and delighting in all of the felicity which wealth can convey. In his love of wealth, he stands in opposition to the pretensions of Christianity, and the behavior of the Christians in the play merits the contempt with which Barabas views them. When they steal his gold, Marlowe tells us in unequivocal terms that Barabas has been wronged. Marlowe's conception in this play seems to involve the pagan superman who is wronged by Christian policy— as Orcanes is in the second part of *Tamburlaine*—and who then seeks by policy in turn to avenge his wrongs, but the very exercise of policy vitiates the superman and destroys his heroic image, reducing him below even those who have sinned against him. He comes finally to be the incarnation of evil, a vehicle for the morality of Satan himself. *The Jew of Malta* represents a movement closer to real tragedy because it portrays the degeneration of a man through the manner in which he reacts to evil. We no longer have the simple movement of an initially complete and static figure as in *Dido* and *Tamburlaine*.

This tragic conception comes through even the crude buffoonery of the final acts, and in the murder of Abigail we are reminded, as we are to be more effectively reminded again in *Edward II*, of the human loss which is the price of policy. In *The Jew of Malta* the limitations of Christianity are exposed, but the failure of policy is given even greater emphasis. Marlowe has begun to question the faith in the power of human mind and will which he had asserted so proudly in *Tamburlaine*.

If we search for the source of Barabas' failure, the collapse of his policy, it is possible to find it in his human need for love. Man cannot be self-sufficient like Tamburlaine. The beginning of Barabas' downfall is in his choice of a companion, Ithamore, and the final destruction of his power comes from his human desire for reconciliation with his enemies, his need to trust those whom the true man of policy would have known could never be trusted. Caricature of the "Machiavel" as Barabas is, he violates the most essential elements of Machiavelli's creed. In this we may find perhaps Marlowe's recognition of the value of those altruistic feelings which might have spared the virgins of Damascus or might have made Æneas the victim of a truly tragic conflict. In this dimension of *The Jew of Malta* is one measure of the distance which Marlowe has traveled.

In *The Jew of Malta* we have the defeat of policy, but we do not have the triumph of its antithesis, for Ferneze the Christian and Calymath the Turk are as guilty as Barabas, and if there is any victory at the end of the play, it certainly is not one of moral principle. Jew, Christian, and Turk in this play all live by the same code, the success of the one following upon the downfall of the other, as each is able to seize the advantage and practice his policy the more efficiently. For the triumph of virtue we must move a step further to *The Massacre at Paris,* and it is because this play seems to supply an element which is missing from *The Jew of Malta* that I would suggest—very tentatively, of course—that it is the play which was written next. We have the self-defeating policy of the Guise, drawn on an even more lavish scale than that of Barabas, without the comic element, with more corpses littering the stage than in any other of Marlowe's plays, to say nothing of the hundreds of whose drowning in the Seine we are told. But we have also in opposition to the Guise the quiet virtue of King Henry of Navarre, and it is this virtue which at the end of the play is triumphant. That Navarre never really comes alive in the play, that his speeches are flat and insipid, consisting of little more than platitudinous moralizing, does not obscure the fact that his role in the play is to stand for anti-clericalism—he specifically allies himself with Queen Elizabeth of England—as the Guise represents the power of the Papacy, and to provide the final victory of a force antithetical to that represented by the Guise. It is difficult to believe that the Navarre of our received text retains much of what must have been the author's original conception. There is, in fact, little other than some speeches of the Guise which sound at all like Marlowe.

These soliloquies reveal the self-reliant man of policy like Barabas, but one who, unlike Barabas, vaunts his deliberate villainy from his first appearance. He seeks a crown by the deliberate exercise of evil, and it is the very danger of the quest which he enjoys. Upon his own power he relies exclusively, using religion only as an instrument of policy. He strives by villainy for the same goal, the "sweet fruition of an earthly crown" which Tamburlaine had sought by strength. Only Navarre stands in his way, and Navarre he must overcome, as Tamburlaine had overcome Mycetes and Bajazeth. In the failure of the Guise to do so is some measure of the difference between these plays.

The action of *The Massacre at Paris* is episodic like that of *Tamburlaine,* the simple detailing of the Guise's villainies until he reaches the height of his power, only to be murdered at last as he outreaches himself. There is also a kind of thematic elaboration in the role of King Henry III, a weak, lascivious practitioner of policy, as the Guise is a cruel and forthright one. Henry comes, however, to a similar end, murdered as his own policy recoils upon him.

We must note that the cause of the Guise's downfall is similar to what destroys Barabas: his inability to cope with the ordinary human emotions, the affections of his wife and his own concern for honor and esteem. We have the ludicrous spectacle in this play of the all-powerful manipulator of kings revealed as a cuckold at home. He incurs the enmity of the king which must at last destroy him when to defend his honor he kills the king's favorite who has been the lover of his wife. The Guise, master of policy, is destroyed when he allows the passions which the man of policy must control to defeat his own policy. In doing so he gives rise to the counterpolicy of Henry III, who lives by a code no different from that of the Guise, and whose murder at the end parallels that of the Guise, emphasizing for a second time the futility of all policy. Henry of Navarre stands in contrast to the other two, the champion of true religion, placing his faith not in policy but in the protection of God, and it is he who comes at last to the French throne.

One might from this suppose that by the time of his writing

The Massacre at Paris Marlowe had returned to the Christian faith of his youth and had been reconciled to the church. Of this we cannot be sure. The religious sentiments which Navarre speaks may bear little relation to what Marlowe originally wrote, and it is, at any rate, to the political rather than doctrinal issues of anti-Catholicism that Marlowe gives his support. But we can be sure that the play does embody a renunciation, even more pronounced than that in *The Jew of Malta,* of the individualist amoral faith of *Tamburlaine.*

The Massacre at Paris, as we have it, is by far the least successful of Marlowe's plays, and there is little in it to arouse the tragic emotions. Marlowe was in his brief career to write only two plays of real tragic scope and intensity, but *Edward II* and *Doctor Faustus* represent a development from all which had gone before, and I would suggest that it would have been difficult for Marlowe to have come to them without the experience of his earlier plays. *Edward II,* which most scholars today regard as the earlier of the final two, recapitulates the career of the Guise in the rise and fall of Mortimer, but there is an important difference in that Mortimer is not evil when the play begins; he is not even amoral like Barabas. Marlowe no longer needs the ready made villain. He can now present a loyal, patriotic gentleman, devoted entirely to the good of his country, and in the process of his decline demonstrate the corrupting force of aspiration to power. He can do so within a truly tragic context, detailing the decline of one man through his own destruction of his human instincts, while in the parallel tragedy of King Edward II he displays the destruction of a man forced by necessity to wield a power which he is incapable of wielding because of his own human instincts. Marlowe holds these two situations in relation to one another, with Edward as he declines in power acquiring to at least some extent a new humility and self-understanding through suffering which wins for him the sympathy of the audience, while Mortimer, rising as Edward falls, is alienated from the audience as it beholds the slow erosion of his humanity.

Marlowe has abandoned his faith in the amoral superman like Tamburlaine. He has shown in *The Jew of Malta* and *The Massacre at Paris* that an egocentric self-reliance may degenerate into a demonic force destructive of itself as well as the social order, and he demonstrates this again in Mortimer. There is no evidence, however, in *Edward II* that he has come to accept the Christian humanist view of order and degree in a divinely controlled and harmonious cosmos, with what Tudor theorists considered to be the role of the king in that system. *Edward II* and *Doctor Faustus* are plays of a terrible pessimism because while they detail the futility of individual aspiration and the corrupting effects of power they offer no alternative which mankind can fully embrace. They are plays without affirmation. If there is any reconciliation at the end of *Edward II*, it may be in the audience's knowledge that the new king, Edward III, did in fact go on to be one of England's greatest kings, that is was possible for at least one king to escape the corrupting effects of power which the play has made clear.

The political setting of *Edward* II involves the same amoral world of *Tamburlaine*, where the events of history represent not the workings of a divine plan for humanity, but the results of human action and human error. There is no mention in *Edward II* of the divine right of kings or of their responsibility to God. A king's power rests only upon his own ability to maintain it in spite of opposition, and when he cannot assert this power, he loses all the attributes of royalty. Edward II is born into a position in which to survive he must be a Machiavellian superman like Tamburlaine, and since he is not he is destroyed. That is his tragedy. But the tragedy of Mortimer is that he is precisely what Edward is not. To be incapable of exercising power like Edward is to be destroyed; to exercise it fully is to destroy one's self like Mortimer. This is the human condition, and man can only meet it by the assertion of the stoic fortitude with which Mortimer accepts his death. The play presents a consistent vision of human experience and a truly tragic one, but the only resolution it can offer is in terms of a classical stoicism.

The only one of Marlowe's plays which is cast in a deliberately Christian context is *Doctor Faustus*. It is obvious that this is a play about human damnation and that the contrary alternative of salvation in specifically Christian terms is always present in the dramatic context. This need not mean that Marlowe expressed his own Christian belief when he wrote this play any more than his authorship of *Dido* need indicate that he was ever a pagan Trojan. Christian doctrine was one of Marlowe's most vital concerns throughout his career. The damnation of Faustus could be taken by the Elizabethan audience, as no doubt it was, as a perfectly orthodox warning to sinners, an *exemplum* in the medieval manner, delineating what the church held to be the mental state of the damned, and dwelling at last upon all of the physical horrors of the soul's being carried off to hell. But Marlowe's *Doctor Faustus* is not a Christian morality play because it contains no affirmation of the goodness or justice of the religious system it portrays. It is rather, a protest against this system, which it reveals as imposing a limitation upon the aspirations of man, holding him in subjection and bondage, denying him at last even the comfort of Christ's blood, and dooming him to the most terrible destruction.

There is an awful warning for humanity in the final chorus. The price of aspiration beyond the ordinary limits of man must be the human deterioration we behold in Faustus, the proud philosopher becoming at last a cowering wretch to be carried off to hell. But the play does not preach a pious submission to divine law. It is a pessimistic statement of the futility of human striving. *Doctor Faustus* is the tragedy of man who will not surrender in return for the promise of salvation those heroic attributes— the craving for knowledge, wealth, power, and delight—for which Marlowe still sees it as in the nature of mankind to yearn. But he has come a long way from *Tamburlaine,* for where he once saw such goals as attainable, he now sees them only as an illusion whose very pursuit must be man's destruction.

Doctor Faustus is the most personal of Marlowe's plays, perhaps of all Elizabethan drama, but we must not confuse the poignant longing for belief, for salvation, perhaps for rescue in orthodox Christianity from the doubts and perplexities which were Marlowe's humanistic heritage, with the signs of acceptance and resignation. The play is a mirror not of Christian certainty, but of agnostic intellectual confusion. The contrary systems of value in *Doctor Faustus* are clear: submission to divine will versus defiant belief in man's own power to control nature. Marlowe's hero does not make the Christian choice, and by his own deterioration and final torture he pays the price of his independence of mind. The play offers little hope for humanity, for the damnation of Faustus leads to no affirmation of order or harmony in the universe; there is no sense of justice, and there is no compensating rebirth of good.

Faustus is the knowing and deliberate apostate who, like Tamburlaine or Barabas, seeks to enlarge the scope of human life so that man on earth may equal the state of the God he envisages in heaven. There is never any doubt in his mind before he makes his bargain that what he seeks is worth the price of damnation. The tragedy lies in that what Faustus receives in exchange for his soul is finally worthless, that wealth, power, and sensual pleasure are revealed to him only as a delusion whose value disappears as soon as they are possessed. The restricting force of Christian submission is made clear in the opening soliloquy; that the alternative is equally without value is the burden of the rest of the play. Faustus can receive no answers to the questions he asks. The broad comic matter which takes up most of the central scenes of the play is probably not from the pen of Marlowe, but these scenes, which follow the source closely, are an essential part of the story, and they must have been a part of the conception of the total play. They are designed in part to illustrate the futility of what Faustus gains, and they are still effective in doing so.

There are three movements in *Doctor Faustus,* following closely the divisions of the source book. First there is the hero's choice of damnation, which springs not only from his awareness of the limitations placed upon him by Christianity, but from his syllogistic conclusion that in Christian doctrine his death through sin already is implicit. The syllogism is a false one because it ignores the atonement of Christ for man's sins and the possibility of salvation through grace, but this is not made clear by Marlowe, and Faustus' view of Christianity is the only one made explicit in the play. The God of *Doctor Faustus* is one singularly without love, a god of terrible justice without mercy. The second movement of the play shows the shallowness of what Faustus receives for his soul, his growing awareness of this shallowness, his own deterioration as he exchanges his heroic aspirations for petty trickery, and the constant pressure he feels to renounce his bargain and accept salvation in Christian terms. In the final movement of the play we have the last stage of Faustus' deterioration as he pleads for the mercy which cannot be granted him, the horror of his destruction, and the realization that it has all been for naught.

The way of repentance is always open to Faustus, as the central scenes constantly make clear. But for Faustus to repent is for him to reject those human aspirations which have led him to make his bargain in the first place, and although again and again he is driven to repentance by fear, the thought of worldly power and delight keeps him steadfast to his bargain. Whether Helen of Troy be a she-devil or not, the lines with which Faustus greets her are still among the most lyrical Marlowe ever wrote, and their poetry alone evokes a sympathetic response to that for which Faustus gives his soul. Although we may pity Faustus and we are horrified by his fate, we may still emotionally identify ourselves with him and feel the magnificence of what he seeks. If Marlowe's final view of Christianity is implicit in this play, it may be that the Christian promise of salvation may be one way out of the human dilemma, but one which he cannot yet bring himself to accept. The tragedy of this play, and of humanity as Marlowe sees it at this point in his career, is that neither Christian submission nor its alternative presents a choice which mankind whole-heartedly can embrace.

The death speech of Faustus reveals none of the stoic resignation with which Mortimer accepts his fate. Marlowe wishes in this play to show the final degeneration of what had been heroic, to reveal a futile longing for faith such as Marlowe himself may have suffered, and to illustrate the final bleak terror of the human situation. We have a poignant pleading by Faustus to escape from what the play has revealed cannot be escaped. The power of Lucifer finally prevails. In the death of Faustus the terror and futility of the human condition are revealed as they never had been before in English drama, with little compensating hope of any kind.

While we keep in mind the many areas of Marlowe's life and thought about which we know nothing, and the impossibility of establishing the chronology of his plays with real certainty, it may be possible still to conclude that he came to the writing of tragedy as he abandoned the optimistic individualism of his early days, but that he did not live long enough to find a faith

.which might replace it. If we assess his final achievement in tragedy, we find that in his last two plays he was able to present a comprehensive view of mankind and to make some statement about the relation of good and evil in the world. He could, however, find no real principle of order in the universe, no hope for human triumph over evil, and the only consolation he could afford to mankind was in the heroic stature of a stoic acceptance and submission to what must be.

The Complete Plays of
Christopher Marlowe

THE
Tragedie of Dido

Queene of Carthage:

Played by the Children of her
Maiesties Chappell.

Written by Christopher Marlowe, and
Thomas Nash. **Gent.**

Actors

Iupiter.	*Ascanius.*
Ganimed.	*Dido.*
Venus.	*Anna.*
Cupid.	*Achates.*
Iuno.	*Ilioneus.*
Mercurie, or	*Iarbas.*
Hermes.	*Cloanthes.*
Æneas.	*Sergestus.*

At London,
Printed, by the Widdowe *Orwin,* for *Thomas Woodcocke,* and
are to be solde at his shop, in Paules Church-yeard, at
the signe of the blacke Beare. 1594.

THE TRAGEDY OF DIDO QUEEN OF CARTHAGE

THE PLAYERS

Jupiter	Æneas	Other Trojans
Ganymede	Ascanius, his son	Iarbas
Mercury, or Hermes	Achates	Carthaginian Lords
Cupid	Ilioneus	Dido
Juno	Cloanthus	Anna, her sister
Venus	Sergestus	Nurse

THE SCENE

Mount Olympus and Carthage

I,i.

Here the Curtains draw. There is discovered Jupiter dandling
Ganymede upon his knee, and Mercury lying asleep.

Jupiter. Come, gentle Ganymede, and play with me.
  I love thee well, say Juno what she will.
Ganymede. I am much better for your worthless love,
  That will not shield me from her shrewish blows.
  Today, whenas I filled into your cups   5
  And held the cloth of pleasance whiles you drank,
  She reached me such a rap for that I spilled,
  As made the blood run down about mine ears.
Jupiter. What! Dares she strike the darling of my thoughts?
  By Saturn's soul and this earth-threat'ning hair,   10
  That, shaken thrice, makes nature's buildings quake,
  I vow, if she but once frown on thee more,
  To hang her, meteor-like, 'twixt heaven and earth
  And bind her hand and foot with golden cords,
  As once I did for harming Hercules.   15
Ganymede. Might I but see that pretty sport afoot,
  O, how would I with Helen's brother laugh
  And bring the gods to wonder at the game.
  Sweet Jupiter, if e'er I pleased thine eye
  Or seemèd fair, walled in with eagle's wings,   20
  Grace my immortal beauty with this boon,
  And I will spend my time in thy bright arms.
Jupiter. What is't, sweet wag, I should deny thy youth,
  Whose face reflects such pleasure to mine eyes,

I,i.
6 *cloth of pleasance* fine gauze.   17 *Helen's brother* Castor or Pollux,
7 *that* that which.   the two brothers of Helen of Troy.

3

As I, exhaled with thy fire-darting beams,   25
Have oft driven back the horses of the night,
Whenas they would have haled thee from my sight.
Sit on my knee and call for thy content;
Control proud fate and cut the thread of time.
Why, are not all the gods at thy command   30
And heaven and earth the bounds of thy delight?
Vulcan shall dance to make thee laughing sport,
And my nine daughters sing when thou art sad.
From Juno's bird I'll pluck her spotted pride
To make thee fans wherewith to cool thy face,   35
And Venus' swans shall shed their silver down
To sweeten out the slumbers of thy bed.
Hermes no more shall show the world his wings,
If that thy fancy in his feathers dwell,
But, as this one, I'll tear them all from him,   40
                    [*He plucks a feather from Mercury's wings.*]
Do thou but say, 'their color pleaseth me.'
Hold here, my little love. These linkèd gems
                                        [*He gives jewels.*]
My Juno ware upon her marriage day,
Put thou about thy neck, my own sweetheart,
And trick thy arms and shoulders with my theft.   45
Ganymede.   I would have a jewel for mine ear
And a fine brooch to put in my hat,
And then I'll hug with you an hundred times.
Jupiter.   And shall have, Ganymede, if thou wilt be my love.
                    Enter Venus.
Venus.   Ay, this is it! You can sit toying there   50
And playing with that female wanton boy,
Whiles my Æneas wanders on the seas
And rests a prey to every billow's pride.
Juno, false Juno, in her chariot's pomp,
Drawn through the heavens by steeds of Boreas' brood,   55
Made Hebe to direct her airy wheels
Into the windy country of the clouds,
Where, finding Æolus entrenched with storms
And guarded with a thousand grisly ghosts,
She humbly did beseech him for our bane,   60
And charged him drown my son with all his train.

25 *exhaled . . . beams* i.e., consumed
with burning passion.

32 *Vulcan . . . sport* Since Vulcan,
the blacksmith of the gods, was lame, his
dancing would provoke laughter.

33 *nine daughters* the muses.

34 *Juno's bird* the peacock.

43 *ware* wore.

45 *trick* adorn.

55 *Boreas* the north wind.

56 *Hebe* goddess of youth, daughter
of Jupiter and Juno.

58 *Æolus* a king of Thessaly to whom
Jupiter had given dominion over the
winds.

Then gan the winds break ope their brazen doors
And all Æolia to be up in arms.
Poor Troy must now be sacked upon the sea,
And Neptune's waves be envious men of war;   65
Epeus' horse, to Ætna's hill transformed,
Preparèd stands to wrack their wooden walls,
And Æolus, like Agamemnon, sounds
The surges, his fierce soldiers, to the spoil.
See how the night, Ulysses-like, comes forth   70
And intercepts the day, as Dolon erst.
Ay me! The stars surprised, like Rhesus' steeds,
Are drawn by darkness forth Astræus' tents.
What shall I do to save thee, my sweet boy,
Whenas the waves do threat our crystal world,   75
And Proteus, raising hills of floods on high,
Intends ere long to sport him in the sky?
False Jupiter, reward'st thou virtue so?
What, is not piety exempt from woe?
Then die Æneas in thine innocence,   80
Since that religion hath no recompense.
Jupiter. Content thee, Cytherea, in thy care,
Since thy Æneas' wandering fate is firm,
Whose weary limbs shall shortly make repose
In those fair walls I promised him of yore.   85
But first in blood must his good fortune bud,
Before he be the lord of Turnus' town,
Or force her smile that hitherto hath frowned.
Three winters shall he with the Rutiles war,
And in the end subdue them with his sword;   90
And full three summers likewise shall he waste
On managing those fierce barbarian minds,
Which once performed, poor Troy, so long suppressed,

---

64 *Poor Troy* i.e., all that remains of
Troy, Æneas and his men.
66 *Epeus'* . . . *transformed* i.e., the
dangers represented at Troy by the
wooden horse built by Epeus are now
represented by the rocks of the Sicilian
coast (Mt. Ætna) which threaten Æneas
and his fleet.
67 *wrack* wreck.
68 *Agamemnon* leader of the Greek
armies.
71 *Dolon* a Trojan spy intercepted by
Ulysses.
72 *Rhesus' steeds* An oracle had declared that Troy would never be taken
if once the horses of Rhesus should
drink from the river Xanthus and feed

upon the Trojan plain. Ulysses and Diomedes slew Rhesus and carried off his
horses before they could do either.
73 *Astræus' tents* where the stars are
kept by Astræus, the Titan husband of
Eos (the dawn) and father of the winds
and stars.
76 *Proteus* a sea deity who constantly
changed his shape as men tried to catch
him.
82 *Cytherea* Venus (who supposedly
rose from the sea near the island of
Cythera).
89 *Rutiles* people ruled over by Turnus at the time of Æneas' arrival in Italy.
92 *managing* bringing under control.

From forth her ashes shall advance her head,
And flourish once again, that erst was dead.   95
But bright Ascanius, beauty's better work,
Who with the sun divides one radiant shape,
Shall build his throne amidst those starry towers
That earth-born Atlas, groaning, underprops.
No bounds but heaven shall bound his empery,   100
Whose azured gates, enchasèd with his name,
Shall make the morning haste her gray uprise
To feed her eyes with his engraven fame.
Thus in stout Hector's race three hundred years
The Roman scepter royal shall remain,   105
Till that a princess-priest, conceived by Mars,
Shall yield to dignity a double birth,
Who will eternish Troy by their attempts.
Venus.   How may I credit these thy flattering terms,
When yet both sea and sands beset their ships,   110
And Phoebus, as in Stygian pools, refrains
To taint his tresses in the Tyrrhene main?
Jupiter.   I will take order for that presently.
Hermes awake, and haste to Neptune's realm,
Whereas the wind-god, warring now with fate,   115
Besiege the offspring of our kingly loins.
Charge him from me to turn his stormy powers
And fetter them in Vulcan's sturdy brass,
That durst thus proudly wrong our kinsman's peace.
                    [*Exit Mercury.*]
Venus, farewell; thy son shall be our care.   120
Come Ganymede, we must about this gear.
                    Exeunt Jupiter and Ganymede.
Venus.   Disquiet seas, lay down your swelling looks,
And court Æneas with your calmy cheer,
Whose beauteous burden well might make you proud,
Had not the heavens, conceived with hell-born clouds,   125
Veiled his resplendent glory from your view.
For my sake pity him, Oceanus,
That erstwhile issued from thy wat'ry loins

---

97 *sun . . . shape* i.e., as handsome as Apollo, the sun god.

99 *Atlas* the Titan, brother of Prometheus and Epimetheus, condemned by Jupiter to bear heaven upon his head and shoulders.

100 *empery* empire.

101 *enchasèd . . . name* with his name written in jewels set in the metal.

107 *double birth* i.e., of Romulus and Remus, founders of Rome, born to the vestal virgin, Rhea Silvia, by the god, Mars.

111–112 *Phoebus . . . main* i.e., the sun refuses to shine over the Tyrrene sea (Mediterranean). The sun's beams were often called the hair of Phoebus, or Apollo.

121 *gear* business.

127–129 *Oceanus . . . froth* Venus had been born out of the ocean.

And had my being from thy bubbling froth.
Triton, I know, hath filled his trump with Troy,   130
And therefore will take pity on his toil,
And call both Thetis and Cymothoe
To succor him in this extremity.
    *Enter Æneas with Ascanius, [Achates, and] with one or two
more.*
What, do I see my son now come on shore?
Venus, how art thou compassed with content,   135
The while thine eyes attract their sought-for joys.
Great Jupiter, still honored may'st thou be
For this so friendly aid in time of need.
Here in this bush disguisèd will I stand,
Whiles my Æneas spends himself in plaints,   140
And heaven and earth with his unrest acquaints. [*She hides.*]
Æneas. You sons of care, companions of my course,
Priam's misfortune follows us by sea,
And Helen's rape doth haunt thee at the heels.
How many dangers have we overpassed!   145
Both barking Scylla and the sounding rocks,
The Cyclops' shelves, and grim Ceraunia's seat
Have you o'ergone and yet remain alive.
Pluck up your hearts, since fate still rests our friend,
And changing heavens may those good days return,   150
Which Pergama did vaunt in all her pride.
Achates. Brave prince of Troy, thou only art our god,
That by thy virtues free'st us from annoy,
And makes our hopes survive to coming joys.
Do thou but smile and cloudy heaven will clear,   155
Whose night and day descendeth from thy brows.
Though we be now in extreme misery
And rest the map of weather-beaten woe,
Yet shall the agèd sun shed forth his hair
To make us live unto our former heat,   160
And every beast the forest doth send forth
Bequeath her young ones to our scanted food.

---

130 *Triton . . . Troy* i.e., Triton's trumpet (used usually to call the winds and waves) has announced instead the fall of Troy. Triton was the son of Neptune and Venus who dwelt in a golden palace at the bottom of the sea.

132 *Thetis and Cymothoe* sea deities. Thetis became the mother of Achilles.

140 *plaints* lamentations.

146 *Scylla* a monster who lived in a cave in a rock (of the same name) between Italy and Sicily. Opposite was the rock under which lived Charybdis, who three times a day swallowed the waters of the sea and three times threw them up again.

147 *Cyclops' shelves* great walls of unhewn stone in Greece and southern Italy, supposedly built by the Cyclops, one-eyed Titans who assisted Vulcan at his forge on Mt. Ætna. *Ceraunia's seat* a range of mountains along the coast of Epirus, famous for thunderstorms.

151 *Pergama* the citadel at Troy, hence Troy itself.

Ascanius.   Father, I faint. Good father, give me meat.
Æneas.   Alas, sweet boy, thou must be still a while,
   Till we have fire to dress the meat we killed.   165
   Gentle Achates, reach the tinder box,
   That we may make a fire to warm us with
   And roast our new found victuals on this shore.
Venus.   See what strange arts necessity finds out.
   How near, my sweet Æneas, art thou driven!   [*Aside.*]   170
Æneas.   Hold; take this candle and go light a fire.
   You shall have leaves and windfall boughs enow,
   Near to these woods, to roast your meat withal.
   Ascanius, go and dry thy drenchèd limbs,
   Whiles I with my Achates rove abroad,   175
   To know what coast the wind hath driven us on,
   Or whether men or beasts inhabit it.
                                        [*Exit Ascanius.*]
Achates.   The air is pleasant, and the soil most fit
   For cities and society's supports;
   Yet much I marvel that I cannot find   180
   No steps of men imprinted in the earth.
Venus.   Now is the time for me to play my part.   [*Aside.*]
   Ho, young men! Saw you as you came
   Any of all my sisters wandering here,
   Having a quiver girded to her side   185
   And clothèd in a spotted leopard's skin?
Æneas.   I neither saw nor heard of any such.
   But what may I, fair virgin, call your name,
   Whose looks set forth no mortal form to view,
   Nor speech bewrays aught human in thy birth?   190
   Thou art a goddess that delud'st our eyes
   And shrouds thy beauty in this borrowed shape,
   But whether thou the sun's bright sister be,
   Or one of chaste Diana's fellow nymphs,
   Live happy in the height of all content,   195
   And lighten our extremes with this one boon,
   As to instruct us under what good heaven
   We breathe as now, and what this world is called
   On which by tempest's fury we are cast.
   Tell us, O, tell us, that are ignorant,   200
   And this right hand shall make thy altars crack
   With mountain-heaps of milk-white sacrifice.
Venus.   Such honor, stranger, do I not affect.
   It is the use for Tyrian maids to wear
   Their bow and quiver in this modest sort   205
   And suit themselves in purple for the nonce,
   That they may trip more lightly o'er the lawnds,

190 *bewrays* betrays.   207 *lawnds* glades.

And overtake the tuskèd boar in chase.
But for the land whereof thou dost inquire,
It is the Punic kingdom, rich and strong,   210
Adjoining on Agenor's stately town,
The kingly seat of Southern Libya,
Whereas Sidonian Dido rules as queen.
But what are you that ask of me these things?
Whence may you come, or whither will you go?   215
Æneas.   Of Troy am I. Æneas is my name,
Who driven by war from forth my native world,
Puts sails to sea to seek out Italy;
And my divine descent from sceptered Jove.
With twice twelve Phrygian ships I plowed the deep   220
And made that way my mother Venus led,
But of them all scarce seven do anchor safe,
And they so wracked and weltered by the waves,
As every tide tilts 'twixt their oaken sides.
And all of them, unburdened of their load,   225
Are ballassèd with billows' watery weight.
But hapless I, God wot, poor and unknown,
Do trace these Libyan deserts all despised,
Exiled forth Europe and wide Asia both,
And have not any coverture but heaven.   230
Venus.   Fortune hath favored thee, whate'er thou be,
In sending thee unto this courteous coast.
A' God's name on, and haste thee to the court,
Where Dido will receive ye with her smiles.
And for thy ships which thou supposest lost,   235
Not one of them hath perished in the storm,
But are arrivèd safe not far from hence.
And so I leave thee to thy fortune's lot,
Wishing good luck unto thy wandering steps.

                                                    Exit.

Æneas.   Achates, 'tis my mother that is fled;   240
I know her by the movings of her feet.
Stay, gentle Venus! Fly not from thy son!
Too cruel, why wilt thou forsake me thus,
Or in these shades deceiv'st mine eyes so oft?
Why talk we not together hand in hand,   245
And tell our griefs in more familiar terms?
But thou art gone and leav'st me here alone
To dull the air with my discoursive moan.

                                                  Exeunt.

---

211 *Agenor's . . . town* Carthage (since Dido was a descendant of Agenor, son of Neptune and King of Phoenicia, the father of Cadmus and Europa).

213 *Sidonian* of Phoenician origin. Sidon was a city of ancient Phoenicia.
226 *ballassèd* ballasted.
227 *hapless* unfortunate.

Enter [Iarbas, followed by Sergestus,] Ilioneus, and Cloanthus,
[and others].

Ilioneus.   Follow, ye Trojans, follow this brave lord,
And plain to him the sum of your distress.
Iarbas.   Why, what are you, or wherefore do you sue?
Ilioneus.   Wretches of Troy, envièd of the winds,
That crave such favor at your honor's feet   5
As poor distressèd misery may plead.
Save, save, O save our ships from cruel fire,
That do complain the wounds of thousand waves,
And spare our lives whom every spite pursues.
We come not, we, to wrong your Libyan gods,   10
Or steal your household Lares from their shrines;
Our hands are not prepared to lawless spoil,
Nor armèd to offend in any kind.
Such force is far from our unweaponed thoughts,
Whose fading weal, of victory forsook,   15
Forbids all hope to harbor near our hearts.
Iarbus.   But tell me, Trojans, Trojans if you be,
Unto what fruitful quarters were ye bound,
Before that Boreas buckled with your sails?
Cloanthus.   There is a place, Hesperia termed by us,   20
An ancient empire, famousèd for arms,
And fertile in fair Ceres' furrowed wealth,
Which now we call Italia, of his name
That in such peace long time did rule the same.
Thither made we,   25
When suddenly gloomy Orion rose
And led our ships into the shallow sands,
Whereas the southern wind with brackish breath
Dispersed them all amongst the wrackful rocks.
From thence a few of us escaped to land;   30
The rest, we fear, are folded in the floods.
Iarbus.   Brave men-at-arms, abandon fruitless fears,
Since Carthage knows to entertain distress.
Sergestus.   Ay, but the barbarous sort do threat our ships
And will not let us lodge upon the sands.   35

I,ii.

11 *Lares* small icons representing the spirits of dead ancestors who watched over households.

20 *Hesperia* Italy.

22 *Ceres* goddess of agriculture, protectress of the harvest.

23 *his name* Italus, an ancient king from whom Italy derives its name.

26 *Orion* a constellation ascendant in November and therefore associated with rain and storms.

29 *wrackful* causing shipwrecks.

31 *folded in the floods* drowned.

In multitudes they swarm unto the shore
And from the first earth interdict our feet.
Iarbus.   Myself will see they shall not trouble ye.
Your men and you shall banquet in our court,
And every Trojan be as welcome here   40
As Jupiter to silly Baucis' house.
Come in with me. I'll bring you to my queen,
Who shall confirm my words with further deeds.
Sergestus.   Thanks, gentle lord, for such unlooked-for grace.
Might we but once more see Æneas' face,   45
Then would we hope to quite such friendly turns
As shall surpass the wonder of our speech.

                                                    [*Exeunt.*]

Enter Æneas, Achates, and Ascanius, [with others].   II,i.
Æneas.   Where am I now? These should be Carthage walls.
Achates.   Why stands my sweet Æneas thus amazed?
Æneas.   O my Achates, Theban Niobe,
Who for her sons' death wept out life and breath
And, dry with grief, was turned into a stone,   5
Had not such passions in her head as I.
Methinks that town there should be Troy, yon Ida's hill,
There Xanthus' stream, because here's Priamus;
And when I know it is not, then I die.
Achates.   And in this humor is Achates too;   10
I cannot choose but fall upon my knees
And kiss his hand. O, where is Hecuba?
Here she was wont to sit, but saving air,
Is nothing here. And what is this but stone?
Æneas.   O, yet this stone doth make Æneas weep!   15
And would my prayers (as Pygmalion's did)
Could give it life, that under his conduct
We might sail back to Troy and be revenged
On these hard-hearted Grecians which rejoice
That nothing now is left of Priamus.   20
O, Priamus is left and this is he!
Come, come aboard; pursue the hateful Greeks.

---

41 *silly* simple. *Baucis' house* Ovid in   **II,i.**
the *Metamorphoses* tells the story of
Baucis and her husband, Philemon, who   13 *Here* next to Priam.
hospitably entertained Jupiter and Mer-   16 *Pygmalion* king of Cyprus who fell
cury.   in love with an ivory statue he had made
                                               and prayed to Venus that it be given
46 **quite** requite.   life. His prayer was granted.

Achates.   What means Æneas?

Æneas.   Achates, though mine eyes say this is stone,
  Yet thinks my mind that this is Priamus,   25
  And when my grievèd heart sighs and says no,
  Then would it leap out to give Priam life.
  O, were I not at all, so thou mightst be!
  Achates, see! King Priam wags his hand!
  He is alive! Troy is not overcome!   30

Achates.   Thy mind, Æneas, that would have it so,
  Deludes thy eyesight. Priamus is dead.

Æneas.   Ah, Troy is sacked and Priamus is dead,
  And why should poor Æneas be alive?

Ascanius.   Sweet father, leave to weep. This is not he,   35
  For were he Priam he would smile on me.

Achates.   Æneas see; here come the citizens.
  Leave to lament, lest they laugh at our fears.
          Enter Cloanthus, Sergestus, Ilioneus, [and others].

Æneas.   Lords of this town, or whatsoever style
  Belongs unto your name, vouchsafe of ruth   40
  To tell us who inhabits this fair town,
  What kind of people and who governs them,
  For we are strangers driven on this shore
  And scarcely know within what clime we are.

Ilioneus.   I hear Æneas' voice, but see him not,   45
  For none of these can be our general.

Achates.   Like Ilioneus speaks this nobleman,
  But Ilioneus goes not in such robes.

Sergestus.   You are Achates, or I deceived.

Achates.   Æneas, see Sergestus or his ghost!   50

Ilioneus.   He names Æneas; let us kiss his feet.

Cloanthus.   It is our captain! See Ascanius!

Sergestus.   Live long Æneas and Ascanius!

Æneas.   Achates speak, for I am overjoyed.

Achates.   O Ilioneus, art thou yet alive?   55

Ilioneus.   Blessed be the time I see Achates' face.

Cloanthus.   Why turns Æneas from his trusty friends?

Æneas.   Sergestus, Ilioneus, and the rest,
  Your sight amazed me. O, what destinies
  Have brought my sweet companions in such plight?   60
  O tell me, for I long to be resolved.

Ilioneus.   Lovely Æneas, these are Carthage walls,
  And here Queen Dido wears th'imperial crown,
  Who for Troy's sake hath entertained us all
  And clad us in these wealthy robes we wear.   65
  Oft hath she asked us under whom we served,
  And when we told her, she would weep for grief,
  Thinking the sea had swallowed up thy ships;
  And now she sees thee, how will she rejoice!

Sergestus.   See where her servitors pass through the hall,   70
  Bearing a banquet. Dido is not far.
Ilioneus.   Look where she comes! Æneas, view her well.
Æneas.   Well may I view her, but she sees not me.
        Enter Dido and her train, [Anna and Iarbas].
Dido.   What stranger art thou that dost eye me thus?
Æneas.   Sometime I was a Trojan, mighty queen,   75
  But Troy is not. What shall I say I am?
Ilioneus.   Renownèd Dido, 'tis our general,
  Warlike Æneas.
Dido.   Warlike Æneas, and in these base robes!
  Go fetch the garment which Sichæus ware.   80
        [Exit an Attendant who returns with a garment
                       which Æneas puts on.]
  Brave prince, welcome to Carthage and to me,
  Both happy that Æneas is our guest.
  Sit in this chair and banquet with a queen.
  Æneas is Æneas, were he clad
  In weeds as bad as ever Irus ware.   85
Æneas.   This is no seat for one that's comfortless.
  May it please your grace to let Æneas wait,
  For though my birth be great, my fortune's mean,
  Too mean to be companion to a queen.
Dido.   Thy fortune may be greater than thy birth.   90
  Sit down, Æneas, sit in Dido's place,
  And if this be thy son, as I suppose,
  Here let him sit. Be merry, lovely child.
Æneas.   This place beseems me not. O, Pardon me.
Dido.   I'll have it so. Æneas, be content.   95
Ascanius.   Madam, you shall be my mother.
Dido.   And so I will, sweet child. Be merry man.
  Here's to thy better fortune and good stars.   *[She drinks.]*
Æneas.   In all humility, I thank your grace.
Dido.   Remember who thou art. Speak like thyself.   100
  Humility belongs to common grooms.
Æneas.   And who so miserable as Æneas is?
Dido.   Lies it in Dido's hands to make thee blessed,
  Then be assured thou art not miserable.
Æneas.   O Priamus! O Troy! O Hecuba!   105
Dido.   May I entreat thee to discourse at large,
  And truly too, how Troy was overcome,
  For many tales go of that city's fall,
  And scarcely do agree upon one point.
  Some say Antenor did betray the town;   110

80 *Sichæus* Dido's uncle and former husband, also called Acerbas. After his murder by her brother, the king of Tyre, Dido fled from Tyre into Africa.

85 *Irus* a beggar in the household of Ulysses.
86 *seat* resting place.

Others report 'twas Sinon's perjury;
But all in this, that Troy is overcome
And Priam dead. Yet how, we hear no news.
Æneas.   A woeful tale bids Dido to unfold,
Whose memory, like pale death's stony mace,   115
Beats forth my senses from this troubled soul
And makes Æneas sink at Dido's feet.
Dido.   What, faints Æneas to remember Troy,
In whose defence he fought so valiantly?
Look up and speak.   120
Æneas.   Then speak, Æneas, with Achilles' tongue,
And Dido and you Carthaginian peers
Hear me, but yet with Myrmidons' harsh ears,
Daily inured to broils and massacres,
Lest you be moved too much with my sad tale.   125
The Grecian soldiers, tired with ten years' war,
Began to cry, 'Let us unto our ships.
Troy is invincible. Why stay we here?'
With whose outcries Atrides being appalled,
Summoned the captains to his princely tent,   130
Who, looking on the scars we Trojans gave,
Seeing the number of their men decreased
And the remainder weak and out of heart,
Gave up their voices to dislodge the camp.
And so in troops all marched to Tenedos,   135
Where when they came, Ulysses on the sand
Assayed with honey words to turn them back.
And as he spoke to further his intent,
The winds did drive huge billows to the shore,
And heaven was darkened with tempestuous clouds.   140
Then he alleged the gods would have them stay,
And prophesied Troy should be overcome;
And therewithal he called false Sinon forth,
A man compact of craft and perjury,
Whose ticing tongue was made of Hermes' pipe,   145
To force an hundred watchful eyes to sleep.
And him—Epeus having made the horse—
With sacrificing wreaths upon his head,
Ulysses sent to our unhappy town,
Who, grovelling in the mire of Xanthus' banks,   150
His hands bound at his back, and both his eyes
Turned up to heaven as one resolved to die,
Our Phrygian shepherds haled within the gates

---

123 *Myrmidons* followers of Achilles.
129 *Atrides* Agamemnon, son of Atreus.
134 *Gave . . . voices* voted.
145 *ticing* enticing. *Hermes' pipe* a
musical instrument with power to en-
chant, as Hermes had with it put to sleep
the hundred-eyed monster, Argus.
150 *Who* i.e., Sinon.

And brought unto the court of Priamus,
To whom he uséd action so pitiful,   155
Looks so remorseful, vows so forcible,
As therewithal the old man, overcome,
Kissed him, embraced him, and unloosed his bands.
And then—O Dido, pardon me!
Dido.   Nay, leave not here. Resolve me of the rest.   160
Æneas.   O, th'enchanting words of that base slave
Made him to think Epeus' pine-tree horse
A sacrifice t'appease Minerva's wrath,
The rather, for that one Laocoön,
Breaking a spear upon his hollow breast,   165
Was with two wingéd serpents stung to death.
Whereat aghast, we were commanded straight
With reverence to draw it into Troy,
In which unhappy work was I employed.
These hands did help to hale it to the gates,   170
Through which it could not enter, 'twas so huge.
O, had it never entered, Troy had stood!
But Priamus, impatient of delay,
Enforced a wide breach in that rampired wall,
Which thousand battering rams could never pierce,   175
And so came in this fatal instrument;
At whose accharséd feet, as overjoyed,
We banqueted till, overcome with wine,
Some surfeited and others soundly slept.
Which Sinon viewing, caused the Greekish spies   180
To haste to Tenedos and tell the camp.
Then he unlocked the horse, and suddenly
From out his entrails Neoptolemus,
Setting his spear upon the ground, leaped forth,
And after him a thousand Grecians more,   185
In whose stern faces shined the quenchless fire
That after burnt the pride of Asia.
By this, the camp was come unto the walls,
And through the breach did march into the streets,
Where, meeting with the rest, 'kill, kill,' they cried.   190
Frighted with this confuséd noise, I rose,
And looking from a turret, might behold
Young infants swimming in their parents' blood,
Headless carcasses piled up in heaps,
Virgins half-dead, dragged by their golden hair   195
And with main force flung on a ring of pikes,
Old men with swords thrust through their agéd sides,
Kneeling for mercy to a Greekish lad,
Who with steel pole-axes dashed out their brains.

183 *Neoptolemus* son of Achilles, also called Pyrrhus.

Then buckled I mine armor, drew my sword,   200
And thinking to go down, came Hector's ghost,
With ashy visage, blueish sulphur eyes,
His arms torn from his shoulders, and his breast
Furrowed with wounds, and—that which made me weep—
Thongs at his heels, by which Achilles' horse   205
Drew him in triumph through the Greekish camp,
Burst from the earth, crying, 'Æneas fly!
Troy is afire! The Grecians have the town!'
Dido.   O Hector, who weeps not to hear thy name?
Æneas.   Yet flung I forth, and desperate of my life,   210
Ran in the thickest throngs, and with this sword
Sent many of their savage ghosts to hell.
At last came Pyrrhus, fell and full of ire,
His harness dropping blood, and on his spear
The mangled head of Priam's youngest son,   215
And after him his band of Myrmidons,
With balls of wild fire in their murdering paws,
Which made the funeral flame that burned fair Troy
All which hemmed me about, crying, 'This is he.'
Dido.   Ah, how could poor Æneas scape their hands?   220
Æneas.   My mother, Venus, jealous of my health,
Conveyed me from their crooked nets and bands.
So I escaped the furious Pyrrhus' wrath,
Who then ran to the palace of the king,
And at Jove's altar finding Priamus,   225
About whose withered neck hung Hecuba,
Folding his hand in hers, and jointly both
Beating their breasts and falling on the ground,
He, with his falchion's point raised up at once,
And with Megæra's eyes, stared in their face,   230
Threat'ning a thousand deaths at every glance.
To whom the agèd king thus, trembling, spoke:
'Achilles' son, remember what I was,
Father of fifty sons, but they are slain;
Lord of my fortune, but my fortune's turned;   235
King of this city, but my Troy is fired;
And now am neither father, lord, nor king.
Yet who so wretched but desires to live?
O, let me live, great Neoptolemus!'
Not moved at all, but smiling at his tears,   240
This butcher, whilst his hands were yet held up,
Treading upon his breast, struck off his hands.
Dido.   O end, Æneas. I can hear no more.

222 *bands* bonds.
230 *Megæra* one of the three Furies
(also called Erinyes and Eumenides)
winged maidens with serpents in their
hair, who visited vengeance on mankind
for sin. Her two sister Furies were Tisiph-
one and Alecto.

Æneas.   At which the frantic queen leaped on his face,
    And in his eyelids hanging by the nails,   245
    A little while prolonged her husband's life.
    At last the soldiers pulled her by the heels
    And swung her howling in the empty air,
    Which sent an echo to the wounded king,
    Whereat he lifted up his bed-rid limbs,   250
    And would have grappled with Achilles' son,
    Forgetting both his want of strength and hands,
    Which he disdaining, whisked his sword about,
    And with the wind thereof the king fell down.
    Then from the navel to the throat at once   255
    He ripped old Priam, at whose latter gasp
    Jove's marble statue gan to bend the brow,
    As loathing Pyrrhus for this wicked act.
    Yet he, undaunted, took his father's flag
    And dipped it in the old king's chill-cold blood,   260
    And then in triumph ran into the streets,
    Through which he could not pass for slaughtered men.
    So, leaning on his sword, he stood stone still,
    Viewing the fire wherewith rich Ilion burned.
    By this, I got my father on my back,   265
    This young boy in mine arms, and by the hand
    Led fair Creusa, my belovèd wife.
    When thou, Achates, with thy sword mad'st way,
    And we were round environed with the Greeks,
    O there I lost my wife, and had not we   270
    Fought manfully, I had not told this tale.
    Yet manhood would not serve. Of force we fled,
    And as we went unto our ships, thou knowest
    We saw Cassandra sprawling in the streets,
    Whom Ajax ravished in Diana's fane,   275
    Her cheeks swollen with sighs, her hair all rent,
    Whom I took up to bear unto our ships.
    But suddenly the Grecians followed us,
    And I, alas, was forced to let her lie.
    Then got we to our ships, and being aboard,   280
    Polyxena cried out, 'Æneas, stay!
    The Greeks pursue me. Stay and take me in!'
    Moved with her voice, I leaped into the sea,
    Thinking to bear her on my back aboard,
    For all our ships were launched into the deep,   285

274 *Cassandra* daughter of Priam, endowed by Apollo with the gift of prophecy and punished by him with the inability to make her words believed.

275 *Diana's fane* the temple of Diana, goddess of chastity. *Ajax* one of the more ferocious of the Greek warriors.

281 *Polyxena* daughter of Priam and Hecuba, beloved by Achilles.

And as I swam, she, standing on the shore,
Was by the cruel Myrmidons surprised
And after by that Pyrrhus sacrificed.
Dido.   I die with melting ruth. Æneas, leave.
Anna.   O, what became of agèd Hecuba?   290
Iarbus.   How got Æneas to the fleet again?
Dido.   But how scaped Helen, she that caused this war?
Æneas.   Achates, speak. Sorrow hath tired me quite.
Achates.   What happened to the queen we cannot show.
We hear they led her captive into Greece.   295
As for Æneas, he swam quickly back,
And Helena betrayed Deiphobus,
Her lover, after Alexander died,
And so was reconciled to Menelaus.
Dido.   O, had that ticing strumpet ne'er been born!   300
Trojan, thy ruthful tale hath made me sad.
Come, let us think upon some pleasing sport
To rid me from these melancholy thoughts.
                    Exeunt all [except Ascanius].

    Enter Venus [with Cupid] at another door and takes Ascanius
            by the sleeve [as he is going off].
Venus.   Fair child, stay thou with Dido's waiting maid.
I'll give thee sugar-almonds, sweet conserves,   305
A silver girdle, and a golden purse,
And this young prince shall be thy playfellow.
Ascanius.   Are you Queen Dido's son?
Cupid.   Ay, and my mother gave me this fine bow.
Ascanius.   Shall I have such a quiver and a bow?   310
Venus.   Such bow, such quiver, and such golden shafts
Will Dido give to sweet Ascanius.
For Dido's sake I take thee in my arms
And stick these spangled feathers in thy hat.
Eat comfits in mine arms and I will sing.   [*She sings.*]   315
Now is he fast asleep, and in this grove
Amongst green brakes I'll lay Ascanius
And strew him with sweet-smelling violets,
Blushing roses, purple hyacinth.
These milk white doves shall be his centronels,   320
Who, if that any seek to do him hurt,
Will quickly fly to Cytherea's fist.

---

288 *Pyrrhus sacrificed* When the Greeks touched the coast of Thrace on their voyage home from Troy, the ghost of Achilles appeared to demand that Polyxena be sacrificed to him. Pyrrhus slew her on his father's tomb.

297 *Deiphobus* son of Priam and Hecuba who married Helen after the death of her lover, Paris. He was slain by Menelaus, Helen's husband, after the fall of Troy.

298 *Alexander* another name for Paris.

320 *centronels* guardians.

Now, Cupid, turn thee to Ascanius' shape
And go to Dido, who, instead of him,
Will set thee on her lap and play with thee.   325
Then touch her white breast with this arrow head,
That she may dote upon Æneas' love,
And by that means repair his broken ships,
Victual his soldiers, give him wealthy gifts,
And he at last depart to Italy,   330
Or else in Carthage make his kingly throne.
Cupid.   I will, fair mother, and so play my part
As every touch shall wound Queen Dido's heart.

                                                 [*Exit.*]

Venus.   Sleep, my sweet nephew, in these cooling shades,
Free from the murmur of these running streams,   335
The cry of beasts, the rattling of the winds,
Or whisking of these leaves. All shall be still
And nothing interrupt thy quiet sleep,
Till I return and take thee hence again.

                                                 Exit.

Enter Cupid alone, [disguised as Ascanius].   III,i.
Cupid.   Now, Cupid, cause the Carthaginian queen
To be enamored of thy brother's looks.
Convey this golden arrow in thy sleeve,
Lest she imagine thou art Venus' son,
And when she strokes thee softly on the head,   5
Then shall I touch her breast and conquer her.
                    Enter Iarbas, Anna, and Dido.
Iarbas.   How long, fair Dido, shall I pine for thee?
'Tis not enough that thou dost grant me love,
But that I may enjoy what I desire.
That love is childish which consists in words.   10
Dido.   Iarbas, know that thou of all my wooers—
And yet have I had many mightier kings—
Hast had the greatest favors I could give.
I fear me, Dido hath been counted light
In being too familiar with Iarbas,   15
Albeit the gods do know no wanton thought
Had ever residence in Dido's breast.
Iarbas.   But Dido is the favor I request.
Dido.   Fear not, Iarbas; Dido may be thine.
Anna.   Look, sister, how Æneas' little son   20
Plays with your garments and embraceth you.
Cupid.   No, Dido will not take me in her arms;

I shall not be her son; she loves me not.
Dido.   Weep not, sweet boy; thou shalt be Dido's son.
Sit in my lap and let me hear thee sing.   25
                                        [Cupid sings.]

No more, my child. Now talk another while,
And tell me where learn'dst thou this pretty song.
Cupid.   My cousin Helen taught it me in Troy.
Dido.   How lovely is Ascanius when he smiles.
Cupid.   Will Dido let me hang about her neck?   30
Dido.   Ay, wag, and give thee leave to kiss her too.
Cupid.   What will you give me now? I'll have this fan.
Dido.   Take it, Ascanius, for thy father's sake.
Iarbas.   Come, Dido, leave Ascanius. Let us walk.
Dido.   Go thou away. Ascanius shall stay.   35
Iarbas.   Ungentle queen, is this thy love to me?
Dido.   O stay, Iarbas, and I'll go with thee.
Cupid.   And if my mother go, I'll follow her.
Dido.   Why stay'st thou here? Thou art no love of mine.
Iarbas.   Iarbas die, seeing she abandons thee.   40
Dido.   No; live Iarbas. What has thou deserved
   That I should say thou art no love of mine?
   Something thou hast deserved. Away, I say!
   Depart from Carthage. Come not in my sight.
Iarbas.   Am I not king of rich Gætulia?   45
Dido.   Iarbas, pardon me and stay awhile.
Cupid.   Mother, look here.
Dido.   What tell'st thou me of rich Gætulia?
   Am I not queen of Libya? Then depart.
Iarbas.   I go to feed the humor of my love,   50
   Yet not from Carthage for a thousand worlds.
Dido.   Iarbas!
Iarbas.   Doth Dido call me back?
Dido.   No; but I charge thee never look on me.
Iarbas.   Then pull out both mine eyes, or let me die.
                                        Exit Iarbas.

Anna.   Wherefore doth Dido bid Iarbas go?   55
Dido.   Because his loathsome sight offends mine eye,
   And in my thoughts is shrined another love.
   O Anna, didst thou know how sweet love were,
   Full soon wouldst thou abjure this single life.
Anna.   Poor soul, I know too well the sour of love.   60
   O, that Iarbas could but fancy me!   *[Aside.]*
Dido.   Is not Æneas fair and beautiful?
Anna.   Yes, and Iarbas foul and favorless.
Dido.   Is he not eloquent in all his speech?
Anna.   Yes, and Iarbas rude and rustical.   65
Dido.   Name not Iarbas. But, sweet Anna, say,

Is not Æneas worthy Dido's love?
Anna.   O sister, were you empress of the world,
  Æneas well deserves to be your love.
  So lovely is he that where'er he goes   70
  The people swarm to gaze him in the face.
Dido.   But tell them none shall gaze on him but I,
  Lest their gross eye-beams taint my lover's cheeks.
  Anna, good sister Anna, go for him,
  Lest with these sweet thoughts I melt clean away.   75
Anna.   Then, sister, you'll abjure Iarbas' love?
Dido.   Yet must I hear that loathsome name again?
  Run for Æneas, or I'll fly to him.
                                                    Exit Anna.
Cupid.   You shall not hurt my father when he comes.
Dido.   No; for thy sake I'll love thy father well.   80
  O dull-conceited Dido, that till now
  Didst never think Æneas beautiful!
  But now, for quittance of this oversight,
  I'll make me bracelets of his golden hair;
  His glistering eyes shall be my looking-glass,   85
  His lips an altar, where I'll offer up
  As many kisses as the sea hath sands.
  Instead of music I will hear him speak.
  His looks shall be my only library,
  And thou, Æneas, Dido's treasury,   90
  In whose fair bosom I will lock more wealth
  Than twenty thousand Indias can afford.
  O, here he comes! Love, love, give Dido leave
  To be more modest than her thoughts admit,
  Lest I be made a wonder to the world.   95
      [*Enter Æneas, Achates, Sergestus, Ilioneus, and Cloanthus.*]
  Achates, how doth Carthage please your lord?
Achates.   That will Æneas show your majesty.
Dido.   Æneas, art thou there?
Æneas.   I understand your highness sent for me.
Dido.   No; but now thou art here, tell me in sooth   100
  In what might Dido highly pleasure thee.
Æneas.   So much have I received at Dido's hands
  As, without blushing, I can ask no more.
  Yet, queen of Afric, are my ships unrigged,
  My sails all rent in sunder with the wind,   105
  My oars broken, and my tackling lost,
  Yea, all my navy split with rocks and shelves;
  Nor stern nor anchor have our maimèd fleet;

III,i.
  107 *shelves* sandbanks.

Our masts the furious winds struck overboard;
Which piteous wants if Dido will supply,   110
We will account her author of our lives.
Dido.   Æneas, I'll repair thy Trojan ships,
Conditionally that thou wilt stay with me
And let Achates sail to Italy.
I'll give thee tackling made of rivelled gold,   115
Wound on the barks of odoriferous trees,
Oars of massy ivory, full of holes
Through which the water shall delight to play.
Thy anchors shall be hewed from crystal rocks
Which, if thou lose, shall shine above the waves;   120
The masts whereon thy swelling sails shall hang,
Hollow pyramidès of silver plate;
The sails of folded lawn, where shall be wrought
The wars of Troy, but not Troy's overthrow.
For ballace, empty Dido's treasury.   125
Take what ye will, but leave Æneas here.
Achates, thou shalt be so meanly clad
As sea-born nymphs shall swarm about thy ships
And wanton mermaids court thee with sweet songs,
Flinging in favors of more sovereign worth   130
Than Thetis hangs about Apollo's neck,
So that Æneas may but stay with me.
Æneas.   Wherefore would Dido have Æneas stay?
Dido.   To war against my bordering enemies.
Æneas, think not Dido is in love,   135
For if that any man could conquer me,
I had been wedded ere Æneas came.
See where the pictures of my suitors hang;
And are not these as fair as fair may be?
Achates.   I saw this man at Troy, ere Troy was sacked.   140
Æneas.   I this in Greece when Paris stole fair Helen.
Ilioneus.   This man and I were at Olympus' games.
Sergestus.   I know this face. He is a Persian born.
I traveled with him to Ætolia.
Cloanthus.   And I in Athens with this gentleman,   145
Unless I be deceived, disputed once.
Dido.   But speak, Æneas; know you none of these?
Æneas.   No, madam, but it seems that these are kings.
Dido.   All these and others which I never saw
Have been most urgent suitors for my love.   150
Some came in person; others sent their legates;
Yet none obtained me; I am free from all,
And yet, God knows, entangled unto one.
This was an orator and thought by words

115 *rivelled* twisted.   125 *ballace* ballast.

To compass me, but yet he was deceived;   155
And this a Spartan courtier, vain and wild,
But his fantastic humors pleased not me.
This was Alcion, a musician,
But played he ne'er so sweet, I let him go.
This was the wealthy king of Thessaly,   160
But I had gold enough and cast him off;
This Meleager's son, a warlike prince,
But weapons gree not with my tender years.
The rest are such as all the world well knows,
Yet now I swear, by heaven and him I love,   165
I was as far from love as they from hate.
Æneas.   O, happy shall he be whom Dido loves.
Dido.   Then never say that thou art miserable,
Because it may be thou shalt be my love.
Yet boast not of it, for I love thee not.   170
And yet I hate thee not. O, if I speak,
I shall betray myself. [*Aside.*] Æneas speak.
We two will go a-hunting in the woods,
But not so much for thee—thou art but one—
As for Achates and his followers.   175

                                               Exeunt.

                    Enter Juno to Ascanius, asleep.   III,ii.
Juno.   Here lies my hate, Æneas' cursèd brat,
The boy wherein false destiny delights,
The heir of fury, the favorite of the Fates,
That ugly imp that shall outwear my wrath
And wrong my deity with high disgrace.   5
But I will take another order now
And race th'eternal register of time.
Troy shall no more call him her second hope,
Nor Venus triumph in his tender youth,
For here, in spite of heaven, I'll murder him   10
And feed infection with his let-out life.
Say, Paris, now shall Venus have the ball?
Say, vengeance, now shall her Ascanius die?

155 *compass* possess.
162 *Meleager's son* The Meleager who
slew the Calydonian boar is not reported
in any Greek legend to have had a son.
163 *gree* agree.
III,ii.
3 *Fates* the Parcae or Moirae, three
sisters (Clotho, Lachesis and Atropos) who
governed human life.
7 *race* raze, erase.
11 *feed . . . life* i.e., cause the air to
be infected by his corpse.

O, no! God wot, I cannot watch my time,
Nor quit good turns with double fee down told.   15
Tut, I am simple, without mind to hurt,
And have no gall at all to grieve my foes,
But lustful Jove and his adulterous child
Shall find it written on confusion's front,
That only Juno rules in Rhamnus' town.   20
                    Enter Venus.
Venus.   What should this mean? My doves are back returned,
Who warn me of such danger prest at hand
To harm my sweet Ascanius' lovely life.
Juno, my mortal foe, what make you here?
Avaunt, old witch, and trouble not my wits.   25
Juno.   Fie, Venus, that such causeless words of wrath
Should e'er defile so fair a mouth as thine.
Are not we both sprung of celestial race
And banquet as two sisters with the gods?
Why is it then displeasure should disjoin   30
Whom kindred and acquaintance co-unites?
Venus.   Out, hateful hag! Thou wouldst have slain my son,
Had not my doves discovered thy intent.
But I will tear thy eyes from forth thy head
And feast the birds with their blood-shotten balls,   35
If thou but lay thy fingers on my boy.
Juno.   Is this then all the thanks that I shall have
For saving him from snakes' and serpents' stings
That would have killed him, sleeping as he lay?
What though I was offended with thy son,   40
And wrought him mickle woe on sea and land,
When, for the hate of Trojan Ganymede
That was advancèd by my Hebe's shame,
And Paris' judgment of the heavenly ball,
I mustered all the winds unto his wrack   45
And urged each element to his annoy.
Yet now I do repent me of his ruth
And wish that I had never wronged him so.
Bootless, I saw, it was to war with fate
That hath so many unresisted friends,   50
Wherefore I changed my counsel with the time
And planted love where envy erst had sprung.

---

20 *Rhamnus' town* Rhamnusia in northern Attica, famous for its temple to Nemesis, and therefore associated with vengeance.

22 *prest* ready.

32 *son* i.e., grandson, Ascanius.

40 *son* Æneas.

41 *mickle* much.

42–43 *Ganymede . . . shame* Hebe, daughter of Juno and Jupiter, had been replaced by Ganymede as cupbearer to the gods.

47 *ruth* pitiful sorrows.

49 *Bootless* in vain.

50 *unresisted* irresistible.

Venus.   Sister of Jove, if that thy love be such
     As these thy protestations do paint forth,
     We two as friends one fortune will divide.   55
     Cupid shall lay his arrows in thy lap
     And to a scepter change his golden shafts;
     Fancy and modesty shall live as mates
     And thy fair peacocks by my pigeons perch.
     Love my Æneas, and desire is thine;   60
     The day, the night, my swans, my sweets are thine.
Juno.   More than melodious are these words to me,
     That overcloy my soul with their content.
     Venus, sweet Venus, how may I deserve
     Such amorous favors at thy beauteous hand?   65
     But that thou mayst more easily perceive
     How highly I do prize this amity,
     Hark to a motion of eternal league,
     Which I will make in quittance of thy love.
     Thy son, thou know'st, with Dido now remains   70
     And feeds his eyes with favors of her court;
     She likewise in admiring spends her time
     And cannot talk nor think of aught but him.
     Why should not they then join in marriage
     And bring forth mighty kings to Carthage town,   75
     Whom casualty of sea hath made such friends?
     And, Venus, let there be a match confirmed
     Betwixt these two whose loves are so alike,
     And both our deities, conjoined in one,
     Shall chain felicity unto their throne.   80
Venus.   Well could I like this reconcilement's means,
     But much I fear my son will ne'er consent,
     Whose armèd soul, already on the sea,
     Darts forth her light to Lavinia's shore.
Juno.   Fair queen of love, I will divorce these doubts   85
     And find the way to weary such fond thoughts.
     This day they both a-hunting forth will ride
     Into these woods adjoining to these walls,
     When in the midst of all their gamesome sports,
     I'll make the clouds dissolve their watery works   90
     And drench Silvanus' dwellings with their showers.
     Then in one cave the queen and he shall meet
     And interchangeably discourse their thoughts,
     Whose short conclusion will seal up their hearts
     Unto the purpose which we now propound.   95
Venus.   Sister, I see you savor of my wiles.
     Be it as you will have it for this once.
     Meantime Ascanius shall be my charge,

60 *desire* i.e., Cupid.   91 *Silvanus' dwellings* the woods.

Whom I will bear to Ida in mine arms,
And couch him in Adonis' purple down.   100

Exeunt.

III,iii.

*Enter Dido, Æneas, Anna, Iarbas, Achates, [Cupid as Ascanius],
and Followers.*

Dido. Æneas, think not but I honor thee
That thus in person go with thee to hunt.
My princely robes, thou see'st, are laid aside,
Whose glittering pomp Diana's shrouds supplies,
All fellows now, disposed alike to sport.   5
The woods are wide, and we have store of game.
Fair Trojan, hold my golden bow awhile
Until I gird my quiver to my side.
Lords, go before. We two must talk alone.
Iarbas. Ungentle, can she wrong Iarbas so?   10
I'll die before a stranger have that grace.
'We two will talk alone'—what words be these?   [*Aside.*]
Dido. What makes Iarbas here of all the rest?
We could have gone without your company.
Æneas. But love and duty led him on perhaps,   15
To press beyond acceptance to your sight.
Iarbas. Why, man of Troy, do I offend thine eyes?
Or art thou grieved thy betters press so nigh?
Dido. How now, Gætulian, are ye grown so brave
To challenge us with your comparisons?   20
Peasant, go seek companions like thyself,
And meddle not with any that I love.
Æneas, be not moved at what he says,
For otherwhile he will be out of joint.
Iarbas. Women may wrong by privilege of love,   25
But should that man of men—Dido except—
Have taunted me in these opprobrious terms,
I would have either drunk his dying blood,
Or else I would have given my life in gage.

99 *Ida* This is the Mt. Ida in Asia Minor where the judgment of Paris took place, and from which the gods watched the war of Troy. It is not to be confused with another Mt. Ida on the isle of Crete, where Jupiter grew up and which was sacred to him.

100 *in . . . down* i.e., among the anemones, purple flowers which, according to legend, had sprung from the blood of the slain Adonis.

III,iii.

4 *Diana's shrouds* costume of a huntress (Diana was goddess of the hunt as well as of the moon and of chastity).

24 *otherwhile* from time to time. *out of joint* distempered, unruly.

29 *in gage* as pledge of sincerity.

Dido.   Huntsmen, why pitch you not your toils apace   30
    And rouse the light-foot deer from forth their lair?
Anna.   Sister, see. See Ascanius in his pomp,
    Bearing his hunt-spear bravely in his hand.
Dido.   Yea, little son, are you so forward now?
Cupid.   Ay, mother. I shall one day be a man   35
    And better able unto other arms;
    Meantime these wanton weapons serve my war,
    Which I will break betwixt a lion's jaws.
Dido.   What! Dar'st thou look a lion in the face?
Cupid.   Ay, and outface him to, do what he can.   40
Anna.   How like his father speaketh he in all.
Æneas.   And mought I live to see him sack rich Thebes
    And load his spear with Grecian princes' heads,
    Then would I wish me with Anchises' tomb
    And dead to honor that hath brought me up.   45
Iarbas.   And might I live to see thee shipped away
    And hoist aloft on Neptune's hideous hills,
    Then would I wish me in fair Dido's arms
    And dead to scorn that hath pursued me so.   [*Aside.*]
Æneas.   Stout friend, Achates, dost thou know this wood?   50
Achates.   As I remember, here you shot the deer
    That saved your famished soldiers' lives from death,
    When first you set your foot upon the shore,
    And here we met fair Venus, virgin-like,
    Bearing her bow and quiver at her back.   55
Æneas.   O, how these irksome labors now delight
    And overjoy my thoughts with their escape.
    Who would not undergo all kind of toil
    To be well stored with such a winter's tale?
Dido.   Æneas, leave these dumps and let's away,   60
    Some to the mountains, some unto the soil,
    You to the valleys—thou [*To Iarbas.*] unto the house.
                              Exeunt all [except Iarbas].
Iarbas.   Ay, this it is which wounds me to the death,
    To see a Phrygian, forfeit to the sea,
    Preferred before a man of majesty.   65
    O love! O hate! O cruel women's hearts,
    That imitate the moon in every change
    And like the planets ever love to range.
    What shall I do, thus wrongèd with disdain?
    Revenge me on Æneas or on her?   70
    On her? Fond man, that were to war 'gainst heaven

---

37 *wanton* childish.
42 *mought* might.
44 *Anchises* the father of Æneas.
61 *soil* water. For a deer, in hunting

terms, to "take soil" was for him to
seek refuge in the water.
64 *forfeit to the sea* i.e., who has been
at the mercy of the sea.

And with one shaft provoke ten thousand darts.
This Trojan's end will be thy envy's aim,
Whose blood will reconcile thee to content
And make love drunken with thy sweet desire.   75
But Dido, that now holdeth him so dear,
Will die with very tidings of his death.
But time will discontinue her content
And mold her mind unto new fancy's shapes.
O God of heaven, turn the hand of fate   80
Unto the happy day of my delight!
And then—what then? Iarbas shall but love.
So doth he now, though not with equal gain.
That resteth in the rival of my pain,
Who ne'er will cease to soar till he be slain.   85

                                                  Exit.

                                                  III,iv.
The storm. Enter Æneas and Dido in the cave, at several times.
Dido.   Æneas!
Æneas.   Dido!
Dido.   Tell me, dear love, how found you out this cave?
Æneas.   By chance, sweet queen, as Mars and Venus met.
Dido.   Why, that was in a net, where we are loose.
    And yet I am not free. O, would I were!   5
Æneas.   Why, what is it that Dido may desire
    And not obtain, be it in human power?
Dido.   The thing that I will die before I ask,
    And yet desire to have before I die.
Æneas.   It is not aught Æneas may achieve?   10
Dido.   Æneas? No—although his eyes do pierce.
Æneas.   What, hath Iarbas angered her in aught,
    And will she be avengèd on his life?
Dido.   Not angered me, except in angering thee.
Æneas.   Who, then, of all so cruel, may he be   15
    That should detain thy eye in his defects.
Dido.   The man that I do eye where'er I am,
    Whose amorous face, like Pæan, sparkles fire,
    Whenas he butts his beams on Flora's bed.
    Prometheus hath put on Cupid's shape,   20

III,iv.

SD *at several times* one after the other.
    4 *in a net* alluding to the well-known
story of the trapping of Mars and Venus
in an iron net forged by Vulcan.

18 *Pæan* Apollo, the sun.
19 *Flora's bed* the earth.
20 *Prometheus* the Titan who brought
fire to man.

And I must perish in his burning arms.
Æneas, O Æneas, quench these flames.
Æneas.   What ails my queen? Is she fall'n sick of late?
Dido.   Not sick, my love—but sick I must conceal
The torment that it boots me not reveal.   [*Aside.*]   25
And yet I'll speak. And yet I'll hold my peace.
Do shame her worst, I will disclose my grief.
Æneas, thou art he. What did I say?
Something it was that now I have forgot.
Æneas.   What means fair Dido by this doubtful speech?   30
Dido.   Nay, nothing. But Æneas loves me not.
Æneas.   Æneas' thoughts dare not ascend so high
As Dido's heart, which monarchs might not scale.
Dido.   It was because I saw no king like thee,
Whose golden crown might balance my content.   35
But now that I have found what to affect,
I follow one that loveth fame for me,
And rather had seem fair in Sirens' eyes
Than to the Carthage queen that dies for him.
Æneas.   If that your majesty can look so low   40
As my despisèd worths that shun all praise,
With this my hand I give to you my heart
And vow by all the gods of hospitality,
By heaven and earth, and my fair brother's bow,
By Paphos, Capys, and the purple sea   45
From whence my radiant mother did descend,
And by this sword that saved me from the Greeks,
Never to leave these new-uprearèd walls,
Whiles Dido lives and rules in Juno's town,
Never to like or love any but her.   50
Dido.   What more than Delian music do I hear,
That calls my soul from forth his living seat
To move unto the measures of delight!
Kind clouds that sent forth such a courteous storm
As made disdain to fly to fancy's lap!   55
Stout love, in mine arms make thy Italy,
Whose crown and kingdom rests at thy command.
Sichæus, not Æneas be thou called,
The king of Carthage, not Anchises' son.
Hold. Take these jewels at thy lover's hand,   60
                                        [*She gives him jewels.*]

---

44 *my fair brother* i.e., Cupid.
45 *Paphos* a town on the Cyprus coast
where Venus was said to have come after
her birth from the sea and where she
had her temple. *Capys* the grandfather
of Æneas.

46 *did descend* was born.
51 *Delian* Delos was the birthplace of
Apollo, god of music.
58 *Sichæus* See note at II,i,80.

These golden bracelets, and this wedding ring
Wherewith my husband wooed me yet a maid,
And be thou king of Libya by my gift.

Exeunt to the cave.

Enter Achates, [Cupid as] Ascanius, Iarbas, and Anna.   IV,i.
Achates.   Did ever men see such a sudden storm,
　Or day so clear so suddenly o'ercast?
Iarbas.   I think some fell enchantress dwelleth here,
　That can call them forth whenas she please
　And dive into black tempests' treasury   5
　Whenas she means to mask the world with clouds.
Anna.   In all my life, I never knew the like.
　It hailed; it snowed; it lightened all at once.
Achates.   I think it was the devil's revelling night,
　There was such hurly-burly in the heavens.   10
　Doubtless Apollo's axle-tree is cracked,
　Or agèd Atlas' shoulder out of joint,
　The motion was so over-violent.
Iarbas.   In all this coil, where have ye left the queen?
Cupid.   Nay, where's my warlike father; can you tell?   15
Anna.   Behold where both of them come forth the cave.
Iarbas.   Come forth the cave? Can heaven endure this sight?
　Iarbas, curse that unrevenging Jove,
　Whose flinty darts slept in Typhœus' den,
　Whiles these adulterers surfeited with sin.   20
　Nature, why mad'st me not some poisonous beast,
　That with the sharpness of my edgèd sting
　I might have staked them both unto the earth,
　Whilst they were sporting in this darksome cave.
　　　　　　[*Enter Æneas and Dido.*]
Æneas.   The air is clear and southern winds are whist.   25
　Come, Dido, let us hasten to the town,
　Since gloomy Æolus doth cease to frown.
Dido.   Achates and Ascanius, well met.
Æneas.   Fair Anna, how escaped you from the shower?
Anna.   As others did, by running to the wood.   30

IV,i.

　4 *them* i.e., the elements which make
up the storm.

　8 *lightened* flashed lightning.

　11 *Apollo's axle-tree* the axis on which
the sun was believed to rotate.

　14 *coil* commotion.

19 *Typhœus' den* Mt. Ætna, where
Jupiter forged his lightning darts, and
beneath which he had imprisoned the
hundred-headed monster Typhœus.

　25 *whist* silent.

　27 *Æolus* See note at I,i,58.

Dido.   But where were you, Iarbas, all this while?
Iarbas.   Not with Æneas in the ugly cave.
Dido.   I see Æneas sticketh in your mind,
But I will soon put by that stumbling-block
And quell those hopes that thus employ your cares.   35

                                    Exeunt.

✳

                 Enter Iarbas to Sacrifice.   IV,ii.
Iarbas.   Come, servants, come; bring forth the sacrifice,
That I may pacify that gloomy Jove
Whose empty altars have enlarged our ills.
    [*Enter servants who bring in the sacrifice and then depart.*]
Eternal Jove, great master of the clouds,
Father of gladness and all frolic thoughts,   5
That with thy gloomy hand corrects the heaven
When airy creatures war amongst themselves,
Hear, hear, O hear Iarbas' plaining prayers,
Whose hideous echoes make the welkin howl
And all the woods Eliza to resound!   10
The woman that thou willed us entertain,
Where, straying in our borders up and down,
She craved a hide of ground to build a town,
With whom we did divide both laws and land,
And all the fruits that plenty else sends forth,   15
Scorning our loves and royal marriage rites,
Yields up her beauty to a stranger's bed,
Who, having wrought her shame, is straightway fled.
Now, if thou beest a pitying god of power,
On whom ruth and compassion ever waits,   20
Redress these wrongs and warn him to his ships,
That now afflicts me with his flattering eyes.
                Enter Anna.
Anna.   How now, Iarbas! At your prayers so hard?
Iarbas.   Ay, Anna. Is there aught you would with me?
Anna.   Nay, no such weighty business of import   25
But may be slacked until another time.

IV,ii.

10 *Eliza* Dido was also known as Elissa, but the use of this name here is probably intended as praise of Queen Elizabeth.

11–13 *woman . . . town* When Dido came to Africa, fleeing from her native kingdom of Tyre, where her husband,

Sichæus had been murdered, she purchased as much land as could be enclosed within the hide of a bull. By cutting the hide into narrow strips, she was able to acquire a considerable plot of land, on which she built the city of Carthage.

26 *slacked* neglected.

Yet, if you would partake with me the cause
Of this devotion that detaineth you,
I would be thankful for such courtesy.
Iarbas.   Anna, against this Trojan do I pray,   30
  Who seeks to rob me of thy sister's love
  And dive into her heart by colored looks.
Anna.   Alas, poor king, that labors so in vain
  For her that so delighteth in thy pain.
  Be ruled by me and seek some other love,   35
  Whose yielding heart may yield thee more relief.
Iarbas.   Mine eye is fixed where fancy cannot start.
  O leave me, leave me to my silent thoughts
  That register the numbers of my ruth,
  And I will either move the thoughtless flint   40
  Or drop out both mine eyes in drizzling tears,
  Before my sorrow's tide have any stint.
Anna.   I will not leave Iarbas, whom I love,
  In this delight of dying pensiveness.
  Away with Dido! Anna be thy song,   45
  Anna that doth admire thee more than heaven.
Iarbas.   I may nor will list to such loathsome change
  That intercepts the course of my desire.
  Servants, come fetch these empty vessels here,
  For I will fly from these alluring eyes   50
  That do pursue my peace where'er it goes.
                    Exit. [*Servants enter and carry out vessels.*]
Anna.   Iarbas, stay! Loving Iarbas, stay,
  For I have honey to present thee with.
  Hard-hearted, wilt not deign to hear me speak?
  I'll follow thee with outcries ne'ertheless   55
  And strew thy walks with my dishevelled hair.
                                                      Exit.

                    Enter Æneas alone.   IV,iii.
Æneas.   Carthage, my friendly host, adieu,
  Since destiny doth call me from the shore.
  Hermes this night, descending in a dream,
  Hath summoned me to fruitful Italy.
  Jove wills it so. My mother wills it so.   5
  Let my Phœnissa grant, and then I go.

37 *fancy cannot start* love cannot be   **IV,iii.**
loosened.   6 *Phoenissa* Phoenician (Dido).
  39 *register . . . ruth* count over my
lamentations.

Grant she or no, Æneas must away,
Whose golden fortunes, clogged with courtly ease,
Cannot ascend to fame's immortal house
Or banquet in bright honor's burnished hall,   10
Till he hath furrowed Neptune's glassy fields
And cut a passage through his topless hills.
Achates, come forth! Sergestus, Ilioneus,
Cloanthus, haste away! Æneas calls.
        Enter Achates, Cloanthus, Sergestus, and Ilioneus.
Achates.   What wills our lord, or wherefore did he call?   15
Æneas.   The dreams, brave mates, that did beset my bed,
When sleep but newly had embraced the night,
Commands me leave these unrenownèd realms,
Whereas nobility abhors to stay,
And none but base Æneas will abide.   20
  Aboard, aboard, since Fates do bid aboard,
And slice the sea with sable-colored ships,
On whom the nimble winds may all day wait,
And follow them, as footmen, through the deep.
Yet Dido casts her eyes like anchors out,   25
To stay my fleet from loosing forth the bay.
'Come back. Come back,' I hear her cry afar,
'And let me link thy body to my lips,
That, tied together by the striving tongues,
We may as one sail into Italy.'   30
Achates.   Banish that ticing dame from forth your mouth,
And follow your foreseeing stars in all.
This is no life for men-at-arms to live,
Where daliance doth consume a soldier's strength,
And wanton motions of alluring eyes   35
Effeminate our minds, inured to war.
Ilioneus.   Why, let us build a city of our own,
And not stand lingering here for amorous looks.
Will Dido raise old Priam forth his grave
And build the town again the Greeks did burn?   40
No, no; she cares not how we sink or swim,
So she may have Æneas in her arms.
Cloanthus.   To Italy, sweet friends, to Italy!
We will not stay a minute longer here.
Æneas.   Trojans aboard, and I will follow you.   45
                        [*Exeunt all but Æneas.*]
I fain would go, yet beauty calls me back.
To leave her so and not once say farewell
Were to transgress against all laws of love,
But if I use such ceremonious thanks
As parting friends accustom on the shore,   50

21 *Fates* See note at III,ii,3.   31 *ticing* enticing.

Her silver arms will coll me round about
And tears of pearl cry, 'Stay, Æneas, stay.'
Each word she says will then contain a crown,
And every speech be ended with a kiss.
I may not dure this female drudgery.   55
To sea, Æneas! Find out Italy!

                                     Exit.

                Enter Dido and Anna.   IV,iv.
Dido.   O, Anna, run unto the water side.
They say Æneas' men are going aboard;
It may be he will steal away with them.
Stay not to answer me. Run, Anna, run.

                              [Exit Anna.]

O foolish Trojans that would steal from hence   5
And not let Dido understand their drift.
I would have given Achates store of gold
And Ilioneus gum and Libyan spice,
The common soldiers rich embroidered coats
And silver whistles to control the winds,   10
Which Circes sent Sichæus when he lived.
Unworthy are they of a queen's reward.
See where they come. How might I do to chide?
      Enter Anna, with Æneas, Achates, Ilioneus, and Sergestus,
               [and Carthaginian Lords].
Anna.   'Twas time to run. Æneas had been gone;
The sails were hoising up and he aboard.   15
Dido.   Is this thy love to me?
Æneas.   O princely Dido, give me leave to speak.
I went to take my farewell of Achates.
Dido.   How haps Achates bid me not farewell?
Achates.   Because I feared your grace would keep me here.   20
Dido.   To rid thee of that doubt, aboard again.
I charge thee put to sea and stay not here.
Achates.   Then let Æneas go aboard with us.
Dido.   Get you aboard. Æneas means to stay.
Æneas.   The sea is rough. The winds blow to the shore.   25
Dido.   O false Æneas! Now the sea is rough,
But when you were aboard, 'twas calm enough.

51 *coll* embrace.
55 *female drudgery* subjection to a woman.

IV,iv.
   6 *drift* intention.

11 *Circes* variant of Circe, the notorious witch. *Sichæus* See note at II,i,80.
15 *hoising* being hoisted.
19 *haps* happens.

Thou and Achates meant to sail away.
Æneas.   Hath not the Carthage queen mine only son?
Thinks Dido I will go and leave him here?   30
Dido.   Æneas pardon me, for I forgot
That young Ascanius lay with me this night.
Love made me jealous. But to make amends,
Wear the imperial crown of Libya.
                              [*She gives him her crown and scepter.*]
Sway thou the Punic scepter in my stead,   35
And punish me, Æneas, for this crime.
Æneas.   This kiss shall be fair Dido's punishment.   [*He kisses her.*]
Dido.   O, how a crown becomes Æneas' head.
Stay here, Æneas, and command as king.
Æneas.   How vain am I to wear this diadem   40
And bear this golden scepter in my hand.
A burgonet of steel and not a crown,
A sword and not a scepter fits Æneas.
Dido.   O keep them still, and let me gaze my fill.
Now looks Æneas like immortal Jove.   45
O where is Ganymede to hold his cup
And Mercury to fly for what he calls?
Ten thousand Cupids hover in the air
And fan it in Æneas' lovely face.
O that the clouds were here, wherein thou fled'st,   50
That thou and I unseen might sport ourselves.
Heavens, envious of our joys, is waxen pale,
And when we whisper, then the stars fall down
To be partakers of our honey talk.
Æneas.   O Dido, patroness of all our lives,   55
When I leave thee, death be my punishment.
Swell, raging seas. Frown wayward destinies.
Blow winds. Threaten ye rocks and sandy shelves.
This is the harbor that Æneas seeks.
Let's see what tempests can annoy me now.   60
Dido.   Not all the world can take thee from mine arms.
Æneas may command as many Moors
As in the sea are little water drops.
And now—to make experience of my love—
Fair sister Anna, lead my lover forth   65
And, seated on my jennet, let him ride
As Dido's husband through the Punic streets,
And will my guard with Mauritanian darts
To wait upon him as their sovereign lord.
Anna.   What if the citizens repine thereat?   70
Dido.   Those that dislike what Dido gives in charge,

42 *burgonet* a light helmet.   70 *repine* protest.
50 *fled'st* i.e., as he fled from Troy.

Command my guard to slay for their offence.
Shall vulgar peasants storm at what I do?
The ground is mine that gives them sustenance,
The air wherein they breathe, the water, fire,   75
All that they have, their lands, their goods, their lives;
And I, the goddess of all these, command
Æneas ride as Carthaginian king.
Achates.   Æneas, for his parentage, deserves
As large a kingdom as is Libya.   80
Æneas.   Ay, and unless the destinies be false,
I shall be planted in as rich a land.
Dido.   Speak of no other land. This land is thine.
Dido is thine; henceforth I'll call thee lord.
Do as I bid thee, sister. Lead the way,   85
And from a turret I'll behold my love.
Æneas.   Then here in me shall flourish Priam's race,
And thou and I, Achates, for revenge
For Troy, for Priam, for his fifty sons,
Our kinsmen's lives, and thousand guiltless souls,   90
Will lead an host against the hateful Greeks
And fire proud Lacedæmon o'er their heads.
                          *Exit, [with the other Trojans. Dido, **Anna,**
                          and the Carthaginian lords remain].*
Dido.   Speaks not Æneas like a conqueror?
O blessèd tempests that did drive him in!
O happy sand that made him run aground!   95
Henceforth you shall be our Carthage gods.
Ay, but it may be he will leave my love
And seek a foreign land called Italy.
O that I had a charm to keep the winds
Within the closure of a golden ball,   100
Or that the Tyrrhene sea were in mine arms,
That he might suffer shipwrack on my breast
As oft as he attempts to hoist up sail.
I must prevent him. Wishing will not serve.
Go, bid my nurse take young Ascanius   105
And bear him in the country to her house.
Æneas will not go without his son.
Yet, lest he should—for I am full of fear—
Bring me his oars, his tackling, and his sails.
                                        [Exit a Lord.]

What if I sink his ships? O, he'll frown.   110
Better he frown than I should die for grief.
I cannot see him frown; it may not be.
Armies of foes resolved to win this town,
Or impious traitors vowed to have my life,
Affright me not; only Æneas' frown   115

92 *Lacedæmon* Sparta.

Is that which terrifies poor Dido's heart.
Not bloody spears, appearing in the air,
Presage the downfall of my empery,
Nor blazing comets threaten Dido's death;
It is Æneas' frown that ends my days.   120
If he forsake me not, I never die,
For in his looks I see eternity,
And he'll make me immortal with a kiss.
      Enter a Lord, [with Attendants carrying tackling,
                    oars and sails].
Lord.   Your nurse is gone with young Ascanius,
And here's Æneas' tackling, oars and sails.   125
Dido.   Are these the sails that, in despite of me,
Packed with the winds to bear Æneas hence?
I'll hang ye in the chamber where I lie;
Drive if you can my house to Italy.
I'll set the casement open that the winds   130
May enter in and once again conspire
Against the life of me, poor Carthage queen.
But though he go, he stays in Carthage still;
And let rich Carthage fleet upon the seas,
So I may have Æneas in mine arms.   135
Is this the wood that grew in Carthage plains,
And would be toiling in the wat'ry billows
To rob their mistress of her Trojan guest?
O cursèd tree, had'st thou but wit or sense
To measure how I prize Æneas' love,   140
Thou wouldst have leaped from out the sailors' hands
And told me that Æneas meant to go.
And yet I blame thee not; thou art but wood.
The water, which our poets term a nymph,
Why did it suffer thee to touch her breast   145
And shrunk not back, knowing my love was there?
The water is an element, no nymph.
Why should I blame Æneas for his flight?
O Dido, blame not him, but break his oars.
These were the instruments which launched him forth.   150
There's not so much as this base tackling too,
But dares to heap up sorrow to my heart.
Was it not you that hoisèd up these sails?
Why burst you not, and they fell in the seas?
For this will Dido tie ye full of knots   155
And shear ye all asunder with her hands.
Now serve to chastise shipboys for their faults;
Ye shall no more offend the Carthage queen.

127 *Packed* conspired.   157 *serve . . . faults* Rope ends were
134 *fleet* float.   used for punishing seamen.
153 *hoisèd* hoisted.

Now let him hang my favors on his masts
And see if those will serve instead of sails.   160
For tackling, let him take the chains of gold
Which I bestowed upon his followers.
Instead of oars, let him use his hands
And swim to Italy. I'll keep these sure.
Come, bear them in.   165

Exit [with the others].

✳

Enter the Nurse, with Cupid for Ascanius.   IV,v.

Nurse. My Lord Ascanius, ye must go with me.
Cupid. Whither must I go? I'll stay with my mother.
Nurse. No, thou shalt go with me unto my house.
     I have an orchard that hath store of plums,
     Brown almonds, services, ripe figs, and dates,   5
     Dewberries, apples, yellow oranges,
     A garden where are bee-hives full of honey,
     Musk-roses, and a thousand sort of flowers;
     And in the midst doth run a silver stream,
     Where thou shalt see the red-gilled fishes leap,   10
     White swans, and many lovely water fowls.
     Now speak, Ascanius, will ye go or no?
Cupid. Come, come, I'll go. How far hence is your house?
Nurse. But hereby, child. We shall go thither straight.
Cupid. Nurse, I am weary; will you carry me?   15
Nurse. Ay, so you'll dwell with me and call me mother.
Cupid. So you'll love me, I care not if I do.
Nurse. That I might live to see this boy a man!
     How prettily he laughs. Go, ye wag!
     You'll be a twigger when you come to age.   20
     Say Dido what she will, I am not old.
     I'll be no more a widow. I am young;
     I'll have a husband or else a lover.
Cupid. A husband, and no teeth?
Nurse. O, what mean I to have such foolish thoughts!   25
     Foolish is love—a toy. O sacred love!
     If there be any heaven in earth, 'tis love,
     Especially in women of your years.
     Blush, blush for shame! Why shouldst thou think of love?
     A grave, and not a lover, fits thy age.   30

---

159 *favors* bits of needlework.

IV,v.

5 *services* pears.

6 *Dewberries* blackberries.

20 *twigger* producer of children. The word was generally applied to ewes who were prolific breeders.

A grave? Why? I may live a hundred years;
Fourscore is but a girl's age. Love is sweet.
My veins are withered and my sinews dry.
Why should I think of love, now I should die?
Cupid. Come, nurse.   35
Nurse. Well, if he come a wooing, he shall speed.
O, how unwise was I to say him nay.

Exeunt.

✳

V,i.

*Enter Æneas with a paper in his hand, drawing the platform
of the city; with him Achates, [Sergestus], Cloanthus, and
Ilioneus.*

Æneas. Triumph, my mates; our travels are at end.
Here will Æneas build a statelier Troy
Than that which grim Atrides overthrew.
Carthage shall vaunt her petty walls no more,
For I will grace them with a fairer frame   5
And clad her in a crystal livery
Wherein the day may evermore delight.
From golden India, Ganges will I fetch,
Whose wealthy streams may wait upon her towers
And triple-wise entrench her round about.   10
The sun from Egypt shall rich odors bring,
Wherewith his burning beams, like laboring bees
That load their thighs with Hybla's honey's spoils,
Shall here unburden their exhalèd sweets
And plant our pleasant suburbs with her fumes.   15
Achates. What length or breadth shall this brave town contain?
Æneas. Not past four thousand paces at the most.
Ilioneus. But what shall it be called? Troy, as before?
Æneas. That have I not determined with myself.
Cloanthus. Let it be termed Ænea, by your name.   20
Sergestus. Rather Ascania, by your little son.
Æneas. Nay, I will have it called Anchisæon,
Of my old father's name.
                    Enter Hermes with Ascanius.
Hermes. Æneas, stay! Jove's herald bids thee stay.
Æneas. What do I see? Jove's wingèd messenger?   25
Welcome to Carthage new-erected town.

V,i.
SD *platform* plan or map.
3 *Atrides* See note at II,i,129.
13 *Hybla* the name of three towns in

Sicily, one of which was famous for its
honey.
14 *exhalèd* breathed out as vapors.

Hermes.   Why, cousin, stand you building cities here
   And beautifying the empire of this queen,
   While Italy is clean out of thy mind?
   Too, too forgetful of thine own affairs,   30
   Why wilt thou so betray thy son's good hap?
   The king of gods sent me from highest heaven
   To sound this angry message in thine ears:
   Vain man, what monarchy expect'st thou here,
   Or with what thought sleep'st thou in Libya shore?   35
   If that all glory hath forsaken thee
   And thou despise the praise of such attempts,
   Yet think upon Ascanius' prophecy,
   And young Iulus' more than thousand years,
   Whom I have brought from Ida where he slept,   40
   And bore young Cupid unto Cyprus isle.
Æneas.   This was my mother that beguiled the queen
   And made me take my brother for my son.
   No marvel, Dido, though thou be in love,
   That daily dandlest Cupid in thine arms.   45
   Welcome, sweet child. Where hast thou been this long?
Ascanius.   Eating sweet comfits with Queen Dido's maid,
   Who ever since hath lulled me in her arms.
Æneas.   Sergestus, bear him hence unto our ships,
   Lest Dido, spying him, keep him for a pledge.   50
                        [*Exit Sergestus with Ascanius.*]
Hermes.   Spendst thou thy time about this little boy,
   And givest not ear unto the charge I bring?
   I tell thee thou must straight to Italy,
   Or else abide the wrath of frowning Jove.
Æneas.   How should I put into the raging deep,   55
   Who have no sails nor tackling for my ships?
   What, would the gods have me, Deucalion-like,
   Float up and down wher'er the billows drive?
   Though she repaired my fleet and gave me ships,
   Yet hath she ta'en away my oars and masts,   60
   And left me neither sail nor stern aboard.
                        Enter to them Iarbas.
Iarbas.   How now, Æneas sad? What means these dumps?
Æneas.   Iarbas, I am clean besides myself.
   Jove hath heaped on me such a desperate charge,
   Which neither art nor reason may achieve,   65
   Nor I devise by what means to contrive.

31 *hap* fortune.
39 *Iulus* Ascanius.
40 *Ida* The poet here mistakenly places
Mt. Ida on the island of Cyprus. See
note at III,ii,99.

47 *comfits* candies.
57 *Deucalion* the Greek Noah who,
when Zeus decided to destory mankind,
built a ship on which he and his wife,
Pyrrha, floated in safety.

Iarbas.   As how, I pray? May I entreat you tell?
Æneas.   With speed he bids me sail to Italy,
   Whenas I want both rigging for my fleet
   And also furniture for these my men.   70
Iarbas.   If that be all, then cheer thy drooping looks,
   For I will furnish thee with such supplies.
   Let some of those thy followers go with me,
   And they shall have what thing soe'er thou need'st.
Æneas.   Thanks, good Iarbas, for thy friendly aid.   75
   Achates and the rest shall wait on thee,
   Whilst I rest thankful for this courtesy.
                          Exit Iarbas and Æneas' train.
   Now will I haste unto Lavinian shore
   And raise a new foundation to old Troy.
   Witness the gods, and witness heaven and earth,   80
   How loath I am to leave these Libyan bounds,
   But that eternal Jupiter commands.
                        Enter Dido.
Dido.   I fear I saw Æneas' little son
   Led by Achates to the Trojan fleet.
   If it be so, his father means to fly.   85
   But here he is. Now, Dido, try thy wit.   [*Aside.*]
   Æneas, wherefore go thy men aboard?
   Why are thy ships new-rigged? Or to what end,
   Launched from the haven, lie they in the road?
   Pardon me, though I ask. Love makes me ask.   90
Æneas.   O, pardon me if I resolve thee why.
   Æneas will not feign with his dear love.
   I must from hence. This day, swift Mercury,
   When I was laying a platform for these walls,
   Sent from his father, Jove, appeared to me,   95
   And in his name rebuked me bitterly
   For lingering here, neglecting Italy.
Dido.   But yet Æneas will not leave his love.
Æneas.   I am commanded by immortal Jove
   To leave this town and pass to Italy,   100
   And therefore must of force.
Dido.   These words proceed not from Æneas' heart.
Æneas.   Not from my heart, for I can hardly go.
   And yet I may not stay. Dido, farewell.
Dido.   Farewell? Is this the mends for Dido's love?   105
   Do Trojans use to quit their lovers thus?
   Fare well may Dido, so Æneas stay;
   I die if my Æneas say farewell.
Æneas.   Then let me go and never say farewell.
Dido.   'Let me go!' 'Farewell!' 'I must from hence!'   110

70 *furniture* military equipment.   105 *mends* amends.

These words are poison to poor Dido's soul.
O speak like my Æneas, like my love.
Why look'st thou toward the sea? The time hath been
When Dido's beauty chained thine eyes to her.
Am I less fair than when thou sawest me first?   115
O, then, Æneas, 'tis for grief of thee.
Say thou wilt stay in Carthage with thy queen,
And Dido's beauty will return again.
Æneas, say, how canst thou take thy leave?
Wilt thou kiss Dido? O, thy lips have sworn   120
To stay with Dido. Canst thou take her hand?
Thy hand and mine have plighted mutual faith.
Therefore, unkind Æneas, must thou say,
'Then let me go, and never say farewell'?
Æneas. O queen of Carthage, wert thou ugly black,   125
Æneas could not choose but hold thee dear.
Yet must he not gainsay the gods' behest.
Dido. The gods? What gods be those that seek my death?
Wherein have I offended Jupiter
That he should take Æneas from mine arms?   130
O, no! The gods weigh not what lovers do.
It is Æneas calls Æneas hence,
And woeful Dido, by these blubbered cheeks,
By this right hand, and by our spousal rites,
Desires Æneas to remain with her.   135
Si bene quid de te merui, fuit aut tibi quidquam
Dulce meum, miserere domus labentis, et istam,
Oro, si quis adhuc precibus lucus, exue mentem.
Æneas. Desine meque tuis incendere teque querelis;
Italiam non sponte sequor.   140
Dido. Hast thou forgot how many neighbor kings
Were up in arms for making thee my love?
How Carthage did rebel, Iarbas storm,
And all the world calls me a second Helen,
For being entangled by a stranger's looks?   145
So thou wouldst prove as true as Paris did,
Would, as fair Troy was, Carthage might be sacked,
And I be called a second Helena.
Had I a son by thee, the grief were less,
That I might see Æneas in his face.   150
Now if thou goest, what canst thou leave behind

133 *blubbered* tear-stained.
136–138 *Si bene . . . mentem* If I have deserved well of you at all, if anything of mine has been sweet to you, have pity on this declining house and put aside your intention, I beg you, if begging may still be of any use. (The lines are from the *Æneid*, IV,317–319.)
139–140 *Desine . . . sequor* Cease to inflame us both with your lamentations. I do not follow after Italy of my own free will. (*Æneid*, IV,360–361.)
146 *So* so that.

But rather will augment than ease my woe?
Æneas.   In vain, my love, thou spend'st thy fainting breath.
   If words might move me, I were overcome.
Dido.   And wilt thou not be moved with Dido's words?   155
   Thy mother was no goddess, perjured man,
   Nor Dardanus the author of thy stock,
   But thou art sprung from Scythian Caucasus,
   And tigers of Hyrcania gave thee suck.
   Ah, foolish Dido, to forbear this long!   160
   Wast thou not wracked upon this Libyan shore,
   And cam'st to Dido like a fisher swain?
   Repaired not I thy ships, made thee a king,
   And all thy needy followers noblemen?
   O serpent that came creeping from the shore   165
   And I for pity harbored in my bosom,
   Wilt thou now slay me with thy venomed sting
   And hiss at Dido for preserving thee?
   Go, go, and spare not. Seek out Italy.
   I hope that that which love forbids me do,   170
   The rocks and sea-gulfs will perform at large,
   And thou shalt perish in the billows' ways,
   To whom poor Dido doth bequeath revenge.
   Ay, traitor, and the waves shall cast thee up
   Where thou and false Achates first set foot.   175
   Which if it chance, I'll give ye burial
   And weep upon your lifeless carcasses,
   Though thou nor he will pity me a whit.
   Why star'st thou in my face? If thou wilt stay,
   Leap in mine arms. Mine arms are open wide.   180
   If not, turn from me, and I'll turn from thee,
   For though thou hast the heart to say farewell,
   I have not power to stay thee.

                                            [*Exit Æneas.*]

                        Is he gone?
   Ay, but he'll come again. He cannot go.
   He loves me too well to serve me so.   185
   Yet he that in my sight would not relent
   Will, being absent, be obdurate still.
   By this is he got to the water side,
   And, see, the sailors take him by the hand,
   But he shrinks back, and now, remembering me,   190
   Returns amain. Welcome, welcome, my love!
   But where's Æneas? Ah, he's gone, he's gone!
                        [*Enter Anna.*]

157 *Dardanus* son of Jupiter and Elec-   159 *Hyrcania* a Persian province on the
tra, the legendary ancestor of the Tro-   shore of the Caspian Sea.
jans.

Anna.   What means my sister, thus to rave and cry?
Dido.   O Anna, my Æneas is aboard,
   And leaving me, will sail to Italy.   195
   Once didst thou go, and he came back again.
   Now bring him back, and thou shalt be a queen,
   And I will live a private life with him.
Anna.   Wicked Æneas.
Dido.   Call him not wicked, sister. Speak him fair,   200
   And look upon him with a mermaid's eye.
   Tell him I never vowed at Aulis' gulf
   The desolation of his native Troy,
   Nor sent a thousand ships unto the walls,
   Nor ever violated faith to him.   205
   Request him gently, Anna, to return.
   I crave but this: he stay a tide or two,
   That I may learn to bear it patiently.
   If he depart thus suddenly, I die.
   Run, Anna, run. Stay not to answer me.   210
Anna.   I go, fair sister. Heavens grant good success.

                                                    Exit Anna.

                         Enter the Nurse.
Nurse.   O Dido, your little son, Ascanius
   Is gone. He lay with me last night,
   And in the morning he was stoll'n from me.
   I think some fairies have beguilèd me.   215
Dido.   O cursèd hag and false dissembling wretch,
   That slay'st me with thy harsh and hellish tale,
   Thou for some petty gift hast let him go,
   And I am thus deluded of my boy.
   Away with her to prison presently,   220
   Traitoress to kind, and cursèd sorceress!
                         [*Enter Attendants.*]
Nurse.   I know not what you mean by treason, I.
   I am as true as any one of yours.
                         Exeunt the Nurse [*and Attendants*].
Dido.   Away with her! Suffer her not to speak.
   My sister comes. I like not her sad looks.   225
                         Enter Anna.
Anna.   Before I came, Æneas was aboard,
   And, spying me, hoist up the sails amain.
   But I cried out, 'Æneas, false Æneas, stay!'
   Then gan he wag his hand, which yet held up,
   Made me suppose he would have heard me speak.   230
   Then gan they drive into the ocean,

   202 *Aulis' gulf* In the harbor of Aulis   **203** *desolation* destruction.
   in Boeotia the Greek fleet assembled be-   **221** *kind* nature, human kind.
   fore sailing to Troy.

Which when I viewed, I cried, 'Æneas, stay!
Dido, fair Dido, wills Æneas stay!'
Yet he, whose heart of adamant or flint,
My tears nor plaints could mollify a whit.   235
Then carelessly I rent my hair for grief,
Which seen to all—though he beheld me not—
They gan to move him to redress my ruth
And stay a while to hear what I could say,
But he, clapped under hatches, sailed away.   240
Dido.   O Anna, Anna, I will follow him.
Anna.   How can ye go when he hath all your fleet?
Dido.   I'll frame me wings of wax like Icarus,
And o'er his ships will soar unto the sun,
That they may melt and I fall in his arms.   245
Or else I'll make a prayer unto the waves
That I may swim to him like Triton's niece.
O Anna, fetch Arion's harp
That I may tice a dolphin to the shore
And ride upon his back unto my love.   250
Look, sister, look! Lovely Æneas' ships!
See, see, the billows heave him up to heaven,
And now down falls the keels into the deep.
O sister, sister, take away the rocks.
They'll break his ships. O Proteus, Neptune, Jove,   255
Save, save Æneas, Dido's liefest love.
Now is he come on shore, safe without hurt.
But see, Achates wills him put to sea,
And all the sailors merry make for joy.
But he, remembering me, shrinks back again.   260
See where he comes. Welcome, welcome, my love.
Anna.   Ah, sister, leave these idle fantasies.
Sweet sister, cease. Remember who you are.
Dido.   Dido I am, unless I be deceived.
And must I rave thus for a runagate?   265
Must I make ships for him to sail away?
Nothing can bear me to him but a ship,
And he hath all my fleet. What shall I do
But die in fury of this oversight?

243 *Icarus* a young man who flew with waxen wings fashioned by his father, Dædalus, but who fell into the sea and perished when he flew too close to the sun and thus caused his wings to melt. This myth seems to have been a favorite one with Marlowe.

247 *Triton's niece* probably Scylla, the daughter of Nisus, king of Megara, who swam after the ship of her lover, Minos. Marlowe seems to have confused her with the monster, Scylla (see note at I,i,146) who was the niece of the sea deity Triton (see note at I,i,130).

248 *Arion's harp* Arion of Methymna in Lesbos was a famous musician who, according to legend, when thrown into the sea by sailors who coveted a treasure he had won in a musical contest, was carried to shore on the back of a dolphin.

265 *runagate* (1) vagabond (2) renegade.

Ay, I must be the murderer of myself.   270
No, but I am not; yet I will be straight.   [*Aside.*]
Anna be glad. Now have I found a mean
To rid me from these thoughts of lunacy.
Not far from hence
There is a woman famousèd for arts,   275
Daughter unto the nymphs Hesperides,
Who willed me sacrifice his ticing relics.
Go, Anna, bid my servants bring me fire.

                                        Exit Anna.

                    Enter Iarbas.

Iarbas.   How long will Dido mourn a stranger's flight,
    That hath dishonored her and Carthage both?   280
    How long shall I with grief consume my days,
    And reap no guerdon for my truest love?
            [*Enter Attendants with wood and torches.*]
Dido.   Iarbas, talk not of Æneas; let him go.
    Lay to thy hands, and help me make a fire
    That shall consume all that this stranger left,   285
    For I intend a private sacrifice
    To cure my mind that melts for unkind love.
Iarbas.   But afterwards, will Dido grant me love?
Dido.   Ay, ay, Iarbas. After this is done,
    None in the world shall have my love but thou.   290
                            [*They build a fire.*]
    So! Leave me now. Let none approach this place.

                                        Exit Iarbas.

    Now, Dido, with these relics burn thyself,
    And make Æneas famous through the world
    For perjury and slaughter of a queen.
    Here lie the sword that in the darksome cave   295
    He drew and swore by to be true to me.
    Thou shalt burn first; thy crime is worse than his.
    Here lie the garment which I clothed him in
    When first he came on shore. Perish thou too.
    These letters, lines, and perjured papers all,   300
    Shall burn to cinders in this precious flame.
    And now, ye gods, that guide the starry frame
    And order all things at your high dispose,
    Grant, though the traitors land in Italy,
    They may be still tormented with unrest.   305
    And from mine ashes let a conqueror rise,
    That may revenge this treason to a queen

276 *Hesperides* nymphs who guarded   306 *a conqueror* Hannibal, who was
the golden apples given by Gea (the   reputedly the descendant of Dido.
earth) to Juno on her marriage to
Jupiter.

By plowing up his countries with the sword.
Betwixt this land and that be never league.
Litora litoribus contraria, fluctibus undas   310
Imprecor, arma armis; pugnent ipsique nepotes.
Live, false Æneas! Truest Dido dies!
Sic, sic juvat ire sub umbras.

       [She throws herself into the flames.]

      Enter Anna.

Anna. **O,** help, Iarbas! Dido in these flames
 Hath burnt herself. Ay me, unhappy me!   315
     Enter Iarbas, running.
Iarbas. Cursèd Iarbas, die to expiate
 The grief that tires upon thine inward soul.
 Dido, I come to thee. Ay me, Æneas!

       [He kills himself.]

Anna. What can my tears or cries prevail me now?
 Dido is dead, Iarbas slain. Iarbas, my dear love!   320
 O sweet Iarbas, Anna's sole delight.
 What fatal destiny envies me thus,
 To see my sweet Iarbas slay himself?
 But Anna now shall honor thee in death
 And mix her blood with thine. This shall I do,   325
 That gods and men may pity this my death
 And rule our ends, senseless of life or breath.
 Now, sweet Iarbas, stay! I come to thee!

       [She kills herself.]

310–311 *Litora . . . nepotes* I invoke sea coast against sea coast, waves against waves, arms against arms. May they and their descendants be forever at war. (*Æneid,* IV,628–629.)

313 *Sic . . . umbras* Thus, thus, it rejoices me to go beneath the shades (to die). (*Æneid,* IV,660.)

Tamburlaine

the Great.

Who, from a Scythian Shepheard*e*,
by his rare and woonderfull Conquests,
became a most puissant and migh-
tye Monarque.

And (for his tyranny, and terrour in
Warre)was tearmed,

The Scourge of God.

Deuided into two Tragicall Dis-
courses, as they were sundrie times
shewed vpon Stages in the Citie
of London.

By the right honorable the Lord
Admyrall, his seruantes.

Now first, and newlie published.

LONDON.
Printed by Richard Ihones: at the signe
of the Rose and Crowne neere Hol-
borne Bridge. 1590.

TO THE GENTLEMEN READERS AND OTHERS THAT
TAKE PLEASURE IN READING HISTORIES:

Gentlemen and courteous readers whosoever, I have here published in print for your sakes the two tragical discourses of the Scythian shepherd Tamburlaine, that became so great a conqueror and so mighty a monarch. My hope is that they will be now no less acceptable unto you to read after your serious affairs and studies than they [5 have been lately delightful for many of you to see, when the same were showed in London upon stages. I have purposely omitted and left out some fond and frivolous gestures, digressing and, in my poor opinion, far unmeet for the matter, which I thought might seem more tedious unto the wise than any way else to be regarded, though haply [10 they have been of some vain, conceited fondlings greatly gaped at, what times they were showed upon the stage in their graced deformities. Nevertheless, now to be mixtured in print with such matter of worth, it would prove a disgrace to so honorable and stately a history. Great folly were it in me to commend unto your wisdoms either the [15 eloquence of the author that writ them or the worthiness of the matter itself. I therefore leave unto your learned censures both the one and the other and myself, the poor printer of them, unto your most courteous and favorable protection, which if you vouchsafe to accept, you shall evermore bind me to employ what travel and service [20 I can to the advancing and pleasuring of your excellent degree.

> Yours, most humble at commandment,
> R[ICHARD] J[ONES], Printer

THE TWO TRAGICAL DISCOURSES OF MIGHTY TAMBURLAINE, THE SCYTHIAN SHEPHERD, ETC.

TAMBURLAINE THE GREAT: PART ONE

THE PLAYERS

Mycetes, King of Persia
Cosroe, his brother
Meander ⎱
Theridamas ⎰
Ortygius ⎬ Persian lords
Ceneus ⎰
Menaphon ⎰
Tamburlaine, A Scythian
  Shepherd

Teschelles ⎱ his followers
Usumcasane ⎰

Bajazeth, Emperor of the Turks
King of Fez
King of Morocco
King of Argier

King of Arabia
Soldan of Egypt
Governor of Damascus

Agydas ⎱ Median lords
Magnetes ⎰

Capolin, an Egyptian
Philemus
Bashaws, Lords, Citizens, Moors,
  Soldiers and Attendants
Zenocrate, daughter of the Soldan
  of Egypt
Anippe, her maid
Zabina, wife of Bajazeth
Ebea, her maid
Virgins of Damascus

THE SCENE
Africa and Asia

THE PROLOGUE

From jigging veins of rhyming mother wits,
And such conceits as clownage keeps in pay,
We'll lead you to the stately tent of war,
Where you shall hear the Scythian Tamburlaine
Threat'ning the world with high astounding terms   5
And scourging kingdoms with his conquering sword.
View but his picture in this tragic glass,
And then applaud his fortunes as you please.

I,i.

[Enter] Mycetes, Cosroe, Meander, Theridamas, Ortygius, Ceneus, [Menaphon,] with others.

Mycetes. Brother Cosroe, I find myself agrieved,
  Yet insufficient to express the same,
  For it requires a great and thund'ring speech.
  Good brother, tell the cause unto my lords;
  I know you have a better wit than I.   5
Cosroe. Unhappy Persia, that in former age
  Hast been the seat of mighty conquerors,
  That in their prowess and their policies
  Have triumphed over Afric and the bounds
  Of Europe, where the sun dares scarce appear   10
  For freezing meteors and congealèd cold,
  Now to be ruled and governed by a man
  At whose birthday Cynthia with Saturn joined,
  And Jove, the sun, and Mercury denied
  To shed their influence in his fickle brain!   15
  Now Turks and Tartars shake their swords at thee,
  Meaning to mangle all thy provinces.
Mycetes. Brother, I see your meaning well enough,
  And through your planets I perceive you think
  I am not wise enough to be a king.   20
  But I refer me to my noblemen
  That know my wit and can be witnesses.
  I might command you to be slain for this.
  Meander, might I not?
Meander. Not for so small a fault, my sovereign lord.   25
Mycetes. I mean it not, but yet I know I might.
  Yet live; yea live; Mycetes wills it so.
  Meander, thou, my faithful counsellor,
  Declare the cause of my conceivèd grief,
  Which is, God knows, about that Tamburlaine,   30
  That, like a fox in midst of harvest-time,
  Doth prey upon my flocks of passengers,
  And, as I hear, doth mean to pull my plumes.
  Therefore 'tis good and meet for to be wise.
Meander. Oft have I heard your majesty complain   35

I,i.

2 *insufficient* unable.

8 *policies* statecraft, diplomacy. See Introduction, p. xxxi.

13–15 *birthday . . . brain* The personality of Mycetes is explained in 16th century astrological terms. Cynthia (the moon) was a traditional symbol of change and fickleness, Saturn of stupidity. The magnanimity of Jove, the artistic nature of Apollo (the sun) and the wit of Mercury have had no share in his composition.

16 *thee* i.e., Persia.

32 *passengers* travelers.

Of Tamburlaine, that sturdy Scythian thief
That robs your merchants of Persepolis,
Treading by land unto the Western Isles,
And in your confines with his lawless train
Daily commits uncivil outrages,   40
Hoping, misled by dreaming prophecies,
To reign in Asia, and with barbarous arms
To make himself the monarch of the East.
But ere he march in Asia or display
His vagrant ensign in the Persian fields,   45
Your grace hath taken order by Theridamas,
Charged with a thousand horse, to apprehend
And bring him captive to your highness' throne.
Mycetes.   Full true thou speak'st, and like thyself, my lord,
Whom I may term a Damon for thy love.   50
Therefore 'tis best, if so it like you all,
To send my thousand horse incontinent
To apprehend that paltry Scythian.
How like you this, my honorable lords?
Is it not a kingly resolution?   55
Cosroe.   It cannot choose, because it comes from you.
Mycetes.   Then hear thy charge, valiant Theridamas,
The chiefest captain of Mycetes' host,
The hope of Persia, and the very legs
Whereon our state doth lean, as on a staff   60
That holds us up and foils our neighbor foes.
Thou shalt be leader of this thousand horse,
Whose foaming gall, with rage and high disdain,
Have sworn the death of wicked Tamburlaine.
Go frowning forth, but come thou smiling home,   65
As did Sir Paris with the Grecian dame.
Return with speed; time passeth swift away.
Our life is frail, and we may die today.

36 *Scythian* The name Scythia has been applied to different areas at different times. The Greek historian, Herodotus, writes of Scythians as nomadic people who lived in southeastern Europe between the Carpathian mountains and the river Don. Later Scythia comes to refer to a large area in northern and central Asia. The historical Tamburlaine was a Mongol, born at Samarkand in Turkestan, and Marlowe's Scythia, according to the maps of Ortelius to which the dramatist referred (see Introduction, p. xxii), was an area on the north shore of the Black Sea, west of Crimea.

37 *Persepolis* the ancient capital of Persia on the Araxis river, some ruins of which still survive.

38 *Western Isles* Britain.

45 *vagrant ensign* nomadic banner.

47 *Charged with* placed in command of.

50 *Damon* with Pythias, a traditional symbol of friendship.

52 *incontinent* at once.

56 *choose* be otherwise.

66 *Grecian dame* i.e., Helen of Troy, stolen from her husband, Menelaus, by the Trojan prince, Paris.

Theridamas.   Before the moon renew her borrowed light,
   Doubt not, my lord and gracious sovereign,   70
   But Tamburlaine and that Tartarian rout
   Shall either perish by our warlike hands
   Or plead for mercy at your highness' feet.
Mycetes.   Go, stout Theridamas; thy words are swords,
   And with thy looks thou conquerest all thy foes.   75
   I long to see thee back return from thence,
   That I may view these milk-white steeds of mine
   All loaden with the heads of killèd men,
   And from their knees even to their hoofs below
   Besmeared with blood; that makes a dainty show.   80
Theridamas.   Then now, my lord, I humbly take my leave.

                                        Exit.

Mycetes.   Theridamas, farewell ten thousand times.
   Ah, Menaphon, why stay'st thou thus behind
   When other men press forward for renown?
   Go, Menaphon, go into Scythia,   85
   And foot by foot follow Theridamas.
Cosroe.   Nay, pray you let him stay. A greater [task]
   Fits Menaphon than warring with a thief.
   Create him prorex of Africa,
   That he may win the Babylonians' hearts,   90
   Which will revolt from Persian government
   Unless they have a wiser king than you.
Mycetes.   Unless they have a wiser king than you?
   These are his words; Meander, set them down.
Cosroe.   And add this to them: that all Asia   95
   Lament to see the folly of their king.
Mycetes.   Well, here I swear by this my royal seat—
Cosroe.   You may do well to kiss it then. [*Aside.*]
Mycetes.   Embossed with silk as best beseems my state,
   To be revenged for these contemptuous words.   100
   O, where is duty and allegiance now?
   Fled to the Caspian or the ocean main?
   What, shall I call thee brother? No, a foe,
   Monster of nature, shame unto thy stock,
   That dar'st presume thy sovereign for to mock.   105
   Meander come. I am abused, Meander.

                    Exit [*Mycetes with his train*].

                  Cosroe and Menaphon remain.
Menaphon.   How now, my lord? What, mated and amazed
   To hear the king thus threaten like himself?

---

71 *Tartarian* used interchangeably with Scythian by Marlowe. Tartary in the maps of Ortelius covered a wide area of central and northern Asia. The Tartar or Mongol empire had, in fact, extended into Europe to include a part of Russia. 78 *loaden* laden.   89 *prorex* viceroy. 107 *mated* confounded.

Cosroe.　Ah, Menaphon, I pass not for his threats.
　The plot is laid by Persian noblemen　　　　　　　　110
　And captains of the Median garrisons
　To crown me emperor of Asia.
　But this it is that doth excruciate
　The very substance of my vexèd soul:
　To see our neighbors that were wont to quake　　　115
　And tremble at the Persian monarch's name
　Now sits and laughs our regiment to scorn;
　And that which might resolve me into tears,
　Men from the farthest equinoctial line
　Have swarmed in troops into the Eastern India,　　120
　Lading their ships with gold and precious stones,
　And made their spoils from all our provinces.
Menaphon.　This should entreat your highness to rejoice,
　Since Fortune gives you opportunity
　To gain the title of a conqueror　　　　　　　　125
　By curing of this maimèd empery.
　Afric and Europe bordering on your land
　And continent to your dominions,
　How easily may you with a mighty host
　Pass into Græcia, as did Cyrus once,　　　　　　130
　And cause them to withdraw their forces home,
　Lest you subdue the pride of Christendom.
　　　　　　　　　　　[*Trumpets sound within.*]
Cosroe.　But, Menaphon, what means this trumpet's sound?
Menaphon.　Behold, my lord, Ortygius and the rest
　Bringing the crown to make you emperor!　　　　135
　　　Enter Ortygius and Ceneus, bearing a crown, with others.
Ortygius.　Magnificent and mighty prince Cosroe,
　We, in the name of other Persian states
　And commons of this mighty monarchy,
　Present thee with th'imperial diadem.
Ceneus.　The warlike soldiers and the gentlemen,　　140
　That heretofore have filled Persepolis
　With Afric captains taken in the field,
　Whose ransom made them march in coats of gold,
　With costly jewels hanging at their ears

109 *pass* care.
117 *regiment* rule, authority.
118 *resolve* dissolve.
119 *equinoctial line* equator.
124 *Fortune* the goddess Fortuna, who with her wheel provided a common classical and medieval symbol of the uncertainty of worldly things.
126 *empery* empire. This is one of Marlowe's favorite words.

128 *continent to* bordering upon.
130 *Græcia* the Greek settlements in Asia Minor. *Cyrus* the elder, the son of Cambises, was the founder of the Persian empire who conquered these Greek settlements.
132 *pride of Christendom* Byzantium or Constantinople.
137 *states* noblemen.

And shining stones upon their lofty crests,   145
Now living idle in the wallèd towns,
Wanting both pay and martial discipline,
Begin in troops to threaten civil war
And openly exclaim against the king.
Therefore, to stay all sudden mutinies,   150
We will invest your highness emperor,
Whereat the soldiers will conceive more joy
Than did the Macedonians at the spoil
Of great Darius and his wealthy host.

Cosroe.   Well, since I see the state of Persia droop   155
And languish in my brother's government,
I willingly receive th'imperial crown
And vow to wear it for my country's good,
In spite of them shall malice my estate.

Ortygius.   And in assurance of desired success,   160
We here do crown thee monarch of the East,
Emperor of Asia and of Persia,
Great lord of Media and Armenia,
Duke of Africa and Albania,
Mesopotamia and of Parthia,   165
East India and the late discovered isles,
Chief lord of all the wide, vast Euxine Sea,
And of the ever-raging Caspian lake.
Long live Cosroe, mighty emperor!

Cosroe.   And Jove may never let me longer live   170
Than I may seek to gratify your love,
And cause the soldiers that thus honor me
To triumph over many provinces;
By whose desires of discipline in arms
I doubt not shortly but to reign sole king,   175
And with the army of Theridamas,
Whither we presently will fly, my lords,
To rest secure against my brother's force.

Ortygius.   We knew, my lord, before we brought the crown,
Intending your investion so near   180
The residence of your despised brother,
The lords would not be too exasperate
To injure or suppress your worthy title.
Or if they would, there are in readiness
Ten thousand horse to carry you from hence   185

153–154 *Macedonians . . . host* Alexander the Great, son of Philip of
Macedon, defeated the Emperor Darius
and his Persian army in 333 B.C. at the
Battle of Issus.

159 *malice* bear malice towards.

166 *late discovered isles* a possible reference to America.

167 *Euxine Sea* Black Sea.

170 *Jove may never* i.e., may Jove
never.

180 *investion* investiture.

182 *exasperate* exasperated.

In spite of all suspected enemies.

Cosroe. I know it well, my lord, and thank you all.

Ortygius. Sound up the trumpets, then. God save the king!

　　　　　　　　　　　　　　　　　　　Exeunt.

✳

　[Enter] Tamburlaine leading Zenocrate, [with] Techelles,
　Usumcasane, [Magnetes, Agydas and] other Lords and Soldiers,
　　　　　　laden with treasure.

Tamburlaine. Come lady, let not this appall your thoughts;
　The jewels and the treasure we have ta'en
　Shall be reserved, and you in better state
　Than if you were arrived in Syria,
　Even in the circle of your father's arms,　　　　　　　5
　The mighty Soldan of Egyptia.
Zenocrate. Ah, shepherd, pity my distressèd plight—
　If, as thou seem'st thou art so mean a man—
　And seek not to enrich thy followers
　By lawless rapine from a silly maid,　　　　　　　10
　Who, travelling with these Median lords
　To Memphis from my uncle's country of Media,
　Where all my youth I have been governèd,
　Have passed the army of the mighty Turk,
　Bearing his privy signet and his hand　　　　　　　15
　To safe conduct us thorough Africa.
Magnetes. And since we have arrived in Scythia,
　Besides rich presents from the puissant Cham,
　We have his highness' letters to command
　Aid and assistance if we stand in need.　　　　　　　20
Tamburlaine. But now you see these letters and commands
　Are countermanded by a greater man,
　And through my provinces you must expect
　Letters of conduct from my mightiness,
　If you intend to keep your treasure safe,　　　　　　　25
　But since I love to live at liberty,
　As easily may you get the Soldan's crown

I,ii.

3 *reserved* safeguarded. *better state* greater honors.

6 *Soldan of Egyptia* None of the wives of the historical Tamburlaine was daughter to the Sultan of Egypt. His chief wife seems to have been a Tartar princess.

10 *silly* childlike, harmless.

15 *hand* signed guarantee of safe-conduct.

18 *Cham* Tartar emperor.

26 *at liberty* with liberality, bounteously.

As any prizes out of my precinct.
For they are friends that help to wean my state,
Till men and kingdoms help to strengthen it,   30
And must maintain my life exempt from servitude.
But tell me, madam, is your grace betrothed?
Zenocrate.   I am, my lord, for so you do import.
Tamburlaine.   I am a lord, for so my deeds shall prove,
And yet a shepherd by my parentage.   35
But, lady, this fair face and heavenly hue
Must grace his bed that conquers Asia
And means to be a terror to the world,
Measuring the limits of his empery
By east and west, as Phœbus doth his course.   40
Lie here, ye weeds that I disdain to wear!

> [*He removes his shepherd's clothes to
> reveal his armor beneath them.*]

This complete armor and this curtle-axe
Are adjuncts more beseeming Tamburlaine.
And madam, whatsoever you esteem
Of this success and loss unvaluèd,   45
Both may invest you empress of the East.
And these, that seem but silly country swains,
May have the leading of so great an host
As with their weight shall make the mountains quake,
Even as when windy exhalations,   50
Fighting for passage, tilt within the earth.
Techelles.   As princely lions when they rouse themselves,
Stretching their paws and threatening herds of beasts,
So in his armor looketh Tamburlaine.
Methinks I see kings kneeling at his feet,   55
And he with frowning brows and fiery looks
Spurning their crowns from off their captive heads.
Usumcasane.   And making thee and me, Techelles, kings,
That even to death will follow Tamburlaine.
Tamburlaine.   Nobly resolved, sweet friends and followers!   60
These lords perhaps do scorn our estimates,
And think we prattle with distempered spirits,
But since they measure our deserts so mean,
That in conceit bear empires on our spears,
Affecting thoughts co-equal with the clouds,   65
They shall be kept our forcèd followers,

---

28 *precinct* province or administrative unit.

29 *wean my state* nurture my greatness, help it to grow.

40 *Phœbus* the sun, Apollo.

41 *weeds* garments.

45 *success* event, i.e., her capture. *unvaluèd* of little value.

47 *these* i.e., his followers. *silly* simple, lowly.

62 *prattle* speak idly.

64 *conceit* imagination.

65 *Affecting* indulging themselves with.

Till with their eyes they view us emperors.
Zenocrate.　The gods, defenders of the innocent,
　Will never prosper your intended drifts,
　That thus oppress poor friendless passengers.　　　　70
　Therefore at least admit us liberty,
　Even as thou hop'st to be eternizèd
　By living Asia's mighty emperor.
Agydas.　I hope our lady's treasure and our own
　May serve for ransom to our liberties.　　　　75
　Return our mules and empty camels back,
　That we may travel into Syria,
　Where her betrothèd lord, Alcidamus,
　Expects th'arrival of her highness' person.
Magnetes.　And wheresoever we repose ourselves,　　　　80
　We will report but well of Tamburlaine.
Tamburlaine.　Disdains Zenocrate to live with me?
　Or you, my lords, to be my followers?
　Think you I weigh this treasure more than you?
　Not all the gold in India's wealthy arms　　　　85
　Shall buy the meanest soldier in my train.
　Zenocrate, lovelier than the love of Jove,
　Brighter than is the silver Rhodope,
　Fairer than whitest snow on Scythian hills,
　Thy person is more worth to Tamburlaine　　　　90
　Than the possession of the Persian crown,
　Which gracious stars have promised at my birth.
　A hundred Tartars shall attend on thee,
　Mounted on steeds swifter than Pegasus.
　Thy garments shall be made of Median silk,　　　　95
　Enchased with precious jewels of mine own,
　More rich and valurous than Zenocrate's.
　With milk-white harts upon an ivory sled,
　Thou shalt be drawn amidst the frozen pools,
　And scale the icy mountains' lofty tops,　　　　100
　Which with thy beauty will be soon resolved.
　My martial prizes, with five hundred men
　Won on the fifty-headed Volga's waves,
　Shall all we offer to Zenocrate,

69 *drifts* purposes.

70 *passengers* travelers.

73 *living* living to become.

88 *silver Rhodope* a snow-capped mountain range in Thrace, regarded by the Greeks as sacred to Dionysius and famous for silver mines.

94 *Pegasus* the famous winged horse of Greek mythology which had sprung from the blood of the gorgon, Medusa.

96 *enchased* adorned. The term was applied usually to the embellishing of metal with jewels and not to the embroidery of silk, as it is here. See note to *Dido* I,i,101.

97 *valurous* valuable.

101 *resolved* melted.

103 *fifty-headed Volga* the delta of the Volga river, with its many streams and tributaries.

And then myself to fair Zenocrate.   105
Techelles.   What now? In love?
Tamburlaine.   Techelles, women must be flatterèd.
  But this is she with whom I am in love.
                          Enter a Soldier.
Soldier.   News, news!
Tamburlaine.   How now? What's the matter?   110
Soldier.   A thousand Persian horsemen are at hand,
  Sent from the king to overcome us all.
Tamburlaine.   How now, my lords of Egypt and Zenocrate?
  Now must your jewels be restored again,
  And I that triumphed so be overcome?   115
  How say you lordings? Is not this your hope?
Agydas.   We hope yourself will willingly restore them.
Tamburlaine.   Such hope, such fortune, have the thousand horse.
  Soft ye, my lords and sweet Zenocrate,
  You must be forcèd from me ere you go.   120
  A thousand horsemen! We five hundred foot!
  An odds too great for us to stand against.
  But are they rich? And is their armor good?
Soldier.   Their plumèd helms are wrought with beaten gold,
  Their swords enamelled, and about their necks   125
  Hangs massy chains of gold down to the waist,
  In every part exceeding brave and rich.
Tamburlaine.   Then shall we fight courageously with them,
  Or look you I should play the orator?
Techelles.   No; cowards and faint-hearted runaways   130
  Look for orations when the foe is near.
  Our swords shall play the orators for us.
Usumcasane.   Come, let us meet them at the mountain foot,
  And with a sudden and an hot alarm
  Drive all their horses headlong down the hill.   135
Techelles.   Come, let us march.
Tamburlaine.   Stay Techelles; ask a parley first.
                    The Soldiers enter.
  Open the mails; yet guard the treasure sure.
  Lay out our golden wedges to the view,
  That their reflections may amaze the Persians,   140
  And look we friendly on them when they come.
  But if they offer word or violence,
  We'll fight, five hundred men-at-arms to one,
  Before we part with our possession.
  And 'gainst the general we will lift our swords,   145
  And either lance his greedy thirsting throat,
  Or take him prisoner, and his chain shall serve
  For manacles till he be ransomed home.

138 *mails* trunks.

Techelles.   I hear them come. Shall we encounter them?
Tamburlaine.   Keep all your standings, and not stir a foot;   150
  Myself will bide the danger of the brunt.
              Enter Theridamas, with others.
Theridamas.   Where is this Scythian, Tamburlaine?
Tamburlaine.   Whom seek'st thou, Persian? I am Tamburlaine.
Theridamas.   Tamburlaine! A Scythian shepherd so embellishèd
  With nature's pride and richest furniture!   155
  His looks do menace heaven and dare the gods.
  His fiery eyes are fixed upon the earth
  As if he now devised some stratagem,
  Or meant to pierce Avernus' darksome vaults
  To pull the triple-headed dog from hell.   160
Tamburlaine.   Noble and mild this Persian seems to be,
  If outward habit judge the inward man.
Techelles.   His deep affections make him passionate.
Tamburlaine.   With what a majesty he rears his looks!
  In thee, thou valiant man of Persia,   165
  I see the folly of thy emperor.
  Art thou but captain of a thousand horse,
  That by characters graven in thy brows,
  And by thy martial face and stout aspect,
  Deserv'st to have the leading of an host?   170
  Forsake thy king and do but join with me,
  And we will triumph over all the world.
  I hold the Fates bound fast in iron chains,
  And with my hand turn Fortune's wheel about,
  And sooner shall the sun fall from his sphere   175
  Then Tamburlaine be slain or overcome.
  Draw forth thy sword, thou mighty man-at-arms,
  Intending but to raze my charmèd skin,
  And Jove himself will stretch his hand from heaven
  To ward the blow and shield me safe from harm.   180
  See how he rains down heaps of gold in showers,
  As if he meant to give my soldiers pay;
  And as a sure and grounded argument
  That I shall be the monarch of the East,
  He sends this Soldan's daughter, rich and brave,   185
  To be my queen and portly emperess.
  If thou wilt stay with me, renownèd man,

155 *furniture* equipment.
159 *Avernus* a dark volcanic lake supposed to lead to the underworld.
160 *triple-headed dog* Cerberus, who
guarded the gates of the underworld.
163 *affections* emotions.
173 *Fates* See note to *Dido*, III,ii,3.
175 *sun . . . sphere* The sun was

conceived, in the Ptolemaic astronomy which Marlowe uses, to move in
an orbit or sphere about the earth.
186 *portly* stately. *emperess* empress.
Here and elsewhere I have retained the
original spelling for the sake of the
meter.

And lead thy thousand horse with my conduct,
Besides thy share of this Egyptian prize,
Those thousand horse shall sweat with martial spoil   190
Of conquered kingdoms and of cities sacked.
Both we will walk upon the lofty clifts,
And Christian merchants, that with Russian stems
Plough up huge furrows in the Caspian Sea,
Shall vail to us as lords of all the lake.   195
Both we will reign as consuls of the earth,
And mighty kings shall be our senators.
Jove sometimes maskèd in a shepherd's weed,
And by those steps that he hath scaled the heavens,
May we become immortal like the gods.   200
Join with me now in this my mean estate—
I call it mean because, being yet obscure,
The nations far removed admire me not—
And when my name and honor shall be spread
As far as Boreas claps his brazen wings,   205
Or fair Boötes sends his cheerful light,
Then shalt thou be competitor with me,
And sit with Tamburlaine in all his majesty.
Theridamas.   Not Hermes, prolocutor to the gods,
Could use persuasions more pathetical.   210
Tamburlaine.   Nor are Apollo's oracles more true
Than thou shalt find my vaunts substantial.
Techelles.   We are his friends, and if the Persian king
Should offer present dukedoms to our state,
We think it loss to make exchange for that   215
We are assured of by our friend's success.
Usumcasane.   And kingdoms at the least we all expect,
Besides the honor in assured conquests,
Where kings shall crouch unto our conquering swords
And hosts of soldiers stand amazed at us,   220
When with their fearful tongues they shall confess
These are the men that all the world admires.
Theridamas.   What strong enchantments tice my yielding soul!
Ah, these resolvèd noble Scythians!
But shall I prove a traitor to my king?   225

188 *conduct* direction.
192 *clifts* cliffs.
193 *stems* ships.
195 *vail* lower their topsails as a token of respect.
198 *maskèd . . . weed* disguised himself as a shepherd.
201 *estate* condition.
205 *as . . . wings* to the farthest reaches of the North.
206 *Boötes* a northern constellation,

known also as the bear, containing the bright star, Arcturus.
207 *competitor* partner.
209 *prolocutor to* spokesman or messenger for; Hermes was the god of eloquence.
210 *pathetical* moving.
214 *offer . . . state* i.e., offer to make us dukes.
223 *tice* entice.
224 *resolvèd* determined.

Tamburlaine. No, but the trusty friend of Tamburlaine.
Theridamas. Won with thy words and conquered with thy looks,
  I yield myself, my men, and horse to thee,
  To be partaker of thy good or ill,
  As long as life maintains Theridamas.   230
Tamburlaine. Theridamas, my friend, take here my hand,
  Which is as much as if I swore by heaven
  And called the gods to witness of my vow.
  Thus shall my heart be still combined with thine,
  Until our bodies turn to elements,   235
  And both our souls aspire celestial thrones.
  Techelles and Casane, welcome him.
Techelles. Welcome, renownèd Persian, to us all.
Usumcasane. Long may Theridamas remain with us.
Tamburlaine. These are my friends in whom I more rejoice   240
  Than doth the king of Persia in his crown;
  And by the love of Pylades and Orestes,
  Whose statues we adore in Scythia,
  Thyself and them shall never part from me
  Before I crown you kings in Asia.   245
  Make much of them, gentle Theridamas,
  And they will never leave thee till the death.
Theridamas. Nor thee, nor them, thrice-noble Tamburlaine,
  Shall want my heart to be with gladness pierced,
  To do you honor and security.   250
Tamburlaine. A thousand thanks, worthy Theridamas.
  And now, fair madam and my noble lords,
  If you will willingly remain with me,
  You shall have honors as your merits be,
  Or else you shall be forced with slavery.   255
Agydas. We yield unto thee, happy Tamburlaine.
Tamburlaine. For you then, madam, I am out of doubt.
Zenocrate. I must be pleased perforce. Wretched Zenocrate!

                                      Exeunt.

234 *still* forever.

235 *elements* i.e., earth, air, fire, and water.

236 *aspire* aspire to.

242 *Pylades and Orestes* When Orestes returned to Argos, his faithful friend, Pylades, accompanied him, and after Orestes had slain his mother, Clytem- nestra, and was pursued by the Furies, Pylades shared the exile and suffering of his friend.

248 *Nor . . . them* neither to thee nor to them.

249 *want* be found lacking.

250 *security* protection.

II,i.

[*Enter*] *Cosroe, Menaphon, Ortygius, Ceneus, with other*
Soldiers.

Cosroe.   Thus far are we towards Theridamas
And valiant Tamburlaine, the man of fame,
The man that in the forehead of his fortune
Bears figures of renown and miracle.
But tell me, that hast seen him, Menaphon,   5
What stature wields he, and what personage?
Menaphon.   Of stature tall, and straightly fashionèd,
Like his desire, lift upwards and divine,
So large of limbs, his joints so strongly knit,
Such breadth of shoulders as might mainly bear   10
Old Atlas' burden. 'Twixt his manly pitch,
A pearl more worth than all the world is placed,
Wherein by curious sovereignty of art
Are fixed his piercing instruments of sight,
Whose fiery circles bear encompassèd   15
A heaven of heavenly bodies in their spheres,
That guides his steps and actions to the throne
Where honor sits invested royally.
Pale of complexion, wrought in him with passion,
Thirsting with sovereignty, with love of arms,   20
His lofty brows in folds do figure death,
And in their smoothness amity and life.
About them hangs a knot of amber hair,
Wrappèd in curls, as fierce Achilles' was,
On which the breath of heaven delights to play,   25
Making it dance with wanton majesty.
His arms and fingers, long and sinewy,
Betokening valor and excess of strength—
In every part proportioned like the man
Should make the world subdued to Tamburlaine.   30
Cosroe.   Well hast thou portrayed in thy terms of life
The face and personage of a wondrous man.
Nature doth strive with Fortune and his stars
To make him famous in accomplished worth,
And well his merits show him to be made   35

II,i.

3–4 *man . . . miracle* It was a part of
Moslem belief that Allah wrote the destiny of a man in secret signs upon his
forehead.

10 *mainly* with strength.

11 *Old Atlas' burden* See note to *Dido*,
I,i,99. *pitch* the width of his shoulders.

12 *pearl* i.e., his head.

15–17 *Whose . . . throne* i.e., within

his eyes there shines a constellation of
such propitious stars as might cause
him to attain the throne. (All human
events were believed to be influenced
by the stars.)

21 *in folds* when furrowed.

26 *wanton* careless.

31 *of life* vivid.

His fortune's master and the king of men,
That could persuade, at such a sudden pinch,
With reasons of his valor and his life,
A thousand sworn and overmatching foes.
Then, when our powers in points of swords are joined,   40
And closed in compass of the killing bullet,
Though strait the passage and the port be made
That leads to palace of my brother's life,
Proud is his fortune if we pierce it not.
And when the princely Persian diadem   45
Shall overweigh his weary witless head
And fall, like mellowed fruit, with shakes of death,
In fair Persia noble Tamburlaine
Shall be my regent and remain as king.
Ortygius. In happy hour we have set the crown   50
Upon your kingly head, that seeks our honor
In joining with the man ordained by heaven
To further every action to the best.
Ceneus. He that with shepherds and a little spoil
Durst, in disdain of wrong and tyranny,   55
Defend his freedom 'gainst a monarchy,
What will he do supported by a king,
Leading a troop of gentlemen and lords,
And stuffed with treasure for his highest thoughts?
Cosroe. And such shall wait on worthy Tamburlaine.   60
Our army will be forty thousand strong,
When Tamburlaine and brave Theridamas
Have met us by the river Araris;
And all conjoined to meet the witless king
That now is marching near to Parthia,   65
And with unwilling soldiers faintly armed,
To seek revenge on me and Tamburlaine,
To whom, sweet Menaphon, direct me straight.
Menaphon. I will, my lord.

                            Exeunt.

[*Enter*] *Mycetes, Meander, with other Lords and Soldiers.* II,ii.
Mycetes. Come, my Meander, let us to this gear.
  I tell you true, my heart is swoll'n with wrath

---

42 *port* entrance.
63 *river Araris* probably the river Araxis which flowed through Armenia to the Caspian Sea.

65 *Parthia* an Asian kingdom, south-east of the Caspian Sea.
II,ii.
  1 *gear* business.

On this same thievish villain, Tamburlaine,
And of that false Cosroe, my traitorous brother.
Would it not grieve a king to be so abused   5
And have a thousand horsemen ta'en away?
And—which is worse—to have his diadem
Sought for by such scald knaves as love him not?
I think it would. Well then, by heavens I swear,
Aurora shall not peep out of her doors,   10
But I will have Cosroe by the head
And kill proud Tamburlaine with point of sword.
Tell you the rest, Meander; I have said.
Meander.   Then, having passed Armenian deserts now,
    And pitched our tents under the Georgian hills,   15
    Whose tops are covered with Tartarian thieves
    That lie in ambush, waiting for a prey,
    What should we do but bid them battle straight
    And rid the world of those detested troops,
    Lest, if we let them linger here a while,   20
    They gather strength by power of fresh supplies.
    This country swarms with vile outrageous men
    That live by rapine and by lawless spoil,
    Fit soldiers for the wicked Tamburlaine.
    And he that could with gifts and promises   25
    Inveigle him that led a thousand horse,
    And make him false his faith unto his king,
    Will quickly win such as are like himself.
    Therefore cheer up your minds; prepare to fight.
    He that can take or slaughter Tamburlaine   30
    Shall rule the province of Albania.
    Who brings that traitor's head, Theridamas,
    Shall have a government in Media,
    Beside the spoil of him and all his train.
    But if Cosroe—as our spials say,   35
    And as we know—remains with Tamburlaine,
    His highness' pleasure is that he should live
    And be reclaimed with princely lenity.
                    [*Enter a Spy.*]
Spy.   An hundred horsemen of my company,
    Scouting abroad upon these champion plains,   40
    Have viewed the army of the Scythians,
    Which make reports it far exceeds the king's.
Meander.   Suppose they be in number infinite,
    Yet being void of martial discipline,

_____

8 *scald* scurvy, contemptible.   27 *false* betray.
10 *Aurora* goddess of the dawn.   35 *spials* spies.
22 *outrageous* fierce, likely to commit   40 *champion* level.
outrages.

All running headlong after greedy spoils, 45
And more regarding gain than victory,
Like to the cruel brothers of the earth,
Sprung of the teeth of dragons venomous,
Their careless swords shall lance their fellows' throats
And make us triumph in their overthrow. 50
Mycetes. Was there such brethren, sweet Meander, say,
That sprung of teeth of dragons venomous?
Meander. So poets say, my lord.
Mycetes. And 'tis a pretty toy to be a poet.
Well, well, Meander, thou art deeply read, 55
And having thee, I have a jewel sure.
Go on, my lord, and give your charge, I say.
Thy wit will make us conquerors today.
Meander. Then, noble soldiers, to entrap these thieves
That live confounded in disordered troops, 60
If wealth or riches may prevail with them,
We have our camels laden all with gold,
Which you that be but common soldiers
Shall fling in every corner of the field,
And while the base-born Tartars take it up, 65
You, fighting more for honor than for gold,
Shall massacre those greedy-minded slaves;
And when their scattered army is subdued,
And you march on their slaughtered carcasses,
Share equally the gold that bought their lives, 70
And live like gentlemen in Persia.
Strike up the drum and march courageously.
Fortune herself doth sit upon our crests.
Mycetes. He tells you true, my masters; so he does.
Drums, why sound ye not when Meander speaks? 75

Exeunt.

II,iii.

[*Enter*] *Cosroe, Tamburlaine, Theridamas, Techelles, Usum-*
casane, Ortygius, with others.
Cosroe. Now, worthy Tamburlaine, have I reposed
In thy approvèd fortunes all my hope.
What think'st thou, man, shall come of our attempts?
For even as from assurèd oracle,

47–48 *cruel . . . venomous* When Cadmus killed the dragon sacred to Mars,
he sowed the teeth, and from the earth
sprang armed soldiers who destroyed
one another until only five were left,
and these founded the city of Thebes.
54 *toy* idle pastime.

I take thy doom for satisfaction. 5
Tamburlaine. And so mistake you not a whit, my lord,
For fates and oracles [of] heaven have sworn
To royalize the deeds of Tamburlaine,
And make them blessed that share in his attempts.
And doubt you not but, if you favor me 10
And let my fortunes and my valor sway
To some direction in your martial deeds,
The world will strive with hosts of men-at-arms
To swarm unto the ensign I support.
The host of Xerxes, which by fame is said 15
To drink the mighty Parthian Araris,
Was but a handful to that we will have.
Our quivering lances shaking in the air
And bullets like Jove's dreadful thunderbolts,
Enrolled in flames and fiery smoldering mists, 20
Shall threat the gods more than Cyclopian wars;
And with our sun-bright armor, as we march
We'll chase the stars from heaven and dim their eyes
That stand and muse at our admirèd arms.
Theridamas. You see, my lord, what working words he hath, 25
But when you see his actions top his speech,
Your speech will stay or so extol his worth
As I shall be commended and excused
For turning my poor charge to his direction.
And these, his two renownèd friends, my lord, 30
Would make one thrust and strive to be retained
In such a great degree of amity.
Techelles. With duty and with amity we yield
Our utmost service to the fair Cosroe.
Cosroe. Which I esteem as portion of my crown. 35
Usumcasane and Techelles both,
When she that rules in Rhamnrs' golden gates
And makes a passage for all prosperous arms
Shall make me solely emperor of Asia,
Then shall your meeds and valors be advanced 40

II,iii.

5 *doom* judgment, opinion. *satisfaction* certainty.

15 *Xerxes* King of Persia, who invaded Greece with the greatest army ever assembled in ancient times (more than two million men, according to Herodotus, although this must be an exaggeration) and was repulsed by the Spartans at Thermopylae.

16 *Parthian Araris* See note at II,i,63. The legend is told by Herodotus, who calls the river Araxis, referring probably to the river Oxus.

21 *Cyclopian wars* Marlowe is identifying the Cyclops with those Titans who warred against Jove. See note to *Dido*, I,i,147.

25 *working words* speech with power to create action.

26 *top* exceed.

37 *she . . . gates* Nemesis, the goddess of revenge. See note to *Dido*, III, ii,20.

To rooms of honor and nobility.
Tamburlaine.   Then haste, Cosroe, to be king alone,
   That I with these my friends and all my men
   May triumph in our long expected fate.
   The king, your brother, is now hard at hand;   45
   Meet with the fool, and rid your royal shoulders
   Of such a burden as outweighs the sands
   And all the craggy rocks of Caspea.
                    [*Enter a Messenger.*]
Messenger.   My lord, we have discoverèd the enemy
   Ready to charge you with a mighty army.   50
Cosroe.   Come, Tamburlaine, now whet thy wingèd sword,
   And lift thy lofty arm into the clouds,
   That it may reach the king of Persia's crown
   And set it safe on my victorious head.
Tamburlaine.   See where it is, the keenest curtle-axe   55
   That e'er made passage thorough Persian arms.
   These are the wings shall make it fly as swift
   As doth the lightning or the breath of heaven,
   And kill as sure as it swiftly flies.
Cosroe.   Thy words assure me of kind success.   60
   Go, valiant soldier, go before and charge
   The fainting army of that foolish king.
Tamburlaine.   Usumcasane and Techelles, come.
   We are enough to scar the enemy,
   And more than needs to make an emperor.   65
                                          [*Exeunt.*]

✻

                                                        II,iv.

   [*Enter Soldiers*] *to the battle and* [*then exeunt*]. *Mycetes comes*
        out alone with his crown in his hand, offering to hide it.
Mycetes.   Accursed be he that first invented war!
   They knew not—ah, they knew not, simple men—
   How those were hit by pelting cannon shot
   Stand staggering like a quivering aspen leaf
   Fearing the force of Boreas' boisterous blasts.   5
   In what a lamentable case were I,
   If nature had not given me wisdom's lore,
   For kings are clouts that every man shoots at,
   Our crown the pin that thousands seek to cleave.

41 *rooms* places.
48 *Caspea* the Caspian Sea.

II,iv.

5 *Boreas* the north wind.

8–9 *kings . . . cleave* The metaphor is
drawn from archery. Clouts are targets.
To cleave the pin is to split the nail in
the center of the target which holds it
in place.

Therefore in policy I think it good   10
To hide it close—a goodly stratagem,
And far from any man that is a fool.
So shall not I be known, or if I be,
They cannot take away my crown from me.
Here will I hide it in this simple hole.   15
                    Enter Tamburlaine.
Tamburlaine.   What, fearful coward! Straggling from the camp,
   When kings themselves are present in the field?
Mycetes.   Thou liest.
Tamburlaine.   Base villain, dar'st thou give the lie?
Mycetes.   Away! I am the king. Go! Touch me not!   20
   Thou break'st the law of arms unless thou kneel
   And cry me, 'Mercy, noble king!'
Tamburlaine.   Are you the witty king of Persia?
Mycetes.   Ay, marry, am I. Have you any suit to me?
Tamburlaine.   I would entreat you to speak but three wise words. 25
Mycetes.   So I can, when I see my time.
Tamburlaine.   Is this your crown?
Mycetes.   Ay. Didst thou ever see a fairer?
                         [*He hands him the crown.*]
Tamburlaine.   You will not sell it, will ye?
Mycetes.   Such another word, and I will have thee executed.   30
   Come, give it me.
Tamburlaine. No; I took it prisoner.
Mycetes.   You lie; I gave it you.
Tamburlaine.   Then 'tis mine.
Mycetes.   No; I mean I let you keep it.   35
Tamburlaine.   Well, I mean you shall have it again.
   Here, take it for a while; I lend it thee
   Till I may see thee hemmed with armèd men.
   Then shalt thou see me pull it from thy head;
   Thou art no match for mighty Tamburlaine.   40
                                        [*Exit.*]
Mycetes.   O gods, is this Tamburlaine the thief?
   I marvel much he stole it not away.
                    Sound trumpets to the battle, and he runs in.

✱

                                                                  II,v.
        [*Enter*] *Cosroe, Tamburlaine, Theridamas, Menaphon, Mean-*
            der, Ortygius, Techelles, Usumcasane, with others.
Tamburlaine.   Hold thee, Cosroe; wear two imperial crowns.
   Think thee invested now as royally,
   Even by the mighty hand of Tamburlaine,

As if as many kings as could encompass thee,
With greatest pomp, had crowned thee emperor.   5
Cosroe.   So do I, thrice renownèd man at arms,
And none shall keep the crown but Tamburlaine.
Thee do I make my regent of Persia
And general lieutenant of my armies.
Meander, you that were our brother's guide   10
And chiefest counsellor in all his acts,
Since he is yielded to the stroke of war,
On your submission we with thanks excuse
And give you equal place in our affairs.
Meander.   Most happy emperor, in humblest terms   15
I vow my service to your majesty,
With utmost virtue of my faith and duty.
Cosroe.   Thanks, good Meander. Then, Cosroe, reign
And govern Persia in her former pomp.
Now send embassage to thy neighbor kings,   20
And let them know the Persian king is changed
From one that knew not what a king should do
To one that can command what 'longs thereto.
And now we will to fair Persepolis
With twenty thousand expert soldiers.   25
The lords and captains of my brother's camp
With little slaughter take Meander's course,
And gladly yield them to my gracious rule.
Ortygius and Menaphon, my trusty friends,
Now will I gratify your former good   30
And grace your calling with a greater sway.
Ortygius.   And as we ever aimed at your behoof,
And sought your state all honor it deserved,
So will we with our powers and our lives
Endeavor to preserve and prosper it.   35
Cosroe.   I will not thank thee, sweet Ortygius;
Better replies shall prove my purposes.
And now, Lord Tamburlaine, my brother's camp
I leave to thee and to Theridamas,
To follow me to fair Persepolis.   40
Then will we march to all those Indian mines
My witless brother to the Christians lost,
And ransom them with fame and usury.
And till thou overtake me, Tamburlaine,
Staying to order all the scattered troops,   45
Farewell, lord regent and his happy friends.
I long to sit upon my brother's throne.

II,v.
32 *behoof* profit.

Menaphon.   Your majesty shall shortly have your wish,
   And ride in triumph through Persepolis.
                    Exeunt [all except] Tamburlaine, Techelles,
                         Theridamas, [and] Usumcasane.
Tamburlaine.   And ride in triumph through Persepolis!   50
   Is it not brave to be a king, Techelles?
   Usumcasane and Theridamas,
   Is it not passing brave to be a king,
   And ride in triumph through Persepolis?
Techelles.   O, my lord, 'tis sweet and full of pomp.   55
Usumcasane.   To be a king is half to be a god.
Theridamas.   A god is not so glorious as a king.
   I think the pleasure they enjoy in heaven
   Can not compare with kingly joys in earth:
   To wear a crown enchased with pearl and gold,   60
   Whose virtues carry with it life and death;
   To ask and have, command and be obeyed;
   When looks breed love, with looks to gain the prize,
   Such power attractive shines in princes' eyes.
Tamburlaine.   Why say, Theridamas, wilt thou be a king?   65
Theridamas.   Nay; though I praise it, I can live without it.
Tamburlaine.   What says my other friends? Will you be kings?
Techelles.   Ay, if I could, with all my heart, my lord.
Tamburlaine.   Why, that's well said, Techelles; so would I.
   And so would you, my masters, would you not?   70
Usumcasane.   What then, my lord?
Tamburlaine.   Why then, Casane, shall we wish for aught
   The world affords in greatest novelty
   And rest attemptless, faint and destitute?
   Methinks we should not. I am strongly moved,   75
   That if I should desire the Persian crown,
   I could attain it with a wondrous ease;
   And would not all our soldiers soon consent,
   If we should aim at such a dignity?
Theridamas.   I know they would with our persuasions.   80
Tamburlaine.   Why then, Theridamas, I'll first assay
   To get the Persian kingdom to myself;
   Then thou for Parthia; they for Scythia and Media;
   And if I prosper, all shall be as sure
   As if the Turk, the Pope, Afric and Greece   85
   Came creeping to us with their crowns apace.
Techelles.   Then shall we send to this triumphing king,
   And bid him battle for his novel crown?
Usumcasane.   Nay, quickly then, before his room be hot.

60 *enchased* See note at I,ii,96.   75 *moved* inwardly convinced.
73 *in greatest novelty* no matter how
rare.

Tamburlaine. 'Twill prove a pretty jest, in faith, my friends.   90
Theridamas. A jest to charge on twenty thousand men?
  I judge the purchase more important far.
Tamburlaine. Judge by thyself, Theridamas, not me,
  For presently Techelles here shall haste
  To bid him battle ere he pass too far   95
  And lose more labor than the game will quite.
  Then shalt thou see the Scythian Tamburlaine
  Make but a jest to win the Persian crown.
  Techelles, take a thousand horse with thee,
  And bid him turn him back to war with us,   100
  That only made him king to make us sport.
  We will not steal upon him cowardly,
  But give him warning and more warriors.
  Haste thee, Techelles; we will follow thee.

                                            [*Exit Techelles.*]

  What saith Theridamas?
Theridamas.   Go on, for me.   105
                                            Exeunt.

                                                                    II,vi.
     [*Enter*] *Cosroe, Meander, Ortygius, Menaphon, with other*
                              Soldiers.
Cosroe. What means this devilish shepherd to aspire
  With such a giantly presumption,
  To cast up hills against the face of heaven,
  And dare the force of angry Jupiter?
  But as he thrust them underneath the hills,   5
  And pressed out fire from their burning jaws,
  So will I send this monstrous slave to hell,
  Where flames shall ever feed upon his soul.
Meander. Some powers divine, or else infernal, mixed
  Their angry seeds at his conception,   10
  For he was never sprung of human race,
  Since with the spirit of his fearful pride,
  He dares so doubtlessly resolve of rule,
  And by profession be ambitious.
Ortygius. What god, or fiend, or spirit of the earth,   15

92 *purchase* what will be gained.
96 *quite* requite, repay.

II,vi.

3 *cast . . . heaven* i.e., as did the
Titans who warred against Jove.
5 *them* i.e., the Titans. Jupiter did
not thrust the rebellious Titans beneath
the hills. It was Typhœus he imprisoned
beneath Mt. Ætna. See note to *Dido,*
IV,i,19.
13 *doubtlessly* without fear or hesita-
tion. *resolve of* determine to.

Or monster turnèd to a manly shape,
Or of what mold or mettle he be made,
What star or state soever govern him,
Let us put on our meet encountering minds,
And in detesting such a devilish thief,   20
In love of honor and defense of right
Be armed against the hate of such a foe,
Whether from earth, or hell, or heaven he grow.
Cosroe.   Nobly resolved, my good Ortygius,
And since we all have sucked one wholesome air,   25
And with the same proportion of elements
Resolve, I hope we are resembled,
Vowing our loves to equal death and life.
Let's cheer our soldiers to encounter him,
That grievous image of ingratitude,   30
That fiery thirster after sovereignty,
And burn him in the fury of that flame
That none can quench but blood and empery.
Resolve, my lords and loving soldiers, now
To save your king and country from decay.   35
Then strike up, drum; and all the stars that make
The loathsome circle of my dated life,
Direct my weapon to his barbarous heart,
That thus opposeth him against the gods
And scorns the powers that govern Persia.   40
                                    [*Exeunt.*]

                                              II,vii.

*Enter [Soldiers] to the battle, and [then exit]. After the battle
enter Cosroe, wounded, Theridamas, Tamburlaine, Techelles,
                Usumcasane, with others.*
Cosroe.   Barbarous and bloody Tamburlaine,
Thus to deprive me of my crown and life!
Treacherous and false Theridamas,
Even at the morning of my happy state,
Scarce being seated in my royal throne,   5
To work my downfall and untimely end!
An uncouth pain torments my grievèd soul,
And death arrests the organ of my voice, |
Who, entering at the breach thy sword hath made,
Sacks every vein and artier of my heart.   10

27 *Resolve* are decomposed (when we   **II,vii.**
die).   10 *artier* artery.

Bloody and insatiate Tamburlaine!
Tamburlaine.   The thirst of reign and sweetness of a crown,
   That caused the eldest son of heavenly Ops
   To thrust his doting father from his chair,
   And place himself in the imperial heaven,   15
   Moved me to manage arms against thy state.
   What better precedent than mighty Jove?
   Nature, that framed us of four elements
   Warring within our breasts for regiment,
   Doth teach us all to have aspiring minds.   20
   Our souls, whose faculties can comprehend
   The wondrous architecture of the world
   And measure every wandering planet's course,
   Still climbing after knowledge infinite,
   And always moving as the restless spheres,   25
   Wills us to wear ourselves and never rest,
   Until we reach the ripest fruit of all,
   That perfect bliss and sole felicity,
   The sweet fruition of an earthly crown.
Theridamas.   And that made me to join with Tamburlaine,   30
   For he is gross and like the massy earth
   That moves not upwards, nor by princely deeds
   Doth mean to soar above the highest sort. .
Techelles.   And that made us, the friends of Tamburlaine,
   To lift our swords against the Persian king.   35
Usumcasane.   For as when Jove did thrust old Saturn down,
   Neptune and Dis gained each of them a crown,
   So do we hope to reign in Asia,
   If Tamburlaine be placed in Persia.
Cosroe.   The strangest men that ever nature made!   40
   I know not how to take their tyrannies.
   My bloodless body waxeth chill and cold,
   And with my blood my life slides through my wound;
   My soul begins to take her flight to hell
   And summons all my senses to depart.   45
   The heat and moisture which did feed each other,
   For want of nourishment to feed them both,
   Is dry and cold; and now doth ghastly death
   With greedy talents gripe my bleeding heart

13–14 *eldest . . . chair*   Jupiter, the son of Saturn and Ops, with his mother's aid deposed his father and made himself king of the gods.

15 *imperial*   The 1590 'Emperiall' may be read also as 'empyreal.' There seems to have been little distinction in Marlowe's time between the two words.

37 *Neptune and Dis* the brothers of Jove, gods of the ocean and underworld respectively.

46–48 *The heat . . . cold* i.e., since his blood, consisting of the qualities of heat and moisture, is departing, what remains is cold and dryness, the composition, according to medieval cosmology, of the earth.

49 *talents* talons.

And like a harpy tires on my life.   50
Theridamas and Tamburlaine, I die—
And fearful vengeance light upon you both!
      [*He dies. Tamburlaine*] *takes the crown and puts it on.*
Tamburlaine.   Not all the curses which the Furies breathe
  Shall make me leave so rich a prize as this.
  Theridamas, Techelles, and the rest,   55
  Who think you now is king of Persia?
All.   Tamburlaine! Tamburlaine!
Tamburlaine.   Though Mars himself, the angry god of arms,
  And all the earthly potentates conspire
  To dispossess me of this diadem,   60
  Yet will I wear it in despite of them,
  As great commander of this eastern world,
  If you but say that Tamburlaine shall reign.
All.   Long live Tamburlaine, and reign in Asia!
Tamburlaine.   So; now it is more surer on my head   65
  Than if the gods had held a parliament,
  And all pronounced me king of Persia.

                                      [*Exeunt.*]

                                       III,i.
  [*Enter*] *Bajazeth, the Kings of Fez, Morocco, and Argier, with*
                others, in great pomp.
Bajazeth.   Great kings of Barbary and my portly bassoes,
  We hear the Tartars and the eastern thieves,
  Under the conduct of one Tamburlaine,
  Presume a bickering with your emperor,
  And thinks to rouse us from our dreadful siege   5
  Of the famous Grecian Constantinople.
  You know our army is invincible;
  As many circumcisèd Turks we have,
  And warlike bands of Christians renièd,
  As hath the ocean or the Terrene sea   10
  Small drops of water when the moon begins
  To join in one her semicircled horns.

---

50 *harpy* one of the mythological birds with heads of women, long claws, and faces pale with hunger. *tires* preys.

53 *Furies* See note to *Dido*, II,i,230.

III,i.

1 *bassoes* bashaws, or pashas. Marlowe prefers this archaic form through-out *Tamburlaine,* and I have retained it in the text, although not in the stage directions.

9 *Christians renièd* apostates.

10 *Terrene sea* Mediterranean.

11–12 *moon . . . horns* i.e., when the moon is full and therefore the tides are high.

Yet would we not be braved with foreign power,
Nor raise our siege before the Grecians yield
Or breathless lie before the city walls.   15
King of Fez. Renownèd emperor and mighty general,
What if you sent the bassoes of your guard
To charge him to remain in Asia,
Or else to threaten death and deadly arms
As from the mouth of mighty Bajazeth?   20
Bajazeth. Hie thee, my basso, fast to Persia.
Tell him thy lord, the Turkish emperor,
Dread lord of Afric, Europe, and Asia,
Great king and conqueror of Græcia,
The ocean, Terrene, and the coal-black sea,   25
The high and highest monarch of the world,
Wills and commands—for say not I entreat—
Not once to set his foot in Africa
Or spread his colors in Græcia,
Lest he incur the fury of my wrath.   30
Tell him I am content to take a truce,
Because I hear he bears a valiant mind;
But if, presuming on his silly power,
He be so mad to manage arms with me,
Then stay thou with him—say, I bid thee so—   35
And if, before the sun have measured heaven
With triple circuit, thou regreet us not,
We mean to take his morning's next arise
For messenger he will not be reclaimed,
And mean to fetch thee in despite of him.   40
Bashaw. Most great and puissant monarch of the earth,
Your basso will accomplish your behest
And show your pleasure to the Persian,
As fits the legate of the stately Turk.
                                          Exit Bashaw.
King of Argier. They say he is the king of Persia;   45
But if he dare attempt to stir your siege,
'Twere requisite he should be ten times more,
For all flesh quakes at your magnificence.
Bajazeth. True, Argier, and tremble at my looks.
King of Morocco. The spring is hindered by your smothering host, 50
For neither rain can fall upon the earth,
Nor sun reflex his virtuous beams thereon,
The ground is mantled with such multitudes.
Bajazeth. All this is true as holy Mahomet,
And all the trees are blasted with our breaths.   55
King of Fez. What thinks your greatness best to be achieved

---

24 **Græcia** See note at I,i,130.   33 *silly* childlike, of little strength.

In pursuit of the city's overthrow?
Bajazeth.   I will the captive pioners of Argier
   Cut off the water that by leaden pipes
   Runs to the city from the mountain Carnon.   60
   Two thousand horse shall forage up and down,
   That no relief or succor come by land,
   And all the sea my galleys countermand.
   Then shall our footmen lie within the trench,
   And with their cannons mouthed like Orcus' gulf,   65
   Batter the walls, and we will enter in;
   And thus the Grecians shall be conquerèd.

Exeunt.

✳

    [*Enter*] *Agydas, Zenocrate, Anippe, with others.*   III,ii
Agydas.   Madam Zenocrate, may I presume
   To know the cause of these unquiet fits
   That work such trouble to your wonted rest?
   'Tis more than pity such a heavenly face
   Should by heart's sorrow wax so wan and pale,   5
   When your offensive rape by Tamburlaine,
   Which of your whole displeasures should be most,
   Hath seemed to be digested long ago.
Zenocrate.   Although it be digested long ago,
   As his exceeding favors have deserved,   10
   And might content the queen of heaven as well
   As it hath changed my first-conceived disdain;
   Yet, since, a farther passion feeds my thoughts
   With ceaseless and disconsolate conceits,
   Which dyes my looks so lifeless as they are,   15
   And might, if my extremes had full events,
   Make me the ghastly counterfeit of death.
Agydas.   Eternal heaven sooner be dissolved,
   And all that pierceth Phœbe's silver eye,
   Before such hap fall to Zenocrate!   20
Zenocrate.   Ah, life and soul, still hover in his breast,
   And leave my body senseless as the earth,
   Or else unite you to his life and soul,
   That I may live and die with Tamburlaine!

III,ii.

58 *pioners* trench-diggers.
63 *countermand* control.
65 *Orcus' gulf* the mouth of hell.
Orcus was one of several Greek names
for Hades.

6 *rape* seizure.
11 *queen of heaven* Juno.
13 *since* since that time.
16 *extremes* violent passions. *events*
expression in action.

Enter, [behind,] Tamburlaine, with Techelles, and others.

Agydas. With Tamburlaine? Ah, fair Zenocrate,   25
  Let not a man so vile and barbarous,
  That holds you from your father in despite
  And keeps you from the honors of a queen,
  Being supposed his worthless concubine,
  Be honored with your love, but for necessity.   30
  So, now the mighty Soldan hears of you,
  Your highness needs not doubt but in short time
  He will, with Tamburlaine's destruction,
  Redeem you from this deadly servitude.
Zenocrate. Leave to wound me with these words,   35
  And speak of Tamburlaine as he deserves.
  The entertainment we have had of him
  Is far from villainy or servitude,
  And might in noble minds be counted princely.
Agydas. How can you fancy one that looks so fierce,   40
  Only disposed to martial stratagems?
  Who, when he shall embrace you in his arms,
  Will tell how many thousand men he slew,
  And, when you look for amorous discourse,
  Will rattle forth his facts of war and blood,   45
  Too harsh a subject for your dainty ears.
Zenocrate. As looks the sun through Nilus' flowing stream,
  Or when the morning holds him in her arms,
  So looks my lordly love, fair Tamburlaine;
  His talk much sweeter than the Muses' song   50
  They sung for honor 'gainst Pierides,
  Or when Minerva did with Neptune strive;
  And higher would I rear my estimate
  Than Juno, sister to the highest god,
  If I were matched with mighty Tamburlaine.   55
Agydas. Yet be not so inconstant in your love,
  But let the young Arabian live in hope,
  After your rescue to enjoy his choice.
  You see, though first the king of Persia,
  Being a shepherd, seemed to love you much,   60
  Now, in his majesty, he leaves those looks,
  Those words of favor, and those comfortings,
  And gives no more than common courtesies.
Zenocrate. Thence rise the tears that so distain my cheeks,
  Fearing his love through my unworthiness.   65

47 *Nilus* the river Nile.
50-51 *Muses' song . . . Pierides* The
nine daughters of Pierus, King of
Emathia in Macedonia, were given the
names of the Muses by their father,
but when they entered a singing contest with the actual Muses were defeated
and transformed into birds.
  52 *Minerva . . . strive* They strug-
gled for control of the government of
Athens.
  65 *Fearing* fearing the loss of.

*Tamburlaine goes to her, and takes her away lovingly by the
hand, looking wrathfully on Agydas, and says nothing. [Exeunt
all except Agydas.]*

Agydas.   Betrayed by fortune and suspicious love,
   Threat'nèd with frowning wrath and jealousy,
   Surprised with fear of hideous revenge,
   I stand aghast; but most astonièd
   To see his choler shut in secret thoughts,   70
   And wrapt in silence of his angry soul.
   Upon his brows was portrayed ugly death,
   And in his eyes the fury of his heart,
   That shine as comets, menacing revenge,
   And casts a pale complexion on his cheeks.   75
   As when the seaman sees the Hyadès
   Gather an army of Cimmerian clouds,
   (Auster and Aquilon with wingèd steeds,
   All sweating, tilt about the watery heavens,
   With shivering spears enforcing thunder-claps,   80
   And from their shields strike flames of lightning)
   All-fearful folds his sails and sounds the main,
   Lifting his prayers to the heavens for aid
   Against the terror of the winds and waves,
   So fares Agydas for the late-felt frowns   85
   That sent a tempest to my daunted thoughts
   And makes my soul divine her overthrow.
      Enter Techelles with a naked dagger, [and Usumcasane.]
Techelles.   See you, Agydas, how the king salutes you.
   He bids you prophesy what it imports.
Agydas.   I prophesied before, and now I prove   90
   The killing frowns of jealousy and love.
   He needed not with words confirm my fear,
   For words are vain where working tools present
   The naked action of my threatened end.
   It says, Agydas, thou shalt surely die,   95
   And of extremities elect the least.
   More honor and less pain it may procure,
   To die by this resolvèd hand of thine
   Than stay the torments he and heaven have sworn.
   Then haste, Agydas, and prevent the plagues   100
   Which thy prolongèd fates may draw on thee.
   Go wander free from fear of tyrant's rage,
   Removèd from the torments and the hell

---

69 *astonièd* astonished.

76 *Hyadès* a constellation of seven stars
which would bring rain if they rose at
the same time as the sun.

77 *Cimmerian* black. The Cimmerii,

a mythical people mentioned by Homer,
lived in total darkness.

78 *Auster* the southwest wind. *Aquilon*
the north wind.

99 *stay* wait for.

Wherewith he may excruciate thy soul,
And let Agydas by Agydas die,   105
And with this stab slumber eternally.   [*He stabs himself.*]
Techelles.   Usumcasane, see how right the man
  Hath hit the meaning of my lord the king.
Usumcasane.   Faith and, Techelles, it was manly done;
  And, since he was so wise and honorable,   110
  Let us afford him now the bearing hence,
  And crave his triple-worthy burial.
Techelles.   Agreed, Casane; we will honor him.
                              [*Exeunt, bearing out the body.*]

✳

                                                            III,iii.
        [*Enter*] *Tamburlaine, Techelles, Usumcasane, Theridamas,* [a]
              Bashaw, Zenocrate, [*Anippe,*] *with others.*
Tamburlaine.   Basso, by this thy lord and master knows
  I mean to meet him in Bithynia.
  See how he comes! Tush, Turks are full of brags
  And menace more than they can well perform.
  He meet me in the field and fetch thee hence!   5
  Alas, poor Turk, his fortune is too weak
  T'encounter with the strength of Tamburlaine.
  View well my camp, and speak indifferently:
  Do not my captains and my soldiers look
  As if they meant to conquer Africa?   10
Bashaw.   Your men are valiant, but their number few,
  And cannot terrify his mighty host.
  My lord, the great commander of the world,
  Besides fifteen contributory kings,
  Hath now in arms ten thousand janissaries,   15
  Mounted on lusty Mauritanian steeds,
  Brought to the war by men of Tripoli;
  Two hundred thousand footmen that have served
  In two set battles fought in Græcia;
  And for the expedition of this war,   20
  If he think good, can from his garrisons
  Withdraw as many more to follow him.
Techelles.   The more he brings, the greater is the spoil,
  For when they perish by our warlike hands,
  We mean to set our footmen on their steeds   25

III,iii.
  2 *Bithynia* a district in Asia Minor   8 *indifferently* without bias.
south of the Black Sea.   15 *janissaries* Turkish infantrymen.

And rifle all those stately janissars.
Tamburlaine.   But will those kings accompany your lord?
Bashaw.   Such as his highness please; but some must stay
  To rule the provinces he late subdued.
Tamburlaine.   Then fight courageously; their crowns are yours.   30
  This hand shall set them on your conquering heads,
  That made me emperor of Asia.
Usumcasane.   Let him bring millions infinite of men,
  Unpeopling Western Africa and Greece,
  Yet we assure us of the victory.   35
Theridamas.   Even he, that in a trice vanquished two kings
  More mighty than the Turkish emperor,
  Shall rouse him out of Europe and pursue
  His scattered army till they yield or die.
Tamburlaine.   Well said, Theridamas! Speak in that mood,   40
  For 'will' and 'shall' best fitteth Tamburlaine,
  Whose smiling stars gives him assurèd hope
  Of martial triumph, ere he meet his foes.
  I that am termed the scourge and wrath of God,
  The only fear and terror of the world,   45
  Will first subdue the Turk, and then enlarge
  Those Christian captives which you keep as slaves,
  Burdening their bodies with your heavy chains,
  And feeding them with thin and slender fare,
  That naked row about the Terrene sea,   50
  And, when they chance to breathe and rest a space,
  Are punished with bastones so grievously
  That they lie panting on the galley's side,
  And strive for life at every stroke they give.
  These are the cruel pirates of Argier,   55
  That damnèd train, the scum of Africa,
  Inhabited with straggling runagates,
  That make quick havoc of the Christian blood.
  But, as I live, that town shall curse the time
  That Tamburlaine set foot in Africa.   60
     Enter Bajazeth with his Bashaws and Contributory Kings,
        [Zabina, and Ebea].
Bajazeth.   Bassoes and janissaries of my guard,
  Attend upon the person of your lord,
  The greatest potentate of Africa.
Tamburlaine.   Techelles and the rest, prepare your swords;
  I mean t'encounter with that Bajazeth.   65
Bajazeth.   Kings of Fez, Morocco, and Argier,
  He calls me Bajazeth, whom you call lord!
  Note the presumption of this Scythian slave!

52 *bastones* cudgels.   57 *runagates* vagabonds, **deserters.**
55 *Argier* Algeria.

I tell thee, villain, those that lead my horse
Have to their names titles of dignity,   70
And dar'st thou bluntly call me Bajazeth?
Tamburlaine. And know thou, Turk, that those which lead my horse
Shall lead thee captive thorough Africa,
And dar'st thou bluntly call me Tamburlaine?
Bajazeth. By Mahomet my kinsman's sepulcher,   75
And by the holy Alcoran I swear,
He shall be made a chaste and lustless eunuch,
And in my sarell tend my concubines;
And all his captains, that thus stoutly stand,
Shall draw the chariot of my emperess,   80
Whom I have brought to see their overthrow.
Tamburlaine. By this my sword that conquered Persia,
Thy fall shall make me famous through the world.
I will not tell thee how I'll handle thee,
But every common soldier of my camp   85
Shall smile to see thy miserable state.
King of Fez. What means the mighty Turkish emperor
To talk with one so base as Tamburlaine?
King of Morocco. Ye Moors and valiant men of Barbary,
How can ye suffer these indignities?   90
King of Argier. Leave words, and let them feel your lances' points,
Which glided through the bowels of the Greeks.
Bajazeth. Well said, my stout contributory kings.
Your threefold army and my hugy host
Shall swallow up these base-born Persians.   95
Techelles. Puissant, renowned, and mighty Tamburlaine,
Why stay we thus prolonging all their lives?
Theridamas. I long to see those crowns won by our swords,
That we may reign as kings of Africa.
Usumcasane. What coward would not fight for such a prize?   100
Tamburlaine. Fight all courageously, and be you kings.
I speak it, and my words are oracles.
Bajazeth. Zabina, mother of three braver boys
Than Hercules, that in his infancy
Did pash the jaws of serpents venomous,   105
Whose hands are made to gripe a warlike lance,
Their shoulders broad, for complete armor fit,
Their limbs more large and of a bigger size
Than all the brats y-sprung from Typhon's loins,
Who, when they come unto their father's age,   110
Will batter turrets with their manly fists—

---

78 *sarell* harem.   phœus (see note to *Dido*, IV,i,19) was
94 *hugy* huge.   the father of the harpies (see note at
105 *pash* crush, dash to pieces.   II,vii,50) as well as of the cruel winds.
109 *brats . . . loins* Typhon or Ty-

Sit here upon this royal chair of state,
And on thy head wear my imperial crown,
Until I bring this sturdy Tamburlaine
And all his captains bound in captive chains.   115
Zabina.   Such good success happen to Bajazeth!
Tamburlaine.   Zenocrate, the loveliest maid alive,
    Fairer than rocks of pearl and precious stone,
    The only paragon of Tamburlaine,
    Whose eyes are brighter than the lamps of heaven   120
    And speech more pleasant than sweet harmony,
    That with thy looks canst clear the darkened sky
    And calm the rage of thundering Jupiter—
    Sit down by her, adornèd with my crown,
    As if thou wert the empress of the world.   125
    Stir not, Zenocrate, until thou see
    Me march victoriously with all my men,
    Triumphing over him and these his kings,
    Which I will bring as vassals to thy feet.
    Till then, take thou my crown, vaunt of my worth,   130
    And manage words with her, as we will arms.
Zenocrate.   And may my love, the king of Persia,
    Return with victory and free from wound!
Bajazeth.   Now shalt thou feel the force of Turkish arms,
    Which lately made all Europe quake for fear.   135
    I have of Turks, Arabians, Moors, and Jews,
    Enough to cover all Bithynia.
    Let thousands die! Their slaughtered carcasses
    Shall serve for walls and bulwarks to the rest;
    And as the heads of Hydra, so my power,   140
    Subdued, shall stand as mighty as before.
    If they should yield their necks unto the sword,
    Thy soldiers' arms could not endure to strike
    So many blows as I have heads for thee.
    Thou know'st not, foolish hardy Tamburlaine,   145
    What 'tis to meet me in the open field,
    That leave no ground for thee to march upon.
Tamburlaine.   Our conquering swords shall marshal us the way
    We use to march upon the slaughtered foe,
    Trampling their bowels with our horses' hoofs,   150
    Brave horses bred on the white Tartarian hills.
    My camp is like to Julius Cæsar's host,
    That never fought but had the victory;
    Nor in Pharsalia was there such hot war
    As these, my followers, willingly would have.   155
    Legions of spirits, fleeting in the air,

140 *Hydra* a hundred-headed monster   154 *Pharsalia* battle in which Julius
killed by Hercules.   Caesar defeated Pompey in 48 B.C.

Direct our bullets and our weapons' points,
And make our strokes to wound the senseless air;
And when she sees our bloody colors spread,
Then Victory begins to take her flight,   160
Resting herself upon my milk-white tent.
But come, my lords, to weapons let us fall;
The field is ours, the Turk, his wife, and all.
                Exit with his followers.

Bajazeth. Come, kings and bassoes, let us glut our swords,
That thirst to drink the feeble Persians' blood.   165
                Exit with his followers.

Zabina. Base concubine, must thou be placed by me
That am the empress of the mighty Turk?
Zenocrate. Disdainful Turkess, and unreverend boss,
Call'st thou me concubine, that am betrothed
Unto the great and mighty Tamburlaine?   170
Zabina. To Tamburlaine, the great Tartarian thief!
Zenocrate. Thou wilt repent these lavish words of thine
When thy great basso-master and thyself
Must plead for mercy at his kingly feet,
And sue to me to be your advocates.   175
Zabina. And sue to thee? I tell thee, shameless girl,
Thou shalt be laundress to my waiting-maid.
How lik'st thou her, Ebea? Will she serve?
Ebea. Madam, she thinks perhaps she is too fine,
But I shall turn her into other weeds   180
And make her dainty fingers fall to work.
Zenocrate. Hear'st thou, Anippe, how thy drudge doth talk,
And how my slave, her mistress, menaceth?
Both for their sauciness shall be employed
To dress the common soldiers' meat and drink,   185
For we will scorn they should come near ourselves.
Anippe. Yet sometimes let your highness send for them
To do the work my chambermaid disdains.
                They sound the battle within.
Zenocrate. Ye gods and powers that govern Persia,
And made my lordly love her worthy king,   190
Now strengthen him against the Turkish Bajazeth,
And let his foes, like flocks of fearful roes
Pursued by hunters, fly his angry looks,
That I may see him issue conqueror.
Zabina. Now, Mahomet, solicit God himself,   195
And make him rain down murdering shot from heaven
To dash the Scythians' brains, and strike them dead

---

168 *boss* fat woman.   180 *weeds* garments.
175 *advocates* possibly "advocatess" (a
feminine form).

That dare to manage arms with him
That offered jewels to thy sacred shrine
When first he warred against the Christians.   200
                    [*They sound within*] *to the battle* **again.**
Zenocrate.   By this the Turks lie weltering in their blood,
And Tamburlaine is lord of Africa.
Zabina.   Thou art deceived. I heard the trumpets sound
As when my emperor overthrew the Greeks
And led them captive into Africa.   205
Straight will I use thee as thy pride deserves;
Prepare thyself to live and die my slave.
Zenocrate.   If Mahomet should come from heaven and swear
My royal lord is slain or conquerèd,
Yet should he not persuade me otherwise   210
But that he lives and will be conqueror.
          [*Enter Bajazeth, pursued by Tamburlaine. They fight briefly
                    and*] *Bajazeth is overcome.*
Tamburlaine.   Now, king of bassoes, who is conqueror?
Bajazeth.   Thou, by the fortune of this damnèd foil.
Tamburlaine.   Where are your stout contributory kings?
                    Enter Techelles, Theridamas, [*and*] *Usumcasane.*
Techelles.   We have their crowns; their bodies strow the field.   215
Tamburlaine.   Each man a crown? Why, kingly fought, i'faith.
Deliver them into my treasury.
Zenocrate.   Now let me offer to my gracious lord
His royal crown again, so highly won.
Tamburlaine.   Nay, take the Turkish crown from her, Zenocrate,   220
And crown me emperor of Africa.
Zabina.   No, Tamburlaine; though now thou gat the best,
Thou shalt not yet be lord of Africa.
Theridamas.   Give her the crown, Turkess, you were best.
                    He takes it from her and gives it [*to*] *Zenocrate.*
Zabina.   Injurious villains, thieves, runagates,   225
How dare you thus abuse my majesty?
Theridamas.   Here, madam, you are empress; she is none.
Tamburlaine.   Not now, Theridamas; her time is past.
The pillars that have bolstered up those terms
Are fall'n in clusters at my conquering feet.   230
Zabina.   Though he be prisoner, he may be ransomèd.
Tamburlaine.   Not all the world shall ransom Bajazeth.
Bajazeth.   Ah, fair Zabina, we have lost the field,
And never had the Turkish emperor
So great a foil by any foreign foe.   235
Now will the Christian miscreants be glad,
Ringing with joy their superstitious bells,

211 *he* i.e., Tamburlaine.   213 *foil* defeat.

And making bonfires for my overthrow.
But ere I die, those foul idolaters
Shall make me bonfires with their filthy bones,　　　　240
For though the glory of this day be lost,
Afric and Greece have garrisons enough
To make me sovereign of the earth again.
Tamburlaine.　Those wallèd garrisons will I subdue,
And write myself great lord of Africa.　　　　245
So from the East unto the furthest West
Shall Tamburlaine extend his puissant arm.
The galleys and those pilling brigandines,
That yearly sail to the Venetian gulf
And hover in the Straits for Christians' wrack,　　　　250
Shall lie at anchor in the Isle Asant,
Until the Persian fleet and men-of-war,
Sailing along the oriental sea,
Have fetched about the Indian continent,
Even from Persepolis to Mexico,　　　　255
And thence unto the Straits of Jubalter,
Where they shall meet and join their force in one,
Keeping in awe the Bay of Portingale
And all the ocean by the British shore;
And by this means I'll win the world at last.　　　　260
Bajazeth.　Yet set a ransom on me, Tamburlaine.
Tamburlaine.　What, think'st thou Tamburlaine esteems thy gold?
I'll make the kings of India, ere I die,
Offer their mines to sue for peace to me,
And dig for treasure to appease my wrath.　　　　265
Come, bind them both, and one lead in the Turk;
The Turkess let my love's maid lead away.
　　　　　　　　　　　　　　　　They bind them.
Bajazeth.　Ah, villains, dare ye touch my sacred arms?
O Mahomet! O sleepy Mahomet!
Zabina.　O cursèd Mahomet, that mak'st us thus　　　　270
The slaves to Scythians rude and barbarous!
Tamburlaine.　Come, bring them in, and for this happy conquest
Triumph, and solemnize a martial feast.
　　　　　　　　　　　　　　　　Exeunt.

248 *pilling* pillaging.
251 *Isle Asant* Zante, an island off the northern coast of Peloponnesus (Achaia).

255 *Persepolis to Mexico* i.e., across the Pacific.
256 *Jubalter* Gibraltar.
258 *Portingale* Biscay.

IV,i.

[Enter the] Soldan of Egypt, with three or four Lords, Capolin,
[and a Messenger].

Soldan. Awake, ye men of Memphis! Hear the clang
  Of Scythian trumpets! Hear the basilisks,
  That roaring shake Damascus' turrets down!
  The rogue of Volga holds Zenocrate,
  The Soldan's daughter, for his concubine,   5
  And with a troop of thieves and vagabonds,
  Hath spread his colors to our high disgrace,
  While you, faint-hearted base Egyptians,
  Lie slumbering on the flowery banks of Nile,
  As crocodiles that unaffrighted rest   10
  While thundering cannons rattle on their skins.
Messenger. Nay, mighty Soldan, did your greatness see
  The frowning looks of fiery Tamburlaine,
  That with his terror and imperious eyes
  Commands the hearts of his associates,   15
  It might amaze your royal majesty.
Soldan. Villain, I tell thee, were that Tamburlaine
  As monstrous as Gorgon, prince of hell,
  The Soldan would not start a foot from him.
  But speak, what power hath he?   20
Messenger. Mighty lord,
  Three hundred thousand men in armor clad,
  Upon their prancing steeds, disdainfully
  With wanton paces trampling on the ground;
  Five hundred thousand footmen threatening shot,   25
  Shaking their swords, their spears, and iron bills,
  Environing their standard round, that stood
  As bristle-pointed as a thorny wood;
  Their warlike engines and munition
  Exceed the forces of their martial men.   30
Soldan. Nay, could their numbers countervail the stars,
  Or ever-drizzling drops of April showers,
  Or withered leaves that autumn shaketh down,
  Yet would the Soldan by his conquering power
  So scatter and consume them in his rage,   35
  That not a man should live to rue their fall.
Capolin. So might your highness, had you time to sort
  Your fighting men and raise your royal host,
  But Tamburlaine by expedition
  Advantage takes of your unreadiness.   40

IV,i.

  2 *basilisks* large cannons.   31 *countervail* equal in number.
  18 *monstrous* unnatural. *Gorgon* Dem-   39 *expedition* speedy action.
ogorgon, a devil.

Soldan.   Let him take all th'advantages he can.
   Were all the world conspired to fight for him,
   Nay, were he devil, as he is no man,
   Yet in revenge of fair Zenocrate,
   Whom he detaineth in despite of us,   45
   This arm should send him down to Erebus,
   To shroud his shame in darkness of the night.
Messenger.   Pleaseth your mightiness to understand,
   His resolution far exceedeth all.
   The first day when he pitcheth down his tents,   50
   White is their hue, and on his silver crest
   A snowy feather spangled-white he bears,
   To signify the mildness of his mind
   That, satiate with spoil, refuseth blood;
   But when Aurora mounts the second time,   55
   As red as scarlet is his furniture;
   Then must his kindled wrath be quenched with blood,
   Not sparing any that can manage arms;
   But if these threats move not submission,
   Black are his colors, black pavilion;   60
   His spear, his shield, his horse, his armor, plumes,
   And jetty feathers menace death and hell;
   Without respect of sex, degree, or age,
   He razeth all his foes with fire and sword.
Soldan.   Merciless villain, peasant ignorant   65
   Of lawful arms or martial discipline!
   Pillage and murder are his usual trades.
   The slave usurps the glorious name of war.
   See Capolin, the fair Arabian king,
   That hath been disappointed by this slave   70
   Of my fair daughter and his princely love,
   May have fresh warning to go war with us,
   And be revenged for her disparagement.

                                                      [*Exeunt.*]

                                                          IV,ii.
[*Enter*] *Tamburlaine, Techelles, Theridamas, Usumcasane,*
   Zenocrate, Anippe, two Moors drawing Bajazeth in his cage,
          and his Wife, [Zabina] following him.
Tamburlaine.   Bring out my footstool.
                    They take Bajazeth out of the cage.

46 *Erebus* the son of Chaos and the
brother of Night, whose name came to
signify the dark region between Earth
and Hades.

55 *Aurora mounts* The dawn comes
up.

56 *furniture* military equipment (tent
and dress, etc.).

Bajazeth.   Ye holy priests of heavenly Mahomet,
      That, sacrificing, slice and cut your flesh,
      Staining his altars with your purple blood,
      Make heaven to frown and every fixèd star   5
      To suck up poison from the moorish fens,
      And pour it in this glorious tyrant's throat!
Tamburlaine.   The chiefest god, first mover of that sphere
      Enchased with thousands ever-shining lamps,
      Will sooner burn the glorious frame of heaven   10
      Than it should so conspire my overthrow.
      But, villain, thou that wishest this to me,
      Fall prostrate on the low disdainful earth,
      And be the footstool of great Tamburlaine,
      That I may rise into my royal throne.   15
Bajazeth.   First shalt thou rip my bowels with thy sword
      And sacrifice my heart to death and hell,
      Before I yield to such a slavery.
Tamburlaine.   Base villain, vassal, slave to Tamburlaine,
      Unworthy to embrace or touch the ground   20
      That bears the honor of my royal weight,
      Stoop, villain, stoop! Stoop, for so he bids
      That may command thee piecemeal to be torn,
      Or scattered like the lofty cedar trees
      Struck with the voice of thundering Jupiter.   25
Bajazeth.   Then, as I look down to the damnèd fiends,
      Fiends, look on me; and thou, dread god of hell,
      With ebon scepter strike this hateful earth,
      And make it swallow both of us at once!
            Tamburlaine gets up upon him [and in]to his chair.
Tamburlaine.   Now clear the triple region of the air,   30
      And let the majesty of heaven behold
      Their scourge and terror tread on emperors.
      Smile stars that reigned at my nativity,
      And dim the brightness of their neighbor lamps;
      Disdain to borrow light of Cynthia,   35
      For I, the chiefest lamp of all the earth,
      First rising in the east with mild aspect,
      But fixèd now in the meridian line,
      Will send up fire to your turning spheres
      And cause the sun to borrow light of you.   40
      My sword struck fire from his coat of steel,
      Even in Bithynia, when I took this Turk,
      As when a fiery exhalation,
      Wrapped in the bowels of a freezing cloud,
      Fighting for passage, makes the welkin crack   45

IV,ii.   35 *Cynthia* the moon.
   7 *glorious* vaunting, boastful.   45 *welkin* world.

And casts a flash of lightning to the earth.
But ere I march to wealthy Persia,
Or leave Damascus and th'Egyptian fields,
As was the fame of Clymene's brain-sick son
That almost brent the axle-tree of heaven,   50
So shall our swords, our lances, and our shot
Fill all the air with fiery meteors.
Then, when the sky shall wax as red as blood,
It shall be said I made it red myself,
To make me think of naught but blood and war.   55
Zabina.   Unworthy king, that by thy cruelty
Unlawfully usurpest the Persian seat,
Dar'st thou, that never saw an emperor
Before thou met my husband in the field,
Being thy captive, thus abuse his state,   60
Keeping his kingly body in a cage,
That roofs of gold and sun-bright palaces
Should have prepared to entertain his grace?
And treading him beneath thy loathsome feet,
Whose feet the kings of Africa have kissed?   65
Techelles.   You must devise some torment worse, my lord,
To make these captives rein their lavish tongues.
Tamburlaine.   Zenocrate, look better to your slave.
Zenocrate.   She is my handmaid's slave, and she shall look
That these abuses flow not from her tongue.   70
Chide her, Anippe.
Anippe.   Let these be warnings for you then, my slave,
How you abuse the person of the king;
Or else I swear to have you whipped stark naked.
Bajazeth.   Great Tamburlaine, great in my overthrow,   75
Ambitious pride shall make thee fall as low,
For treading on the back of Bajazeth,
That should be horsèd on four mighty kings.
Tamburlaine.   Thy names and titles and thy dignities
Are fled from Bajazeth and remain with me,   80
That will maintain it against a world of kings.
Put him in again.
                              [*They put him into the cage.*]
Bajazeth.   Is this a place for mighty Bajazeth?
Confusion light on him that helps thee thus.
Tamburlaine.   There, whiles he lives, shall Bajazeth be kept,   85
And where I go be thus in triumph drawn;
And thou, his wife, shalt feed him with the scraps

---

49 *Clymene's brain-sick son* Phaëthon, son of Apollo and Clymene, who drove the chariot of his father, the sun, but was unable to control the horses.   50 *brent* burned. *axle-tree of heaven* the axis of the universe on which all of the heavenly spheres were believed to turn.   60 *state* royal position.

My servitors shalt bring thee from my board,
For he that gives him other food than this
Shall sit by him and starve to death himself.   90
This is my mind, and I will have it so.
Not all the kings and emperors of the earth,
If they would lay their crowns before my feet,
Shall ransom him or take him from his cage.
The ages that shall talk of Tamburlaine,   95
Even from this day to Plato's wondrous year,
Shall talk how I have handled Bajazeth.
These Moors, that drew him from Bithynia
To fair Damascus, where we now remain,
Shall lead him with us wheresoe'er we go.   100
Techelles, and my loving followers,
Now may we see Damascus' lofty towers,
Like to the shadows of Pyramidès
That with their beauties graced the Memphian fields.
The golden stature of their feathered bird,   105
That spreads her wings upon the city walls,
Shall not defend it from our battering shot.
The townsmen mask in silk and cloth of gold,
And every house is as a treasury;
The men, the treasure, and the town is ours.   110
Theridamas.   Your tents of white now pitched before the gates,
And gentle flags of amity displayed,
I doubt not but the governor will yield,
Offering Damascus to your majesty.
Tamburlaine.   So shall he have his life, and all the rest.   115
But if he stay until the bloody flag
Be once advanced on my vermilion tent,
He dies, and those that kept us out so long.
And when they see me march in black array,
With mournful streamers hanging down their heads,   120
Were in that city all the world contained,
Not one should 'scape, but perish by our swords.
Zenocrate.   Yet would you have some pity for my sake,
Because it is my country's and my father's.
Tamburlaine.   Not for the world, Zenocrate, if I have sworn.   125
Come, bring in the Turk.

                                        Exeunt.

96 *Plato's wondrous year* a time when
the irregularities in the universe caused
by the movement of planets are all regularized, all being in the same position
at the end of the year as at the beginning. This concept, which Plato refers
to in his *Timæus,* was commonplace in
medieval and Renaissance thought.

105 *stature* statue. *bird* the ibis, a
bird sacred to the Egyptians.

[*Enter*] *Soldan,* [*King of*] *Arabia, Capolin, with streaming*
colours; and Soldiers.

Soldan. Methinks we march as Meleager did,
  Environèd with brave Argolian knights,
  To chase the savage Calydonian boar,
  Or Cephalus, with lusty Theban youths,
  Against the wolf that angry Themis sent   5
  To waste and spoil the sweet Aonian fields.
  A monster of five hundred thousand heads,
  Compact of rapine, piracy, and spoil,
  The scum of men, the hate and scourge of God,
  Raves in Egyptia and annoyeth us.   10
  My lord, it is the bloody Tamburlaine,
  A sturdy felon, and a base-bred thief,
  By murder raisèd to the Persian crown,
  That dares control us in our territories.
  To tame the pride of this presumptuous beast,   15
  Join your Arabians with the Soldan's power;
  Let us unite our royal bands in one
  And hasten to remove Damascus' siege.
  It is a blemish to the majesty
  And high estate of mighty emperors,   20
  That such a base usurping vagabond
  Should brave a king or wear a princely crown.
King of Arabia. Renownèd Soldan, have ye lately heard
  The overthrow of mighty Bajazeth
  About the confines of Bithynia?   25
  The slavery wherewith he persecutes
  The noble Turk and his great emperess?
Soldan. I have, and sorrow for his bad success.
  But, noble lord of great Arabia,
  Be so persuaded that the Soldan is   30
  No more dismayed with tidings of his fall,
  Than in the haven when the pilot stands
  And views a stranger's ship rent in the winds
  And shiverèd against a craggy rock.
  Yet in compassion of his wretched state,   35
  A sacred vow to heaven and him I make,

IV,iii.

ι *Meleager* a Greek hero who slew the
giant boar which laid waste his native
Calydon.

2 *Argolian* of Argos.

4 *Cephalus* a hunter beloved by Eos,
the dawn, and possessed of a spear which
never missed its mark.

5 *Themis* daughter of Uranus and
Gea and married to Zeus; stands for order and justice in the universe. She is
the mother of the nymphs.

6 *Aonian* Greek.

Confirming it with Ibis' holy name,
That Tamburlaine shall rue the day, the hour,
Wherein he wrought such ignominious wrong
Unto the hallowed person of a prince, 40
Or kept the fair Zenocrate so long,
As concubine, I fear, to feed his lust.
King of Arabia. Let grief and fury hasten on revenge.
Let Tamburlaine for his offences feel
Such plagues as heaven and we can pour on him. 45
I long to break my spear upon his crest
And prove the weight of his victorious arm;
For fame, I fear, hath been too prodigal
In sounding through the world his partial praise.
Soldan. Capolin, hast thou surveyed our powers? 50
Capolin. Great emperors of Egypt and Arabia,
The number of your hosts united is
A hundred and fifty thousand horse,
Two hundred thousand foot, brave men-at-arms,
Courageous and full of hardiness, 55
As frolic as the hunters in the chase
Of savage beasts amid the desert woods.
King of Arabia. My mind presageth fortunate success,
And, Tamburlaine, my spirit doth foresee
The utter ruin of thy men and thee. 60
Soldan. Then rear your standards; let your sounding drums
Direct our soldiers to Damascus' walls.
Now, Tamburlaine, the mighty Soldan comes
And leads with him the great Arabian king
To dim thy baseness and obscurity, 65
Famous for nothing but for theft and spoil;
To raze and scatter thy inglorious crew
Of Scythians and slavish Persians.

Exeunt.

IV,iv.

*The banquet [is set out] and to it come Tamburlaine, all in
scarlet, [Zenocrate], Theridamas, Techelles, Usumcasane,
[Bajazeth], the Turk, [drawn in his cage, Zabina], with others.*
Tamburlaine. Now hang our bloody colors by Damascus,
Reflexing hues of blood upon their heads,
While they walk quivering on their city walls,
Half dead for fear before they feel my wrath.

37 *Ibis' holy name* See note at IV,ii,   47 *prove* test.
105.

Then let us freely banquet and carouse   5
Full bowls of wine unto the god of war,
That means to fill your helmets full of gold,
And make Damascus' spoils as rich to you
As was to Jason Colchos' golden fleece.
And now, Bajazeth, hast thou any stomach?   10

Bajazeth.   Ay, such a stomach, cruel Tamburlaine, as I could willingly
feed upon thy blood-raw heart.

Tamburlaine.   Nay, thine own is easier to come by. Pluck out that, and
'twill serve thee and thy wife. Well, Zenocrate, Techelles, and the
rest, fall to your victuals.   15

Bajazeth.   Fall to, and never may your meat digest!
Ye Furies, that can mask invisible,
Dive to the bottom of Avernus' pool,
And in your hands bring hellish poison up,
And squeeze it in the cup of Tamburlaine!   20
Or, wingèd snakes of Lerna, cast your stings,
And leave your venoms in this tyrant's dish!

Zabina.   And may this banquet prove as ominous
As Progne's to th'adulterous Thracian king
That fed upon the substance of his child.   25

Zenocrate.   My lord, how can you suffer these
Outrageous curses by these slaves of yours?

Tamburlaine.   To let them see, divine Zenocrate,
I glory in the curses of my foes,
Having the power from the imperial heaven   30
To turn them all upon their proper heads.

Techelles.   I pray you, give them leave, madam; this speech is a goodly
refreshing to them.

Theridamas.   But, if his highness would let them be fed, it would do
them more good.   35

Tamburlaine.   Sirrah, why fall you not to? Are you so daintily brought
up, you cannot eat your own flesh?

Bajazeth.   First, legions of devils shall tear thee in pieces.

Usumcasane.   Villain, knowest thou to whom thou speakest?

Tamburlaine.   Oh, let him alone. Here; eat, sir; take it from my   [40
sword's point, or I'll thrust it to thy heart.

[Bajazeth] takes [the food,] and stamps upon it.

IV,iv.

9 *Jason* Greek hero who with his
Argonauts journeyed to Colchos in quest
of the golden fleece.

10 *stomach* (1) appetite (2) anger
(since choler was produced in the stomach).

18 **Furies** See note to *Dido,* II,i,230.
19 *Avernus' pool* See note at I,ii,159.
21 *Lerna* region near Argos where

Hercules killed the Hydra, a nine-headed
monster.

24-25 *Progne . . . child* After Tereus,
king of Thrace, had ravished Philomela,
her sister, Progne, sought vengeance
upon the king, her husband, by murdering their child, Itys, and tricking
Tereus into eating the body.

30 *imperial* See note at II,vii,15.

Theridamas.   He stamps it under his feet, my lord.

Tamburlaine.   Take it up, villain, and eat it, or I will make thee slice the brawns of thy arms into carbonadoes and eat them.

Usumcasane.   Nay, 'twere better he killed his wife, and then she   [45 shall be sure not to be starved, and he be provided for a month's victual beforehand.

Tamburlaine.   Here is my dagger. Dispatch her while she is fat, for if she live but a while longer, she will fall into a consumption with fretting, and then she will not be worth the eating.   50

Theridamas.   Dost thou think that Mahomet will suffer this?

Techelles.   'Tis like he will, when he cannot let it.

Tamburlaine.   Go to; fall to your meat. What, not a bit? Belike he hath not been watered to-day; give him some drink.

> *They give [Bajazeth] water to drink, and he flings*
>   *it on the ground.*

Fast, and welcome, sir, while hunger make you eat. How now,   [55 Zenocrate, doth not the Turk and his wife make a goodly show at a banquet?

Zenocrate.   Yes, my lord.

Theridamas.   Methinks 'tis a great deal better than a consort of music.

Tamburlaine.   Yet music would do well to cheer up Zenocrate.   [60 Pray thee tell, why art thou so sad? If thou wilt have a song, the Turk shall strain his voice. But why is it?

Zenocrate.   My lord, to see my father's town besieged,
The country wasted, where myself was born,
How can it but afflict my very soul?   65
If any love remain in you, my lord,
Or if my love unto your majesty
May merit favor at your highness' hands,
Then raise your siege from fair Damascus' walls,
And with my father take a friendly truce.   70

Tamburlaine.   Zenocrate, were Egypt Jove's own land,
Yet would I with my sword make Jove to stoop.
I will confute those blind geographers
That make a triple region in the world,
Excluding regions which I mean to trace,   75
And with this pen reduce them to a map,
Calling the provinces, cities, and towns,
After my name and thine, Zenocrate.
Here at Damascus will I make the point
That shall begin the perpendicular.   80

---

44 *brawns* muscles. *carbonadoes* thin
strips of meat (like rashers of bacon).
52 *let* hinder.
55 *while* until.
59 *consort* company of musicians.

74 *triple region* i.e., Asia, Africa, and
Europe.
76 *this pen* i.e., his sword.
79–80 *Here . . . perpendicular* The
sense of this difficult passage is that

And wouldst thou have me buy thy father's love
With such a loss? Tell me, Zenocrate.
Zenocrate.   Honor still wait on happy Tamburlaine;
Yet give me leave to plead for him, my lord.
Tamburlaine.   Content thyself; his person shall be safe,   85
And all the friends of fair Zenocrate,
If with their lives they will be pleased to yield,
Or may be forced to make me emperor;
For Egypt and Arabia must be mine.
     Feed, you slave; thou mayst think thyself happy to be fed   [90
from my trencher. [*To Bajazeth.*]
Bajazeth.   My empty stomach, full of idle heat,
Draws bloody humors from my feeble parts,
Preserving life by hasting cruel death.
My veins are pale, my sinews hard and dry,   95
My joints benumbed; unless I eat, I die.
Zabina.   Eat, Bajazeth. Let us live in spite of them, looking some happy
power will pity and enlarge us.
Tamburlaine.   Here, Turk; wilt thou have a clean trencher?
Bajazeth.   Ay, tyrant, and more meat.   100
Tamburlaine.   Soft, sir, you must be dieted; too much eating will make
you surfeit.
Theridamas.   So it would, my lord, 'specially having so small a walk
and so little exercise.
                    Enter a second course of crowns.
Tamburlaine.   Theridamas, Techelles, and Casane, here are the   [105
cates you desire to finger, are they not?
Theridamas.   Ay, my lord, but none save kings must feed with these.
Techelles.   'Tis enough for us to see them, and for Tamburlaine only
to enjoy them.
Tamburlaine.   Well, here is now to the Soldan of Egypt, the King   [110
of Arabia, and the Governor of Damascus. Now, take these three
crowns, and pledge me, my contributory kings. I crown you here,
Theridamas, King of Argier; Techelles, King of Fez; and Usumcasane,
King of Morocco. How say you to this, Turk? These are not your
contributory kings.   115
Bajazeth.   Nor shall they long be thine, I warrant them.
Tamburlaine.   Kings of Argier, Morocco, and of Fez,
You that have marched with happy Tamburlaine
As far as from the frozen place of heaven

Tamburlaine will make Damascus the
center of the new world he will create
by making its meridian the first meridian. It will, in other words, occupy the
position on the map which Greenwich,
England occupies today.

83 *still* forever.
97 *looking* hoping that.
99 *trencher* flat wooden dish.
106 *cates* delicacies.

Unto the wat'ry morning's ruddy bower,   120
And thence by land unto the torrid zone,
Deserve these titles I endow you with
By valor and by magnanimity.
Your births shall be no blemish to your fame,
For virtue is the fount whence honor springs,   125
And they are worthy she investeth kings.
Theridamas.   And since your highness hath so well vouchsafed,
If we deserve them not with higher meeds
Than erst our states and actions have retained,
Take them away again, and make us slaves.   130
Tamburlaine.   Well said, Theridamas. When holy Fates
Shall 'stablish me in strong Egyptia,
We mean to travel to th'antarctic pole,
Conquering the people underneath our feet,
And be renowned as never emperors were.   135
Zenocrate, I will not crown thee yet,
Until with greater honors I be graced.

                                        [*Exeunt.*]

                                                          V,i.
[*Enter*] *the Governor of Damascus with three or four Citizens,*
        and four Virgins with branches of laurel in their hands.
Governor.   Still doth this man, or rather god of war,
Batter our walls and beat our turrets down;
And to resist with longer stubbornness
Or hope of rescue from the Soldan's power,
Were but to bring our wilful overthrow,   5
And make us desperate of our threat'nèd lives.
We see his tents have now been alterèd
With terrors to the last and cruel'st hue.
His coal-black colors, everywhere advanced,
Threaten our city with a general spoil;   10
And if we should with common rites of arms
Offer our safeties to his clemency,
I fear the custom proper to his sword,
Which he observes as parcel of his fame,
Intending so to terrify the world,   15
By any innovation or remorse
Will never be dispensed with till our deaths.
Therefore, for these our harmless virgins' sakes,

                        V,i.

124 *births* humble origins.   14 *parcel of* an essential **part of.**
126 *they* they that.   16 *innovation* alteration.

    Whose honors and whose lives rely on him,
    Let us have hope that their unspotted prayers,   20
    Their blubbered cheeks, and hearty humble moans
    Will melt his fury into some remorse,
    And use us like a loving conqueror.
First Virgin.   If humble suits or imprecations—
    Uttered with tears of wretchedness and blood   25
    Shed from the heads and hearts of all our sex,
    Some made your wives, and some your children—
    Might have entreated your obdurate breasts
    To entertain some care of our securities
    Whiles only danger beat upon our walls,   30
    These more than dangerous warrants of our death
    Had never been erected as they be,
    Nor you depend on such weak helps as we.
Governor.   Well, lovely virgins, think our country's care,
    Our love of honor, loath to be enthralled   35
    To foreign powers and rough imperious yokes,
    Would not with too much cowardice or fear,
    Before all hope of rescue were denied,
    Submit yourselves and us to servitude.
    Therefore, in that your safeties and our own,   40
    Your honors, liberties, and lives were weighed
    In equal care and balance with our own,
    Endure as we the malice of our stars,
    The wrath of Tamburlaine and power of wars,
    Or be the means the overweighing heavens   45
    Have kept to qualify these hot extremes,
    And bring us pardon in your cheerful looks.
Second Virgin.   Then here, before the majesty of heaven
    And holy patrons of Egyptia,
    With knees and hearts submissive we entreat   50
    Grace to our words and pity to our looks
    That this device may prove propitious,
    And through the eyes and ears of Tamburlaine
    Convey events of mercy to his heart.
    Grant that these signs of victory we yield   55
    May bind the temples of his conquering head
    To hide the folded furrows of his brows,
    And shadow his displeasèd countenance
    With happy looks of ruth and lenity.
    Leave us, my lord, and loving countrymen.   60
    What simple virgins may persuade, we will.
Governor.   Farewell, sweet virgins, on whose safe return
    Depends our city, liberty, and lives.

                Exeunt [all except the Virgins].

21 *blubbered* tear-stained.   54 *events* results.

V,ii.

[*Enter*] *Tamburlaine, Techelles, Theridamas, Usumcasane,*
    with others; Tamburlaine all in black, and very melancholy.
Tamburlaine.   What, are the turtles frayed out of their nests?
    Alas, poor fools, must you be first shall feel
    The sworn destruction of Damascus?
    They know my custom; could they not as well
    Have sent ye out when first my milk-white flags,   5
    Through which sweet Mercy threw her gentle beams,
    Reflexing them on your disdainful eyes,
    As now when fury and incensèd hate
    Flings slaughtering terror from my coal-black tents,
    And tells for truth submissions comes too late?   10
First Virgin.   Most happy king and emperor of the earth,
    Image of honor and nobility,
    For whom the powers divine have made the world
    And on whose throne the holy Graces sit,
    In whose sweet person is comprised the sum   15
    Of nature's skill and heavenly majesty,
    Pity our plights! O, pity poor Damascus!
    Pity old age, within whose silver hairs
    Honor and reverence evermore have reigned.
    Pity the marriage-bed, where many a lord,   20
    In prime and glory of his loving joy,
    Embraceth now with tears of ruth and blood
    The jealous body of his fearful wife,
    Whose cheeks and hearts, so punished with conceit
    To think thy puissant never-stayèd arm   25
    Will part their bodies and prevent their souls
    From heavens of comfort yet their age might bear,
    Now wax all pale and withered to the death,
    As well for grief our ruthless governor
    Have thus refused the mercy of thy hand,   30
    Whose scepter angels kiss and Furies dread,
    As for their liberties, their loves, or lives.
    Oh, then, for these, and such as we ourselves,
    For us, for infants, and for all our bloods,

V,ii.

Although the virgins remain on stage
and no change of place is indicated, I
have followed the 1590 direction, *Actus
5 Scæna 2,* in indicating a new scene
here.
    1 *turtles frayed* frightened turtle-
doves.
    2 *fools* helpless ones.

14 *Graces* three daughters of Jupiter
(Euphrosyne, Aglaia, and Thalia) who
lend their charms to whatever elevates
man, poetry in particular; for they live
in harmony with the Muses on Mt.
Olympus.
    24 *conceit* foreboding.
    31 *Furies* See note to *Dido,* II,i,230.

That never nourished thought against thy rule,   35
Pity, O pity, sacred emperor,
The prostrate service of this wretched town;
And take in sign thereof this gilded wreath,
Whereto each man of rule hath given his hand,
And wished, as worthy subjects, happy means   40
To be investers of thy royal brows
Even with the true Egyptian diadem.
Tamburlaine.   Virgins, in vain ye labor to prevent
That which mine honor swears shall be performed.
Behold my sword; what see you at the point?   45
First Virgin.   Nothing but fear and fatal steel, my lord.
Tamburlaine.   Your fearful minds are thick and misty then,
For there sits Death; there sits imperious Death,
Keeping his circuit by the slicing edge.
But I am pleased you shall not see him there.   50
He now is seated on my horsemen's spears,
And on their points his fleshless body feeds.
Techelles, straight go charge a few of them
To charge these dames and show my servant, Death,
Sitting in scarlet on their armèd spears.   55
Virgins.   Oh, pity us!
Tamburlaine.   Away with them, I say, and show them Death.
                                        They take them away.
I will not spare these proud Egyptians,
Nor change my martial observations
For all the wealth of Gihon's golden waves,   60
Or for the love of Venus, would she leave
The angry god of arms and lie with me.
They have refused the offer of their lives;
And know my customs are as peremptory
As wrathful planets, death or destiny.   65
                        Enter Techelles.
What, have your horsemen shown the virgins Death?
Techelles.   They have, my lord, and on Damascus' walls
Have hoisted up their slaughtered carcasses.
Tamburlaine.   A sight as baneful to their souls, I think,
As are Thessalian drugs or mithridate.   70
But go, my lords, put the rest to the sword.
                        Exeunt [all except Tamburlaine].

49 *circuit* sphere of action.
52 *fleshless body* Death is conceived of, in the medieval manner, as a skeleton. He is also a judge whose circuit is equal to that reached by the edge of Tamburlaine's sword.
59 *observations* customary practices.
60 *Gihon* one of the traditional four rivers of Eden.
62 *god of arms* i.e., Mars, the beloved of Venus.
70 *mithridate* Although generally used as an antidote against poisons, it is here referred to as a poison itself.

Ah, fair Zenocrate! Divine Zenocrate!
Fair is too foul an epithet for thee,
That in thy passion for thy country's love,
And fear to see thy kingly father's harm,   75
With hair dishevelled wip'st thy watery cheeks;
And, like to Flora in her morning's pride,
Shaking her silver tresses in the air,
Rain'st on the earth resolvèd pearl in showers,
And sprinklest sapphires on thy shining face,   80
Where Beauty, mother to the Muses, sits,
And comments volumes with her ivory pen,
Taking instructions from thy flowing eyes,
Eyes, when that Ebena steps to heaven,
In silence of thy solemn evening's walk,   85
Making the mantle of the richest night,
The moon, the planets, and the meteors, light.
There angels in their crystal armors fight
A doubtful battle with my tempted thoughts
For Egypt's freedom and the Soldan's life,   90
His life that so consumes Zenocrate,
Whose sorrows lay more siege unto my soul
Than all my army to Damascus' walls;
And neither Persians' sovereign nor the Turk
Troubled my senses with conceit of foil   95
So much by much as doth Zenocrate.
What is beauty, saith my sufferings, then?
If all the pens that ever poets held
Had fed the feeling of their masters' thoughts,
And every sweetness that inspired their hearts,   100
Their minds, and muses on admirèd themes;
If all the heavenly quintessence they still
From their immortal flowers of poesy,
Wherein, as in a mirror, we perceive
The highest reaches of a human wit;   105
If these had made one poem's period,
And all combined in beauty's worthiness,
Yet should there hover in their restless heads
One thought, one grace, one wonder, at the least,
Which into words no virtue can digest.   110
But how unseemly is it for my sex,
My discipline of arms and chivalry,

74 *passion* sorrow.
77 *Flora* goddess of springtime and flowers.
79 *resolvèd pearl* i.e., tears.
84 *Ebena* There is no such classical deity, and where Marlowe derived the name has been much debated. The sense of the passage (84–87) is that Zenocrate's eyes at evening lend light to the moon, stars, and planets.
95 *conceit of foil* conception of defeat.
102 *still* distill.

My nature, and the terror of my name,
To harbor thoughts effeminate and faint!
Save only that in beauty's just applause,　　　　　　　115
With whose instinct the soul of man is touched;
And every warrior that is rapt with love
Of fame, of valor, and of victory,
Must needs have beauty beat on his conceits.
I thus conceiving and subduing both,　　　　　　　120
That which hath stopped the tempest of the gods,
Even from the fiery-spangled veil of heaven,
To feel the lovely warmth of shepherds' flames
And march in cottages of strowèd weeds,
Shall give the world to note, for all my birth,　　　　　125
That virtue solely is the sum of glory,
And fashions men with true nobility.
Who's within there?
　　　　　　Enter two or three [Attendants].
Hath Bajazeth been fed to-day?
Attendant.　Ay, my lord.　　　　　　　　　　　130
Tamburlaine.　Bring him forth. And let us know if the town be ran-
　sacked.
　　　　　　　　　　　　　[Exeunt Attendants.]

　　　Enter Techelles, Theridamas, Usumcasane, and others.
Techelles.　The town is ours, my lord, and fresh supply
　Of conquest and of spoil is offered us.
Tamburlaine.　That's well, Techelles. What's the news?　　135
Techelles.　The Soldan and the Arabian king together
　March on us with such eager violence
　As if there were no way but one with us.
Tamburlaine.　No more there is not, I warrant thee, Techelles.
　　　*They bring in [Bajazeth], the Turk [in his cage, followed by
　　　　　　　　　　Zabina].*
Theridamas.　We know the victory is ours, my lord,　　　140
　But let us save the reverend Soldan's life
　For fair Zenocrate that so laments his state.
Tamburlaine.　That will we chiefly see unto, Theridamas,
　For sweet Zenocrate, whose worthiness
　Deserves a conquest over every heart.　　　　　　145
　And now, my footstool, if I lose the field,
　You hope of liberty and restitution.
　Here let him stay, my masters, from the tents,
　Till we have made us ready for the field.

121–124 *That . . . weeds* a very obscure passage which has been much
emended. The sense seems to be that
beauty has eased the fury of the gods
and caused them to assume the guise of
shepherds, as Jove and Apollo did when
courting mortal women.

Pray for us, Bajazeth; we are going.   150
                    Exeunt [all except Bajazeth and Zabina].
Bajazeth.   Go, never to return with victory!
    Millions of men encompass thee about,
    And gore thy body with as many wounds!
    Sharp forkèd arrows light upon thy horse!
    Furies from the black Cocytus lake,   155
    Break up the earth, and with their firebrands
    Enforce thee run upon the baneful pikes!
    Volleys of shot pierce through thy charmèd skin,
    And every bullet dipped in poisoned drugs!
    Or roaring cannons sever all thy joints,   160
    Making thee mount as high as eagles soar!
Zabina.   Let all the swords and lances in the field
    Stick in his breast as in their proper rooms!
    At every pore let blood come dropping forth,
    That lingering pains may massacre his heart   165
    And madness send his damnèd soul to hell!
Bajazeth.   Ah, fair Zabina, we may curse his power,
    The heavens may frown, the earth for anger quake,
    But such a star hath influence in his sword
    As rules the skies and countermands the gods   170
    More than Cimmerian Styx or Destiny.
    And then shall we in this detested guise,
    With shame, with hunger, and with horror—ay,
    Griping our bowels with retorquèd thoughts—
    And have no hope to end our ecstasies.   175
Zabina.   Then is there left no Mahomet, no God,
    No fiend, no fortune, nor no hope of end
    To our infamous, monstrous slaveries?
    Gape earth, and let the fiends infernal view
    A hell as hopeless and as full of fear   180
    As are the blasted banks of Erebus,
    Where shaking ghosts with ever-howling groans
    Hover about the ugly ferryman
    To get a passage to Elysium!
    Why should we live? Oh, wretches, beggars, slaves!   185
    Why live we, Bajazeth, and build up nests
    So high within the region of the air,
    By living long in this oppression,
    That all the world will see and laugh to scorn
    The former triumphs of our mightiness   190

---

155 *Cocytus* a river leading into the underworld; it was a tributary of Avernus (see note at I,ii,159).

171 *Cimmerian* black (see note at III, ii,77). *Styx* the chief river of Hades.

174 *retorquèd* frustrated, bent and twisted back upon itself.

181 *Erebus* See note at IV,i,46.

183 *ferryman* Charon, who conveyed the dead across the river Styx.

 In this obscure infernal servitude?
Bajazeth. O life more loathsome to my vexèd thoughts
 Than noisome parbreak of the Stygian snakes,
 Which fills the nooks of hell with standing air,
 Infecting all the ghosts with cureless griefs!   195
 O dreary engines of my loathèd sight,
 That sees my crown, my honor, and my name
 Thrust under yoke and thraldom of a thief,
 Why feed ye still on day's accursèd beams,
 And sink not quite into my tortured soul?   200
 You see my wife, my queen, and emperess,
 Brought up and proppèd by the hand of Fame,
 Queen of fifteen contributory queens,
 Now thrown to rooms of black abjection,
 Smeared with blots of basest drudgery,   205
 And villainess to shame, disdain, and misery.
 Accursèd Bajazeth, whose words of ruth,
 That would with pity cheer Zabina's heart,
 And make our souls resolve in ceaseless tears,
 Sharp hunger bites upon and gripes the root   210
 From whence the issues of my thoughts do break.
 O poor Zabina! O my queen, my queen!
 Fetch me some water for my burning breast,
 To cool and comfort me with longer date,
 That in the shortened sequel of my life   215
 I may pour forth my soul into thine arms
 With words of love, whose moaning intercourse
 Hath hitherto been stayed with wrath and hate
 Of our expressless banned inflictions.
Zabina. Sweet Bajazeth, I will prolong thy life   220
 As long as any blood or spark of breath
 Can quench or cool the torments of my grief.

             She goes out.

Bajazeth. Now, Bajazeth, abridge thy baneful days,
 And beat thy brains out of thy conquered head,
 Since other means are all forbidden me,   225
 That may be ministers of my decay.
 O highest lamp of ever-living Jove,
 Accursèd day, infected with my griefs,
 Hide now thy stainèd face in endless night,
 And shut the windows of the lightsome heavens.   230
 Let ugly Darkness with her rusty coach
 Engirt with tempests, wrapped in pitchy clouds,
 Smother the earth with never-fading mists,
 And let her horses from their nostrils breathe

193 *parbreak* vomit.   209 *resolve* dissolve.
196 *engines* instruments.

Rebellious winds and dreadful thunder claps,   235
That in this terror Tamburlaine may live,
And my pined soul, resolved in liquid air,
May still excruciate his tormented thoughts!
Then let the stony dart of senseless cold
Pierce through the center of my withered heart,   240
And make a passage for my loathèd life!
                        He brains himself against the cage.

                        Enter Zabina.
Zabina.   What do mine eyes behold? My husband dead!
His skull all riven in twain, his brains dashed out!
The brains of Bajazeth, my lord and sovereign!
O, Bajazeth, my husband and my lord!   245
O Bajazeth! O Turk! O emperor!
Give him his liquor? Not I. Bring milk and fire, and my blood I
bring him again. Tear me in pieces. Give me the sword with a ball
of wild-fire upon it. Down with him! Down with him! Go to, my
child. Away, away, away! Ah, save that infant! Save him, save |250
him! I, even I, speak to her. The sun was down—streamers white, red,
black. Here, here, here! Fling the meat in his face! Tamburlaine,
Tamburlaine! Let the soldiers be buried. Hell, death, Tamburlaine,
hell! Make ready my coach, my chair, my jewels. I come, I come, I
come!   255
            She runs against the cage and brains herself.

                [Enter] Zenocrate with Anippe.
Zenocrate.   Wretched Zenocrate, that livest to see
Damascus' walls dyed with Egyptian blood,
Thy father's subjects and thy countrymen;
Thy streets strowed with dissevered joints of men,
And wounded bodies gasping yet for life;   260
But most accursed, to see the sun-bright troop
Of heavenly virgins and unspotted maids,
Whose looks might make the angry god of arms
To break his sword and mildly treat of love,
On horsemen's lances to be hoisted up,   265
And guiltlessly endure a cruel death.
For every fell and stout Tartarian steed,
That stamped on others with their thundering hoofs,
When all their riders charged their quivering spears,
Began to check the ground and rein themselves,   270
Gazing upon the beauty of their looks.
Ah, Tamburlaine, wert thou the cause of this,
That term'st Zenocrate thy dearest love?
Whose lives were dearer to Zenocrate
Than her own life, or aught save thine own love?   275

263 *god of arms* Mars.   **270** *check* stamp upon.

But see, another bloody spectacle!
Ah, wretched eyes, the enemies of my heart,
How are ye glutted with these grievous objects,
And tell my soul more tales of bleeding ruth!
See, see, Anippe, if they breathe or no.   280
Anippe.   No breath, nor sense, nor motion in them both.
Ah, madam, this their slavery hath enforced,
And ruthless cruelty of Tamburlaine.
Zenocrate.   Earth, cast up fountains from thy entrails,
And wet thy cheeks for their untimely deaths.   285
Shake with their weight in sign of fear and grief.
Blush heaven, that gave them honor at their birth
And let them die a death so barbarous.
Those that are proud of fickle empery
And place their chiefest good in earthly pomp,   290
Behold the Turk and his great emperess!
Ah, Tamburlaine my love, sweet Tamburlaine,
That fights for scepters and for slippery crowns,
Behold the Turk and his great emperess!
Thou, that in conduct of thy happy stars,   295
Sleep'st every night with conquest on thy brows,
And yet wouldst shun the wavering turns of war,
In fear and feeling of the like distress,
Behold the Turk and his great emperess!
Ah, mighty Jove and holy Mahomet,   300
Pardon my love! Oh, pardon his contempt
Of earthly fortune and respect of pity,
And let not conquest, ruthlessly pursued,
Be equally against his life incensed
In this great Turk and hapless emperess!   305
And pardon me that was not moved with ruth
To see them live so long in misery!
Ah, what may chance to thee, Zenocrate?
Anippe.   Madam, content yourself, and be resolved,
Your love hath Fortune so at his command,   310
That she shall stay and turn her wheel no more,
As long as life maintains his mighty arm
That fights for honor to adorn your head.
               Enter [Philemus], a Messenger.
Zenocrate.   What other heavy news now brings Philemus?
Philemus.   Madam, your father and th'Arabian king,   315
The first affecter of your excellence,
Comes now, as Turnus 'gainst Æneas did,
Armèd with lance into the Egyptian fields,

289 *empery* imperial power.   Æneas married Lavinia, who had once
317 *Turnus* the foe of Æneas (see note   been betrothed to Turnus.
to *Dido*, I,i,89) whose enmity began when

    Ready for battle 'gainst my lord the king.

Zenocrate.   Now shame and duty, love and fear presents   320
    A thousand sorrows to my martyred soul.
    Whom should I wish the fatal victory,
    When my poor pleasures are divided thus,
    And racked by duty from my cursèd heart?
    My father and my first-betrothèd love   325
    Must fight against my life and present love,
    Wherein the change I use condemns my faith
    And makes my deeds infamous through the world.
    But as the gods, to end the Trojans' toil,
    Prevented Turnus of Lavinia   330
    And fatally enriched Æneas' love,
    So, for a final issue to my griefs,
    To pacify my country and my love,
    Must Tamburlaine by their resistless powers,
    With virtue of a gentle victory,   335
    Conclude a league of honor to my hope;
    Then, as the powers divine have pre-ordained,
    With happy safety of my father's life
    Send like defense of fair Arabia.
       They sound to the battle [within], and Tamburlaine enjoys
       the victory, after [which, the King of] Arabia enters wounded.

King of Arabia.   What cursèd power guides the murdering hands   340
    Of this infamous tyrant's soldiers,
    That no escape may save their enemies,
    Nor fortune keep themselves from victory?
    Lie down Arabia, wounded to the death,
    And let Zenocrate's fair eyes behold   345
    That, as for her thou bear'st these wretched arms,
    Even so for her thou diest in these arms,
    Leaving thy blood for witness of thy love.

Zenocrate.   Too dear a witness for such love, my lord.
    Behold Zenocrate, the cursed object   350
    Whose fortunes never masterèd her griefs.
    Behold her wounded in conceit for thee,
    As much as thy fair body is for me!

King of Arabia.   Then shall I die with full contented heart,
    Having beheld divine Zenocrate,   355
    Whose sight with joy would take away my life,
    As now it bringeth sweetness to my wound,
    If I had not been wounded as I am.
    Ah, that the deadly pangs I suffer now
    Would lend an hour's licence to my tongue,   360
    To make discourse of some sweet accidents
    Have chanced thy merits in this worthless bondage,

352 *conceit* imagination.

And that I might be privy to the state
Of thy deserved contentment and thy love.
But, making now a virtue of thy sight,   365
To drive all sorrow from my fainting soul,
Since death denies me further cause of joy,
Deprived of care, my heart with comfort dies,
Since thy desired hand shall close mine eyes.

                                                      [*He dies.*]

Enter Tamburlaine, leading the Soldan; Techelles, Theri-
          damas, Usumcasane, with others.

Tamburlaine.   Come, happy father of Zenocrate,   370
   A title higher than thy Soldan's name.
   Though my right hand have thus enthrallèd thee,
   Thy princely daughter here shall set thee free,
   She that hath calmed the fury of my sword,
   Which had ere this been bathed in streams of blood   375
   As vast and deep as Euphrates or Nile.
Zenocrate.   O sight thrice-welcome to my joyful soul,
   To see the king my father issue safe
   From dangerous battle of my conquering love!
Soldan.   Well met, my only dear Zenocrate,   380
   Though with the loss of Egypt and my crown.
Tamburlaine.   'Twas I, my lord, that gat the victory,
   And therefore grieve not at your overthrow,
   Since I shall render all into your hands,
   And add more strength to your dominions   385
   Than ever yet confirmed th'Egyptian crown.
   The god of war resigns his room to me,
   Meaning to make me general of the world.
   Jove, viewing me in arms, looks pale and wan,
   Fearing my power should pull him from his throne.   390
   Where'er I come the Fatal Sisters sweat,
   And grisly Death, by running to and fro
   To do their ceaseless homage to my sword.
   And here in Afric, where it seldom rains,
   Since I arrived with my triumphant host,   395
   Have swelling clouds, drawn from wide-gasping wounds,
   Been oft resolved in bloody purple showers,
   A meteor that might terrify the earth,
   And make it quake at every drop it drinks.
   Millions of souls sit on the banks of Styx,   400
   Waiting the back-return of Charon's boat;
   Hell and Elysium swarm with ghosts of men
   That I have sent from sundry foughten fields

To spread my fame through hell and up to heaven.
And see, my lord, a sight of strange import,   405
Emperors and kings lie breathless at my feet.
The Turk and his great empress, as it seems,
Left to themselves while we were at the fight,
Have desperately dispatched their slavish lives;
With them Arabia too hath left his life;   410
All sights of power to grace my victory.
And such are objects fit for Tamburlaine,
Wherein, as in a mirror, may be seen
His honor, that consists in shedding blood
When men presume to manage arms with him.   415
Soldan.   Mighty hath God and Mahomet made thy hand,
Renownèd Tamburlaine, to whom all kings
Of force must yield their crowns and emperies;
And I am pleased with this my overthrow,
If, as beseems a person of thy state,   420
Thou hast with honor used Zenocrate.
Tamburlaine.   Her state and person wants no pomp, you see,
And for all blot of foul unchastity,
I record heaven, her heavenly self is clear.
Then let me find no further time to grace   425
Her princely temples with the Persian crown;
But here these kings that on my fortunes wait,
And have been crowned for provèd worthiness
Even by this hand that shall establish them,
Shall now, adjoining all their hands with mine,   430
Invest her here my Queen of Persia.
What saith the noble Soldan and Zenocrate?
Soldan.   I yield with thanks and protestations
Of endless honor to thee for her love.
Tamburlaine.   Then doubt I not but fair Zenocrate   435
Will soon consent to satisfy us both.
Zenocrate.   Else should I much forget myself, my lord.
Theridamas.   Then let us set the crown upon her head,
That long hath lingered for so high a seat.
Techelles.   My hand is ready to perform the deed,   440
For now her marriage-time shall work us rest.
Usumcasane.   And here's the crown, my lord; help set it on.
Tamburlaine.   Then sit thou down, divine Zenocrate,
And here we crown thee Queen of Persia,
And all the kingdoms and dominions   445
That late the power of Tamburlaine subdued.
As Juno, when the giants were suppressed,
That darted mountains at her brother Jove,

447–448 *Juno . . . Jove* Juno actually   war of the Titans against Jove.
had no part in classical accounts of the

So looks my love, shadowing in her brows
Triumphs and trophies for my victories;   450
Or as Latona's daughter, bent to arms,
Adding more courage to my conquering mind.
To gratify thee, sweet Zenocrate,
Egyptians, Moors, and men of Asia,
From Barbary unto the Western Indie,   455
Shall pay a yearly tribute to thy sire;
And from the bounds of Afric to the banks
Of Ganges shall his mighty arm extend.
And now, my lords and loving followers,
That purchased kingdoms by your martial deeds,   460
Cast off your armor, put on scarlet robes,
Mount up your royal places of estate,
Environèd with troops of noblemen,
And there make laws to rule your provinces.
Hang up your weapons on Alcides' post,   465
For Tamburlaine takes truce with all the world.
Thy first-betrothèd love, Arabia,
Shall we with honor, as beseems, entomb
With this great Turk and his fair emperess.
Then, after all these solemn exequies,   470
We will our rites of marriage solemnise.

                                                        [*Exeunt.*]

451 *Latona's daughter* Diana (whose   465 *Alcides' post* the door post of the
arms were the bow and arrow used for   temple of Hercules (Alcides).
hunting, not for warfare).

TAMBURLAINE THE GREAT: PART TWO

THE PLAYERS

Tamburlaine, King of Persia

Calyphas ⎫
Amyras ⎬ his sons
Celebinus ⎭

Theridamas, King of Argier
Techelles, King of Fez
Usumcasane, King of Morocco
Orcanes, King of Natolia
King of Trebizon
King of Soria
King of Jerusalem
King of Amasia
Gazellus, Viceroy of Byron
Uribassa
Sigismund, King of Hungary

Frederick ⎫ lords of Buda and Bo-
Baldwin ⎬ hemia

Callapine, son to Bajazeth, and prisoner to Tamburlaine
Almeda, his keeper

Governor of Babylon
Captain of Balsera
His Son
Another Captain
Maximus, Perdicas, Physicians, Lords, Citizens, Messengers, Soldiers, and Attendants
Zenocrate, wife to Tamburlaine

Olympia, wife to the Captain of Balsera

Turkish Concubines

THE SCENE

Asia and Africa

The Second Part of The Bloody Conquests of Mighty Tamburlaine. With his impassionate fury, for the death of his lady and love, fair Zenocrate: his form of exhortation and discipline to his three sons, and the manner of his own death.

Prologue.

THE PROLOGUE

THE general welcomes Tamburlaine received,
When he arrivèd last upon our stage,
Hath made our poet pen his Second Part,
Where death cuts off the progress of his pomp
And murderous Fates throws all his triumphs down.   5
But what became of fair Zenocrate,
And with how many cities' sacrifice
He celebrated her sad funeral,
Himself in presence shall unfold at large.

I,i.

[*Enter*] *Orcanes, King of Natolia, Gazellus, Viceroy of Byron,*
Uribassa, and their train, with drums and trumpets.

Orcanes. Egregious viceroys of these eastern parts,
Placed by the issue of great Bajazeth,
And sacred lord, the mighty Callapine,
Who lives in Egypt prisoner to that slave
Which kept his father in an iron cage,   5
Now have we marched from fair Natolia
Two hundred leagues, and on Danubius' banks
Our warlike host in complete armor rest,
Where Sigismund, the king of Hungary,
Should meet our person to conclude a truce.   10
What! Shall we parle with the Christian,
Or cross the stream and meet him in the field?
Gazellus. King of Natolia, let us treat of peace.
We all are glutted with the Christians' blood,
And have a greater foe to fight against,   15
Proud Tamburlaine, that now in Asia,
Near Guyron's head, doth set his conquering feet
And means to fire Turkey as he goes.
'Gainst him, my lord, must you address your power.
Uribassa. Besides, King Sigismund hath brought from Christendom   20
More than his camp of stout Hungarians—
Slavonians, Almains, Rutters, Muffs, and Danes,
That with the halberd, lance, and murdering axe,
Will hazard that we might with surety hold.
Orcanes. Though from the shortest northern parallel,   25
Vast Gruntland, compassed with the frozen sea,
Inhabited with tall and sturdy men,
Giants as big as hugy Polypheme,
Millions of soldiers cut the arctic line,
Bringing the strength of Europe to these arms,   30
Our Turkey blades shall glide through all their throats,
And make this champion mead a bloody fen.
Danubius' stream, that runs to Trebizon,

I,i.

1 *Egregious* distinguished.

17 *Guyron's head* a town on the upper
Euphrates river, northeast of Aleppo.

22 *Slavonians* Slavs. *Almains* Germans.
Rutters horsemen. *Muffs* Swiss.

24 *that* that which.

26 *Gruntland* Greenland. *frozen sea*
Arctic ocean.

28 *hugy* huge. *Polypheme* one of the
Cyclops (see note to *Dido*, I,i,147) who
fell in love with the nymph, Galatea and
who was blinded by Ulysses.

32 *champion mead* level plain.

33–41 *Danubius'* . . . *argosies.* The waters of the Danube are conceived of
here as flowing from the river mouth in
two currents, the one going across the
Black sea to Trebizond, the other going

Shall carry, wrapped within his scarlet waves,
As martial presents to our friends at home,   35
The slaughtered bodies of these Christians.
The Terrene main, wherein Danubius falls,
Shall by this battle be the bloody sea.
The wandering sailors of proud Italy
Shall meet those Christians, fleeting with the tide,   40
Beating in heaps against their argosies,
And make fair Europe, mounted on her bull,
Trapped with the wealth and riches of the world,
Alight and wear a woeful mourning weed.
Gazellus.   Yet, stout Orcanes, prorex of the world,   45
Since Tamburlaine hath mustered all his men,
Marching from Cairon northward with his camp,
To Alexandria and the frontier towns,
Meaning to make a conquest of our land,
'Tis requisite to parle for a peace   50
With Sigismund, the king of Hungary,
And save our forces for the hot assaults
Proud Tamburlaine intends Natolia.
Orcanes.   Viceroy of Byron, wisely hast thou said.
My realm, the center of our empery,   55
Once lost, all Turkey would be overthrown;
And for that cause the Christians shall have peace.
Slavonians, Almains, Rutters, Muffs, and Danes,
Fear not Orcanes, but great Tamburlaine,
Nor he, but Fortune that hath made him great.   60
We have revolted Grecians, Albanese,
Sicilians, Jews, Arabians, Turks, and Moors,
Natolians, Sorians, black Egyptians,
Illyrians, Thracians, and Bithynians,
Enough to swallow forceless Sigismund,   65
Yet scarce enough t'encounter Tamburlaine.
He brings a world of people to the field:
From Scythia to the oriental plage
Of India, where raging Lantchidol

south to the Mediterranean (Terrene Main) and then into the Aegean. Each of these currents will carry the bodies of Christian soldiers which will beat against the merchant ships (argosies) of Christian seamen.

42 *Europe . . . bull* Europa, daughter of Agenor, king of Phoenicia, was wooed by Jupiter in the form of a bull. When she mounted his back, the bull plunged into the sea and swam with her

to Crete. She gave her name to the continent of Europe.

44 *weed* garment.

45 *prorex* viceroy.

55 *empery* empire.

59 *Fear* frighten.

60 *Fortune* See note to *I Tamb.*, I,i, 124.

61 *revolted* renegade.

68 *oriental plage* eastern shore.

69 *Lantchidol* an arm of the Indian ocean.

Beats on the regions with his boisterous blows,   70
That never seaman yet discoverèd,
All Asia is in arms with Tamburlaine.
Even from the midst of fiery Cancer's tropic
To Amazonia under Capricorn,
And thence as far as Archipelago,   75
All Afric is in arms with Tamburlaine;
Therefore, viceroys, the Christians must have peace.

I,ii.

*[Enter] Sigismund, Frederick, Baldwin, and their train, with
drums and trumpets.*

Sigismund.   Orcanes, as our legates promised thee,
    We, with our peers, have crossed Danubius' stream
    To treat of friendly peace or deadly war.
    Take which thou wilt; for, as the Romans used,
    I here present thee with a naked sword.   5
    Wilt thou have war, then shake this blade at me;
    If peace, restore it to my hands again,
    And I will sheathe it to confirm the same.
Orcanes.   Stay, Sigismund. Forgett'st thou I am he
    That with the cannon shook Vienna walls   10
    And made it dance upon the continent,
    As when the massy substance of the earth
    Quiver about the axle-tree of heaven?
    Forgett'st thou that I sent a shower of darts,
    Minglèd with powdered shot and feathered steel   15
    So thick upon the blink-eyed burghers' heads,
    That thou thyself, then County Palatine,
    The King of Boheme, and the Austric Duke,
    Sent heralds out, which basely on their knees,
    In all your names desired a truce of me?   20
    Forgett'st thou that to have me raise my siege,
    Wagons of gold were set before my tent,
    Stamped with the princely fowl that in her wings
    Carries the fearful thunderbolts of Jove?
    How canst thou think of this and offer war?   25

73–74 *from . . . Capricorn* i.e., from the Canary islands (the center of the Tropic of Cancer) to a region known on ancient maps as *Amazonum regio* around the source of the Nile. Marlowe seems to see this territory as extending below the tropic of Capricorn.

75 *thence . . . Archipelago* northward to the Mediterranean islands.

I,ii.

The 1590 indication of a scene divi-

sion is retained here (*Act. I Scæna* 2.) even though there is no change of place, and Orcanes and his followers are left standing on the stage. Such scene division was common in classical drama and may reflect Marlowe's intention.

13 *axle-tree of heaven* See note to *I Tamb.*, IV,ii,50.

16 *blink-eyed* probably wide-eyed with amazement.

18 *Austric* Austrian.

23 *princely fowl* eagle.

Sigismund.   Vienna was besieged, and I was there,
  Then County Palatine, but now a king,
  And what we did was in extremity.
  But now, Orcanes, view my royal host
  That hides these plains and seems as vast and wide   30
  As doth the desert of Arabia
  To those that stand on Badgeth's lofty tower,
  Or as the ocean to the traveler
  That rests upon the snowy Appenines,
  And tell me whether I should stoop so low,   35
  Or treat of peace with the Natolian king.
Gazellus.   Kings of Natolia and of Hungary,
  We came from Turkey to confirm a league,
  And not to dare each other to the field.
  A friendly parle might become ye both.   40
Frederick.   And we from Europe to the same intent,
  Which if your general refuse or scorn,
  Our tents are pitched, our men stand in array,
  Ready to charge you ere you stir your feet.
Orcanes.   So prest are we; but yet, if Sigismund   45
  Speak as a friend, and stand not upon terms,
  Here is his sword; let peace be ratified
  On these conditions specified before,
  Drawn with advice of our ambassadors.
Sigismund.   Then here I sheathe it and give thee my hand,   50
  Never to draw it out or manage arms
  Against thyself or thy confederates,
  But whilst I live will be at truce with thee.
Orcanes.   But, Sigismund, confirm it with an oath,
  And swear in sight of heaven and by thy Christ.   55
Sigismund.   By Him that made the world and saved my soul,
  The Son of God and issue of a maid,
  Sweet Jesus Christ, I solemnly protest
  And vow to keep this peace inviolable.
Orcanes.   By sacred Mahomet, the friend of God,   60
  Whose holy Alcoran remains with us,
  Whose glorious body, when he left the world,
  Closed in a coffin mounted up the air
  And hung on stately Mecca's temple roof,
  I swear to keep this truce inviolable.   65
  Of whose conditions and our solemn oaths,
  Signed with our hands, each shall retain a scroll
  As memorable witness of our league.
  Now, Sigismund, if any Christian king

30 *hides* covers.   45 *prest* ready.
32 *Badgeth's lofty tower* Bagdad's tall-
est minaret.

    Encroach upon the confines of thy realm,   70
    Send word, Orcanes of Natolia
    Confirmed this league beyond Danubius' stream,
    And they will, trembling, sound a quick retreat;
    So am I feared among all nations.
Sigismund. If any heathen potentate or king   75
    Invade Natolia, Sigismund will send
    A hundred thousand horse trained to the war,
    And backed by stout lancèrs of Germany,
    The strength and sinews of the imperial seat.
Orcanes. I thank thee, Sigismund; but, when I war,   80
    All Asia Minor, Africa, and Greece
    Follow my standard and my thundering drums.
    Come, let us go and banquet in our tents.
    I will dispatch chief of my army hence
    To fair Natolia and to Trebizon,   85
    To stay my coming 'gainst proud Tamburlaine.
    Friend Sigismund and peers of Hungary,
    Come, banquet and carouse with us a while,
    And then depart we to our territories.

                                       Exeunt.

         [Enter] Callapine, *with* Almeda, *his keeper.*   I,iii.
Callapine. Sweet Almeda, pity the ruthful plight
    Of Callapine, the son of Bajazeth,
    Born to be monarch of the western world,
    Yet here detained by cruel Tamburlaine.
Almeda. My lord, I pity it, and with my heart   5
    Wish your release; but he whose wrath is death,
    My sovereign lord, renownèd Tamburlaine,
    Forbids you further liberty than this.
Callapine. Ah, were I now but half so eloquent
    To paint in words what I'll perform in deeds,   10
    I know thou wouldst depart from hence with me.
Almeda. Not for all Afric; therefore move me not.
Callapine. Yet hear me speak, my gentle Almeda.
Almeda. No speech to that end, by your favor, sir.
Callapine. By Cairo runs—   15
Almeda. No talk of running, I tell you, sir.
Callapine. A little further, gentle Almeda.
Almeda. Well, sir, what of this?
Callapine. By Cairo runs to Alexandria bay
                        I,iii.

86 *stay* await.   3 *western world* Turkish empire.

Darotes' streams, wherein at anchor lies   20
A Turkish galley of my royal fleet,
Waiting my coming to the river side,
Hoping by some means I shall be released;
Which, when I come aboard, will hoist up sail
And soon put forth into the Terrene sea,   25
Where, 'twixt the isles of Cyprus and of Crete,
We quickly may in Turkish seas arrive.
Then shalt thou see a hundred kings and more,
Upon their knees, all bid me welcome home.
Amongst so many crowns of burnished gold,   30
Choose which thou wilt; all are at thy command.
A thousand galleys, manned with Christian slaves,
I freely give thee, which shall cut the Straits,
And bring armadoes from the coasts of Spain,
Fraughted with gold of rich America.   35
The Grecian virgins shall attend on thee,
Skillful in music and in amorous lays,
As fair as was Pygmalion's ivory girl
Or lovely Iö metamorphosèd.
With naked negroes shall thy coach be drawn,   40
And as thou rid'st in triumph through the streets,
The pavement underneath thy chariot wheels
With Turkey carpets shall be coverèd,
And cloth of Arras hung about the walls,
Fit objects for thy princely eye to pierce.   45
A hundred bassoes, clothed in crimson silk,
Shall ride before thee on Barbarian steeds;
And, when thou goest, a golden canopy
Enchased with precious stones, which shine as bright
As that fair veil that covers all the world,   50
When Phœbus, leaping from his hemisphere,
Descendeth downward to th'Antipodes—
And more than this, for all I cannot tell.
Almeda.   How far hence lies the galley, say you?
Callapine.   Sweet Almeda, scarce half a league from hence.   55
Almeda.   But need we not be spièd going aboard?
Callapine.   Betwixt the hollow hanging of a hill

---

20 *Darotes' streams* the Nile from
Cairo to Alexandria, which runs by the
town of Darote.
  22 *Waiting* awaiting.
  25 *Terrene sea* Mediterranean.
  34 *armadoes* warships.
  35 *Fraughted* laden.
  38 *Pygmalion's ivory girl* Galatea. See
note to *Dido*, II,i,16.
  39 *Iö* the daughter of Inachus, king

of Argus, who was loved by Jupiter and
transformed into a heifer out of fear of
Juno.
  49 *Enchased* adorned. See note to
Dido, I,i,101.
  52 *Antipodes* a small group of islands
in the Western Pacific, among whom the
sun was believed to set.
  56 *need we not* shall we not inevitably.

And crooked bending of a craggy rock,
The sails wrapped up, the mast and tacklings down,
She lies so close that none can find her out.   60
Almeda.   I like that well. But tell me, my lord, if I should let you go,
would you be as good as your word? Shall I be made a king for my
labor?
Callapine.   As I am Callapine the emperor,
And by the hand of Mahomet I swear,   65
Thou shalt be crowned a king, and be my mate.
Almeda.   Then here I swear, as I am Almeda,
Your keeper under Tamburlaine the Great,
—For that's the style and title I have yet—
Although he sent a thousand armèd men   70
To intercept this haughty enterprise,
Yet would I venture to conduct your grace
And die before I brought you back again!
Callapine.   Thanks, gentle Almeda. Then let us haste,
Lest time be past and lingering let us both.   75
Almeda.   When you will, my lord, I am ready.
Callapine.   Even straight; and farewell, cursèd Tamburlaine.
Now go I to revenge my father's death.

                                                    Exeunt.

                                                              I,iv.
*[Enter] Tamburlaine with Zenocrate, and his three sons,
Calyphas, Amyras, and Celebinus, with drums and trumpets.*
Tamburlaine.   Now, bright Zenocrate, the world's fair eye,
Whose beams illuminate the lamps of heaven,
Whose cheerful looks do clear the cloudy air
And clothe it in a crystal livery,
Now rest thee here on fair Larissa plains,   5
Where Egypt and the Turkish empire parts,
Between thy sons that shall be emperors,
And every one commander of a world.
Zenocrate.   Sweet Tamburlaine, when wilt thou leave these arms
And save thy sacred person free from scathe   10
And dangerous chances of the wrathful war?
Tamburlaine.   When heaven shall cease to move on both the poles,
And when the ground, whereon my soldiers march,

                          I,iv.
66 *mate* equal.   5 *Larissa* a sea-coast town south of
75 *let* hinder.   Gaza, the present-day El Arish.

Shall rise aloft and touch the hornèd moon,
And not before, my sweet Zenocrate.   15
Sit up, and rest thee like a lovely queen.
So, now she sits in pomp and majesty,
When these, my sons, more precious in mine eyes
Than all the wealthy kingdoms I subdued,
Placed by her side, look on their mother's face.   20
But yet methinks their looks are amorous,
Not martial as the sons of Tamburlaine.
Water and air, being symbolized in one,
Argue their want of courage and of wit;
Their hair, as white as milk, and soft as down—   25
Which should be like the quills of porcupines,
As black as jet, and hard as iron or steel—
Bewrays they are too dainty for the wars;
Their fingers made to quaver on a lute,
Their arms to hang about a lady's neck,   30
Their legs to dance and caper in the air,
Would make me think them bastards, not my sons,
But that I know they issued from thy womb,
That never looked on man but Tamburlaine.
Zenocrate.   My gracious lord, they have their mother's looks, 35
But when they list, their conquering father's heart.
This lovely boy, the youngest of the three,
Not long ago bestrid a Scythian steed,
Trotting the ring, and tilting at a glove,
Which when he tainted with his slender rod,   40
He reined him straight and made him so curvet
As I cried out for fear he should have fall'n.
Tamburlaine.   Well done, my boy! Thou shalt have shield and lance,
Armor of proof, horse, helm, and curtle-axe,
And I will teach thee how to charge thy foe   45
And harmless run among the deadly pikes.
If thou wilt love the wars and follow me,
Thou shalt be made a king and reign with me,
Keeping in iron cages emperors.
If thou exceed thy elder brothers' worth,   50
And shine in complete virtue more than they,
Thou shalt be king before them, and thy seed
Shall issue crownèd from their mother's womb.

21 *amorous* loving, gentle.

23–24 *Water . . . wit* Tamburlaine is explaining the weak temperaments of his sons in terms of the physiology of Marlowe's day. Being overbalanced in the phlegmatic (chiefly water) and sanguine (blood) humours, the boys lack the necessary black bile (chiefly earth) and choler (chiefly fire) which might give them courage and wit.

28 *Bewrays* betrays, reveals.

40 *tainted* struck (a technical term used in tilting).

44 *proof* metal which has been tested.

Celebinus.   Yes, father; you shall see me, if I live,
  Have under me as many kings as you,   55
  And march with such a multitude of men
  As all the world shall tremble at their view.
Tamburlaine.   These words assure me, boy, thou art my son.
  When I am old and cannot manage arms,
  Be thou the scourge and terror of the world.   60
Amyras.   Why may not I, my lord, as well as he,
  Be termed the scourge and terror of the world?
Tamburlaine.   Be all a scourge and terror to the world,
  Or else you are not sons of Tamburlaine.
Calyphas.   But while my brothers follow arms, my lord,   65
  Let me accompany my gracious mother.
  They are enough to conquer all the world,
  And you have won enough for me to keep.
Tamburlaine.   Bastardly boy, sprung from some coward's loins,
  And not the issue of great Tamburlaine!   70
  Of all the provinces I have subdued
  Thou shalt not have a foot, unless thou bear
  A mind courageous and invincible;
  For he shall wear the crown of Persia
  Whose head hath deepest scars, whose breast most wounds,   75
  Which being wroth sends lightning from his eyes,
  And in the furrows of his frowning brows
  Harbors revenge, war, death, and cruelty;
  For in a field, whose superficies
  Is covered with a liquid purple veil   80
  And sprinkled with the brains of slaughtered men,
  My royal chair of state shall be advanced;
  And he that means to place himself therein,
  Must armèd wade up to the chin in blood.
Zenocrate.   My lord, such speeches to our princely sons   85
  Dismays their minds before they come to prove
  The wounding troubles angry war affords.
Celebinus.   No, madam, these are speeches fit for us,
  For if his chair were in a sea of blood,
  I would prepare a ship and sail to it,   90
  Ere I would lose the title of a king.
Amyras.   And I would strive to swim through pools of blood
  Or make a bridge of murdered carcasses,
  Whose arches should be framed with bones of Turks,
  Ere I would lose the title of a king.   95
Tamburlaine.   Well, lovely boys, you shall be emperors both,
  Stretching your conquering arms from east to west.
  And, sirrah, if you mean to wear a crown,
  When we shall meet the Turkish deputy

And all his viceroys, snatch it from his head,   100
And cleave his pericranion with thy sword.
Calyphas.   If any man will hold him, I will strike
And cleave him to the channel with my sword.
Tamburlaine.   Hold him, and cleave him too, or I'll cleave thee;
For we will march against them presently.   105
Theridamas, Techelles, and Casane
Promised to meet me on Larissa plains
With hosts apiece against this Turkish crew;
For I have sworn by sacred Mahomet
To make it parcel of my empery.   110
The trumpets sound, Zenocrate; they come.

                                                                  I,v.
    Enter Theridamas, and his train, with drums and trumpets.
Tamburlaine.   Welcome Theridamas, king of Argier.
Theridamas.   My lord, the great and mighty Tamburlaine,
Arch-monarch of the world, I offer here
My crown, myself, and all the power I have,
In all affection at thy kingly feet.   5
Tamburlaine.   Thanks, good Theridamas.
Theridamas.   Under my colors march ten thousand Greeks,
And of Argier and Afric's frontier towns
Twice twenty thousand valiant men-at-arms,
All which have sworn to sack Natolia.   10
Five hundred brigandines are under sail,
Meet for your service on the sea, my lord,
That, launching from Argier to Tripoli,
Will quickly ride before Natolia
And batter down the castles on the shore.   15
Tamburlaine.   Well said, Argier; receive thy crown again.

    Enter Techelles and Usumcasane together.   I,vi.
Tamburlaine.   Kings of Morocco and of Fez, welcome.
Usumcasane.   Magnificent and peerless Tamburlaine,
I and my neighbor king of Fez have brought,
To aid thee in this Turkish expedition,
A hundred thousand expert soldiers;   5
From Azamor to Tunis near the sea
Is Barbary unpeopled for thy sake,

103 *channel* collar bone.

I,vi.

I,v.
  See note at I,ii.
  11 *brigandines* light vessels which
could be either sailed or rowed.

See note at I,ii and I,v.
  6 *Azamor* town in North Africa.

And all the men in armor under me,
Which with my crown I gladly offer thee.
Tamburlaine.   Thanks, king of Morocco; take your crown again.   10
Techelles.   And, mighty Tamburlaine, our earthly god,
   Whose looks make this inferior world to quake,
   I here present thee with the crown of Fez,
   And with an host of Moors trained to the war,
   Whose coal-black faces make their foes retire   15
   And quake for fear, as if infernal Jove,
   Meaning to aid thee in these Turkish arms,
   Should pierce the black circumference of hell,
   With ugly Furies bearing fiery flags,
   And millions of his strong tormenting spirits;   20
   From strong Tesella unto Biledull
   All Barbary is unpeopled for thy sake.
Tamburlaine.   Thanks, king of Fez; take here thy crown again.
   Your presence, loving friends and fellow kings,
   Makes me to surfeit in conceiving joy.   25
   If all the crystal gates of Jove's high court
   Were opened wide, and I might enter in
   To see the state and majesty of heaven,
   It could not more delight me than your sight.
   Now will we banquet on these plains a while,   30
   And after march to Turkey with our camp,
   In number more than are the drops that fall
   When Boreas rents a thousand swelling clouds;
   And proud Orcanes of Natolia
   With all his viceroys shall be so afraid,   35
   That though the stones, as at Deucalion's flood,
   Were turned to men, he should be overcome.
   Such lavish will I make of Turkish blood,
   That Jove shall send his wingèd messenger
   To bid me sheathe my sword and leave the field;   40
   The sun, unable to sustain the sight,
   Shall hide his head in Thetis' watery lap
   And leave his steeds to fair Boötes' charge;
   For half the world shall perish in this fight.
   But now, my friends, let me examine ye;   45
   How have ye spent your absent time from me?
Usumcasane.   My lord, our men of Barbary have marched
   Four hundred miles with armor on their backs,

---

21 *Tesella . . . Biledull*   towns   in
North Africa.
   33 *Boreas* the north wind.
   36 *Deucalion's flood* See note to *Dido*,
V,i,57.

39 *wingèd messenger* Mercury.
42 *Thetis* See note to *Dido*, I,i,132.
43 *steeds* i.e., of his chariot. *Boötes*
See note to *I Tamb.*, I,ii,206.

And lain in leaguer fifteen months and more;
For, since we left you at the Soldan's court,   50
We have subdued the southern Guallatia
And all the land unto the coast of Spain.
We kept the narrow Strait of Gibraltar,
And made Canaria call us kings and lords;
Yet never did they recreate themselves,   55
Or cease one day from war and hot alarms;
And therefore let them rest a while, my lord.
Tamburlaine.   They shall, Casane, and 'tis time, i'faith.
Techelles.   And I have marched along the river Nile
    To Machda, where the mighty Christian priest,   60
    Called John the Great, sits in a milk-white robe,
    Whose triple mitre I did take by force,
    And made him swear obedience to my crown.
    From thence unto Cazates did I march,
    Where Amazonians met me in the field,   65
    With whom, being women, I vouchsafed a league,
    And with my power did march to Zanzibar,
    The western part of Afric, where I viewed
    The Ethiopian sea, rivers and lakes,
    But neither man nor child in all the land.   70
    Therefore I took my course to Manico,
    Where, unresisted, I removed my camp;
    And, by the coast of Byather, at last
    I came to Cubar, where the negroes dwell,
    And, conquering that, made haste to Nubia.   75
    There, having sacked Borno, the kingly seat,
    I took the king and led him bound in chains
    Unto Damascus, where I stayed before.
Tamburlaine.   Well done, Techelles. What saith Theridamas?
Theridamas.   I left the confines and the bounds of Afric,   80
    And made a voyage into Europe,

---

49 *in leaguer* in camp.

51 *Guallatia* Gualata, a province in North Africa.

54 *Canaria* the Canary islands.

60 *Machda* an Abyssinian town on a tributary of the Nile.

64 *Cazates* a town in *Amazonum regio* (see note at I,i,73–74) where the Nile rises out of the great body of water we today call Lake Victoria.

65 *Amazonians* warlike women supposed to inhabit *Amazonum regio*, although according to Greek legendry they came from the Caucasus and settled in Asia Minor.

67–68 *Zanzibar . . . Afric*   Marlowe, following the maps of Ortelius, takes Zanzibar as the entire west coast of Africa.

69 *Ethiopian sea* the ocean separating West Africa from South America.

71–76 *Manico . . . Borno*   The campaign of Techelles can actually be followed on the maps of Ortelius. He moved from the province of Manicongo (Manico) to Biafar (Byather), another province whose chief town is Gubar (Cubar) and on to Borno, the chief town of the province of Nubia on Lake Borno.

Where by the river Tyros I subdued
Stoka, Padalia, and Codemia;
Then crossed the sea and came to Oblia
And Nigra Silva, where the devils dance,   85
Which, in despite of them, I set on fire.
From thence I crossed the gulf called by the name
Mare Majore of th'inhabitants.
Yet shall my soldiers make no period
Until Natolia kneel before your feet.   90
Tamburlaine.   Then we will triumph, banquet, and carouse.
Cooks shall have pensions to provide us cates
And glut us with the dainties of the world;
Lachryma Christi and Calabrian wines
Shall common soldiers drink in quaffing bowls,   95
Ay, liquid gold, when we have conquered him,
Minglèd with coral and with orient pearl.
Come, let us banquet and carouse the whiles.

Exeunt.

II,i.

[Enter] Sigismund, Frederick, *[and]* Baldwin, *with their train.*
Sigismund.   Now say, my lords of Buda and Bohemia,
What motion is it that enflames your thoughts,
And stirs your valors to such sudden arms?
Frederick.   Your majesty remembers, I am sure,
What cruel slaughter of our Christian bloods   5
These heathenish Turks and pagans lately made
Betwixt the city Zula and Danubius;
How through the midst of Varna and Bulgaria,
And almost to the very walls of Rome,
They have, not long since, massacred our camp.   10
It resteth now, then, that your majesty
Take all advantages of time and power

82–90 *Tyros . . . Natolia* The march of Theridamas in Eastern Europe can also be traced on the maps of Ortelius. He moved along the river Dniester (Tyros) which serves as the southern boundary of the province of Podolia (Padalia). He subdued the city of Stoko (Stoka) on the river and the city of Codemia close by it on another stream. Between Codemia and Olbia (Oblia) is an area called the Nigra Silva or Black Forest, but what sea he had to cross here is not clear. From the general region of present-day Odessa he then crossed the Black Sea (Mare Majore) and so passed into Asia Minor.

92 *cates* delicacies.

94 *Lachryma Christi* a sweet wine made in southern Italy.

II,i.

7 *Zula* a city which the maps of Ortelius locate north of the Danube river.

9 *Rome* possibly Roumania.

And work revenge upon these infidels.
Your highness knows, for Tamburlaine's repair,
That strikes a terror to all Turkish hearts,   15
Natolia hath dismissed the greatest part
Of all his army pitched against our power
Betwixt Cutheia and Orminius' mount,
And sent them marching up to Belgasar,
Acantha, Antioch, and Cæsarea,   20
To aid the kings of Soria and Jerusalem.
Now then, my lord, advantage take hereof
And issue suddenly upon the rest,
That in the fortune of their overthrow
We may discourage all the pagan troop   25
That dare attempt to war with Christians.
Sigismund.   But calls not then your grace to memory
    The league we lately made with King Orcanes,
    Confirmed by oath and articles of peace,
    And calling Christ for record of our truths?   30
    This should be treachery and violence
    Against the grace of our profession.
Baldwin.   No whit, my lord; for with such infidels,
    In whom no faith nor true religion rests,
    We are not bound to those accomplishments   35
    The holy laws of Christendom enjoin;
    But as the faith which they profanely plight
    Is not by necessary policy
    To be esteemed assurance for ourselves,
    So what we vow to them should not infringe   40
    Our liberty of arms and victory.
Sigismund.   Though I confess the oaths they undertake
    Breed little strength to our security,
    Yet those infirmities that thus defame
    Their faiths, their honors, and their religion   45
    Should not give us presumption to the like.
    Our faiths are sound, and must be consummate,
    Religious, righteous, and inviolate.
Frederick.   Assure your grace, 'tis superstition
    To stand so strictly on dispensive faith;   50
    And should we lose the opportunity
    That God hath given to venge our Christians' death
    And scourge their foul blasphemous paganism,

---

14 *repair* return.
18-20 *Betwixt . . . Cæsarea* The passage describes the movement of Orcanes'
army through various places in Asia
Minor.

35 *accomplishments* performance of
obligations.
47 *consummate* perfect, of the highest quality.
50 *dispensive faith* faith which may
be set aside by special dispensation.

As fell to Saul, to Balaam, and the rest,
That would not kill and curse at God's command,   55
So surely will the vengeance of the Highest,
And jealous anger of his fearful arm,
Be poured with rigor on our sinful heads,
If we neglect this offered victory.

Sigismund.   Then arm, my lords, and issue suddenly,   60
Giving commandment to our general host,
With expedition to assail the pagan,
And take the victory our God hath given.

                                        Exeunt.

                                        II,ii.

   [Enter] Orcanes, Gazellus, [and] Uribassa, with their train.
Orcanes.   Gazellus, Uribassa, and the rest,
Now we will march from proud Orminius' mount
To fair Natolia, where our neighbor kings
Expect our power and our royal presence,
T'encounter with the cruel Tamburlaine,   5
That nigh Larissa sways a mighty host,
And with the thunder of his martial tools
Makes earthquakes in the hearts of men and heaven.

Gazellus.   And now come we to make his sinews shake
With greater power than erst his pride hath felt.   10
An hundred kings, by scores, will bid him arms,
And hundred thousands subjects to each score;
Which, if a shower of wounding thunderbolts
Should break out of the bowels of the clouds
And fall as thick as hail upon our heads,   15
In partial aid of that proud Scythian,
Yet should our courages and steelèd crests,
And numbers more than infinite of men,
Be able to withstand and conquer him.

Uribassa.   Methinks I see how glad the Christian king   20
Is made for joy of your admitted truce,
That could not but before be terrified
With unacquainted power of our host.

                    Enter a Messenger.

II,ii.

54 *Balaam* Marlowe's biblical allusion is somewhat confused, for Balaam was ordered by God not to curse the children of Israel. See Numbers, XXII.

62 *expedition* speed.

2 *Orminius' mount* Mount Horminius in Asia Minor.

6 *Larissa* See note at I,iv,5.

11 *bid him arms* challenge him to combat.

Messenger.   Arm, dread sovereign, and my noble lords!
   The treacherous army of the Christians,   25
   Taking advantage of your slender power,
   Comes marching on us and determines straight
   To bid us battle for our dearest lives.
Orcanes.   Traitors, villains, damnèd Christians!
   Have I not here the articles of peace   30
   And solemn covenants we have both confirmed,
   He by his Christ and I by Mahomet?
Gazellus.   Hell and confusion light upon their heads,
   That with such treason seek our overthrow,
   And cares so little for their prophet Christ!   35
Orcanes.   Can there be such deceit in Christians
   Or treason in the fleshly heart of man,
   Whose shape is figure of the highest God?
   Then if there be a Christ, as Christians say,
   But in their deeds deny him for their Christ,   40
   If he be son to everliving Jove,
   And hath the power of his outstretchèd arm,
   If he be jealous of his name and honor
   As is our holy prophet Mahomet,
   Take here these papers as our sacrifice   45
   And witness of Thy servant's perjury.
                  [*He tears to pieces the articles of peace.*]
   Open, thou shining veil of Cynthia,
   And make a passage from the imperial heaven,
   That He that sits on high and never sleeps,
   Nor in one place is circumscriptible,   50
   But everywhere fills every continent
   With strange infusion of His sacred vigor,
   May, in His endless power and purity,
   Behold and venge this traitor's perjury!
   Thou Christ that art esteemed omnipotent,   55
   If thou wilt prove thyself a perfect God,
   Worthy the worship of all faithful hearts,
   Be now revenged upon this traitor's soul,
   And make the power I have left behind—
   Too little to defend our guiltless lives—   60
   Sufficient to discomfort and confound
   The trustless force of those false Christians.
   To arms, my lords! On Christ still let us cry.
   If there be Christ, we shall have victory.
                                        [*Exeunt.*]

48 *imperial* See note at *I Tamb.,* II, vii,15 and IV,iv,30.

Sound to the battle, and Sigismund comes out wounded.

Sigismund.   Discomfited is all the Christian host,
And God hath thundered vengeance from on high
For my accursed and hateful perjury.
O just and dreadful punisher of sin,
Let the dishonor of the pains I feel   5
In this my mortal well-deservèd wound
End all my penance in my sudden death!
And let this death, wherein to sin I die,
Conceive a second life in endless mercy!

                                          [He dies.]

Enter Orcanes, Gazellus, Uribassa, with others.

Orcanes.   Now lie the Christians bathing in their bloods,   10
And Christ or Mahomet hath been my friend.

Gazellus.   See here the perjured traitor Hungary,
Bloody and breathless for his villainy.

Orcanes.   Now shall his barbarous body be a prey
To beasts and fowls, and all the winds shall breathe   15
Through shady leaves of every senseless tree,
Murmurs and hisses for his heinous sin.
Now scalds his soul in the Tartarian streams
And feeds upon the baneful tree of hell,
That Zoacum, that fruit of bitterness,   20
That in the midst of fire is engraffed,
Yet flourisheth as Flora in her pride,
With apples like the heads of damnèd fiends.
The devils there, in chains of quenchless flame,
Shall lead his soul through Orcus' burning gulf,   25
From pain to pain, whose change shall never end.
What say'st thou yet, Gazellus, to his foil,
Which we referred to justice of his Christ
And to His power, which here appears as full
As rays of Cynthia to the clearest sight?   30

Gazellus.   'Tis but the fortune of the wars, my lord,
Whose power is often proved a miracle.

Orcanes.   Yet in my thoughts shall Christ be honorèd,
Not doing Mahomet an injury,
Whose power had share in this our victory;   35
And since this miscreant hath disgraced his faith
And died a traitor both to heaven and earth,

II,iii.

20 *Zoacum* (or Ezecum) a tree of hell described in the thirty-seventh chapter of the Koran.

22 *Flora* the goddess of springtime and flowers.

25 *Orcus* the Greek Hades. Marlowe in this passage fuses Moslem, Christian, and Greek notions of hell.

27 *foil* disgrace.

We will both watch and ward shall keep his trunk
Amidst these plains for fowls to prey upon.
Go, Uribassa, give it straight in charge.   40
Uribassa.   I will, my lord.

Exit Uribassa.

Orcanes.   And now, Gazellus, let us haste and meet
Our army, and our brother of Jerusalem,
Of Soria, Trebizon, and Amasia,
And happily, with full Natolian bowls   45
Of Greekish wine, now let us celebrate
Our happy conquest and his angry fate.

Exeunt.

II,iv.

The arras is drawn, and Zenocrate lies in her bed of state,
[with] Tamburlaine *sitting by her, three Physicians about her*
bed, tempering potions, [and] Theridamas, Techelles, Usum-*
casane and the three sons.

Tamburlaine.   Black is the beauty of the brightest day;
The golden ball of heaven's eternal fire,
That danced with glory on the silver waves,
Now wants the fuel that inflamed his beams,
And all with faintness and for foul disgrace,   5
He binds his temples with a frowning cloud,
Ready to darken earth with endless night.
Zenocrate, that gave him light and life,
Whose eyes shot fire from their ivory bowers,
And tempered every soul with lively heat,   10
Now by the malice of the angry skies,
Whose jealousy admits no second mate,
Draws in the comfort of her latest breath,
All dazzled with the hellish mists of death.
Now walk the angels on the walls of heaven,   15
As sentinels to warn th'immortal souls
To entertain divine Zenocrate.
Apollo, Cynthia, and the ceaseless lamps
That gently looked upon this loathsome earth
Shine downwards now no more, but deck the heavens   20
To entertain divine Zenocrate.
The crystal springs, whose taste illuminates
Refinèd eyes with an eternal sight,

II,iv.

4 *inflamed* filled with flame.   9 *bowers* i.e., places wherein her eyes
                                         are set.

Like trièd silver runs through Paradise
To entertain divine Zenocrate.   25
The cherubins and holy seraphins,
That sing and play before the King of Kings,
Use all their voices and their instruments
To entertain divine Zenocrate.
And in this sweet and curious harmony,   30
The god that tunes this music to our souls
Holds out his hand in highest majesty
To entertain divine Zenocrate.
Then let some holy trance convey my thoughts
Up to the palace of th'imperial heaven,   35
That this my life may be as short to me
As are the days of sweet Zenocrate.
Physicians, will no physic do her good?
First Physician.   My lord, your majesty shall soon perceive,
    And if she pass this fit, the worst is past.   40
Tamburlaine.   Tell me, how fares my fair Zenocrate?
Zenocrate.   I fare, my lord, as other empresses,
    That, when this frail and transitory flesh
    Hath sucked the measure of that vital air
    That feeds the body wth his dated health,   45
    Wane with enforced and necessary change.
Tamburlaine.   May never such a change transform my love,
    In whose sweet being I repose my life,
    Whose heavenly presence, beautified with health,
    Gives light to Phœbus and the fixèd stars,   50
    Whose absence makes the sun and moon as dark
    As when, opposed in one diameter,
    Their spheres are mounted on the serpent's head,
    Or else descended to his winding train.
    Live still, my love, and so conserve my life,   55
    Or, dying, be the author of my death.
Zenocrate.   Live still, my lord! Oh, let my sovereign live!
    And sooner let the fiery element
    Dissolve and make your kingdom in the sky,
    Than this base earth should shroud your majesty;   60
    For, should I but suspect your death by mine,
    The comfort of my future happiness
    And hope to meet your highness in the heavens,
    Turned to despair, would break my wretched breast,
    And fury would confound my present rest.   65

35 *imperial* See note at II,ii,48.
45 *dated* limited.
52 *opposed in one diameter* in eclipse, the moon being exactly opposite to the sun, with the earth between them.
53-54 *spheres . . . train* i.e., when, as part of the eclipse, either the head or the tail of the constellation Scorpio (the serpent) falls in the same plane as the earth, sun, and moon. Why Marlowe considers this phenomenon as necessary to an eclipse is not clear.

But let me die, my love; yet let me die;
With love and patience let your true love die.
Your grief and fury hurts my second life.
Yet let me kiss my lord before I die,
And let me die with kissing of my lord.   70
But since my life is lengthened yet a while,
Let me take leave of these my loving sons,
And of my lords, whose true nobility
Have merited my latest memory.
Sweet sons, farewell! In death resemble me,   75
And in your lives your father's excellency.
Some music, and my fit will cease, my lord.

They call [for] music.

Tamburlaine.   Proud fury and intolerable fit,
That dares torment the body of my love
And scourge the scourge of the immortal God!   80
Now are those spheres where Cupid used to sit,
Wounding the world with wonder and with love,
Sadly supplied with pale and ghastly death,
Whose darts do pierce the center of my soul.
Her sacred beauty hath enchanted heaven,   85
And had she lived before the siege of Troy,
Helen, whose beauty summoned Greece to arms
And drew a thousand ships to Tenedos,
Had not been named in Homer's Iliads;
Her name had been in every line he wrote.   90
Or, had those wanton poets, for whose birth
Old Rome was proud, but gazed a while on her,
Nor Lesbia nor Corinna had been named;
Zenocrate had been the argument
Of every epigram or elegy.   95

The music sounds, and she dies.

What, is she dead? Techelles, draw thy sword
And wound the earth, that it may cleave in twain
And we descend into th'infernal vaults,
To hale the Fatal Sisters by the hair
And throw them in the triple moat of hell,   100
For taking hence my fair Zenocrate.
Casane and Theridamas, to arms!
Raise cavalieros higher than the clouds,
And with the cannon break the frame of heaven.
Batter the shining palace of the sun,   105

88 *Tenedos* an island in the Aegean sea to which the Greeks withdrew their fleet in order to make the Trojans think they had departed.
90 *Her* i.e., Zenocrate's.
93 *Lesbia . . . Corinna* ladies cele-brated in the Latin love poetry of Ovid, Horace, and Catullus.
99 *Fatal Sisters* See note to *Dido*, III, ii,3.
103 *cavalieros* mounds on which cannon were placed.

And shiver all the starry firmament,
For amorous Jove hath snatched my love from hence,
Meaning to make her stately queen of heaven.
What god soever holds thee in his arms,
Giving thee nectar and ambrosia,   110
Behold me here, divine Zenocrate,
Raving, impatient, desperate, and mad,
Breaking my steelèd lance, with which I burst
The rusty beams of Janus' temple doors,
Letting out death and tyrannising war,   115
To march with me under this bloody flag!
And, if thou pitiest Tamburlaine the Great,
Come down from heaven, and live with me again!
Theridamas.   Ah, good my lord, be patient. She is dead,
And all this raging cannot make her live.   120
If words might serve, our voice hath rent the air;
If tears, our eyes have watered all the earth;
If grief, our murdered hearts have strained forth blood.
Nothing prevails, for she is dead, my lord.
Tamburlaine.   For she is dead! Thy words do pierce my soul!   125
Ah, sweet Theridamas, say so no more.
Though she be dead, yet let me think she lives
And feed my mind that dies for want of her.
Where'er her soul be, thou [*to the body*] shalt stay with me,
Embalmed with cassia, ambergris, and myrrh,   130
Not lapped in lead, but in a sheet of gold,
And till I die thou shalt not be interred.
Then in as rich a tomb as Mausolus'
We both will rest and have one epitaph
Writ in as many several languages   135
As I have conquered kingdoms with my sword.
This cursed town will I consume with fire,
Because this place bereft me of my love;
The houses, burnt, will look as if they mourned;
And here will I set up her statue   140
And march about it with my mourning camp,
Drooping and pining for Zenocrate.

               The arras is drawn.

114 *Janus' temple doors* The doors of the temple of Janus in Rome stood open in time of war and were closed in time of peace.

133 *Mausolus* king of Caria, whose wife (also his sister) Artemisia built a costly tomb for him after his death, called the Mausoleum.

III,i.

Enter the Kings of Trebizon and Soria, one bringing a sword
and another a scepter. [Enter] next [Orcanes, King of] Natolia,
and [the King of] Jerusalem, with the imperial crown. After
[them, enter] Callapine, and after him [Almeda] and other
Lords. Orcanes and [the King of] Jerusalem crown Callapine,
and the other[s] give him the scepter.

Orcanes.   Callapinus Cyricelibes, otherwise Cybelius, son and successive
heir to the late mighty emperor, Bajazeth, by the aid of God and his
friend Mahomet, Emperor of Natolia, Jerusalem, Trebizon, Soria,
Amasia, Thracia, Illyria, Carmonia, and all the hundred and thirty
kingdoms late contributory to his mighty father. Long live [5
Callapinus, Emperor of Turkey!

Callapine.   Thrice worthy kings, of Natolia and the rest,
  I will requite your royal gratitudes
  With all the benefits my empire yields;
  And were the sinews of th'imperial seat   10
  So knit and strengthened as when Bajazeth,
  My royal lord and father, filled the throne,
  Whose cursèd fate hath so dismembered it,
  Then should you see this thief of Scythia,
  This proud usurping king of Persia,   15
  Do us such honor and supremacy,
  Bearing the vengeance of our father's wrongs,
  As all the world should blot our dignities
  Out of the book of base born infamies.
  And now I doubt not but your royal cares   20
  Hath so provided for this cursèd foe,
  That, since the heir of mighty Bajazeth—
  An emperor so honored for his virtues—
  Revives the spirits of true Turkish hearts,
  In grievous memory of his father's shame,   25
  We shall not need to nourish any doubt,
  But that proud Fortune, who hath followed long
  The martial sword of mighty Tamburlaine,
  Will now retain her old inconstancy
  And raise our honors to as high a pitch,   30
  In this our strong and fortunate encounter;
  For so hath heaven provided my escape
  From all the cruelty my soul sustained,
  By this my friendly keeper's happy means,
  That Jove, surcharged wth pity of our wrongs,   35
  Will pour it down in showers on our heads,
  Scourging the pride of cursèd Tamburlaine.
Orcanes.   I have a hundred thousand men in arms,
  Some, that in conquest of the perjured Christian,

Being a handful to a mighty host,   40
Think them in number yet sufficient
To drink the river Nile or Euphrates,
And for their power enow to win the world.
King of Jerusalem.   And I as many from Jerusalem,
Judæa, Gaza, and Scalonians' bounds,   45
That on mount Sinai, with their ensigns spread,
Look like the parti-colored clouds of heaven
That show fair weather to the neighbor morn.
King of Trebizon.   And I as many bring from Trebizon,
Chio, Famastro, and Amasia,   50
All bordering on the Mare Major Sea,
Riso, Sancina, and the bordering towns
That touch the end of famous Euphrates,
Whose courages are kindled with the flames
The cursèd Scythian sets on all their towns,   55
And vow to burn the villain's cruel heart.
King of Soria.   From Soria with seventy thousand strong,
Ta'en from Aleppo, Soldino, Tripoli,
And so unto my city of Damascus,
I march to meet and aid my neighbor kings,   60
All which will join against this Tamburlaine
And bring him captive to your highness' feet.
Orcanes.   Our battle then, in martial manner pitched,
According to our ancient use, shall bear
The figure of the semicircled moon,   65
Whose horns shall sprinkle through the tainted air
The poisoned brains of this proud Scythian.
Callapine.   Well, then, my noble lords, for this my friend
That freed me from the bondage of my foe,
I think it requisite and honorable   70
To keep my promise and to make him king,
That is a gentleman, I know, at least.
Almeda.   That's no matter, sir, for being a king, for Tamburlaine
came up of nothing.
King of Jerusalem.   Your majesty may choose some 'pointed time,   75
Performing all your promise to the full.
'Tis naught for your majesty to give a kingdom.

III,i.

43 *enow* enough.

45 *Scalonians* men of Ascalon, often called Scalona on ancient maps.

51 *Mare Major Sea* Black Sea.

57–59 *From Soria . . . Damascus* The movement is from Aleppo southward to the sea coast near Cyprus, passing Soldino and Tripoli, and then inland to Damascus.

63–65 *battle . . . moon* The crescent-shaped battle formation was a favorite among the ancients.

Callapine. Then will I shortly keep my promise, Almeda.
Almeda. Why, I thank your majesty.

                                                        Exeunt.

[*Enter*] *Tamburlaine, with Usumcasane and his three sons;
four* [*Attendants*] *bearing the hearse of Zenocrate, and the
drums sounding a doleful march; the town burning.*
Tamburlaine. So, burn the turrets of this cursèd town,
    Flame to the highest region of the air,
    And kindle heaps of exhalations
    That, being fiery meteors, may presage
    Death and destruction to th'inhabitants!   5
    Over my zenith hang a blazing star,
    That may endure till heaven be dissolved,
    Fed with the fresh supply of earthly dregs,
    Threatening a dearth and famine to this land!
    Flying dragons, lightning, fearful thunder-claps,   10
    Singe these fair plains, and make them seem as black
    As is the island where the Furies mask,
    Compassed with Lethe, Styx, and Phlegethon,
    Because my dear Zenocrate is dead.
Calyphas. This pillar, placed in memory of her,   15
    Where in Arabian, Hebrew, Greek, is writ,
    This town, being burnt by Tamburlaine the Great,
·   *Forbids the world to build it up again.*
Amyras. And here this mournful streamer shall be placed,
    Wrought with the Persian and Egyptian arms,   20
    To signify she was a princess born
    And wife unto the monarch of the East.
Celebinus. And here this table as a register
    Of all her virtues and perfections.
Tamburlaine. And here the picture of Zenocrate,   25
    To show her beauty which the world admired;

III,ii.

2–9 *Flame . . . land* i.e., may the
flames of the burning town rise as high
as the uppermost limit of the atmosphere,
believed in Ptolemaic astronomy to be next
to the sphere of the moon, and may these
flames create meteors which—since meteors traditionally were regarded as signs
of coming disasters—might give prophecy of the death and destruction to
follow. At the same time, in a direct
line over Tamburlaine's head, may a
burning star hang, to be kept in flame
by the continuing fires of destruction
which he will light on earth, and may
this star also presage death and famine
on earth.

13 *Lethe, Styx and Phlegethon* the
rivers of the Greek underworld.

20 *Wrought* embroidered.

Sweet picture of divine Zenocrate,
That, hanging here, will draw the gods from heaven
And cause the stars fixed in the southern arc,
Whose lovely faces never any viewed   30
That have not passed the center's latitude,
As pilgrims travel to our hemisphere,
Only to gaze upon Zenocrate.
Thou shalt not beautify Larissa plains,
But keep within the circle of mine arms;   35
At every town and castle I besiege,
Thou shalt be set upon my royal tent;
And when I meet an army in the field,
Those looks will shed such influence in my camp,
As if Bellona, goddess of the war,   40
Threw naked swords and sulphur balls of fire
Upon the heads of all our enemies.
And now, my lords, advance your spears again.
Sorrow no more, my sweet Casane, now.
Boys, leave to mourn; this town shall ever mourn,   45
Being burnt to cinders for your mother's death.
Calyphas.   If I had wept a sea of tears for her,
It would not ease the sorrows I sustain.
Amyras.   As is that town, so is my heart consumed
With grief and sorrow for my mother's death.   50
Celebinus.   My mother's death hath mortified my mind,
And sorrow stops the passage of my speech.
Tamburlaine.   But now, my boys, leave off and list to me,
That mean to teach you rudiments of war.
I'll have you learn to sleep upon the ground,   55
March in your armor thorough watery fens,
Sustain the scorching heat and freezing cold,
Hunger and thirst, right adjuncts of the war,
And after this, to scale a castle wall,
Besiege a fort, to undermine a town,   60
And make whole cities caper in the air.
Then next, the way to fortify your men,
In champion grounds what figure serves you best,
For which the quinque-angle form is meet,
Because the corners there may fall more flat   65
Whereas the fort may fittest be assailed,

29–32 *stars . . . hemisphere* i.e., the southern stars, seen only by those who have passed below the equator (center's latitude), will travel to the northern half of the globe (hemisphere) in order to see Zenocrate.

34 *Larissa* See note at I,iv,5.

40 *Bellona* Roman goddess of war, usually regarded as the sister or wife of Mars.

41 *sulphur balls of fire* probably the primitive ancestors of our hand grenades.

63 *champion* level.

64 *quinque-angle form* star-shaped fort

66 *Whereas* where.

And sharpest where th'assault is desperate.
The ditches must be deep, the counterscarps
Narrow and steep, the walls made high and broad,
The bulwarks and the rampires large and strong, 70
With cavalieros and thick counterforts,
And room within to lodge six thousand men.
It must have privy ditches, countermines,
And secret issuings to defend the ditch.
It must have high argins and covered ways 75
To keep the bulwark fronts from battery,
And parapets to hide the musketeers,
Casemates to place the great artillery,
And store of ordnance, that from every flank
May scour the outward curtains of the fort, 80
Dismount the cannon of the adverse part,
Murder the foe, and save the walls from breach.
When this is learned for service on the land,
By plain and easy demonstration
I'll teach you how to make the water mount, 85
That you may dry-foot march through lakes and pools,
Deep rivers, havens, creeks, and little seas,
And make a fortress in the raging waves,
Fenced with the concave of a monstrous rock,
Invincible by nature of the place. 90
When this is done, then are ye soldiers
And worthy sons of Tamburlaine the Great.
Calyphas. My lord, but this is dangerous to be done;
We may be slain or wounded ere we learn.
Tamburlaine. Villain, art thou the son of Tamburlaine, 95
And fear'st to die, or with a curtle-axe
To hew thy flesh and make a gaping wound?
Hast thou beheld a peal of ordnance strike
A ring of pikes, minglèd with shot and horse,
Whose shattered limbs, being tossed as high as heaven, 100
Hang in the air as thick as sunny motes,
And canst thou, coward, stand in fear of death?
Hast thou not seen my horsemen charge the foe,
Shot through the arms, cut overthwart the hands,
Dyeing their lances with their streaming blood, 105
And yet at night carouse within my tent,
Filling their empty veins with airy wine,

68 *counterscarps* walls of the ditches facing a fort.
70 *rampires* ramparts.
71 *cavalieros* See note at II,iv,103.
75 *argins* earthworks. *covered ways* protected passages between earthworks and counterscarps.
78 *Casemates* vaulted chambers within the ramparts of a fortress.
80 *curtains of the fort* walls connecting the fortress towers.
101 *sunny motes* particles of dust in the sunlight.

That, being concocted, turns to crimson blood,
And wilt thou shun the field for fear of wounds?
View me, thy father, that hath conquered kings,   110
And with his host marched round about the earth,
Quite void of scars and clear from any wound,
That by the wars lost not a dram of blood,
And see him lance his flesh to teach you all.

He cuts his arm.

A wound is nothing, be it ne'er so deep;   115
Blood is the god of war's rich livery.
Now look I like a soldier, and this wound
As great a grace and majesty to me,
As if a chair of gold enamellèd,
Enchased with diamonds, sapphires, rubies,   120
And fairest pearl of wealthy India,
Were mounted here under a canopy,
And I sat down, clothed with the massy robe
That late adorned the Afric potentate,
Whom I brought bound unto Damascus' walls.   125
Come, boys, and with your fingers search my wound,
And in my blood wash all your hands at once,
While I sit smiling to behold the sight.
Now, my boys, what think you of a wound?

Calyphas.   I know not what I should think of it. Methinks 'tis a   [130
pitiful sight.
Celebinus.   'Tis nothing. Give me a wound, father.
Amyras.   And me another, my lord.
Tamburlaine.   Come, sirrah, give me your arm.
Celebinus.   Here, father, cut it bravely, as you did your own.   135
Tamburlaine.   It shall suffice thou dar'st abide a wound.
My boy, thou shalt not lose a drop of blood
Before we meet the army of the Turk;
But then run desperate through the thickest throngs,
Dreadless of blows, of bloody wounds, and death;   140
And let the burning of Larissa walls,
My speech of war, and this my wound you see,
Teach you, my boys, to bear courageous minds,
Fit for the followers of great Tamburlaine.
Usumcasane, now come let us march   145
Towards Techelles and Theridamas,
That we have sent before to fire the towns,
The towers and cities of these hateful Turks,
And hunt that coward faint-heart runaway,
With that accursèd traitor, Almeda,   150
Till fire and sword have found them at a bay.
Usumcasane.   I long to pierce his bowels with my sword,

124 *Afric potentate* i.e., Bajazeth.

    That hath betrayed my gracious sovereign,
    That cursed and damnèd traitor, Almeda.
Tamburlaine.   Then let us see if coward Callapine   155
    Dare levy arms against our puissance,
    That we may tread upon his captive neck,
    And treble all his father's slaveries.

                                      Exeunt.

       [Enter] Techelles, Theridamas, *and their train.*   III,iii.
Theridamas.   Thus have we marched northward from Tamburlaine,
    Unto the frontier point of Soria,
    And this is Balsera, their chiefest hold,
    Wherein is all the treasure of the land.
Techelles.   Then let us bring our light artillery,   5
    Minions, falc'nets, and sakers, to the trench,
    Filling the ditches with the walls' wide breach,
    And enter in to seize upon the gold.
    How say ye, soldiers; shall we not?
Soldiers.   Yes, my lord, yes; come, let's about it.   10
Theridamas.   But stay a while; summon a parle, drum.
    It may be they will yield it quietly,
    Knowing two kings, the friends to Tamburlaine,
    Stand at the walls with such a mighty power.
      [A] Summon[*s to*] *the battle* [*is sounded*]. [*The*] Captain, *with*
      [*Olympia*], *his wife and* [*their young*] *son* [*appear on the walls*].
Captain.   What require you, my masters?   15
Theridamas.   Captain, that thou yield up thy hold to us.
Captain.   To you! Why, do you think me weary of it?
Techelles.   Nay, captain, thou art weary of thy life
    If thou withstand the friends of Tamburlaine.
Theridamas.   These pioners of Argier in Africa   20
    Even in the cannon's face shall raise a hill
    Of earth and faggots higher than thy fort,
    And over thy argins and covered ways
    Shall play upon the bulwarks of thy hold
    Volleys of ordnance, till the breach be made   25
    That with his ruin fills up all the trench;
    And, when we enter in, not heaven itself
    Shall ransom thee, thy wife, and family.

III,iii.

  3 *Balsera* probably Passera, a town in
Natolia indicated on the maps of Ortelius.
  6 *Minions, falc'nets, and sakers* small
ordnance pieces.

  20 *pioners* trench diggers. *Argier* Algeria.
  23 *argins . . . ways* See note at III.
ii,75.

Techelles.   Captain, these Moors shall cut the leaden pipes
   That bring fresh water to thy men and thee,   30
   And lie in trench before thy castle walls,
   That no supply of victual shall come in,
   Nor [any] issue forth but they shall die;
   And, therefore, captain, yield it quietly.
Captain.   Were you, that are the friends of Tamburlaine,   35
   Brothers to holy Mahomet himself,
   I would not yield it; therefore do your worst.
   Raise mounts, batter, intrench, and undermine,
   Cut off the water, all convoys that can,
   Yet I am resolute; and so, farewell.   40
        [*The Captain, Olympia, and their son retire from the walls.*]
Theridamas.   Pioners, away! And where I struck the stake,
   Intrench with those dimensions I prescribed;
   Cast up the earth towards the castle wall,
   Which, till it may defend you, labor low,
   And few or none shall perish by their shot.   45
Pioners. We will, my lord.
                                        Exeunt [Pioners].
Techelles.   A hundred horse shall scout about the plains
   To spy what force comes to relieve the hold.
   Both we, Theridamas, will intrench our men,
   And with the Jacob's staff measure the height   50
   And distance of the castle from the trench,
   That we may know if our artillery
   Will carry full point blank unto their walls.
Theridamas.   Then see the bringing of our ordinance
   Along the trench into the battery,   55
   Where we will have gabions of six foot broad,
   To save our cannoneers from musket shot;
   Betwixt which shall our ordnance thunder forth,
   And with the breach's fall, smoke, fire, and dust,
   The crack, the echo, and the soldier's cry,   60
   Make deaf the air and dim the crystal sky.
Techelles.   Trumpets and drums, alarum presently!
   And, soldiers, play the men; the hold is yours!
                                        [*Exeunt.*]

---

38 *intrench* dig trenches.
50 *Jacob's staff* an instrument for measuring heights and distances.
54 *ordinance* Here and elsewhere the

archaic spelling of the 1590 text is retained for the sake of the meter.
56 *gabions* great baskets filled with earth, used to steady cannons.

III,iv.

[*Alarms within.*] *Enter the Captain, with Olympia, and* [*their*]
                                    son.

Olympia.   Come, good my lord, and let us haste from hence
    Along the cave that leads beyond the foe.
    No hope is left to save this conquered hold.
Captain.   A deadly bullet gliding through my side
    Lies heavy on my heart; I cannot live.   5
    I feel my liver pierced, and all my veins,
    That there begin and nourish every part,
    Manglèd and torn, and all my entrails bathed
    In blood that straineth from their orifex.
    Farewell, sweet wife! Sweet son, farewell! I die.   10
                                    [*He dies.*]
Olympia.   Death, whither art thou gone, that both we live?
    Come back again, sweet Death, and strike us both!
    One minute end our days, and one sepulcher
    Contain our bodies! Death, why com'st thou not?
    Well, this must be the messenger for thee.   15
                                [*She draws a dagger.*]
    Now, ugly Death, stretch out thy sable wings
    And carry both our souls where his remains.
    Tell me, sweet boy, art thou content to die?
    These barbarous Scythians, full of cruelty,
    And Moors, in whom was never pity found,   20
    Will hew us piecemeal, put us to the wheel,
    Or else invent some torture worse than that;
    Therefore die by thy loving mother's hand,
    Who gently now will lance thy ivory throat
    And quickly rid thee both of pain and life.   25
Son.   Mother, dispatch me, or I'll kill myself;
    For think ye I can live and see him dead?
    Give me your knife, good mother, or strike home;
    The Scythians shall not tyrannize on me.
    Sweet mother, strike, that I may meet my father.   30
                                She stabs him, [*and he dies*].
Olympia.   Ah, sacred Mahomet, if this be sin,
    Entreat a pardon of the God of heaven,
    And purge my soul before it come to thee.
                [*She burns the bodies of her husband and son, and
                        then attempts to kill herself.*]

            Enter Theridamas, Techelles, and all their train.
Theridamas.   How now, madam, what are you doing?
Olympia.   Killing myself, as I have done my son,   35

III,iv.
    9 *orifex* orifice.

Whose body, with his father's, I have burnt,
Lest cruel Scythians should dismember him.
Techelles. 'Twas bravely done, and like a soldier's wife.
  Thou shalt with us to Tamburlaine the Great,
  Who, when he hears how resolute thou wert,   40
  Will match thee with a viceroy or a king.
Olympia. My lord deceased was dearer unto me
  Than any viceroy, king, or emperor;
  And for his sake here will I end my days.
Theridamas. But, lady, go with us to Tamburlaine,   45
  And thou shalt see a man greater than Mahomet,
  In whose high looks is much more majesty
  Than from the concave superficies
  Of Jove's vast palace, the imperial orb,
  Unto the shining bower where Cynthia sits,   50
  Like lovely Thetis, in a crystal robe;
  That treadeth fortune underneath his feet
  And makes the mighty god of arms his slave;
  On whom Death and the Fatal Sisters wait
  With naked swords and scarlet liveries;   55
  Before whom, mounted on a lion's back,
  Rhamnusia bears a helmet full of blood
  And strows the way with brains of slaughtered men;
  By whose proud side the ugly Furies run,
  Hearkening when he shall bid them plague the world;   60
  Over whose zenith, clothed in windy air,
  And eagle's wings joined to her feathered breast,
  Fame hovereth, sounding of her golden trump,
  That to the adverse poles of that straight line
  Which measureth the glorious frame of heaven   65
  The name of mighty Tamburlaine is spread;
  And him, fair lady, shall thy eyes behold.
  Come.
Olympia. Take pity of a lady's ruthful tears,
  That humbly craves upon her knees to stay   70
  And cast her body in the burning flame
  That feeds upon her son's and husband's flesh.
Techelles. Madam, sooner shall fire consume us both
  Than scorch a face so beautiful as this,

47–51 *In whose . . . robe* i.e., in whose looks there is more majesty than may be found in all of heaven, from the hollow roof (concave superficies) of Jove's palace itself to the bower where the moon (Cynthia) sits, like the sea-deity Thetis, wearing a veil of crystal.

53 *god of arms* Mars.

54 *Fatal Sisters* the Parcae. See note to *Dido,* III,ii,3.

57 *Rhamnusia* Nemesis. See note to *Dido,* III,ii,20.

58 *strows* strews.

59 *Furies* See note to *Dido,* II,i,230.

61 *zenith* crest, or head.

64–65 *adverse . . . heaven* the diameter of the sphere of heaven.

In frame of which nature hath showed more skill   75
Than when she gave eternal chaos form,
Drawing from it the shining lamps of heaven.
Theridamas.   Madam, I am so far in love with you
That you must go with us—no remedy.
Olympia.   Then carry me, I care not, where you will,   80
And let the end of this my fatal journey
Be likewise end to my accursèd life.
Techelles.   No, madam, but the beginning of your joy.
Come willingly, therefore.
Theridamas.   Soldiers, now let us meet the general,   85
Who by this time is at Natolia,
Ready to charge the army of the Turk.
The gold, the silver, and the pearl ye got,
Rifling this fort, divide in equal shares:
This lady shall have twice so much again   90
Out of the coffers of our treasury.

                                         Exeunt.

                                                            III,v.

[*Enter*] *Callapine, Orcanes,* [*the Kings of*] *Jerusalem, Trebizon,*
        and Soria, with their train, Almeda, [*and a Messenger*].
Messenger.   Renownèd emperor, mighty Callapine,
God's great lieutenant over all the world,
Here at Aleppo, with an host of men,
Lies Tamburlaine, this king of Persia,
In number more than are the quivering leaves   5
Of Ida's forest, where your highness' hounds
With open cry pursues the wounded stag,
Who means to girt Natolia's walls with siege,
Fire the town, and over-run the land.
Callapine.   My royal army is as great as his,   10
That, from the bounds of Phrygia to the sea
Which washeth Cyprus with his brinish waves,
Covers the hills, the valleys and the plains.
Viceroys and peers of Turkey, play the men.
Whet all your swords to mangle Tamburlaine,   15
His sons, his captains, and his followers.
By Mahomet, not one of them shall live.
The field wherein this battle shall be fought
For ever term the Persians' sepulcher,
In memory of this our victory.   20

III,v.
   6 *Ida's forest* probably on Mt. Ida in Crete. See note to *Dido,* III,ii,99.

Orcanes. Now he that calls himself the scourge of Jove,
   The emperor of the world, and earthly god,
   Shall end the warlike progress he intends
   And travel headlong to the lake of hell,
   Where legions of devils, knowing he must die   25
   Here in Natolia by your highness' hands,
   All brandishing their brands of quenchless fire,
   Stretching their monstrous paws, grin with their teeth
   And guard the gates to entertain his soul.
Callapine. Tell me, viceroys, the number of your men,   30
   And what our army royal is esteemed.
King of Jerusalem. From Palestina and Jerusalem,
   Of Hebrews three score thousand fighting men
   Are come, since last we showed your majesty.
Orcanes. So from Arabia desert, and the bounds   35
   Of that sweet land whose brave metropolis
   Re-edified the fair Semiramis,
   Came forty thousand warlike foot and horse,
   Since last we numbered to your majesty.
King of Trebizon. From Trebizon in Asia the Less,   40
   Naturalizèd Turks and stout Bithynians
   Came to my bands full fifty thousand more,
   That, fighting, knows not what retreat doth mean,
   Nor e'er return but with the victory,
   Since last we numbered to your majesty.   45
King of Soria. Of Sorians from Halla is repaired,
   And neighbor cities of your highness' land,
   Ten thousand horse and thirty thousand foot,
   Since last we numbered to your majesty;
   So that the army royal is esteemed   50
   Six hundred thousand valiant fighting men.
Callapine. Then welcome, Tamburlaine, unto thy death.
   Come, puissant viceroys, let us to the field,
   The Persians' sepulcher, and sacrifice
   Mountains of breathless men to Mahomet,   55
   Who now, with Jove, opens the firmament
   To see the slaughter of our enemies.
     [*Enter*] *Tamburlaine with his three sons, Usumcasane, **with***
                other[s].
Tamburlaine. How now, Casane! See, a knot of kings,
   Sitting as if they were a-telling riddles.
Usumcasane. My lord, your presence makes them pale and wan.   60
   Poor souls, they look as if their deaths were near.

36–37 *sweet land . . . Semiramis* i.e., Babylon, whose walls supposedly were built by Semiramis.

40 *Asia the Less* Asia Minor.

46 *Halla* a town to the southeast of Aleppo.

Tamburlaine.   Why, so he is, Casane; I am here.
   But yet I'll save their lives and make them slaves.
   Ye petty kings of Turkey, I am come,
   As Hector did into the Grecian camp,   65
   To overdare the pride of Græcia
   And set his warlike person to the view
   Of fierce Achilles, rival of his fame.
   I do you honor in the simile;
   For, if I should, as Hector did Achilles,   70
   The worthiest knight that ever brandished sword,
   Challenge in combat any of you all,
   I see how fearfully ye would refuse,
   And fly my glove as from a scorpion.
Orcanes.   Now thou art fearful of thy army's strength,   75
   Thou wouldst with overmatch of person fight.
   But, shepherd's issue, base born Tamburlaine,
   Think of thy end; this sword shall lance thy throat.
Tamburlaine.   Villain, the shepherd's issue, at whose birth
   Heaven did afford a gracious aspect,   80
   And joined those stars that shall be opposite
   Even till the dissolution of the world,
   And never meant to make a conqueror
   So famous as is mighty Tamburlaine,
   Shall so torment thee and that Callapine,   85
   That, like a roguish runaway, suborned
   That villain there, that slave, that Turkish dog,
   To false his service to his sovereign,
   As ye shall curse the birth of Tamburlaine.
Callapine.   Rail not, proud Scythian. I shall now revenge   90
   My father's vile abuses and mine own.
King of Jerusalem.   By Mahomet, he shall be tied in chains,
   Rowing with Christians in a brigandine
   About the Grecian isles to rob and spoil,
   And turn him to his ancient trade again.   95
   Methinks the slave should make a lusty thief.
Callapine.   Nay, when the battle ends, all we will meet
   And sit in council to invent some pain
   That most may vex his body and his soul.

65–68 *As Hector . . . fame* No such
episode appears in the *Iliad* of Homer.
It does occur, however, in Lydgate's
Troy Book and in other medieval accounts of the Trojan war.
   66 *Græcia* Greece.
   74 *glove* i.e., thrown down as a challenge.
   80–82 *Heaven . . . world* i.e., heaven

never again will cause the stars to come
into a relationship similar to that at
Tamburlaine's birth, and therefore the
world will never see another like him. It
was commonly believed that a man's
life was determined by the conjunction of
stars at his birth.
   88 *false* betray.
   93 *brigandine* See note at I,v,11.

Tamburlaine.   Sirrah Callapine, I'll hang a clog about your neck   [100
   for running away again. You shall not trouble me thus to come and
   fetch you.
   But as for you, viceroy, you shall have bits,
   And, harnessed like my horses, draw my coach;
   And, when ye stay, be lashed with whips of wire.   105
   I'll have you learn to feed on provender
   And in a stable lie upon the planks.
Orcanes.   But, Tamburlaine, first thou shalt kneel to us
   And humbly crave a pardon for thy life.
King of Trebizon.   The common soldiers of our mighty host   110
   Shall bring thee bound unto the general's tent.
King of Soria.   And all have jointly sworn thy cruel death,
   Or bind thee in eternal torments' wrath.
Tamburlaine.   Well, sirs, diet yourselves; you know I shall have occa-
   sion shortly to journey you.   115
Celebinus.   See, father, how Almeda the jailor looks upon us.
Tamburlaine.   Villain, traitor, damnèd fugitive.
   I'll make thee wish the earth had swallowed thee.
   See'st thou not death within my wrathful looks?
   Go, villain, cast thee headlong from a rock,   120
   Or rip thy bowels and rend out thy heart
   T'appease my wrath; or else I'll torture thee,
   Searing thy hateful flesh with burning irons
   And drops of scalding lead, while all thy joints
   Be racked and beat asunder with the wheel;   125
   For if thou liv'st, not any element
   Shall shroud thee from the wrath of Tamburlaine.
Callapine.   Well, in despite of thee, he shall be king.
   Come, Almeda, receive this crown of me.
   I here invest thee king of Ariadan,   130
   Bordering on Mare Roso, near to Mecca.
Orcanes.   What! Take it, man.
Almeda.   Good my lord, let me take it.
Callapine.   Dost thou ask him leave? Here; take it.
Tamburlaine.   Go to, sirrah, take your crown, and make up the   [135
   half dozen. So, sirrah, now you are a king you must give arms.
Orcanes.   So he shall, and wear thy head in his scutcheon.
Tamburlaine.   No; let him hang a bunch of keys on his standard, to
   put him in remembrance he was a jailor, that, when I take him, I may
   knock out his brains with them, and lock you in the stable,   [140
   when you shall come sweating from my chariot.
King of Trebizon.   Away; let us to the field, that the villain may be
   slain.
Tamburlaine.   Sirrah, prepare whips, and bring my chariot to my tent;

   101 *for* to prevent   131 *Mare Roso* the Red Sea.

for, as soon as the battle is done, I'll ride in triumph through   [145
the camp.
         Enter Theridamas, Techelles, and their train.
How now, ye petty kings? Lo, here are bugs
Will make the hair stand upright on your heads,
And cast your crowns in slavery at their feet.
Welcome, Theridamas and Techelles, both.   150
See ye this rout, and know ye this same king?
Theridamas.   Ay, my lord; he was Callapine's keeper.
Tamburlaine.   Well now you see he is a king. Look to him, Theri-
damas, when we are fighting, lest he hide his crown as the foolish king
of Persia did.   155
King of Soria.   No, Tamburlaine; he shall not be put to that exigent,
I warrant thee.
Tamburlaine.   You know not, sir.
But now, my followers and my loving friends,
Fight as you ever did, like conquerors;   160
The glory of this happy day is yours.
My stern aspect shall make fair Victory,
Hovering betwixt our armies, light on me,
Loaden with laurel wreaths to crown us all.
Techelles.   I smile to think how when this field is fought   165
And rich Natolia ours, our men shall sweat
With carrying pearl and treasure on their backs.
Tamburlaine.   You shall be princes all, immediately.
Come, fight, ye Turks, or yield us victory.
Orcanes.   No; we will meet thee, slavish Tamburlaine.   170
                                        Exeunt.

✱

IV,i.

     Alarm[s within]. Amyras and Celebinus issue from the tent
              where Calyphas sits asleep.
Amyras.   Now in their glories shine the golden crowns
Of these proud Turks, much like so many suns
That half dismay the majesty of heaven.
Now, brother, follow we our father's sword,
That flies with fury swifter than our thoughts   5
And cuts down armies with his conquering wings.
Celebinus.   Call forth our lazy brother from the tent,
For if my father miss him in the field,
Wrath, kindled in the furnace of his breast,
Will send a deadly lightning to his heart.   10

---

147 *bugs* bugbears.   **164** *Loaden* laden.

Amyras.   Brother, ho! What, given so much to sleep,
    You cannot leave it when our enemies' drums
    And rattling cannons thunder in our ears
    Our proper ruin and our father's foil?
Calyphas.   Away, ye fools! My father needs not me,   15
    Nor you, in faith, but that you will be thought
    More childish-valorous than manly-wise.
    If half our camp should sit and sleep with me,
    My father were enough to scar the foe.
    You do dishonor to his majesty,   20
    To think our helps will do him any good.
Amyras.   What, dar'st thou then be absent from the fight,
    Knowing my father hates thy cowardice
    And oft hath warned thee to be still in field,
    When he himself amidst the thickest troops   25
    Beats down our foes to flesh our taintless swords?
Calyphas.   I know, sir, what it is to kill a man;
    It works remorse of conscience in me.
    I take no pleasure to be murderous,
    Nor care for blood when wine will quench my thirst.   30
Celebinus.   O cowardly boy! Fie, for shame, come forth!
    Thou dost dishonor manhood and thy house.
Calyphas.   Go, go, tall stripling, fight you for us both,
    And take my other toward brother here,
    For person like to prove a second Mars.   35
    'Twill please my mind as well to hear both you
    Have won a heap of honor in the field
    And left your slender carcasses behind,
    As if I lay with you for company.
Amyras.   You will not go, then?   40
Calyphas.   You say true.
Amyras.   Were all the lofty mounts of Zona Mundi
    That fill the midst of farthest Tartary
    Turned into pearl and proffered for my stay,
    I would not bide the fury of my father,   45
    When, made a victor in these haughty arms,
    He comes and finds his sons have had no shares
    In all the honors he proposed for us.
Calyphas.   Take you the honor, I will take my ease;
    My wisdom shall excuse my cowardice.   50
    I go into the field before I need?
        [An] alarm [is sounded] and Amyras and Celebinus run in.
    The bullets fly at random where they list;
    And should I go and kill a thousand men,

IV,i.

14 *proper* own. *foil* disgrace.   42 *Zona Mundi* a mountain range in
33 *tall* brave.   Tartary.

I were as soon rewarded with a shot,
And sooner far than he that never fights;   55
And should I go and do nor harm nor good,
I might have harm, which all the good I have,
Joined with my father's crown, would never cure.
I'll to cards. Perdicas!

[Enter Perdicas.]

Perdicas.   Here, my lord.   60
Calyphas.   Come, thou and I will go to cards to drive away the time.
Perdicas.   Content, my lord; but what shall we play for?
Calyphas.   Who shall kiss the fairest of the Turks' concubines first,
    when my father hath conquered them.
Perdicas.   Agreed, i'faith.   *They play.* 65
Calyphas.   They say I am a coward, Perdicas, and I fear as little their
    taratantaras, their swords, or their cannons as I do a naked lady in a
    net of gold, and, for fear I should be afraid, would put it off and come
    to bed with me.
Perdicas.   Such a fear, my lord, would never make ye retire.   70
Calyphas.   I would my father would let me be put in the front of such
    a battle once, to try my valor. *Alarm[s within]*. What a coil they keep!
    I believe there will be some hurt done anon amongst them.

                                                        [Exeunt.]

                                                                 IV,ii.

    Enter Tamburlaine, Theridamas, Techelles, Usumcasane, Amy-
    ras [and] Celebinus leading [in] the Turkish Kings; [and
                        Soldiers].

Tamburlaine.   See now, ye slaves, my children stoops your pride
    And leads your glories sheep-like to the sword.
    Bring them, my boys, and tell me if the wars
    Be not a life that may illustrate gods,
    And tickle not your spirits with desire   5
    Still to be trained in arms and chivalry?
Amyras.   Shall we let go these kings again, my lord,
    To gather greater numbers 'gainst our power,
    That they may say it is not chance doth this,
    But matchless strength and magnanimity?   10
Tamburlaine.   No, no, Amyras; tempt not Fortune so.
    Cherish thy valor still with fresh supplies,
    And glut it not with stale and daunted foes.
    But where's this coward villain, not my son,

IV,ii.

67 *taratantaras* bugle calls.   1 *stoops* bends.
72 *coil* commotion.   4 *illustrate* adorn, render illustrious.

But traitor to my name and majesty?   15
                    He goes in and brings Calyphas out.
Image of sloth, and picture of a slave,
The obloquy and scorn of my renown!
How may my heart, thus firèd with mine eyes,
Wounded with shame and killed with discontent,
Shroud any thought may hold my striving hands   20
From martial justice on thy wretched soul?
Theridamas.   Yet pardon him, I pray your majesty.
Techelles and Usumcasane.   Let all of us entreat your highness' pardon.
                                        [*They kneel.*]
Tamburlaine.   Stand up, ye base, unworthy soldiers!
Know ye not yet the argument of arms?   25
Amyras.   Good my lord, let him be forgiven for once,
And we will force him to the field hereafter.
                                     [*The Sons kneel.*]
Tamburlaine.   Stand up, my boys, and I will teach ye arms,
And what the jealousy of wars must do.
O Samarcanda, where I breathèd first,   30
And joyed the fire of this martial flesh,
Blush, blush, fair city, at thine honor's foil,
And shame of nature, which Jaertis' stream,
Embracing thee with deepest of his love,
Can never wash from thy distainèd brows!   35
Here, Jove, receive his fainting soul again,
A form not meet to give that subject essence
Whose matter is the flesh of Tamburlaine,
Wherein an incorporeal spirit moves,
Made of the mould whereof thyself consists,   40
Which makes me valiant, proud, ambitious,
Ready to levy power against thy throne,
That I might move the turning spheres of heaven,
For earth and all this airy region
Cannot contain the state of Tamburlaine.   45
                                  [*He stabs Calyphas.*]
By Mahomet, thy mighty friend, I swear,
In sending to my issue such a soul,
Created of the massy dregs of earth,

25 *argument of arms* necessity of military life.
29 *jealousy of wars* military zeal.
30 *Samarcanda* Samarkand, Tamburlaine's birthplace.
32 *foil* disgrace.
33 *Jaertis' stream* the river Jarartes
which flows east from Tartary to the
Caspian Sea.
37–38 *A form . . . Tamburlaine* i.e.,

the spirit (form) of Calyphas is not
worthy (meet) to serve as the immortal
part (essence) of that mortal being (subject) which is Tamburlaine. The terms
are derived from sixteenth century Aris-
totelian logic. He is saying, in effect,
that Calyphas is unworthy to be his
son and thereby carry on his spirit to
posterity.
    40 *thyself* i.e., Jove.

The scum and tartar of the elements,
Wherein was neither courage, strength, or wit,   50
But folly, sloth, and damnèd idleness,
Thou hast procured a greater enemy
Than he that darted mountains at thy head,
Shaking the burden mighty Atlas bears,
Whereat thou trembling hidd'st thee in the air,   55
Clothed with a pitchy cloud for being seen.
And now, ye cankered curs of Asia,
That will not see the strength of Tamburlaine,
Although it shine as brightly as the sun,
Now you shall feel the strength of Tamburlaine,   60
And, by the state of his supremacy,
Approve the difference 'twixt himself and you.
Orcanes.   Thou show'st the difference 'twixt ourselves and thee,
In this thy barbarous damnèd tyranny.
King of Jerusalem.   Thy victories are grown so violent,   65
That shortly heaven, filled with the meteors
Of blood and fire thy tyrannies have made,
Will pour down blood and fire on thy head,
Whose scalding drops will pierce thy seething brains,
And, with our bloods, revenge our bloods on thee.   70
Tamburlaine.   Villains, these terrors and these tyrannies—
If tyrannies war's justice ye repute—
I execute, enjoined me from above,
To scourge the pride of such as heaven abhors;
Nor am I made arch-monarch of the world,   75
Crowned and invested by the hand of Jove,
For deeds of bounty or nobility;
But since I exercise a greater name,
The scourge of God and terror of the world,
I must apply myself to fit those terms,   80
In war, in blood, in death, in cruelty,
And plague such peasants as resist in me
The power of heaven's eternal majesty.
Theridamas, Techelles, and Casane,
Ransack the tents and the pavilions   85
Of these proud Turks, and take their concubines,
Making them bury this effeminate brat;
For not a common soldier shall defile
His manly fingers with so faint a boy.
Then bring those Turkish harlots to my tent,   90
And I'll dispose them as it likes me best.
Meanwhile, take him in.

49 *tartar* dregs (as of a wine cask).   54 *burden . . . bears* i.e., **heaven.**
53 *he . . . head* the Titans who warred   56 *for being seen* to avoid being **seen.**
against Jove.   89 *faint* faint-hearted, cowardly.

Soldiers.   We will, my lord.

                 [*Exeunt Soldiers with the body of Calyphas.*]

King of Jerusalem.   O damnèd monster, nay, a fiend of hell,
   Whose cruelties are not so harsh as thine,   95
   Nor yet imposed with such a bitter hate!
Orcanes.   Revenge it, Rhadamanth and Æacus,
   And let your hates, extended in his pains,
   Excel the hate wherewith he pains our souls!
King of Trebizon.   May never day give virtue to his eyes,   100
   Whose sight, composed of fury and of fire,
   Doth send such stern affections to his heart!
King of Soria.   May never spirit, vein, or artier, feed
   The cursèd substance of that cruel heart;
   But, wanting moisture and remorseful blood,   105
   Dry up with anger, and consume with heat!
Tamburlaine.   Well, bark, ye dogs. I'll bridle all your tongues
   And bind them close with bits of burnished steel,
   Down to the channels of your hateful throats;
   And, with the pains my rigor shall inflict,   110
   I'll make ye roar, that earth may echo forth
   The far-resounding torments ye sustain;
   As when an herd of lusty Cimbrian bulls
   Run mourning round about the females' miss,
   And, stung with fury of their following,   115
   Fill all the air with troublous bellowing.
   I will, with engines never exercised,
   Conquer, sack, and utterly consume
   Your cities and your golden palaces,
   And with the flames that beat against the clouds,   120
   Incense the heavens and make the stars to melt,
   As if they were the tears of Mahomet,
   For hot consumption of his country's pride.
   And, till by vision or by speech I hear
   Immortal Jove say 'Cease, my Tamburlaine,'   125
   I will persist a terror to the world,
   Making the meteors, that like armèd men
   Are seen to march upon the towers of heaven,
   Run tilting round about the firmament
   And break their burning lances in the air,   130

    97 *Rhadamanth and Æacus* with Minos, the judges of the Greek underworld.
   102 *affections* emotions.
   103 *artier* artery.
   105 *remorseful* compassionate
   113 *Cimbrian* possibly referring to the Cimbri, a celtic people who defeated several Roman armies in the second century B.C. but these people had no particular relation to bulls, and Marlowe's allusion defies explanation.
   114 *females' miss* i.e., loss of their mates.

For honor of my wondrous victories.
Come, bring them in to our pavilion.

Exeunt.

IV,iii.

                        [*Enter*] *Olympia, alone.*
Olympia.   Distressed Olympia, whose weeping eyes
    Since thy arrival here beheld no sun,
    But, closed within the compass of a tent,
    Have stained thy cheeks and made thee look like death,
    Devise some means to rid thee of thy life,   5
    Rather than yield to his detested suit,
    Whose drift is only to dishonor thee;
    And since this earth, dewed with thy brinish tears,
    Affords no herbs whose taste may poison thee,
    Nor yet this air, beat often with thy sighs,   10
    Contagious smells and vapors to infect thee,
    Nor thy close cave a sword to murder thee,
    Let this invention be the instrument.
                        Enter Theridamas.
Theridamas.   Well met, Olympia. I sought thee in my tent,
    But when I saw the place obscure and dark,   15
    Which with thy beauty thou wast wont to light,
    Enraged, I ran about the fields for thee,
    Supposing amorous Jove had sent his son,
    The wingèd Hermes, to convey thee hence.
    But now I find thee, and that fear is past.   20
    Tell me, Olympia, wilt thou grant my suit?
Olympia.   My lord and husband's death, with my sweet son's,
    With whom I buried all affections
    Save grief and sorrow, which torment my heart,
    Forbids my mind to entertain a thought   25
    That tends to love, but meditate on death,
    A fitter subject for a pensive soul.
Theridamas.   Olympia, pity him in whom thy looks
    Have greater operation and more force
    Than Cynthia's in the watery wilderness,   30
    For with thy view my joys are at the full,
    And ebb again as thou depart'st from me.
Olympia.   Ah, pity me, my lord, and draw your sword,

IV,iii.
  7 *drift* intention.

  30 *Cynthia's . . . wilderness* i.e., the
power of the moon to govern the tides.

Making a passage for my troubled soul,
Which beats against this prison to get out   35
And meet my husband and my loving son.
Theridamas.   Nothing but still thy husband and thy son?
Leave this, my love, and listen more to me:
Thou shalt be stately queen of fair Argier,
And, clothed in costly cloth of massy gold,   40
Upon the marble turrets of my court
Sit like to Venus in her chair of state,
Commanding all thy princely eye desires;
And I will cast off arms and sit with thee,
Spending my life in sweet discourse of love.   45
Olympia.   No such discourse is pleasant in mine ears,
But that where every period ends with death,
And every line begins with death again.
I cannot love, to be an emperess.
Theridamas.   Nay lady, then, if nothing will prevail,   50
I'll use some other means to make you yield.
Such is the sudden fury of my love,
I must and will be pleased, and you shall yield.
Come to the tent again.
Olympia.   Stay, good my lord, and, will you save my honor, 55
I'll give your grace a present of such price
As all the world cannot afford the like.
Theridamas.   What is it?
Olympia.   An ointment which a cunning alchemist
Distillèd from the purest balsamum   60
And simplest extracts of all minerals,
In which the essential form of marble stone,
Tempered by science metaphysical,
And spells of magic from the mouths of spirits,
With which if you but 'noint your tender skin,   65
Nor pistol, sword, nor lance, can pierce your flesh.
Theridamas.   Why, madam, think ye to mock me thus palpably?
Olympia.   To prove it, I will 'noint my naked throat,
Which when you stab, look on your weapon's point,
And you shall see't rebated with the blow.   70
Theridamas.   Why gave you not your husband some of it,
If you loved him, and it so precious?
Olympia.   My purpose was, my lord, to spend it so,
But was prevented by his sudden end;
And for a present easy proof hereof,   75
That I dissemble not, try it on me.
Theridamas.   I will, Olympia, and will keep it for

---

61 *simplest extracts* in alchemy, the   62 *essential form* fundamental quality
elemental parts.   of a spirit.
                                               70 *rebated* blunted.

The richest present of this eastern world.

She anoints her throat.

Olympia.   Now stab, my lord, and mark your weapon's point,
That will be blunted if the blow be great.   80
Theridamas.   Here, then, Olympia.   [*He stabs her. She dies.*]
What, have I slain her? Villain, stab thyself!
Cut off this arm that murderèd my love,
In whom the learnèd rabbis of this age
Might find as many wondrous miracles   85
As in the theoria of the world.
Now hell is fairer than Elysium;
A greater lamp than that bright eye of heaven,
From whence the stars do borrow all their light,
Wanders about the black circumference;   90
And now the damnèd souls are free from pain,
For every Fury gazeth on her looks.
Infernal Dis is courting of my love,
Inventing masks and stately shows for her,
Opening the doors of his rich treasury   95
To entertain this queen of chastity,
Whose body shall be tombed with all the pomp
The treasure of my kingdom may afford.

Exit, taking her [body] away.

[*Enter*] *Tamburlaine, drawn in his chariot by* [*the Kings of*]
*Trebizon and Soria, with bits in their mouths, reins in his left
hand, and in his right hand a whip with which he scourgeth
them; Techelles, Theridamas, Usumcasane, Amyras, Celebinus;*
[*Orcanes, King of*] *Natolia, and* [*the King of*] *Jerusalem, led
by five or six common Soldiers.*

Tamburlaine.   Holla, ye pampered jades of Asia!
What, can ye draw but twenty miles a day,
And have so proud a chariot at your heels,
And such a coachman as great Tamburlaine,
But from Asphaltis, where I conquered you,   5
To Byron here, where thus I honor you?
The horse that guide the golden eye of heaven

IV,iv.

84 *rabbis* learned men in general, and
not merely Jewish teachers.

93 *Dis* Pluto, god of the underworld.

94 *masks* lavish entertainments.

5 *Asphaltis* a bituminous lake near
Babylon.

6 *Byron* a city near Babylon.

And blow the morning from their nosterils,
Making their fiery gait above the clouds,
Are not so honored in their governor   10
As you, ye slaves, in mighty Tamburlaine.
The headstrong jades of Thrace Alcides tamed,
That King Ægeus fed with human flesh
And made so wanton that they knew their strengths,
Were not subdued with valor more divine   15
Than you by this unconquered arm of mine.
To make you fierce and fit my appetite,
You shall be fed with flesh as raw as blood
And drink in pails the strongest muscadel.
If you can live with it, then live, and draw   20
My chariot swifter than the racking clouds;
If not, then die like beasts, and fit for naught
But perches for the black and fatal ravens.
Thus am I right the scourge of highest Jove,
And see the figure of my dignity,   25
By which I hold my name and majesty!
Amyras.   Let me have coach, my lord, that I may ride,
And thus be drawn with these two idle kings.
Tamburlaine.   Thy youth forbids such ease, my kingly boy.
They shall to-morrow draw my chariot,   30
While these their fellow-kings may be refreshed.
Orcanes.   O thou that sway'st the region under earth
And art a king as absolute as Jove,
Come as thou didst in fruitful Sicily,
Surveying all the glories of the land,   35
And as thou took'st the fair Proserpina,
Joying the fruit of Ceres' garden-plot,
For love, for honor, and to make her queen,
So, for just hate, for shame, and to subdue
This proud contemner of thy dreadful power,   40
Come once in fury and survey his pride,
Haling him headlong to the lowest hell.
Theridamas.   Your majesty must get some bits for these,
To bridle their contemptuous cursing tongues,
That, like unruly never-broken jades,   45
Break through the hedges of their hateful mouths

---

8 *nosterils* nostrils. The 1590 spelling
is retained for the sake of the meter.
12–13 *headstrong . . . flesh* One of the
twelve labors of Hercules (Alcides) was
to capture the wild mares, fed with
human flesh, of Ægeus or Diomedes,
king of the Bistones in Thrace. Hercules
fed them the flesh of their master, after
which they became tame.

21 *racking* scudding before the wind.
32 *thou . . . earth* i.e., Pluto, god of
the underworld, who had carried off
Proserpina, daughter of Ceres, goddess
of the harvest, and made her his queen
in Hades.
40 *contemner* holder in contempt.
46 *hedges . . . mouths* i.e., teeth.

And pass their fixèd bounds exceedingly.
Techelles.   Nay, we will break the hedges of their mouths
   And pull their kicking colts out of their pastures.
Usumcasane.   Your majesty already hath devised   50
   A mean, as fit as may be, to restrain
   These coltish coach-horse tongues from blasphemy.
Celebinus.   How like you that, sir king? Why speak you not?
King of Jerusalem.   Ah, cruel brat, sprung from a tyrant's loins!
   How like his cursèd father he begins   55
   To practice taunts and bitter tyrannies!
Tamburlaine.   Ay, Turk, I tell thee, this same boy is he
   That must, advanced in higher pomp than this,
   Rifle the kingdoms I shall leave unsacked,
   If Jove, esteeming me too good for earth,   60
   Raise me to match the fair Aldeboran,
   Above the threefold astracism of heaven,
   Before I conquer all the triple world.
   Now fetch me out the Turkish concubines.
   I will prefer them for the funeral   65
   They have bestowed on my abortive son.
                              The Concubines are brought in.
   Where are my common soldiers now, that fought
   So lion-like upon Asphaltis' plains?
Soldiers.   Here, my lord.
Tamburlaine.   Hold ye, tall soldiers; take ye queens apiece—   70
   I mean such queens as were kings' concubines.
   Take them; divide them, and their jewels too,
   And let them equally serve all your turns.
Soldiers.   We thank your majesty.
Tamburlaine.   Brawl not, I warn you, for your lechery,   75
   For every man that so offends shall die.
Orcanes.   Injurious tyrant, wilt thou so defame
   The hateful fortunes of thy victory,
   To exercise upon such guiltless dames
   The violence of thy common soldiers' lust?   80
Tamburlaine.   Live continent, then, ye slaves, and meet not me
   With troops of harlots at your slothful heels.
Concubines.   O pity us, my lord, and save our honors.
Tamburlaine.   Are ye not gone, ye villains, with your spoils?
                              The Soldiers run away with the Ladies.
King of Jerusalem.   O, merciless, infernal cruelty!   85
Tamburlaine.   Save your honors! 'Twere but time indeed,
   Lost long before you knew what honor meant.
Theridamas.   It seems they meant to conquer us, my lord,

61 *Aldeboran* a star in the constellation   62 *astracism* constellation.
of Taurus, one of the fixed stars of   70 *tall* brave.
heaven.

And make us jesting pageants for their trulls.
Tamburlaine.   And now themselves shall make our pageant,   90
And common soldiers jest with all their trulls.
Let them take pleasure soundly in their spoils,
Till we prepare our march to Babylon,
Whither we next make expedition.
Techelles.   Let us not be idle then, my lord,   95
But presently be prest to conquer it.
Tamburlaine.   We will, Techelles. Forward, then, ye jades.
Now crouch, ye kings of greatest Asia,
And tremble when ye hear this scourge will come
That whips down cities and controlleth crowns,   100
Adding their wealth and treasure to my store.
The Euxine sea, north to Natolia,
The Terrene, west, the Caspian, north-north-east,
And on the south, Sinus Arabicus,
Shall all be loaden with the martial spoils   105
We will convey with us to Persia.
Then shall my native city Samarcanda,
And crystal waves of fresh Jaertis' stream,
The pride and beauty of her princely seat,
Be famous through the furthest continents;   110
For there my palace royal shall be placed,
Whose shining turrets shall dismay the heavens
And cast the fame of Ilion's tower to hell.
Thorough the streets, with troops of conquered kings,
I'll ride in golden armor like the sun,   115
And in my helm a triple plume shall spring,
Spanglèd with diamonds, dancing in the air,
To note me emperor of the three-fold world;
Like to an almond-tree y-mounted high
Upon the lofty and celestial mount   120
Of ever-green Selinus, quaintly decked
With blooms more white than Erycina's brows,
Whose tender blossoms tremble every one
At every little breath that thorough heaven is blown.
Then in my coach, like Saturn's royal son   125
Mounted his shining chariot gilt with fire,
And drawn with princely eagles through the path
Paved with bright crystal and enchased with stars,
When all the gods stand gazing at his pomp,
So will I ride through Samarcanda streets,   130

96 *prest* ready.
102 *Euxine* Black.
108 *Jaertis' stream* See note at IV,ii,
33.
118 *three-fold world* consisting of Europe, Asia, and Africa.

121 *Selinus* town in Sicily located on a river of the same name.
122 *Erycina* Venus (who was worshipped at a temple on Mt. Eryx in western Sicily).
125 *Saturn's royal son* i.e., Jove.

Until my soul, dissevered from this flesh,
Shall mount the milk-white way, and meet Him there.
To Babylon, my lords, to Babylon!

Exeunt.

V,i.

*Enter the Governor of Babylon, upon the walls, with [Maxi-
mus and] others.*

Governor.   What saith Maximus?
Maximus.   My lord, the breach the enemy hath made
  Gives such assurance of our overthrow,
  That little hope is left to save our lives
  Or hold our city from the conqueror's hands.   5
  Then hang out flags, my lord, of humble truce,
  And satisfy the people's general prayers,
  That Tamburlaine's intolerable wrath
  May be suppressed by our submission.
Governor.   Villain, respects thou more thy slavish life   10
  Than honor of thy country or thy name?
  Is not my life and state as dear to me,
  The city and my native country's weal,
  As any thing of price with thy conceit?
  Have we not hope, for all our battered walls,   15
  To live secure and keep his forces out,
  When this our famous lake of Limnasphaltis
  Makes walls afresh with every thing that falls
  Into the liquid substance of his stream,
  More strong than are the gates of death or hell?   20
  What faintness should dismay our courages,
  When we are thus defensed against our foe,
  And have no terror but his threatening looks?
     Enter another [Citizen], kneeling to the Governor.
Citizen.   My lord, if ever you did deed of ruth,
  And now will work a refuge to our lives,   25
  Offer submission, hang up flags of truce,
  That Tamburlaine may pity our distress
  And use us like a loving conqueror.
  Though this be held his last day's dreadful siege,
  Wherein he spareth neither man nor child,   30

V,i.

14 *As . . . conceit* as anything which
may be of value in your thoughts.
17 *Limnasphaltis* the bituminous lake
of Babylon, of whose fabulous properties
Marlowe may have read in Herodotus.

Yet are there Christians of Georgia here,
Whose state he ever pitied and relieved,
Will get his pardon, if your grace would send.
Governor.   How is my soul environèd!
And this eternized city Babylon   35
Filled with a pack of faint-heart fugitives
That thus entreat their shame and servitude!
                    [*Enter, a Second Citizen.*]
Second Citizen.   My lord, if ever you will win our hearts,
Yield up the town, save our wives and children;
For I will cast myself from off these walls   40
Or die some death of quickest violence,
Before I bide the wrath of Tamburlaine.
Governor.   Villains, cowards, traitors to our state,
Fall to the earth, and pierce the pit of hell,
That legions of tormenting spirits may vex   45
Your slavish bosoms with continual pains!
I care not, nor the town will never yield
As long as any life is in my breast.
          Enter Theridamas and Techelles, with other Soldiers.
Theridamas.   Thou desperate governor of Babylon,
To save thy life, and us a little labor,   50
Yield speedily the city to our hands,
Or else be sure thou shalt be forced with pains
More exquisite than ever traitor felt.
Governor.   Tyrant, I turn the traitor in thy throat,
And will defend it in despite of thee.   55
Call up the soldiers to defend these walls.
Techelles.   Yield, foolish governor; we offer more
Than ever yet we did to such proud slaves
As durst resist us till our third day's siege.
Thou seest us prest to give the last assault,   60
And that shall bide no more regard of parley.
Governor.   Assault and spare not; we will never yield.
                    Alarm; and they scale the walls.

          Enter Tamburlaine [drawn in his chariot by the Kings of Tre-
          bizon and Soria]; with Usumcasane, Amyras, and Celebinus;
          [Orcanes, the King of Natolia, and the King of Jerusalem, led
                    by soldiers; and others].
Tamburlaine.   The stately buildings of fair Babylon,
Whose lofty pillars, higher than the clouds,
Were wont to guide the seaman in the deep,   65
Being carried thither by the cannon's force,
Now fill the mouth of Limnasphaltis' lake
And make a bridge unto the battered walls.

60 *prest* ready.

Where Belus, Ninus, and great Alexander
Have rode in triumph, triumphs Tamburlaine,   70
Whose chariot-wheels have burst th'Assyrians' bones,
Drawn with these kings on heaps of carcasses.
Now in the place where fair Semiramis,
Courted by kings and peers of Asia,
Hath trod the measures, do my soldiers march,   75
And in the streets where brave Assyrian dames
Have rid in pomp like rich Saturnia,
With furious words and frowning visages
My horsemen brandish their unruly blades.

Enter Theridamas and Techelles, bringing [in] the Governor
of Babylon.

Who have ye there, my lords?   80
Theridamas.   The sturdy governor of Babylon,
That made us all the labor for the town
And used such slender reck'ning of your majesty.
Tamburlaine.   Go, bind the villain; he shall hang in chains
Upon the ruins of this conquered town.   85
Sirrah, the view of our vermilion tents
Which threatened more than if the region
Next underneath the element of fire
Were full of comets and of blazing stars,
Whose flaming trains should reach down to the earth,   90
Could not affright you; no, nor I myself,
The wrathful messenger of mighty Jove,
That with his sword hath quailed all earthly kings,
Could not persuade you to submission,
But still the ports were shut. Villain, I say,   95
Should I but touch the rusty gates of hell,
The triple headed Cerberus would howl
And make black Jove to crouch and kneel to me;
But I have sent volleys of shot to you,
Yet could not enter till the breach was made.   100
Governor.   Nor if my body could have stopped the breach,
Shouldst thou have entered, cruel Tamburlaine.
'Tis not thy bloody tents can make me yield,
Nor yet thyself, the anger of the Highest,
For though thy cannon shook the city walls,   105
My heart did never quake or courage faint.
Tamburlaine.   Well, now I'll make it quake. Go, draw him up;

69 *Belus . . . Alexander* Belus, son
of Neptune, was the legendary founder
of Babylon; Ninus, the founder of
Nineveh, married Simiramis, who built
the walls of Babylon; Alexander the
Great of Macedon conquered Babylon
in 331 B.C.

71 *burst* broken.
77 *Saturnia* Juno, queen of the gods.
95 *ports* gates.
97 *Cerberus* the three-headed dog of
Hades.
98 *black Jove* Pluto.

Hang him up in chains upon the city walls,
And let my soldiers shoot the slave to death.

Governor. Vile monster, born of some infernal hag   110
And sent from hell to tyrannize on earth,
Do all thy worst; nor death, nor Tamburlaine,
Torture, or pain, can daunt my dreadless mind.

Tamburlaine. Up with him, then; his body shall be scarred.

Governor. But, Tamburlaine, in Limnasphaltis' lake   115
There lies more gold than Babylon is worth,
Which, when the city was besieged, I hid.
Save but my life, and I will give it thee.

Tamburlaine. Then, for all your valor, you would save your life?
Whereabout lies it?   120

Governor. Under a hollow bank, right opposite
Against the western gate of Babylon.

Tamburlaine. Go thither, some of you, and take his gold.
                    [*Exeunt some Attendants.*]
The rest forward with execution.
Away with him hence; let him speak no more.   125
I think I make your courage something quail.
          [*Exeunt Attendants with the Governor of Babylon.*]
When this is done, we'll march from Babylon
And make our greatest haste to Persia.
These jades are broken winded and half tired;
Unharness them, and let me have fresh horse.   130
          [*Attendants unharness the Kings of Trebizon and Soria.*]
So; now their best is done to honor me,
Take them and hang them both up presently.

King of Trebizon. Vild tyrant! Barbarous bloody Tamburlaine!

Tamburlaine. Take them away, Theridamas; see them dispatched.

Theridamas. I will, my lord.   135
          [*Exit Theridamas with the Kings of Trebizon and Soria.*]

Tamburlaine. Come, Asian viceroys; to your tasks awhile,
And take such fortune as your fellows felt.

Orcanes. First let thy Scythian horse tear both our limbs,
Rather than we should draw thy chariot,
And, like base slaves, abject our princely minds   140
To vile and ignominious servitude.

King of Jerusalem. Rather lend me thy weapon, Tamburlaine.
That I may sheathe it in this breast of mine.
A thousand deaths could not torment our hearts
More than the thought of this doth vex our souls.   145

Amyras. They will talk still, my lord, if you do not bridle them.

Tamburlaine. Bridle them, and let me to my coach.
          [*Attendants bridle Orcanes King of Natolia, and the King of
          Jerusalem, and harness them to the chariot. The Governor of*

133 *Vild* vile.   140 *abject* abase.

Babylon appears hanging in chains on the walls. Enter Theri-
damas.]

Amyras. See, now, my lord, how brave the captain hangs.

Tamburlaine. 'Tis brave indeed, my boy. Well done!
  Shoot first, my lord, and then the rest shall follow.   150

Theridamas. Then have at him, to begin withal.

                                    Theridamas shoots.

Governor. Yet save my life, and let this wound appease
  The mortal fury of great Tamburlaine.

Tamburlaine. No, though Asphaltis' lake were liquid gold,
  And offered me as ransom for thy life,   155
  Yet shouldst thou die. Shoot at him all at once.

                                    They shoot.

  So, now he hangs like Bagdet's governor,
  Having as many bullets in his flesh
  As there be breaches in her battered wall.
  Go now, and bind the burghers hand and foot,   160
  And cast them headlong in the city's lake.
  Tartars and Persians shall inhabit there;
  And, to command the city, I will build
  A citadel, that all Africa,
  Which hath been subject to the Persian king,   165
  Shall pay me tribute for in Babylon.

Techelles. What shall be done with their wives and children, my lord?

Tamburlaine. Techelles, drown them all, man, woman, and child;
  Leave not a Babylonian in the town.

Techelles. I will about it straight. Come, soldiers.   170

                          Exit [Techelles with Soldiers].

Tamburlaine. Now, Casane, where's the Turkish Alcoran
  And all the heaps of superstitious books
  Found in the temples of that Mahomet
  Whom I have thought a god? They shall be burnt.

Usumcasane. Here they are, my lord.   175

Tamburlaine. Well said; let there be a fire presently.

                                    [*They light a fire.*]

  In vain, I see, men worship Mahomet.
  My sword hath sent millions of Turks to hell,
  Slew all his priests, his kinsmen, and his friends,
  And yet I live untouched by Mahomet.   180
  There is a God, full of revenging wrath,
  From whom the thunder and the lightning breaks,
  Whose scourge I am, and Him will I obey.
  So, Casane; fling them in the fire.   [*They burn the books.*]
  Now, Mahomet, if thou have any power,   185
  Come down thyself and work a miracle.
  Thou are not worthy to be worshippèd

157 *Bagdet's* Bagdad's.

That suffers flames of fire to burn the writ
Wherein the sum of thy religion rests.
Why send'st thou not a furious whirlwind down   190
To blow thy Alcoran up to thy throne,
Where men report thou sitt'st by God himself?
Or vengeance on the head of Tamburlaine
That shakes his sword against thy majesty
And spurns the abstracts of thy foolish laws?   195
Well, soldiers, Mahomet remains in hell;
He cannot hear the voice of Tamburlaine.
Seek out another godhead to adore—
The God that sits in heaven, if any god,
For He is God alone, and none but He.   200
                    [*Enter Techelles.*]
Techelles. I have fulfilled your highness' will, my lord.
    Thousands of men, drowned in Asphaltis' lake,
    Have made the water swell above the banks,
    And fishes, fed by human carcasses,
    Amazed, swim up and down upon the waves,   205
    As when they swallow asafœtida,
    Which makes them fleet aloft and gasp for air.
Tamburlaine. Well, then, my friendly lords, what now remains,
    But that we leave sufficient garrison
    And presently depart to Persia,   210
    To triumph after all our victories?
Theridamas. Ay, good my lord, let us in haste to Persia;
    And let this captain be removed the walls
    To some high hill about the city here.
Tamburlaine. Let it be so; about it, soldiers.   215
    But stay; I feel myself distempered suddenly.
Techelles. What is it dares distemper Tamburlaine?
Tamburlaine. Something, Techelles, but I know not what.
    But, forth, ye vassals! Whatsoe'er it be,
    Sickness or death can never conquer me.   220
                                            Exeunt.

                                                            V,ii
    Enter Callapine, [*King of*] *Amasia,* [*and train,*] *with* **drums**
                    and trumpets.
Callapine. King of Amasia, now our mighty host
    Marcheth in Asia Major, where the streams
    Of Euphrates and Tigris swiftly runs;

206 *asafœtida* a concreted resinous gum   207 *fleet* float.
with a strong odor, used in medicine
as an anti-spasmodic.

And here may we behold great Babylon,
Circlèd about with Limnasphaltis' lake,   5
Where Tamburlaine with all his army lies,
Which being faint and weary with the siege,
We may lie ready to encounter him
Before his host be full from Babylon,
And so revenge our latest grievous loss,   10
If God or Mahomet send any aid.
King of Amasia.   Doubt not, my lord, but we shall conquer him.
The monster that hath drunk a sea of blood
And yet gapes still for more to quench his thirst,
Our Turkish swords shall headlong send to hell;   15
And that vile carcass, drawn by warlike kings,
The fowls shall eat; for never sepulcher
Shall grace that base-born tyrant Tamburlaine.
Callapine.   When I record my parents' slavish life,
Their cruel death, mine own captivity,   20
My viceroys' bondage under Tamburlaine,
Methinks I could sustain a thousand deaths
To be revenged of all his villany.
Ah, sacred Mahomet, thou that hast seen
Millions of Turks perish by Tamburlaine,   25
Kingdoms made waste, brave cities sacked and burnt,
And but one host is left to honor thee,
Aid thy obedient servant Callapine,
And make him, after all these overthrows,
To triumph over cursèd Tamburlaine.   30
King of Amasia.   Fear not, my lord. I see great Mahomet,
Clothèd in purple clouds, and on his head
A chaplet brighter than Apollo's crown,
Marching about the air with armèd men,
To join with you against this Tamburlaine.   35
Renownèd general, mighty Callapine,
Though God himself and holy Mahomet
Should come in person to resist your power,
Yet might your mighty host encounter all,
And pull proud Tamburlaine upon his knees   40
To sue for mercy at your highness' feet.
Callapine.   Captain, the force of Tamburlaine is great,
His fortune greater, and the victories
Wherewith he hath so sore dismayed the world
Are greatest to discourage all our drifts;   45
Yet when the pride of Cynthia is at full,
She wanes again, and so shall his, I hope;

V,ii.
19 *record* call to mind.   45 *drifts* purposes.

For we have here the chief selected men
Of twenty several kingdoms at the least.
Nor ploughman, priest, nor merchant, stays at home;   50
All Turkey is in arms with Callapine;
And never will we sunder camps and arms
Before himself or his be conquerèd.
This is the time that must eternize me
For conquering the tyrant of the world.   55
Come, soldiers, let us lie in wait for him,
And if we find him absent from his camp,
Or that it be rejoined again at full,
Assail it and be sure of victory.

Exeunt.

[*Enter*] *Theridamas, Techelles, and Usumcasane.*   V,iii.
Theridamas.   Weep, heavens, and vanish into liquid tears!
Fall, stars that govern his nativity,
And summon all the shining lamps of heaven
To cast their bootless fires to the earth
And shed their feeble influence in the air.   5
Muffle your beauties with eternal clouds,
For Hell and Darkness pitch their pitchy tents,
And Death, with armies of Cimmerian spirits,
Gives battle 'gainst the heart of Tamburlaine.
Now in defiance of that wonted love   10
Your sacred virtues poured upon his throne,
And made his state an honor to the heavens,
These cowards invisibly assail his soul
And threaten conquest on our sovereign.
But if he die, your glories are disgraced,   15
Earth droops and says that hell in heaven is placed.
Techelles.   Oh, then, ye powers that sway eternal seats
And guide this massy substance of the earth,
If you retain desert of holiness,
As your supreme estates instruct our thoughts,   20
Be not inconstant, careless of your fame,
Bear not the burden of your enemies' joys,
Triumphing in his fall whom you advanced,
But as his birth, life, health, and majesty
Were strangely blessed and governèd by heaven,   25

V,iii.
4 *bootless* unavailing.   12 *state* throne.
8 *Cimmerian* black, coming from the
underworld.

So honor, heaven, till heaven dissolvèd be,
His birth, his life, his health, and majesty!
Usumcasane.   Blush, heaven, to lose the honor of thy name,
  To see thy footstool set upon thy head;
  And let no baseness in thy haughty breast   30
  Sustain a shame of such inexcellence,
  To see the devils mount in angels' thrones,
  And angels dive into the pools of hell.
  And though they think their painful date is out
  And that their power is puissant as Jove's,   35
  Which makes them manage arms against thy state,
  Yet make them feel the strength of Tamburlaine,
  Thy instrument and note of majesty,
  Is greater far than they can thus subdue;
  For, if he die, thy glory is disgraced,   40
  Earth droops and says that hell in heaven is placed.
      [*Enter Tamburlaine, drawn in his chariot by Orcanes King of*
      Natolia, and the King of Jerusalem; Amyras, Celebinus, and
                    Physicans.]
Tamburlaine.   What daring god torments my body thus
  And seeks to conquer mighty Tamburlaine?
  Shall sickness prove me now to be a man,
  That have been termed the terror of the world?   45
  Techelles and the rest, come, take your swords,
  And threaten him whose hand afflicts my soul.
  Come, let us march against the powers of heaven
  And set black streamers in the firmament
  To signify the slaughter of the gods.   50
  Ah, friends, what shall I do? I cannot stand.
  Come, carry me to war against the gods,
  That thus envy the health of Tamburlaine.
Theridamas.   Ah, good my lord, leave these impatient **words**
  Which add much danger to your malady.   55
Tamburlaine.   Why, shall I sit and languish in this pain?
  No, strike the drums, and, in revenge of this,
  Come, let us charge our spears and pierce his breast
  Whose shoulders bear the axis of the world,
  That if I perish, heaven and earth may fade.   60
  Theridamas, haste to the court of Jove;
  Will him to send Apollo hither straight
  To cure me, or I'll fetch him down myself.
Techelles.   Sit still, my gracious lord; this grief will cease
  And cannot last, it is so violent.   65
Tamburlaine.   Not last, Techelles? No, for I shall die.

38 *note* distinguishing mark.   to Greek legend, and not the axis of
59 *Whose . . . world* Atlas, who bears   the earth.
the heavens upon his shoulders according

See where my slave, the ugly monster Death,
Shaking and quivering, pale and wan for fear,
Stands aiming at me with his murdering dart,
Who flies away at every glance I give,   70
And when I look away, comes stealing on.
Villain, away, and hie thee to the field!
I and mine army come to load thy bark
With souls of thousand mangled carcasses.
Look, where he goes! But see, he comes again   75
Because I stay. Techelles, let us march
And weary Death with bearing souls to hell.
First Physician.   Pleaseth your majesty to drink this potion,
Which will abate the fury of your fit
And cause some milder spirits govern you.   80
Tamburlaine.   Tell me, what think you of my sickness now?
First Physician.   I viewed your urine, and the hypostasis,
Thick and obscure, doth make your danger great.
Your veins are full of accidental heat,
Whereby the moisture of your blood is dried.   85
The humidum and calor, which some hold
Is not a parcel of the elements,
But of a substance more divine and pure,
Is almost clean extinguishèd and spent,
Which, being the cause of life, imports your death.   90
Besides, my lord, this day is critical,
Dangerous to those whose crisis is as yours.
Your artiers, which alongst the veins convey
The lively spirits which the heart engenders,
Are parched and void of spirit, that the soul,   95
Wanting those organons by which it moves,
Cannot endure by argument of art.
Yet, if your majesty may escape this day,
No doubt but you shall soon recover all.
Tamburlaine.   Then will I comfort all my vital parts,   100
And live, in spite of death, above a day.

                                                    Alarm within.

[Enter a Messenger.]

Messenger.   My lord, young Callapine, that lately fled from your
majesty, hath now gathered a fresh army, and hearing your absence
in the field, offers to set upon us presently.

82 *hypostasis* accumulation of solids
within a fluid.
84 *accidental* in excess of the proper
amount.
86 *humidum and calor* moisture and
heat, which in combination form the
sanguine humor.

91 *day is critical* i.e., the stars are
not in a proper conjunction for effecting
a cure. Medicine and astrology were
closely linked.
96 *organons* instruments.

Tamburlaine.   See, my physicians, now, how Jove hath sent   105
A present medicine to recure my pain.
My looks shall make them fly; and might I follow,
There should not one of all the villain's power
Live to give offer of another fight.
Usumcasane.   I joy, my lord, your highness is so strong,   110
That can endure so well your royal presence,
Which only will dismay the enemy.
Tamburlaine.   I know it will, Casane. Draw, you slaves!
In spite of death, I will go show my face.

> *Alarm. Tamburlaine goes in, and comes out again
> with all the rest.*

Tamburlaine.   Thus are the villains, cowards fled for fear,   115
Like summer's vapors vanished by the sun;
And could I but a while pursue the field,
That Callapine should be my slave again.
But I perceive my martial strength is spent.
In vain I strive and rail against those powers   120
That mean t'invest me in a higher throne,
As much too high for this disdainful earth.
Give me a map; then let me see how much
Is left for me to conquer all the world,
That these, my boys, may finish all my wants.   125

> *One brings a map.*

Here I began to march towards Persia,
Along Armenia and the Caspian Sea,
And thence unto Bithynia, where I took
The Turk and his great empress prisoners.
Then marched I into Egypt and Arabia;   130
And here, not far from Alexandria,
Whereas the Terrene and the Red Sea meet,
Being distant less than full a hundred leagues,
I meant to cut a channel to them both,
That men might quickly sail to India.   135
From thence to Nubia near Borno lake,
And so along the Ethiopian sea,
Cutting the tropic line of Capricorn,
I conquered all as far as Zanzibar.
Then, by the northern part of Africa,   140
I came at last to Græcia, and from thence
To Asia, where I stay against my will;
Which is from Scythia, where I first began,
Backward and forwards near five thousand leagues.

106 *recure* cure.
134 *cut a channel* build a canal. He is, of course, indicating the site of the present day Suez canal, a project which several kings had attempted to execute before Marlowe's time.

Look here, my boys; see what a world of ground   145
Lies westward from the midst of Cancer's line
Unto the rising of this earthly globe,
Whereas the sun, declining from our sight,
Begins the day with our Antipodes.
And shall I die, and this unconquerèd?   150
Lo, here, my sons, are all the golden mines,
Inestimable drugs and precious stones,
More worth than Asia and the world beside;
And from th'Antarctic Pole eastward behold
As much more land, which never was descried,   155
Wherein are rocks of pearl that shine as bright
As all the lamps that beautify the sky.
And shall I die, and this unconquerèd?
Here, lovely boys; what death forbids my life,
That let your lives command in spite of death.   160
Amyras.   Alas, my lord, how should our bleeding hearts,
Wounded and broken with your highness' grief,
Retain a thought of joy or spark of life?
Your soul gives essence to our wretched subjects,
Whose matter is incorporate in your flesh.   165
Celebinus.   Your pains do pierce our souls; no hope survives,
For by your life we entertain our lives.
Tamburlaine.   But, sons, this subject, not of force enough
To hold the fiery spirit it contains,
Must part, imparting his impressions   170
By equal portions into both your breasts.
My flesh, divided in your precious shapes,
Shall still retain my spirit, though I die,
And live in all your seeds immortally.
Then now remove me, that I may resign   175
My place and proper title to my son.
First, take my scourge and my imperial crown,
And mount my royal chariot of estate,
That I may see thee crowned before I die.
Help me, my lords, to make my last remove.   180
[*They help Tamburlaine out of his chariot.*]
Theridamas.   A woeful change, my lord, that daunts our thoughts
More than the ruin of our proper souls.

149 *Antipodes* people who live in the region of the setting sun. See note at I,iii,52.

154–155 *And from . . . descried* Australia, of which rumors were current in Marlowe's time, although the continent had not yet been discovered.

164–165 *Your soul . . . flesh* i.e., the soul of Tamburlaine has bequeathed a spirit (essence) to the bodies (subjects) of his sons, since their bodies are parts of his flesh.

168–171 *this subject . . . breasts* i.e., this body, unable longer to contain its spirit, must divide that spirit equally among its sons.

182 *proper* own.

Tamburlaine. Sit up, my son; let me see how well
   Thou wilt become thy father's majesty.

                                   They crown Amyras.

Amyras. With what a flinty bosom should I joy   185
   The breath of life and burden of my soul,
   If not resolved into resolvèd pains,
   My body's mortifièd lineaments
   Should exercise the motions of my heart,
   Pierced with the joy of any dignity!   190
   O father, if the unrelenting ears
   Of death and hell be shut against my prayers,
   And that the spiteful influence of heaven
   Deny my soul fruition of her joy,
   How should I step or stir my hateful feet   195
   Against the inward powers of my heart,
   Leading a life that only strives to die,
   And plead in vain unpleasing sovereignty?
Tamburlaine. Let not thy love exceed thine honor, son,
   Nor bar thy mind that magnanimity   200
   That nobly must admit necessity.
   Sit up, my boy, and with these silken reins
   Bridle the steelèd stomachs of those jades.
Theridamas. My lord, you must obey his majesty,
   Since fate commands and proud necessity.   205
Amyras. Heavens witness me with what a broken heart

                     [*Mounting the chariot.*]

   And damnèd spirit I ascend this seat,
   And send my soul, before my father die,
   His anguish and his burning agony!
Tamburlaine. Now fetch the hearse of fair Zenocrate.   210
   Let it be placed by this my fatal chair
   And serve as parcel of my funeral.
Usumcasane. Then feels your majesty no sovereign ease,
   Nor may our hearts, all drowned in tears of blood,
   Joy any hope of your recovery?   215
Tamburlaine. Casane, no. The monarch of the earth,
   And eyeless monster that torments my soul,
   Cannot behold the tears ye shed for me,
   And therefore still augments his cruelty.
Techelles. Then let some god oppose his holy power   220
   Against the wrath and tyranny of Death,
   That his tear-thirsty and unquenchèd hate
   May be upon himself reverberate!

          They bring in the hearse [*of Zenocrate*].

Tamburlaine. Now, eyes, enjoy your latest benefit,

185 *joy* enjoy.

And when my soul hath virtue of your sight,   225
Pierce through the coffin and the sheet of gold,
And glut your longings with a heaven of joy.
So, reign, my son; scourge and control those slaves,
Guiding thy chariot with thy father's hand.
As precious is the charge thou undertak'st   230
As that which Clymene's brain-sick son did guide,
When wandering Phœbe's ivory cheeks were scorched,
And all the earth, like Ætna, breathing fire.
Be warned by him; then learn with awful eye
To sway a throne as dangerous as his;   235
For if thy body thrive not full of thoughts
As pure and fiery as Phyteus' beams,
The nature of these proud rebelling jades
Will take occasion by the slenderest hair
And draw thee piecemeal, like Hippolytus,   240
Through rocks more steep and sharp than Caspian cliffs.
The nature of thy chariot will not bear
A guide of baser temper than myself,
More than heaven's coach the pride of Phaëton.
Farewell, my boys! My dearest friends, farewell!   245
My body feels, my soul doth weep to see
Your sweet desires deprived my company,
For Tamburlaine, the scourge of God, must die.

                                        [*He dies.*]

Amyras.   Meet heaven and earth, and here let all things end,
For earth hath spent the pride of all her fruit,   250
And heaven consumed his choicest living fire.
Let earth and heaven his timeless death deplore,
For both their worths will equal him no more.

                                        [*Exeunt.*]

225 *when . . . sight* i.e., when, after death, his spirit, freed from the body and thus from the limitations of mortality, will be able to see the spirit of Zenocrate with unclouded vision.

231 *Clymene's brain-sick son* See note to *I Tamb.*, IV,ii,49.

232 *Phœbe* the moon.

237 *Phyteus'* Apollo's.

240 *Hippolytus* the son of Theseus by Hippolyta. When Theseus remarried, his new wife, Phaedra, fell in love with her stepson and when he repulsed her advances, accused him of attempting to dishonor her. Theseus caused his son to be destroyed; his body was mutilated as it was dragged along the ground by the horses of his overturned carriage.

244 *Phaëton* the son of Apollo. See note to *I Tamb.*, IV,ii,49.

The Famous

TRAGEDY

OF

THE RICH IEVV

OF *MALTA.*

AS IT WAS PLAYD

BEFORE THE KING AND
QVEENE, IN HIS MAJESTIES
Theatre at *White-Hall,* by her Majesties
Servants at the *Cock-pit.*

Written by CHRISTOPHER MARLO,

LONDON;
Printed by *I. B.* for *Nicholas Vavasour,* and are to be sold
at his Shop in the Inner-Temple, neere the
Church. 1 6 3 3,

TO MY WORTHY FRIEND, MASTER THOMAS HAMMON
OF GRAY'S INN, ETC.

This play, composed by so worthy an author as Master Marlowe, and the part of the Jew presented by so inimitable an actor as Master Alleyn, being in this later age commended to the stage; as I ushered it unto the court and presented it to the Cockpit with these prologues and epilogues here inserted, so now being newly brought to the [5 press, I was loath it should be published without the ornament of an Epistle, making choice of you unto whom to devote it, than whom—of all those gentlemen and acquaintance within the compass of my long knowledge—there is none more able to tax ignorance or attribute right to merit. Sir, you have been pleased to grace some of mine own [10 works with your courteous patronage. I hope this will not be the worse accepted because commended by me, over whom none can claim more power or privilege than yourself. I had no better a new year's gift to present you with; receive it therefore as a continuance of that inviolable obligement by which he rests still engaged, who, as he ever hath, [15 shall always remain,

Tuissimus,
THOMAS HEYWOOD.

Dedication.

2–3 *Master Alleyn* Edward Alleyn (1566–1626) the celebrated tragic actor who starred as Barabas when the play was performed by the Lord Admiral's Men.

4 *Cockpit* a theater in Drury Lane, known also as the Phoenix.

9 *tax* censure.

THE JEW OF MALTA

THE PLAYERS

Ferneze, **Governor** of Malta
Lodowick, his son
Selim Calymath, son to the Grand
  Seignior
Martin Del Bosco, vice-admiral of
  Spain
Mathias
Barabas, the Jew of Malta
Ithamore, his slave
Jacomo ⎱ friars
Barnardine ⎰
Pilia-Borza, a bully

Two Merchants
Three Jews
Knights, Bashaws, Officers, **Guard,**
  Slaves, Messenger and **Carpen-**
  ters

Katherine, mother of Mathias
Abigail, daughter of Barabas
Bellamira, a courtesan
Abbess
Nun
Machiavel, the **Prologue-speaker**

THE SCENE
Malta

THE PROLOGUE SPOKEN AT COURT

Gracious and great, that we so boldly dare,
'Mongst other plays that now in fashion are,
To present this, writ many years agone,
And in that age thought second unto none,
We humbly crave your pardon. We pursue   5
The story of a rich and famous Jew
Who lived in Malta. You shall find him still,
In all his projects, a sound Machiavel,
And that's his character. He that hath passed
So many censures is now come at last   10
To have your princely ears. Grace you him, then
You crown the action, and renown the pen.

EPILOGUE [SPOKEN AT COURT]

It is our fear, dread sovereign, we have been
Too tedious; neither can't be less than sin
To wrong your princely patience. If we have,
Thus low dejected, we your pardon crave.
And if ought here offend your ear or sight,   5
We only act and speak what others write.

177

THE PROLOGUE TO THE STAGE
At the Cockpit

We know not how our play may pass this stage,
But by the best of poets in that age
The Malta Jew had being and was made,
And he then by the best of actors played.
In *Hero and Leander* one did gain   5
A lasting memory. In *Tamburlaine,*
This *Jew,* with others many, th'other wan
The attribute of peerless, being a man
Whom we may rank with—doing no one wrong—
Proteus for shapes and Roscius for a tongue,   10
So could he speak, so vary. Nor is't hate
To merit in him who doth personate
Our Jew this day; nor is it his ambition
To exceed or equal, being of condition
More modest. This is all that he intends—   15
And that too at the urgence of some friends—
To prove his best, and, if none here gainsay it,
The part he hath studied and intends to play it.

EPILOGUE [TO THE STAGE
At the Cockpit]

In graving, with Pygmalion to contend,
Or painting, with Apelles, doubtless the end
Must be disgrace. Our actor did not so;
He only aimed to go, but not out-go.
Nor think that this day any prize was played;   5
Here were no bets at all, no wagers laid.
All the ambition that his mind doth swell,
Is but to hear from you—by me—'twas well.

Prologue.

[*Enter Machiavel.*]

Machiavel.   Albeit the world think Machiavel is dead,
Yet was his soul but flown beyond the Alps,

Prologue to the Stage.

2 *best of poets* In the margin of the 1633 quarto appears the name "Marlo."
4 *best of actors* "Allin" appears in the 1633 margin.
5 *Hero and Leander* See Introduction, p. xv.
7 *wan* won.
10 *Proteus* See note to *Dido,* I,i,76. *Roscius* a famous Roman actor of comic roles.
12 *in him* The name "Perkins" appears in the 1633 margin. This is

Richard Perkins, a well-known actor member of Queen Henrietta's men who starred in the revival of the play which is referred to.

Epilogue to the Stage.

1 *Pygmalion* See note to *Dido,* II,i,16.
2 *Apelles* a Greek painter in the service of King Alexander the Great.

Prologue.

1 *Machiavel* Niccolò Machiavelli (1469–1527), Florentine statesman and political theorist, whose work was distorted in

And, now the Guise is dead, is come from France
To view this land and frolic with his friends.
To some perhaps my name is odious,   5
But such as love me guard me from their tongues,
And let them know that I am Machiavel,
And weigh not men, and therefore not men's words.
Admired I am of those that hate me most.
Though some speak openly against my books,   10
Yet will they read me and thereby attain
To Peter's chair; and, when they cast me off,
Are poisoned by my climbing followers.
I count religion but a childish toy
And hold there is no sin but ignorance.   15
Birds of the air will tell of murders past;
I am ashamed to hear such fooleries.
Many will talk of title to a crown;
What right had Caesar to the empery?
Might first made kings, and laws were then most sure   20
When, like the Draco's, they were writ in blood.
Hence comes it that a strong built citadel
Commands much more than letters can import;
Which maxim had Phalaris observèd,
H'had never bellowed in a brazen bull   25
Of great one's envy. O' the poor petty wights
Let me be envied and not pitièd.
But whither am I bound? I come not, I,
To read a lecture here in Britain,
But to present the tragedy of a Jew   30
Who smiles to see how full his bags are crammed,
Which money was not got without my means.
I crave but this: grace him as he deserves,
And let him not be entertained the worse
Because he favors me.   [*Exit.*] 35

popular interpretation until he began
to appear upon the stage, as here, as a
burlesque figure standing for fraud and
dissimulation in political affairs, and
gloating over villainy for its own sake.
Marlowe's lines here are based upon a
Latin poem by Gabriel Harvey which
reflects the popular distortion of Machiavelli's views.

3 *Guise* Henry of Lorraine, third
Duke of Guise (1550–1588), the subject
of Marlowe's *Massacre at Paris*, was
active in the St. Bartholomew Massacre
of 1572, and thus among English Protestants was regarded as the epitome of
evil. He was assassinated by order of
King Henry III of France on December
23, 1588.

21 *Draco* an Athenian legislator of
the seventh century B.C., known for the
severity of his laws.

24 *Phalaris* a Sicilian tyrant of the
sixth century B.C., known for his extreme
cruelty. He is said to have roasted his
victims alive in a brazen bull, in which
he himself finally was burned after his
own overthrow.

35 *favors* resembles.

Enter Barabas in his counting-house, with heaps of gold before
him.

Barabas.   So that of thus much that return was made;
And of the third part of the Persian ships
There was the venture summed and satisfied.
As for those Samnites and the men of Uz
That bought my Spanish oils and wines of Greece,   5
Here have I pursed their paltry silverlings.
Fie, what a trouble 'tis to count this trash!
Well fare the Arabians, who so richly pay
The things they traffic for with wedge of gold,
Whereof a man may easily in a day   10
Tell that which may maintain him all his life.
The needy groom that never fingered groat
Would make a miracle of thus much coin,
But he whose steel-barred coffers are crammed full,
And all his life-time hath been tired   15
Wearying his fingers' ends with telling it,
Would in his age be loath to labor so,
And for a pound to sweat himself to death.
Give me the merchants of the Indian mines
That trade in metal of the purest mold,   20
The wealthy Moor that in the eastern rocks
Without control can pick his riches up
And in his house heap pearl like pebble-stones,
Receive them free and sell them by the weight.
Bags of fiery opals, sapphires, amethysts,   25
Jacinths, hard topaz, grass-green emeralds,
Beauteous rubies, sparkling diamonds,
And seld-seen costly stones of so great price
As one of them, indifferently rated
And of a carat of this quantity,   30
May serve in peril of calamity
To ransom great kings from captivity—
This is the ware wherein consists my wealth.
And thus methinks should men of judgment frame
Their means of traffic from the vulgar trade,   35

I,i.

4 *Samnites* probably a people who had once lived in the mountains of central Italy. The quarto reading "Samintes" has been much emended and debated. *Uz* biblical land in the general region of Palestine. Marlowe is using these names for their exotic connotations, rather than for reference to specific geographic locales.

9 *wedge of gold* ingots.

11 *Tell* count.

12 *groat* a small silver coin, worth fourpence.

22 *control* restriction, check.

29 *indifferently rated* appraised without bias.

And as their wealth increaseth, so enclose
Infinite riches in a little room.
But now how stands the wind?
Into what corner peers my halcyon's bill?
Ha! To the east? Yes; see how stands the vanes!   40
East and by south; why then I hope my ships
I sent for Egypt and the bordering isles
Are gotten up by Nilus' winding banks.
Mine argosy from Alexandria,
Loaden with spice and silks, now under sail,   45
Are smoothly gliding down by Candy shore
To Malta, through our Mediterranean sea.
But who comes here?

Enter a Merchant.

How now?

Merchant.   Barabas, thy ships are safe,
Riding in Malta road, and all the merchants   50
With other merchandise are safe arrived,
And have sent me to know whether yourself
Will come and custom them.

Barabas.   The ships are safe thou say'st, and richly fraught?

Merchant.   They are.

Barabas.   Why, then go bid them come ashore,   55
And bring with them their bills of entry.
I hope our credit in the custom house
Will serve as well as I were present there.
Go send 'em threescore camels, thirty mules,
And twenty wagons to bring up the ware.   60
But art thou master in a ship of mine,
And is thy credit not enough for that?

Merchant.   The very custom barely comes to more
Than many merchants of the town are worth,
And therefore far exceeds my credit, sir.   65

Barabas.   Go tell 'em the Jew of Malta sent thee, man.
Tush, who amongst 'em knows not Barabas?

Merchant.   I go.

Barabas.   So, then, there's somewhat come.
Sirrah, which of my ships art thou master of?

Merchant.   Of the *Speranza,* sir.

Barabas.   And saw'st thou not   70
Mine argosy at Alexandria?
Thou couldst not come from Egypt or by Caire,

---

39 *halcyon's bill* It was an old belief
that if the dead body of a kingfisher
(halcyon) were hung up by the bill, it
would serve as a weather vane, changing
its position with the wind.

46 *Candy* Candia was the Italian name
for the Greek island of Crete.

53 *custom them* see them through the
customs house.

But at the entry there into the sea,
Where Nilus pays his tribute to the main,
Thou needs must sail by Alexandria.   75
Merchant.   I neither saw them nor inquired of them.
But this we heard some of our seamen say:
They wondered how you durst with so much wealth
Trust such a crazèd vessel, and so far.
Barabas.   Tush, they are wise. I know her and her strength.   80
But go; go thou thy ways; discharge my ship,
And bid my factor bring his loading in.

                                        [*Exit Merchant.*]

And yet I wonder at this argosy.
                    Enter a Second Merchant.
Second Merchant.   Thine argosy from Alexandria,
Know Barabas, doth ride in Malta road,   85
Laden with riches and exceeding store
Of Persian silks, of gold, and orient pearl.
Barabas.   How chance you came not with those other ships
That sailed by Egypt?
Second Merchant.   Sir, we saw 'em not.
Barabas.   Belike they coasted round by Candy shore   90
About their oils or other businesses.
But 'twas ill done of you to come so far
Without the aid or conduct of their ships.
Second Merchant.   Sir, we were wafted by a Spanish fleet
That never left us till within a league,   95
That had the galleys of the Turk in chase.
Barabas.   O, they were going up to Sicily. Well, go
And bid the merchants and my men dispatch
And come ashore, and see the fraught discharged.
Second Merchant.   I go.   100

                                                        Exit.

Barabas.   Thus trowls our fortune in by land and sea,
And thus are we on every side enriched.
These are the blessings promised to the Jews,
And herein was old Abram's happiness.
What more may heaven do for earthly man   105
Than thus to pour out plenty in their laps,
Ripping the bowels of the earth for them,
Making the sea their servants, and the winds
To drive their substance with successful blasts?
Who hateth me but for my happiness?   110
Or who is honored now but for his wealth?
Rather had I, a Jew, be hated thus,
Than pitied in a Christian poverty;

82 *factor* agent.   99 *fraught* cargo.
94 *wafted* escorted.   101 *trowls* flows abundantly.

For I can see no fruits in all their faith,
But malice, falsehood, and excessive pride,   115
Which methinks fits not their profession.
Haply some hapless man hath conscience,
And for his conscience lives in beggary.
They say we are a scattered nation.
I cannot tell, but we have scambled up   120
More wealth by far than those that brag of faith.
There's Kirriah Jairim, the great Jew of Greece,
Obed in Bairseth, Nones in Portugal,
Myself in Malta, some in Italy,
Many in France, and wealthy every one,   125
Ay, wealthier far than any Christian.
I must confess we come not to be kings.
That's not our fault. Alas, our number's few,
And crowns come either by succession
Or urged by force, and nothing violent,   130
Oft have I heard tell, can be permanent.
Give us a peaceful rule; make Christians kings,
That thirst so much for principality.
I have no charge, nor many children,
But one sole daughter, whom I hold as dear   135
As Agamemnon did his Iphigen;
And all I have is hers. But who comes here?
                    Enter three Jews.
First Jew.   Tush, tell not me; 'twas done of policy.
Second Jew.   Come, therefore, let us go to Barabas,
For he can counsel best in these affairs;   140
And here he comes.
Barabas.   Why, how now, countrymen?
Why flock you thus to me in multitudes?
What accident's betided to the Jews?
First Jew.   A fleet of warlike galleys, Barabas,
Are come from Turkey and lie in our road,   145
And they this day sit in the council-house
To entertain them and their embassy.
Barabas.   Why, let 'em come, so they come not to war,
Or let 'em war, so we be conquerors.
Nay, let 'em combat, conquer, and kill all,   150

116 *profession* belief; what they profess.

117 *Haply* by good fortune. *hapless* unfortunate.

120 *scambled* scrambled, gathered.

136 *Agamemnon . . . Iphigen* When Agamemnon and his Greek fleet, for offending Diana, were becalmed at Aulis on the way to Troy, the goddess could only be appeased by the sacrifice of Agamemnon's beloved daughter, Iphigenia. She was, in fact, rescued by Diana, in whose temple she became a priestess.

138 *policy* underhanded dealings. See Introduction, p. xxxi.

146 *they* i.e., the Maltese governor · his council.

147 *them* i.e., the Turks.

So they spare me, my daughter, and my wealth.   *Aside.*
First Jew.   Were it for confirmation of a league,
 They would not come in warlike manner thus.
Second Jew.   I fear their coming will afflict us all.
Barabas.   Fond men, what dream you of their multitudes?   155
 What need they treat of peace that are in league?
 The Turks and those of Malta are in league.
 Tut, tut, there is some other matter in't.
First Jew.   Why, Barabas, they come for peace or war.
Barabas.   Haply for neither, but to pass along   160
 Towards Venice by the Adriatic sea,
 With whom they have attempted many times,
 But never could effect their stratagem.
Third Jew.   And very wisely said; it may be so.
Second Jew.   But there's a meeting in the senate-house,   165
 And all the Jews in Malta must be there.
Barabas.   Hum, all the Jews in Malta must be there.
 Ay, like enough. Why then, let every man
 Provide him and be there for fashion sake.
 If anything shall there concern our state,   170
 Assure yourselves I'll look—unto myself.   *Aside.*
First Jew.   I know you will. Well, brethren, let us go.
Second Jew.   Let's take our leaves. Farewell, good Barabas.
Barabas.   Do so. Farewell, Zaareth; farewell, Temainte.
            [*Exeunt Jews.*]

And, Barabas, now search this secret out.   175
Summon thy senses; call thy wits together.
These silly men mistake the matter clean.
Long to the Turk did Malta contribute,
Which tribute—all in policy, I fear—
The Turks have let increase to such a sum   180
As all the wealth of Malta cannot pay,
And now by that advantage thinks, belike,
To seize upon the town; ay, that he seeks.
Howe'er the world go, I'll make sure for one,
And seek in time to intercept the worst,   185
Warily guarding that which I ha' got.
Ego mihimet sum semper proximus.
Why, let 'em enter; let 'em take the town.
              [*Exit.*]

155 *Fond* foolish.   177 *silly* simple.
160 *Haply* perhaps.   187 *Ego . . . proximus* I am always
162 *whom* i.e., the Venetians. closest to myself.

Enter [Ferneze,] Governor of Malta, Knights, [and Officers,]
met by Bashaws of the Turk [and] Calymath.

Ferneze. Now, bassoes, what demand you at our hands?

First Bashaw. Know, knights of Malta, that we came from Rhodes,
From Cyprus, Candy, and those other isles
That lie betwixt the Mediterranean seas.

Ferneze. What's Cyprus, Candy, and those other isles   5
To us or Malta? What at our hands demand ye?

Calymath. The ten years' tribute that remains unpaid.

Ferneze. Alas, my lord, the sum is over-great.
I hope your highness will consider us.

Calymath. I wish, grave governor, 'twere in my power   10
To favor you, but 'tis my father's cause,
Wherein I may not, nay I dare not dally.

Ferneze. Then give us leave, great Selim Calymath.

Calymath. Stand all aside, and let the knights determine,
And send to keep our galleys under sail,   15
For happily we shall not tarry here.
Now, governor, how are you resolved?

Ferneze. Thus: since your hard conditions are such
That you will needs have ten years' tribute past,
We may have time to make collection   20
Amongst the inhabitants of Malta for't.

First Bashaw. That's more than is in our commission.

Calymath. What, Callapine, a little courtesy!
Let's know their time; perhaps it is not long;
And 'tis more kingly to obtain by peace   25
Than to enforce conditions by constraint.
What respite ask you, governor?

Ferneze.   But a month.

Calymath. We grant a month, but see you keep your promise.
Now launch our galleys back again to sea,
Where we'll attend the respite you have ta'en   30
And for the money send our messenger.
Farewell, great governor and brave knights of Malta.

Exeunt [Calymath and Bashaws].

Ferneze. And all good fortune wait on Calymath.
Go one and call those Jews of Malta hither.
Were they not summoned to appear today?   35

First Officer. They were, my lord, and here they come.

Enter Barabas and three Jews.

First Knight. Have you determined what to say to them?

I,ii.

1 *bassoes* See note to *I Tamb.*, III,i,1.
This form appears commonly in the

first two acts of *The Jew of Malta.*
Bashaw is used in the final acts.
16 *happily* haply, perhaps.

Ferneze. Yes; give me leave—and Hebrews, now come near.
  From the Emperor of Turkey is arrived
  Great Selim Calymath, his highness' son,   40
  To levy of us ten years' tribute past.
  Now, then, here know that it concerneth us.
Barabas. Then, good my lord, to keep your quiet still,
  Your lordship shall do well to let them have it.
Ferneze. Soft, Barabas, there's more 'longs to't than so.   45
  To what this ten years' tribute will amount,
  That we have cast, but cannot compass it
  By reason of the wars that robbed our store;
  And therefore are we to request your aid.
Barabas. Alas, my lord, we are no soldiers;   50
  And what's our aid against so great a prince?
First Knight. Tut, Jew, we know thou art no soldier.
  Thou art a merchant and a moneyed man,
  And 'tis thy money, Barabas, we seek.
Barabas. How, my lord? My money?
Ferneze.   Thine and the rest;   55
  For, to be short, amongst you 't must be had.
First Jew. Alas, my lord, the most of us are poor.
Ferneze. Then let the rich increase your portions.
Barabas. Are strangers with your tribute to be taxed?
Second Knight. Have strangers leave with us to get their wealth?   60
  Then let them with us contribute.
Barabas. How? Equally?
Ferneze.   No, Jew, like infidels;
  For through our sufferance of your hateful lives,
  Who stand accursèd in the sight of heaven,
  These taxes and afflictions are befall'n;   65
  And therefore thus we are determinèd:
  Read there the articles of our decrees.
Officer. [*reads*] First, the tribute money of the Turks shall all be
  levied amongst the Jews, and each of them to pay one half of his
  estate.   70
Barabas. How, half his estate? I hope you mean not mine. [*Aside.*]
Ferneze. Read on.
Officer. [*reads*] Secondly, he that denies to pay shall straight become
  a Christian.
Barabas. How, a Christian? Hum, what's here to do? [*Aside.*]   75
Officer. [*reads*] Lastly, he that denies this shall absolutely lose all he
  has.
All Three Jews. O my lord, we will give half.
Barabas. O earth-mettled villains, and no Hebrews born!
  And will you basely thus submit yourselves   80
  To leave your goods to their arbitrament?

  47 *cast* computed. *compass* obtain.   76 *denies* refuses.

Ferneze. Why, Barabas, wilt thou be christenèd?
Barabas. No, governor, I will be no convertite.
Ferneze. Then pay thy half.
Barabas. Why, know you what you did by this device?   85
   Half of my substance is a city's wealth.
   Governor, it was not got so easily,
   Nor will I part so slightly therewithal.
Ferneze. Sir, half is the penalty of our decree.
   Either pay that, or we will seize on all.   90
                    [*Exeunt Officers on a sign from Ferneze.*]
Barabas. *Corpo di Dio!* Stay! You shall have half.
   Let me be used but as my brethren are.
Ferneze. No, Jew. Thou hast denied the articles,
   And now it cannot be recalled.
Barabas. Will you then steal my goods?   95
   Is theft the ground of your religion?
Ferneze. No, Jew. We take particularly thine
   To save the ruin of a multitude,
   And better one want for a common good
   Than many perish for a private man.   100
   Yet, Barabas, we will not banish thee,
   But here in Malta, where thou gott'st thy wealth,
   Live still, and if thou canst, get more.
Barabas. Christians, what or how can I multiply?
   Of nought is nothing made.   105
First Knight. From nought at first thou cam'st to little wealth,
   From little unto more, from more to most.
   If your first curse fall heavy on thy head
   And make thee poor and scorned of all the world,
   'Tis not our fault, but thy inherent sin.   110
Barabas. What, bring you Scripture to confirm your wrongs?
   Preach me not out of my possessions.
   Some Jews are wicked, as all Christians are;
   But say the tribe that I descended of
   Were all in general cast away for sin,   115
   Shall I be tried by their transgression?
   The man that dealeth righteously shall live.
   And which of you can charge me otherwise?
Ferneze. Out, wretched Barabas!
   Sham'st thou not thus to justify thy self,   120
   As if we knew not thy profession?
   If thou rely upon thy righteousness,
   Be patient, and thy riches will increase.
   Excess of wealth is cause of covetousness,
   And covetousness, O, 'tis a monstrous sin.   125

91 *Corpo di Dio* body of God.   121 *profession* (1) religious belief (2)
                                        vocation.

Barabas. Ay, but theft is worse. Tush, take not from me then,
 For that is theft. And if you rob me thus,
 I must be forced to steal and compass more.
First Knight. Grave governor, list not to his exclaims.
 Convert his mansion to a nunnery;   130
 His house will harbor many holy nuns.
Ferneze. It shall be so.

Enter Officers.

      Now, officers, have you done?
First Officer. Ay, my lord, we have seized upon the goods
 And wares of Barabas, which, being valuèd,
 Amount to more than all the wealth in Malta.   135
 And of the other we have seizèd half.
Ferneze. Then we'll take order for the residue.
Barabas. Well, then, my lord, say, are you satisfied?
 You have my goods, my money, and my wealth,
 My ships, my store, and all that I enjoyed.   140
 And, having all, you can request no more,
 Unless your unrelenting flinty hearts
 Suppress all pity in your stony breasts,
 And now shall move you to bereave my life.
Ferneze. No, Barabas. To stain our hands with blood   145
 Is far from us and our profession.
Barabas. Why, I esteem the injury far less
 To take the lives of miserable men
 Than be the causers of their misery.
 You have my wealth, the labor of my life,   150
 The comfort of mine age, my children's hope,
 And therefore ne'er distinguish of the wrong.
Ferneze. Content thee, Barabas; thou has nought but right.
Barabas. Your extreme right does me exceeding wrong.
 But take it to you, i' the devil's name!   155
Ferneze. Come, let us in and gather of these goods
 The money for this tribute of the Turk.
First Knight. 'Tis necessary that be looked unto,
 For if we break our day, we break the league,
 And that will prove but simple policy.   160

Exeunt [all but Barabas and the other Jews].

Barabas. Ay, policy; that's their profession,
 And not simplicity, as they suggest.
 The plagues of Egypt and the curse of heaven,
 Earth's barrenness and all men's hatred
 Inflict upon them, thou great *Primus Motor!*   165
 And here upon my knees, striking the earth,
 I ban their souls to everlasting pains

165 *Primus Motor* first mover, or God.   167 *ban* curse.

And extreme tortures of the fiery deep,
That thus have dealt with me in my distress.
First Jew.   O yet be patient, gentle Barabas.   170
Barabas.   O silly brethren, born to see this day,
  Why stand you thus unmoved with my laments?
  Why weep you not to think upon my wrongs?
  Why pine not I and die in this distress?
First Jew.   Why, Barabas, as hardly can we brook   175
  The cruel handling of ourselves in this.
  Thou seest they have taken half our goods.
Barabas.   Why did you yield to their extortion?
  You were a multitude and I but one,
  And of me only have they taken all.   180
First Jew.   Yet, brother Barabas, remember Job.
Barabas.   What tell you me of Job? I wot his wealth
  Was written thus: he had seven thousand sheep,
  Three thousand camels, and two hundred yoke
  Of laboring oxen, and five hundred   185
  She asses. But for every one of those,
  Had they been valued at indifferent rate,
  I had at home and in mine argosy
  And other ships that came from Egypt last,
  As much as would have bought his beasts and him   190
  And yet have kept enough to live upon;
  So that not he, but I, may curse the day,
  Thy fatal birthday, forlorn Barabas,
  And henceforth wish for an eternal night,
  That clouds of darkness may enclose my flesh   195
  And hide these extreme sorrows from mine eyes,
  For only I have toiled to inherit here
  The months of vanity and loss of time,
  And painful nights have been appointed me.
Second Jew.   Good Barabas, be patient.   200
Barabas.   Ay, ay. Pray leave me in my patience. You that
  Were ne'er possessed of wealth are pleased with want.
  But give him liberty at least to mourn,
  That in a field amidst his enemies
  Doth see his soldiers slain, himself disarmed,   205
  And knows no means of his recovery.
  Ay, let me sorrow for this sudden chance.
  'Tis in the trouble of my spirit I speak:
  Great injuries are not so soon forgot.
First Jew.   Come, let us leave him. In his ireful mood   210
  Our words will but increase his ecstasy.

187 *indifferent* impartial, fair.   211 *ecstasy* mental disturbance, madness.

Second Jew.   On then. But, trust me, 'tis a misery
  To see a man in such affliction.
  Farewell, Barabas.

                                       Exeunt [Jews].

Barabas.   Ay, fare you well.
  See the simplicity of these base slaves,   215
  Who—for the villains have no wit themselves—
  Think me to be a senseless lump of clay
  That will with every water wash to dirt.
  No, Barabas is born to better chance
  And framed of finer mold than common men   220
  That measure nought but by the present time.
  A reaching thought will search his deepest wits
  And cast with cunning for the time to come,
  For evils are apt to happen every day.
  But whither wends my beauteous Abigail?   225

            Enter Abigail, the Jew's daughter.

  O, what has made my lovely daughter sad?
  What, woman! Moan not for a little loss.
  Thy father has enough in store for thee.
Abigail.   Not for my self, but agèd Barabas,
  Father, for thee lamenteth Abigail.   230
  But I will learn to leave these fruitless tears,
  And, urged thereto with my afflictions,
  With fierce exclaims run to the senate-house,
  And in the senate reprehend them all,
  And rent their hearts with tearing of my hair,   235
  Till they reduce the wrongs done to my father.
Barabas.   No, Abigail. Things past recovery
  Are hardly cured with exclamations.
  Be silent, daughter. Sufferance breeds ease,
  And time may yield us an occasion,   240
  Which on the sudden cannot serve the turn.
  Besides, my girl, think me not all so fond
  As negligently to forgo so much
  Without provision for thyself and me.
  Ten thousand portagues, besides great pearls,   245
  Rich costly jewels, and stones infinite,
  Fearing the worst of this before it fell,
  I closely hid.
Abigail.   Where, father?
Barabas.   In my house, my girl.

---

215 *simplicity* folly.   235 *rent* rend.
222 *reaching thought* far-seeing wis-   236 *reduce* diminish.
dom.   242 *fond* foolish.
223 *cast* prepare.   245 *portagues* Portuguese **gold coins.**
233 *exclaims* outcries.

Abigail.   Then shall they ne'er be seen of Barabas,   250
  For they have seized upon thy house and wares.
Barabas.   But they will give me leave once more, I trow,
  To go into my house.
Abigail   That may they not,
  For there I left the governor placing nuns,
  Displacing me, and of thy house they mean   255
  To make a nunnery, where none but their own sect
  Must enter in, men generally barred.
Barabas.   My gold, my gold, and all my wealth is gone.
  You partial heavens, have I deserved this plague?
  What, will you thus oppose me, luckless stars,   260
  To make me desperate in my poverty?
  And knowing me impatient in distress,
  Think me so mad as I will hang myself,
  That I may vanish o'er the earth in air
  And leave no memory that e'er I was?   265
  No, I will live; nor loathe I this my life.
  And since you leave me in the ocean thus
  To sink or swim, and put me to my shifts,
  I'll rouse my senses and awake myself.
  Daughter, I have it. Thou perceiv'st the plight   270
  Wherein these Christians have oppressèd me.
  Be ruled by me, for in extremity
  We ought to make bar of no policy.
Abigail.   Father, whate'er it be, to injure them
  That have so manifestly wrongèd us,   275
  What will not Abigail attempt?
Barabas.   Why, so.
  Then thus: thou told'st me they have turned my house
  Into a nunnery, and some nuns are there?
Abigail.   I did.
Barabas.   Then, Abigail, there must my girl
  Entreat the abbess to be entertained.   280
Abigail.   How? As a nun?
Barabas.   Ay, daughter, for religion
  Hides many mischiefs from suspicion.
Abigail.   Ay, but father, they will suspect me there.
Barabas.   Let 'em suspect, but be thou so precise
  As they may think it done of holiness.   285
  Entreat 'em fair, and give them friendly speech,
  And seem to them as if thy sins were great,
  Till thou hast gotten to be entertained.
Abigail.   Thus, father, shall I much dissemble.
Barabas.   Tush!
  As good dissemble that thou never mean'st   290

256 *sect* sex.   284 *precise* pious, puritanical.

As first mean truth and then dissemble it.
A counterfeit profession is better
Than unseen hypocrisy.
Abigail.   Well, father, say I be entertained,
What then shall follow?
Barabas.   This shall follow then: 295
There have I hid, close underneath the plank
That runs along the upper-chamber floor,
The gold and jewels which I kept for thee.
But here they come. Be cunning, Abigail.
Abigail.   Then, father, go with me.
Barabas.   No, Abigail, in this   300
It is not necessary I be seen,
For I will seem offended with thee for't.
Be close, my girl, for this must fetch my gold.

                                        [*They retire.*]

    Enter [*Friar Jacomo, Friar Barnardine, Abbess and a Nun*].
Friar Jacomo.   Sisters,
We now are almost at the new-made nunnery.   305
Abbess.   The better; for we love not to be seen.
'Tis thirty winters long since some of us
Did stray so far amongst the multitude.
Friar Jacomo.   But, madam, this house
And waters of this new-made nunnery   310
Will much delight you.
Abbess.   It may be so. But who comes here?

                            [*Abigail comes forward.*]

Abigail.   Grave abbess, and you, happy virgin's guide,
Pity the state of a distressèd maid.
Abbess.   What art thou, daughter?   315
Abigail.   The hopeless daughter of a hapless Jew,
The Jew of Malta, wretched Barabas,
Sometimes the owner of a goodly house,
Which they have now turned to a nunnery.
Abbess.   Well, daughter, say, what is thy suit with us?   320
Abigail.   Fearing the afflictions which my father feels
Proceed from sin or want of faith in us,
I'd pass away my life in penitence
And be a novice in your nunnery
To make atonement for my laboring soul.   325
Friar Jacomo.   No doubt, brother, but this proceedeth of the spirit.
Friar Barnardine.   Ay, and of a moving spirit too, brother; but come,
Let us entreat she may be entertained.
Abbess.   Well, daughter, we admit you for a nun.

---

303 *close* secret.   325 *laboring* struggling (against evil).

Abigail. First let me as a novice learn to frame   330
    My solitary life to your strait laws,
    And let me lodge where I was wont to lie.
    I do not doubt, by your divine precepts
    And mine own industry, but to profit much.
Barabas. As much, I hope, as all I hid is worth. *Aside.*   335
Abbess. Come, daughter, follow us.
Barabas. [*coming forward*] Why, how now, Abigail!
    What mak'st thou amongst these hateful Christians?
Friar Jacomo. Hinder her not, thou man of little faith,
    For she has mortified herself.
Barabas.   How! Mortified!   340
Friar Jacomo. And is admitted to the sisterhood.
Barabas. Child of perdition, and thy father's shame,
    What wilt thou do among these hateful fiends?
    I charge thee on my blessing that thou leave
    These devils and their damnèd heresy.   345
Abigail. Father, give me—
Barabas.   Nay, back, Abigail!
    And think upon the jewels and the gold;
    The board is markèd thus that covers it. *Whispers to her.*
    Away, accursèd, from thy father's sight!
Friar Jacomo. Barabas, although thou art in misbelief   350
    And wilt not see thine own afflictions,
    Yet let thy daughter be no longer blind.
Barabas. Blind, friar? I reck not thy persuasions—
    The board is markèd thus that covers it— [*Aside to her.*]
    For I had rather die than see her thus.   355
    Wilt thou forsake me too in my distress,
    Seducèd daughter? Go, forget not. *Aside to her.*
    Becomes it Jews to be so credulous?
    Tomorrow early I'll be at the door. *Aside to her.*
    No, come not at me. If thou wilt be damned,   360
    Forget me, see me not, and so be gone.
    Farewell; remember tomorrow morning. *Aside* [*to her*].
    Out, out, thou wretch!
                    [*Exit Barabas on one side. Exeunt the others on
                        the opposite side. As they are leaving,*] enter
                                                        Mathias.
Mathias. Who's this? Fair Abigail, the rich Jew's daughter,
    Become a nun? Her father's sudden fall   365
    Has humbled her and brought her down to this.
    Tut, she were fitter for a tale of love
    Than to be tired out with orisons,
    And better would she far become a bed,

340 *Mortified* dead in so far as the world is concerned, because she is a nun.

Embracèd in a friendly lover's arms,   370
Than rise at midnight to a solemn mass.

Enter Lodowick.

Lodowick.   Why, how now, Don Mathias, in a dump?
Mathias.   Believe me, noble Lodowick, I have seen
   The strangest sight, in my opinion,
   That ever I beheld.
Lodowick.   What was't, 1 prithee?   375
Mathias.   A fair young maid, scarce fourteen years of age,
   The sweetest flower in Cytherea's field,
   Cropped from the pleasures of the fruitful earth
   And strangely metamorphosed nun.
Lodowick.   But say, what was she?
Mathias.   Why, the rich Jew's daughter.   380
Lodowick.   What? Barabas, whose goods were lately seized?
   Is she so fair?
Mathias.   And matchless beautiful,
   As, had you seen her, 'twould have moved your heart,
   Though countermured with walls of brass, to love
   Or, at the least, to pity.   385
Lodowick.   And if she be so fair as you report,
   'Twere time well spent to go and visit her.   .
   How say you? Shall we?
Mathias.   I must and will, sir; there's no remedy.
Lodowick.   And so will I too, or it shall go hard.   390
   Farewell, Mathias.
Mathias.   Farewell, Lodowick.

                                        Exeunt.

Enter Barabas, with a light.   II,i.

Barabas.   Thus, like the sad presaging raven that tolls
   The sick man's passport in her hollow beak,
   And in the shadow of the silent night
   Doth shake contagion from her sable wings,
   Vexed and tormented runs poor Barabas   5
   With fatal curses towards these Christians.
   The uncertain pleasures of swift-footed time
   Have ta'en their flight and left me in despair,
   And of my former riches rests no more
   But bare remembrance, like a soldier's scar   10
   That has no further comfort for his maim.

---

372 *dump* fit of abstraction.
377 *Cytherea* Venus, goddess of love.

384 *countermured* protected by double
walls (a term used in military fortification).

O Thou that with a fiery pillar led'st
The sons of Israel through the dismal shades,
Light Abraham's offspring, and direct the hand
Of Abigail this night, or let the day   15
Turn to eternal darkness after this.
No sleep can fasten on my watchful eyes,
Nor quiet enter my distempered thoughts,
Till I have answer of my Abigail.

Enter Abigail above.

Abigail.   Now have I happily espied a time   20
To search the plank my father did appoint,
And here behold, unseen, where I have found
The gold, the pearls, and jewels which he hid.
Barabas.   Now I remember those old women's words,
Who, in my wealth, would tell me winter's tales,   25
And speak of spirits and ghosts that glide by night
About the place where treasure hath been hid;
And now methinks that I am one of those,
For whilst I live, here lives my soul's sole hope,
And when I die, here shall my spirit walk.   30
Abigail.   Now that my father's fortune were so good
As but to be about this happy place!
'Tis not so happy. Yet when we parted last,
He said he would attend me in the morn.
Then, gentle sleep, where'er his body rests,   35
Give charge to Morpheus that he may dream
A golden dream, and of the sudden walk,
Come, and receive the treasure I have found.
Barabas.   *Bueno para todos mi ganado no era.*
As good go on, as sit so sadly thus.   40
But stay! What star shines yonder in the east?
The lodestar of my life, if Abigail.
Who's there?
Abigail.   Who's that?
Barabas.   Peace, Abigail, 'tis I.
Abigail.   Then, father, here receive thy happiness.
Barabas.   Hast thou't?   45
Abigail.   Here. [*She*] *throws down bags.* Hast thou't?
There's more, and more, and more.
Barabas.   O my girl,
My gold, my fortune, my felicity,

II,i

25 *in my wealth* in the days of my
prosperity. *winter's tales* stories of fantasy and enchantment.

36 *Morpheus* the son of sleep and god
of dreams.

37 *walk* wake (an old Scottish form).
39 *Bueno . . . era* My flock (or wealth)
is not good for everyone.

Strength to my soul, death to mine enemy,
Welcome, the first beginner of my bliss.   50
O Abigail, Abigail, that I had thee here too,
Then my desires were fully satisfied.
But I will practice thy enlargement thence.
O girl! O gold! O beauty! O my bliss!   [*He*] *hugs his bags.*
Abigail.   Father, it draweth towards midnight now,   55
And 'bout this time the nuns begin to wake.
To shun suspicion, therefore, let us part.
Barabas.   Farewell, my joy, and by my fingers take
A kiss from him that sends it from his soul.

                                      [*Exit Abigail above.*]

Now, Phoebus, ope the eyelids of the day,   60
And for the raven wake the morning lark,
That I may hover with her in the air,
Singing o'er these as she does o'er her young.
Hermoso placer de los dineros.

                                                    Exit.

Enter *Ferneze, Martin del Bosco, Knights,* [*and Officers*].   II,ii.
Ferneze.   Now, captain, tell us whither thou art bound,
Whence is thy ship that anchors in our road,
And why thou cam'st ashore without our leave.
Bosco.   Governor of Malta, hither am I bound.
My ship, the Flying Dragon, is of Spain,   5
And so am I. Del Bosco is my name,
Vice-admiral unto the Catholic king.
First Knight.   'Tis true, my lord; therefore entreat him well.
Bosco.   Our fraught is Grecians, Turks, and Afric Moors;
For late upon the coast of Corsica,   10
Because we vailed not to the Turkish fleet,
Their creeping galleys had us in the chase;
But suddenly the wind began to rise,
And then we luffed and tacked and fought at ease.
Some have we fired and many have we sunk,   15
But one amongst the rest became our prize.
The captain's slain; the rest remain our slaves,
Of whom we would make sale in Malta here.
Ferneze.   Martin del Bosco, I have heard of thee.

64 *Hermoso . . . dineros* How beautiful is money.

II,ii.
8 *entreat* treat.
9 *fraught* cargo.

11 *vailed* lowered topsails as a sign
of respect.
14 *luffed* turned the ship's head into
the wind. *tacked* changed course. (nau-
tical terms).

Welcome to Malta and to all of us.   20
But to admit a sale of these thy Turks
We may not—nay, we dare not—give consent,
By reason of a tributary league.
First Knight.   Del Bosco, as thou lov'st and honor'st us,
Persuade our governor against the Turk.   25
This truce we have is but in hope of gold,
And with that sum he craves might we wage war.
Bosco.   Will knights of Malta be in league with Turks,
And buy it basely too for sums of gold?
My lord, remember that, to Europe's shame,   30
The Christian Isle of Rhodes, from whence you came,
Was lately lost, and you were stated here
To be at deadly enmity with Turks.
Ferneze.   Captain, we know it, but our force is small.
Bosco.   What is the sum that Calymath requires?   35
Ferneze.   A hundred thousand crowns.
Bosco.   My lord and king hath title to this isle,
And he means quickly to expel you hence;
Therefore be ruled by me and keep the gold.
I'll write unto his majesty for aid,   40
And not depart until I see you free.
Ferneze.   On this condition shall thy Turks be sold.
Go, officers, and set them straight in show.
                                        [*Exeunt Officers.*]
Bosco, thou shalt be Malta's general.
We and our warlike knights will follow thee   45
Against these barbarous misbelieving Turks.
Bosco.   So shall you imitate those you succeed;
For when their hideous force environed Rhodes,
Small though the number was that kept the town,
They fought it out, and not a man survived   50
To bring the hapless news to Christendom.
Ferneze.   So will we fight it out. Come, let's away.
Proud daring Calymath, instead of gold
We'll send thee bullets wrapped in smoke and fire.
Claim tribute where thou wilt; we are resolved.   55
Honor is bought with blood and not with gold.
                                            Exeunt.

31 *Rhodes* the headquarters of the   expelled by the Turks in 1522. From
Knights of the Order of the Hospital of   Rhodes the Christian knights came to
St. John of Jerusalem until they were   Malta.

Enter Officers with [Ithamore and other] Slaves.   **II,iii.**

First Officer.   This is the market place; here let 'em stand.
  Fear not their sale, for they'll be quickly bought.
Second Officer.   Every one's price is written on his back,
  And so much must they yield, or not be sold.
First Officer.   Here comes the Jew. Had not his goods been seized,   5
  He'd give us present money for them all.

Enter Barabas.

Barabas.   In spite of these swine-eating Christians,
  Unchosen nation, never circumcised,
  Such as—poor villains—were ne'er thought upon
  Till Titus and Vespasian conquered us,   10
  Am I become as wealthy as I was.
  They hoped my daughter would ha' been a nun,
  But she's at home, and I have bought a house
  As great and fair as is the governor's;
  And there, in spite of Malta, will I dwell,   15
  Having Ferneze's hand, whose heart I'll have—
  Ay, and his son's too—or it shall go hard.
  I am not of the tribe of Levi, I,
  That can so soon forget an injury.
  We Jews can fawn like spaniels when we please,   20
  And when we grin, we bite; yet are our looks
  As innocent and harmless as a lamb's.
  I learned in Florence how to kiss my hand,
  Heave up my shoulders when they call me dog,
  And duck as low as any barefoot friar,   25
  Hoping to see them starve upon a stall,
  Or else be gathered for in our synagogue,
  That when the offering-basin comes to me,
  Even for charity I may spit into't.
  Here comes Don Lodowick, the governor's son,   30
  One that I love for his good father's sake.

Enter Lodowick.

Lodowick.   I hear the wealthy Jew walkèd this way.
  I'll seek him out and so insinuate
  That I may have a sight of Abigail,
  For Don Mathias tells me she is fair.   35
Barabas.   Now will I show myself to have more of the serpent than the
  dove; that is, more knave than fool.   [*Aside.*]
Lodowick.   Yond' walks the Jew. Now for fair Abigail.
Barabas.   Ay, ay, no doubt but she's at your command.   [*Aside.*]

II,iii.

6 *present money* ready cash.
10 *Titus and Vespasian* Roman emperors who conquered Judea between 66 and 70 A.D. Titus, who finally captured Jerusalem, was the son of Vespasian, who had begun the campaign.
27 *be gathered for* be the object of charitable donations.

Lodowick.   Barabas, thou know'st I am the governor's son.   40
Barabas.   I would you were his father too, sir! That's all the harm I
  wish you. The slave looks like a hog's cheek new singed.   [*Aside.*]
Lodowick.   Whither walk'st thou, Barabas?
Barabas.   No further. 'Tis a custom held with us
  That when we speak with Gentiles like to you,   45
  We turn into the air to purge ourselves,
  For unto us the promise doth belong.
Lodowick.   Well, Barabas, canst help me to a diamond?
Barabas.   O, sir, your father had my diamonds;
  Yet I have one left that will serve your turn.   50
  I mean my daughter, but ere he shall have her,
  I'll sacrifice her on a pile of wood.
  I ha' the poison of the city for him,
  And the white leprosy.   *Aside.*
Lodowick.   What sparkle does it give without a foil?   55
Barabas.   The diamond that I talk of ne'er was foiled.
  But when he touches it, it will be foiled.   [*Aside.*]
  Lord Lodowick, it sparkles bright and fair.
Lodowick.   Is it square or pointed? Pray, let me know?
Barabas.   Pointed it is, good sir. But not for you.   *Aside.*   60
Lodowick.   I like it much the better.
Barabas.   So do I too.
Lodowick.   How shows it by night?
Barabas.   Outshines Cynthia's rays.
  You'll like it better far 'a nights than days.   *Aside.*
Lodowick.   And what's the price?
Barabas.   Your life, and if you have it. [*Aside.*] O my lord,   65
  We will not jar about the price. Come to my house
  And I will giv't your honor—with a vengeance!   *Aside.*
Lodowick.   No, Barabas; I will deserve it first.
Barabas.   Good sir,
  Your father has deserved it at my hands,
  Who, of mere charity and Christian ruth,   70
  To bring me to religious purity,
  And, as it were, in catechising sort,
  To make me mindful of my mortal sins,
  Against my will, and whether I would or no,
  Seized all I had, and thrust me out o' doors,   75
  And made my house a place for nuns most chaste.
Lodowick.   No doubt your soul shall reap the fruit of it.
Barabas.   Ay, but my lord, the harvest is far off.
  And yet I know the prayers of those nuns

---

54 *white leprosy* It was believed that
leprosy was most contagious when white,
flaky scales appeared on the skin of the
victim.

55 *foil* dull background to set off the
brilliance of a jewel.
56 *foiled* defiled.

And holy friars, having money for their pains,   80
Are wondrous—and indeed do no man good.   *Aside.*
And seeing they are not idle, but still doing,
'Tis likely they in time may reap some fruit—
I mean in fulness of perfection.
Lodowick.   Good Barabas, glance not at our holy nuns.   85
Barabas.   No, but I do it through a burning zeal—
Hoping ere long to set the house afire,
For though they do a while increase and multiply,
I'll have a saying to that nunnery.   *Aside.*
As for the diamond, sir, I told you of,   90
Come home, and there's no price shall make us part,
Even for your honorable father's sake.
It shall go hard, but I will see your death.   *Aside.*
But now I must be gone to buy a slave.
Lodowick.   And, Barabas, I'll bear thee company.   95
Barabas.   Come then. Here's the market place. What's the price of this
slave? Two hundred crowns? Do the Turks weigh so much?
First Officer.   Sir, that's his price.
Barabas.   What? Can he steal, that you demand so much?
Belike he has some new trick for a purse;   100
And if he has, he is worth three hundred plates,
So that, being bought, the town seal might be got
To keep him for his lifetime from the gallows.
The sessions day is critical to thieves,
And few or none 'scape but by being purged.   105
Lodowick.   Rat'st thou this Moor but at two hundred plates?
First Officer.   No more, my lord.
Barabas.   Why should this Turk be dearer than that Moor?
First Officer.   Because he is young and has more qualities.
Barabas.   What? Hast the philosopher's stone? And thou hast,   [110
break my head with it, I'll forgive thee.
Slave.   No, sir; I can cut and shave.
Barabas.   Let me see, sirrah. Are you an old shaver?
Slave.   Alas, sir, I am a very youth.
Barabas.   A youth! I'll buy you and marry you to Lady Vanity if   [115
you do well.
Slave.   I will serve you, sir.
Barabas.   Some wicked trick or other. It may be, under color of shav-
ing, thou'lt cut my throat for my goods. Tell me, hast thou thy health
well?   120
Slave.   Ay, passing well.

---

89 *have a saying* have something to
say.
101 *plates* Spanish silver coins.
105 *purged* acquitted of charges.
110 *philosopher's stone* a substance
sought by the alchemists for a supposed
ability to change base metals into gold:

it was believed also to be a cure for all
illnesses.
113 *old shaver* a term of contempt
applied originally to monks and friars
because of their shaven crowns.
118 *color* pretense.

Barabas. So much the worse. I must have one that's sickly, and be but
  for sparing victuals. 'Tis not a stone of beef a day will maintain you
  in these chops. Let me see one that's somewhat leaner.
First Officer. Here's a leaner. How like you him.   125
Barabas. Where was thou born?
Ithamore. In Thrace, brought up in Arabia.
Barabas. So much the better. Thou art for my turn.
  An hundred crowns? I'll have him; there's the coin.
                                                    [*He gives money.*]
First Officer. Then mark him, sir, and take him hence.   130
Barabas. Ay, mark him, you were best; for this is he
  That by my help shall do much villainy. [*Aside.*]
  My lord, farewell. Come, sirrah, you are mine.
  As for the diamond, it shall be yours.
  I pray, sir, be no stranger at my house;   135
  All that I have shall be at your command.
             Enter Mathias [and Katherine, his Mother].
Mathias. What makes the Jew and Lodowick so private?
  I fear me 'tis about fair Abigail. [*Aside.*]
Barabas. Yonder comes Don Mathias. Let us stay.
  He loves my daughter, and she holds him dear,   140
  But I have sworn to frustrate both their hopes,
                                              [*Exit Lodowick.*]
  And be revenged upon the—governor. [*Aside.*]
Katherine. This Moor is comeliest, is he not? Speak, son.
Mathias. No, this is the better, mother; view him well.
Barabas. Seem not to know me here before your mother,   145
  Lest she mistrust the match that is in hand.
  When you have brought her home, come to my house.
  Think of me as thy father. Son, farewell.
Mathias. But wherefore talked Don Lodowick with you?
Barabas. Tush man, we talked of diamonds, not of Abigail.   150
Katherine. Tell me, Mathias, is not that the Jew?
Barabas. As for the comment on the Maccabees,
  I have it, sir, and 'tis at your command.
Mathias. Yes, madam, and my talk with him was
  About the borrowing of a book or two.   155
Katherine. Converse not with him; he is cast off from heaven.
  Thou hast thy crowns, fellow. Come, let's away.
Mathias. Sirrah, Jew, remember the book.
Barabas.   Marry, will I, sir.
                          Exeunt [Katherine and Mathias].
First Officer. Come, I have made a reasonable market. Let's away.
                          [*Exeunt Officers with Slaves.*]
Barabas. Now let me know thy name, and therewithal   160

124 *chops* fat cheeks.
152 *Maccabees* Jewish heroes whose
exploits, the subject of voluminous com-

mentary, are celebrated in the feast of
Hanukkah.

Thy birth, condition, and profession.

Ithamore. Faith, sir, my birth is but mean. My name's Ithamore, my
    profession what you please.

Barabas. Hast thou no trade? Then listen to my words,
    And I will teach that shall stick by thee.   165
    First, be thou void of these affections:
    Compassion, love, vain hope, and heartless fear.
    Be moved at nothing. See thou pity none,
    But to thyself smile when the Christians moan.

Ithamore. O, brave master! I worship your nose for this.   170

Barabas. As for myself, I walk abroad 'a nights
    And kill sick people groaning under walls.
    Sometimes I go about and poison wells,
    And now and then, to cherish Christian thieves,
    I am content to lose some of my crowns   175
    That I may, walking in my gallery,
    See 'em go pinioned along by my door.
    Being young, I studied physic and began
    To practice first upon the Italian.
    There I enriched the priests with burials   180
    And always kept the sexton's arms in ure
    With digging graves and ringing dead men's knells.
    And after that I was an engineer,
    And in the wars 'twixt France and Germany,
    Under pretense of helping Charles the Fifth,   185
    Slew friend and enemy with my stratagems.
    Then after that I was an usurer,
    And with extorting, cozening, forfeiting,
    And tricks belonging unto brokery,
    I filled the jails with bankrouts in a year,   190
    And with young orphans planted hospitals,
    And every moon made some or other mad,
    And now and then one hang himself for grief,
    Pinning upon his breast a long great scroll,
    How I with interest tormented him.   195
    But mark how I am blessed for plaguing them:
    I have as much coin as will buy the town.
    But tell me now, how hast thou spent thy time?

Ithamore. Faith, master,
    In setting Christian villages on fire,   200
    Chaining of eunuchs, binding galley slaves.
    One time I was an hostler in an inn,
    And in the night time secretly would I steal
    To travelers' chambers and there cut their throats.
    Once at Jerusalem where the pilgrims kneeled,   205
    I strewèd powder on the marble stones,

181 *ure* use.   190 *bankrouts* bankrupts.

And therewithal their knees would rankle so
That I have laughed a-good to see the cripples
Go limping home to Christendom on stilts.
Barabas.   Why this is something. Make account of me   210
As of thy fellow; we are villains both.
Both circumcisèd, we hate Christians both.
Be true and secret; thou shalt want no gold.
But stand aside. Here comes Don Lodowick.
                    Enter Lodowick.
Lodowick.   O Barabas, well met.   215
Where is the diamond you told me of?
Barabas.   I have it for you, sir. Please you walk in with me.
What, ho, Abigail! Open the door, I say.
                    Enter Abigail.
Abigail.   In good time, father. Here are letters come
From Ormus, and the post stays here within.   220
Barabas.   Give me the letters. Daughter, do you hear?
Entertain Lodowick, the governor's son,
With all the courtesy you can afford,
Provided that you keep your maidenhead.
Use him as if he were a—Philistine.   225
Dissemble, swear, protest, vow to love him;
He is not of the seed of Abraham.   *Aside.*
I am a little busy, sir. Pray, pardon me.
Abigail, bid him welcome for my sake.
Abigail.   For your sake and his own he's welcome hither.   230
Barabas.   Daughter, a word more. Kiss him, speak him fair,
And like a cunning Jew so cast about
That ye be both made sure ere you come out.   *[Aside to her.]*
Abigail.   O father, Don Mathias is my love.   *[Aside to him.]*
Barabas.   I know it. Yet I say make love to him.   235
Do; it is requisite it should be so.   *[Aside to her.]*
Nay, on my life, it is my factor's hand.
But go you in. I'll think upon the account.
                    [Exeunt Abigail and Lodowick.]
The account is made, for Lodowick dies.
My factor sends me word a merchant's fled   240
That owes me for a hundred tun of wine.
I weigh it thus much *[snapping his fingers]*. I have wealth enough.
For now by this has he kissed Abigail,
And she vows love to him and he to her.
As sure as heaven rained manna for the Jews,   245
So sure shall he and Don Mathias die.

209 *stilts* crutches.   233 *made sure* betrothed.
220 *Ormus* a city on the Persian Gulf, 237 *factor's hand* agent's handwriting.
famous for its trade in spices, drugs, and
jewels.

His father was my chiefest enemy.

Enter Mathias.

Whither goes Don Mathias? Stay a while.

Mathias.   Whither, but to my fair love, Abigail?

Barabas.   Thou know'st, and heaven can witness it is true,   250
That I intend my daughter shall be thine.

Mathias.   Ay, Barabas, or else thou wrong'st me much.

Barabas.   O, heaven forbid I should have such a thought.
Pardon me though I weep. The governor's son
Will, whether I will or no, have Abigail.   255
He sends her letters, bracelets, jewels, rings.

Mathias.   Does she receive them?

Barabas.   She? No, Mathias, no, but sends them back,
And when he comes, she locks herself up fast.
Yet through the keyhole will he talk to her,   260
While she runs to the window, looking out
When you should come and hale him from the door.

Mathias.   O treacherous Lodowick!

Barabas.   Even now, as I came home, he slipped me in,
And I am sure he is with Abigail.   265

Mathias.   I'll rouse him thence.

Barabas.   Not for all Malta; therefore sheathe your sword.
If you love me, no quarrels in my house,
But steal you in, and seem to see him not.
I'll give him such a warning ere he goes   270
As he shall have small hopes of Abigail.
Away, for here they come.

Enter Lodowick [and] Abigail.

Mathias.   What, hand in hand! I cannot suffer this.

Barabas.   Mathias, as thou lov'st me, not a word.

Mathias.   Well, let it pass; another time shall serve.   275

Exit.

Lodowick.   Barabas, is not that the widow's son?

Barabas.   Ay, and take heed, for he hath sworn your death.

Lodowick.   My death? What, is the base-born peasant mad?

Barabas.   No, no; but happily he stands in fear
Of that which you, I think, ne'er dream upon,   280
My daughter here, a paltry silly girl.

Lodowick.   Why, loves she Don Mathias?

Barabas.   Doth she not with her smiling answer you?

Abigail.   He has my heart; I smile against my will.   [*Aside.*]

Lodowick.   Barabas, thou know'st I have loved thy daughter **long**.   285

Barabas.   And so has she done you, even from a child.

Lodowick.   And now I can no longer hold my mind.

Barabas.   Nor I the affection that I bear to you.

Lodowick.   This is thy diamond; tell me, shall I have it?

279 *happily* perhaps.   **281** *silly* simple.

Barabas.   Win it and wear it; it is yet unsoiled.   290
  O, but I know your lordship would disdain
  To marry with the daughter of a Jew,
  And yet I'll give her many a golden cross
  With Christian posies round about the ring.
Lodowick.   'Tis not thy wealth, but her that I esteem.   295
  Yet crave I thy consent.
Barabas.   And mine you have; yet let me talk to her.
  This offspring of Cain, this Jebusite
  That never tasted of the Passover,
  Nor e'er shall see the land of Canaan,   300
  Nor our Messias that is yet to come,
  This gentle maggot—Lodowick, I mean—
  Must be deluded. Let him have thy hand,
  But keep thy heart till Don Mathias comes.   *Aside [to her].*
Abigail.   What? Shall I be betrothed to Lodowick?   305
                              [Aside to him.]
Barabas.   It is no sin to deceive a Christian,
  For they themselves hold it a principle,
  Faith is not to be held with heretics;
  But all are heretics that are not Jews.
  This follows well, and therefore, Daughter, fear not.   310
                              [Aside to her.]
  I have entreated her, and she will grant.
Lodowick.   Then, gentle Abigail, plight thy faith to me.
Abigail.   I cannot choose, seeing my father bids.
  Nothing but death shall part my love and me.
Lodowick.   Now have I that for which my soul hath longed.   315
Barabas.   So have not I; but yet I hope I shall.   *Aside.*
Abigail.   O wretched Abigail, what hast thou done?   *[Aside.]*
Lodowick.   Why on the sudden is your color changed?
Abigail.   I know not. But farewell; I must be gone.
Barabas.   Stay her, but let her not speak one word more.   320
Lodowick.   Mute o' the sudden! Here's a sudden change.
Barabas.   O muse not at it. 'Tis the Hebrews' guise
  That maidens new-betrothed should weep a while.
  Trouble her not. Sweet Lodowick, depart.
  She is thy wife, and thou shalt be mine heir.   325
Lodowick.   O, is't the custom? Then I am resolved.
  But rather let the brightsome heavens be dim
  And nature's beauty choke with stifling clouds,
  Than my fair Abigail should frown on me.
  There comes the villain; now I'll be revenged.   330

293 *golden cross* gold coin stamped
with a cross.
294 *posies* mottoes in verse, inscribed
often within rings.

298 *Jebusite* member of a tribe of
Canaanites driven from Jerusalem by
King David.
322 *guise* custom.

Enter Mathias.

Barabas.   Be quiet, Lodowick. It is enough
  That I have made thee sure to Abigail.
Lodowick.   Well, let him go.

                                        Exit.

Barabas.   Well, but for me, as you went in at doors
  You had been stabbed. But not a word on't now.   335
  Here must no speeches pass, nor swords be drawn.
Mathias.   Suffer me, Barabas, but to follow him.
Barabas.   No; so shall I, if any hurt be done,
  Be made an accessory of your deeds.
  Revenge it on him when you meet him next.   340
Mathias.   For this I'll have his heart.
Barabas.   Do so. Lo, here I give thee Abigail.
Mathias.   What greater gift can poor Mathias have?
  Shall Lodowick rob me of so fair a love?
  My life is not so dear as Abigail.   345
Barabas.   My heart misgives me that to cross your love
  He's with your mother. Therefore, after him.
Mathias.   What? Is he gone unto my mother?
Barabas.   Nay, if you will, stay till she comes herself.
Mathias.   I cannot stay, for if my mother come,   350
  She'll die with grief.

                                        Exit.

Abigail.   I cannot take my leave of him for tears.
  Father, why have you thus incensed them both?
Barabas.   What's that to thee?
Abigail.   I'll make 'em friends again.
Barabas.   You'll make 'em friends? Are there not Jews enow   355
  In Malta, but thou must dote upon a Christian?
Abigail.   I will have Don Mathias; he is my love.
Barabas.   Yes, you shall have him. Go put her in.
Ithamore.   Ay, I'll put her in. [*He puts her in.*]
Barabas.   Now tell me, Ithamore, how lik'st thou this?   360
Ithamore.   Faith, master, I think by this
  You purchase both their lives. Is it not so?
Barabas.   True, and it shall be cunningly performed.
Ithamore.   O, master, that I might have a hand in this!
Barabas.   Ay, so thou shalt; 'tis thou must do the deed.   365
  Take this and bear it to Mathias straight, [*He gives a letter.*]
  And tell him that it comes from Lodowick.
Ithamore.   'Tis poisoned, is it not?
Barabas.   No, no; and yet it might be done that way.
  It is a challenge feigned from Lodowick.   370
Ithamore.   Fear not. I'll so set his heart a-fire,
  That he shall verily think it comes from him.
Barabas.   I cannot choose but like thy readiness.

Yet be not rash, but do it cunningly.
Ithamore.　As I behave myself in this, employ me hereafter.　　　375
Barabas.　Away then!

　　　　　　　　　　　　　　　　　　　Exit [Ithamore].

So, now will I go in to Lodowick,
And, like a cunning spirit, feign some lie,
Till I have set 'em both at enmity.

　　　　　　　　　　　　　　　　　　　　　Exit.

✳

　　　　Enter [Bellamira,] a Courtesan.　　　　III,i.
Bellamira.　Since this town was besieged, my gain grows cold.
　The time has been that but for one bare night
　A hundred ducats have been freely given,
　But now against my will I must be chaste.
　And yet I know my beauty doth not fail.　　　　　　　5
　From Venice merchants, and from Padua
　Were wont to come rare-witted gentlemen—
　Scholars, I mean—learnèd and liberal,
　And now, save Pilia-Borza, comes there none,
　And he is very seldom from my house.　　　　　　　10
　And here he comes.
　　　　　　　Enter Pilia-Borza.
Pilia-Borza.　Hold thee, wench; there's something for thee to spend.
　　　　　　　　　　　　[He shows a bag of silver.]
Bellamira.　'Tis silver; I disdain it.
Pilia-Borza.　Ay, but the Jew has gold,
　And I will have it, or it shall go hard.　　　　　　　15
Bellamira.　Tell me, how cam'st thou by this?
Pilia-Borza.　Faith, walking the back lanes through the gardens, I
　chanced to cast mine eye up to the Jew's counting-house where I
　saw some bags of money, and in the night I clambered up with my
　hooks; and as I was taking my choice, I heard a rumbling in the　[20
　house; so I took only this and run my way. But here's the Jew's man.
　　　　　　　Enter Ithamore.
Bellamira.　Hide the bag.
Pilia-Borza.　Look not towards him. Let's away. Zoons, what a looking
　thou keep'st; thou'lt betray's anon.
　　　　　　[Exeunt Bellamira and Pilia-Borza.]
Ithamore.　O, the sweetest face that ever I beheld! I know she is　[25
　a courtesan by her attire. Now would I give a hundred of the Jew's
　crowns that I had such a concubine.

III,i.
　20 *hooks* implements used by burglars.

Well, I have delivered the challenge in such sort,
As meet they will and fighting die—brave sport.

Exit.

Enter Mathias. III,ii.

Mathias.   This is the place. Now Abigail shall see
Whether Mathias holds her dear or no.

Enter Lodowick.

What, dares the villain write in such base terms?
Lodowick.   I did it—and revenge it, if thou dar'st.

[*They*] *fight.*

Enter Barabas, above.

Barabas.   O, bravely fought! And yet they thrust not home.   5
Now, Lodowick! Now, Mathias! So!   [*They both fall.*]
So, now they have showed themselves to be tall fellows.
[*Cries from*] *within.*   Part 'em. Part 'em!
Barabas.   Ay, part 'em, now they are dead. Farewell. Farewell.

Exit.

Enter Ferneze, Katherine, [and Attendants].

Ferneze.   What sight is this? My Lodowick slain!   10
These arms of mine shall be thy sepulcher.
Katherine.   Who is this? My son Mathias slain!
Ferneze.   O Lodowick, hadst thou perished by the Turk,
Wretched Ferneze might have venged thy death.
Katherine.   Thy son slew mine, and I'll revenge his death.   15
Ferneze.   Look, Katherine, look! Thy son gave mine these wounds.
Katherine.   O, leave to grieve me; I am grieved enough.
Ferneze.   O, that my sighs could turn to lively breath,
And these my tears to blood, that he might live.
Katherine.   Who made them enemies?   20
Ferneze.   I know not, and that grieves me most of all.
Katherine.   My son loved thine.
Ferneze.   And so did Lodowick him.
Katherine.   Lend me that weapon that did kill my son,
And it shall murder me.
Ferneze.   Nay, madam, stay. That weapon was my son's,   25
And on that rather should Ferneze die.
Katherine.   Hold; let's inquire the causers of their deaths,
That we may venge their blood upon their heads.
Ferneze.   Then take them up, and let them be interred
Within one sacred monument of stone,   30

III,ii.
   7 *tall* brave.

Upon which altar I will offer up
My daily sacrifice of sighs and tears,
And with my prayers pierce impartial heavens,
Till they [reveal] the causers of our smarts,
Which forced their hands divide united hearts.   35
Come, Katherine, our losses equal are;
Then of true grief let us take equal share.
                        Exeunt [bearing out the bodies].

                Enter Ithamore.   III,iii.
Ithamore.   Why, was there ever seen such villainy,
    So neatly plotted and so well performed?
    Both held in hand, and flatly both beguiled?
                Enter Abigail.
Abigail.   Why, how now, Ithamore! Why laugh'st thou so?
Ithamore.   O mistress! Ha, ha, ha!   5
Abigail.   Why, what ail'st thou?
Ithamore.   O, my master!
Abigail.   Ha!
Ithamore.   O, mistress, I have the bravest, gravest, secret, subtle, bottle-
    nosed knave to my master, that ever gentleman had.   10
Abigail.   Say, knave, why rail'st upon my father thus?
Ithamore.   O, my master has the bravest policy.
Abigail.   Wherein?
Ithamore.   Why, know you not?
Abigail.   Why, no.   15
Ithamore.   Know you not of Mathias' and Don Lodowick's disaster?
Abigail.   No. What was it?
Ithamore.   Why the devil invented a challenge, my master writ it, and
    I carried it, first to Lodowick, and *imprimis* to Mathias.
    And then they met, [and] as the story says,   20
    In doleful wise they ended both their days.
Abigail.   And was my father furtherer of their deaths?
Ithamore.   Am I Ithamore?
Abigail.   Yes.
Ithamore.   So sure did your father write and I carry the challenge.   25
Abigail.   Well, Ithamore, let me request thee this:
    Go to the new made nunnery and inquire
    For any of the friars of St. Jaques,
    And say I pray them come and speak with me.
Ithamore.   I pray, mistress, will you answer me to one question?   30

III,iii.

12 *policy* See note at I,i,138.

Abigail.   Well, sirrah, what is't?

Ithamore.   A very feeling one. Have not the nuns fine sport with the
friars now and then?

Abigail.   Go to, sirrah sauce. Is this your question? Get ye gone.

Ithamore.   I will, forsooth, mistress.   35

                                                                Exit.

Abigail.   Hard-hearted father, unkind Barabas,
   Was this the pursuit of thy policy,
   To make me show them favor severally,
   That by my favor they should both be slain?
   Admit thou lov'dst not Lodowick for his sire,   40
   Yet Don Mathias ne'er offended thee.
   But thou wert set upon extreme revenge
   Because the sire dispossessed thee once,
   And couldst not venge it but upon his son,
   Nor on his son but by Mathias' means,   45
   Nor on Mathias but by murdering me.
   But I perceive there is no love on earth,
   Pity in Jews, nor piety in Turks.
   But here comes cursèd Ithamore with the friar.

                     Enter Ithamore [with] Friar [Jacomo].

Friar Jacomo.   Virgo, salve.   50

Ithamore.   When duck you?

Abigail.   Welcome, grave friar. Ithamore, begone.

                                                Exit [Ithamore].

   Know, holy sir, I am bold to solicit thee.

Friar Jacomo.   Wherein?

Abigail.   To get me be admitted for a nun.   55

Friar Jacomo.   Why, Abigail, it is not yet long since
   That I did labor thy admission,
   And then thou didst not like that holy life.

Abigail.   Then were my thoughts so frail and unconfirmed,
   And I was chained to follies of the world,   60
   But now experience, purchasèd with grief,
   Has made me see the difference of things.
   My sinful soul, alas, hath paced too long
   The fatal labyrinth of misbelief,
   Far from the Son that gives eternal life.   65

Friar Jacomo.   Who taught thee this?

Abigail.   The abbess of the house,
   Whose zealous admonition I embrace.
   O, therefore, Jacomo, let me be one,
   Although unworthy, of that sisterhood.

---

50 *Virgo, salve* virgin, hail.
51 *duck* bow in reverence (a term of
contempt applied often to friars).
57 *labor* work for.

65 *Son* This is the quarto reading,
but "sun" is equally possible. Marlowe
may be punning upon both meanings.

Friar Jacomo.   Abigail, I will. But see thou change no more,   70
  For that will be most heavy to thy soul.
Abigail.   That was my father's fault.
Friar Jacomo.   Thy father's? How?
Abigail.   Nay, you shall pardon me. O Barabas,
  Though thou deservest hardly at my hands,
  Yet never shall these lips bewray thy life.   [*Aside.*]   75
Friar Jacomo.   Come, shall we go?
Abigail.   My duty waits on you.

                                                               Exeunt.

                       ✳

                Enter Barabas, reading a letter.   III,iv.
Barabas.   What, Abigail become a nun again?
  False and unkind! What, hast thou lost thy father?
  And, all unknown and unconstrained of me,
  Art thou again got to the nunnery?
  Now here she writes and wills me to repent.   5
  Repentance! *Spurca!* What pretendeth this?
  I fear she knows—'tis so—of my device
  In Don Mathias' and Lodovico's deaths.
  If so, 'tis time that it be seen into,
  For she that varies from me in belief   10
  Gives great presumption that she loves me **not**,
  Or loving, doth dislike of something done.
  But who comes here?
               [*Enter Ithamore.*]
             O Ithamore, come near.
  Come near, my love; come near, thy master's life,
  My trusty servant, nay, my second self,   15
  For I have now no hope but even in thee,
  And on that hope my happiness is built.
  When saw'st thou Abigail?
Ithamore.   Today.
Barabas.   With whom?
Ithamore.   A friar.
Barabas.   A friar! False villain, he hath done the deed.   20
Ithamore.   How, sir?
Barabas.   Why, made mine Abigail a nun.
Ithamore.   That's no lie, for she sent me for him.
Barabas.   O unhappy day!
  False, credulous, inconstant Abigail!

                       III,iv.

             6 *Spurca* an imprecation of Latin origin, probably meaning filthy.

But let 'em go. And Ithamore, from hence   25
Ne'er shall she grieve me more with her disgrace;
Ne'er shall she live to inherit aught of mine,
Be blessed of me, nor come within my gates,
But perish underneath my bitter curse,
Like Cain by Adam, for his brother's death.   30
Ithamore.   O master!
Barabas.   Ithamore, entreat not for her. I am moved,
And she is hateful to my soul and me,
And 'less thou yield to this that I entreat,
I cannot think but that thou hat'st my life.   35
Ithamore.   Who, I, master? Why, I'll run to some rock,
And throw myself headlong into the sea.
Why, I'll do anything for your sweet sake.
Barabas.   O trusty Ithamore, no servant, but my friend,
I here adopt thee for mine only heir.   40
All that I have is thine when I am dead,
And whilst I live use half. Spend as myself.
Here take my keys—I'll give 'em thee anon.
Go buy thee garments, but thou shalt not want.
Only know this, that thus thou art to do.   45
But first go fetch me in the pot of rice
That for our supper stands upon the fire.
Ithamore.   I hold my head my master's hungry.
I go sir.

                                                Exit.

Barabas.   Thus every villain ambles after wealth,   50
Although he ne'er be richer than in hope.
But, husht!
                    Enter Ithamore with the pot.
Ithamore.   Here 'tis, master.
Barabas.   Well said, Ithamore.
What, hast thou brought the ladle with thee too?
Ithamore.   Yes sir. The proverb says he that eats with the devil had
need of a long spoon. I have brought you a ladle.   55
Barabas.   Very well, Ithamore. Then now be secret,
And for thy sake, whom I so dearly love,
Now shalt thou see the death of Abigail,
That thou mayst freely live to be my heir.
Ithamore.   Why, master, will you poison her with a mess of rice   [60
porridge? That will preserve life, make her round and plump, and
batten more than you are aware.
Barabas.   Ay, but Ithamore, seest thou this?
It is a precious powder that I bought
Of an Italian in Ancona once,   65
Whose operation is to bind, infect,

62 *batten* fatten.

And poison deeply, yet not appear
In forty hours after it is ta'en.
Ithamore.   How, master?
Barabas.   Thus, Ithamore: 70
This even they use in Malta here—'tis called
Saint Jaques' Even—and then, I say, they use
To send their alms unto the nunneries.
Amongst the rest bear this, and set it there.
There's a dark entry where they take it in,   75
Where they must neither see the messenger,
Nor make inquiry who hath sent it them.
Ithamore.   How so?
Barabas.   Belike there is some ceremony in't.
There, Ithamore, must thou go place this pot.   80
Stay; let me spice it first.
Ithamore.   Pray do, and let me help you, master.
Pray, let me taste first.
Barabas.   Prithee do. [*Ithamore tastes.*] What say'st thou now?
Ithamore.   Troth, master, I'm loath such a pot of pottage should   [85
be spoiled.
Barabas.   Peace, Ithamore; 'tis better so than spared.
                                        [*He pours powder into pot.*]
Assure thyself thou shalt have broth by the eye.
My purse, my coffer, and myself is thine.
Ithamore.   Well, master, I go.   90
Barabas.   Stay! First let me stir it, Ithamore.
                                                  [*He stirs.*]
As fatal be it to her as the draught
Of which great Alexander drunk and died,
And with her let it work like Borgia's wine,
Whereof his sire, the Pope, was poisonèd.   95
In few, the blood of Hydra, Lerna's bane,
The juice of Hebon, and Cocytus' breath,
And all the poisons of the Stygian pool
Break from the fiery kingdom, and in this
Vomit your venom, and envenom her   100
That like a fiend hath left her father thus.

88 *by the eye* in great quantity.

93 *Alexander* the Greek conqueror who, according to Plutarch, died of a fever brought on by excessive drinking of wine.

94–95 *Borgia's wine . . . poisonèd* The Borgias, Lucretia, Cesare, and their father, Pope Alexander VI, were associated in the popular imagination with the skillful use of poisons. The pope himself is said to have died of poison-ing, although this is discounted by modern historians.

96 *Hydra* a nine-headed monster which ravaged the country of Lerna; slain by Hercules as the second of his twelve labors.

97 *Hebon* probably henbane, a common source of poison. *Cocytus* one of the rivers of the Greek Hades.

98 *Stygian pool* the river Styx, principal river of Hades.

99 *fiery kingdom* Hell.

Ithamore. What a blessing has he given't! Was ever **pot of** rice
  porridge so sauced? What shall I do with it?
Barabas. O my sweet Ithamore, go set it down,
  And come again as soon as thou hast done,   105
  For I have other business for thee.
Ithamore. Here's a drench to poison a whole stable of Flanders mares.
  I'll carry't to the nuns with a powder.
Barabas. And the horse pestilence to boot. Away!
Ithamore. I am gone.   110
  Pay me my wages, for my work is done.

                                                            Exit.

Barabas. I'll pay thee with a vengeance, Ithamore.

                                                            Exit.

✳

III,v.

        Enter Ferneze, [Martin Del] Bosco, Knights [and] Bashaw.
Ferneze. Welcome, great Bashaw. How fares Calymath?
  What wind drives you thus into Malta road?
Bashaw. The wind that bloweth all the world besides,
  Desire of gold.
Ferneze.   Desire of gold, great sir?
  That's to be gotten in the Western Inde;   5
  In Malta are no golden minerals.
Bashaw. To you of Malta thus saith Calymath:
  The time you took for respite is at hand
  For the performance of your promise past;
  And for the tribute money I am sent.   10
Ferneze. Bashaw, in brief, shalt have no tribute here,
  Nor shall the heathens live upon our spoil.
  First will we race the city walls ourselves,
  Lay waste the island, hew the temples down,
  And shipping off our goods to Sicily,   15
  Open an entrance for the wasteful sea,
  Whose billows, beating the resistless banks,
  Shall overflow it with their refluence.
Bashaw. Well, governor, since thou hast broke the league
  By flat denial of the promised tribute,   20
  Talk not of racing down your city walls.
  You shall not need to trouble yourselves so far,
  For Selim Calymath shall come himself,

III,v.

107 *drench* dose of medicine (applied
usually to animals).

13 *race* raze.
18 *refluence* backward movement of
the waters.

And with brass bullets batter down your towers,
And turn proud Malta to a wilderness   25
For these intolerable wrongs of yours.
And so, farewell.
Ferneze.   Farewell.   [*Exit Bashaw.*]
And now, you men of Malta, look about,
And let's provide to welcome Calymath.
Close your portcullis; charge your basilisks,   30
And as you profitably take up arms,
So now courageously encounter them,
For by this answer broken is the league,
And nought is to be looked for now but wars,
And nought to us more welcome is than wars.   35
                                        Exeunt.

✱

                Enter Friar Jacomo and Friar Barnardine.   III,vi.
Friar Jacomo.   O brother, brother, all the nuns are sick,
    And physic will not help them; they must die.
Friar Barnardine.   The abbess sent for me to be confessed.
    O, what a sad confession will there be.
Friar Jacomo.   And so did fair Maria send for me.   5
    I'll to her lodging; hereabouts she lies.
                                        Exit.
                Enter Abigail.
Friar Barnardine.   What, all dead save only Abigail?
Abigail.   And I shall die too, for I feel death coming.
    Where is the friar that conversed with me?
Friar Barnardine.   O, he is gone to see the other nuns.   10
Abigail.   I sent for him, but seeing you are come,
    Be you my ghostly father. And first know
    That in this house I lived religiously,
    Chaste, and devout, much sorrowing for my sins.
    But, ere I came—
Friar Barnardine.   What then?   15
Abigail.   I did offend high heaven so grievously
    As I am almost desperate for my sins,
    And one offense torments me more than all.
    You knew Mathias and Don Lodowick?
Friar Barnardine.   Yes, what of them?   20
Abigail.   My father did contract me to 'em both:
    First to Don Lodowick; him I never loved.
    Mathias was the man that I held dear,
    And for his sake did I become a nun.

30 *basilisks* large brazen cannon.   31 *profitably* for your own profits.

Friar Barnardine. So say, how was their end?   25
Abigail. Both, jealous of my love, envied each other,
  And by my father's practice—which is there

                                        [*She gives him a paper.*]

  Set down at large—the gallants were both slain.
Friar Barnardine. O, monstrous villainy!
Abigail. To work my peace, this I confess to thee.   30
  Reveal it not, for then my father dies.
Friar Barnardine. Know that confession must not be revealed.
  The canon law forbids it, and the priest
  That makes it known, being degraded first,
  Shall be condemned and then sent to the fire.   35
Abigail. So I have heard. Pray, therefore, keep it close.
  Death seizeth on my heart. Ah, gentle friar,
  Convert my father that he may be saved,
  And witness that I die a Christian. [*She dies.*]
Friar Barnardine. Ay, and a virgin, too—that grieves me most.   40
  But I must to the Jew and exclaim on him
  And make him stand in fear of me.
                    Enter Friar [Jacomo].
Friar Jacomo. O brother, all the nuns are dead. Let's bury them.
Friar Barnardine. First help to bury this. Then go with me,
  And help me to exclaim against the Jew.   45
Friar Jacomo. Why, what has he done?
Friar Barnardine. A thing that makes me tremble to unfold.
Friar Jacomo. What, has he crucified a child?
Friar Barnardine. No, but a worse thing. 'Twas told me in shrift.
  Thou know'st 'tis death and if it be revealed.   50
  Come, let's away.

                                                    Exeunt.

                Enter Barabas [and] Ithamore. Bells within.   IV,i.
Barabas. There is no music to a Christian's knell.
  How sweet the bells ring now the nuns are dead,
  That sound at other times like tinkers' pans.
  I was afraid the poison had not wrought,
  Or though it wrought, it would have done no good,   5
  For every year they swell, and yet they live.
  Now all are dead; not one remains alive.
Ithamore. That's brave, master. But think you it will not be known?

III,vi.   **IV,i.**
  27 *practice* treachery.   1 *to* equal to.
  41 *exclaim on* accuse.   6 *swell* become pregnant.

Barabas.   How can it, if we two be secret?
Ithamore.   For my part, fear you not.   10
Barabas.   I'd cut thy throat if I did.
Ithamore.   And reason too.
  But here's a royal monast'ry hard by;
  Good master, let me poison all the monks.
Barabas.   Thou shalt not need, for now the nuns are dead,
  They'll die with grief.   15
Ithamore.   Do you not sorrow for your daughter's death?
Barabas.   No, but I grieve because she lived so long,
  An Hebrew born and would become a Christian.
           Enter Friar Jacomo and Friar Barnardine.
  Cazzo Diabolo!
Ithamore.   Look, look, master. Here come two religious cater-   [20
  pillars.
Barabas.   I smelt 'em ere they came.
Ithamore.   God-a-mercy, nose. Come, let's begone.
Friar Barnardine.   Stay, wicked Jew. Repent, I say, and stay.
Friar Jacomo.   Thou hast offended, therefore must be damned.   25
Barabas.   I fear they know we sent the poisoned broth.
Ithamore.   And so do I, master; therefore speak 'em fair.
Friar Barnardine.   Barabas, thou hast—
Friar Jacomo.   Ay, that thou hast—
Barabas.   True, I have money. What, though I have?   30
Friar Barnardine.   Thou art a—
Friar Jacomo.   Ay, that thou art a—
Barabas.   What needs all this? I know I am a Jew.
Friar Barnardine.   Thy daughter—
Friar Jacomo.   Ay, thy daughter—   35
Barabas.   O, speak not of her; then I die with grief.
Friar Barnardine.   Remember that—
Friar Jacomo.   Ay, remember that—
Barabas.   I must needs say that I have been a great usurer.
Friar Barnardine.   Thou hast committed—   40
Barabas.   Fornication? But that
  Was in another country, and besides
  The wench is dead.
Friar Barnardine.   Ay, but Barabas,
  Remember Mathias and Don Lodowick.   45
Barabas.   Why, what of them?
Friar Barnardine.   I will not say that by a forged challenge they met.
Barabas.   She has confessed, and we are both undone,
  My bosom intimates. But I must dissemble.   *Aside [to Ithamore].*
  O holy friars, the burden of my sins   50
  Lie heavy on my soul. Then, pray you, tell me,
  Is't not too late now to turn Christian?

19 *Cazzo Diabolo* an Italian imprecation.

I have been zealous in the Jewish faith,
Hard-hearted to the poor, a covetous wretch
That would for lucre's sake have sold my soul.   55
A hundred for a hundred I have ta'en,
And now for store of wealth may I compare
With all the Jews in Malta. But what is wealth?
I am a Jew, and therefore am I lost.
Would penance serve for this my sin,   60
I could afford to whip myself to death.
Ithamore.   And so could I, but penance will not serve.
Barabas.   To fast, to pray, and wear a shirt of hair,
And on my knees creep to Jerusalem.
Cellars of wine and sollars full of wheat,   65
Warehouses stuffed with spices and with drugs,
Whole chests of gold in bullion and in coin,
Besides I know not how much weight in pearl,
Orient and round, have I within my house;
At Alexandria merchandise unsold.   70
But yesterday two ships went from this town;
Their voyage will be worth ten thousand crowns.
In Florence, Venice, Antwerp, London, Seville,
Frankfort, Lubeck, Moscow, and where not,
Have I debts owing, and in most of these   75
Great sums of money lying in the banco.
All this I'll give to some religious house,
So I may be baptized and live therein.
Friar Jacomo.   O good Barabas, come to our house.
Friar Barnardine.   O no, good Barabas, come to our house.   80
And Barabas, you know—
Barabas.   I know that I have highly sinned.
You shall convert me. You shall have all my wealth.
Friar Jacomo.   O Barabas, their laws are strict.
Barabas.   I know they are, and I will be with you.   85
Friar Jacomo.   They wear no shirts, and they go barefoot too.
Barabas.   Then 'tis not for me, and I am resolved
You shall confess me and have all my goods.
Friar Jacomo.   Good Barabas, come to me.
Barabas.   You see, I answer him, and yet he stays.   90
Rid him away, and go you home with me.
Friar Jacomo.   I'll be with you tonight.
Barabas.   Come to my house at one o'clock this night.
Friar Jacomo.   You hear your answer, and you may be gone.
Friar Barnardine.   Why go, get you away.   95
Friar Jacomo.   I will not go for thee.
Friar Barnardine.   Not? Then, I'll make thee, rogue.

56 *hundred . . . ta'en* i.e., as usuri-   65 *sollars* granaries on the upper floors
ous interest.   of houses.

Friar Jacomo.   How! Dost call me rogue?

                                       [They] fight.

Ithamore.   Part 'em, master, part 'em.

Barabas.   This is mere frailty. Brethren, be content—   100

    Friar Barnardine go you with Ithamore.

    You know my mind; let me alone with him.

Friar Jacomo.   Why does he go to thy house? Let him be gone.

Barabas.   I'll give him something and so stop his mouth.

                    Exit [Friar Barnardine with Ithamore].

    I never heard of any man but he   105

    Maligned the order of the Jacobins.

    But do you think that I believe his words?

    Why, brother, you converted Abigail,

    And I am bound in charity to requite it.

    And so I will. O Jacomo, fail not, but come.   110

Friar Jacomo.   But, Barabas, who shall be your godfathers?

    For presently you shall be shrived.

Barabas.   Marry, the Turk shall be one of my godfathers,

    But not a word to any of your convent.

Friar Jacomo.   I warrant thee, Barabas.   115

                                      Exit.

Barabas.   So now the fear is past and I am safe,

    For he that shrived her is within my house.

    What if I murdered him ere Jacomo comes?

    Now I have such a plot for both their lives

    As never Jew nor Christian knew the like.   120

    One turned my daughter; therefore he shall die.

    The other knows enough to have my life;

    Therefore 'tis not requisite he should live.

    But are not both these wise men to suppose

    That I will leave my house, my goods, and all,   125

    To fast and be well whipped? I'll none of that.

    Now, Friar Barnardine, I come to you.

    I'll feast you, lodge you, give you fair words,

    And after that, I and my trusty Turk—

    No more, but so. It must and shall be done.   130

                                [Exit.]

                    [Enter Barabas.]   **IV,ii.**

Barabas.   Ithamore, tell me, is the friar asleep?

                  Enter Ithamore.

Ithamore.   Yes, and I know not what the reason is.

    Do what I can, he will not strip himself,

---

106 *Jacobins* Dominican friars.   113 *Turk* i.e., Ithamore.

Nor go to bed, but sleeps in his own clothes.
I fear me he mistrusts what we intend. 5
Barabas. No; 'tis an order which the friars use.
Yet, if he knew our meanings, could he 'scape?
Ithamore. No; none can hear him, cry he ne'er so loud.
Barabas. Why, true; therefore did I place him there.
The other chambers open towards the street. 10
Ithamore. You loiter, master. Wherefore stay we thus?
O, how I long to see him shake his heels.
Barabas. Come on, sirrah.
Off with your girdle. Make a handsome noose.
[*Ithamore makes a noose with his girdle.*]

Friar, awake! [*They put the noose around the Friar's neck.*] 15
Friar Barnardine. What! Do you mean to strangle me?
Ithamore. Yes, 'cause you use to confess.
Barabas. Blame not us, but the proverb, 'Confess and be hanged.' Pull
hard.
Friar Barnardine. What, will you have my life? 20
Barabas. Pull hard, I say. You would have had my goods.
Ithamore. Ay, and our lives too. Therefore pull amain.
[*They strangle him.*]
'Tis neatly done, sir. Here's no print at all.
Barabas. Then is it as it should be. Take him up.
Ithamore. Nay, master, be ruled by me a little. So, let him lean [25
upon his staff. Excellent! He stands as if he were begging of bacon.
Barabas. Who would not think but that this friar lived?
What time o' night is't now, sweet Ithamore?
Ithamore. Towards one.
Barabas. Then will not Jacomo be long from hence. 30
[*Exeunt*]

Enter [*Friar*] *Jacomo.* IV,iii.
Friar Jacomo. This is the hour wherein I shall proceed—
O happy hour—wherein I shall convert
An infidel and bring his gold into our treasury.
But soft! Is not this Barnardine? It is;
And understanding I should come this way, 5
Stands here a purpose, meaning me some wrong,
And intercept my going to the Jew.

IV,ii.
12 *shake his heels* i.e., be hanged.
17 *use* are accustomed to. *confess* hear
confessions.

23 *print* mark of the cord.

IV,iii.
1 *proceed* prosper.

Barnardine!
Wilt thou not speak? Thou think'st I see thee not?
Away, I'd wish thee, and let me go by.   10
No, wilt thou not? Nay, then I'll force my way.
And see, a staff stands ready for the purpose.
As thou lik'st that, stop me another time.

        [He] strikes [Barnardine, who] falls.

        Enter Barabas [and Ithamore].

Barabas.   Why, how now, Jacomo! What hast thou done?
Friar Jacomo.   Why, stricken him that would have struck at me.   15
Barabas.   Who is it? Barnardine? Now out, alas, he is slain.
Ithamore.   Ay, master, he's slain. Look how his brains drop out on's
nose.
Friar Jacomo.   Good sirs, I have done't, but nobody knows it but you
two. I may escape.   20
Barabas.   So might my man and I hang with you for company.
Ithamore.   No; let us bear him to the magistrates.
Friar Jacomo.   Good Barabas, let me go.
Barabas.   No, pardon me. The law must have his course.
I must be forced to give in evidence   25
That being importuned by this Barnardine
To be a Christian, I shut him out,
And there he sat. Now I, to keep my word
And give my goods and substance to your house,
Was up thus early with intent to go   30
Unto your friary because you stayed.
Ithamore.   Fie upon 'em, master. Will you turn Christian, when holy
friars turn devils and murder one another?
Barabas.   No; for this example I'll remain a Jew.
Heaven bless me! What, a friar a murderer?   35
When shall you see a Jew commit the like?
Ithamore.   Why, a Turk could ha' done no more.
Barabas.   Tomorrow is the sessions; you shall to it.
Come, Ithamore, let's help to take him hence.
Friar Jacomo.   Villains, I am a sacred person. Touch me not.   40
Barabas.   The law shall touch you. We'll but lead you, we.
'Las, I could weep at your calamity.
Take in the staff too, for that must be shown.
Law wills that each particular be known.

        Exeunt.

        Enter Bellamira and Pilia-Borza.   IV,iv.
Bellamira.   Pilia-Borza, didst thou meet with Ithamore?

17 *on's* o^ his.   31 *stayed* delayed in coming.

Pilia-Borza. I did.

Bellamira. And didst thou deliver my letter?

Pilia-Borza. I did.

Bellamira. And what think'st thou? Will he come?   5

Pilia-Borza. I think so. And yet I cannot tell, for at the reading of the letter he looked like a man of another world.

Bellamira. Why so?

Pilia-Borza. That such a base slave as he should be saluted by such a tall man as I am, from such a beautiful dame as you.   10

Bellamira. And what said he?

Pilia-Borza. Not a wise word—only gave me a nod, as who should say, 'Is it even so?' And so I left him, being driven to a non-plus at the critical aspect of my terrible countenance.

Bellamira. And where didst meet him?   15

Pilia-Borza. Upon mine own free-hold, within forty foot of the gallows, conning his neck-verse, I take it, looking of a friar's execution— whom I saluted with an old hempen proverb, *Hodie tibi, cras mihi,* and so I left him to the mercy of the hangman. But, the exercise being done, see where he comes.   20

Enter Ithamore.

Ithamore. I never knew a man take his death so patiently as this friar. He was ready to leap off ere the halter was about his neck. And when the hangman had put on his hempen tippet, he made such haste to his prayers, as if he had had another cure to serve. Well, go whither he will, I'll be none of his followers in haste. And now I think   [25 on't, going to the execution, a fellow met me with muschatoes like a raven's wing and a dagger with a hilt like a warming pan, and he gave me a letter from one Madam Bellamira, saluting me in such sort as if he had meant to make clean my boots with his lips. The effect was that I should come to her house. I wonder what the reason   [30 is. It may be she sees more in me than I can find in myself, for she writes further that she loves me ever since she saw me. And who would not requite such love? Here's her house, and here she comes, and now would I were gone. I am not worthy to look upon her.

Pilia-Borza. This is the gentleman you writ to.   35

Ithamore. Gentleman! He flouts me. What gentry can be in a poor Turk of ten pence? I'll be gone. [*Aside.*]

Bellamira. Is't not a sweet-faced youth, Pilia?

IV,iv.

10 *tall* brave.

13 *non-plus* state of confusion.

17 *neck-verse* a Latin passage which criminals who claimed benefit of clergy to escape hanging were obliged to read.

18 *hempen* referring to the hangman's rope. *Hodie . . . mihi* Today you, tomorrow me.

19 *exercise* i.e., the hanging.

23 *tippet* scarf, i.e., the hangman's rope.

26 *muschatoes* moustaches (one of many variant forms).

Ithamore. Again, sweet youth. [*Aside.*] Did not you, sir, bring the sweet
youth a letter?   40
Pilia-Borza. I did, sir, and from this gentlewoman who, as myself and
the rest of the family, stand or fall at your service.
Bellamira. Though woman's modesty should hale me back, I can with-
hold no longer. Welcome, sweet love.
Ithamore. Now am I clean—or rather, foully—out of the way.   45
                                                                [*Aside.*]
Bellamira. Whither so soon?
Ithamore. I'll go steal some money from my master to make me hand-
some. [*Aside.*] Pray, pardon me; I must go see a ship discharged.
Bellamira. Canst thou be so unkind to leave me thus?
Pilia-Borza. And ye did but know how she loves you, sir!   50
Ithamore. Nay, I care not how much she loves me.
   Sweet Bellamira, would I had my master's wealth for thy sake!
Pilia-Borza. And you can have it, sir, and if you please.
Ithamore. If 'twere above ground, I could and would have it, but he
hides and buries it up as partridges do their eggs, under the   [55
earth.
Pilia-Borza. And is't not possible to find it out?
Ithamore. By no means possible.
Bellamira. What shall we do with this base villain then?
                                                [*Aside to Pilia-Borza.*]
Pilia-Borza. Let me alone; do but you speak him fair.   60
                                                          [*Aside to her.*]
   But you know some secrets of the Jew,
   Which, if they were revealed, would do him harm?
Ithamore. Ay, and such as—go to, no more! I'll make him send me
half he has and glad he 'scapes so too. Pen and ink. I'll write unto
him. We'll have money straight.   65
Pilia-Borza. Send for a hundred crowns at least.
Ithamore. Ten hundred thousand crowns. *He writes.* 'Master Barabas—'
Pilia-Borza. Write not so submissively, but threatening him.
Ithamore. [*writing*] 'Sirrah Barabas, send me a hundred crowns.'
Pilia-Borza. Put in two hundred at least.   70
Ithamore. [*writing*] 'I charge thee send me three hundred by this
bearer, and this shall be your warrant. If you do not, no more, but so.'
Pilia-Borza. Tell him you will confess.
Ithamore. [*writing*] 'Otherwise, I'll confess all.' Vanish, and return in a
twinkle. [*He gives letter to Pilia-Borza.*]   75
Pilia-Borza. Let me alone. I'll use him in his kind.
                                                      [*Exit Pilia-Borza.*]
Ithamore. Hang him, Jew!
Bellamira. Now, gentle Ithamore, lie in my lap.
   Where are my maids? Provide a running banquet.
79 *running* hastily prepared.

Send to the merchant; bid him bring me silks.   80
  Shall Ithamore, my love, go in such rags?

Ithamore.   And bid the jeweller come hither too.

Bellamira.   I have no husband, sweet; I'll marry thee.

Ithamore.   Content, but we will leave this paltry land
  And sail from hence to Greece, to lovely Greece.   85
  I'll be thy Jason, thou my golden fleece.
  Where painted carpets o'er the meads are hurled,
  And Bacchus' vineyards overspread the world,
  Where woods and forests go in goodly green,
  I'll be Adonis; thou shalt be Love's queen.   90
  The meads, the orchards, and the primrose lanes,
  Instead of sedge and reed, bear sugar canes.
  Thou in those groves, by Dis above,
  Shalt live with me, and be my love.

Bellamira.   Whither will I not go with gentle Ithamore?   95
                   Enter Pilia-Borza.

Ithamore.   How now? Hast thou the gold?

Pilia-Borza.   Yes.

Ithamore.   But came it freely? Did the cow give down her milk freely?

Pilia-Borza.   At reading of the letter, he stared and stamped and
turned aside. I took him by the beard and looked upon him [100
thus, told him he were best to send it. Then he hugged and embraced
me.

Ithamore.   Rather for fear than love.

Pilia-Borza.   Then, like a Jew, he laughed and jeered, and told me he
loved me for your sake, and said what a faithful servant you [105
had been.

Ithamore.   The more villain he to keep me thus. Here's goodly 'parel,
is there not?

Pilia-Borza.   To conclude, he gave me ten crowns.

Ithamore.   But ten? I'll not leave him worth a gray groat. Give [110
me a ream of paper. We'll have a kingdom of gold for't.

Pilia-Borza.   Write for five hundred crowns.

Ithamore. [*writing*]   'Sirrah Jew, as you love your life, send me five hundred crowns and give the bearer a hundred.' Tell him I must have't.

Pilia-Borza.   I warrant, your worship shall have't.   115

Ithamore.   And if he ask why I demand so much, tell him I scorn to
write a line under a hundred crowns.

Pilia-Borza.   You'd make a rich poet, sir. I am gone.

                             Exit.

---

86 *Jason* Greek hero who sailed to
Colchos in quest of the golden fleece.
88 *Bacchus* god of wine.
90 *Adonis* a Greek youth beloved by
Venus (Love's queen); he was killed by
a boar. Venus mourned for him so much

that the god of Hades permitted him
to return to earth for six months of
every year to be with her.

93 *Dis* another name for **Pluto**, god
of Hades. Ithamore reveals his ignorance
by placing him "above."

Ithamore.   Take thou the money; spend it for my sake.
Bellamira.   'Tis not thy money, but thyself I weigh.   120
   Thus Bellamira esteems of gold.   [*She casts it aside.*]
   But thus of thee.   [*She*] *kisse*[*s*] *him.*
Ithamore.   That kiss again. She runs division of my lips.
   What an eye she casts on me! It twinkles like a star.
Bellamira.   Come, my dear love; let's in and sleep together.   125
Ithamore.   O, that ten thousand nights were put in one,
   That we might sleep seven years together afore we wake.
Bellamira.   Come, amorous wag; first banquet, and then sleep.
                                           [*Exeunt.*]

                Enter Barabas, reading a letter.   IV,v.
Barabas.   'Barabas, send me three hundred crowns.'
   Plain Barabas? O, that wicked courtesan!
   He was not wont to call me Barabas.
   'Or else I will confess.' Ay, there it goes.
   But, if I get him, *coupe de gorge* for that.   5
   He sent a shaggy, tottered, staring slave,
   That when he speaks draws out his grisly beard
   And winds it twice or thrice about his ear,
   Whose face has been a grindstone for men's swords—
   His hands are hacked, some fingers cut quite off—   10
   Who when he speaks grunts like a hog, and looks
   Like one that is employed in catzerie
   And cross-biting—such a rogue
   As is the husband to a hundred whores—
   And I by him must send three hundred crowns.   15
   Well, my hope is he will not stay there still;
   And when he comes—O, that he were but here!
                   Enter Pilia-Borza.
Pilia-Borza.   Jew, I must ha' more gold.
Barabas.   Why? Want'st thou any of thy tale?
Pilia-Borza.   No, but three hundred will not serve his turn.   20
Barabas.   Not serve his turn, sir?
Pilia-Borza.   No, sir, and therefore I must have five hundred more.
Barabas.   I'll rather—
Pilia-Borza.   O, good words, sir, and send it you were best.
   See, there's his letter.   [*He gives the letter.*]   25

---

123 *runs division* plays a rapid pas-   6 *tottered* tattered.
sage of music, i.e., she is kissing him   12 *catzerie* roguery.
with rapidity and variety.   13 *cross-biting* swindling.
IV,v.   19 *tale* reckoning.
   5 *coupe de gorge* a slit throat.

Barabas.   Might he not as well come as send? Pray, bid him come and
fetch it. What he writes for you, ye shall have straight.

Pilia-Borza.   Ay, and the rest too, or else—

Barabas.   I must make this villain away. [*Aside.*] Please you dine with
me, sir? And you shall be most heartily poisoned.   *Aside.*   30

Pilia-Borza.   No, God-a-mercy. Shall I have these crowns?

Barabas.   I cannot do it; I have lost my keys.

Pilia-Borza.   O, if that be all, I can pick ope your locks.

Barabas.   Or climb up to my counting-house window? You know my
meaning?   35

Pilia-Borza.   I know enough, and therefore talk not to me of your
counting-house. The gold—or know, Jew, it is in my power to hang
thee.

Barabas.   I am betrayed. [*Aside.*]

'Tis not five hundred crowns that I esteem.   40
I am not moved at that. This angers me,
That he who knows I love him as myself
Should write in this imperious vein. Why, sir,
You know I have no child, and unto whom
Should I leave all but unto Ithamore?   45

Pilia-Borza.   Here's many words, but no crowns. The crowns!

Barabas.   Commend me to him, sir, most humbly,
And unto your good mistress as unknown.

Pilia-Borza.   Speak; shall I have 'em, sir?

Barabas.   Sir, here they are.
O, that I should part with so much gold! [*Aside.*]   50
Here, take 'em, fellow, with as good a will—
As I would see thee hanged. [*Aside.*] O, love stops my breath.
Never loved man servant as I do Ithamore.

Pilia-Borza.   I know it, sir.

Barabas.   Pray, when, sir, shall I see you at my house?   55

Pilia-Borza.   Soon enough to your cost sir. Fare you well.

                                                          Exit.

Barabas.   Nay, to thine own cost, villain, if thou com'st.
Was ever Jew tormented as I am?
To have a shag-rag knave to come—
Three hundred crowns—and then five hundred crowns!   60
Well, I must seek a means to rid 'em all,
And presently; for in his villainy
He will tell all he knows, and I shall die for't.
I have it.
I will in some disguise go see the slave,   65
And how the villain revels with my gold.

                                                          Exit.

Enter Bellamira, Ithamore, [and] Pilia-Borza.   IV,vi.

Bellamira.   I'll pledge thee, love, and therefore drink it off.

Ithamore.   Say'st thou me so? Have at it! And do you hear?

                                       [He whispers.]

Bellamira.   Go to; it shall be so.

Ithamore.   Of that condition I will drink it up.

  Here's to thee.

Bellamira.   Nay, I'll have all or none.   5

Ithamore.   There. If thou lov'st me, do not leave a drop.

Bellamira.   Love thee? Fill me three glasses.

Ithamore.   Three and fifty dozen! I'll pledge thee.

Pilia-Borza.   Knavely spoke, and like a knight-at-arms.

Ithamore.   Hey, *Rivo Castiliano!* A man's a man.   10

Bellamira.   Now to the Jew.

Ithamore.   Ha! To the Jew! And send me money you were best.

Pilia-Borza.   What wouldst thou do if he should send thee none?

Ithamore.   Do nothing, but I know what I know. He's a murderer.

Bellamira.   I had not thought he had been so brave a man.   15

Ithamore.   You knew Mathias and the governor's son. He and I killed

  'em both and yet never touched 'em.

Pilia-Borza.   O, bravely done!

Ithamore.   I carried the broth that poisoned the nuns, and he and I—

  snickle hand too fast—strangled a friar.   20

Bellamira.   You two alone?

Ithamore.   We two. And 'twas never known, nor never shall be for me.

Pilia-Borza.   This shall with me unto the governor.

                              [Aside to Bellamira.]

Bellamira.   And fit it should. But first let's ha' more gold.

                            [Aside to Pilia-Borza.]

  Come, gentle Ithamore, lie in my lap.   25

Ithamore.   'Love me little, love me long.' Let music rumble,

  Whilst I in thy incony lap do tumble.

            Enter Barabas, with a lute, disguised.

Bellamira.   A French musician! Come, let's hear your skill.

Barabas.   Must tuna my lute for sound, twang, twang, first.

Ithamore.   Wilt drink, Frenchman? Here's to thee with a—   30

  Pox on this drunken hiccup!

Barabas.   Gramercy, monsieur.

Bellamira.   Prithee, Pilia-Borza, bid the fiddler give me the posy in his

  hat there.

IV,vi.

4 *Of* on.

10 *Rivo Castiliano* a drinking expression of uncertain meaning, though probably of Spanish origin.

12 *you* Most editors have amended this to "he," but there is no need to do so. Ithamore, drunk and swelling in his sense of power, sees himself addressing his master in these imperious terms.

20 *snickle . . . fast* has never been explained satisfactorily. To snickle, in Northern English dialect, means to snare with a noose.

27 *incony* sweet, lovable.

Pilia-Borza.   Sirrah, you must give my mistress your posy.   35
Barabas.   *A votre commandement, madame.*
Bellamira.   How sweet, my Ithamore, the flowers smell.
Ithamore.   Like thy breath, sweetheart; no violet like 'em.
Pilia-Borza.   Foh! Methinks they stink like a hollyhock.
Barabas.   So now I am revenged upon 'em all.   40
    The scent thereof was death; I poisoned it.   [*Aside.*]
Ithamore.   Play, fiddler, or I'll cut your cat's guts into chitterlings.
Barabas.   *Pardonnez moi.* Be no in tune yet. So now, now all be in.
Ithamore.   Give him a crown, and fill me out more wine.
Pilia-Borza.   There's two crowns for thee. Play.   45
Barabas.   How liberally the villain gives me mine own gold.   *Aside.*
Pilia-Borza.   Methinks he fingers very well.
Barabas.   So did you when you stole my gold.   *Aside.*
Pilia-Borza.   How swift he runs.
Barabas.   You run swifter when you threw my gold out of my   [50
    window.   *Aside.*
Bellamira.   Musician, hast been in Malta long?
Barabas.   Two, three, four month, madam.
Ithamore.   Dost not know a Jew, one Barabas?
Barabas.   Very mush, monsieur. You no be his man?   55
Pilia-Borza.   His man!
Ithamore.   I scorn the peasant; tell him so.
Barabas.   He knows it already.   [*Aside.*]
Ithamore.   'Tis a strange thing of that Jew: he lives upon pickled grass-
    hoppers and sauced mushrumbs.   60
Barabas.   What a slave's this! The governor feeds not as I do.
                                                        Aside.
Ithamore.   He never put on clean shirt since he was circumcised.
Barabas.   O rascal! I change myself twice a day.   *Aside.*
Ithamore.   The hat he wears, Judas left under the elder when he
    hanged himself.   65
Barabas.   'Twas sent me for a present from the great Cham.
                                                        Aside.
Pilia-Borza.   A nasty slave he is. Whither now, fiddler?
Barabas.   *Pardonnez moi, monsieur.* Me be no well.
                                                        Exit.
Pilia-Borza.   Farewell, fiddler. One letter more to the Jew.
Bellamira.   Prithee, sweet love, one more, and write it sharp.   70
Ithamore.   No, I'll send by word of mouth now. Bid him deliver
    thee a thousand crowns by the same token, that the nuns loved rice,
    that Friar Barnardine slept in his own clothes. Any of 'em will do it.
Pilia-Borza.   Let me alone to urge it, now I know the meaning.
Ithamore.   The meaning has a meaning. Come, let's in.   75

---

42 *chitterlings* animal **intestines used**   60 *mushrumbs* **mushrooms.**
in sausage making.

To undo a Jew is charity, and not sin.

                            Exeunt.

Enter Ferneze, Knights, Martin Del Bosco, [and Officers].   V,i.
Ferneze. Now, gentlemen, betake you to your arms,
  And see that Malta be well fortified.
  And it behoves you to be resolute,
  For Calymath, having hovered here so long,
  Will win the town or die before the walls.   5
First Knight. And die he shall, for we will never yield.
              Enter Bellamira, [and] Pilia-Borza.
Bellamira. O, bring us to the governor.
Ferneze. Away with her! She is a courtesan.
Bellamira. Whate'er I am, yet, governor, hear me speak.
  I bring thee news by whom thy son was slain.   10
  Mathias did it not; it was the Jew.
Pilia-Borza. Who, besides the slaughter of these gentlemen,
  Poisoned his own daughter and the nuns,
  Stranglèd a friar, and I know not what
  Mischief beside.
Ferneze.   Had we but proof of this—   15
Bellamira. Strong proof, my lord. His man's now at my lodging
  That was his agent; he'll confess it all.
Ferneze. Go fetch him straight.
                        [Exeunt Officers.]
                I always feared that Jew.
      Enter Barabas [and] Ithamore, [with Officers].
Barabas. I'll go alone. Dogs, do not hale me thus.
Ithamore. Nor me neither. I cannot out-run you, constable.   20
  O, my belly!
Barabas. One dram of powder more had made all sure.
  What a damned slave was I! *[Aside.]*
Ferneze. Make fires! Heat irons! Let the rack be fetched!
First Knight. Nay, stay, my lord; 't may be he will confess.   25
Barabas. Confess? What mean you, lords? Who should confess?
Ferneze. Thou and thy Turk; 'twas you that slew my son.
Ithamore. Guilty, my lord, I confess. Your son and Mathias were both
  contracted unto Abigail. [He] forged a counterfeit challenge.
Barabas. Who carried that challenge?   30
Ithamore. I carried it, I confess. But who writ it? Marry, even he that
  strangled Barnardine, poisoned the nuns and his own daughter.
Ferneze. Away with him! His sight is death to me.
Barabas. For what? You men of Malta, hear me speak.

She is a courtesan and he a thief,   35
And he my bondman. Let me have law,
For none of this can prejudice my life.

Ferneze. Once more, away with him! You shall have law.

Barabas. Devils do your worst. I live in spite of you.   [*Aside.*]
As these have spoke, so be it to their souls!   40
I hope the poisoned flowers will work anon.   [*Aside.*]
      Exit [*with Ithamore, Bellamira, Pilia-Borza, and Officers*].

                    Enter Katherine.

Katherine. Was my Mathias murdered by the Jew?
Ferneze, 'twas thy son that murdered him.

Ferneze. Be patient, gentle madam; it was he.
He forged the daring challenge made them fight.   45

Katherine. Where is the Jew? Where is that murderer?

Ferneze. In prison till the law has passed on him.

                    Enter Officer.

Officer. My lord, the courtesan and her man are dead;
So is the Turk and Barabas the Jew.

Ferneze. Dead?   50

Officer. Dead, my lord, and here they bring his body.

Bosco. This sudden death of his is very strange.
      [*Enter Officers, carrying Barabas as dead.*]

Ferneze. Wonder not at it, sir; the heavens are just.
Their deaths were like their lives; then think not of 'em.
Since they are dead, let them be burièd.   55
For the Jew's body, throw that o'er the walls
To be a prey for vultures and wild beasts.
So, now away and fortify the town.

                    Exeunt [*all but Barabas*].

Barabas. [*rising*] What, all alone? Well fare, sleepy drink!
I'll be revenged on this accursèd town,   60
For by my means Calymath shall enter in.
I'll help to slay their children and their wives,
To fire the churches, pull their houses down,
Take my goods too, and seize upon my lands.
I hope to see the governor a slave   65
And, rowing in a galley, whipped to death.

                    Enter Calymath, Bashaws, [*and*] *Turks.*

Calymath. Whom have we there? A spy?

Barabas. Yes, my good lord, one that can spy a place
Where you may enter and surprise the town.
My name is Barabas; I am a Jew.   70

Calymath. Art thou that Jew whose goods we heard were sold
For tribute money?

Barabas.   The very same, my lord.
And since that time they have hired a slave, my man,
To accuse me of a thousand villainies.

I was imprisonèd but 'scaped their hands.   75
Calymath.   Didst break prison?
Barabas.   No, no.
  I drank of poppy and cold mandrake juice,
  And being asleep, belike they thought me dead
  And threw me o'er the walls. So—or how else—   80
  The Jew is here and rests at your command.
Calymath.   'Twas bravely done. But tell me, Barabas,
  Canst thou, as thou report'st, make Malta ours?
Barabas.   Fear not, my lord, for here against the sluice,
  The rock is hollow and of purpose digged   85
  To make a passage for the running streams
  And common channels of the city.
  Now, whilst you give assault unto the walls,
  I'll lead five hundred soldiers through the vault
  And rise with them i' th' middle of the town,   90
  Open the gates for you to enter in,
  And by this means the city is your own.
Calymath.   If this be true, I'll make thee governor.
Barabas.   And if it be not true, then let me die.
Calymath.   Thou'st doomed thyself. Assault it presently.   95

                                         Exeunt.

    Alarums [within]. Enter [Calymath, Bashaws,] Turks, [and]
      Barabas, [with] Ferneze, and Knights [led as] prisoners.
Calymath.   Now vail your pride, you captive Christians,
  And kneel for mercy to your conquering foe.
  Now where's the hope you had of haughty Spain?
  Ferneze, speak. Had it not been much better
  To kept thy promise than be thus surprised?   5
Ferneze.   What should I say? We are captives and must yield.
Calymath.   Ay, villains, you must yield, and under Turkish yokes
  Shall groaning bear the burden of our ire.
  And Barabas, as erst we promised thee,
  For thy desert we make thee governor.   10
  Use them at thy discretion.
Barabas.   Thanks, my lord.
Ferneze.   O fatal day! To fall into the hands

V,i.

  78 *poppy . . . mandrake* plants fa-   95 *doomed* sentenced.
mous for their soporific and narcotic
qualities.   **V,ii.**
  87 *channels* gutters, sewers.   1 *vail* lower.

Of such a traitor and unhallowed Jew!
What greater misery could heaven inflict?
Calymath.   'Tis our command. And Barabas, we give   15
    To guard thy person, these our Janissaries.
    Entreat them well, as we have usèd thee.
    And now, brave bashaws, come. We'll walk about
    The ruined town and see the wrack we made.
    Farewell, brave Jew. Farewell, great Barabas.   20
                    Exeunt [Calymath and Bashaws].
Barabas.   May all good fortune follow Calymath.
    And now, as entrance to our safety,
    To prison with the governor and these
    Captains, his consorts and confederates.
Ferneze.   O villain, heaven will be revenged on thee.   25
                    Exeunt [Ferneze and Knights, under guard].
Barabas.   Away! No more! Let him not trouble me.
    Thus hast thou gotten by thy policy
    No simple place, no small authority.
    I now am governor of Malta. True,
    But Malta hates me, and in hating me   30
    My life's in danger. And what boots it thee,
    Poor Barabas, to be the governor,
    Whenas thy life shall be at their command?
    No, Barabas, this must be looked into;
    And since by wrong thou gott'st authority,   35
    Maintain it bravely by firm policy;
    At least, unprofitably lose it not,
    For he that liveth in authority,
    And neither gets him friends nor fills his bags,
    Lives like the ass that Æsop speaketh of,   40
    That labors with a load of bread and wine
    And leaves it off to snap on thistle tops.
    But Barabas will be more circumspect.
    Begin betimes; occasion's bald behind.
    Slip not thine opportunity, for fear too late   45
    Thou seek'st too much, but canst not compass it.
    Within here!
                    Enter Ferneze with a Guard.
Ferneze.   My lord?
Barabas.   Ay, lord! Thus slaves will learn.
    Now, governor— Stand by there; wait within—   50
                            [Exit Guard.]

16 *Janissaries* Turkish footsoldiers.   the statue by Lysippus (ca. 370 B.C.) in
17 *Entreat* treat.   which Opportunity carries a razor and
31 *boots* avails.   flies on the wings of the wind, the back
44 *occasion's bald behind* i.e., oppor-   of his head shaven smooth, although
tunity depends upon time (Father Time   that Marlowe could have known about
was traditionally pictured as bald). See   this statue is not clear.

This is the reason that I sent for thee:
Thou seest thy life and Malta's happiness
Are at my arbitrament, and Barabas
At his discretion may dispose of both.
Now tell me, governor, and plainly too,   55
What think'st thou shall become of it and thee?
Ferneze.   This, Barabas: since things are in thy power,
I see no reason but of Malta's wrack,
Nor hope of thee but extreme cruelty,
Nor fear I death, nor will I flatter thee.   60
Barabas.   Governor, good words. Be not so furious.
'Tis not thy life which can avail me aught;
Yet you do live, and live for me you shall.
And as for Malta's ruin, think you not
'Twere slender policy for Barabas   65
To dispossess himself of such a place?
For sith, as once you said, within this isle,
In Malta here, that I have got my goods,
And in this city still have had success,
And now at length am grown your governor,   70
Yourselves shall see it shall not be forgot;
For, as a friend not known but in distress,
I'll rear up Malta, now remediless.
Ferneze.   Will Barabas recover Malta's loss?
Will Barabas be good to Christians?   75
Barabas.   What wilt thou give me, governor, to procure
A dissolution of the slavish bands
Wherein the Turk hath yoked your land and you?
What will you give me if I render you
The life of Calymath, surprise his men,   80
And in an out-house of the city shut
His soldiers till I have consumed 'em all with fire?
What will you give him that procureth this?
Ferneze.   Do but bring this to pass which thou pretendest,
Deal truly with us as thou intimatest,   85
And I will send amongst the citizens
And by my letters privately procure
Great sums of money for thy recompense.
Nay more, do this, and live thou governor still.
Barabas.   Nay, do thou this, Ferneze, and be free.   90
Governor, I enlarge thee. Live with me.
Go walk about the city; see thy friends.
Tush, send not letters to 'em; go thyself,
And let me see what money thou canst make.
Here is my hand that I'll set Malta free;   95

65 *slender* weak.   69 *still* always.
67 *sith* since.   84 *pretendest* propose.

And thus we cast it: to a solemn feast
I will invite young Selim Calymath,
Where be thou present only to perform
One stratagem that I'll impart to thee,
Wherein no danger shall betide thy life,　　　　　100
And I will warrant Malta free forever.

Ferneze.　　Here is my hand. Believe me, Barabas,
I will be there and do as thou desirest.
When is the time?

Barabas.　　　　　Governor, presently;
For Calymath, when he hath viewed the town,　　　　　105
Will take his leave and sail toward Ottoman.

Ferneze.　　Then will I, Barabas, about this coin,
And bring it with me to thee in the evening.

Barabas.　　Do so, but fail not. Now farewell, Ferneze.

　　　　　　　　　　　　　　[Exit Ferneze.]

And thus far roundly goes the business.　　　　　110
Thus, loving neither, will I live with both,
Making a profit of my policy,
And he from whom my most advantage comes
Shall be my friend.
This is the life we Jews are used to lead—　　　　　115
And reason too, for Christians do the like.
Well, now about effecting this device:
First to surprise great Selim's soldiers,
And then to make provision for the feast,
That at one instant all things may be done.　　　　　120
My policy detests prevention.
To what event my secret purpose drives
I know—and they shall witness with their lives.

　　　　　　　　　　　　　　Exit.

　　　　　　　Enter Calymath [and] Bashaws.　　　　　V,iii.

Calymath.　　Thus have we viewed the city, seen the sack,
And caused the ruins to be new-repaired,
That with our bombard's shot and basilisk
We rent in sunder at our entry.
And now I see the situation,　　　　　5
And how secure this conquered island stands,

V,iii.

96 *cast* contrive.
110 *roundly* successfully.
121 *prevention* forestalling, anticipation.

3 *bombard's . . . basilisk* varieties of cannon.

Environed with the Mediterranean sea,
Strong countermured with other petty isles,
And, toward Calabria, backed by Sicily,
Where Syracusian Dionysius reigned,   10
Two lofty turrets that command the town;
I wonder how it could be conquered thus.
                      Enter a Messenger.
Messenger.   From Barabas, Malta's governor, I bring
    A message unto mighty Calymath.
    Hearing his sovereign was bound for sea,   15
    To sail to Turkey, to great Ottoman,
    He humbly would entreat your majesty
    To come and see his homely citadel
    And banquet with him ere thou leav'st the isle.
Calymath.   To banquet with him in his citadel?   20
    I fear me, messenger, to feast my train
    Within a town of war so lately pillaged
    Will be too costly and too troublesome;
    Yet would I gladly visit Barabas,
    For well has Barabas deserved of us.   25
Messenger.   Selim, for that, thus saith the governor:
    That he hath in store a pearl so big,
    So precious, and withal so orient,
    As, be it valued but indifferently,
    The price thereof will serve to entertain   30
    Selim and all his soldiers for a month.
    Therefore he humbly would entreat your highness
    Not to depart till he has feasted you.
Calymath.   I cannot feast my men in Malta walls,
    Except he place his tables in the streets.   35
Messenger.   Know, Selim, that there is a monastery
    Which standeth as an out-house of the town;
    There will he banquet them, but thee at home,
    With all thy bashaws and brave followers.
Calymath.   Well, tell the governor we grant his suit.   40
    We'll in this summer evening feast with him.
Messenger.   I shall, my lord.
                                                        Exit.
Calymath.   And now, bold bashaws, let us to our tents,
    And meditate how we may grace us best
    To solemnize our governor's great feast.   45
                                                      Exeunt.

---

8 *countermured* See note at I,ii,384.   in Sicily, who lived from 430 to 367 B.C.
10 *Dionysius* famed tyrant of Syracuse

Enter Ferneze, Knights, [and Martin] Del Bosco.   V,iv.

Ferneze.   In this, my countrymen, be ruled by me.
  Have special care that no man sally forth
  Till you shall hear a culverin discharged
  By him that bears the linstock, kindled thus.
  Then issue out and come to rescue me,   5
  For happily I shall be in distress,
  Or you releasèd of this servitude.
First Knight.   Rather than thus to live as Turkish thralls,
  What will we not adventure?
Ferneze.   On, then; be gone.   10
Knights.   Farewell, brave governor.

                                    [Exeunt.]

                                    V,v.

*Enter [Barabas] with a hammer, above, very busy, [and Car-
penters].*

Barabas.   How stand the cords? How hang these hinges? Fast?
  Are all the cranes and pulleys sure?
First Carpenter.   All fast.
Barabas.   Leave nothing loose, all levelled to my mind.
  Why, now I see that you have art indeed.
  There, carpenters, divide that gold amongst you.   5
                        [He gives them gold.]
  Go, swill in bowls of sack and muscadine.
  Down to the cellar; taste of all my wines.
First Carpenter.   We shall, my lord, and thank you.
                        Exeunt [Carpenters].
Barabas.   And if you like them, drink your fill and die!
  For, so I live, perish may all the world!   10
  Now, Selim Calymath, return me word
  That thou wilt come, and I am satisfied.
                        Enter Messenger.
  Now, sirrah; what, will he come?
Messenger.   He will; and has commanded all his men
  To come ashore and march through Malta streets,   15
  That thou may'st feast them in thy citadel.
Barabas.   Then now are all things as my wish would have 'em.

V,iv.
  3 *culverin* a long-barrelled cannon.
  4 *linstock* pole used to fire the cannon.
  6 *happily* perhaps.

V,v.
  3 *levelled to my mind* in accordance
  with my plans.
  6 *sack* a white Spanish wine. *muscadine*
  muscatel, a strong sweet wine.
  10 *so* so that.

There wanteth nothing but the governor's pelf,
And see, he brings it.

Enter Ferneze.

Now, governor, the sum?

Ferneze.   With free consent, a hundred thousand pounds.   20
Barabas.   Pounds, say'st thou, governor? Well, since it is no more,
I'll satisfy myself with that. Nay, keep it still,
For if I keep not promise, trust not me.
And, governor, now partake my policy:
First, for his army, they are sent before,   25
Entered the monastery, and underneath
In several places are field-pieces pitched,
Bombards, whole barrels full of gunpowder,
That on the sudden shall dissever it
And batter all the stones about their ears,   30
Whence none can possibly escape alive.
Now, as for Calymath and his consorts,
Here have I made a dainty gallery,
The floor whereof, this cable being cut,
Doth fall asunder, so that it doth sink   35
Into a deep pit past recovery.
Here, hold that knife. And when thou seest he comes
And with his bashaws shall be blithely set,
A warning piece shall be shot off from the tower
To give thee knowledge when to cut the cord   40
And fire the house. Say, will not this be brave?

Ferneze.   O, excellent! Here, hold thee, Barabas.
I trust thy word; take what I promised thee.

Barabas.   No, governor. I'll satisfy thee first;
Thou shalt not live in doubt of anything.   45
Stand close, for here they come.

[*Ferneze retires.*]

Why, is not this
A kingly kind of trade, to purchase towns
By treachery and sell 'em by deceit?
Now tell me, worldlings, underneath the sun
If greater falsehood ever has been done?   50

Enter Calymath and Bashaws.

Calymath.   Come, my companion bashaws. See, I pray,
How busy Barabas is there above
To entertain us in his gallery.
Let us salute him. Save thee, Barabas!

Barabas.   Welcome, great Calymath.   55

Ferneze.   How the slave jeers at him.   [*Aside.*]

Barabas.   Will't please thee, mighty Selim Calymath,

18 *pelf* money.   49 *worldings* those devoted to worldly
24 *partake* share in the knowledge of.   values, e.g., money.

To ascend our homely stairs?
Calymath.   Ay Barabas.
    Come, bashaws, attend.
Ferneze.   [*coming forward*] Stay Calymath!   60
    For I will show thee greater courtesy
    Than Barabas would have afforded thee.
Knight. [*within*] Sound a charge there!
        A charge [*is sounded within*]. *The cable* [*is*] *cut* [*by Ferneze.*
        The floor of the gallery collapses, and Barabas falls into] *a*
        caldron [*which is*] *discovered* [*below. Enter Knights and Martin*
                        Del Bosco].
Calymath.   How now! What means this?
Barabas.   Help, help me, Christians, help.   65
Ferneze.   See, Calymath. This was devised for thee.
Calymath.   Treason, treason! Bashaws, fly!
Ferneze.   No, Selim, do not fly.
    See his end first, and fly then if thou canst.
Barabas.   O, help me, Selim! Help me, Christians!   70
    Governor, why stand you all so pitiless?
Ferneze.   Should I in pity of thy plaints or thee,
    Accursèd Barabas, base Jew, relent?
    No, thus I'll see thy treachery repaid,
    But wish thou hadst behaved thee otherwise.   75
Barabas.   You will not help me, then?
Ferneze.   No, villain, no.
Barabas.   And, villains, know you cannot help me now.
    Then, Barabas, breathe forth thy latest fate,
    And in the fury of thy torments strive
    To end thy life with resolution.   80
    Know, governor, 'twas I that slew thy son.
    I framed the challenge that did make them meet.
    Know, Calymath, I aimed thy overthrow,
    And had I but escaped this stratagem,
    I would have brought confusion on you all,   85
    Damned Christians, dogs, and Turkish infidels!
    But now begins the extremity of heat
    To pinch me with intolerable pangs.
    Die, life! Fly, soul! Tongue, curse thy fill, and die!
                                            [*He dies.*]
Calymath.   Tell me, you Christians, what doth this portend?   90
Ferneze.   This train he laid to have entrapped thy life.
    Now, Selim, note the unhallowed deeds of Jews.
    Thus he determined to have handlèd thee,
    But I have rather chose to save thy life.
Calymath.   Was this the banquet he prepared for us?   95
    Let's hence, lest further mischief be pretended.
    96 *pretended* intended.

Ferneze.   Nay, Selim, stay, for since we have thee here,
  We will not let thee part so suddenly.
  Besides, if we should let thee go, all's one,
  For with thy galleys couldst thou not get hence,   100
  Without fresh men to rig and furnish them.
Calymath.   Tush, governor, take thou no care for that.
  My men are all aboard
  And do attend my coming there by this.
Ferneze.   Why, heard'st thou not the trumpet sound a charge?   105
Calymath.   Yes; what of that?
Ferneze.   Why, then the house was fired,
  Blown up, and all thy soldiers massacred.
Calymath.   O, monstrous treason!
Ferneze.   A Jew's courtesy;
  For he that did by treason work our fall
  By treason hath delivered thee to us.   110
  Know, therefore, till thy father hath made good
  The ruins done to Malta and to us,
  Thou canst not part. For Malta shall be freed,
  Or Selim ne'er return to Ottoman.
Calymath.   Nay, rather, Christians, let me go to Turkey,   115
  In person there to meditate your peace.
  To keep me here will nought advantage you.
Ferneze.   Content thee, Calymath; here thou must stay
  And live in Malta prisoner, for come all the world
  To rescue thee, so will we guard us now,   120
  As sooner shall they drink the ocean dry
  Than conquer Malta or endanger us.
  So, march away, and let due praise be given
  Neither to fate nor fortune, but to heaven.

                                   [Exeunt.]

THE
MASSACRE
AT PARIS:

With the Death of the Duke
of Guise.

**As it was plaide by t'e right honourable the
Lord high _Admirall_ his Seruants.**

Written by _Christopher Marlow._

AT LONDON
Printed by _E. A._ for _Edward White_,dwelling neere
the little North doore of S.Paules
Church,at the signe of
the Gun.

THE MASSACRE AT PARIS

THE PLAYERS

Charles the Ninth, King of France
Duke of Anjou, his brother, after-
   wards King Henry the Third
King Henry of Navarre
Prince of Condé, his brother
Duke of Guise ⎫
Duke Dumaine ⎬ brothers
Cardinal of Lorraine ⎭
Son to the Duke of Guise
The Lord High Admiral
Duke Joyeux
Epernoun
Pleshé
Bartus
Two Lords of Poland
Gonzago
Retes
Mountsorrell
Mugeroun
A Cutpurse
Loreine, A Protestant preacher

Seroune
Ramus
Taleus
Friar
Surgeon
English Agent
Apothecary
Cossin, Captain of the guard
Protestants, Schoolmasters,
   Soldiers, Murderers,
   Attendants, etc.

Catherine, the Queen-Mother of
   France
Margaret, her daughter, wife of
   the King of Navarre
The Old Queen of Navarre
Duchess of Guise
Wife to Seroune
Maid to the Duchess of Guise

THE SCENE
Paris, Navarre.

Scene i.

Enter Charles, the French king; [Catherine,] the Queen-
Mother; [Henry,] the King of Navarre; [Margaret, Queen of
Navarre]; the Prince of Condé; the Lord High Admiral; and
the [old] Queen of Navarre; with others.

Charles. Prince of Navarre, my honorable brother,
  Prince Condé, and my good Lord Admiral,
  I wish this union and religious league,
  Knit in these hands, thus joined in nuptial rites,
  May not dissolve till death dissolve our lives;   5

i.

2 *Lord Admiral* Gaspard de Coligny
(1519–1572), a Huguenot leader who was
killed at the St. Bartholomew Day Massacre.

3–4 *union . . . rites* The marriage on
August 18, 1572, with which the play

opens, between King Henry of Navarre
and Margaret of Valois, sister of King
Charles IX of France, was designed to
end the struggle between the French
crown and the Huguenots, of whom
Henry was a leader.

And that the native sparks of princely love
That kindled first this motion in our hearts
May still be fuelled in our progeny.
Navarre.   The many favors that your grace hath shown
From time to time, but specially in this,   10
Shall bind me ever to your highness' will
In what Queen-Mother or your grace commands.
Catherine.   Thanks, son Navarre. You see we love you well,
That link you in marriage with our daughter here.
And, as you know, our difference in religion   15
Might be a means to cross you in your love.
Charles.   Well, madam, let that rest.
And now, my lords, the marriage rites performed,
We think it good to go and consummate
The rest with hearing of a holy mass.   20
Sister, I think yourself will bear us company.
Margaret.   I will, my good lord.
Charles.   The rest that will not go, my lords, may stay.
Come, mother,
Let us go to honor this solemnity.   25
Catherine.   Which I'll dissolve with blood and cruelty.   [*Aside.*]

> [*Exeunt all except*] *Navarre, the Prince of Condé,*
> *and the Lord High Admiral.*

Navarre.   Prince Condé and my good Lord Admiral,
Now Guise may storm, but do us little hurt,
Having the king, Queen-Mother on our sides,
To stop the malice of his envious heart,   30
That seeks to murder all the Protestants.
Have you not heard of late how he decreed—
If that the king had given consent thereto—
That all the Protestants that are in Paris
Should have been murderèd the other night?   35
Admiral.   My lord, I marvel that th'aspiring Guise
Dares once adventure, without the king's consent,
To meddle or attempt such dangerous things.
Condé.   My lord, you need not marvel at the Guise,
For what he doth the Pope will ratify—   40
In murder, mischief, or in tyranny.
Navarre.   But he that sits and rules above the clouds
Doth hear and see the prayers of the just,
And will revenge the blood of innocents
That Guise hath slain by treason of his heart   45
And brought by murder to their timeless ends.
Admiral.   My lord, but did you mark the Cardinal,

---

7 *motion* impulse.   16 *cross* frustrate.
8 *still* forever.   46 *timeless* premature.

The Guise's brother, and the Duke Dumaine,
How they did storm at these your nuptial rites,
Because the house of Bourbon now comes in   50
And joins your lineage to the crown of France?
Navarre.   And that's the cause that Guise so frowns at us
And beats his brains to catch us in his trap,
Which he hath pitched within his deadly toil.
Come, my lords, let's go to the church and pray   55
That God may still defend the right of France
And make His gospel flourish in this land.

                                          Exeunt.

✳

                    Enter the Duke of Guise.   ii.
Guise.   If ever Hymen loured at marriage rites
And had his altars decked with dusky lights,
If ever sun stained heaven with bloody clouds
And made it look with terror on the world,
If ever day were turned to ugly night   5
And night made semblance of the hue of hell,
This day, this hour, this fatal night
Shall fully show the fury of them all.
Apothecary!
                    Enter the Apothecary.
Apothecary.   My lord?   10
Guise.   Now shall I prove and guerdon to the full
The love thou bear'st unto the house of Guise.
Where are those perfumed gloves which I sent
To be poisoned? Hast thou done them? Speak!
Will every savor breed a pang of death?   15
Apothecary.   See where they be, my good lord,
And he that smells but to them dies.
Guise.   Then thou remainest resolute?
Apothecary.   I am, my lord, in what your grace commands,
Till death.   20
Guise.   Thanks, my good friend. I will requite thy love.
Go, then, present them to the Queen Navarre,
For she is that huge blemish in our eye
That makes these upstart heresies in France.
Be gone, my friend; present them to her straight.   25
                                          Exit Apothecary.
Soldier!

                              ii.

54 *pitched . . . toil* i.e., set within a   1 *Hymen* Greek god of marriage.
dangerous net.   11 *guerdon* reward.

Enter a Soldier.

Soldier.   My lord?

Guise.   Now come thou forth and play thy tragic part.
  Stand in some window opening near the street,
  And when thou seest the Admiral ride by,   30
  Discharge thy musket and perform his death.
  And then I'll guerdon thee with store of crowns.

Soldier.   I will, my lord.   *Exit Soldier.*

Guise.   Now, Guise, begins those deep-engendered thoughts
  To burst abroad those never-dying flames   35
  Which cannot be extinguished but by blood.
  Oft have I levelled, and at last have learned
  That peril is the chiefest way to happiness,
  And resolution honor's fairest aim.
  What glory is there in a common good   40
  That hangs for every peasant to achieve?
  That like I best that flies beyond my reach.
  Set me to scale the high pyramidès
  And thereon set the diadem of France;
  I'll either rend it with my nails to naught   45
  Or mount the top with my aspiring wings,
  Although my downfall be the deepest hell.
  For this I wake, when others think I sleep;
  For this I wait, that scorns attendance else;
  For this my quenchless thirst—whereon I build—   50
  Hath often pleaded kindred to the king;
  For this, this head, this heart, this hand, and sword
  Contrives, imagines, and fully executes
  Matters of import aimèd at by many,
  Yet understood by none;   55
  For this hath heaven engendered me of earth;
  For this, this earth sustains my body's weight,
  And with this weight I'll counterpoise a crown,
  Or with seditions weary all the world;
  For this from Spain the stately Catholics   60
  Sends Indian gold to coin me French ecues;
  For this have I a largess from the Pope,
  A pension and a dispensation too,
  And by that privilege to work upon,
  My policy hath framed religion.   65
  Religion! *O Diabole!*
  Fie, I am ashamed, however that I seem,
  To think a word of such a simple sound
  Of so great a matter should be made the ground.
  The gentle king, whose pleasure uncontrolled   70

---

37 *levelled* guessed at.   58 *counterpoise* balance by an oppos-
49 *wait* serve in attendance at court.   ing weight (that of his body).
                                      61 *French ecues* gold coins.

Weakeneth his body and will waste his realm
If I repair not what he ruinates,
Him, as a child, I daily win with words,
So that for proof he barely bears the name.
I execute, and he sustains the blame.　　　　　　75
The Mother-Queen works wonders for my sake,
And in my love entombs the hope of France,
Rifling the bowels of her treasury
To supply my wants and necessity.
Paris hath full five hundred colleges,　　　　　　80
As monasteries, priories, abbeys, and halls,
Wherein are thirty thousand able men,
Besides a thousand sturdy student Catholics,
And more. Of my knowledge, in one cloister keeps
Five hundred fat Franciscan friars and priests—　　85
All this and more, if more may be comprised,
To bring the will of our desires to end.
Then, Guise,
Since thou hast all the cards within thy hands,
To shuffle or cut, take this as surest thing,　　　　90
That, right or wrong, thou deal thyself a king.
Ay, but Navarre!
Navarre? 'Tis but a nook of France,
Sufficient yet for such a petty king,
That, with a rabblement of his heretics,
Blinds Europe's eyes and troubleth our estate.　　　95
Him will we— *Pointing to his sword.*
But first let's follow those in France
That hinder our possession to the crown.
As Caesar to his soldiers, so say I:
Those that hate me will I learn to loathe.　　　　100
Give me a look that, when I bend the brows,
Pale death may walk in furrows of my face,
A hand that with a grasp may gripe the world,
An ear to hear what my detractors say,　　　　　105
A royal seat, a scepter, and a crown,
That those which do behold, they may become
As men that stand and gaze against the sun.
The plot is laid, and things shall come to pass
Where resolution strives for victory.　　　*Exit.* 110

74 *for proof* i.e., of his statement.
92–93 *Ay . . . Navarre* Because of the
corrupt state of the text, it is impossible
to be certain of Marlowe's intention here.
Most editors have omitted the second
'Navarre' as a compositor's error. It is
more likely, however, that the first
'Navarre' refers to the king (echoing
'Guise' of line 88) and that the second
'Navarre' refers to the country, which
is but 'a nook of France.'

Enter the King of Navarre and Queen [Margaret], and his
Mother, [the old] Queen [of Navarre], the Prince of Condé,
the Admiral, and the Apothecary, [who meets them] with the
gloves, and gives them to the Old Queen.

Apothecary.   Madam, I beseech your grace to accept this simple gift.
Old Queen.   Thanks, my good friend. Hold, take thou this reward.
                              [*She gives him a purse.*]
Apothecary.   I humbly thank your majesty.
                              Exit Apothecary.
Old Queen.   Methinks the gloves have a very strong perfume,
    The scent whereof doth make my head to ache.   5
Navarre.   Doth not your grace know the man that gave them you?
Old Queen.   Not well, but do remember such a man.
Admiral.   Your grace was ill advised to take them then,
    Considering of these dangerous times.
Old Queen.   Help, son Navarre! I am poisonèd!   10
Margaret.   The heavens forbid your highness such mishap.
Navarre.   The late suspicion of the Duke of Guise
    Might well have moved your highness to beware
    How you did meddle with such dangerous gifts.
Margaret.   Too late it is, my lord, if that be true,   15
    To blame her highness, but I hope it be
    Only some natural passion makes her sick.
Old Queen.   O, no, sweet Margaret. The fatal poison
    Works within my head. My brain-pan breaks.
    My heart doth faint. I die.   *She dies.*   20
Navarre.   My mother poisoned here before my face!
    O gracious God, what times are these!
    O grant, sweet God, my days may end with hers,
    That I with her may die and live again.
Margaret.   Let not this heavy chance, my dearest lord—   25
    For whose effects my soul is massacred—
    Infect thy gracious breast with fresh supply
    To aggravate our sudden misery.
Admiral.   Come, my lords. Let us bear her body hence,
    And see it honored with just solemnity.   30
                    As they are going [out], the Soldier dischargeth his
                              musket at the Lord Admiral.
Condé.   What, are you hurt, my Lord High Admiral?
Admiral.   Ay, my good lord, shot through the arm.
Navarre.   We are betrayèd. Come my lords,
    And let us go tell the king of this.
Admiral.   These are

---

iii.
17 *natural passion* an ordinary physical
disorder (not caused by poisoning).

24 *live again* i.e., in heaven.
26 *effects* accomplishment.

The cursèd Guisians that do seek our death.   35
O, fatal was this marriage to us all.
They bear away the [Old] Queen and go out.

iv.

Enter King [Charles, Catherine, the] Queen-Mother, Duke of
Guise, Duke Anjou, Duke Dumaine.
Catherine. My noble son, and princely Duke of Guise,
  Now have we got the fatal straggling deer
  Within the compass of a deadly toil,
  And as we late decreed we may perform.
Charles. Madam, it will be noted through the world   5
  An action bloody and tyrannical,
  Chiefly since under safety of our word
  They justly challenge their protection.
  Besides, my heart relents that noblemen,
  Only corrupted in religion,   10
  Ladies of honor, knights and gentlemen,
  Should, for their conscience, taste such ruthless ends.
Anjou. Though gentle minds should pity others' pains,
  Yet will the wisest note their proper griefs,
  And rather seek to scourge their enemies   15
  Than be themselves base subjects to the whip.
Guise. Methinks my Lord Anjou hath well advised
  Your highness to consider of the thing,
  And rather choose to seek your country's good
  Than pity or relieve these upstart heretics.   20
Catherine. I hope these reasons may serve my princely son
  To have some care for fear of enemies.
Charles. Well, madam, I refer it to your majesty
  And to my nephew here, the Duke of Guise.
  What you determine, I will ratify.   25
Catherine. Thanks to my princely son. Then tell me, Guise,
  What order will you set down for the massacre?
Guise. Thus, madam:
  They that shall be actors in this massacre
  Shall wear white crosses on their burgonets   30
  And tie white linen scarfs about their arms.
  He that wants these and is suspect of heresy
  Shall die, be he king or emperor. Then I'll have

iv.
  2 *fatal* fated for death.   24 *nephew* i.e., blood relative.
  3 *toil* net.   30 *burgonets* helmets.
  14 *proper* own.

A peal of ordnance shot from the tower, at which
They all shall issue out and set the streets.   35
And then,
The watchword being given, a bell shall ring,
Which when they hear, they shall begin to kill,
And never cease until that bell shall cease;
Then breathe a while.

Enter the Admiral's Man.

Charles.   How now, fellow! What news?   40
Man.   And it please your grace, the Lord High Admiral,
   Riding the streets, was traitorously shot,
   And most humbly entreats your majesty
   To visit him, sick in his bed.
Charles.   Messenger, tell him I will see him straight.   45

                              Exit Messenger.

What shall we do now with the Admiral?
Catherine.   Your majesty were best go visit him
   And make a show as if all were well.
Charles.   Content; I will go visit the Admiral.
Guise.   And I will go take order for his death.   50

                              Exit Guise.

Enter the Admiral in his bed.

Charles.   How fares it with my Lord High Admiral?
   Hath he been hurt with villains in the street?
   I vow and swear, as I am king of France,
   To find and to repay the man with death,
   With death delayed and torments never used,   55
   That durst presume for hope of any gain
   To hurt the nobleman their sovereign loves.
Admiral.   Ah, my good lord, these are the Guisians,
   That seek to massacre our guiltless lives.
Charles.   Assure yourself, my good Lord Admiral,   60
   I deeply sorrow for your treacherous wrong;
   And that I am not more secure myself
   Than I am careful you should be preserved—
   Cossin! Take twenty of our strongest guard,
   And, under your direction, see they keep   65
   All treacherous violence from our noble friend,
   Repaying all attempts with present death
   Upon the cursèd breakers of our peace.
   And so be patient, good Lord Admiral,
   And every hour I will visit you.   70

35 *set* beset.
50, SD *Enter . . . bed* On the Elizabethan stage, the bed was literally thrust
out upon the stage already occupied by
the other characters.

52 *with* by.
62–63 *And . . . preserved* i.e., my concern for my own security is no greater
than my care for yours.

Admiral.   I humbly thank your royal majesty.

Exeunt

*Enter Guise, Anjou, Dumaine, Gonzago, Retes, Mountsorrell,
and Soldiers, to the massacre.*

Guise.   Anjou, Dumaine, Gonzago, Retes, swear
  By the argent crosses in your burgonets
  To kill all that you suspect of heresy.

Dumaine.   I swear by this to be unmerciful.

Anjou.   I am disguised, and none knows who I am,   5
  And therefore mean to murder all I meet.

Gonzago.   And so will I.

Retes.   And I.

Guise.   Away then! Break into the Admiral's house.

Retes.   Ay, let the Admiral be first dispatched.   10

Guise.   The Admiral,
  Chief standard-bearer to the Lutherans,
  Shall in the entrance of this massacre
  Be murdered in his bed.
  Gonzago, conduct them thither; and then   15
  Beset his house that not a man may live.

Anjou.   That charge is mine. Switzers, keep you the streets;
  And at each corner shall the king's guard stand.

Gonzago.   Come, sirs, follow me.

Exit Gonzago and others with him.

Anjou.   Cossin, the captain of the Admiral's guard,   20
  Placed by my brother, will betray his lord.
  Now, Guise, shall Catholics flourish once again;
  The head being off, the members cannot stand.

Retes.   But look, my lord; there's some in the Admiral's house.
[*The Admiral is discovered in his bed above; Gonzago and
others are with him.*]

Anjou.   In lucky time. Come, let us keep this lane   25
  And slay his servants that shall issue out.

Gonzago.   Where is the Admiral?

Admiral.   O, let me pray before I die.

Gonzago.   Then pray unto our Lady; kiss this cross.
[*They*] *stab him.*

v.

24, SD *The Admiral . . . him* The
staging here is difficult to determine,
but perhaps the curtains of the upper
stage opened to reveal the admiral lying
in his bed with the murderers around

him. Anjou and Guise remain upon the
platform below. The octavo SD reads
*Enter into the Admiral's house, and he
in his bed.*

Admiral.   O God, forgive my sins. [*He dies.*]   30
Guise.   Gonzago, what, is he dead?
Gonzago.   Ay, my lord.
Guise.   Then throw him down.
                    [*The Admiral's body is thrown down.*]
Anjou.   Now, cousin, view him well. It may be it is some other, and he
     escaped.   35
Guise.   Cousin, 'tis he; I know him by his look.
     See where my soldier shot him through the arm.
     He missed him near, but we have struck him now.
     Ah, base Chatillon and degenerate,
     Chief standard-bearer to the Lutherans,   40
     Thus, in despite of thy religion,
     The Duke of Guise stamps on thy lifeless bulk.
Anjou.   Away with him! Cut off his head and hands,
     And send them for a present to the Pope.
     And when this just revenge is finishèd,   45
     Unto Mount Faucon will we drag his corpse;
     And he that living hated so the cross
     Shall, being dead, be hanged thereon in chains.
Guise.   Anjou, Gonzago, Retes, if that you three
     Will be as resolute as I and Dumaine,   50
     There shall not a Huguenot breathe in France.
Anjou.   I swear by this cross, we'll not be partial,
     But slay as many as we can come near.
Guise.   Mountsorrell, go shoot the ordnance off,
     That they which have already set the street   55
     May know their watchword. Then toll the bell,
     And so let's forward to the massacre.
Mountsorrell.   I will, my lord.
                                         Exit Mountsorrell.
Guise.   And now, my lords, let us closely to our business.
Anjou.   Anjou will follow thee.   60
Dumaine.   And so will Dumaine.
                    The ordnance being shot off, the bell tolls.
Guise.   Come, then, let's away.
                                            Exeunt.

                                                                       vi.

The Guise enters again, with all the rest, with their swords
drawn, chasing the Protestants.

39 *Chatillon* the family name of Coli-   where the bodies of criminals commonly
gny, the Lord Admiral.   hung from gibbets.
46 *Mount Faucon* a hill near Paris   55 *set* beset.

Guise.   *Tuez, tuez, tuez!*
   Let none escape! Murder the Huguenots!
Anjou.   Kill them! Kill them!

                                                           Exeunt.
      Enter Loreine running, the Guise and the rest pursuing him.
Guise.   Loreine, Loreine! Follow Loreine! Sirrah,
   Are you a preacher of these heresies?   5
Loreine.   I am a preacher of the word of God,
   And thou a traitor to thy soul and him.
Guise.   'Dearly belovèd brother'—thus 'tis written. *He stabs him.*
Anjou.   Stay, my lord. Let me begin the psalm.
Guise.   Come, drag him away, and throw him in a ditch.   10
                  Exeunt [with the body of Loreine].

      Enter Mountsorrell and knocks at Seroune's door.   vii.
Seroune's Wife. [*within*] Who is that which knocks there?
Mountsorrell.   Mountsorrell, from the Duke of Guise.
Seroune's Wife. [*within*] Husband, come down. Here's one would
   speak with you from the Duke of Guise.
                        Enter Seroune.
Seroune.   To speak with me? From such a man as he?   5
Mountsorrell.   Ay, ay, for this, Seroune; and thou shalt ha't.
                              Showing his dagger.
Seroune.   O, let me pray before I take my death.
Mountsorrell.   Dispatch, then, quickly.
Seroune.   O Christ, my Savior!
Mountsorrell.   Christ, villain!   10
   Why darest thou presume to call on Christ
   Without the intercession of some saint?
   Sanctus Jacobus, he's my saint. Pray to him.
Seroune.   O, let me pray unto my God.
Mountsorrell.   Then take this with you.   15
         [*He*] *stab*[*s*] *him.* [*Seroune dies.*] *Exit* [*Mountsorrell*].

      Enter Ramus, in his study.   viii.
Ramus.   What fearful cries comes from the river Seine,

viii.

SD *Enter . . . study* Probably the curtains of the inner stage open to reveal
Ramus in his study. Petrus Ramus, or
Pierre de la Ramée (1515–1572), was a
logician who challenged the authority of
Aristotle, and whose writings Marlowe
may well have read at Cambridge, where
Ramus' system was the subject of much
controversy.

That frights poor Ramus sitting at his book!
I fear the Guisians have passed the bridge
And mean once more to menace me.
                    Enter Taleus.
Taleus.   Fly, Ramus, fly, if thou wilt save thy life.   5
Ramus.   Tell me, Taleus, wherefore should I fly?
Taleus.   The Guisians are
    Hard at thy door and mean to murder us.
    Hark, hark, they come! I'll leap out at the window.
Ramus.   Sweet Taleus, stay.   10
        *Enter Gonzago and Retes. [They stop Taleus as he is going
                    out.]*
Gonzago.   Who goes there?
Retes.   'Tis Taleus, Ramus' bedfellow.
Gonzago.   What art thou?
Taleus.   I am, as Ramus is, a Christian.
Retes.   O, let him go; he is a Catholic.   15
                                        Exit Taleus.
Gonzago.   Come, Ramus, more gold, or thou shalt have the stab.
Ramus.   Alas, I am a scholar. How should I have gold?
    All that I have is but my stipend from the king,
    Which is no sooner received but it is spent.
        *Enter the Guise and Anjou, [Dumaine, Mountsorrell, and
                    Soldiers].*
Anjou.   Who have you there?   20
Retes.   'Tis Ramus, the king's professor of logic.
Guise.   Stab him.
Ramus.   O, good, my lord,
    Wherein hath Ramus been so offensious?
Guise.   Marry, sir, in having a smack in all,
    And yet didst never sound anything to the depth.   25
    Was it not thou that scoff'dst the *Organon*
    And said it was a heap of vanities?
    He that will be a flat dichotomist
    And seen in nothing but epitomes
    Is in your judgment thought a learnèd man.   30
    And he, forsooth, must go and preach in Germany,
    Excepting against doctors' axioms,

---

6 *Taleus* Omer Talon (1510?–1610), who survived the massacre, was professor of rhetoric at Paris and a friend of Ramus.

15 The octavo SD *Enter Ramus* is omitted by all editors, as impossible to reconcile with any conception of how the scene might have been staged.

23 *offensious* offensive.

24 *smack in* superficial knowledge of.

26 *Organon* Aristotle's book of formal logic.

28 *dichotomist* logician who divides one class into two subclasses which are mutually exclusive of one another.

29 *seen in* versed in. *epitomes* abstracts or condensed versions.

32 *Excepting against* challenging in disagreement with.

And *ipse dixi* with this quiddity,
Argumentum testimonii est inartificiale.
To contradict which, I say Ramus shall die.　　　35
How answer you that? Your *nego argumentum*
Cannot serve, sirrah. Kill him.
Ramus.　O, good my lord, let me but speak a word.
Anjou.　Well, say on.
Ramus.　Not for my life do I desire this pause,　　　40
But in my latter hour to purge myself,
In that I know the things that I have wrote,
Which, as I hear, one Scheckius takes it ill
Because my places, being but three, contain all his.
I knew the *Organon* to be confused,　　　45
And I reduced it into better form.
And this for Aristotle will I say,
That he that despiseth him can ne'er
Be good in logic or philosophy.
And that's because the blockish Sorbonnists　　　50
Attribute as much unto their works
As to the service of the eternal God.
Guise.　Why suffer you that peasant to declaim?
Stab him, I say, and send him to his friends in hell.
Anjou.　Ne'er was there collier's son so full of pride.　　　55
　　　　　　　　　　　[He] kill[s] Ramus.
Guise.　My lord of Anjou, there are a hundred Protestants
Which we have chased into the river Seine,
That swim about and so preserve their lives.
How may we do? I fear me they will live.
Dumaine.　Go place some men upon the bridge　　　60
With bows and darts, to shoot them as they see,
And sink them in the river as they swim.
Guise.　'Tis well advised, Dumaine. Go see it straight be done.
　　　　　　　　　　　[Exit Dumaine.]
And in the meantime, my lord, could we devise
To get those pedants from the King Navarre,　　　65
That are tutors to him and the Prince of Condé—
Anjou.　For that, let me alone. Cousin, stay you here,
And when you see me in, then follow hard.

33 *ipse dixi* I have said it myself. *quiddity* quibble, nicety of argument.

34 *Argumentum . . . inartificiale* The argument of the evidence is not according to the rules.

36 *nego argumentum* I deny the argument.

43 *Scheckius* Jacob Schegk, a scholar of the university of Tubingen, with whom Ramus corresponded.

44 *places* grounds of proof in scholastic argument.

50 *Sorbonnists* students at the Sorbonne, then seat of the theological faculty of the University of Paris.

53 *peasant* Ramus was the son of a collier.

68, SD Probably Anjou moves to the door at the side and knocks, while Guise and the others remain in the back-

He knocketh [at the door], and enter the King of Navarre and
Prince of Condé, with their Schoolmasters.

How now, my lords! How fare you?

Navarre. My lord, they say that all the Protestants are massacred.   70

Anjou. Ay, so they are. But yet, what remedy?
I have done what I could to stay this broil.

Navarre. But yet, my lord, the report doth run,
That you were one that made this massacre.

Anjou. Who, I? You are deceived. I rose but now.   75

[Guise, who has been in the background, now comes forward,
with Gonzago, Retes, Mountsorrell and Soldiers.]

Guise. Murder the Huguenots! Take those pedants hence!

Navarre. Thou traitor, Guise, lay off thy bloody hands.

Condé. Come, let us go tell the king.

Exeunt [Condé and Navarre].

Guise. Come, sirs, I'll whip you to death with my poniard's point.

He kills [the Schoolmasters].

Anjou. Away with them both!   80

Exit Anjou [with the Soldiers bearing the bodies].

Guise. And now, sirs, for this night let our fury stay.
Yet will we not that the massacre shall end.
Gonzago, post you to Orleans,
Retes to Dieppe, Mountsorrell unto Rouen,
And spare not one that you suspect of heresy.   85
And now stay
That bell that to the devil's matins rings.
Now every man put off his burgonet,
And so convey him closely to his bed.

Enter Anjou, with two Lords of Poland.   ix.

Anjou. My lords of Poland, I must needs confess
The offer of your Prince Electors far
Beyond the reach of my deserts,
For Poland is, as I have been informed,
A martial people, worthy such a king   5
As hath sufficient counsel in himself
To lighten doubts and frustrate subtle foes,

---

ground of the inner stage. Navarre,
Condé (actually the young Prince of
Condé, confused by Marlowe with his
father, who was introduced earlier in
the play), and the schoolmasters come
through the side door on to the platform stage where they are murdered.
Guise and the others move forward at
line 76.

89 *closely* secretly.

And such a king whom practice long hath taught
To please himself with manage of the wars,
The greatest wars within our Christian bounds— 10
I mean our wars against the Muscovites,
And, on the other side, against the Turk,
Rich princes both, and mighty emperors.
Yet by my brother Charles, our king of France,
And by his grace's council, it is thought 15
That if I undertake to wear the crown
Of Poland, it may prejudice their hope
Of my inheritance to the crown of France—
For if th'Almighty take my brother hence,
By due descent the regal seat is mine. 24
With Poland, therefore, must I covenant thus:
That if, by death of Charles, the diadem
Of France be cast on me, then with your leaves
I may retire me to my native home.
If your commission serve to warrant this, 25
I thankfully shall undertake the charge
Of you and yours, and carefully maintain
The wealth and safety of your kingdom's right.
First Lord. All this and more, your highness shall command
For Poland's crown and kingly diadem. 30
Anjou. Then come, my lords, let's go.

✱

Exeunt.

Enter two [Men] with the Admiral's body. x.

First Man. Now, sirrah, what shall we do with the Admiral?
Second Man. Why, let us burn him for an heretic.
First Man. O, no! His body will infect the fire, and the fire the air,
and so we shall be poisoned with him.
Second Man. What shall we do then? 5
First Man. Let's throw him into the river.
Second Man. O, 'twill corrupt the water, and the water the fish, and
by the fish ourselves, when we eat them.
First Man. Then throw him into the ditch.
Second Man. No, no. To decide all doubts, be ruled by me. Let's [10
hang him here upon this tree.
First Man. Agreed. *They hang him [and then exeunt].*

*Enter the Duke of Guise, and [Catherine], the Queen-Mother,
and the Cardinal [of Lorraine, with Attendants].*

Guise. Now, madam, how like you our lusty Admiral?
Catherine. Believe me, Guise, he becomes the place so well
As I could long ere this have wished him there. 15
But come,
Let's walk aside. The air's not very sweet.

Guise.   No, by my faith, madam.
   Sirs, take him away and throw him in some ditch.
              [The Attendants] carry away the dead body.
   And now, madam, as I understand,   20
   There are a hundred Huguenots and more
   Which in the woods do hold their synagogue
   And daily meet about this time of day;
   And thither will I to put them to the sword.
Catherine.   Do so, sweet Guise. Let us delay no time,   25
   For if these stragglers gather head again
   And disperse themselves throughout the realm of France,
   It will be hard for us to work their deaths.
   Be gone. Delay no time, sweet Guise.
Guise.   Madam,
   I go as whirlwinds rage before a storm.   30
                      Exit Guise.
Catherine.   My lord of Lorraine, have you marked of late
   How Charles, our son, begins for to lament
   For the late night's work which my lord of Guise
   Did make in Paris amongst the Huguenots?
Cardinal.   Madam, I have heard him solemnly vow   35
   With the rebellious King of Navarre,
   For to revenge their deaths upon us all.
Catherine.   Ay, but, my lord, let me alone for that,
   For Catherine must have her will in France.
   As I do live, so surely shall he die,   40
   And Henry then shall wear the diadem.
   And if he grudge or cross his mother's will,
   I'll disinherit him and all the rest,
   For I'll rule France, but they shall wear the crown,
   And if they storm, I then may pull them down.   45
   Come, my lord, let us go.
                      Exeunt.

   Enter five or six Protestants with books, and kneel together.
     [Then] enter also the Guise [and others].
Guise.   Down with the Huguenots! Murder them!
First Protestant.   O Monsieur de Guise, hear me but speak.
Guise.   No, villain. That tongue of thine,
   That hath blasphemed the holy church of Rome,

x.

22 *synagogue* place of religious as-   26 *gather head* assemble their forces.
sembly.   42 *grudge* object to, complain about.

Shall drive no plaint into the Guise's ears,   5
To make the justice of my heart relent.
Tuez, tuez, tuez! Let none escape.
                              [*They*] *kill* [*all the Protestants*].
So, drag them away.
                              Exeunt [*with the bodies*].

✳

Enter King Charles, Navarre and Epernoun staying him. Enter
[Catherine], the Queen-Mother, [Pleshé], and the Cardinal [of
Lorraine, with Attendants].

Charles.   O, let me stay and rest me here a while.
   A griping pain hath seized upon my heart,
   A sudden pang, the messenger of death.
Catherine.   O, say not so. Thou kill'st thy mother's heart.
Charles.   I must say so. Pain forceth me complain.   5
Navarre.   Comfort yourself, my lord, and have no doubt
   But God will sure restore you to your health.
Charles.   O no, my loving brother of Navarre.
   I have deserved a scourge, I must confess;
   Yet is their patience of another sort   10
   Than to misdo the welfare of their king.
   God grant my nearest friends may prove no worse.
   O, hold me up! My sight begins to fail!
   My sinews shrink; my brains turn upside down;
   My heart doth break. I faint and die.   *He dies.*   15
Catherine.   What, art thou dead, sweet son? Speak to thy mother.
   O no, his soul is fled from out his breast,
   And he nor hears nor sees us what we do.
   My lords, what resteth there now for to be done,
   But that we presently dispatch ambassadors   20
   To Poland, to call Henry back again
   To wear his brother's crown and dignity.
   Epernoun, go see it presently be done,
   And bid him come without delay to us.
Epernoun.   Madam, I will.   25
                              Exit Epernoun.
Catherine.   And now, my lords, after these funerals be done,
   We will, with all the speed we can, provide
   For Henry's coronation from Polony.

xii.

10–11 *Yet . . . king* i.e., the patience   them) will not permit them to murder
(feelings) of those by whom I deserve to   their king.
be scourged (because I have wronged

Come, let us take his body hence.

All go out, [bearing the body of King Charles] but
Navarre and Pleshé [who remain].

Navarre.   And now, Navarre, whilst that these broils do last,   30
My opportunity may serve me fit
To steal from France and hie me to my home,
For here's no safety in the realm for me.
And now that Henry is called from Poland,
It is my due, by just succession.   35
And therefore, as speedily as I can perform,
I'll muster up my army secretly,
For fear that Guise, joined with the king of Spain,
Might seek to cross me in mine enterprise.
But God, that always doth defend the right,   40
Will show his mercy and preserve us still.

Pleshé.   The virtues of our true religion
Cannot but march with many graces more,
Whose army shall discomfort all your foes,
And, at the length, in Pampelonia crown—   45
In spite of Spain and all the popish power
That holds it from your highness wrongfully—
Your majesty her rightful lord and sovereign.

Navarre.   Truth, Pleshé; and God so prosper me in all,
As I intend to labor for the truth   50
And true profession of his holy word.
Come Pleshé, let's away whilst time doth serve.

Exeunt.

Sound trumpets within, and then all cry 'Vive le Roi' two or
three times. Enter Anjou, crowned [as King Henry the Third],
Queen [Catherine], Cardinal [of Lorraine], Duke of Guise,
Epernoun, [Mugeroun], a Cutpurse and others.

All.   Vive le Roi! Vive le Roi!   *Sound trumpets.*

Catherine.   Welcome from Poland, Henry, once again.
Welcome to France, thy father's royal seat.
Here hast thou a country void of fears,
A warlike people to maintain thy right,   5
A watchful senate for ordaining laws,

---

30 *Navarre* Most editors have considered this a compositor's error and
emended to 'Pleshé,' but Navarre may be
communing with himself. *broils* discords.
42 *Pleshé* This is Philippe Du-Plessis-

Mornay, the Huguenot leader, and friend
of Sir Philip Sidney.
45 *Pampelonia* Pamplona, the capital
city of Navarre.

A loving mother to preserve thy state,
And all things that a king may wish besides;
All this and more hath Henry with his crown.
Cardinal.   And long may Henry enjoy all this, and more!   10
All.   *Vive le Roi! Vive le Roi!*   *Sound trumpets.*
Henry.   Thanks to you all. The guider of all crowns
  Grant that our deeds may well deserve your loves.
  And so they shall, if fortune speed my will,
  And yield your thoughts to height of my deserts.   15
  What says our minions? Think they Henry's heart
  Will not both harbor love and majesty?
  Put off that fear; they are already joined.
  No person, place, or time, or circumstance
  Shall slack my love's affection from his bent.   20
  As now you are, so shall you still persist,
  Removeless from the favors of your king.
Mugeroun.   We know that noble minds change not their thoughts
  For wearing of a crown, in that your grace
  Hath worn the Poland diadem before   25
  You were invested in the crown of France.
Henry.   I tell thee, Mugeroun, we will be friends,
  And fellows too, whatever storms arise.
Mugeroun.   Then may it please your majesty to give me leave
  To punish those that do profane this holy feast.   30
Henry.   How meanst thou that?
              [Mugeroun] cuts off the Cutpurse's ear, for cutting
                            the gold buttons off his cloak.
Cutpurse.   **O** Lord, mine ear!
Mugeroun.   Come, sir, give me my buttons and here's your ear.
Guise.   Sirrah, take him away.
Henry.   Hands off, good fellow. I will be his bail   35
  For this offence. Go, sirrah, work no more
  Till this our coronation day be past.
  And now,
  Our solemn rites of coronation done,
  What now remains but for a while to feast   40
  And spend more days in barriers, tourney, tilt,
  And like disports, such as do fit the court?
  Let's go, my lords; our dinner stays for us.
            Exeunt all but [Catherine], the Queen-[Mother], and
                        the Cardinal [of Lorraine].
Catherine.   My Lord Cardinal of Lorraine, tell me,
  How likes your grace my son's pleasantness?   45

---

xiii.

16 *minions* favorites.
20 *bent* purpose, inclination.

41 *barriers, tourney, tilt* various military sports performed before spectators.
42 *disports* entertainments.

His mind, you see, runs on his minions,
And all his heaven is to delight himself.
And whilst he sleeps securely thus in ease,
Thy brother Guise and we may now provide
To plant ourselves with such authority   50
As not a man may live without our leaves.
Then shall the Catholic faith of Rome
Flourish in France and none deny the same.
Cardinal.   Madam, as in secrecy I was told,
My brother Guise hath gathèrèd a power of men   55
Which are, he saith, to kill the Puritans,
But 'tis the house of Bourbon that he means.
Now, madam, must you insinuate with the king
And tell him that 'tis for his country's good
And common profit of religion.   60
Catherine.   Tush, man, let me alone with him
To work the way to bring this thing to pass.
And if he do deny what I do say,
I'll dispatch him with his brother presently,
And then shall Monsieur wear the diadem.   65
Tush, all shall die unless I have my will,
For while she lives, Catherine will be queen.
Come, my lord, let us go seek the Guise
And then determine of this enterprise.

                                             Exeunt.

Duchess.   Go fetch me pen and ink—
Maid.   I will, madam.

                                          Exit Maid.

Duchess.   That I may write unto my dearest lord.
Sweet Mugeroun, 'tis he that hath my heart,
And Guise usurps it 'cause I am his wife.
Fain would I find some means to speak with him,   5
But cannot, and therefore am enforced to write,
That he may come and meet me in some place
Where we may one enjoy the other's sight.
          Enter the Maid with [pen], ink and paper.
So, set it down and leave me to myself.
               [Exit Maid. The Duchess] writes.
O, would to God this quill that here doth write   10
Had late been plucked from out fair Cupid's wing,
That it might print these lines within his heart.
<hr>
65 *Monsieur* her son, François duc d'Alençon.

Enter the Guise.

Guise.   What, all alone, my love? And writing too?
  I prithee, say to whom thou writes.
Duchess.   To such
  A one, my lord, as when she reads my lines   15
  Will laugh, I fear me, at their good array.
Guise.   I pray thee, let me see.
Duchess.   O, no, my lord. A woman only must
  Partake the secrets of my heart.
Guise.   But, madam, I must see. *He [seizes the paper].*   20
  Are these your secrets that no man must know?
Duchess.   O, pardon me, my lord!
Guise.   Thou trothless and unjust! What lines are these?
  Am I grown old, or is thy lust grown young,
  Or hath my love been so obscured in thee
  That others need to comment on my text?   25
  Is all my love forgot, which held thee dear,
  Ay, dearer than the apple of mine eye?
  Is Guise's glory but a cloudy mist
  In sight and judgment of thy lustful eye?   30
  Mort Dieu! Wert not the fruit within thy womb,
  Of whose increase I set some longing hope,
  This wrathful hand should strike thee to the heart.
  Hence strumpet! Hide thy head for shame,
  And fly my presence, if thou look to live.   35
                                    Exit [Duchess].

  O wicked sex, perjurèd and unjust!
  Now do I see that from the very first
  Her eyes and looks sowed seeds of perjury.
  But villain, he to whom these lines should go,
  Shall buy her love even with his dearest blood.   *Exit.* 40

Enter the King of Navarre, Pleshé and Bartus, and their train,
                    with drums and trumpets.

Navarre.   My lords, sith in a quarrel just and right
  We undertake to manage these our wars
  Against the proud disturbers of the faith—
  I mean the Guise, the Pope, and king of Spain—
  Who set themselves to tread us under foot   5
  And rent our true religion from this land;
  But for you know our quarrel is no more

xv.

1 *sith* since.   6 *rent* rend, tear.

But to defend their strange inventions,
Which they will put us to with sword and fire,
We must with resolute minds resolve to fight   10
In honor of our God and country's good.
Spain is the council-chamber of the Pope;
Spain is the place where he makes peace and war,
And Guise for Spain hath now incensed the king
To send his power to meet us in the field.   15

Bartus.   Then in this bloody brunt they may behold
The sole endeavor of your princely care,
To plant the true succession of the faith,
In spite of Spain and all his heresies.

Navarre.   The power of vengeance now encamps itself   20
Upon the haughty mountains of my breast,
Plays with her gory colors of revenge,
Whom I respect as leaves of boasting green,
That change their color when the winter comes,
When I shall vaunt as victor in revenge.   25

Enter a Messenger.

How now, sirrah! What news?

Messenger.   My lord, as by our scouts we understand,
A mighty army comes from France with speed,
Which are already mustered in the land,
And means to meet your highness in the field.   30

Navarre.   In God's name, let them come!
This is the Guise that hath incensed the king
To levy arms and make these civil broils.
But canst thou tell who is their general?

Messenger.   Not yet, my lord, for thereon do they stay;   35
But, as report doth go, the Duke of Joyeux
Hath made great suit unto the king therefor.

Navarre.   It will not countervail his pains, I hope.
I would the Guise in his stead might have come,
But he doth lurk within his drowsy couch   40
And makes his footstool on security.
So he be safe, he cares not what becomes
Of king or country—no, not for them both.
But come, my lords, let us away with speed
And place ourselves in order for the fight.   45

Exeunt.

8 *defend* repel.
19 *Spain* i.e., the king of Spain.
36 *Duke of Joyeux* Anne de Joyeuse,
a favorite of King Henry III; in 1586
he led the campaign against the Huguenots in Guienne. He was slain when his
army was defeated at Coutras in 1587.
   38 *countervail his pains* be worth his
efforts.

Enter King Henry, Duke of Guise, Epernoun, and Duke
Joyeux.

Henry.   My sweet Joyeux, I make thee general
Of all my army now in readiness
To march against the rebellious King Navarre.
At thy request I am content thou go,
Although my love to thee can hardly suffer,   5
Regarding still the danger of thy life.

Joyeux.   Thanks to your majesty. And so I take my leave.
Farewell to my lord of Guise and Epernoun.

Guise.   Health and hearty farewell to my Lord Joyeux.

                                              Exit Joyeux.

Henry.   So kindly, cousin of Guise, you and your wife   10
Do both salute our lovely minions.
Remember you the letter, gentle sir,
Which your wife writ
To my dear minion and her chosen friend?

                          He makes horns at the Guise.

Guise.   How now, my lord! Faith, this is more than need.   15
Am I thus to be jested at and scorned?
'Tis more than kingly or imperious;
And sure, if all the proudest kings
In Christendom should bear me such derision,
They should know how I scorned them and their mocks.   20
I love your minions! Dote on them yourself!
I know none else but holds them in disgrace.
And here, by all the saints in heaven, I swear
That villain for whom I bear this deep disgrace,
Even for your words that have incensed me so,   25
Shall buy that strumpet's favor with his blood.
Whether he have dishonored me or no,
Par la mort de Dieu, il mourra.

                                                    Exit.

Henry.   Believe me, this jest bites sore.

Epernoun.   My lord, 'twere good to make them friends,   30
For his oaths are seldom spent in vain.

                      Enter Mugeroun.

Henry.   How now, Mugeroun! Met'st thou not the Guise at the door?

Mugeroun.   Not I, my lord. What if I had?

Henry.   Marry, if thou hadst, thou mightst have had the stab,
For he hath solemnly sworn thy death.   35

xvi.

5 *suffer* permit it.   17 *imperious* fitting for an emperor.
14, SD *makes horns* makes a conven-   28 *Par . . . mourra* By God's death,
tional gesture which accuses the Guise he shall die.
of being a cuckold.

Mugeroun.   I may be stabbed and live till he be dead,
    But wherefore bears he me such deadly hate?
Henry.   Because his wife bears thee such kindly love.
Mugeroun.   If that be all, the next time that I meet her
    I'll make her shake off love with her heels.   40
    But which way is he gone? I'll go make a walk
    On purpose from the court to meet with him.

                                                          Exit.

Henry.   I like not this. Come, Epernoun,
    Let's go seek the duke and make them friends.

                                                          Exeunt.

                                                          xvii.

Alarums within, [*and a cry,*] '*The Duke Joyeux* [*is*] **slain.**'
    Enter the King of Navarre, [*Bartus,*] *and his train.*
Navarre.   The duke is slain and all his power dispersed,
    And we are graced with wreaths of victory.
    Thus God, we see, doth ever guide the right,
    To make His glory great upon the earth.
Bartus.   The terror of this happy victory,   5
    I hope, will make the king surcease his hate,
    And either never manage army more,
    Or else employ them in some better cause.
Navarre.   How many noblemen have lost their lives
    In prosecution of these cruel arms   10
    Is ruth and almost death to call to mind.
    But God, we know, will always put them down
    That lift themselves against the perfect truth,
    Which I'll maintain so long as life doth last,
    And with the queen of England join my force   15
    To beat the papal monarch from our lands
    And keep those relics from our countries' coasts.
    Come, my lords. Now that this storm is overpassed,
    Let us away with triumph to our tents.

                                                          Exeunt.

xvii.

   6 *surcease* give up.
   15 *queen of England* i.e., Queen Elizabeth, with whom Henry of Navarre
sought constantly to ally himself against
the Catholic powers.

   17 *relics* possibly (1) the religious relics
worshipped by Catholics, or (2) the Catholics themselves as relics of a former
era. The exact meaning is uncertain.

Enter a Soldier with a musket. [He conceals himself.]

Soldier. Now sir, to you that dares make a duke a cuckold and use a
counterfeit key to his privy chamber: though you take out none but
your own treasure, yet you put in that displeases him, and fill up his
room that he should occupy. Herein, sir, you forestall the market and
set up your standing where you should not. But you will say you   [5
leave him room enough besides. That's no answer. He's to have the
choice of his own free land. If it be not too free—there's the question!
Now, sir, where he is your landlord, you take upon you to be his and
will needs enter by default. What though you were once in possession? Yet coming upon you unawares, he frayed you out again.   [10
Therefore your entry is mere intrusion. This is against the law, sir,
and though I come not to keep possession—as I would I might—yet
I come to keep you out, sir. [*He sees Mugeroun coming.*] You are
welcome, sir. Have at you.

Enter Mugeroun. The Soldier shoots him.

Mugeroun. Traitorous Guise! Ah, thou hast murdered me.   15
            [*He dies.*]

Enter Guise [with Attendants].

Guise. Hold thee, tall soldier. Take this and fly.
     [*He gives the Soldier a purse. Exit Soldier.*]
Thus fall, imperfect exhalation
Which our great sun of France could not effect,
A fiery meteor in the firmament.
Lie there, the king's delight and Guise's scorn!   20
Revenge it, Henry, if thou list or dar'st;
I did it only in despite of thee.
Fondly hast thou incensed the Guise's soul,
That of itself was hot enough to work
Thy just digestion with extremest shame.   25
The army I have gathered now shall aim
More at thy end than extirpation,
And when thou think'st I have forgotten this
And that thou most reposest on my faith,
Then will I wake thee from thy foolish dream   30
And let thee see thyself my prisoner.
   Exeunt [with Attendants bearing out the body].

Enter King [Henry] and Epernoun.

Henry. My lord of Guise, we understand
That you have gatherèd a power of men.

---

xviii.

The text from the opening of this
scene to line 31 follows the 'Collier
Leaf.' See Textual Notes, p. 423.

3 *that* that which.

5 *standing* position, with a possible
secondary meaning which may be a rare
instance of Marlovian bawdry.

10 *frayed* frightened.

16 *tall* brave.

What your intent is yet we cannot learn,
But we presume it is not for our good.   35
Guise.   Why, I am no traitor to the crown of France.
What I have done, 'tis for the Gospel's sake.
Epernoun.   Nay, for the Pope's sake and thine own benefit.
What peer in France but thou, aspiring Guise,
Durst be in arms without the king's consent?   40
I challenge thee for treason in the cause.
Guise.   Ah, base Epernoun! Were not his highness here,
Thou shouldst perceive the Duke of Guise is moved.
Henry.   Be patient, Guise, and threat not Epernoun,
Lest thou perceive the king of France be moved.   45
Guise.   Why, I am a prince of the Valois's line,
Therefore an enemy to the Bourbonites;
I am a juror in the holy league,
And therefore hated of the Protestants.
What should I do but stand upon my guard?   50
And being able, I'll keep an host in pay.
Epernoun.   Thou able to maintain an host in pay,
That livest by foreign exhibition!
The Pope and king of Spain are thy good friends;
Else all France knows how poor a duke thou art.   55
Henry.   Ay, those are they that feed him with their gold
To countermand our will and check our friends.
Guise.   My lord, to speak more plainly, thus it is:
Being animated by religious zeal,
I mean to muster all the power I can   60
To overthrow those factious Puritans.
And know, my lord, the Pope will sell his triple crown,
Ay, and the Catholic Philip, king of Spain,
Ere I shall want, will cause his Indians
To rip the golden bowels of America.   65
Navarre, that cloaks them underneath his wings,
Shall feel the house of Lorraine is his foe.
Your highness needs not fear mine army's force;
'Tis for your safety and your enemies' wrack.
Henry.   Guise, wear our crown and be thou king of France,   70
And, as dictator, make or war or peace,
Whilst I cry *placet* like a senator.

46 *Valois* the ruling family of France.
The Guise, however, was not a member
of this family, but rather of the house
of Lorraine.

47 *Bourbonites* Bourbons, family of
King Henry of Navarre who succeeded
the Valois dynasty upon the French
throne.

48 *holy league* a religious and political
organization headed by the Guise family,
designed to destroy the Huguenots and
to re-establish Catholic unity in France.

51 *host* army.

53 *exhibition* support. The Guise received large sums of money from Spain
and the Papacy.

57 *check* keep under control.

66 *them* i.e., the Huguenots, protected
by Navarre.

69 *wrack* destruction.

I cannot brook thy haughty insolence.
Dismiss thy camp, or else by our edict
Be thou proclaimed a traitor throughout France.   75
Guise.   The choice is hard; I must dissemble.   [*Aside.*]
My lord, in token of my true humility
And simple meaning to your majesty,
I kiss your grace's hand and take my leave,
Intending to dislodge my camp with speed.   80
Henry.   Then farewell, Guise. The king and thou are friends.
                                             Exit Guise.
Epernoun.   But trust him not my lord; for had your highness
Seen with what a pomp he entered Paris,
And how the citizens with gifts and shows
Did entertain him   85
And promisèd to be at his command—
Nay, they feared not to speak in the streets
That the Guise durst stand in arms against the king
For not effecting of his holiness' will.
Henry.   Did they of Paris entertain him so?   90
Then means he present treason to our state.
Well, let me alone. Who's within there?
          Enter [an Attendant], with a pen and ink.
Make a discharge of all my council straight,
And I'll subscribe my name and seal it straight.
                              [*The Attendant writes.*]
My head shall be my council. They are false.   95
And, Epernoun, I will be ruled by thee.
Epernoun.   My lord,
I think, for safety of your royal person,
It would be good the Guise were made away,
And so to quit your grace of all suspect.   100
Henry.   First, let us set our hand and seal to this.   *He writes.*
And then I'll tell thee what I mean to do.
So; convey this to the council presently.
                              Exit [Attendant].
And, Epernoun, though I seem mild and calm,
Think not but I am tragical within.   105
I'll secretly convey me unto Blois,
For now that Paris takes the Guise's part,
Here is no staying for the king of France,
Unless he mean to be betrayed and die.
But as I live, so sure the Guise shall die.   110
                              Exeunt.

89 *effecting* carrying out.   105 *tragical* full of strong passion.
100 *quit* free. *suspect* suspicion.

Enter the King of Navarre, reading a letter, and Bartus.   xix.

Navarre.   My lord, I am advertisèd from France
  That the Guise hath taken arms against the king
  And that Paris is revolted from his grace.
Bartus.   Then hath your grace fit opportunity
  To show your love unto the king of France,   5
  Offering him aid against his enemies,
  Which cannot but be thankfully received.
Navarre.   Bartus, it shall be so. Post then to France,
  And there salute his highness in our name.
  Assure him all the aid we can provide   10
  Against the Guisians and their 'complices.
  Bartus, be gone. Commend me to his grace,
  And tell him, ere it be long, I'll visit him.
Bartus.   I will, my lord.

                                            Exit.

                     Enter Pleshé.

Navarre.   Pleshé.   15
Pleshé.   My lord.
Navarre.   Pleshé, go muster up our men with speed,
  And let them march away to France amain,
  For we must aid the king against the Guise.
  Be gone, I say; 'tis time that we were there.   20
Pleshé.   I go, my lord.

                                         [Exit.]

Navarre.   That wicked Guise, I fear me much, will be
  The ruin of that famous realm of France,
  For his aspiring thoughts aim at the crown,
  And takes his vantage on religion,   25
  To plant the Pope and popelings in the realm
  And bind it wholly to the see of Rome.
  But if that God do prosper mine attempts
  And send us safely to arrive in France,
  We'll beat him back and drive him to his death,   30
  That basely seeks the ruin of his realm.

                                         Exit.

                                             xx.

Enter [Cossin], the Captain of the Guard and three Murderers.
Cossin.   Come on, sirs. What, are you resolutely bent
  Hating the life and honor of the Guise?

xix.
  11 *'complices* accomplices.
  18 *amain* with haste.
  25 *vantage* opportunity.

xx.
  1 *resolutely bent* determined absolutely.

What, will you not fear, when you see him come?
First Murderer.   Fear him, said you? Tush, were he here, we would kill
   him presently.   5
Second Murderer.   O, that his heart were leaping in my hand.
Third Murderer.   But when will he come, that we may murder him?
Cossin.   Well, then, I see you are resolute.
First Murderer.   Let us alone; I warrant you.
Cossin.   Then, sirs, take your standings within this chamber,   10
   For anon the Guise will come.
All Three Murderers.   You will give us our money?
Cossin.   Ay, ay, fear not. Stand close. So; be resolute.
   Now falls the star whose influence governs France,
   Whose light was deadly to the Protestants.   15
   Now must he fall and perish in his height.
         Enter King [Henry] and Epernoun.
Henry.   Now, captain of my guard, are these murderers ready?
Cossin.   They be, my good lord.
Henry.   But are they resolute and armed to kill,
   Hating the life and honor of the Guise?   20
Cossin.   I warrant ye, my lord.
                                [Exit.]
Henry.   Then come, proud Guise, and here disgorge thy breast,
   Surcharged with surfeit of ambitious thoughts.
   Breathe out that life wherein my death was hid,
   And end thy endless treasons with thy death.   25
         Enter the Guise and knocketh.
Guise.   Holà, varlet, hé! Epernoun, where is the king?
Epernoun.   Mounted his royal cabinet.
Guise.   I prithee, tell him that the Guise is here.
Epernoun.   And please your grace, the Duke of Guise
   Doth crave access unto your highness.   30
Henry.   Let him come in.
   Come, Guise, and see thy traitorous guile outreached,
   And perish in the pit thou mad'st for me.
            The Guise comes to the King.
Guise.   Good morrow to your majesty.
Henry.   Good morrow to my loving cousin of Guise.   35
   How fares it this morning with your excellence?
Guise.   I heard your majesty was scarcely pleased
   That in the court I bear so great a train.
Henry.   They were to blame that said I was displeased,
   And you, good cousin, to imagine it.   40
   'Twere hard with me if I should doubt my kin

---

10 *standings* positions.
27 *Mounted . . . cabinet* probably sitting upon a raised dais in his throne room. The stage business here is very confused, but probably King Henry has retired to the rear of the stage and is seated upon his throne when the Guise enters upon the platform stage and knocks.

Or be suspicious of my dearest friends.
Cousin, assure you I am resolute,
Whatsoever any whisper 'in mine ears,
Not to suspect disloyalty in thee.   45
And so, sweet coz, farewell.

        Exit King [Henry, with Epernoun].

Guise. So;
Now sues the king for favor to the Guise,
And all his minions stoop when I command.
Why, this 'tis to have an army in the field.   50
Now by the holy sacrament I swear,
As ancient Romans o'er their captive lords,
So will I triumph o'er this wanton king,
And he shall follow my proud chariot's wheels.
Now do I but begin to look about,   55
And all my former time was spent in vain.
Hold, sword,
For in thee is the Duke of Guise's hope.

        Enter Third Murderer.

Villain, why dost thou look so ghastly? Speak.
Third Murderer. O, pardon me, my Lord of Guise.   60
Guise. Pardon thee? Why, what hast thou done?
Third Murderer. O, my lord, I am one of them that is set **to murder**
you.
Guise. To murder me, villain?
Third Murderer. Ay, my lord. The rest have ta'en their standings [65
in the next room; therefore, good my lord, go not forth.
Guise. Yet Caesar shall go forth.
Let mean conceits and baser men fear death.
Tut, they are peasants; I am Duke of Guise,
And princes with their looks engender fear.   70
First Murderer. [within] Stand close; he is coming. I know him by his
voice.
Guise. As pale as ashes? Nay, then 'tis time to look about.

      [Enter First and Second Murderers.]

All the Murderers. Down with him! Down with him!

        They stab him.

Guise. O, I have my death's wound. Give me leave to speak.   75
Second Murderer. Then pray to God, and ask forgiveness of the king.
Guise. Trouble me not. I ne'er offended him,
Nor will I ask forgiveness of the king.
O, that I have not power to stay my life,
Nor immortality to be revenged!   80
To die by peasants, what a grief is this!
Ah, Sixtus, be revenged upon the king!

---

53 *wanton* careless, effeminate.   82 *Sixtus* Pope Sixtus V.
68 *mean conceits* men of lowly mind.

Philip and Parma, I am slain for you!
Pope excommunicate, Philip depose
The wicked branch of cursed Valois his line.   85
Vive la messe! Perish Huguenots!
Thus Caesar did go forth, and thus he died.

                                       He dies.

           Enter [Cossin,] the Captain of the Guard.
Cossin.   What, have you done?
  Then stay a while, and I'll go call the king.
  But see where he comes.   90
       [Enter King Henry, Epernoun, and Attendants.]
  My lord, see where the Guise is slain.
Henry.   Ah, this sweet sight is physic to my soul.
  Go fetch his son for to behold his death.

                           [Exit an Attendant.]

  Surcharged with guilt of thousand massacres,
  Monsieur of Lorraine, sink away to hell.   95
  And in remembrance of those bloody broils
  To which thou didst allure me, being alive,
  And here in presence of you all, I swear
  I ne'er was king of France until this hour.
  This is the traitor that hath spent my gold   100
  In making foreign wars and civil broils.
  Did he not draw a sort of English priests
  From Douai to the seminary at Rheims,
  To hatch forth treason 'gainst their natural queen?
  Did he not cause the king of Spain's huge fleet   105
  To threaten England and to menace me?
  Did he not injure Monsieur that's deceased?
  Hath he not made me, in the Pope's defense,
  To spend the treasure that should strength my land
  In civil broils between Navarre and me?   110
  Tush, to be short, he meant to make me monk,
  Or else to murder me, and so be king.
  Let Christian princes that shall hear of this—
  As all the world shall know our Guise is dead—
  Rest satisfied with this: that here I swear,   115
  Ne'er was there king of France so yoked as I.

---

83 *Philip* King Philip II of Spain. *Parma* Alexander Ferneze, Prince of Parma, leader of the Spanish forces in the low countries.

86 *la messe* the Catholic mass.

103 *Douai . . . Rheims* English colleges had been established at Douai and Rheims for the training of Catholic exiles. These were the centers of Anglo-Catholic activity on the Continent, and from them Jesuit priests were sent on missions into England.

104 *hatch . . . queen* Marlowe is probably referring to the Babington conspiracy against Queen Elizabeth which was uncovered in 1586.

105 *Spain's huge fleet* the Spanish Armada, destroyed by the English in 1588.

107 *Monsieur* François duc d'Alençon, who had died in 1584.

Epernoun.   My lord, here is his son.
Enter the Guise's Son.
Henry.   Boy, look where your father lies.
Guise's Son.   My father slain! Who hath done this deed?
Henry.   Sirrah, 'twas I that slew him and will slay   120
 Thee too, and thou prove such a traitor.
Guise's Son.   Art thou king, and hast done this bloody deed?
 I'll be revenged.   *He offers to throw his dagger.*
Henry.   Away to prison with him! I'll clip his wings
 Or e'er he pass my hands. Away with him!   125
Exit [Guise's Son with Attendants].
 But what availeth that this traitor's dead,
 When Duke Dumaine, his brother, is alive,
 And that young cardinal that is grown so proud?
 Go to the governor of Orleans
 And will him, in my name, to kill the duke.   [*To Cossin.*]   130
 Get you away, and strangle the cardinal.   [*To the Murderers.*]

[*Exeunt Cossin and Murderers.*]
 These two will make one entire Duke of Guise,
 Especially with our old mother's help.
Epernoun.   My lord, see where she comes, as if she drooped
 To hear these news.   135
Henry.   And let her droop; my heart is light enough.
Enter [Catherine, the] Queen-Mother.
 Mother, how like you this device of mine?
 I slew the Guise because I would be king.
Catherine.   King! Why, so thou wert before!
 Pray God thou be a king now this is done.   140
Henry.   Nay, he was king and countermanded me.
 But now I will be king and rule myself
 And make the Guisians stoop that are alive.
Catherine.   I cannot speak for grief. When thou wast born,
 I would that I had murdered thee, my son.   145
 My son! Thou art a changeling, not my son!
 I curse thee and exclaim thee miscreant,
 Traitor to God and to the realm of France.
Henry.   Cry out! Exclaim! Howl till thy throat be hoarse!
 The Guise is slain, and I rejoice therefore.   150
 And now will I to arms. Come, Epernoun,
 And let her grieve her heart out if she will.
Exit King [Henry] and Epernoun.
Catherine.   Away! Leave me alone to meditate.
[*Exeunt Attendants.*]
 Sweet Guise, would he had died, so thou wert here.

---

146 *changeling* child, usually deformed, supposedly substituted by fairies in the cradle of a child they had kidnapped (an old folk superstition).
147 *exclaim* cry out against, accuse.

To whom shall I bewray my secrets now,   155
Or who will help to build religion?
The Protestants will glory and insult;
Wicked Navarre will get the crown of France;
The Popedom cannot stand; all goes to wrack;
And all for thee, my Guise. What may I do?   160
But sorrow seize upon my toiling soul,
For since the Guise is dead, I will not live.

                                                        Exit.

    Enter two [Murderers], dragging in the Cardinal.   xxi.
Cardinal.   Murder me not; I am a cardinal.
First Murderer.   Wert thou the Pope, thou mightst not 'scape from us.
Cardinal.   What, will you 'file your hands with churchmen's blood?
Second Murderer.   Shed your blood? O Lord, no, for we intend to
    strangle you.   5
Cardinal.   Then there is no remedy, but I must die?
First Murderer.   No remedy; therefore prepare yourself.
Cardinal.   Yet lives my brother, Duke Dumaine, and many moe,
   To revenge our deaths upon that cursèd king,
   Upon whose heart may all the furies gripe,   10
   And with their paws drench his black soul in hell.
First Murderer.   Yours, my Lord Cardinal, you should have said.
                  Now they strangle him.
  So, pluck amain.
  He is hard-hearted; therefore pull with violence.
  Come, take him away.   15
          Exeunt [with the Cardinal's body].

    Enter Duke Dumaine, reading a letter; with others.   xxii.
Dumaine.   My noble brother murdered by the king!
  O, what may I do for to revenge thy death?
  The king's alone, it cannot satisfy.
  Sweet Duke of Guise, our prop to lean upon,
  Now thou art dead, here is no stay for us.   5

---

155 *bewray* confide.   8 *moe* more.
161 *toiling* struggling.   **xxii.**
xxi.   3 *the king's* i.e., the king's death.
  3 *'file* defile.

I am thy brother, and I'll revenge thy death,
And root Valois his line from forth of France,
And beat proud Bourbon to his native home,
That basely seeks to join with such a king,
Whose murderous thoughts will be his overthrow.   10
He willed the governor of Orleans, in his name,
That I with speed should have been put to death,
But that's prevented, for to end his life,
And all those traitors to the church of Rome
That durst attempt to murder noble Guise.   15

Enter the Friar.

Friar.   My lord, I come to bring you news that your brother, the cardi-
nal of Lorraine, by the king's consent, is lately strangled unto death.
Dumaine.   My brother cardinal slain, and I alive?
O words of power to kill a thousand men.
Come, let us away and levy men;   20
'Tis war that must assuage this tyrant's pride.
Friar.   My lord, hear me but speak.
I am a friar of the order of the Jacobins,
That for my conscience' sake will kill the king.
Dumaine.   But what doth move thee above the rest to do the deed?   [25
Friar.   O, my lord, I have been a great sinner in my days, and the deed
is meritorious.
Dumaine.   But how wilt thou get opportunity?
Friar.   Tush, my lord, let me alone for that.
Dumaine.   Friar, come with me;   30
We will go talk more of this within.

Exeunt.

xxiii.

*Sound drum and trumpets, and enter [Henry,] the King of
France, and Navarre, Epernoun, Bartus, Pleshé, [Attendants]
and Soldiers.*

Henry.   Brother of Navarre, I sorrow much
That ever I was proved your enemy,
And that the sweet and princely mind you bear
Was ever troubled with injurious wars.
I vow, as I am lawful king of France,   5
To recompense your reconcilèd love
With all the honors and affections

---

7 *Valois* See note at xviii, 46.
8 *Bourbon* See note at xviii, 47.
23 *Jacobins* Dominicans.

27 *meritorious* to be rewarded by ab-
solution from sin. The murder of King
Henry III had been justified by Pope
Sixtus V.

That ever I vouchsafed my dearest friends.

Navarre.   It is enough if that Navarre may be
Esteemèd faithful to the king of France,   10
Whose service he may still command till death.

Henry.   Thanks to my kingly brother of Navarre
Then here we'll lie before Lutetia walls,
Girting this strumpet city with our siege
Till, surfeiting with our afflicting arms,   15
She cast her hateful stomach to the earth.

Enter a Messenger.

Messenger.   And it please your majesty, here is a friar of the order of
the Jacobins, sent from the President of Paris, that craves access unto
your grace.

Henry.   Let him come in.   20

[Exit Messenger.]

Enter Friar with a letter.

Epernoun.   I like not this friar's look.
'Twere not amiss, my lord, if he were searched.

Henry.   Sweet Epernoun, our friars are holy men
And will not offer violence to their king
For all the wealth and treasure of the world.   25
Friar, thou dost acknowledge me thy king?

Friar.   Ay, my good lord, and will die therein.

Henry.   Then come thou near, and tell what news thou bringst.

Friar.   My lord, the President of Paris greets your grace and sends his
duty by these speedy lines, humbly craving your gracious reply. [30

[He gives the letter.]

Henry.   I'll read them, friar, and then I'll answer thee.

Friar.   *Sancte Jacobe,* now have mercy on me!

*He stabs the King with a knife as he reads the letter,
and then the King gets the knife and kills him.*

Epernoun.   O, my lord, let him live a while!

Henry.   No, let the villain die and feel in hell
Just torments for his treachery.   35

Navarre.   What, is your highness hurt?

Henry.   Yes, Navarre; but not to death, I hope.

Navarre.   God shield your grace from such a sudden death.
Go call a surgeon hither straight.

[Exit an Attendant.]

Henry.   What irreligious pagans' parts be these,   40
Of such as hold them of the holy church!

xxiii.

13 *Lutetia* Paris.
14 *Girting* encircling.
16 *stomach* proud resistance, with a
double meaning: to 'cast stomach' is to
vomit.

18 *President of Paris* leader of the
parliament at Paris.
40 *parts* attributes.

Take hence that damnèd villain from my sight.

[Attendants carry out the Friar's body.]

Epernoun.   Ah, had your highness let him live,
  We might have punished him to his deserts.

Henry.   Sweet Epernoun, all rebels under heaven   45
  Shall take example by his punishment,
  How they bear arms against their sovereign.
  Go, call the English agent hither straight.

[Exit an Attendant.]

  I'll send my sister England news of this,
  And give her warning of her treacherous foes.   50

[Enter a Surgeon.]

Navarre.   Pleaseth your grace to let the surgeon search your wound?

Henry.   The wound, I warrant ye, is deep, my lord.
  Search, surgeon, and resolve me what thou see'st.

The Surgeon searches [the wound].

Enter the English Agent.

  Agent for England, send thy mistress word
  What this detested Jacobin hath done.   55
  Tell her, for all this, that I hope to live,
  Which if I do, the papal monarch goes
  To wrack, and antichristian kingdom falls.
  These bloody hands shall tear his triple crown
  And fire accursèd Rome about his ears.   60
  I'll fire his crazèd buildings and enforce
  The papal towers to kiss the lowly earth.
  Navarre, give me thy hand. I here do swear
  To ruinate that wicked church of Rome
  That hatcheth up such bloody practices,   65
  And here protest eternal love to thee
  And to the Queen of England specially,
  Whom God hath blessed for hating papistry.

Navarre.   These words revive my thoughts and comfort me,
  To see your highness in this virtuous mind.   70

Henry.   Tell me, surgeon, shall I live?

Surgeon.   Alas, my lord, the wound is dangerous,
  For you are stricken with a poisoned knife.

Henry.   A poisoned knife! What, shall the French king die,
  Wounded and poisoned, both at once?

Epernoun.   O, that   75
  That damnèd villain were alive again,
  That we might torture him with some new-found death.

Bartus.   He died a death too good. The devil of hell torture his wicked
  soul.

Henry.   Ah, curse him not, sith he is dead. O, the fatal poison   [80

65 *practices* plots.

works within my breast. Tell me, surgeon, and flatter not; may I live?
Surgeon.   Alas, my lord, your highness cannot live.
Navarre.   Surgeon, why say'st thou so? The king may live.
Henry.   O, no, Navarre. Thou must be king of France.
Navarre.   Long may you live and still be king of France.   85
Epernoun.   Or else, die Epernoun!
Henry.   Sweet Epernoun, thy king must die. My lords,
　Fight in the quarrel of this valiant prince,
　For he is your lawful king and my next heir;
　Valois's line ends in my tragedy.   90
　Now let the house of Bourbon wear the crown,
　And may it never end in blood as mine hath done.
　Weep not, sweet Navarre, but revenge my death.
　Ah, Epernoun, is this thy love to me?
　Henry, thy king, wipes off these childish tears   95
　And bids thee whet thy sword on Sixtus' bones,
　That it may keenly slice the Catholics.
　He loves me not that sheds most tears,
　But he that makes most lavish of his blood.
　Fire Paris, where these treacherous rebels lurk.   100
　I die, Navarre. Come bear me to my sepulcher.
　Salute the queen of England in my name,
　And tell her Henry dies her faithful friend.   *He dies.*
Navarre.   Come, lords, take up the body of the king,
　That we may see it honorably interred.   105
　And then I vow for to revenge his death
　As Rome and all those popish prelates there
　Shall curse the time that e'er Navarre was king
　And ruled in France by Henry's fatal death.
　　　　They march out, with the body of the King lying on four
　　　　　　men's shoulders, with a dead march, drawing weapons
　　　　　　　　　　　　on the ground.

88 *prince* i.e., Navarre.

The troublesome

raigne and lamentable death of
Edward *the second, King of*
England: with the tragicall
fall of proud Mortimer:

As it was sundrie times publiquely acted
in the honourable citie of London, by the
right honourable the Earle of Pem-
brooke his seruants.

Written by Chri. Marlow *Gent.*

Imprinted at London for *William Iones*
dwelling neere Holbourne conduit, at the
signe of the Gunne. 1 5 9 4.

THE TROUBLESOME REIGN AND LAMENTABLE DEATH OF EDWARD THE SECOND

THE PLAYERS

King Edward the Second
Prince Edward, his Son, afterwards King Edward the Third
Earl of Kent, Brother of King Edward the Second
Gaveston
Warwick
Lancaster
Pembroke
Arundel
Leicester
Berkeley
Mortimer senior
Mortimer junior, his Nephew
Spencer senior
Spencer junior, his Son
Archbishop of Canterbury
Bishop of Coventry
Bishop of Winchester

Baldock
Beaumont
Trussel
Gurney
Matrevis
Lightborn
Sir John of Hainault
Levune
Rice ap Howell
Abbot, Monks, Herald, Lords, Poor Men, James, Mower, Champion, Messengers, Soldiers, and Attendants
Queen Isabella, Wife of King Edward the Second
Niece to King Edward the Second, daughter of the Duke of Gloucester
Ladies

THE SCENE
England, France.

I,i.

Enter Gaveston, reading on a letter that was brought him from the king.

Gaveston. 'My father is deceased. Come, Gaveston,
And share the kingdom with thy dearest friend.'
Ah, words that make me surfeit with delight!
What greater bliss can hap to Gaveston
Than live and be the favorite of a king?   5
Sweet prince, I come; these, these thy amorous lines
Might have enforced me to have swum from France,
And, like Leander, gasped upon the sand,

I,i.

1 *Gaveston* Son of a Gascon knight in the service of King Edward I, he had been brought up as a childhood friend of Edward II.

7 *France* Gaveston had been banished to his native Gascony by King Edward I.

The young Edward II's first act upon becoming king was to call his friend home in 1307.

8 *Leander* hero of the Greek love story who nightly swam the Hellespont to be with his beloved Hero; he finally

So thou wouldst smile and take me in thy arms.
The sight of London to my exiled eyes   10
Is as Elysium to a new-come soul;
Not that I love the city or the men,
But that it harbors him I hold so dear,
The king, upon whose bosom let me die,
And with the world be still at enmity.   15
What need the arctic people love starlight,
To whom the sun shines both by day and night?
Farewell base stooping to the lordly peers.
My knee shall bow to none but to the king.
As for the multitude that are but sparks,   20
Raked up in embers of their poverty—
Tanti; I'll fawn first on the wind
That glanceth at my lips and flieth away.
But how now, what are these?
                Enter three Poor Men.
Poor Men.   Such as desire your worship's service.   25
Gaveston.   What canst thou do?
First Poor Man.   I can ride.
Gaveston.   But I have no horses. What art thou?
Second Poor Man.   A traveler.
Gaveston.   Let me see—thou wouldst do well   30
   To wait at my trencher and tell me lies at dinner time,
   And as I like your discoursing, I'll have you.
   And what art thou?
Third Poor Man.   A soldier, that hath served against the Scot.
Gaveston.   Why, there are hospitals for such as you.   35
   I have no war, and therefore, sir, be gone.
Third Poor Man.   Farewell, and perish by a soldier's hand,
   That wouldst reward them with an hospital.
Gaveston.   Ay, ay, these words of his move me as much
   As if a goose should play the porpentine   40
   And dart her plumes, thinking to pierce my breast.
   But yet it is no pain to speak men fair.
   I'll flatter these and make them live in hope.   [*Aside.*]
   You know that I came lately out of France,
   And yet I have not viewed my lord the king.   45
   If I speed well, I'll entertain you all.

drowned. Marlowe retold the story in
his poem *Hero and Leander.*

14 *die* swoon with joy. There is little
justification for the emendation, 'lie'
adopted by some modern editors.

20–21 *sparks . . . poverty* Fires were
kept alive overnight by raking ashes over
the live embers.

22 *Tanti* So much for that (an expression of contempt).

31 *trencher* a flat wooden dish on
which food was served.

35 *hospitals* homes for disabled soldiers.

40 *porpentine* porcupine (supposed in
popular superstition to be able to dart
its quills).

Poor Men. We thank your worship.

Gaveston. I have some business; leave me to myself.

Poor Men. We will wait here about the court.

                                Exeunt [Poor Men].

Gaveston. Do. These are not men for me.   50
  I must have wanton poets, pleasant wits,
  Musicians, that with touching of a string
  May draw the pliant king which way I please.
  Music and poetry is his delight;
  Therefore I'll have Italian masks by night,   55
  Sweet speeches, comedies, and pleasing shows;
  And in the day, when he shall walk abroad,
  Like sylvan nymphs my pages shall be clad.
  My men, like satyrs grazing on the lawns,
  Shall with their goat-feet dance an antic hay.   60
  Sometime a lovely boy in Dian's shape,
  With hair that gilds the water as it glides,
  Crownets of pearl about his naked arms,
  And in his sportful hands an olive tree,
  To hide those parts which men delight to see,   65
  Shall bathe him in a spring; and there, hard by,
  One like Actæon peeping through the grove,
  Shall by the angry goddess be transformed,
  And running in the likeness of an hart,
  By yelping hounds pulled down, and seem to die— 70
  Such things as these best please his majesty.
  My lord! Here comes the king and the nobles
  From the parliament. I'll stand aside.

                                [He retires.]

Enter King [Edward], Lancaster, Mortimer Senior, Mortimer Junior, Edmund, Earl of Kent, Guy, Earl of Warwick, [and others].

King Edward. Lancaster!

51 *wanton* amorous.

55 *Italian masks* elaborate Elizabethan entertainments involving disguises, thought in the sixteenth century to have come from Italy, but actually of obscure origins, although certainly influenced by Italian customs. Marlowe here is anachronistic, since there were no masks in Edward's time.

59 *grazing* strolling.

60 *antic hay* an old-fashioned dance.

61 *Dian* the Greek goddess of chastity and the hunt (to be portrayed by a boy, as were all women's parts in Elizabethan entertainments).

63 *Crownets* bracelets.

67 *Actæon* a hunter, in Greek mythology, transformed by Diana into a stag after having seen her bathing, and then killed by his own hounds. The story is in Ovid's *Metamorphoses.*

73 SD *Edmund* an anachronism, since Edmund of Woodstock, Earl of Kent, Edward's half-brother, was not born until 1301, and thus was only six years old at the time of Gaveston's recall in 1307. The Mortimers, similarly, had no actual part in the opposition to Gaveston. Thomas, Earl of Lancaster, grandson of Henry III, was a powerful opponent of Gaveston, the Spencers, and Edward II.

Lancaster.   My lord.   75
Gaveston.   That Earl of Lancaster do I abhor.   [*Aside.*]
King Edward.   Will you not grant me this? In spite of them
   I'll have my will, and these two Mortimers,
   That cross me thus, shall know I am displeased.   [*Aside.*]
Mortimer Senior.   If you love us, my lord, hate Gaveston.   80
Gaveston.   That villain Mortimer! I'll be his death.   [*Aside.*]
Mortimer Junior.   Mine uncle here, this earl, and I myself
   Were sworn to your father at his death,
   That he should ne'er return into the realm.
   And know, my lord, ere I will break my oath,   85
   This sword of mine, that should offend your foes,
   Shall sleep within the scabbard at thy need,
   And underneath thy banners march who will,
   For Mortimer will hang his armor up.
Gaveston.   *Mort Dieu!*   [*Aside.*]   90
King Edward.   Well, Mortimer, I'll make thee rue these words.
   Beseems it thee to contradict thy king?
   Frown'st thou thereat, aspiring Lancaster?
   The sword shall plane the furrows of thy brows,
   And hew these knees that now are grown so stiff.   95
   I will have Gaveston, and you shall know
   What danger 'tis to stand against your king.
Gaveston.   Well done, Ned!   [*Aside.*]
Lancaster.   My lord, why do you thus incense your peers,
   That naturally would love and honor you   100
   But for that base and obscure Gaveston?
   Four earldoms have I besides Lancaster—
   Derby, Salisbury, Lincoln, Leicester;
   These will I sell to give my soldiers pay,
   Ere Gaveston shall stay within the realm;   105
   Therefore, if he be come, expel him straight.
Kent.   Barons and earls, your pride hath made me mute,
   But now I'll speak, and to the proof, I hope.
   I do remember in my father's days,
   Lord Percy of the north, being highly moved,   110
   Braved Mowbery in presence of the king;
   For which, had not his highness loved him well,
   He should have lost his head; but with his look
   The undaunted spirit of Percy was appeased,
   And Mowbery and he were reconciled.   115
   Yet dare you brave the king unto his face?
   Brother, revenge it, and let these their heads
   Preach upon poles for trespass of their tongues.
Warwick.   O, our heads!
King Edward.   Ay, yours; and therefore I would wish you grant—   120

108 *to the proof* irrefutably.   111 *Braved* challenged.

Warwick.   Bridle thy anger, gentle Mortimer.
Mortimer Junior.   I cannot, nor I will not; I must speak.
   Cousin, our hands I hope shall fence our heads
   And strike off his that makes you threaten us.
   Come, uncle, let us leave the brainsick king   125
   And henceforth parley with our naked swords.
Mortimer Senior.   Wiltshire hath men enough to save our heads.
Warwick.   All Warwickshire will love him for my sake.
Lancaster.   And northward Gaveston hath many friends.
   Adieu, my lord, and either change your mind,   130
   Or look to see the throne, where you should sit,
   To float in blood, and at thy wanton head
   The glozing head of thy base minion thrown.
                              Exeunt [all but King Edward, Kent,
                                   Gaveston and Attendants].
King Edward.   I cannot brook these haughty menaces.
   Am I a king, and must be overruled?   135
   Brother, display my ensigns in the field;
   I'll bandy with the barons and the earls,
   And either die or live with Gaveston.
Gaveston.   I can no longer keep me from my lord.
                                   [*He comes forward.*]
King Edward.   What, Gaveston! Welcome! Kiss not my hand;   140
   Embrace me, Gaveston, as I do thee.
   Why shouldst thou kneel? Knowest thou not who I am?
   Thy friend, thyself, another Gaveston!
   Not Hylas was more mourned of Hercules
   Than thou hast been of me since thy exile.   145
Gaveston.   And since I went from hence, no soul in hell
   Hath felt more torment than poor Gaveston.
King Edward.   I know it. Brother, welcome home my friend.
   Now let the treacherous Mortimers conspire,
   And that high minded Earl of Lancaster!   150
   I have my wish in that I joy thy sight,
   And sooner shall the sea o'erwhelm my land,
   Than bear the ship that shall transport thee hence.
   I here create thee Lord High Chamberlain,
   Chief Secretary to the state and me,   155
   Earl of Cornwall, King and Lord of Man.

---

123 *Cousin* any relative outside the immediate family. Mortimer was very distantly related to the king.

132 *wanton* irresponsible.

133 *glozing* flattering. *minion* favorite.

137 *bandy* exchange blows.

144 *Hylas . . . Hercules* Hylas was a youth who accompanied Hercules with Jason on the quest for the golden fleece and was carried off by Nymphs when he went ashore at Nysia to draw water. Hercules mourned and searched for him but could find only an echo.

156 *King and Lord of Man* Rulers of the Isle of Man, between England and Ireland, had certain sovereign rights and were called kings.

Gaveston.   My lord, these titles far exceed my worth.
Kent.   Brother, the least of these may well suffice
  For one of greater birth than Gaveston.
King Edward.   Cease, brother, for I cannot brook these words.   160
  Thy worth, sweet friend, is far above my gifts;
  Therefore, to equal it, receive my heart.
  If for these dignities thou be envied,
  I'll give thee more; for but to honor thee,
  Is Edward pleased with kingly regiment.   165
  Fearst thou thy person? Thou shalt have a guard.
  Wantest thou gold? Go to my treasury.
  Wouldst thou be loved and feared? Receive my seal;
  Save or condemn, and in our name command
  Whatso thy mind affects or fancy likes.   170
Gaveston.   It shall suffice me to enjoy your love,
  Which whiles I have, I think myself as great
  As Caesar riding in the Roman street,
  With captive kings at his triumphant car.
                    Enter the Bishop of Coventry.
King Edward.   Whither goes my lord of Coventry so fast?   175
Coventry.   To celebrate your father's exequies.
  But is that wicked Gaveston returned?
King Edward.   Ay, priest, and lives to be revenged on thee,
  That wert the only cause of his exile.
Gaveston.   'Tis true, and but for reverence of these robes,   180
  Thou shouldst not plod one foot beyond this place.
Coventry.   I did no more than I was bound to do;
  And, Gaveston, unless thou be reclaimed,
  As then I did incense the parliament,
  So will I now, and thou shalt back to France.   185
Gaveston.   Saving your reverence, you must pardon me.
King Edward.   Throw off his golden mitre, rend his stole,
  And in the channel christen him anew.
Kent.   Ah, brother, lay not violent hands on him,
  For he'll complain unto the see of Rome.   190
Gaveston.   Let him complain unto the see of hell;
  I'll be revenged on him for my exile.
King Edward.   No, spare his life, but seize upon his goods.
  Be thou lord bishop and receive his rents,
  And make him serve thee as thy chaplain.   195
  I give him thee—here, use him as thou wilt.
Gaveston.   He shall to prison and there die in bolts.
King Edward.   Ay, to the Tower, the Fleet, or where thou wilt.
Coventry.   For this offence, be thou accursed of God!
King Edward.   Who's there? Convey this priest to the Tower.   200

  188 *channel* open gutter through which   198 *Fleet* a London prison.
sewage flowed.

Coventry.　True, true.
King Edward.　But in the meantime, Gaveston, away,
　And take possession of his house and goods.
　Come, follow me, and thou shalt have my guard
　To see it done and bring thee safe again.　　　　　　　　205
Gaveston.　What should a priest do with so fair a house?
　A prison may beseem his holiness.

　　　　　　　　　　　　　　　　　　　　　　[Exeunt.]

✱

　　　　　Enter both the Mortimers, Warwick and Lancaster.　I,ii.
Warwick.　'Tis true, the bishop is in the Tower,
　And goods and body given to Gaveston.
Lancaster.　What! Will they tyrannise upon the church?
　Ah, wicked king! Accursèd Gaveston!
　This ground, which is corrupted with their steps,　　　　5
　Shall be their timeless sepulcher or mine.
Mortimer Junior.　Well, let that peevish Frenchman guard him sure;
　Unless his breast be sword-proof he shall die.
Mortimer Senior.　How now! Why droops the Earl of Lancaster?
Mortimer Junior.　Wherefore is Guy of Warwick discontent?　　10
Lancaster.　That villain Gaveston is made an earl.
Mortimer Senior.　An earl!
Warwick.　Ay, and besides Lord Chamberlain of the realm,
　And Secretary too, and Lord of Man.
Mortimer Senior.　We may not, nor we will not suffer this.　　15
Mortimer Junior.　Why post we not from hence to levy men?
Lancaster.　'My Lord of Cornwall,' now at every word!
　And happy is the man whom he vouchsafes,
　For vailing of his bonnet, one good look.
　Thus, arm in arm, the king and he doth march.　　　　20
　Nay more, the guard upon his lordship waits,
　And all the court begins to flatter him.
Warwick.　Thus leaning on the shoulder of the king,
　He nods, and scorns, and smiles at those that pass.
Mortimer Senior.　Doth no man take exceptions at the slave?　　25
Lancaster.　All stomach him, but none dare speak a word.
Mortimer Junior.　Ah, that bewrays their baseness, Lancaster!
　Were all the earls and barons of my mind,

I,ii.

1 *Warwick* Guy, Earl of Warwick, historically was the most persistent foe of Gaveston and Edward II.

6 *timeless* premature.

19 *vailing of his bonnet* lifting his hat.

25 *take exceptions at* object to.

26 *stomach* are angry at (the stomach was regarded as the producer of choler, and therefore the seat of anger).

27 *bewrays* reveals.

We'll hale him from the bosom of the king,
And at the court gate hang the peasant up,   30
Who, swoll'n with venom of ambitious pride,
Will be the ruin of the realm and us.

Enter the [Arch]bishop of Canterbury [and an Attendant].

Warwick.   Here comes my lord of Canterbury's grace.
Lancaster.   His countenance bewrays he is displeased.
Canterbury.   First were his sacred garments rent and torn,   35
Then laid they violent hands upon him; next
Himself imprisoned, and his goods asseized.
This certify the Pope; away, take horse.

[Exit Attendant.]

Lancaster.   My lord, will you take arms against the king?
Canterbury.   What need I? God himself is up in arms,   40
When violence is offered to the church.
Mortimer Junior.   Then will you join with us that be his peers,
To banish or behead that Gaveston?
Canterbury.   What else, my lords? For it concerns me near;
The bishopric of Coventry is his.   45

Enter Queen [Isabella].

Mortimer Junior.   Madam, whither walks your majesty so fast?
Queen Isabella.   Unto the forest, gentle Mortimer,
To live in grief and baleful discontent,
For now my lord the king regards me not,
But dotes upon the love of Gaveston.   50
He claps his cheeks and hangs about his neck,
Smiles in his face and whispers in his ears,
And when I come, he frowns, as who should say,
'Go whither thou wilt, seeing I have Gaveston.'
Mortimer Senior.   Is it not strange that he is thus bewitched?   55
Mortimer Junior.   Madam, return unto the court again.
That sly inveigling Frenchman we'll exile
Or lose our lives; and yet, ere that day come,
The king shall lose his crown, for we have power,
And courage too, to be revenged at full.   60
Canterbury.   But yet lift not your swords against the king.
Lancaster.   No, but we'll lift Gaveston from hence.
Warwick.   And war must be the means, or he'll stay still.
Queen Isabella.   Then let him stay; for rather than my lord
Shall be oppressed by civil mutinies,   65
I will endure a melancholy life,
And let him frolic with his minion.
Canterbury.   My lords, to ease all this, but hear me speak:

---

37 *asseized* taken possession of.
45. SD *Queen Isabella* Daughter of King Philip the Fair of France, she was born in 1292 and married king Edward in 1308. Her affair with Mortimer occurred much later.
47 *forest* wilderness (the queen is speaking figuratively).

We and the rest that are his counselors
Will meet and with a general consent   70
  Confirm his banishment with our hands and seals.
Lancaster.   What we confirm the king will frustrate.
Mortimer Junior.   Then may we lawfully revolt from him.
Warwick.   But say, my lord, where shall this meeting be?
Canterbury.   At the New Temple.   75
Mortimer Junior.   Content.
Canterbury.   And, in the meantime, I'll entreat you all
  To cross to Lambeth and there stay with me.
Lancaster.   Come then, let's away.
Mortimer Junior.   Madam, farewell.   80
Queen Isabella.   Farewell, sweet Mortimer, and for my sake
  Forbear to levy arms against the king.
Mortimer Junior.   Ay, if words will serve; if not, I must.

                                          [*Exeunt.*]

                Enter Gaveston and the Earl of Kent.   I,iii.
Gaveston.   Edmund, the mighty prince of Lancaster,
  That hath more earldoms than an ass can bear,
  And both the Mortimers, two goodly men,
  With Guy of Warwick, that redoubted knight,
  Are gone towards Lambeth. There let them remain.   5

                                          [*Exeunt.*]

                              I,iv.

Enter [Lancaster, Warwick, Pembroke, Mortimer Senior, Morti-
    mer Junior, the Archbishop of Canterbury and Attendants].
Lancaster.   Here is the form of Gaveston's exile;
  May it please your lordship to subscribe your name.
Canterbury.   Give me the paper.
                [He subscribes, as do the others after him.]
Lancaster.   Quick, quick, my lord; I long to write my name.
Warwick.   But I long more to see him banished hence.   5
Mortimer Junior.   The name of Mortimer shall fright the king,
  Unless he be declined from that base peasant.
            Enter King [Edward, Kent,] and Gaveston.
King Edward.   What? Are you moved that Gaveston sits here?
  It is our pleasure; we will have it so.

75 *New Temple* house founded by the   78 *Lambeth* a palace held by the
Knights Templar.   Archbishops of Canterbury since 1179.

Lancaster.   Your grace doth well to place him by your side,   10
   For nowhere else the new earl is so safe.
Mortimer Senior.   What man of noble birth can brook this sight?
   Quam male conveniunt!
   See what a scornful look the peasant casts.
Pembroke.   Can kingly lions fawn on creeping ants?   15
Warwick.   Ignoble vassal, that like Phaeton
   Aspir'st unto the guidance of the sun.
Mortimer Junior.   Their downfall is at hand, their forces down.
   We will not thus be faced and over-peered.
King Edward.   Lay hands on that traitor Mortimer!   20
Mortimer Senior.   Lay hands on that traitor Gaveston!
Kent.   Is this the duty that you owe your king?
Warwick.   We know our duties; let him know his peers.
King Edward.   Whither will you bear him? Stay, or ye shall die.
Mortimer Senior.   We are no traitors; therefore threaten not.   25
Gaveston.   No, threaten not, my lord, but pay them home!
   Were I a king—
Mortimer Junior.   Thou villain, wherefore talks thou of a king,
   That hardly art a gentleman by birth?
King Edward.   Were he a peasant, being my minion,   30
   I'll make the proudest of you stoop to him.
Lancaster.   My lord, you may not thus disparage us.
   Away, I say, with hateful Gaveston!
Mortimer Senior.   And with the Earl of Kent that favors him.
                    [*Attendants remove Kent and Gaveston.*]
King Edward.   Nay, then lay violent hands upon your king.   35
   Here, Mortimer, sit thou in Edward's throne.
   Warwick and Lancaster, wear you my crown.
   Was ever king thus over-ruled as I?
Lancaster.   Learn then to rule us better and the realm.
Mortimer Junior.   What we have done, our heart-blood shall main-
      tain.   40
Warwick.   Think you that we can brook this upstart pride?
King Edward.   Anger and wrathful fury stops my speech.
Canterbury.   Why are you moved? Be patient, my lord,
   And see what we your counselors have done.
Mortimer Junior.   My lords, now let us all be resolute,   45
   And either have our wills or lose our lives.
King Edward.   Meet you for this, proud overdaring peers?
   Ere my sweet Gaveston shall part from me,

I,iv.

13 *Quam male conveniunt.* How badly
they suit one another.
16 *Phaeton* See note *I Tamb.* IV,ii,49.
19 *faced and over-peered* bullied and

looked down upon (with a probable pun
on 'peer').
28 *villain* (1) scoundrel (2) peasant
bound to the land.
32 *disparage* vilify.

This isle shall fleet upon the ocean
And wander to the unfrequented Inde.   50
Canterbury.   You know that I am legate to the Pope;
  On your allegiance to the see of Rome,
  Subscribe as we have done to his exile.
Mortimer Junior.   Curse him if he refuse, and then may we
  Depose him and elect another king.   55
King Edward.   Ay, there it goes! But yet I will not yield;
  Curse me, depose me, do the worst you can.
Lancaster.   Then linger not, my lord, but do it straight.
Canterbury.   Remember how the bishop was abused.
  Either banish him that was the cause thereof,   60
  Or I will presently discharge these lords
  Of duty and allegiance due to thee.
King Edward.   It boots me not to threat; I must speak **fair.**
  The legate of the Pope will be obeyed.   [*Aside.*]
  My lord, you shall be Chancellor of the realm,   65
  Thou, Lancaster, High Admiral of our fleet;
  Young Mortimer and his uncle shall be earls,
  And you, Lord Warwick, President of the North,
  And thou of Wales. If this content you not,
  Make several kingdoms of this monarchy   70
  And share it equally amongst you all,
  So I may have some nook or corner left
  To frolic with my dearest Gaveston.
Canterbury.   Nothing shall alter us; we are resolved.
Lancaster.   Come, come, subscribe.   75
Mortimer Junior.   Why should you love him whom the **world** hates so?
King Edward.   Because he loves me more than all the world.
  Ah, none but rude and savage-minded men
  Would seek the ruin of my Gaveston;
  You that be noble-born should pity him.   80
Warwick.   You that are princely-born should shake him **off.**
  For shame subscribe, and let the lown depart.
Mortimer Senior.   Urge him, my lord.
Canterbury.   Are you content to banish him the realm?
King Edward.   I see I must, and therefore am content. 85
  Instead of ink I'll write it with my tears.

                                   [*He subscribes*].
Mortimer Junior.   The king is love-sick for his minion.
King Edward.   'Tis done, and now, accursèd hand, fall off!
Lancaster.   Give it me; I'll have it published in the streets.
Mortimer Junior.   I'll see him presently dispatched away.   90
Canterbury.   Now is my heart at ease.
Warwick.   And so is mine.

49 *fleet* float.   63 *boots* avails.
50 *Inde* India.   82 *lown* peasant.

Pembroke.   This will be good news to the common sort.
Mortimer Senior.   Be it or no, he shall not linger here.

Exeunt [all except King Edward].

King Edward.   How fast they run to banish him I love.
  They would not stir, were it to do me good.   95
  Why should a king be subject to a priest?
  Proud Rome, that hatchest such imperial grooms,
  For these thy superstitious taper-lights,
  Wherewith thy antichristian churches blaze,
  I'll fire thy crazèd buildings and enforce   100
  The papal towers to kiss the lowly ground.
  With slaughtered priests may Tiber's channel swell,
  And banks raised higher with their sepulchers.
  As for the peers that back the clergy thus,
  If I be king, not one of them shall live.   105

Enter Gaveston.

Gaveston.   My lord, I hear it whispered everywhere
  That I am banished and must fly the land.
King Edward.   'Tis true, sweet Gaveston—O, were it false!
  The legate of the Pope will have it so,
  And thou must hence, or I shall be deposed.   110
  But I will reign to be revenged of them,
  And therefore, sweet friend, take it patiently.
  Live where thou wilt, I'll send thee gold enough;
  And long thou shalt not stay, or if thou dost,
  I'll come to thee; my love shall ne'er decline.   115
Gaveston.   Is all my hope turned to this hell of grief?
King Edward.   Rend not my heart with thy too-piercing words.
  Thou from this land, I from myself am banished.
Gaveston.   To go from hence grieves not poor Gaveston,
  But to forsake you, in whose gracious looks   120
  The blessedness of Gaveston remains;
  For nowhere else seeks he felicity.
King Edward.   And only this torments my wretched soul,
  That, whether I will or no, thou must depart.
  Be governor of Ireland in my stead,   125
  And there abide till fortune call thee home.
  Here take my picture, and let me wear thine;

[They exchange pictures.]

  O, might I keep thee here as I do this,
  Happy were I, but now most miserable.
Gaveston.   'Tis something to be pitied of a king.   130
King Edward.   Thou shalt not hence; I'll hide thee, Gaveston.
Gaveston.   I shall be found, and then 'twill grieve me more.
King Edward.   Kind words and mutual talk makes our grief greater;
  Therefore, with dumb embracement, let us part—

100 *crazèd* ruined.

Stay, Gaveston, I cannot leave thee thus.   135
Gaveston.   For every look my lord drops down a tear;
  Seeing I must go, do not renew my sorrow.
King Edward.   The time is little that thou hast to stay,
  And therefore give me leave to look my fill.
  But come, sweet friend, I'll bear thee on thy way.   140
Gaveston.   The peers will frown.
King Edward.   I pass not for their anger. Come, let's go.
  O that we might as well return as go.
Enter Queen Isabella.
Queen Isabella.   Whither goes my lord?
King Edward.   Fawn not on me, French strumpet; get thee gone.   145
Queen Isabella.   On whom but on my husband should I fawn?
Gaveston.   On Mortimer, with whom, ungentle queen—
  I say no more; judge you the rest, my lord.
Queen Isabella.   In saying this, thou wrong'st me, Gaveston.
  Is't not enough that thou corrupts my lord   150
  And art a bawd to his affections,
  But thou must call mine honor thus in question?
Gaveston.   I mean not so; your grace must pardon me.
King Edward.   Thou art too familiar with that Mortimer,
  And by thy means is Gaveston exiled.   155
  But I would wish thee reconcile the lords,
  Or thou shalt ne'er be reconciled to me.
Queen Isabella.   Your highness knows it lies not in my power.
King Edward.   Away then; touch me not. Come, Gaveston.
Queen Isabella.   Villain, 'tis thou that robb'st me of my lord.   160
Gaveston.   Madam, 'tis you that rob me of my lord.
King Edward.   Speak not unto her; let her droop and pine.
Queen Isabella.   Wherein, my lord, have I deserved these words?
  Witness the tears that Isabella sheds,
  Witness this heart, that sighing for thee breaks,   165
  How dear my lord is to poor Isabel.
King Edward.   And witness heaven how dear thou art to me.
  There weep; for till my Gaveston be repealed,
  Assure thyself thou com'st not in my sight.
Exeunt [King] Edward and Gaveston.
Queen Isabella.   O miserable and distressèd queen!   170
  Would, when I left sweet France and was embarked,
  That charming Circes, walking on the waves,
  Had changed my shape, or at the marriage-day
  The cup of Hymen had been full of poison,
  Or with those arms that twined about my neck   175

---

140 *bear* accompany.
142 *pass* care.
151 *affections* idle inclinations.

172 *charming* having power to en-
chant. *Circes* variant of Circe, the enchantress of Homer's *Odyssey*.
174 *Hymen* Greek god of marriage

I had been stifled, and not lived to see
The king my lord thus to abandon me.
Like frantic Juno will I fill the earth
With ghastly murmur of my sighs and cries,
For never doted Jove on Ganymede   180
So much as he on cursèd Gaveston.
But that will more exasperate his wrath;
I must entreat him, I must speak him fair,
And be a means to call home Gaveston.
And yet he'll ever dote on Gaveston,   185
And so am I for ever miserable.

*Enter [Lancaster, Warwick, Pembroke, Mortimer Senior, and
Mortimer Junior].*

Lancaster.   Look where the sister of the king of France
Sits wringing of her hands and beats her breast.
Warwick.   The king, I fear, hath ill entreated her.
Pembroke.   Hard is the heart that injures such a saint.   190
Mortimer Junior.   I know 'tis 'long of Gaveston she weeps.
Mortimer Senior.   Why? He is gone.
Mortimer Junior.   Madam, how fares your grace?
Queen Isabella.   Ah, Mortimer! Now breaks the king's hate forth,
And he confesseth that he loves me not.
Mortimer Junior.   Cry quittance, madam, then, and love not him.   195
Queen Isabella.   No, rather will I die a thousand deaths,
And yet I love in vain; he'll ne'er love me.
Lancaster.   Fear ye not, madam; now his minion's gone,
His wanton humor will be quickly left.
Queen Isabella.   O never, Lancaster! I am enjoined   200
To sue unto you all for his repeal.
This wills my lord, and this must I perform,
Or else be banished from his highness' presence.
Lancaster.   For his repeal, madam? He comes not back,
Unless the sea cast up his shipwrack body.   205
Warwick.   And to behold so sweet a sight as that,
There's none here but would run his horse to death.
Mortimer Junior.   But, madam, would you have us call him home?
Queen Isabella.   Ay, Mortimer, for till he be restored,
The angry king hath banished me the court;   210
And therefore, as thou lovest and tender'st me,
Be thou my advocate unto these peers.
Mortimer Junior.   What, would ye have me plead for Gaveston?

178–180 *Juno . . . Ganymede*   Juno,
queen of the gods, was enraged when
her husband, Jove, carried off the handsome boy, Ganymede to be his cupbearer and favorite. The story is told in
Ovid's *Metamorphoses*.
    186, SD *Pembroke* Aymer de Valence,

at first opposed Edward and Gaveston,
but joined the king's party after a
quarrel with Lancaster and Warwick.
He died in 1324, while serving as the
king's envoy in France.
    189 *entreated* treated.
    191 *'long of* because of.

Mortimer Senior.   Plead for him he that will; I am resolved.
Lancaster.   And so am I, my lord. Dissuade the queen.   215
Queen Isabella.   O Lancaster, let him dissuade the king,
  For 'tis against my will he should return.
Warwick.   Then speak not for him; let the peasant go.
Queen Isabella.   'Tis for myself I speak, and not for him.
Pembroke.   No speaking will prevail, and therefore cease.   220
Mortimer Junior.   Fair queen, forbear to angle for the fish
  Which, being caught, strikes him that takes it dead.
  I mean that vile torpedo, Gaveston,
  That now, I hope, floats on the Irish seas.
Queen Isabella.   Sweet Mortimer, sit down by me awhile,   225
  And I will tell thee reasons of such weight
  As thou wilt soon subscribe to his repeal.
Mortimer Junior.   It is impossible, but speak your mind.
Queen Isabella.   Then thus, but none shall hear it but ourselves.
                     [*She talks to Mortimer Junior apart.*]
Lancaster.   My lords, albeit the queen win Mortimer,   230
  Will you be resolute and hold with me?
Mortimer Senior.   Not I, against my nephew.
Pembroke.   Fear not, the queen's words cannot alter him.
Warwick.   No? Do but mark how earnestly she pleads.
Lancaster.   And see how coldly his looks make denial.   235
Warwick.   She smiles; now for my life his mind is changed.
Lancaster.   I'll rather lose his friendship, I, than grant.
Mortimer Junior.   Well, of necessity it must be so.
  My lords, that I abhor base Gaveston,
  I hope your honors make no question,   240
  And therefore, though I plead for his repeal,
  'Tis not for his sake, but for our avail;
  Nay for the realm's behoof, and for the king's.
Lancaster.   Fie, Mortimer, dishonor not thyself!
  Can this be true, 'twas good to banish him?   245
  And is this true, to call him home again?
  Such reasons make white black and dark night day.
Mortimer Junior.   My lord of Lancaster, mark the respect.
Lancaster.   In no respect can contraries be true.
Queen Isabella.   Yet, good my lord, hear what he can allege.   250
Warwick.   All that he speaks is nothing; we are resolved.
Mortimer Junior.   Do you not wish that Gaveston were dead?
Pembroke.   I would he were.
Mortimer Junior.   Why then, my lord, give me but leave to speak.
Mortimer Senior.   But, nephew, do not play the sophister.   255
Mortimer Junior.   This which I urge is of a burning zeal

223 *torpedo* cramp-fish or electric ray.   255 *play the sophister* use false argu-
248 *respect* consideration of a special   ments.
situation.

To mend the king and do our country good.
Know you not Gaveston hath store of gold,
Which may in Ireland purchase him such friends
As he will front the mightiest of us all?   260
And whereas he shall live and be beloved,
'Tis hard for us to work his overthrow.
Warwick.   Mark you but that, my lord of Lancaster.
Mortimer Junior.   But were he here, detested as he is,
How easily might some base slave be suborned   265
To greet his lordship with a poniard,
And none so much as blame the murderer,
But rather praise him for that brave attempt
And in the chronicle enrol his name
For purging of the realm of such a plague.   270
Pembroke.   He saith true.
Lancaster.   Ay, but how chance this was not done before?
Mortimer Junior.   Because, my lords, it was not thought upon.
Nay, more, when he shall know it lies in us
To banish him and then to call him home,   275
'Twill make him vail the top-flag of his pride,
And fear to offend the meanest nobleman.
Mortimer Senior.   But how if he do not, nephew?
Mortimer Junior.   Then may we with some color rise in arms;
For howsoever we have borne it out,   280
'Tis treason to be up against the king;
So shall we have the people of our side,
Which for his father's sake lean to the king,
But cannot brook a night-grown mushrump,
Such a one as my lord of Cornwall is,   285
Should bear us down of the nobility.
And when the commons and the nobles join,
'Tis not the king can buckler Gaveston.
We'll pull him from the strongest hold he hath.
My lords, if to perform this I be slack,   290
Think me as base a groom as Gaveston.
Lancaster.   On that condition, Lancaster will grant.
Warwick.   And so will Pembroke and I.
Mortimer Senior.   And I.
Mortimer Junior.   In this I count me highly gratified,
And Mortimer will rest at your command.   295
Queen Isabella.   And when this favor Isabel forgets,
Then let her live abandoned and forlorn.
But see, in happy time, my lord the king,
Having brought the Earl of Cornwall on his way,

279 *color* pretext, excuse.   288 *buckler* protect (**literally with a**
284 *mushrump* mushroom (one of many   **shield).**
variant forms).

Is new returned. This news will glad him much,   300
Yet not so much as me. I love him more
Than he can Gaveston; would he loved me
But half so much, then were I treble-blessed!

Enter King Edward, mourning.

King Edward. He's gone, and for his absence thus I mourn.
Did never sorrow go so near my heart   305
As doth the want of my sweet Gaveston;
And could my crown's revenue bring him back,
I would freely give it to his enemies
And think I gained, having bought so dear a friend.

Queen Isabella. Hark, how he harps upon his minion.   310

King Edward. My heart is as an anvil unto sorrow,
Which beats upon it like the Cyclops' hammers
And with the noise turns up my giddy brain
And makes me frantic for my Gaveston.
Ah, had some bloodless Fury rose from hell   315
And with my kingly scepter struck me dead,
When I was forced to leave my Gaveston.

Lancaster. *Diablo!* What passions call you these?

Queen Isabella. My gracious lord, I come to bring you news.

King Edward. That you have parlèd with your Mortimer.   320

Queen Isabella. That Gaveston, my lord, shall be repealed.

King Edward. Repealed? The news is too sweet to be true.

Queen Isabella. But will you love me, if you find it so?

King Edward. If it be so, what will not Edward do?

Queen Isabella. For Gaveston, but not for Isabel.   325

King Edward. For thee, fair queen, if thou lovest Gaveston;
I'll hang a golden tongue about thy neck,
Seeing thou hast pleaded with so good success.

Queen Isabella. No other jewels hang about my neck
Than these, my lord; nor let me have more wealth   330
Than I may fetch from this rich treasury.
O how a kiss revives poor Isabel!

King Edward. Once more receive my hand, and let this be
A second marriage 'twixt thyself and me.

Queen Isabella. And may it prove more happy than the first.   335
My gentle lord, bespeak these nobles fair,
That wait attendance for a gracious look
And on their knees salute your majesty.

King Edward. Courageous Lancaster, embrace thy king.
And, as gross vapors perish by the sun,   340
Even so let hatred with thy sovereign's smile.
Live thou with me as my companion.

Lancaster. This salutation overjoys my heart.

King Edward. Warwick shall be my chiefest counselor.

312 *Cyclops* See note to *Dido* I,i,147.   330 *these* i.e., Edward's arms.

These silver hairs will more adorn my court   345
Than gaudy silks or rich embroidery.
Chide me, sweet Warwick, if I go astray.
Warwick.   Slay me, my lord, when I offend your grace.
King Edward.   In solemn triumphs and in public shows,
Pembroke shall bear the sword before the king.   350
Pembroke.   And with this sword Pembroke will fight for you.
King Edward.   But wherefore walks young Mortimer aside?
Be thou commander of our royal fleet;
Or, if that lofty office like thee not,
I make thee here Lord Marshal of the realm.   355
Mortimer Junior.   My lord, I'll marshal so your enemies,
As England shall be quiet and you safe.
King Edward.   And as for you, Lord Mortimer of Chirke,
Whose great achievements in our foreign war
Deserves no common place, nor mean reward,   360
Be you the general of the levied troops
That now are ready to assail the Scots.
Mortimer Senior.   In this your grace hath highly honored me,
For with my nature war doth best agree.
Queen Isabella.   Now is the king of England rich and strong, 365
Having the love of his renownèd peers.
King Edward.   Ay, Isabel, ne'er was my heart so light.
Clerk of the crown, direct our warrant forth
For Gaveston to Ireland.
                    [*Enter Beaumont.*]
                    Beaumont, fly
As fast as Iris or Jove's Mercury.   370
Beaumont.   It shall be done, my gracious lord.
                                                    [*Exit.*]
King Edward.   Lord Mortimer, we leave you to your charge.
Now let us in and feast it royally.
Against our friend the Earl of Cornwall comes,
We'll have a general tilt and tournament,   375
And then his marriage shall be solemnized;
For wot you not that I have made him sure
Unto our cousin, the Earl of Gloucester's heir?
Lancaster.   Such news we hear, my lord.
King Edward.   That day, if not for him. yet for my sake,   380
Who in the triumph will be challenger,
Spare for no cost; we will requite your love.

---

358 *Chirke* border city between Shrop-
shire and Wales, of which the elder
Mortimer was lord.

370 *Iris . . . Mercury* Iris was the
messenger of Juno, as Mercury was that
of Jove.

374 *Against* in preparation for the
time when. *Earl of Cornwall* i.e., Gaveston.

378 *Earl . . . heir* Gilbert de Clare,
eighth Earl of Gloucester, was married
to King Edward's sister. Their daughter,
Margaret, became the wife of Gaveston.

Warwick.   In this or ought your highness shall command us.
King Edward.   Thanks, gentle Warwick. Come, let's in and revel.
                              Exeunt all except the Mortimers.
Mortimer Senior.   Nephew, I must to Scotland; thou stayest here.   385
  Leave now to oppose thyself against the king.
  Thou seest by nature he is mild and calm,
  And, seeing his mind so dotes on Gaveston,
  Let him without controlment have his will.
  The mightiest kings have had their minions.   390
  Great Alexander loved Hephaestion;
  The conquering Hercules for Hylas wept,
  And for Patroclus stern Achilles drooped.
  And not kings only, but the wisest men:
  The Roman Tully loved Octavius,   395
  Grave Socrates, wild Alcibiades.
  Then let his grace, whose youth is flexible
  And promiseth as much as we can wish,
  Freely enjoy that vain, light-headed earl,
  For riper years will wean him from such toys.   400
Mortimer Junior.   Uncle, his wanton humor grieves not me;
  But this I scorn, that one so basely born
  Should by his sovereign's favor grow so pert
  And riot it with the treasure of the realm.
  While soldiers mutiny for want of pay,   405
  He wears a lord's revenue on his back,
  And, Midas-like, he jets it in the court
  With base outlandish cullions at his heels,
  Whose proud fantastic liveries make such show,
  As if that Proteus, god of shapes, appeared.   410
  I have not seen a dapper Jack so brisk.
  He wears a short Italian hooded cloak,
  Larded with pearl, and in his Tuscan cap
  A jewel of more value than the crown.
  While others walk below, the king and he   415
  From out a window laugh at such as we,
  And flout our train, and jest at our attire.

391 *Hephaestion* the close friend and companion of Alexander the Great.

392 *Hylas* See note at I,i,144.

393 *Patroclus* the friend of Achilles, whose slaying by Hector finally aroused Achilles to action and brought an end to the Trojan war.

395 *Tully* Marcus Tullius Cicero, the great Roman orator and statesman. He had no relation to the Emperor Augustus Caesar (Octavius) comparable to that of Gaveston to Edward.

396 *Alcibiades* a somewhat rakish young man of noble birth and good looks befriended by the Greek philosopher, Socrates.

400 *toys* foolish pastimes.

407 *Midas-like* like Midas, the mythical king endowed by Dionysius with the power to turn all he touched to gold. *jets it* struts.

408 *outlandish cullions* foreign scoundrels.

410 *Proteus* a sea deity who changed his shape whenever men tried to restrain him.

Uncle, 'tis this that makes me impatient.

Mortimer Senior.   But, nephew, now you see the king is changed.

Mortimer Junior.   Then so am I, and live to do him service.   420
But whiles I have a sword, a hand, a heart,
I will not yield to any such upstart.
You know my mind; come, uncle, let's away.

                                                  Exeunt.

＊

Enter Spencer [Junior] and Baldock.   II,i.

Baldock.   Spencer,
Seeing that our lord th' Earl of Gloucester's dead,
Which of the nobles dost thou mean to serve?

Spencer Junior.   Not Mortimer, nor any of his side,
Because the king and he are enemies.   5
Baldock, learn this of me: a factious lord
Shall hardly do himself good, much less us,
But he that hath the favor of a king
May with one word advance us while we live.
The liberal Earl of Cornwall is the man   10
On whose good fortune Spencer's hope depends.

Baldock.   What, mean you then to be his follower?

Spencer Junior.   No, his companion, for he loves me well
And would have once preferred me to the king.

Baldock.   But he is banished; there's small hope of him.   15

Spencer Junior.   Ay, for a while; but, Baldock, mark the end.
A friend of mine told me in secrecy
That he's repealed and sent for back again,
And even now a post came from the court
With letters to our lady from the king,   20
And as she read she smiled, which makes me think
It is about her lover Gaveston.

Baldock.   'Tis like enough, for since he was exiled
She neither walks abroad nor comes in sight.
But I had thought the match had been broke off   25
And that his banishment had changed her mind.

Spencer Junior.   Our lady's first love is not wavering;
My life for thine she will have Gaveston.

II,i.

SD *Spencer Junior* Hugh le Despenser, who married the elder sister of Gaveston's wife, daughter of the Earl of Gloucester. Always a strong partisan of King Edward, he was executed at Hereford in November, 1326, one month after the execution of his father. *Baldock* Robert of Baldock, keeper of the king's privy seal, fled with King Edward, was captured in November, 1326, and died the following year.

Baldock.   Then hope I by her means to be preferred,
Having read unto her since she was a child.   30
Spencer Junior.   Then, Baldock, you must cast the scholar off
And learn to court it like a gentleman.
'Tis not a black coat and a little band,
A velvet-caped cloak, faced before with serge,
And smelling to a nosegay all the day,   35
Or holding of a napkin in your hand,
Or saying a long grace at a table's end,
Or making low legs to a nobleman,
Or looking downward with your eyelids close,
And saying, 'Truly, an't may please your honor,'   40
Can get you any favor with great men;
You must be proud, bold, pleasant, resolute,
And now and then stab, as occasion serves.
Baldock.   Spencer, thou knowest I hate such formal toys
And use them but of mere hypocrisy.   45
Mine old lord whiles he lived was so precise
That he would take exceptions at my buttons,
And being like pin's heads, blame me for the bigness;
Which made me curate-like in mine attire,
Though inwardly licentious enough   50
And apt for any kind of villainy.
I am none of these common pedants, I,
That cannot speak without *propterea quod.*
Spencer Junior.   But one of those that saith *quandoquidem*
And hath a special gift to form a verb.   55
Baldock.   Leave off this jesting, here my lady comes.
                    Enter the King's Niece.
Niece.   The grief for his exile was not so much
As is the joy of his returning home.
This letter came from my sweet Gaveston.
What needst thou, love, thus to excuse thyself?   60
I know thou couldst not come and visit me.
'I will not long be from thee, though I die.'   [*She reads.*]
This argues the entire love of my lord.
'When I forsake thee, death seize on my heart.'   [*She reads.*]
But rest thee here where Gaveston shall sleep.   65
                    [*She places the letter in her bosom.*]
Now to the letter of my lord the king.
He wills me to repair unto the court
And meet my Gaveston. Why do I stay,
Seeing that he talks thus of my marriage day?
Who's there? Baldock!   70

---

33 *black coat* the traditional garb of   *dem* Both are terms meaning 'because'
the scholar.   and used in formal rhetoric.
53–54 *propterea quod . . . quandoqui-*   55 *form a verb* use language eloquently.

See that my coach be ready; I must hence.
Baldock. It shall be done, madam.
Niece. And meet me at the park-pale presently.

                                          Exit [Baldock].

Spencer, stay you and bear me company,
For I have joyful news to tell thee of.   75
My lord of Cornwall is a-coming over
And will be at the court as soon as we.
Spencer Junior. I knew the king would have him home again.
Niece. If all things sort out as I hope they will,
Thy service, Spencer, shall be thought upon.   80
Spencer Junior. I humbly thank your ladyship.
Niece. Come, lead the way; I long till I am there.

                                           [Exeunt.]

✳

                                               II,ii.

    Enter [King] Edward, Queen [Isabella], Lancaster, Mortimer
      [Junior], Warwick, Pembroke, Kent [and] Attendants.
King Edward. The wind is good; I wonder why he stays;
  I fear me he is wracked upon the sea.
Queen Isabella. Look, Lancaster, how passionate he is,
  And still his mind runs on his minion.
Lancaster. My lord—   5
King Edward. How now! What news? Is Gaveston arrived?
Mortimer Junior. Nothing but Gaveston! What means your grace?
  You have matters of more weight to think upon;
  The king of France sets foot in Normandy.
King Edward. A trifle! We'll expel him when we please.   10
  But tell me, Mortimer, what's thy device
  Against the stately triumph we decreed?
Mortimer Junior. A homely one, my lord, not worth the telling.
King Edward. Prithee let me know it.
Mortimer Junior. But seeing you are so desirous, thus it is: 15
  A lofty cedar tree, fair flourishing,
  On whose top-branches kingly eagles perch,
  And by the bark a canker creeps me up
  And gets unto the highest bough of all;
  The motto, *Æque tandem.*   20
King Edward. And what is yours, my lord of Lancaster?

---

71 *coach* an anachronism, since coaches were not introduced into England until the middle of the sixteenth century.

II,ii.

2 *wracked* shipwrecked.

11 *device* a painting on a shield, accompanied by a motto.
18 *canker* canker-worm, a striped green caterpillar which destroys plants.
20 *Æque tandem* equally at last (the sense being that Gaveston, the canker,

Lancaster.   My lord, mine's more obscure than Mortimer's.
  Pliny reports there is a flying fish
  Which all the other fishes deadly hate,
  And therefore, being pursued, it takes the air.   25
  No sooner is it up, but there's a fowl
  That seizeth it; this fish, my lord, I bear;
  The motto this: *Undique mors est.*
King Edward.   Proud Mortimer! Ungentle Lancaster!
  Is this the love you bear your sovereign?   30
  Is this the fruit your reconcilement bears?
  Can you in words make show of amity,
  And in your shields display your rancorous minds?
  What call you this but private libelling
  Against the Earl of Cornwall and my brother?   35
Queen Isabella.   Sweet husband, be content; they all love you.
King Edward.   They love me not that hate my Gaveston.
  I am that cedar, shake me not too much;
  And you the eagles; soar ye ne'er so high,
  I have the jesses that will pull you down;   40
  And *Æque tandem* shall that canker cry
  Unto the proudest peer of Britainy.
  Though thou compar'st him to a flying fish,
  And threatenest death whether he rise or fall,
  'Tis not the hugest monster of the sea,   45
  Nor foulest harpy, that shall swallow him.
Mortimer Junior.   If in his absence thus he favors him,
  What will he do whenas he shall be present?
Lancaster.   That shall we see; look where his lordship comes.
              Enter Gaveston.
King Edward.   My Gaveston!   50
  Welcome to Tynemouth! Welcome to thy friend!
  Thy absence made me droop and pine away;
  For, as the lovers of fair Danaë,
  When she was locked up in a brazen tower,
  Desired her more and waxed outrageous,   55
  So did it sure with me. And now thy sight
  Is sweeter far than was thy parting hence

---

will finally reach the top of the tree
and be equal with the eagle, Edward).

23 *Pliny* Gaius Plinius Secundus, or
Pliny the Elder, Roman author of the
Naturalis Historia. Actually there is no
such account in Pliny, although there
is a description similar to Marlowe's in
Sir John Hawkins' account of his second
voyage to Guiana, published in 1565.

28 *Undique mors est* Death is on all
sides.

40 *jesses* short straps, usually of leather,
tied to the legs of trained hawks and
used to control them.

46 *harpy* legendary bird with the head
of a woman.

53 *Danaë* legendary Greek heroine who,
although locked up in a tower by her
father, was wooed by Zeus in the form
of a shower of gold. Greek mythology
does not record that she had other lovers.

Bitter and irksome to my sobbing heart.
Gaveston.   Sweet lord and king, your speech preventeth mine,
  Yet have I words left to express my joy.   60
  The shepherd nipped with biting winter's rage
  Frolics not more to see the painted spring,
  Than I do to behold your majesty.
King Edward.   Will none of you salute my Gaveston?
Lancaster.   Salute him? Yes. Welcome Lord Chamberlain.   65
Mortimer Junior.   Welcome is the good Earl of Cornwall.
Warwick.   Welcome, Lord Governor of the Isle of Man.
Pembroke.   Welcome, Master Secretary.
Kent.   Brother, do you hear them?
King Edward.   Still will these earls and barons use me thus?   70
Gaveston.   My lord, I cannot brook these injuries.
Queen Isabella.   Ay me, poor soul, when these begin to jar.
                                                    [*Aside.*]
King Edward.   Return it to their throats; I'll be thy warrant.
Gaveston.   Base, leaden earls, that glory in your birth,
  Go sit at home and eat your tenants' beef,   75
  And come not here to scoff at Gaveston,
  Whose mounting thoughts did never creep so low
  As to bestow a look on such as you.
Lancaster.   Yet I disdain not to do this for you.
                                      [*He draws his sword.*]
King Edward.   Treason, treason! Where's the traitor?   80
Pembroke.   Here! Here!
King Edward.   Convey hence Gaveston; they'll murder him.
Gaveston.   The life of thee shall salve this foul disgrace.
Mortimer Junior.   Villain, thy life unless I miss mine aim.
                                      [*He wounds Gaveston.*]
Queen Isabella.   Ah, furious Mortimer, what hast thou done?   85
Mortimer Junior.   No more than I would answer, were he slain.
                          [*Exit Gaveston with Attendants.*]
King Edward.   Yes, more than thou canst answer, though he live.
  Dear shall you both aby this riotous deed.
  Out of my presence; come not near the court.
Mortimer Junior.   I'll not be barred the court for Gaveston.   90
Lancaster.   We'll hale him by the ears unto the block.
King Edward.   Look to your own heads; his is sure enough.
Warwick.   Look to your own crown, if you back him thus.
Kent.   Warwick, these words do ill beseem thy years.
King Edward.   Nay, all of them conspire to cross me thus,   95
  But if I live, I'll tread upon their heads
  That think with high looks thus to tread me down.
  Come, Edmund, let's away and levy men;
  'Tis war that must abate these barons' pride.
            Exit King [Edward with Queen Isabella and Kent].
62 *painted* adorned with flowers.   88 *aby* pay for.

Warwick.   Let's to our castles, for the king is moved.   100
Mortimer Junior.   Moved may he be, and perish in his wrath!
Lancaster.   Cousin, it is no dealing with him now.
   He means to make us stoop by force of arms,
   And therefore let us jointly here protest
   To prosecute that Gaveston to the death.   105
Mortimer Junior.   By heaven, the abject villain shall not live.
Warwick.   I'll have his blood or die in seeking it.
Pembroke.   The like oath Pembroke takes.
Lancaster.   And so doth Lancaster.
   Now send our heralds to defy the king,
   And make the people swear to put him down.   110
                    Enter a Messenger.
Mortimer Junior.   Letters? From whence?
Messenger.   From Scotland, my lord.
                    [*He gives letters to Mortimer, who reads.*]
Lancaster.   Why, how now, cousin, how fares all our friends?
Mortimer Junior.   My uncle's taken prisoner by the Scots.
Lancaster.   We'll have him ransomed, man; be of good cheer.
Mortimer Junior.   They rate his ransom at five thousand pound.   115
   Who should defray the money but the king,
   Seeing he is taken prisoner in his wars?
   I'll to the king.
Lancaster.   Do, cousin, and I'll bear thee company.
Warwick.   Meantime, my lord of Pembroke and myself   120
   Will to Newcastle here and gather head.
Mortimer Junior.   About it then, and we will follow you.
Lancaster.   Be resolute and full of secrecy.
Warwick.   I warrant you.
                    [*Exeunt all but Mortimer Junior and Lancaster.*]
Mortimer Junior.   Cousin, and if he will not ransom him,   125
   I'll thunder such a peal into his ears
   As never subject did unto his king.
Lancaster.   Content, I'll bear my part. Holla! Who's there?
                    [*Enter a Guard.*]
Mortimer Junior.   Ay, marry, such a guard as this doth well.
Lancaster.   Lead on the way.   130
Guard.   Whither will your lordships?
Mortimer Junior.   Whither else but to the king?
Guard.   His highness is disposed to be alone.
Lancaster.   Why, so he may, but we will speak to him.
Guard.   You may not in, my lord.   135
Mortimer Junior.   May we not?
                    [*Enter King Edward and Kent.*]
King Edward.   How now! What noise is this?

104 *protest* vow.   113 *uncle's . . . Scots* There is no his-
109 *defy* renounce allegiance to.   torical basis for this episode.
                                        121 *gather head* raise an army.

Who have we there? Is't you?

                                      [*Going.*]

Mortimer Junior. Nay, stay, my lord, I come to bring you news;
  Mine uncle's taken prisoner by the Scots.   140
King Edward. Then ransom him.
Lancaster. 'Twas in your wars; you should ransom him.
Mortimer Junior. And you shall ransom him, or else—
Kent. What, Mortimer! You will not threaten him?
King Edward. Quiet yourself; you shall have the broad seal   145
  To gather for him thoroughout the realm.
Lancaster. Your minion Gaveston hath taught you this.
Mortimer Junior. My lord, the family of the Mortimers
  Are not so poor, but, would they sell their land,
  Would levy men enough to anger you.   150
  We never beg, but use such prayers as these.

                              [*He grasps his sword.*]

King Edward. Shall I still be haunted thus?
Mortimer Junior. Nay, now you are here alone, I'll speak my mind.
Lancaster. And so will I, and then, my lord, farewell.
Mortimer Junior. The idle triumphs, masks, lascivious shows,   155
  And prodigal gifts bestowed on Gaveston,
  Have drawn thy treasure dry and made thee weak,
  The murmuring commons overstretchèd hath.
Lancaster. Look for rebellion; look to be deposed.
  Thy garrisons are beaten out of France,   160
  And, lame and poor, lie groaning at the gates.
  The wild O'Neil, with swarms of Irish kerns,
  Lives uncontrolled within the English pale.
  Unto the walls of York the Scots made road
  And unresisted drave away rich spoils.   165
Mortimer Junior. The haughty Dane commands the narrow seas,
  While in the harbor ride thy ships unrigged.
Lancaster. What foreign prince sends thee ambassadors?
Mortimer Junior. Who loves thee, but a sort of flatterers?
Lancaster. Thy gentle queen, sole sister to Valois,   170
  Complains that thou hast left her all forlorn.
Mortimer Junior. Thy court is naked, being bereft of those
  That makes a king seem glorious to the world;
  I mean the peers, whom thou shouldst dearly love.
  Libels are cast again thee in the street,   175
  Ballads and rhymes made of thy overthrow.

145–146 *broad seal . . . realm* royal
license to collect alms (as a beggar) for
him. The king is being contemptuous
and insulting.
  152 *haunted* pursued.
  162 *O'Neil* Shane O'Neil was an Irish

leader of Marlowe's own day. *kerns* footsoldiers.
  170 *Valois* See note to *Massacre at
Paris*, xviii,46. Queen Isabella's brothers
actually were not of the house of Valois,
although her cousin, Philip of Valois, did
eventually become king of France.

Lancaster.　The Northern borderers, seeing their houses burnt,
　　Their wives and children slain, run up and down,
　　Cursing the name of thee and Gaveston.
Mortimer Junior.　When wert thou in the field with banner spread?　180
　　But once, and then thy soldiers marched like players,
　　With garish robes, not armor, and thyself,
　　Bedaubed with gold, rode laughing at the rest,
　　Nodding and shaking of thy spangled crest,
　　Where women's favors hung like labels down.　185
Lancaster.　And thereof came it that the fleering Scots,
　　To England's high disgrace, have made this jig:

　　　　　Maids of England, sore may you mourn,
　　　　　　For your lemans you have lost at Bannocksbourn,
　　　　　　　With a heave and a ho!　190
　　　　　　What weeneth the King of England,
　　　　　　So soon to have won Scotland?
　　　　　　　With a rombelow!

Mortimer Junior.　Wigmore shall fly to set my uncle free.
Lancaster.　And when 'tis gone, our swords shall purchase more.　195
　　If ye be moved, revenge it as you can.
　　Look next to see us with our ensigns spread.
　　　　　　　　　　　[*Exit with Mortimer Junior.*]
King Edward.　My swelling heart for very anger breaks.
　　How oft have I been baited by these peers,
　　And dare not be revenged, for their power is great!
　　Yet, shall the crowing of these cockerels　200
　　Affright a lion? Edward, unfold thy paws,
　　And let their lives' blood slake thy fury's hunger.
　　If I be cruel and grow tyrannous,
　　Now let them thank themselves and rue too late.　205
Kent.　My lord, I see your love to Gaveston
　　Will be the ruin of the realm and you,
　　For now the wrathful nobles threaten wars,
　　And therefore, brother, banish him for ever.
King Edward.　Art thou an enemy to my Gaveston?　210
Kent.　Ay, and it grieves me that I favored him.
King Edward.　Traitor, begone! Whine thou with Mortimer.
Kent.　So will I, rather than with Gaveston.
King Edward.　Out of my sight, and trouble me no more.
Kent.　No marvel though thou scorn thy noble peers,　215

185 *labels* pieces of parchment used to affix seals to documents.
186 *fleering* jeering.
187 *jig* mocking song.
189 *lemans* sweethearts. *Bannocksbourn* battle against the Scots, fought on June

21, 1314, in which the English suffered a crushing defeat.
193 *rombelow* a meaningless term used in refrains.
194 *Wigmore* Mortimer Junior's estate. *shall fly* i.e., will be sold.
201 *cockerels* young roosters.

When I thy brother am rejected thus.
King Edward. Away!

                                                    Exit [Kent].

Poor Gaveston, that hast no friend but me,
Do what they can, we'll live in Tynemouth here,
And so I walk with him about the walls,   220
What care I though the earls begirt us round?
Here comes she that's cause of all these jars.

        Enter Queen [Isabella, with the King's Niece, two] Ladies,
                [Gaveston,] Baldock, and Spencer [Junior].

Queen Isabella. My lord, 'tis thought the earls are up in arms.
King Edward. Ay, and 'tis likewise thought you favor 'em.
Queen Isabella. Thus do you still suspect me without cause?   225
Niece. Sweet uncle, speak more kindly to the queen.
Gaveston. My lord, dissemble with her; speak her fair.

                                    [Aside to King Edward.]

King Edward. Pardon me, sweet, I forgot myself.
Queen Isabella. Your pardon is quickly got of Isabel.
King Edward. The younger Mortimer is grown so brave   230
That to my face he threatens civil wars.
Gaveston. Why do you not commit him to the Tower?
King Edward. I dare not, for the people love him well.
Gaveston. Why, then we'll have him privily made away.
King Edward. Would Lancaster and he had both caroused   235
A bowl of poison to each other's health.
But let them go, and tell me what are these.
Niece. Two of my father's servants whilst he lived.
May't please your grace to entertain them now?
King Edward. Tell me, where wast thou born? What is thine
    arms?   240
Baldock. My name is Baldock, and my gentry
I fetched from Oxford, not from heraldry.
King Edward. The fitter art thou, Baldock, for my turn.
Wait on me, and I'll see thou shalt not want.
Baldock. I humbly thank your majesty.   245
King Edward. Knowest thou him, Gaveston?
Gaveston.   Ay, my lord;
His name is Spencer; he is well allied.
For my sake, let him wait upon your grace.
Scarce shall you find a man of more desert.
King Edward. Then, Spencer, wait upon me; for his sake   250
I'll grace thee with a higher style ere long.
Spencer Junior. No greater titles happen unto me
Than to be favored of your majesty.
King Edward. Cousin, this day shall be your marriage feast.
And, Gaveston, think that I love thee well,   255
To wed thee to our niece, the only heir

Unto the Earl of Gloucester late deceased.
Gaveston.   I know, my lord, many will stomach me,
But I respect neither their love nor hate.
King Edward.   The headstrong barons shall not limit me;   260
He that I list to favor shall be great.
Come, let's away; and when the marriage ends,
Have at the rebels and their 'complices.

Exeunt.

✳

Enter Lancaster, Mortimer [Junior,] Warwick, Pembroke, Kent
[and others].

Kent.   My lords, of love to this our native land
I come to join with you and leave the king,
And in your quarrel and the realm's behoof
Will be the first that shall adventure life.
Lancaster.   I fear me you are sent of policy,   5
To undermine us with a show of love.
Warwick.   He is your brother; therefore have we cause
To cast the worst and doubt of your revolt.
Kent.   Mine honor shall be hostage of my truth;
If that will not suffice, farewell, my lords.   10
Mortimer Junior.   Stay, Edmund; never was Plantagenet
False of his word, and therefore trust we thee.
Pembroke.   But what's the reason you should leave him now?
Kent.   I have informed the Earl of Lancaster.
Lancaster.   And it sufficeth. Now, my lords, know this,   15
That Gaveston is secretly arrived
And here in Tynemouth frolics with the king.
Let us with these our followers scale the walls
And suddenly surprise them unawares.
Mortimer Junior.   I'll give the onset.
Warwick.   And I'll follow thee.   20
Mortimer Junior.   This tottered ensign of my ancestors,
Which swept the desert shore of that Dead Sea
Whereof we got the name of Mortimer,
Will I advance upon these castle walls.
Drums, strike alarum, raise them from their sport,   25
And ring aloud the knell of Gaveston.
Lancaster.   None be so hardy as to touch the king,

258 *stomach* take offense at.

II,iii.
5 *policy* political deception.

8 *cast* anticipate.
21 *tottered* tattered.

But neither spare you Gaveston nor his friends.

Exeunt.

✻

    Enter King [Edward] and Spencer [Junior].   II,iv.
King Edward.   O tell me, Spencer, where is Gaveston?
Spencer Junior.   I fear me he is slain, my gracious lord.
King Edward.   No, here he comes. Now let them spoil and kill.
    [Enter] to them [Queen Isabella, the King's Niece,] Gaveston,
                    [and Others].
Fly, fly, my lords, the earls have got the hold;
Take shipping and away to Scarborough;   5
Spencer and I will post away by land.
Gaveston.   O stay, my lord, they will not injure you.
King Edward.   I will not trust them. Gaveston, away.
Gaveston.   Farewell, my lord.
King Edward.   Lady, farewell.   10
Niece.   Farewell, sweet uncle, till we meet again.
King Edward.   Farewell, sweet Gaveston, and farewell, niece.
Queen Isabella.   No farewell to poor Isabel thy queen?
King Edward.   Yes, yes, for Mortimer, your lover's sake.
Queen Isabella.   Heavens can witness I love none but you.   15
                  Exeunt [all but Queen] Isabella.
From my embracements thus he breaks away.
O that mine arms could close this isle about,
That I might pull him to me where I would,
Or that these tears that drizzle from mine eyes
Had power to mollify his stony heart,   20
That when I had him we might never part.
    Enter [Lancaster, Warwick, Mortimer Junior, and Others].
                Alarums [within].
Lancaster.   I wonder how he 'scaped?
Mortimer Junior.   Who's this? The queen!
Queen Isabella.   Ay, Mortimer, the miserable queen,
Whose pining heart her inward sighs have blasted,
And body with continual mourning wasted.   25
These hands are tired with haling of my lord
From Gaveston, from wicked Gaveston,
And all in vain, for when I speak him fair,
He turns away and smiles upon his minion.
Mortimer Junior.   Cease to lament, and tell us where's the king?   30
Queen Isabella.   What would you with the king? Is't him you seek?
Lancaster.   No madam, but that cursèd Gaveston.
Far be it from the thought of Lancaster
To offer violence to his sovereign.

We would but rid the realm of Gaveston.   35
Tell us where he remains, and he shall die.
Queen Isabella.   He's gone by water unto Scarborough;
  Pursue him quickly, and he cannot 'scape;
  The king hath left him, and his train is small.
Warwick.   Forslow no time. Sweet Lancaster, let's march.   40
Mortimer Junior.   How comes it that the king and he is parted?
Queen Isabella.   That this your army, going several ways,
  Might be of lesser force, and with the power
  That he intendeth presently to raise,
  Be easily suppressed; and therefore be gone.   45
Mortimer Junior.   Here in the river rides a Flemish hoy;
  Let's all aboard and follow him amain.
Lancaster.   The wind that bears him hence will fill our sails.
  Come, come aboard; 'tis but an hour's sailing.
Mortimer Junior.   Madam, stay you within this castle here.   50
Queen Isabella.   No, Mortimer, I'll to my lord the king.
Mortimer Junior.   Nay, rather sail with us to Scarborough.
Queen Isabella.   You know the king is so suspicious,
  As if he hear I have but talked with you,
  Mine honor will be called in question;   55
  And therefore, gentle Mortimer, be gone.
Mortimer Junior.   Madam, I cannot stay to answer you,
  But think of Mortimer as he deserves.
                  [Exeunt all but Queen Isabella.]
Queen Isabella.   So well hast thou deserved, sweet Mortimer,
  As Isabel could live with thee forever.   60
  In vain I look for love at Edward's hand,
  Whose eyes are fixed on none but Gaveston;
  Yet once more I'll importune him with prayers.
  If he be strange and not regard my words,
  My son and I will over into France   65
  And to the king my brother there complain
  How Gaveston hath robbed me of his love.
  But yet I hope my sorrows will have end,
  And Gaveston this blessèd day be slain.

                                    Exit.

         Enter Gaveston, pursued.   II,v.
Gaveston.   Yet, lusty lords, I have escaped your hands,
  Your threats, your 'larums, and your hot pursuits;

II,iv.   **II,v.**
40 *Forslow* waste.   2 *'larums* alarms.
46 *Flemish hoy* a small fishing vessel
used in the North Sea.

And though divorcèd from King Edward's eyes,
Yet liveth Pierce of Gaveston unsurprised,
Breathing, in hope—*malgrado* all your beards,   5
That muster rebels thus against your king—
To see his royal sovereign once again.

> *Enter [Warwick, Lancaster, Pembroke, Mortimer Junior, Sol-
> diers, James, and other Attendants of Pembroke].*

Warwick.   Upon him, soldiers; take away his weapons.
Mortimer Junior.   Thou proud disturber of thy country's peace,
Corrupter of thy king, cause of these broils,   10
Base flatterer, yield! And were it not for shame,
Shame and dishonor to a soldier's name,
Upon my weapon's point here shouldst thou fall
And welter in thy gore.
Lancaster.   Monster of men,
That, like the Greekish strumpet, trained to arms   15
And bloody wars so many valiant knights,
Look for no other fortune, wretch, than death.
King Edward is not here to buckler thee.
Warwick.   Lancaster, why talk'st thou to the slave?
Go, soldiers, take him hence, for, by my sword,   20
His head shall off. Gaveston, short warning
Shall serve thy turn. It is our country's cause
That here severely we will execute
Upon thy person. Hang him at a bough.
Gaveston.   My lord—   25
Warwick.   Soldiers, have him away.
But for thou wert the favorite of a king,
Thou shalt have so much honor at our hands.
Gaveston.   I thank you all, my lords. Then I perceive
That heading is one, and hanging is the other,   30
And death is all.

> *Enter Earl of Arundel.*

Lancaster.   How now, my lord of Arundel?
Arundel.   My lords, King Edward greets you all by me.
Warwick.   Arundel, say your message.
Arundel.   His majesty,
Hearing that you had taken Gaveston,   35
Entreateth you by me, yet but he may
See him before he dies; for why, he says,

---

5 *malgrado* in spite of.
15 *Greekish strumpet* Helen of Troy.
trained enticed.
18 *buckler* See note at I,iv,288.
28 *so much honor* Gentlemen were
beheaded, hanging being reserved for
common thieves.

31, SD *Arundel* Edmund Fitzalan, Earl
of Arundel, at first opposed King Edward, but later joined the king's part
and was executed by Mortimer in November, 1326.
37 *for why* because.

And sends you word, he knows that die he shall;
And if you gratify his grace so far,
He will be mindful of the courtesy.   40
Warwick. How now?
Gaveston.   Renownèd Edward, how thy name
  Revives poor Gaveston.
Warwick.   No, it needeth not.
  Arundel, we will gratify the king
  In other matters; he must pardon us in this.
  Soldiers, away with him.   45
Gaveston. Why, my lord of Warwick,
  Will not these delays beget my hopes?
  I know it, lords, it is this life you aim at;
  Yet grant King Edward this.
Mortimer Junior.   Shalt thou appoint
  What we shall grant? Soldiers, away with him.   50
  Thus we'll gratify the king;
  We'll send his head by thee; let him bestow
  His tears on that, for that is all he gets
  Of Gaveston, or else his senseless trunk.
Lancaster. Not so, my lord, lest he bestow more cost   55
  In burying him than he hath ever earned.
Arundel. My lords, it is his majesty's request,
  And in the honor of a king he swears,
  He will but talk with him and send him back.
Warwick. When, can you tell? Arundel, no; we wot   60
  He that the care of realm remits
  And drives his nobles to these exigents
  For Gaveston, will, if he sees him once,
  Violate any promise to possess him.
Arundel. Then if you will not trust his grace in keep,   65
  My lords, I will be pledge for his return.
Mortimer Junior. It is honorable in thee to offer this,
  But for we know thou art a noble gentleman,
  We will not wrong thee so, to make away
  A true man for a thief.   70
Gaveston. How mean'st thou, Mortimer? That is over-base.
Mortimer Junior. Away, base groom, robber of king's renown.
  Question with thy companions and thy mates.
Pembroke. My lord Mortimer, and you, my lords, each one,
  To gratify the king's request therein,   75
  Touching the sending of this Gaveston,
  Because his majesty so earnestly
  Desires to see the man before his death,
  I will upon mine honor undertake
  To carry him and bring him back again;   80

61 *remits* abandons.

Provided this, that you my lord of Arundel
Will join with me.
Warwick.   Pembroke, what wilt thou do?
Cause yet more bloodshed? Is it not enough
That we have taken him, but must we now
Leave him on 'had I wist,' and let him go?   85
Pembroke.   My lords, I will not over-woo your honors,
But if you dare trust Pembroke with the prisoner,
Upon mine oath, I will return him back.
Arundel.   My lord of Lancaster, what say you in this?
Lancaster.   Why, I say, let him go on Pembroke's word.   90
Pembroke.   And you, Lord Mortimer?
Mortimer Junior.   How say you, my lord of Warwick?
Warwick.   Nay, do your pleasures; I know how 'twill prove.
Pembroke.   Then give him me.
Gaveston.   Sweet sovereign, yet I come
To see thee ere I die.
Warwick.   Yet not perhaps,   95
If Warwick's wit and policy prevail.   [*Aside.*]
Mortimer Junior.   My lord of Pembroke, we deliver him you;
Return him on your honor. Sound, away!
          Exeunt [*all except*] *Pembroke,* [*Arundel,*] *Gaveston,*
                    [*James, and other Attendants of Pembroke*].
Pembroke.   My lord, you shall go with me.
My house is not far hence, out of the way   100
A little, but our men shall go along.
We that have pretty wenches to our wives,
Sir, must not come so near and balk their lips.
Arundel.   'Tis very kindly spoke, my lord of Pembroke.
Your honor hath an adamant of power   105
To draw a prince.
Pembroke.   So, my lord. Come hither, James.
I do commit this Gaveston to thee.
Be thou this night his keeper; in the morning
We will discharge thee of thy charge. Be gone.
Gaveston.   Unhappy Gaveston, whither goest thou now?   110
          Exit [*Pembroke with Attendants*].
Horse-boy.   My lord, we'll quickly be at Cobham.
                    Exeunt.

III,i.

Enter Gaveston mourning, [*James, and others of*] *the Earl of
Pembroke's Men.*

105 *adamant* magnet.

Gaveston.   O treacherous Warwick, thus to wrong thy friend.
James.   I see it is your life these arms pursue.
Gaveston.   Weaponless must I fall, and die in bands?
  O, must this day be period of my life?
  Center of all my bliss! And ye be men,   5
  Speed to the king.
          Enter Warwick and his company [of Soldiers].
Warwick.   My lord of Pembroke's men,
  Strive you no longer; I will have that Gaveston.
James.   Your lordship doth dishonor to yourself,
  And wrong our lord, your honorable friend.
Warwick.   No, James, it is my country's cause I follow.   10
  Go, take the villain; soldiers, come away.
  We'll make quick work. Commend me to your master,
  My friend, and tell him that I watched it well.
  Come, let thy shadow parley with King Edward.
Gaveston.   Treacherous earl, shall I not see the king?   15
Warwick.   The king of heaven perhaps, no other king.
  Away!
        Exeunt Warwick and his Men with Gaveston.
James.   Come, fellows, it booted not for us to strive;
  We will in haste go certify our lord.
             Exeunt.

    *Enter King Edward and Spencer [Junior, Baldock, and Nobles
    of the King's side, and Soldiers] with drums and fifes.*
King Edward.   I long to hear an answer from the barons
  Touching my friend, my dearest Gaveston.
  Ah, Spencer, not the riches of my realm
  Can ransom him; ah, he is marked to die.
  I know the malice of the younger Mortimer.   5
  Warwick I know is rough, and Lancaster
  Inexorable, and I shall never see
  My lovely Pierce, my Gaveston again.
  The barons overbear me with their pride.
Spencer Junior.   Were I King Edward, England's sovereign,   10
  Son to the lovely Eleanor of Spain.

III,i.

  3 *bands* bondage.
  5 *Center . . . bliss* i.e., the day of **his**
reunion with the king, which was to
be the firm center of his happiness, as
the middle of the earth was considered
to be the center of the universe.
  14 *shadow* ghost.
  18 *booted not* was of no avail.

Great Edward Longshanks' issue, would I bear
These braves, this rage, and suffer uncontrolled
These barons thus to beard me in my land,
In mine own realm? My lord, pardon my speech.   15
Did you retain your father's magnanimity,
Did you regard the honor of your name,
You would not suffer thus your majesty
Be counterbuffed of your nobility.
Strike off their heads, and let them preach on poles.   20
No doubt, such lessons they will teach the rest,
As by their preachments they will profit much
And learn obedience to their lawful king.
King Edward.   Yea, gentle Spencer, we have been too mild,
Too kind to them; but now have drawn our sword,   25
And if they send me not my Gaveston,
We'll steel it on their crest and poll their tops.
Baldock.   This haught resolve becomes your majesty,
Not to be tied to their affection,
As though your highness were a schoolboy still,   30
And must be awed and governed like a child.
          Enter Spencer Senior with his truncheon and Soldiers.
Spencer Senior.   Long live my sovereign, the noble Edward,
In peace triumphant, fortunate in wars!
King Edward.   Welcome, old man. Com'st thou in Edward's aid?
Then tell thy prince of whence and what thou art.   35
Spencer Senior.   Lo, with a band of bowmen and of pikes,
Brown bills and targeteers, four hundred strong,
Sworn to defend King Edward's royal right,
I come in person to your majesty,
Spencer, the father of Hugh Spencer there,   40
Bound to your highness everlastingly,
For favors done, in him, unto us all.
King Edward.   Thy father, Spencer?
Spencer Junior.   True, and it like your grace,
That pours, in lieu of all your goodness shown,
His life, my lord, before your princely feet.   45
King Edward.   Welcome ten thousand times, old man, again.
Spencer, this love, this kindness to thy king,

III,ii.

12 *Edward Longshanks* King Edward I.

13 *braves* insults.

20 *poles* The heads of traitors were placed on poles and exhibited on Londdon bridge.

22 *preachments* sermons.

27 *poll their tops* behead them (as the tops of trees are trimmed).

29 *their affection* what they affect, or desire.

31 *Spencer Senior* Hugh le Despenser, a strong supporter of Edward II, executed at Bristol in 1326.

37 *Brown bills* bronzed halberds.

Argues thy noble mind and disposition.
Spencer, I here create thee Earl of Wiltshire,
And daily will enrich thee with our favor,   50
That as the sunshine shall reflect o'er thee.
Beside, the more to manifest our love,
Because we hear Lord Bruce doth sell his land
And that the Mortimers are in hand withal,
Thou shalt have crowns of us t'outbid the barons.   55
And, Spencer, spare them not, but lay it on.
Soldiers, a largess, and thrice welcome all.
Spencer Junior.   My lord, here comes the queen.
    Enter Queen [Isabella] and her son, [Prince Edward,] and
                Levune, a Frenchman.
King Edward.   Madam, what news?
Queen Isabella.   News of dishonor, lord, and discontent.
Our friend Levune, faithful and full of trust,   60
Informeth us by letters and by words
That Lord Valois our brother, king of France,
Because your highness hath been slack in homage,
Hath seizèd Normandy into his hands.
These be the letters, this the messenger.   65
King Edward.   Welcome, Levune. Tush, Sib, if this be all,
Valois and I will soon be friends again.
But to my Gaveston; shall I never see,
Never behold thee now? Madam, in this matter
We will employ you and your little son;   70
You shall go parley with the king of France.
Boy, see you bear you bravely to the king,
And do your message with a majesty.
Prince Edward.   Commit not to my youth things of more weight
Than fits a prince so young as I to bear,   75
And fear not, lord and father, heaven's great beams
On Atlas' shoulder shall not lie more safe
Than shall your charge committed to my trust.
Queen Isabella.   Ah, boy, this towardness makes thy mother fear
Thou art not marked to many days on earth.   80
King Edward.   Madam, we will that you with speed be shipped,
And this our son; Levune shall follow you
With all the haste we can dispatch him hence.
Choose of our lords to bear you company,
And go in peace; leave us in wars at home.   85
Queen Isabella.   Unnatural wars, where subjects brave their king;

49 *Spencer . . . Wiltshire* Young Spen-   77 *Atlas* the Titan of Greek mythology
cer historically was never Earl of Wilt-   condemned by Zeus to bear the heavens
shire. This is Marlowe's invention.   upon his shoulders.
66 *Sib* wife.

God end them once! My lord, I take my leave
To make my preparation for France.

[*Exit with Prince Edward.*]

Enter Arundel.

King Edward.　What, Lord Arundel, dost thou come alone?
Arundel.　Yea, my good lord, for Gaveston is dead.　　　　90
King Edward.　Ah, traitors! Have they put my friend to death?
　Tell me, Arundel, died he ere thou cam'st,
　Or didst thou see my friend to take his death?
Arundel.　Neither, my lord, for as he was surprised,
　Begirt with weapons and with enemies round,　　　　95
　I did your highness' message to them all,
　Demanding him of them, entreating rather,
　And said, upon the honor of my name,
　That I would undertake to carry him
　Unto your highness and to bring him back.　　　　100
King Edward.　And tell me, would the rebels deny me that?
Spencer Junior.　Proud recreants.
King Edward.　　　　　　　　　　Yea, Spencer, traitors all.
Arundel.　I found them at the first inexorable.
　The Earl of Warwick would not bide the hearing,
　Mortimer hardly; Pembroke and Lancaster　　　　105
　Spake least. And when they flatly had denied,
　Refusing to receive me pledge for him,
　The Earl of Pembroke mildly thus bespake:
　'My lords, because our sovereign sends for him
　And promiseth he shall be safe returned,　　　　110
　I will this undertake, to have him hence
　And see him re-delivered to your hands.'
King Edward.　Well, and how fortunes that he came not?
Spencer Junior.　Some treason or some villainy was cause.
Arundel.　The Earl of Warwick seized him on his way;　　　　115
　For being delivered unto Pembroke's men,
　Their lord rode home thinking his prisoner safe;
　But ere he came, Warwick in ambush lay,
　And bare him to his death, and in a trench
　Strake off his head, and marched unto the camp.　　　　120
Spencer Junior.　A bloody part, flatly against law of arms.
King Edward.　O shall I speak, or shall I sigh and die!
Spencer Junior.　My lord, refer your vengeance to the sword
　Upon these barons; hearten up your men;
　Let them not unrevenged murder your friends.　　　　125
　Advance your standard, Edward, in the field,
　And march to fire them from their starting holes.

---

120 *Strake* struck.
127 *starting holes* holes in which wild　animals might take refuge from hunters, usually to be driven out by fire.

King Edward.   By earth, the common mother of us all,   *He kneels.*
  By heaven, and all the moving orbs thereof,
  By this right hand, and by my father's sword,   130
  And all the honors 'longing to my crown,
  I will have heads and lives for him as many
  As I have manors, castles, towns, and towers.
                                    [*He rises.*]
  Treacherous Warwick! Traitorous Mortimer!
  If I be England's king, in lakes of gore   135
  Your headless trunks, your bodies will I trail,
  That you may drink your fill, and quaff in blood,
  And stain my royal standard with the same,
  That so my bloody colors may suggest
  Remembrance of revenge immortally   140
  On your accursèd traitorous progeny,
  You villains that have slain my Gaveston!
  And in this place of honor and of trust,
  Spencer, sweet Spencer, I adopt thee here,
  And merely of our love we do create thee   145
  Earl of Gloucester and Lord Chamberlain,
  Despite of times, despite of enemies.
Spencer Junior.   My lord, here's a messenger from the barons
  Desires access unto your majesty.
King Edward.   Admit him near.   150
      Enter the Herald from the Barons, with his coat of arms.
Herald.   Long live King Edward, England's lawful lord.
King Edward.   So wish not they, I wis, that sent thee hither.
  Thou com'st from Mortimer and his 'complices;
  A ranker rout of rebels never was.
  Well, say thy message.   155
Herald.   The barons up in arms by me salute
  Your highness with long life and happiness,
  And bid me say, as plainer to your grace,
  That if without effusion of blood
  You will this grief have ease and remedy,   160
  That from your princely person you remove
  This Spencer, as a putrifying branch
  That deads the royal vine, whose golden leaves
  Empale your princely head, your diadem,
  Whose brightness such pernicious upstarts dim,   165
  Say they; and lovingly advise your grace
  To cherish virtue and nobility,
  And have old servitors in high esteem,
  And shake off smooth dissembling flatterers.

---

131 *'longing* belonging.
146 *Earl of Gloucester* Being married to
the Earl of Gloucester's daughter, young

Spencer did in fact succeed to the title
following the death of his wife's brother.
158 *plainer* complainant.

This granted, they, their honors, and their lives,   170
Are to your highness vowed and consecrate.
Spencer Junior.   Ah, traitors, will they still display their pride?
King Edward.   Away, tarry no answer, but be gone.
  Rebels, will they appoint their sovereign
  His sports, his pleasures, and his company?   175
  Yet, ere thou go, see how I do divorce
                             [He] embrace[s] Spencer.
  Spencer from me. Now get thee to thy lords,
  And tell them I will come to chastise them
  For murdering Gaveston. Hie thee, get thee gone.
  Edward with fire and sword follows at thy heels.   180
                         [Exit Herald.]
  My lord, perceive you how these rebels swell?
  Soldiers, good hearts, defend your sovereign's right,
  For now, even now, we march to make them stoop.
  Away!
                   Exeunt. Alarums, excursions, a great
                   fight, and a retreat [sounded within].

                                      III,iii.
    Enter King [Edward], Spencer Senior, Spencer Junior, and the
             Noblemen of the King's side.
King Edward.   Why do we sound retreat? Upon them, lords!
  This day I shall pour vengeance with my sword
  On those proud rebels that are up in arms
  And do confront and countermand their king.
Spencer Junior.   I doubt it not, my lord, right will prevail.   5
Spencer Senior.   'Tis not amiss, my liege, for either part
  To breathe awhile; our men, with sweat and dust
  All choked well near, begin to faint for heat,
  And this retire refresheth horse and man.
Spencer Junior.   Here come the rebels.   10
    Enter the Barons, Mortimer [Junior,] Lancaster, Warwick,
             Pembroke and others.
Mortimer Junior.   Look, Lancaster, yonder is Edward
  Among his flatterers.
Lancaster.   And there let him be
  Till he pay dearly for their company.
Warwick.   And shall, or Warwick's sword shall smite in vain.
King Edward.   What, rebels, do you shrink and sound retreat?   15
Mortimer Junior.   No, Edward, no; thy flatterers faint and fly.
Lancaster.   Thou'd best betimes forsake them, and their trains,
  For they'll betray thee, traitors as they are.

Spencer Junior.   Traitor on thy face, rebellious Lancaster!
Pembroke.   Away, base upstart, brav'st thou nobles thus?   20
Spencer Senior.   A noble attempt and honorable deed,
  Is it not, trow ye, to assemble aid
  And levy arms against your lawful king?
King Edward.   For which ere long their heads shall satisfy,
  T'appease the wrath of their offended king.   25
Mortimer Junior.   Then, Edward, thou wilt fight it to the last
  And rather bathe thy sword in subjects' blood
  Than banish that pernicious company.
King Edward.   Ay, traitors all, rather than thus be braved,
  Make England's civil towns huge heaps of stones   30
  And ploughs to go about our palace gates.
Warwick.   A desperate and unnatural resolution.
  Alarum to the fight! St. George for England,
  And the barons' right.
King Edward.   Saint George for England, and King Edward's right.   35
               [Alarums. Exeunt the two parties severally.]

   Enter [King] Edward [and his followers,] with the Barons [and
              Kent,] captives.

King Edward.   Now, lusty lords, now, not by chance of war,
  But justice of the quarrel and the cause,
  Vailed is your pride. Methinks you hang the heads,
  But we'll advance them, traitors. Now 'tis time
  To be avenged on you for all your braves   40
  And for the murder of my dearest friend,
  To whom right well you knew our soul was knit,
  Good Pierce of Gaveston, my sweet favorite.
  Ah, rebels, recreants, you made him away!
Kent.   Brother, in regard of thee and of thy land,   45
  Did they remove that flatterer from thy throne.
King Edward.   So, sir, you have spoke; away, avoid our presence.
                      [Exit Kent.]
  Accursèd wretches, was't in regard of us,
  When we had sent our messenger to request
  He might be spared to come to speak with us,   50
  And Pembroke undertook for his return,
  That thou, proud Warwick, watched the prisoner,
  Poor Pierce, and headed him against law of arms?
  For which thy head shall overlook the rest,
  As much as thou in rage outwent'st the rest.   55
Warwick.   Tyrant, I scorn thy threats and menaces;

III,iii.
33 *St. George* an anachronism, since St.   saint of England until the reign of
George was not adopted as the patron   Edward III.
                    53 *headed* beheaded.

'Tis but temporal that thou canst inflict.

Lancaster.   The worst is death, and better die to live
   Than live in infamy under such a king.

King Edward.   Away with them, my lord of Winchester!   60
   These lusty leaders, Warwick and Lancaster,
   I charge you roundly, off with both their heads!
   Away!

Warwick.   Farewell, vain world.

Lancaster.   Sweet Mortimer, farewell.   65

Mortimer Junior.   England, unkind to thy nobility,
   Groan for this grief. Behold how thou art maimed.

King Edward.   Go, take that haughty Mortimer to the Tower;
   There see him safe bestowed; and for the rest,
   Do speedy execution on them all.   70
   Be gone!

Mortimer Junior.   What, Mortimer, can raggèd stony walls
   Immure thy virtue that aspires to heaven?
   No, Edward, England's scourge, it may not be;
   Mortimer's hope surmounts his fortune far.   75

                    [*Exit under guard with the other
                              captive Barons.*]

King Edward.   Sound, drums and trumpets! March with me, my friends.
   Edward this day hath crowned him king anew.

                    Exit [*with all except*] *Spencer Junior,
                              Levune and Baldock.*

Spencer Junior.   Levune, the trust that we repose in thee
   Begets the quiet of King Edward's land.
   Therefore be gone in haste, and with advice   80
   Bestow that treasure on the lords of France,
   That, therewith all enchanted, like the guard
   That suffered Jove to pass in showers of gold
   To Danaë, all aid may be denied
   To Isabel the queen, that now in France   85
   Makes friends, to cross the seas with her young son
   And step into his father's regiment.

Levune.   That's it these barons and the subtle queen
   Long leveled at.

Baldock.   Yea, but, Levune, thou seest
   These barons lay their heads on blocks together;   90
   What they intend, the hangman frustrates clean.

Levune.   Have you no doubts, my lords, I'll clap so close
   Among the lords of France with England's gold,
   That Isabel shall make her plaints in vain,

---

57 *temporal . . . inflict* i.e., you can
only harm my body (not my soul).

83–84 *Jove . . . Danaë* See note at II,
ii,53.

87 *regiment* royal authority.
89 *levelled* aimed.
92 *clap so close* work so secretly.

And France shall be obdurate with her tears.   95
Spencer Junior.   Then make for France amain. Levune, away.
  Proclaim King Edward's wars and victories.

                                                    Exeunt.

                    Enter Kent.   IV,i.
Kent.   Fair blows the wind for France. Blow, gentle gale,
  Till Edmund be arrived for England's good.
  Nature, yield to my country's cause in this.
  A brother, no, a butcher of thy friends,
  Proud Edward, dost thou banish me thy presence?   5
  But I'll to France and cheer the wrongèd queen,
  And certify what Edward's looseness is.
  Unnatural king, to slaughter noblemen
  And cherish flatterers. Mortimer, I stay
  Thy sweet escape. Stand gracious, gloomy night,   10
  To his device.
                Enter Mortimer [Junior,] disguised.
Mortimer Junior.   Holla! Who walketh there?
  Is't you, my lord?
Kent.   Mortimer, 'tis I;
  But hath thy potion wrought so happily?
Mortimer Junior.   It hath, my lord; the warders all asleep,
  I thank them, gave me leave to pass in peace.   15
  But hath your grace got shipping unto France?
Kent.   Fear it not.
                                                    Exeunt.

        Enter Queen [Isabella] and her son, [Prince Edward].   IV,ii.
Queen Isabella.   Ah, boy, our friends do fail us all in France.
  The lords are cruel and the king unkind.
  What shall we do?
Prince Edward.   Madam, return to England
  And please my father well, and then a fig
  For all my uncle's friendship here in France.   5
  I warrant you, I'll win his highness quickly;
  'A loves me better than a thousand Spencers.
Queen Isabella.   Ah, boy, thou art deceived, at least in this,
  To think that we can yet be tuned together.
  No, no, we jar too far. Unkind Valois,   10
  Unhappy Isabel, when France rejects,

Whither, oh, whither dost thou bend thy steps?

Enter Sir John of Hainault.

Sir John.   Madam, what cheer?

Queen Isabella.   Ah, good Sir John of Hainault,
Never so cheerless, nor so far distressed.

Sir John.   I hear, sweet lady, of the king's unkindness,   15
But droop not, madam; noble minds contemn
Despair. Will your grace with me to Hainault,
And there stay time's advantage with your son?
How say you, my lord, will you go with your friends,
And share of all our fortunes equally?   20

Prince Edward.   So pleaseth the queen, my mother, me it likes.
The king of England, nor the court of France,
Shall have me from my gracious mother's side,
Till I be strong enough to break a staff;
And then have at the proudest Spencer's head.   25

Sir John.   Well said, my lord.

Queen Isabella.   O, my sweet heart, how do I moan thy wrongs,
Yet triumph in the hope of thee, my joy.
Ah, sweet Sir John, even to the utmost verge
Of Europe or the shore of Tanais,   30
Will we with thee to Hainault, so we will.
The marquis is a noble gentleman;
His grace, I dare presume, will welcome me.
But who are these?

Enter Kent and Mortimer [Junior].

Kent.   Madam, long may you live,
Much happier than your friends in England do.   35

Queen Isabella.   Lord Edmund and Lord Mortimer alive!
Welcome to France. The news was here, my lord,
That you were dead or very near your death.

Mortimer Junior.   Lady, the last was truest of the twain,
But Mortimer, reserved for better hap,   40
Hath shaken off the thraldom of the Tower
And lives t'advance your standard, good my lord.

Prince Edward.   How mean you, and the king, my father, lives?
No, my Lord Mortimer, not I, I trow.

Queen Isabella.   Not, son! Why not? I would it were no worse.   45
But, gentle lords, friendless we are in France.

Mortimer Junior.   Monsieur le Grand, a noble friend of yours,
Told us, at our arrival, all the news—
How hard the nobles, how unkind the king

IV,ii.

12, SD *Sir John of Hainault* uncle of
the Princess Philippa, who was to be
the wife of King Edward III.

16 *contemn* hold in contempt.

30 *Tanais* the river Don, regarded by
Elizabethans as dividing Europe from
Asia.

43 *and* if.

Hath showed himself. But, madam, right makes room 50
Where weapons want; and though a many friends
Are made away, as Warwick, Lancaster,
And others of our party and faction,
Yet have we friends, assure your grace, in England
Would cast up caps and clap their hands for joy, 55
To see us there appointed for our foes.
Kent. Would all were well and Edward well reclaimed,
For England's honor, peace, and quietness.
Mortimer Junior. But by the sword, my lord, it must be deserved;
The king will ne'er forsake his flatterers. 60
Sir John. My lords of England, sith the ungentle king
Of France refuseth to give aid of arms
To this distressèd queen his sister here,
Go you with her to Hainault. Doubt ye not
We will find comfort, money, men and friends 65
Ere long, to bid the English king a base.
How say, young prince, what think you of the match?
Prince Edward. I think King Edward will outrun us all.
Queen Isabella. Nay, son, not so; and you must not discourage
Your friends that are so forward in your aid. 70
Kent. Sir John of Hainault, pardon us, I pray;
These comforts that you give our woeful queen
Bind us in kindness all at your command.
Queen Isabella. Yea, gentle brother, and the God of heaven
Prosper your happy motion, good Sir John. 75
Mortimer Junior. This noble gentleman, forward in arms,
Was born, I see, to be our anchor-hold.
Sir John of Hainault, be it thy renown,
That England's queen and nobles in distress
Have been by thee restored and comforted. 80
Sir John. Madam, along, and you, my lord, with me,
That England's peers may Hainault's welcome see.

                             [Exeunt.]

                               IV,iii.

   Enter King [Edward], Arundel, the two Spencers, with Others.
King Edward. Thus after many threats of wrathful war,
Triumpheth England's Edward with his friends;

---

51 *a many* many (a common Elizabethan usage).
56 *appointed for* ready for battle with.
66 *bid . . . base* i.e., challenge the English king. Prisoner's base was a boys'
game in which a runner was chased from
base to base by another player. To 'bid
a base' is to challenge a player to a run.
67 *match* i.e., the game of prisoner's
base.

And triumph, Edward, with his friends uncontrolled.
My lord of Gloucester, do you hear the news?
Spencer Junior.   What news, my lord?   5
King Edward.   Why, man, they say there is great execution
  Done through the realm. My lord of Arundel,
  You have the note, have you not?
Arundel.   From the lieutenant of the Tower, my lord.
King Edward.   I pray let us see it. [*He takes the note.*] What have we
      there?   10
      Read it, Spencer.   [*He hands it to*] Spencer [*Junior, who*]
                                          reads their names.

Why so; they barked apace a month ago.
Now, on my life, they'll neither bark nor bite.
Now, sirs the news from France? Gloucester, I trow
The lords of France love England's gold so well   15
As Isabel gets no aid from thence.
What now remains? Have you proclaimed, my lord,
Reward for them can bring in Mortimer?
Spencer Junior.   My lord, we have; and if he be in England,
  'A will be had ere long, I doubt it not.   20
King Edward.   If, dost thou say? Spencer, as true as death,
  He is in England's ground; our portmasters
  Are not so careless of their king's command.
                          Enter a Messenger.
  How now, what news with thee? From whence come these?
Messenger.   Letters, my lord, and tidings forth of France;   25
  To you, my lord of Gloucester, from Levune.
                  [*He gives letters to Spencer Junior.*]
King Edward.   Read.
Spencer Junior.   [*reads*]   My duty to your honor premised, &c. I have,
  according to instructions in that behalf, dealt with the king of France
  his lords, and effected that the queen, all discontented and dis-   [30
  comforted, is gone; whither, if you ask, with Sir John of Hainault,
  brother to the marquis, into Flanders. With them are gone Lord Edmund and the Lord Mortimer, having in their company divers of
  your nation, and others; and as constant report goeth, they intend to
  give King Edward battle in England sooner than he can look for   [35
  them. This is all the news of import.
          Your honor's in all service, Levune.
King Edward.   Ah, villains, hath that Mortimer escaped?
  With him is Edmund gone associate?
  And will Sir John of Hainault lead the round?   40
  Welcome, a God's name, madam, and your son;

IV,iii.
  12 *barked* embarked.   40 *round* dance.

England shall welcome you and all your rout.
Gallop apace, bright Phœbus, through the sky,
And dusky night, in rusty iron car,
Between you both shorten the time, I pray,   45
That I may see that most desirèd day
When we may meet these traitors in the field.
Ah, nothing grieves me but my little boy
Is thus misled to countenance their ills.
Come, friends, to Bristow, there to make us strong;   50
And, winds, as equal be to bring them in,
As you injurious were to bear them forth.

                                        [*Exeunt.*]

                                                            IV,iv.

Enter Queen [Isabella,] *her son,* [Prince Edward,] *Kent, Morti-*
            mer Junior, and Sir John [of Hainault].
Queen Isabella.   Now, lords, our loving friends and countrymen,
    Welcome to England all, with prosperous winds.
    Our kindest friends in Belgia have we left,
    To cope with friends at home; a heavy case
    When force to force is knit, and sword and glaive   5
    In civil broils makes kin and countrymen
    Slaughter themselves in others, and their sides
    With their own weapons gored. But what's the help?
    Misgoverned kings are cause of all this wrack;
    And, Edward, thou art one among them all   10
    Whose looseness hath betrayed thy land to spoil
    And made the channels overflow with blood.
    Of thine own people patron shouldst thou be,
    But thou—
Mortimer Junior.   Nay, madam, if you be a warrior,   15
    You must not grow so passionate in speeches.
    Lords, sith that we are by sufferance of heaven
    Arrived and armèd in this prince's right,
    Here for our country's cause swear we to him
    All homage, fealty, and forwardness;   20
    And for the open wrongs and injuries
    Edward hath done to us, his queen and land,

43 *Phœbus* the sun god (Apollo) who   4 *cope* fight.
drove the chariot of the sun across the   5 *glaive* lance.
sky.   9 *wrack* disaster.
                                            12 *channels* street   gutters   through
IV,iv.   which sewage flowed.
    3 *Belgia* the Netherlands.

We come in arms to wreck it with the swords,
That England's queen in peace may repossess
Her dignities and honors; and withal   25
We may remove these flatterers from the king,
That havocs England's wealth and treasury.
Sir John.   Sound trumpets, my lord, and forward let us march.
Edward will think we come to flatter him.
Kent.   I would he never had been flattered more.   30

                                                       [Exeunt.]

                                                             IV,v.

*Enter King [Edward,] Baldock, and Spencer Junior, flying
about the stage.*
Spencer Junior.   Fly, fly, my lord, the queen is over-strong;
Her friends do multiply, and yours do fail.
Shape we our course to Ireland, there to breathe.
King Edward.   What, was I born to fly and run away,
And leave the Mortimers conquerors behind?   5
Give me my horse, and let's r'enforce our troops,
And in this bed of honor die with fame.
Baldock.   O no, my lord, this princely resolution
Fits not the time; away, we are pursued.

                                                           [Exeunt.]

        [Enter] Kent alone, with a sword and target.
Kent.   This way he fled, but I am come too late.   10
Edward, alas, my heart relents for thee.
Proud traitor, Mortimer, why dost thou chase
Thy lawful king, thy sovereign, with thy sword?
Vile wretch, and why hast thou, of all unkind,
Borne arms against thy brother and thy king?   15
Rain showers of vengeance on my cursèd head,
Thou God, to whom in justice it belongs
To punish this unnatural revolt.
Edward, this Mortimer aims at thy life.
O fly him, then! But, Edmund, calm this rage;   20
Dissemble, or thou diest, for Mortimer
And Isabel do kiss while they conspire;
And yet she bears a face of love forsooth.
Fie on that love that hatcheth death and hate.
Edmund, away. Bristow to Longshanks' blood   25
Is false; be not found single for suspect.

                                             IV,v.

23 *wreck it* cause destruction.   14 *unkind* contrary to nature.
27 *havocs* causes havoc with.   25 *Longshanks* See note at III,ii,12.

Proud Mortimer pries near into thy walks.

   Enter Queen [Isabella], Mortimer [Junior], the young Prince
       [Edward], and Sir John of Hainault.

Queen Isabella.   Successful battles gives the God of kings

  To them that fight in right and fear His wrath.

  Since then successfully we have prevailed,   30

  Thanks be heaven's great architect, and you.

  Ere farther we proceed, my noble lords,

  We here create our well-belovèd son,

  Of love and care unto his royal person,

  Lord Warden of the realm, and sith the fates   35

  Have made his father so unfortunate,

  Deal you, my lords, in this, my loving lords,

  As to your wisdoms fittest seems in all.

Kent.   Madam, without offence, if I may ask,

  How will you deal with Edward in his fall?   40

Prince Edward.   Tell me, good uncle, what Edward do you mean?

Kent.   Nephew, your father; I dare not call him king.

Mortimer Junior.   My lord of Kent, what needs these questions?

  'Tis not in her controlment, nor in ours,

  But as the realm and parliament shall please,   45

  So shall your brother be disposèd of.

  I like not this relenting mood in Edmund.

  Madam, 'tis good to look to him betimes.

                        [Aside to Queen Isabella.]

Queen Isabella.   My lord, the Mayor of Bristow knows our mind.

Mortimer Junior.   Yea, madam, and they scape not easily   50

  That fled the field.

Queen Isabella.   Baldock is with the king.

  A goodly chancellor, is he not my lord?

Sir John.   So are the Spencers, the father and the son.

Kent.   This, Edward, is the ruin of the realm.

   Enter Rice ap Howell and the Mayor of Bristow, with Spencer
       Senior, [prisoner, and Attendants].

Rice.   God save Queen Isabel and her princely son.   55

  Madam, the mayor and citizens of Bristow,

  In sign of love and duty to this presence,

  Present by me this traitor to the state,

  Spencer, the father to that wanton Spencer,

  That, like the lawless Catiline of Rome,   60

  Revelled in England's wealth and treasury.

Queen Isabella.   We thank you all.

---

44 *controlment* power.

54 SD *Rice ap Howell* a partisan of the barons, commissioned by Queen Isabella to stir up opposition to King Edward in Wales and to capture him if possible.

60 *Catiline* Lucius Sergius Catilina, a Roman noble whose famous conspiracy was defeated largely through the efforts of Cicero.

Mortimer Junior.   Your loving care in this
  Deserveth princely favors and rewards.
  But where's the king and the other Spencer fled?
Rice.   Spencer the son, created Earl of Gloucester,   65
  Is with that smooth-tongued scholar Baldock gone
  And shipped but late for Ireland with the king.
Mortimer Junior.   Some whirlwind fetch them back or sink them all.
                                                        [*Aside.*]

  They shall be started thence, I doubt it not.
Prince Edward.   Shall I not see the king my father yet?   70
Kent.   Unhappy is Edward, chased from England's bounds.
                                                        [*Aside.*]

Sir John.   Madam, what resteth? Why stand ye in a muse?
Queen Isabella.   I rue my lord's ill-fortune; but alas,
  Care of my country called me to this war.
Mortimer Junior.   Madam, have done with care and sad complaint;   75
  Your king hath wronged your country and himself,
  And we must seek to right it as we may.
  Meanwhile, have hence this rebel to the block.
  Your lordship cannot privilege your head.
Spencer Senior.   Rebel is he that fights against his prince;   80
  So fought not they that fought in Edward's right.
Mortimer Junior.   Take him away; he prates.
                  [*Exeunt Attendants with Spencer Senior.*]
                                  You, Rice ap Howell,
  Shall do good service to her majesty,
  Being of countenance in your country here,
  To follow these rebellious runagates.   85
  We in meanwhile, madam, must take advice,
  How Baldock, Spencer, and their 'complices,
  May in their fall be followed to their end.
                                          Exeunt.

*

                                                        IV,vi.

    Enter the Abbot, Monks, [King] Edward, Spencer [Junior,]
              and Baldock, [the three latter disguised].
Abbot.   Have you no doubt, my lord; have you no fear;
  As silent and as careful will we be
  To keep your royal person safe with us,
  Free from suspect, and fell invasion
  Of such as have your majesty in chase,   5
  Yourself, and those your chosen company,

---

  69 *started* driven from hiding (a   84 *countenance* authority.
hunting term).   85 *runagates* runaways.

As danger of this stormy time requires.
King Edward.   Father, thy face should harbor no deceit.
   O, hadst thou ever been a king, thy heart,
   Piercèd deeply with sense of my distress,   10
   Could not but take compassion of my state.
   Stately and proud, in riches and in train,
   Whilom I was powerful and full of pomp;
   But what is he whom rule and empery
   Have not in life or death made miserable?   15
   Come, Spencer; come, Baldock, come, sit down by me;
   Make trial now of that philosophy
   That in our famous nurseries of arts
   Thou sucked'st from Plato and from Aristotle.
   Father, this life contemplative is heaven.   20
   O that I might this life in quiet lead.
   But we, alas, are chased, and you, my friends,
   Your lives and my dishonor they pursue.
   Yet, gentle monks, for treasure, gold nor fee,
   Do you betray us and our company.   25
Monks.   Your grace may sit secure, if none but we
   Do wot of your abode.
Spencer Junior.   Not one alive, but shrewdly I suspect
   A gloomy fellow in a mead below.
   'A gave a long look after us, my lord,   30
   And all the land I know is up in arms,
   Arms that pursue our lives with deadly hate.
Baldock.   We were embarked for Ireland, wretched we,
   With awkward winds and sore tempests driven
   To fall on shore, and here to pine in fear   35
   Of Mortimer and his confederates.
King Edward.   Mortimer! Who talks of Mortimer?
   Who wounds me with the name of Mortimer,
   That bloody man? Good father, on thy lap
   Lay I this head, laden with mickle care.   40
   O might I never open these eyes again,
   Never again lift up this drooping head,
   O never more lift up this dying heart!
Spencer Junior.   Look up, my lord. Baldock, this drowsiness
   Betides no good; here even we are betrayed.   45
      Enter, with Welsh hooks, Rice ap Howell, a Mower, and the
                  Earl of Leicester.
Mower.   Upon my life, those be the men ye seek.

IV,vi.

40 *mickle* much.

45, **SD** *Leicester* Henry, Earl of
Leicester, younger brother to Thomas,
Earl of Lancaster and, like his brother,
a foe of Edward and the Spencers. *Welsh
hooks* partisans, with cross pieces below
their blades.

Rice.   Fellow, enough. My lord, I pray be short;
   A fair commission warrants what we do.
Leicester.   The queen's commission, urged by Mortimer.
   What cannot gallant Mortimer with the queen?   50
   Alas, see where he sits, and hopes unseen
   T'escape their hands that seek to reave his life.
   Too true it is, *Quem dies vidit veniens superbum,*
   Hunc dies vidit fugiens jacentem.
   But, Leicester, leave to grow so passionate.   55
   Spencer and Baldock, by no other names,
   I arrest you of high treason here.
   Stand not on titles, but obey th'arrest;
   'Tis in the name of Isabel the queen.
   My lord, why droop you thus?   60
King Edward.   O day! The last of all my bliss on earth,
   Center of all misfortune! O my stars,
   Why do you lour unkindly on a king?
   Comes Leicester, then, in Isabella's name
   To take my life, my company from me?   65
   Here, man, rip up this panting breast of mine,
   And take my heart in rescue of my friends.
Rice.   Away with them.
Spencer Junior.   It may become thee yet
   To let us take our farewell of his grace.
Abbot.   My heart with pity earns to see this sight,   70
   A king to bear these words and proud commands.
King Edward.   Spencer, ah, sweet Spencer, thus then must we part.
Spencer Junior.   We must, my lord, so will the angry heavens.
King Edward.   Nay, so will hell and cruel Mortimer;
   The gentle heavens have not to do in this.   75
Baldock.   My lord, it is in vain to grieve or storm.
   Here humbly of your grace we take our leaves.
   Our lots are cast; I fear me, so is thine.
King Edward.   In heaven we may, in earth never shall we meet.
   And, Leicester, say, what shall become of us?   80
Leicester.   Your majesty must go to Killingworth.
King Edward.   Must! 'Tis somewhat hard, when kings must go.
Leicester.   Here is a litter ready for your grace,
   That waits your pleasure, and the day grows old.
Rice.   As good be gone as stay and be benighted.   85
King Edward.   A litter hast thou? Lay me in a hearse,
   And to the gates of hell convey me hence.
   Let Pluto's bells ring out my fatal knell

53–54 *Quem . . . jacentem* Whom the coming day (dawn) saw in his pride, the departing day (evening) saw cast down. (The lines are from Seneca's *Thyestes.*)

70 *earns* grieves.
81 *Killingworth* Kenilworth castle.
88 *Pluto* Greek god of the underworld.

And hags howl for my death at Charon's shore,
For friends hath Edward none but these and these,   90
And these must die under a tyrant's sword.
Rice.   My lord, be going; care not for these,
For we shall see them shorter by the heads.
King Edward.   Well, that shall be, shall be. Part we must.
Sweet Spencer, gentle Baldock, part we must.   95
Hence feignèd weeds! Unfeignèd are my woes.
                                        [*He throws off his disguise.*]
Father, farewell. Leicester, thou stay'st for me,
And go I must. Life, farewell, with my friends.
                                Exeunt King Edward and Leicester.
Spencer Junior.   O, is he gone? Is noble Edward gone,
Parted from hence, never to see us more?   100
Rent, sphere of heaven, and, fire, forsake thy orb!
Earth, melt to air! Gone is my sovereign,
Gone, gone, alas, never to make return.
Baldock.   Spencer, I see our souls are fleeted hence;
We are deprived the sunshine of our life.   105
Make for a new life, man; throw up thy eyes
And heart and hand to heaven's immortal throne;
Pay nature's debt with cheerful countenance.
Reduce we all our lessons unto this,
To die, sweet Spencer, therefore live we all;   110
Spencer, all live to die, and rise to fall.
Rice.   Come, come, keep these preachments till you come to the place
appointed. You, and such as you are, have made wise work in Eng-
land. Will your lordships away?
Mower.   Your worship, I trust, will remember me?   115
Rice.   Remember thee, fellow? What else? Follow me to the town.
                                        [*Exeunt.*]

✳

*Enter King [Edward], Leicester, [the] Bishop [of Winchester,
and Trussel].*
Leicester.   Be patient, good my lord, cease to lament.
Imagine Killingworth Castle were your court
And that you lay for pleasure here a space,
Not of compulsion or necessity.
King Edward.   Leicester, if gentle words might comfort me,   5
Thy speeches long ago had eased my sorrows,
For kind and loving hast thou always been.

89 *Charon* boatman who conveyed de-   96 *weeds* clothes.
parted spirits across the river Styx.   101 *Rent* rend.

The griefs of private men are soon allayed,
But not of kings. The forest deer, being struck,
Runs to an herb that closeth up the wounds,   10
But when the imperial lion's flesh is gored,
He rends and tears it with his wrathful paw,
And highly scorning that the lowly earth
Should drink his blood, mounts up into the air.
And so it fares with me, whose dauntless mind   15
The ambitious Mortimer would seek to curb,
And that unnatural queen, false Isabel,
That thus hath pent and mewed me in a prison;
For such outrageous passions cloy my soul,
As with the wings of rancor and disdain   20
Full often am I soaring up to heaven,
To plain me to the gods against them both.
But when I call to mind I am a king,
Methinks I should revenge me of the wrongs
That Mortimer and Isabel have done.   25
But what are kings when regiment is gone,
But perfect shadows in a sunshine day?
My nobles rule, I bear the name of king;
I wear the crown, but am controlled by them,
By Mortimer and my unconstant queen,   30
Who spots my nuptial bed with infamy,
Whilst I am lodged within this cave of care,
Where sorrow at my elbow still attends,
To company my heart with sad laments,
That bleeds within me for this strange exchange.   35
But tell me, must I now resign my crown,
To make usurping Mortimer a king?
Winchester.   Your grace mistakes; it is for England's good
And princely Edward's right we crave the crown.
King Edward.   No, 'tis for Mortimer, not Edward's head; 40
For he's a lamb, encompassèd by wolves,
Which in a moment will abridge his life.
But if proud Mortimer do wear this crown,
Heavens turn it to a blaze of quenchless fire;
Or like the snaky wreath of Tisiphon,   45
Engirt the temples of his hateful head;

V,i.

10 *herb* dittany, or Dictanum, supposed according to legend to possess heal-
ing powers known to wild animals by
instinct.

14 *mounts . . . air* i.e., the lion.

22 *plain me* complain.

26 *regiment* rule, authority.

44 *blaze . . . fire* i.e., like the crown
which Medea gave to Creusa, for whom
Jason had deserted her. When Creusa
placed it upon her head, it burst into
flames, and although the metal melted
it could not be removed.

45 *Tisiphon* See note to *Dido,* II,i,230.

So shall not England's vine be perishèd,
But Edward's name survives, though Edward dies.
Leicester.   My lord, why waste you thus the time away?
  They stay your answer; will you yield your crown?   50
King Edward.   Ah, Leicester, weigh how hardly I can brook
  To lose my crown and kingdom without cause,
  To give ambitious Mortimer my right,
  That like a mountain overwhelms my bliss,
  In which extreme my mind here murdered is.   55
  But what the heavens appoint, I must obey.
  Here, take my crown; the life of Edward too;
                         [He takes off the crown.]
  Two kings in England cannot reign at once.
  But stay awhile; let me be king till night,
  That I may gaze upon this glittering crown;   60
  So shall my eyes receive their last content,
  My head, the latest honor due to it,
  And jointly both yield up their wishèd right.
  Continue ever thou celestial sun;
  Let never silent night possess this clime.   65
  Stand still you watches of the element;
  All times and seasons, rest you at a stay,
  That Edward may be still fair England's king.
  But day's bright beams doth vanish fast away,
  And needs I must resign my wishèd crown.   70
  Inhuman creatures, nursed with tiger's milk,
  Why gape you for your sovereign's overthrow?
  My diadem I mean, and guiltless life.
  See, monsters, see, I'll wear my crown again.
                       [He puts on the crown.]
  What, fear you not the fury of your king?   75
  But, hapless Edward, thou art fondly led;
  They pass not for thy frowns as late they did,
  But seeks to make a new-elected king;
  Which fills my mind with strange despairing thoughts,
  Which thoughts are martyrèd with endless torments,   80
  And in this torment comfort find I none,
  But that I feel the crown upon my head,
  And therefore let me wear it yet awhile.
Trussel.   My lord, the parliament must have present news,
  And therefore say, will you resign or no?   85
                      The King rageth.
King Edward.   I'll not resign, but whilst I live—
  Traitors, be gone, and join you with Mortimer!
  Elect, conspire, install, do what you will;

47 *England's vine* the symbolic vine   66 *element* sky.
on the English crown.   77 *pass* care.

Their blood and yours shall seal these treacheries.
Winchester. This answer we'll return, and so farewell.   90
Leicester. Call them again, my lord, and speak them fair,
  For if they go, the prince shall lose his right.
King Edward. Call thou them back; I have no power to speak.
Leicester. My lord, the king is willing to resign.
Winchester. If he be not, let him choose.   95
King Edward. O would I might, but heavens and earth conspire
  To make me miserable. Here receive my crown.
  Receive it? No, these innocent hands of mine
  Shall not be guilty of so foul a crime.
  He of you all that most desires my blood   100
  And will be called the murderer of a king,
  Take it. What, are you moved? Pity you me?
  Then send for unrelenting Mortimer
  And Isabel, whose eyes, being turned to steel,
  Will sooner sparkle fire than shed a tear.   105
  Yet stay, for rather than I will look on them,
  Here, here! [*He gives the crown.*]
           Now, sweet God of heaven,
  Make me despise this transitory pomp
  And sit for aye enthronizèd in heaven.
  Come, death, and with thy fingers close my eyes,   110
  Or if I live, let me forget myself.
Winchester. My lord—
King Edward. Call me not lord! Away—out of my sight!
  Ah, pardon me; grief makes me lunatic.
  Let not that Mortimer protect my son;   115
  More safety is there in a tiger's jaws
  Than his embracements. Bear this to the queen,
  Wet with my tears, and dried again with sighs.
              [*He gives a handkerchief.*]
  If with the sight thereof she be not moved,
  Return it back and dip it in my blood.   120
  Commend me to my son, and bid him rule
  Better than I. Yet how have I transgressed,
  Unless it be with too much clemency?
Trussel. And thus most humbly do we take our leave.
      [*Exeunt the Bishop of Winchester and Trussel*
                     with the crown.]
King Edward. Farewell; I know the next news that they bring   125
  Will be my death, and welcome shall it be.
  To wretched men death is felicity.
      [*Enter Berkeley, who gives a paper to Leicester.*]

127, SD *Berkeley* Sir Thomas Berkeley, who had been deprived of his inheritance by Spencer Junior because of his father's support of Lancaster. Berkeley castle was restored to him by Queen Isabella after she had captured it.

Leicester.   Another post. What news brings he?

King Edward.   Such news as I expect. Come, Berkeley, come,

And tell thy message to my naked breast.   130

Berkeley.   My lord, think not a thought so villainous

Can harbor in a man of noble birth.

To do your highness service and devoir

And save you from your foes, Berkeley would die.

Leicester.   My lord, the council of the queen commands   135

That I resign my charge.

King Edward.   And who must keep me now? Must you, my lord?

Berkeley.   Ay, my most gracious lord, so 'tis decreed.

King Edward. [*taking the paper*]   By Mortimer, whose name is written

here.

Well may I rent his name that rends my heart!   140

[*He tears the paper.*]

This poor revenge hath something eased my mind.

So may his limbs be torn as is this paper.

Hear me, immortal Jove, and grant it too.

Berkeley.   Your grace must hence with me to Berkeley straight.

King Edward.   Whither you will; all places are alike,   145

And every earth is fit for burial.

Leicester.   Favor him, my lord, as much as lieth in you.

Berkeley.   Even so betide my soul as I use him.

King Edward.   Mine enemy hath pitied my estate,

And that's the cause that I am now removed.   150

Berkeley.   And thinks your grace that Berkeley will be cruel?

King Edward.   I know not; but of this am I assured,

That death ends all, and I can die but once.

Leicester, farewell.

Leicester.   Not yet, my lord; I'll bear you on your way.   155

Exeunt.

Enter Mortimer [Junior] and Queen Isabella.   V,ii.

Mortimer Junior.   Fair Isabel, now have we our desire;

The proud corrupters of the light-brained king

Have done their homage to the lofty gallows,

And he himself lies in captivity.

Be ruled by me, and we will rule the realm.   5

In any case take heed of childish fear,

For now we hold an old wolf by the ears,

V,ii.

140 *rent* rend.   7 *an old wolf by the ears* a popular
144 *Berkeley* Berkeley castle in Glouces-   proverb.
tershire.

That, if he slip, will seize upon us both,
And gripe the sorer, being griped himself.
Think therefore, madam, that imports us much   10
To erect your son with all the speed we may,
And that I be protector over him,
For our behoof will bear the greater sway
Whenas a king's name shall be under writ.
Queen Isabella.   Sweet Mortimer, the life of Isabel,   15
  Be thou persuaded that I love thee well,
  And therefore, so the prince my son be safe,
  Whom I esteem as dear as these mine eyes,
  Conclude against his father what thou wilt,
  And I myself will willingly subscribe.   20
Mortimer Junior.   First would I hear news that he were deposed,
  And then let me alone to handle him.
                    Enter Messenger.
  Letters! From whence?
Messenger.   From Killingworth, my lord.
Queen Isabella.   How fares my lord the king?
Messenger.   In health, madam, but full of pensiveness.   25
Queen Isabella.   Alas, poor soul, would I could ease his grief.
        [*Enter the Bishop of Winchester with the crown.*]
  Thanks, gentle Winchester. Sirrah, be gone.
                              [*Exit Messenger.*]
Winchester.   The king hath willingly resigned his crown.
Queen Isabella.   O happy news! Send for the prince, my son.
Winchester.   Further, ere this letter was sealed, Lord Berkeley came,   30
  So that he now is gone from Killingworth;
  And we have heard that Edmund laid a plot
  To set his brother free; no more but so.
  The lord of Berkeley is so pitiful
  As Leicester that had charge of him before.   35
Queen Isabella.   Then let some other be his guardian.
Mortimer Junior.   Let me alone, here is the privy seal.
                    [*Exit the Bishop of Winchester.*]
  Who's there? Call hither Gurney and Matrevis.
                         [*To Attendants within.*]
  To dash the heavy-headed Edmund's drift,
  Berkeley shall be discharged, the king removed,   40
  And none but we shall know where he lieth.
Queen Isabella.   But, Mortimer, as long as he survives,
  What safety rest for us or for my son?

---

11 *erect* establish on the throne.
34 *pitiful* full of pity, easily moved.
38 *Gurney and Matrevis* Thomas Gour-
nay fled the country after King Edward's
murder, was captured at Marseilles, and

died mysteriously on his way back to
England; he was probably murdered to
prevent his revealing his accomplices. Sir
John Maltravers was Edward's jailor.
39 *dash* ruin. *drift* design or plot.

Mortimer Junior.   Speak, shall he presently be dispatched and die?
Queen Isabella.   I would he were, so it were not by my means.   45
    Enter Matrevis and Gurney.
Mortimer Junior.   Enough.
 Matrevis, write a letter presently
 Unto the lord of Berkeley from ourself
 That he resign the king to thee and Gurney,
 And when 'tis done we will subscribe our name.   50
Matrevis.   It shall be done, my lord.   [*He writes.*]
Mortimer Junior.   Gurney.
Gurney.   My lord.
Mortimer Junior.   As thou intendest to rise by Mortimer,
 Who now makes Fortune's wheel turn as he please,
 Seek all the means thou canst to make him droop,
 And neither give him kind word nor good look.   55
Gurney.   I warrant you, my lord.
Mortimer Junior.   And this above the rest: because we hear
 That Edmund casts to work his liberty,
 Remove him still from place to place by night,
 Till at the last he come to Killingworth,   60
 And then from thence to Berkeley back again.
 And by the way, to make him fret the more,
 Speak curstly to him; and in any case
 Let no man comfort him if he chance to weep,
 But amplify his grief with bitter words.   65
Matrevis.   Fear not, my lord. we'll do as you command.
Mortimer Junior.   So now away; post thitherwards amain.
Queen Isabella.   Whither goes this letter? To my lord the king?
 Commend me humbly to his majesty,
 And tell him that I labor all in vain   70
 To ease his grief and work his liberty,
 And bear him this as witness of my love.
       [*She gives a ring.*]
Matrevis.   I will, madam.
     Exeunt Matrevis and Gurney.
Mortimer Junior.   Finely dissembled. Do so still, sweet queen.
 Here comes the young prince with the Earl of Kent.   75
Queen Isabella.   Something he whispers in his childish ears.
Mortimer Junior.   If he have such access unto the prince,
 Our plots and stratagems will soon be dashed.
Queen Isabella.   Use Edmund friendly as if all were well.
  Enter the young Prince [Edward] and the Earl of Kent talking
      with him.
Mortimer Junior.   How fares my honorable lord of Kent?   80
Kent.   In health, sweet Mortimer. How fares your grace?

44 *presently* immediately.   63 *curstly* harshly.
58 *casts* plots

Queen Isabella.   Well, if my lord your brother were enlarged.
Kent.   I hear of late he hath deposed himself.
Queen Isabella.   The more my grief.
Mortimer Junior.   And mine.   85
Kent.   Ah, they do dissemble.   [*Aside.*]
Queen Isabella.   Sweet son, come hither; I must talk with thee.
Mortimer Junior.   Thou being his uncle and the next of blood,
  Do look to be protector over the prince?
Kent.   Not I, my lord. Who should protect the son,   90
  But she that gave him life? I mean the queen.
Prince Edward.   Mother, persuade me not to wear the crown.
  Let him be king. I am too young to reign.
Queen Isabella.   But be content, seeing it is his highness' pleasure.
Prince Edward.   Let me but see him first, and then I will.   95
Kent.   Ay, do, sweet nephew.
Queen Isabella.   Brother, you know it is impossible.
Prince Edward.   Why, is he dead?
Queen Isabella.   No, God forbid.
Kent.   I would those words proceeded from your heart.   100
Mortimer Junior.   Inconstant Edmund, dost thou favor him,
  That wast a cause of his imprisonment?
Kent.   The more cause have I now to make amends.
Mortimer Junior.   I tell thee, 'tis not meet that one so false
  Should come about the person of a prince.   105
  My lord, he hath betrayed the king his brother,
  And therefore trust him not.
Prince Edward.   But he repents and sorrows for it now.
Queen Isabella.   Come, son, and go with this gentle lord and me.
Prince Edward.   With you I will, but not with Mortimer.   110
Mortimer Junior.   Why, youngling, 'sdain'st thou so of Mortimer?
  Then I will carry thee by force away.
Prince Edward.   Help, uncle Kent; Mortimer will wrong me.
Queen Isabella.   Brother Edmund, strive not; we are his frien's.
  Isabel is nearer than the Earl of Kent.   115
Kent.   Sister, Edward is my charge; redeem him.
Queen Isabella.   Edward is my son, and I will keep him.
Kent.   Mortimer shall know that he hath wrongèd me.
  Hence will I haste to Killingworth Castle
  And rescue agèd Edward from his foes,   120
  To be revenged on Mortimer and thee.
                    Exeunt [*on one side Queen Isabella, Prince Edward,*
                        and Mortimer Junior; on the other, Kent].

82 *enlarged* liberated.

Enter Matrevis and Gurney [and Soldiers, with King Edward].
Matrevis. My lord, be not pensive; we are your friends.
  Men are ordained to live in misery.
  Therefore come; dalliance dangereth our lives.
King Edward. Friends, whither must unhappy Edward go?
  Will hateful Mortimer appoint no rest?   5
  Must I be vexèd like the nightly bird
  Whose sight is loathsome to all wingèd fowls?
  When will the fury of his mind assuage?
  When will his heart be satisfied with blood?
  If mine will serve, unbowel straight this breast,   10
  And give my heart to Isabel and him;
  It is the chiefest mark they level at.
Gurney. Not so, my liege; the queen hath given this charge
  To keep your grace in safety.
  Your passions make your dolors to increase.   15
King Edward. This usage makes my misery increase.
  But can my air of life continue long
  When all my senses are annoyed with stench?
  Within a dungeon England's king is kept,
  Where I am starved for want of sustenance.   20
  My daily diet is heart-breaking sobs,
  That almost rents the closet of my heart.
  Thus lives old Edward not relieved by any,
  And so must die, though pitièd by many.
  O, water, gentle friends, to cool my thirst   25
  And clear my body from foul excrements.
Matrevis. Here's channel water, as our charge is given.
  Sit down, for we'll be barbers to your grace.
King Edward. Traitors, away! What, will you murder me,
  Or choke your sovereign with puddle water?   30
Gurney. No, but wash your face and shave away your beard,
  Lest you be known and so be rescuèd.
Matrevis. Why strive you thus? Your labor is in vain.
King Edward. The wren may strive against the lion's strength,
  But all in vain; so vainly do I strive   35
  To seek for mercy at a tyrant's hand.
      They wash him with puddle water, and shave his beard away.
  Immortal powers, that knows the painful cares
  That waits upon my poor distressèd soul,
  O level all your looks upon these daring men,
  That wrongs their liege and sovereign, England's king.   40
  O Gaveston, it is for thee that I am wronged;
  For me both thou and both the Spencers died,

6 *nightly bird* owl.   27 *channel* See note at IV,iv,12.

And for your sakes a thousand wrongs I'll take.
The Spencers' ghosts, wherever they remain,
Wish well to mine; then tush, for them I'll die.   45
Matrevis.   'Twixt theirs and yours shall be no enmity.
Come, come away. Now put the torches out;
We'll enter in by darkness to Killingworth.
                    Enter Kent.
Gurney.   How now, who comes there?
Matrevis.   Guard the king sure; it is the Earl of Kent.   50
King Edward.   O gentle brother, help to rescue me.
Matrevis.   Keep them asunder; thrust in the king.
Kent.   Soldiers, let me but talk to him one word.
Gurney.   Lay hands upon the earl for this assault.
Kent.   Lay down your weapons, traitors; yield the king.   55
Matrevis.   Edmund, yield thou thyself, or thou shalt die.
Kent.   Base villains, wherefore do you gripe me thus?
Gurney.   Bind him and so convey him to the court.
Kent.   Where is the court but here? Here is the king,
   And I will visit him. Why stay you me?   60
Matrevis.   The court is where Lord Mortimer remains;
   Thither shall your honor go; and so farewell.
         Exeunt Matrevis and Gurney, with King [Edward].
Kent.   O miserable is that commonweal, where lords
   Keep courts, and kings are locked in prison!
Soldier.   Wherefore stay we? On, sirs, to the court.   65
Kent.   Ay, lead me whither you will, even to my death,
   Seeing that my brother cannot be released.
                                        Exeunt.

✳

         Enter Mortimer [Junior] alone.   V,iv.
Mortimer Junior.   The king must die, or Mortimer goes down;
   The commons now begin to pity him.
   Yet he that is the cause of Edward's death
   Is sure to pay for it when his son is of age,
   And therefore will I do it cunningly.   5
   This letter, written by a friend of ours,
   Contains his death, yet bids them save his life.

                                        [He reads.]

   '*Edwardum occidere nolite timere bonum est;*
   Fear not to kill the king, 'tis good he die.'
   But read it thus, and that's another sense: 10
   '*Edwardum occidere nolite timere bonum est;*
   Kill not the king, 'tis good to fear the worst.'

Unpointed as it is, thus shall it go,
That, being dead, if it chance to be found,
Matrevis and the rest may bear the blame,   15
And we be quit that caused it to be done.
Within this room is locked the messenger
That shall convey it and perform the rest.
And by a secret token that he bears,
Shall he be murdered when the deed is done.   20
Lightborn, come forth!
                         [*Enter Lightborn.*]
Art thou as resolute as thou wast?
Lightborn.   What else, my lord? And far more resolute.
Mortimer Junior.   And hast thou cast how to accomplish it?
Lightborn.   Ay, ay, and none shall know which way he died.   25
Mortimer Junior.   But at his looks, Lightborn, thou wilt relent.
Lightborn.   Relent! Ha, ha! I use much to relent.
Mortimer Junior.   Well, do it bravely, and be secret.
Lightborn.   You shall not need to give instructions;
'Tis not the first time I have killed a man.   30
I learned in Naples how to poison flowers,
To strangle with a lawn thrust through the throat,
To pierce the windpipe with a needle's point,
Or whilst one is asleep, to take a quill
And blow a little powder in his ears,   35
Or open his mouth and pour quicksilver down.
But yet I have a braver way than these.
Mortimer Junior.   What's that?
Lightborn.   Nay, you shall pardon me; none shall know my tricks.
Mortimer Junior.   I care not how it is, so it be not spied.   40
Deliver this to Gurney and Matrevis.   [*He gives a letter.*]
At every ten miles' end thou hast a horse.
Take this. [*He gives money.*] Away, and never see me more.
Lightborn.   No.
Mortimer Junior.   No,   45
Unless thou bring me news of Edward's death.
Lightborn.   That will I quickly do. Farewell, my lord.
                                             [*Exit.*]
Mortimer Junior.   The prince I rule, the queen do I command,
And with a lowly congé to the ground,
The proudest lords salute me as I pass;   50
I seal, I cancel, I do what I will.
Feared am I more than loved; let me be feared,
And when I frown, make all the court look pale.

V,iv.

13 *Unpointed* without punctuation.   24 *cast* See note at II,iii,8.
21 *Lightborn* The name, invented by   32 *lawn* thread.
Marlowe, may be a translation of Lucifer.   49 *congé* bow.

I view the prince with Aristarchus' eyes,
Whose looks were as a breeching to a boy.   55
They thrust upon me the protectorship
And sue to me for that that I desire.
While at the council-table, grave enough,
And not unlike a bashful Puritan,
First I complain of imbecility,   60
Saying it is *onus quam gravissimum;*
Till, being interrupted by my friends,
Suscepi that *provinciam* as they term it;
And to conclude, I am Protector now.
Now is all sure; the queen and Mortimer   65
Shall rule the realm, the king, and none rule us.
Mine enemies will I plague, my friends advance,
And what I list command who dare control?
Major sum quam cui possit fortuna nocere.
And that this be the coronation day,   70
It pleaseth me, and Isabel the queen.
                          [*Trumpets sound within.*]
The trumpets sound; I must go take my place.
     Enter the young King, [Edward III], [the] Bishop [of Canter-
          bury,] Champion, Nobles, [and] Queen [Isabella].
Canterbury.   Long live King Edward, by the grace of God,
king of England and lord of Ireland.
Champion.   If any Christian, Heathen, Turk, or Jew,   75
Dares but affirm that Edward's not true king,
And will avouch his saying with the sword,
I am the champion that will combat him.
Mortimer Junior.   None comes, sound trumpets.
                          [*Trumpets sound.*]
King Edward III.   Champion, here's to thee.
                          [*He gives a purse.*]
Queen Isabella.   Lord Mortimer, now take him to your charge.   80
          Enter Soldiers, with the Earl of Kent prisoner.
Mortimer Junior.   What traitor have we there with blades and bills?
Soldier.   Edmund, the Earl of Kent.
King Edward III.   What hath he done?
Soldier.   'A would have taken the king away perforce,
As we were bringing him to Killingworth.
Mortimer Junior.   Did you attempt his rescue, Edmund? Speak.   85
Kent.   Mortimer, I did; he is our king,
And thou compell'st this prince to wear the crown.

---

54 *Aristarchus* Greek grammarian and
schoolmaster of the second century B.C.
55 *breeching* beating.
60 *imbecility* weakness.

61 *onus quam gravissimum* a very heavy
load.
63 *Suscepi that provinciam* I accepted
that province (undertook the task).
69 *Major . . . nocere* I am too great
for fortune to harm me.

Mortimer Junior.   Strike off his head! He shall have martial law.
Kent.   Strike off my head! Base traitor, I defy thee.
King Edward III.   My lord, he is my uncle and shall live.   90
Mortimer Junior.   My lord, he is your enemy and shall die.
Kent.   Stay, villains!
King Edward III.   Sweet mother, if I cannot pardon him,
 Entreat my Lord Protector for his life.
Queen Isabella.   Son, be content; I dare not speak a word.   95
King Edward III.   Nor I, and yet methinks I should command;
 But, seeing I cannot, I'll entreat for him.
 My lord, if you will let my uncle live,
 I will requite it when I come to age.
Mortimer Junior.   'Tis for your highness' good and for the realm's.   100
 How often shall I bid you bear him hence?
Kent.   Art thou king? Must I die at thy command?
Mortimer Junior.   At our command. Once more away with him.
Kent.   Let me but stay and speak; I will not go.
 Either my brother or his son is king,   105
 And none of both them thirst for Edmund's blood.
 And therefore, soldiers, whither will you hale me?
      [*Soldiers*] *hale Kent away, and carry him to be beheaded.*
King Edward III.   What safety may I look for at his hands,
 If that my uncle shall be murdered thus?
Queen Isabella.   Fear not, sweet boy, I'll guard thee from thy foes.   110
 Had Edmund lived, he would have sought thy death.
 Come, son, we'll ride a-hunting in the park.
King Edward III.   And shall my uncle Edmund ride with us?
Queen Isabella.   He is a traitor; think not on him; come.
                                              Exeunt.

              Enter Matrevis and Gurney.   V,v.
Matrevis.   Gurney, I wonder the king dies not,
 Being in a vault up to the knees in water,
 To which the channels of the castle run,
 From whence a damp continually ariseth,
 That were enough to poison any man,   5
 Much more a king brought up so tenderly.
Gurney.   And so do I, Matrevis. Yesternight
 I opened but the door to throw him meat,
 And I was almost stifled with the savor.
Matrevis.   He hath a body able to endure   10
 More than we can inflict, and therefore now
 Let us assail his mind another while.
Gurney.   Send for him out thence, and I will anger him.

Matrevis. But stay, who's this?

Enter Lightborn.

Lightborn.   My Lord Protector greets you.

[He gives letter.]

Gurney. What's here? I know not how to conster it.   15
Matrevis. Gurney, it was left unpointed for the nonce;
  '*Edwardum occidere nolite timere,*'
  That's his meaning.
Lightborn. Know you this token? I must have the king.

[He gives token.]

Matrevis. Ay, stay awhile; thou shalt have answer straight.   20
  This villain's sent to make away the king. [*Aside.*]
Gurney. I thought as much. [*Aside.*]
Matrevis.   And when the murder's done,
  See how he must be handled for his labor.
  Pereat iste! Let him have the king. [*Aside.*]
  What else? Here is the key, this is the lake;   25
  Do as you are commanded by my lord.
Lightborn. I know what I must do. Get you away.
  Yet be not far off; I shall need your help.
  See that in the next room I have a fire,
  And get me a spit, and let it be red-hot.   30
Matrevis. Very well.
Gurney.   Need you anything besides?
Lightborn. What else? A table and a feather-bed.
Gurney. That's all?
Lightborn. Ay, ay; so, when I call you, bring it in.
Matrevis. Fear not you that.   35
Gurney. Here's a light to go into the dungeon.

[He gives a light, and then exit with Matrevis.]

Lightborn. So now
  Must I about this gear. Ne'er was there any
  So finely handled as this king shall be.
  Foh, here's a place indeed, with all my heart.   40
King Edward. Who's there? What light is that? Wherefore comes thou?
Lightborn. To comfort you and bring you joyful news.
King Edward. Small comfort finds poor Edward in thy looks.
  Villain, I know thou com'st to murder me.
Lightborn. To murder you, my most gracious lord?   45
  Far is it from my heart to do you harm.
  The queen sent me to see how you were used,
  For she relents at this your misery.
  And what eyes can refrain from shedding tears
  To see a king in this most piteous state?   50

V,v.
  24 *Pereat iste* Let him perish.   38 *gear* business.
  25 *lake* pit or dungeon.

King Edward.   Weep'st thou already? List awhile to me
    And then thy heart, were it as Gurney's is,
    Or as Matrevis', hewn from the Caucasus,
    Yet will it melt ere I have done my tale.
    This dungeon where they keep me is the sink   55
    Wherein the filth of all the castle falls.
Lightborn.   O villains!
King Edward.   And there in mire and puddle have I stood
    This ten days' space; and, lest that I should sleep,
    One plays continually upon a drum.   60
    They give me bread and water, being a king;
    So that, for want of sleep and sustenance,
    My mind's distempered, and my body's numbed,
    And whether I have limbs or no I know not.
    O, would my blood dropped out from every vein,   65
    As doth this water from my tattered robes.
    Tell Isabel, the queen, I looked not thus,
    When for her sake I ran at tilt in France
    And there unhorsed the Duke of Cleremont.
Lightborn.   O speak no more, my lord; this breaks my heart.   70
    Lie on this bed, and rest yourself awhile.
King Edward.   These looks of thine can harbor nought but death.
    I see my tragedy written in thy brows.
    Yet stay awhile; forbear thy bloody hand,
    And let me see the stroke before it comes,   75
    That even then when I shall lose my life,
    My mind may be more steadfast on my God.
Lightborn.   What means your highness to mistrust me thus?
King Edward.   What means thou to dissemble with me thus?
Lightborn.   These hands were never stained with innocent blood, 80
    Nor shall they now be tainted with a king's.
King Edward.   Forgive my thought for having such a thought.
    One jewel have I left; receive thou this.
                                        [*He gives a jewel.*]
    Still fear I, and I know not what's the cause,
    But every joint shakes as I give it thee.   85
    O, if thou harbor'st murder in thy heart,
    Let this gift change thy mind and save thy soul.
    Know that I am a king. O, at that name
    I feel a hell of grief! Where is my crown?
    Gone, gone, and do I remain alive?   90
Lightborn.   You're overwatched, my lord; lie down and rest.
King Edward.   But that grief keeps me waking, I should sleep;
    For not these ten days have these eyes' lids closed.
    Now as I speak they fall, and yet with fear
    Open again. O wherefore sits thou here?   95

91 *overwatched* exhausted from lack of sleep.

Lightborn.   If you mistrust me, I'll be gone, my lord.
King Edward.   No, no, for if thou mean'st to murder me,
    Thou wilt return again, and therefore stay.   [*He sleeps.*]
Lightborn.   He sleeps.
King Edward.   [*waking*]   O let me not die yet. Stay, O stay a while!   100
Lightborn.   How now, my lord?
King Edward.   Something still buzzeth in mine ears
    And tells me if I sleep I never wake.
    This fear is that which makes me tremble thus;
    And therefore tell me, wherefore art thou come?   105
Lightborn.   To rid thee of thy life. Matrevis, come!
                    [*Enter Matrevis and Gurney.*]
King Edward.   I am too weak and feeble to resist.
    Assist me, sweet God, and receive my soul!
Lightborn.   Run for the table.
King Edward.   O spare me, or dispatch me in a trice.   110
                    [*Matrevis brings in a table.*]
Lightborn.   So, lay the table down, and stamp on it,
    But not too hard, lest that you bruise his body.
                    [*King Edward is murdered.*]
Matrevis.   I fear me that this cry will raise the town,
    And therefore let us take horse and away.
Lightborn.   Tell me, sirs, was it not bravely done?   115
Gurney.   Excellent well. Take this for thy reward.
                    Gurney stabs Lightborn, [*who dies*].
    Come, let us cast the body in the moat,
    And bear the king's to Mortimer our lord.
    Away!
                    Exeunt [*with the bodies*].

                    Enter Mortimer [*Junior*] *and Matrevis.*   V,vi.
Mortimer Junior.   Is't done, Matrevis, and the murderer dead?
Matrevis.   Ay, my good lord; I would it were undone.
Mortimer Junior.   Matrevis, if thou now growest penitent
    I'll be thy ghostly father; therefore choose
    Whether thou wilt be secret in this   5
    Or else die by the hand of Mortimer.
Matrevis.   Gurney, my lord, is fled, and will, I fear,
    Betray us both; therefore let me fly.
Mortimer Junior.   Fly to the savages.
Matrevis.   I humbly thank your honor.   10
                                            [*Exit.*]

V,vi.
    4 *ghostly father* priest (who brings sacraments to one about to die).

Mortimer Junior.　As for myself, I stand as Jove's huge tree,
And others are but shrubs compared to me.
All tremble at my name, and I fear none;
Let's see who dare impeach me for his death.

　　　　　Enter Queen [Isabella].

Queen Isabella.　Ah, Mortimer, the king my son hath news　　　15
His father's dead, and we have murdered him!
Mortimer Junior.　What if he have? The king is yet a child.
Queen Isabella.　Ay, ay, but he tears his hair, and wrings his hands,
And vows to be revenged upon us both.
Into the council chamber he is gone　　　　20
To crave the aid and succor of his peers.
Ay me, see where he comes, and they with him.
Now, Mortimer, begins our tragedy.

　　　Enter King [Edward the Third,] with the Lords, [and Attendants].

First Lord.　Fear not, my lord; know that you are a king.
King Edward III.　Villain!　　　　25
Mortimer Junior.　How now, my lord?
King Edward III.　Think not that I am frighted with thy words.
My father's murdered through thy treachery,
And thou shalt die, and on his mournful hearse
Thy hateful and accursèd head shall lie　　　30
To witness to the world that by thy means
His kingly body was too soon interred.
Queen Isabella.　Weep not, sweet son.
King Edward III.　Forbid not me to weep; he was my father;
And had you loved him half so well as I,　　　35
You could not bear his death thus patiently.
But you, I fear, conspired with Mortimer.
First Lord.　Why speak you not unto my lord the king?
Mortimer Junior.　Because I think scorn to be accused.
Who is the man dare say I murdered him?　　　40
King Edward III.　Traitor, in me my loving father speaks
And plainly saith, 'twas thou that murdered'st him.
Mortimer Junior.　But hath your grace no other proof than this?
King Edward III.　Yes, if this be the hand of Mortimer.

　　　　　　　　　　　　[He shows letter.]

Mortimer Junior.　False Gurney hath betrayed me and himself.　45

　　　　　　　　　　　　　[Aside.]

Queen Isabella.　I feared as much; murder cannot be hid.

　　　　　　　　　　　　　[Aside.]

Mortimer Junior.　'Tis my hand; what gather you by this?
King Edward III.　That thither thou didst send a murderer.
Mortimer Junior.　What murderer? Bring forth the man I sent.
King Edward III.　Ah, Mortimer, thou knowest that he is slain;　　50

11 *Jove's huge tree* the oak.

And so shalt thou be too. Why stays he here?
Bring him unto a hurdle, drag him forth;
Hang him, I say, and set his quarters up;
But bring his head back presently to me.

Queen Isabella.   For my sake, sweet son, pity Mortimer.   55
Mortimer Junior.   Madam, entreat not; I will rather die
Than sue for life unto a paltry boy.
King Edward III.   Hence with the traitor, with the murderer!
Mortimer Junior.   Base Fortune, now I see that in thy wheel
There is a point, to which when men aspire,   60
They tumble headlong down. That point I touched,
And, seeing there was no place to mount up higher,
Why should I grieve at my declining fall?
Farewell, fair queen; weep not for Mortimer,
That scorns the world, and, as a traveler,   65
Goes to discover countries yet unknown.
King Edward III.   What! Suffer you the traitor to delay?

> [*Mortimer Junior is taken away by the First Lord
> and Attendants.*]

Queen Isabella.   As thou received'st thy life from me,
Spill not the blood of gentle Mortimer!
King Edward III.   This argues that you spilt my father's blood;   70
Else would you not entreat for Mortimer.
Queen Isabella.   I spill his blood? No!
King Edward III.   Ay, madam, you; for so the rumor runs.
Queen Isabella.   That rumor is untrue; for loving thee,
Is this report raised on poor Isabel.   75
King Edward III.   I do not think her so unnatural.
Second Lord.   My lord, I fear me it will prove too true.
King Edward III.   Mother, you are suspected for his death,
And therefore we commit you to the Tower
Till further trial may be made thereof;   80
If you be guilty, though I be your son,
Think not to find me slack or pitiful.
Queen Isabella.   Nay, to my death, for too long have I lived,
Whenas my son thinks to abridge my days.
King Edward III.   Away with her. Her words enforce these tears,   85
And I shall pity her if she speak again.
Queen Isabella.   Shall I not mourn for my belovèd lord,
And with the rest accompany him to his grave?
Second Lord.   Thus, madam; 'tis the king's will you shall hence.
Queen Isabella.   He hath forgotten me; stay, I am his mother.   90
Second Lord.   That boots not; therefore, gentle madam, go.
Queen Isabella.   Then come, sweet death, and rid me of this grief.

> [*Exit with Second Lord.*]

---

52 *hurdle* cart on which condemned   91 *boots* avails.
criminals were taken to the gallows.

[*Enter First Lord, with the head of Mortimer Junior.*]

First Lord.   My lord, here is the head of Mortimer.

King Edward III.   Go fetch my father's hearse where it shall lie,
And bring my funeral robes.

[*Exeunt Attendants.*]

Accursèd head,   95
Could I have ruled thee then, as I do now,
Thou hadst not hatched this monstrous treachery!
Here comes the hearse; help me to mourn, my lords.

[*Re-enter Attendants with the hearse and funeral robes.*]

Sweet father, here unto thy murdered ghost
I offer up this wicked traitor's head,   100
And let these tears, distilling from mine eyes,
Be witness of my grief and innocency.

[*Exeunt.*]

101 *distilling* falling slowly.

The Tragicall Hiſtory
of the Life and Death
of *Doctor Fauſtus.*

Written by *Ch. Marklin.*

LONDON,
Printed for *Iohn Wright*, and are to be ſold at his ſhop
without Newgate, at the ſ ... of the
Bib' 1616.

THE TRAGICAL HISTORY OF THE LIFE AND DEATH OF DOCTOR FAUSTUS

THE PLAYERS

The Chorus
Doctor Faustus
Wagner, his student
    and servant
Valdes
Cornelius
Three Scholars
An Old Man.

Pope Adrian
Raymond, King of
    Hungary
Bruno, the rival Pope
Two Cardinals
The Archbishop of Rheims
Charles V, Emperor of Germany
Martino ⎫
Frederick ⎬ Gentlemen of the
Benvolio ⎭ Emperor's court
Beëlzebub
Duke of Saxony
Duke of Anholt
Duchess of Anholt

Robin, the clown, an hostler
Dick
A Vintner
A Horse-Courser
A Carter
Hostess

Good Angel
Bad Angel
Lucifer
Mephistophilis
Pride ⎫
Covetousness
Envy
Wrath ⎬ The Seven
Gluttony ⎪ Deadly Sins
Sloth
Lechery ⎭
Alexander, the Great
His Paramour
Darius, King of Persia
Helen of Troy
Two Cupids
Devils, Bishops, Monks,
Friars, Soldiers

THE SCENE

Wittenberg, Rome, The Emperor's court at Innsbruck, court
of the Duke of Anholt, and the neighboring countryside.

Enter Chorus.   Prologue.

Chorus.   Not marching in the fields of Trasimene
Where Mars did mate the warlike Carthagens,
Nor sporting in the dalliance of love
In courts of kings where state is overturned,

Prologue.

1-2 *Trasimene . . . Carthagens* (modern spelling—Carthaginians) This may be an allusion to a lost play on the subject of the Carthaginian, Hannibal, who

achieved one of his greatest victories at Lake Trasimene in 217 B.C. *mate* rival (in military prowess).
    4 *state* government.

357

Nor in the pomp of proud audacious deeds   5
Intends our muse to vaunt his heavenly verse.
Only this, gentles: we must now perform
The form of Faustus' fortunes, good or bad.
And now to patient judgments we appeal,
And speak for Faustus in his infancy.   10
Now is he born, of parents base of stock,
In Germany, within a town called Rhode.
At riper years to Wittenberg he went,
Whereas his kinsmen chiefly brought him up.
So much he profits in divinity,   15
The fruitful plot of scholarism graced,
That shortly he was graced with doctor's name,
Excelling all whose sweet delight disputes
In th'heavenly matters of theology,
Till swoll'n with cunning of a self-conceit,   20
His waxen wings did mount above his reach,
And melting, heavens conspired his overthrow;
For, falling to a devilish exercise
And glutted now with learning's golden gifts,
He surfeits upon cursèd necromancy.   25
Nothing so sweet as magic is to him,
Which he prefers before his chiefest bliss;
And this the man that in his study sits.

I,i.

Faustus in his study.
Faustus.   Settle thy studies, Faustus, and begin
   To sound the depth of that thou wilt profess.
   Having commenced, be a divine in show;
   Yet level at the end of every art,
   And live and die in Aristotle's works.   5
   Sweet Analytics, 'tis thou hast ravished me!
   Bene disserere est finis logices.
   Is to dispute well logic's chiefest end?

12 *Rhode* or Roda, a town in the
Duchy of Saxe-Altenburg, Germany.

16. *fruitful plot . . . graced* i.e., he
adorned the university.

18 *whose . . . disputes* whose sweet
delight it was to dispute.

21 *waxen wings* See note to *Dido*, V,
i,243.

I,i.

SD *Faustus . . . study* The chorus-
speaker probably draws the curtains of
the inner stage to reveal Faustus in his
study at Wittenberg.

3 *commenced* taken a degree.

4 *level* aim.

7 *Bene . . . logices* The end of logic
is to dispute well. This notion is part
of the anti-Aristotelian system of Petrus
Ramus, introduced at Cambridge while
Marlowe was a student there. See note
to *Massacre at Paris*, viii, SD.

Affords this art no greater miracle?
Then read no more; thou hast attained that end.   10
A greater subject fitteth Faustus' wit!
Bid *On cay mae on* farewell; Galen come.
Seeing *ubi desinit philosophus ibi incipit medicus,*
Be a physician, Faustus; heap up gold,
And be eternized for some wondrous cure.   15
Summum bonum medicinae sanitas.
The end of physic is our body's health.
Why, Faustus, hast thou not attained that end?
Is not thy common talk sound aphorisms?
Are not thy bills hung up as monuments,   20
Whereby whole cities have escaped the plague,
And divers desperate maladies been cured?
Yet art thou still but Faustus and a man.
Couldst thou make men to live eternally,
Or, being dead, raise them to life again,   25
Then this profession were to be esteemed.
Physic, farewell! Where is Justinian?
Si una eademque res legatus duobus,   [*He reads.*]
Alter rem, alter valorem rei, etc.
A petty case of paltry legacies!   30
Exhæreditare filium non potest pater nisi—   [*He reads.*]
Such is the subject of the Institute
And universal body of the law.
This study fits a mercenary drudge
Who aims at nothing but external trash,   35
Too servile and illiberal for me.
When all is done, divinity is best.
Jeromè's Bible, Faustus, view it well:
Stipendium peccati mors est. Ha! *Stipendium, etc.*   [*He reads.*]
The reward of sin is death. That's hard.   40
Si peccasse negamus, fallimur   [*He reads.*]
Et nulla est in nobis veritas.
If we say that we have no sin,
We deceive ourselves, and there's no truth in us.
Why then belike we must sin,   45

12 *On cay mae on* Aristotle's being or
not being (as Bullen seems to be the
first to have perceived). *Galen* a Greek
physician regarded throughout the Middle
Ages as a medical authority.
13 *ubi . . . medicus* Where the philosopher stops the doctor begins.
20 *bills* medical prescriptions.
27 *Justinian* Roman emperor of Constantinople (527–565) responsible for as-
sembling the Roman law; he was famous
throughout the Middle Ages as a jurist.

28–29 *Si . . . rei, etc.* If the same object is willed to two persons, let one have
the thing itself and the other its value,
etc. This is an incorrect version of one of
the rules in Justinian's *Institutes.*
31 *Exhæreditare . . . nisi* The father
cannot disinherit the son except (another
of Justinian's rules, roughly paraphrased).
38 *Jeromè's Bible* the Vulgate, translated by St. Jerome.
39 *Stipendium . . . est* Romans, VI,23.
41–42 *Si . . . veritas* St. John, I,8.

And so consequently die.
Ay, we must die an everlasting death.
What doctrine call you this? *Che serà, serà:*
What will be, shall be! Divinity, adieu!
These metaphysics of magicians   50
And necromantic books are heavenly.
Lines, circles, signs, letters, and characters—
Ay, these are those that Faustus most desires.
O, what a world of profit and delight,
Of power, of honor, of omnipotence   55
Is promised to the studious artisan!
All things that move between the quiet poles
Shall be at my command. Emperors and kings
Are but obeyed in their several provinces,
Nor can they raise the wind or rend the clouds,   60
But his dominion that exceeds in this
Stretcheth as far as doth the mind of man.
A sound magician is a demi-god.
Here try thy brains to get a deity!
Wagner!

Enter Wagner.

Commend me to my dearest friends,   65
The German Valdes and Cornelius;
Request them earnestly to visit me.
Wagner.   I will sir.

Exit.

Faustus.   Their conference will be a greater help to me
Than all my labors, plod I ne'er so fast.   70

Enter the Good Angel and the Evil Angel.

Good Angel.   O, Faustus, lay that damnèd book aside,
And gaze not on it, lest it tempt thy soul
And heap God's heavy wrath upon thy head.
Read, read the Scriptures. That is blasphemy.
Bad Angel.   Go forward, Faustus, in that famous art   75
Wherein all nature's treasury is contained.
Be thou on earth as Jove is in the sky,
Lord and commander of these elements.

Exeunt Angels.

Faustus.   How am I glutted with conceit of this!
Shall I make spirits fetch me what I please,   80
Resolve me of all ambiguities,
Perform what desperate enterprise I will?
I'll have them fly to India for gold,
Ransack the ocean for orient pearl,
And search all corners of the new-found world   85
For pleasant fruits and princely delicates.

79 *conceit* the conception of attaining.   81 *Resolve me of* explain to me.

I'll have them read me strange philosophy
And tell the secrets of all foreign kings;
I'll have them wall all Germany with brass
And make swift Rhine circle fair Wittenberg.   90
I'll have them fill the public schools with silk
Wherewith the students shall be bravely clad.
I'll levy soldiers with the coin they bring
And chase the Prince of Parma from our land
And reign sole king of all the provinces.   95
Yea, stranger engines for the brunt of war
Than was the fiery keel at Antwerp's bridge
I'll make my servile spirits to invent.
Come, German Valdes and Cornelius,   [*He calls within.*]
And make me blessed with your sage conference!   100
                    Enter Valdes and Cornelius.
Valdes, sweet Valdes, and Cornelius,
Know that your words have won me at the last
To practice magic and concealèd arts;
Yet not your words only, but mine own fantasy
That will receive no object, for my head   105
But ruminates on necromantic skill.
Philosophy is odious and obscure;
Both law and physic are for petty wits;
Divinity is basest of the three,
Unpleasant, harsh, contemptible and vile.   110
'Tis magic, magic, that hath ravished me.
Then, gentle friends, aid me in this attempt,
And I, that have with subtle syllogisms
Gravelled the pastors of the German church,
And made the flowering pride of Wittenberg   115
Swarm to my problems as th'infernal spirits
On sweet Musæus when he came to hell,
Will be as cunning as Agrippa was,
Whose shadows made all Europe honor him.
Valdes. Faustus, these books, thy wit, and our experience   120
Shall make all nations to canonize us.

---

90 *Rhine . . . Wittenberg* Wittenberg
is actually on the Elbe river, not the
Rhine.

94 *Prince of Parma* See note to *Massacre at Paris,* xx,83.

95 *provinces* i.e., of the Netherlands.

97 *fiery . . . bridge* In April, 1584, the
Dutch used a fire-ship to destroy a bridge
built across the Scheldt river by the
Prince of Parma in an attempt to block-
ade Antwerp.

114 *Gravelled* puzzled and amazed.

116 *problems* public disputations.

117 *Musæus* a semi-mythical Greek
poet whose name appears on a Greek
poem about the love of Hero and
Leander, but which actually was written
after his time. Marlowe, following Virgil,
has him visit hell like the mythical
Orpheus.

118–119 *Agrippa . . . shadows* Cornelius Agrippa (1486?–1535) a German physician and student of the occult, was
said to have had power to raise spirits
(shadows) from the dead.

As Indian Moors obey their Spanish lords,
So shall the spirits of every element
Be always serviceable to us three.
Like lions shall they guard us when we please,   125
Like Almain rutters with their horsemen's staves
Or Lapland giants trotting by our sides,
Sometimes like women or unwedded maids,
Shadowing more beauty in their airy brows
Than in the white breasts of the queen of love.   130
From Venice shall they drag huge argosies,
And from America the golden fleece
That yearly stuffs old Philip's treasury,
If learnèd Faustus will be resolute.
Faustus.   Valdes, as resolute am I in this   135
As thou to live; therefore object it not.
Cornelius.   The miracles that magic will perform
Will make thee vow to study nothing else.
He that is grounded in astrology,
Enriched with tongues, well seen in minerals,   140
Hath all the principles magic doth require.
Then doubt not, Faustus, but to be renowned
And more frequented for this mystery
Than heretofore the Delphian oracle.
The spirits tell me they can dry the sea   145
And fetch the treasure of all foreign wracks,
Yea, all the wealth that our forefathers hid
Within the massy entrails of the earth.
Then tell me, Faustus, what shall we three want?
Faustus.   Nothing, Cornelius. O, this cheers my soul!   150
Come, show me some demonstrations magical,
That I may conjure in some lusty grove
And have these joys in full possession.
Valdes.   Then haste thee to some solitary grove,
And bear wise Bacon's and Abanus' works,   155
The Hebrew Psalter, and New Testament;
And whatsoever else is requisite
We will inform thee ere our conference cease.
Cornelius.   Valdes, first let him know the words of art,
And then, all other ceremonies learned,   160
Faustus may try his cunning by himself.
Valdes.   First I'll instruct thee in the rudiments,

122 *Indian Moors* American Indians.
126 *Almain rutters* German cavalrymen.
129 *Shadowing* harboring, sheltering.
140 *Enriched . . . tongues* learned in
Latin (the language traditionally used
for communicating with spirits).
144 *Delphian oracle* the high priest to

Apollo at Delphos who had power to
foretell the future.

155 *Bacon's . . . works* Roger Bacon
(1214?–1294) and Pietro D'Abano (1250–
1316) were famous in the Middle Ages
for their feats of magic.

And then wilt thou be perfecter than I.

Faustus.   Then come and dine with me, and after meat
    We'll canvass every quiddity thereof,   165
    For ere I sleep I'll try what I can do.
    This night I'll conjure, though I die therefore.

                                   Exeunt.

✳

                 Enter two Scholars.   I,ii.

First Scholar.   I wonder what's become of Faustus, that was wont to
make our schools ring with *sic probo.*

                  Enter Wagner.

Second Scholar.   That shall we presently know; here comes his boy.

First Scholar.   How now sirrah! Where's thy master?

Wagner.   God in heaven knows.

Second Scholar.   Why, dost not thou know then?   5

Wagner.   Yes, I know, but that follows not.

First Scholar.   Go to, sirrah! Leave your jesting and tell us where he is.

Wagner.   That follows not by force of argument, which you, being
licentiates, should stand upon; therefore acknowledge your error [10
and be attentive.

Second Scholar.   Then you will not tell us?

Wagner.   You are deceived, for I will tell you. Yet if you were not
dunces, you would never ask me such a question. For is he not
corpus naturale, and is not that *mobile?* Then wherefore should [15
you ask me such a question? But that I am by nature phlegmatic, slow
to wrath, and prone to lechery—to love, I would say—it were not
for you to come within forty foot of the place of execution, although
I do not doubt but to see you both hanged the next sessions. Thus
having triumphed over you, I will set my countenance like a [20
precisian and begin to speak thus: Truly, my dear brethren, my master is within at dinner with Valdes and Cornelius, as this wine, if it
could speak, would inform your worships. And so, the Lord bless you,
preserve you, and keep you, my dear brethren.

                                   Exit.

First Scholar.   O Faustus, then I fear that which I have long sus-
      pected.   25
    That thou art fall'n into that damnèd art
    For which they two are infamous through the world.

Second Scholar.   Were he a stranger, not allied to me,

---

165 *quiddity* essential element (a term
from scholastic logic).

I,ii.

2 *sic probo* thus I prove (a form used
in scholastic argument).

15 *corpus naturale* The subject matter
of physics, in scholastic terms, was
Corpus naturale seu mobile.
21 *precisian* puritan.

The danger of his soul would make me mourn.
But come, let us go and inform the rector.   30
It may be his grave counsel may reclaim him.
First Scholar.   I fear me nothing will reclaim him now.
Second Scholar.   Yet let us see what we can do.

                                                    Exeunt.

      Thunder. Enter [above] Lucifer and four Devils.   I,iii.
                  Enter Faustus to conjure.
Faustus.   Now that the gloomy shadow of the night,
      Longing to view Orion's drizzling look,
      Leaps from th'Antarctic world unto the sky
      And dims the welkin with her pitchy breath,
      Faustus begin thine incantations,   5
      And try if devils will obey thy hest,
      Seeing thou hast prayed and sacrificed to them.
      Within this circle is Jehovah's name,
      Forward and backward anagrammatized,
      Th'abbreviated names of holy saints,   10
      Figures of every adjunct to the heavens,
      And characters of signs and erring stars,
      By which the spirits are enforced to rise.
      Then fear not, Faustus, to be resolute,
      And try the utmost magic can perform.   *Thunder.*   15
Sint mihi Dei Acherontis propitii! Valeat numen triplex Jehovae.
Ignei, aerii, aquatani spiritus, salvete! Orientis princeps, Beëlzebub,
inferni ardentis monarcha, et Demogorgon, propitiamus vos, ut
appareat et surgat Mephistophilis. Quid tu moraris? Per Jehovam
Gehennam, et consecratam aquam quam nunc spargo, signum-   [20
que crucis quod nunc facio, et per vota nostra, ipse nunc surgat
nobis dicatus Mephistophilis.
                  Enter [Mephistophilis,] a Devil.
I charge thee to return and change thy shape;

30 *rector* head of the university.

I,iii.

4 *welkin* world.
12 *erring* wandering.
16–22 *Sint . . . Mephistophilis* May
the gods of Acheron be propitious to
me. Let the triple name of Jehova (the
trinity) be gone. Hail spirits of fire, air,
and water. Prince of the East, Beëlzebub,
monarch of burning hell, and Demogorgon, we petition you that Mephistophilis may appear and rise. Why do you
linger? By Jehova, Gehenna and the holy
water which I now sprinkle and the
sign of the cross which I now make and
by our vows, let Mephistophilis himself
now rise to serve us.

Boas has held that the word *Dragon*
(here omitted) which appears before
quod tumeraris in the 1616 text may be
the fragment of a stage direction, indicating that at this point a dragon appears in the air. The suggestion, followed
by Greg, is very plausible.

Thou art too ugly to attend on me.
Go, and return an old Franciscan friar;   25
That holy shape becomes a devil best.

                                                  Exit Devil.

I see there's virtue in my heavenly words.
Who would not be proficient in this art?
How pliant is this Mephistophilis,
Full of obedience and humility.   30
Such is the force of magic and my spells.
Now Faustus, thou art conjuror laureate,
That canst command great Mephistophilis.
Quin redis Mephistophilis fratris imagine.
     Enter Mephistophilis [dressed like a Franciscan friar].
Mephistophilis. Now Faustus, what wouldst thou have me do?   35
Faustus. I charge thee wait upon me whilst I live,
To do whatever Faustus shall command,
Be it to make the moon drop from her sphere
Or the ocean to overwhelm the world.
Mephistophilis. I am a servant to great Lucifer   40
And may not follow thee without his leave.
No more than he commands must we perform.
Faustus. Did not he charge thee to appear to me?
Mephistophilis. No, I came hither of mine own accord.
Faustus. Did not my conjuring speeches raise thee? Speak.   45
Mephistophilis. That was the cause, but yet *per accidens,*
For when we hear one rack the name of God,
Abjure the Scriptures and his Savior Christ,
We fly in hope to get his glorious soul;
Nor will we come unless he use such means   50
Whereby he is in danger to be damned.
Therefore the shortest cut for conjuring
Is stoutly to abjure the Trinity
And pray devoutly to the prince of hell.
Faustus. So Faustus hath   55
Already done, and holds this principle:
There is no chief but only Beëlzebub,
To whom Faustus doth dedicate himself.
This word 'damnation' terrifies not me,
For I confound hell in Elysium.   60
My ghost be with the old philosophers!
But leaving these vain trifles of men's souls,
Tell me what is that Lucifer thy lord?
Mephistophilis. Arch-regent and commander of all spirits.
Faustus. Was not that Lucifer an angel once?   65

---

34 *Quin . . . imagine* Return, Meph-   46 *cause . . . per accidens* The terms
istophilis, in the shape of a friar.   are from scholastic logic.
                                   61 *ghost* spirit.

Mephistophilis.   Yes Faustus, and most dearly loved of God.
Faustus.   How comes it then that he is prince of devils?
Mephistophilis.   O, by aspiring pride and insolence,
   For which God threw him from the face of heaven.
Faustus.   And what are you that live with Lucifer?   70
Mephistophilis.   Unhappy spirits that fell with Lucifer,
   Conspired against our God with Lucifer,
   And are for ever damned with Lucifer.
Faustus.   Where are you damned?
Mephistophilis.   In hell.
Faustus.   How comes it then that thou art out of hell?   75
Mephistophilis.   Why this is hell, nor am I out of it.
   Think'st thou that I who saw the face of God
   And tasted the eternal joys of heaven
   Am not tormented with ten thousand hells
   In being deprived of everlasting bliss?   80
   O Faustus, leave these frivolous demands
   Which strike a terror to my fainting soul.
Faustus.   What, is great Mephistophilis so passionate
   For being deprivèd of the joys of heaven?
   Learn thou of Faustus manly fortitude,   85
   And scorn those joys thou never shalt possess.
   Go bear these tidings to great Lucifer:
   Seeing Faustus hath incurred eternal death
   By desperate thoughts against Jove's deity,
   Say he surrenders up to him his soul,   90
   So he will spare him four and twenty years,
   Letting him live in all voluptuousness,
   Having thee ever to attend on me,
   To give me whatsoever I shall ask,
   To tell me whatsoever I demand,   95
   To slay mine enemies, and aid my friends,
   And always be obedient to my will.
   Go, and return to mighty Lucifer,
   And meet me in my study at midnight,
   And then resolve me of thy master's mind.   100
Mephistophilis.   I will, Faustus.

                                        Exit.

Faustus.   Had I as many souls as there be stars,
   I'd give them all for Mephistophilis.
   By him I'll be great emperor of the world,
   And make a bridge thorough the moving air,   105
   To pass the ocean with a band of men.
   I'll join the hills that bind the Afric shore,
   And make that country continent to Spain,
   And both contributory to my crown.

107 *bind* enclose.

The Emperor shall not live but by my leave,   110
Nor any potentate of Germany.
Now that I have obtained what I desire,
I'll live in speculation of this art
Till Mephistophilis return again.

Exit.

Enter Wagner and [Robin,] the Clown.   I,iv.

Wagner. Come hither, sirrah boy.

Robin. Boy! O disgrace to my person. Zounds, boy in your face! You
have seen many boys with such pickedevants, I am sure.

Wagner. Sirrah, hast thou no comings in?

Robin. Yes, and goings out too, you may see, sir.   5

Wagner. Alas, poor slave! See how poverty jests in his nakedness. I
know the villain's out of service, and so hungry that I know he would
give his soul to the devil for a shoulder of mutton, though it were
blood-raw.

Robin. Not so neither. I had need to have it well roasted, and   [10
good sauce to it, if I pay so dear, I can tell you.

Wagner. Sirrah, wilt thou be my man and wait on me, and I will
make thee go like *Qui mihi discipulus?*

Robin. What, in verse?

Wagner. No slave; in beaten silk and staves-acre.   15

Robin. Staves-acre? That's good to kill vermin. Then, belike, if I serve
you I shall be lousy.

Wagner. Why, so thou shalt be, whether thou dost it or no; for,
sirrah, if thou dost not presently bind thyself to me for seven years,
I'll turn all the lice about thee into familiars and make them   [20
tear thee in pieces.

Robin. Nay sir, you may save yourself a labor, for they are as familiar
with me as if they paid for their meat and drink, I can tell you.

Wagner. Well, sirrah, leave your jesting and take these guilders.

Robin. Yes, marry sir, and I thank you too.   25

Wagner. So, now thou art to be at an hour's warning, whensoever and
wheresoever the devil shall fetch thee.

Robin. Here, take your guilders again. I'll none of 'em.

Wagner. Not I. Thou art pressed. Prepare thyself, for I will presently

I,iv.

3 *pickedevants* pointed beards.

4 *comings in* earnings.

13 *Qui . . . discipulus* who is my
disciple (the opening words of a Latin
poem by William Lyly, well known to
Elizabethan schoolboys).

15 *beaten* embroidered with metal.
staves-acre a plant used for killing
vermin.

20 *familiars* attendant evil spirits.

29 *pressed* enlisted into service in exchange for money.

raise up two devils to carry thee away. Banio! Belcher!   30
Robin.   Belcher? And Belcher come here, I'll belch him. I am not
afraid of a devil.

     Enter two Devils.

Wagner.   How now, sir? Will you serve me now?
Robin.   Ay, good Wagner; take away the devil then.
Wagner.   Spirits away! Now, sirrah, follow me.   35

        [Exeunt Devils.]

Robin.   I will sir. But hark you, master, will you teach me this conjuring occupation?
Wagner.   Ay, sirrah. I'll teach thee to turn thyself to a dog, or a cat,
or a mouse, or a rat, or any thing.
Robin.   A dog, or a cat, or a mouse, or a rat! O brave Wagner!   40
Wagner.   Villain, call me Master Wagner, and see that you walk at-
tentively, and let your right eye be always diametrally fixed upon my
left heel, that thou may'st *quasi vestigias nostras insistere.*
Robin.   Well, sir, I warrant you.

          Exeunt.

     Enter Faustus in his Study.   II,i.
Faustus.   Now Faustus must thou needs be damned,
 And canst thou not be saved.
 What boots it then to think on God or heaven?
 Away with such vain fancies, and despair;
 Despair in God, and trust in Beëlzebub.   5
 Now go not backward; Faustus, be resolute.
 Why waver'st thou? O, something soundeth in mine ear:
 'Abjure this magic; turn to God again.'
 Ay, and Faustus will turn to God again!
 To God? He loves thee not.
 The God thou serv'st is thine own appetite,
 Wherein is fixed the love of Beëlzebub.
 To him I'll build an altar and a church,
 And offer lukewarm blood of new-born babes.
     Enter the two Angels.
Bad Angel.   Go forward, Faustus, in that famous **art.**   15
Good Angel.   Sweet Faustus, leave that execrable art.
Faustus.   Contrition, prayer, repentance—what of these?
Good Angel.   O, they are means to bring thee unto heaven.
Bad Angel.   Rather illusions, fruits of lunacy,

      II,i.
42 *diametrally* in a straight line. 3 *boots* avails.
43 *quasi . . . insistere* as if to walk
in our tracks.

That make men foolish that do use them most.   20
Good Angel.   Sweet Faustus, think of heaven and heavenly things.
Bad Angel.   No Faustus; think of honor and wealth.
Exeunt Angels.
Faustus.   Wealth? Why, the signory of Emden shall be mine.
   When Mephistophilis shall stand by me,
   What power can hurt me? Faustus thou art safe.   25
   Cast no more doubts. Mephistophilis, come
   And bring glad tidings from great Lucifer.
   Is't not midnight? Come, Mephistophilis.
   Veni, veni, Mephistophile.
Enter Mephistophilis.
   Now tell me what saith Lucifer, thy lord?   30
Mephistophilis.   That I shall wait on Faustus whilst he lives,
   So he will buy my service with his soul.
Faustus.   Already Faustus hath hazarded that for thee.
Mephistophilis.   But now thou must bequeath it solemnly
   And write a deed of gift with thine own blood,   35
   For that security craves great Lucifer.
   If thou deny it, I must back to hell.
Faustus.   Stay, Mephistophilis! Tell me what good
   Will my soul do thy lord.
Mephistophilis.   Enlarge his kingdom.
Faustus.   Is that the reason why he tempts us thus?   40
Mephistophilis.   *Solamen miseris socios habuisse doloris.*
Faustus.   Why, have you any pain that torture others?
Mephistophilis.   As great as have the human souls of men.
   But tell me, Faustus, shall I have thy soul?
   And I will be thy slave and wait on thee   45
   And give thee more than thou hast wit to ask.
Faustus.   Ay, Mephistophilis, I'll give it him.
Mephistophilis.   Then Faustus, stab thy arm courageously,
   And bind thy soul that at some certain day
   Great Lucifer may claim it as his own,   50
   And then be thou as great as Lucifer.
Faustus. [*stabbing his arm*]   Lo, Mephistophilis, for love of thee,
   I cut mine arm, and with my proper blood
   Assure my soul to be great Lucifer's,
   Chief lord and regent of perpetual night.   55
   View here this blood that trickles from mine arm,
   And let it be propitious for my wish.
Mephistophilis.   But Faustus,
   Write it in manner of a deed of gift.

---

23 *Emden* the chief city of East Fries-
land, near the mouth of the river Ems,
which had considerable trade relations
with Elizabethan England.

41 *Solamen . . . doloris* It is a consolation in misery to have a fellow
sufferer.

53 *proper* own.

Faustus.   Ay, so I do. [*He writes.*] But Mephistophilis,   60
  My blood congeals, and I can write no more.
Mephistophilis.   I'll fetch thee fire to dissolve it straight.

                                      Exit.

Faustus.   What might the staying of my blood portend?
  Is it unwilling I should write this bill?
  Why streams it not that I may write afresh?   65
  'Faustus gives to thee his soul.' Ah, there it stayed.
  Why shouldst thou not? Is not thy soul thine own?
  Then write again: 'Faustus gives to thee his soul.'
       Enter Mephistophilis with the chafer of fire.
Mephistophilis.   See Faustus, here is fire. Set it on.
Faustus.   So. Now the blood begins to clear again.   70
  Now will I make an end immediately.   [*He writes.*]
Mephistophilis.   What will not I do to obtain his soul?   [*Aside.*]
Faustus.   *Consummatum est;* this bill is ended,
  And Faustus hath bequeathed his soul to Lucifer.
  But what is this inscription on mine arm?   75
  Homo fuge! Whither should I fly?
  If unto God, he'll throw me down to hell.
  My senses are deceived; here's nothing writ.
  O yes, I see it plain. Even here is writ
  Homo fuge! Yet shall not Faustus fly.   80
Mephistophilis.   I'll fetch him somewhat to delight his mind.
                                    [*Aside.*]
                                    Exit.

    Enter Devils, giving crowns and rich apparel to Faustus. They
      dance and then depart. Enter Mephistophilis.
Faustus.   What means this show? Speak Mephistophilis.
Mephistophilis.   Nothing, Faustus, but to delight thy mind
  And let thee see what magic can perform.
Faustus.   But may I raise such spirits when I please?   85
Mephistophilis.   Ay Faustus, and do greater things than these.
Faustus.   Then, Mephistophilis, receive this scroll,
  A deed of gift of body and of soul,
  But yet conditionally that thou perform
  All covenants and articles between us both.   90
Mephistophilis.   Faustus, I swear by hell and Lucifer
  To effect all promises between us made.
Faustus.   Then hear me read it Mephistophilis.
  On these conditions following:
  First, that Faustus may be a spirit in form and substance;   95
  Secondly, that Mephistophilis shall be his servant and be at his com-
  mand;

69 *Set it on* i.e., set the dish of blood   73 *Consummatum est* It is completed
on the fire.   (St. John, XIX,30).
                                    76 *Homo fuge* Man fly.

Thirdly, that Mephistophilis shall do for him and bring him what-
soever;
Fourthly, that he shall be in his chamber or house invisible;   100
Lastly, that he shall appear to the said John Faustus at all times, in
what form or shape soever he please:
I, John Faustus, of Wittenberg, doctor, by these presents, do give
both body and soul to Lucifer, Prince of the East, and his minister,
Mephistophilis; and furthermore grant unto them that four [105
and twenty years being expired, the articles above written inviolate,
full power to fetch or carry the said John Faustus, body and soul,
flesh, blood, or goods, into their habitation wheresoever.
                              By me, John Faustus.

Mephistophilis.   Speak Faustus. Do you deliver this as your deed? [110
Faustus.   Ay, take it, and the devil give thee good of it.
Mephistophilis.   So now, Faustus, ask me what thou wilt.
Faustus.   First will I question with thee about hell.
   Tell me, where is the place that men call hell?
Mephistophilis.   Under the heavens.   115
Faustus.   Ay, so are all things else. But whereabouts?
Mephistophilis.   Within the bowels of these elements,
   Where we are tortured and remain for ever.
   Hell hath no limits, nor is circumscribed
   In one self place, but where we are is hell,   120
   And where hell is, there must we ever be.
   And, to be short, when all the world dissolves
   And every creature shall be purified,
   All places shall be hell that is not heaven.
Faustus.   I think hell's a fable.   125
Mephistophilis.   Ay, think so still, till experience change thy mind.
Faustus.   Why, dost thou think that Faustus shall be damned?
Mephistophilis.   Ay, of necessity, for here's the scroll
   In which thou hast given thy soul to Lucifer.
Faustus.   Ay, and body too. But what of that?   130
   Think'st thou that Faustus is so fond to imagine
   That after this life there is any pain?
   No, these are trifles and mere old wives' tales.
Mephistophilis.   But I am an instance to prove the contrary,
   For I tell thee I am damned and now in hell.   135
Faustus.   Nay, and this be hell, I'll willingly be damned.
   What? Sleeping, eating, walking and disputing?
   But, leaving off this, let me have a wife,
   The fairest maid in Germany,
   For I am wanton and lascivious,   140
   And cannot live without a wife.
Mephistophilis.   I prithee, Faustus, talk not of a wife.
Faustus.   Nay, sweet Mephistophilis, fetch me one, for I will have one.
  131 *fond* foolish.

Mephistophilis.   Well, Faustus, thou shalt have a wife.
    Sit there till I come.   *[Exit.]*   145
        Enter [Mephistophilis] with a Devil dressed like a woman,
                        with fireworks.
Faustus.   What sight is this?
Mephistophilis.   Now Faustus, how dost thou like thy wife?
Faustus.   Here's a hot whore indeed! No, I'll no wife.
Mephistophilis.   Marriage is but a ceremonial toy,
    And if thou lovest me, think no more of it.   150
    I'll cull thee out the fairest courtesans
    And bring them every morning to thy bed.
    She whom thine eye shall like, thy heart shall have,
    Were she as chaste as was Penelope,
    As wise as Saba, or as beautiful   155
    As was bright Lucifer before his fall.
    Hold; take this book; peruse it thoroughly.
    The iterating of these lines brings gold;
    The framing of this circle on the ground
    Brings thunder, whirlwinds, storm and lightning.   160
    Pronounce this thrice devoutly to thyself,
    And men in harness shall appear to thee,
    Ready to execute what thou command'st.
Faustus.   Thanks, Mephistophilis, for this sweet book.
    This will I keep as chary as my life.   165
                                            Exeunt.

        Enter Faustus in his study and Mephistophilis.   II,ii.
Faustus.   When I behold the heavens, then I repent
    And curse thee, wicked Mephistophilis,
    Because thou hast deprived me of those joys.
Mephistophilis.   'Twas thine own seeking, Faustus; thank thyself.
    But think'st thou heaven is such a glorious thing?   5
    I tell thee, Faustus, 'tis not half so fair
    As thou, or any man that breathes on earth.
Faustus.   How prov'st thou that?
Mephistophilis.   'Twas made for man; then he's more excellent.
Faustus.   If heaven was made for man, 'twas made for me.   10
    I will renounce this magic and repent.
                    Enter the two Angels.
Good Angel.   Faustus repent; yet God will pity thee.
Bad Angel.   Thou art a spirit; God cannot pity thee.

II,ii.

154 *Penelope* the faithful wife of
Ulysses in Homer's *Odyssey.*
155 *Saba* the Queen of Sheba.
162 *harness* armor.

13 *spirit* devil (indicating that Faustus
by his apostasy is already a damned soul
in hell).

Faustus.   Who buzzeth in mine ears I am a spirit?
  Be I a devil, yet God may pity me;   15
  Yea, God will pity me if I repent.
Bad Angel.   Ay, but Faustus never shall repent.

                                                    Exeunt Angels.

Faustus.   My heart is hardened; I cannot repent.
  Scarce can I name salvation, faith, or heaven,
  But fearful echoes thunder in mine ears: 20
  'Faustus, thou art damned!' Then swords and knives,
  Poison, guns, halters, and envenomed steel
  Are laid before me to dispatch myself;
  And long ere this I should have done the deed,
  Had not sweet pleasure conquered deep despair.   25
  Have not I made blind Homer sing to me
  Of Alexander's love and Oenon's death?
  And hath not he, that built the walls of Thebes
  With ravishing sound of his melodious harp,
  Made music with my Mephistophilis?   30
  Why should I die then, or basely despair?
  I am resolved; Faustus shall not repent.
  Come, Mephistophilis, let us dispute again
  And reason of divine astrology.
  Speak; are there many spheres above the moon?   35
  Are all celestial bodies but one globe,
  As is the substance of this centric earth?
Mephistophilis.   As are the elements, such are the heavens,
  Even from the moon unto the empyreal orb,
  Mutually folded in each others' spheres,   40
  And jointly move upon one axle-tree,
  Whose terminè is termed the world's wide pole;
  Nor are the names of Saturn, Mars, or Jupiter
  Feigned, but are erring stars.
Faustus.   But have they all
  One motion, both *situ et tempore?*   45
Mephistophilis.   All move from east to west in four and twenty hours
  upon the poles of the world, but differ in their motions upon the
  poles of the zodiac.
Faustus.   These slender questions Wagner can decide.
  Hath Mephistophilis no greater skill?   50

---

27 *Alexander . . . death* Paris, or
Alexander as he was sometimes called,
loved the nymph Oenone when he lived
as a shepherd on Mt. Ida. She died of
a broken heart when he left her.

28-29 *he . . . harp* Amphion, son of
Zeus and Antiope, caused stones to move
and build the walls of Thebes simply by

playing upon the lyre given to him by
Hermes.

42 *terminè* limit.

44 *erring stars* planets.

45 *situ et tempore* in position (the
direction of their movements) and in the
time they take to revolve about the earth.

Who knows not the double motion of the planets?
That the first is finished in a natural day?
The second thus? Saturn in thirty years?
Jupiter in twelve; Mars in four; the sun, Venus and Mercury in a
year; the moon in twenty eight days? These are freshmen's sup-   [55
positions. But tell me, hath every sphere a dominion or *intelligentia?*
Mephistophilis.   Ay.
Faustus.   How many heavens or spheres are there?
Mephistophilis.   Nine—the seven planets, the firmament, and the em-
pyreal heaven.   60
Faustus.   But is there not *coelum igneum, et crystallinum?*
Mephistophilis.   No, Faustus, they be but fables.
Faustus.   Resolve me then in this one question: why are not conjunc-
tions, oppositions, aspects, eclipses all at one time, but in some years
we have more, in some less?   65
Mephistophilis.   *Per inaequalem motum respectu totius.*
Faustus.   Well, I am answered. Now tell me who made the world.
Mephistophilis.   I will not.
Faustus.   Sweet Mephistophilis, tell me.
Mephistophilis.   Move me not, Faustus.   70
Faustus.   Villain, have not I bound thee to tell me any thing?
Mephistophilis.   Ay, that is not against our kingdom.
This is. Thou art damned. Think thou of hell.
Faustus.   Think, Faustus, upon God that made the world.
Mephistophilis.   Remember this.   75

Exit.

Faustus.   Ay, go accursèd spirit to ugly hell.
'Tis thou hast damned distressèd Faustus' soul.
Is't not too late?

Enter the two Angels.

Bad Angel.   Too late.
Good Angel.   Never too late, if Faustus will repent.   80
Bad Angel.   If thou repent, devils will tear thee in pieces.
Good Angel.   Repent, and they shall never raze thy skin.

Exeunt Angels.

Faustus.   O Christ, my Savior, my Savior,
Help to save distressèd Faustus' soul.

Enter Lucifer, Beëlzebub, and Mephistophilis.

Lucifer.   Christ cannot save thy soul, for he is just.   85
There's none but I have interest in the same.

---

56 *dominion or intelligentia* govern-
ing angel.

61 *coelum . . . crystallinum* the fiery
and the crystaline spheres of Ptolemaic
astronomy.

63–64 *conjunctions* seeming proximities
of heavenly bodies. *oppositions* diver-
gences of heavenly bodies. *aspects* any

other relations of such bodies to one
another. *eclipses* the blottings out of
one heavenly body by another.

66 *Per . . . totius* By their unequal
movements in respect to the whole (i.e.,
the different speeds of the various planets
within the total cosmos).

Faustus. O, what art thou that look'st so terribly?
Lucifer. I am Lucifer,
   And this is my companion prince in hell.
Faustus. O, Faustus, they are come to fetch thy soul.   90
Beëlzebub. We are come to tell thee thou dost injure us.
Lucifer. Thou call'st on Christ, contrary to thy promise.
Beëlzebub. Thou shouldst not think on God.
Lucifer. Think on the devil.
Beëlzebub. And his dam too.   95
Faustus. Nor will I henceforth. Pardon me in this,
   And Faustus vows never to look to heaven,
   Never to name God, or to pray to him,
   To burn his Scriptures, slay his ministers,
   And make my spirits pull his churches down.   100
Lucifer. So shalt thou show thyself an obedient servant,
   And we will highly gratify thee for it.
Beëlzebub. Faustus, we are come from hell in person to show thee
   some pastime. Sit down, and thou shalt behold the Seven Deadly Sins
   appear to thee in their own proper shapes and likeness.   105
Faustus. That sight will be as pleasant to me as Paradise was to Adam
   the first day of his creation.
Lucifer. Talk not of Paradise or creation, but mark the show. Go,
   Mephistophilis, fetch them in.

                              [*Exit Mephistophilis.*]

         Enter the Seven Deadly Sins, [with Mephistophilis,
                     led by a Piper].

Beëlzebub. Now Faustus, question them of their names and dis-   [110
   positions.
Faustus. That shall I soon. What art thou, the first?
Pride. I am Pride. I disdain to have any parents. I am like to Ovid's
   flea: I can creep into every corner of a wench. Sometimes, like a peri-
   wig, I sit upon her brow. Next, like a necklace, I hang about   [115
   her neck. Then, like a fan of feathers, I kiss her lips, and then, turning myself to a wrought smock, do what I list. But fie, what a smell
   is here! I'll not speak another word unless the ground be perfumed
   and covered with cloth of Arras.
Faustus. Thou art a proud knave indeed. What art thou, the   [120
   second?
Covetousness. I am Covetousness, begotten of an old churl in a leather
   bag, and might I now obtain my wish, this house, you and all, should
   turn to gold, that I might lock you safe into my chest. O my sweet
   gold!   125
Faustus. And what art thou, the third?

113–114 *Ovid's flea* The medieval   119 *cloth of Arras* Flemish cloth used
poem, *Carmine de Pulice* was generally   generally for tapestries.
attributed to Ovid.

Envy. I am Envy, begotten of a chimney-sweeper and an oyster-wife.
I cannot read and therefore wish all books burned. I am lean with
seeing others eat. O, that there would come a famine over all the
world, that all might die, and I live alone; then thou shouldst   [130
see how fat I'd be. But must thou sit and I stand? Come down, with
a vengeance.

Faustus.   Out envious wretch! But what are thou, the fourth?

Wrath.   I am Wrath. I had neither father nor mother. I leaped out of
a lion's mouth when I was scarce an hour old, and ever since   [135
have run up and down the world with this case of rapiers, wounding
myself when I could get none to fight withal. I was born in hell, and
look to it, for some of you shall be my father.

Faustus.   And what are you, the fifth?

Gluttony.   I am Gluttony. My parents are all dead, and the devil   [140
a penny they have left me but a small pension, and that buys me
thirty meals a day and ten bevers—a small trifle to suffice nature. I
come of a royal pedigree. My father was a gammon of bacon, and my
mother was a hogshead of claret wine. My godfathers were these:
Peter Pickled-herring and Martin Martlemas-beef. But my god-   [145
mother, O, she was a jolly gentlewoman, and well beloved in every
good town and city; her name was Mistress Margery March-beer. Now
Faustus, thou hast heard all my progeny; wilt thou bid me to a supper.

Faustus.   Not I. Thou wilt eat up all my victuals.   150

Gluttony.   Then the devil choke thee.

Faustus.   Choke thyself, glutton. What art thou, the sixth?

Sloth.   Heigh ho! I am Sloth. I was begotten on a sunny bank, where
I have lain ever since, and you have done me great injury to bring
me from thence. Let me be carried thither again by Gluttony   [155
and Lechery. Heigh ho! I'll not speak a word more for a king's ransom.

Faustus.   And what are you Mistress Minx, the seventh and last?

Lechery.   Who, I, sir? I am one that loves an inch of raw mutton better
than an ell of fried stockfish, and the first letter of my name   [160
begins with lechery.

Lucifer.   Away to hell! Away! On piper!

                    Exeunt the seven Sins [and the Piper].

Faustus.   O, how this sight doth delight my soul!

Lucifer.   But Faustus, in hell is all manner of delight.

Faustus.   O, might I see hell and return again safe, how happy   [165
were I then!

142 *bevers* light snacks taken between regular meals.

145 *Martlemas-beef* salted meat hung for the winter on Martinmas, November 11.

147 *March-beer* a fine ale, made in the springtime and not drunk until it has been aged for two years.

159 *raw mutton* common slang for whore.

160 *stockfish* dried codfish.

Lucifer. Faustus, thou shalt. At midnight I will send for thee. Meanwhile peruse this book and view it thoroughly, and thou shalt turn thyself into what shape thou wilt.

Faustus. Thanks, mighty Lucifer.   170
This will I keep as chary as my life.

Lucifer. Now Faustus, farewell.

Faustus. Farewell, great Lucifer. Come, Mephistophilis.

Exeunt, several ways.

Enter the clown, [Robin, holding a book].   II,iii.

Robin. What, Dick, look to the horses there till I come again. I have gotten one of Doctor Faustus' conjuring books, and now we'll have such knavery as't passes.

Enter Dick.

Dick. What, Robin, you must come away and walk the horses.

Robin. I walk the horses? I scorn't, 'faith. I have other matters in   [5
hand. Let the horses walk themselves and they will. [*He reads.*] *A per se a; t, h, e, the; o per se o; deny orgon, gorgon.* Keep further from me, O thou illiterate and unlearned hostler.

Dick. 'Snails, what hast thou got there? A book? Why, thou canst not tell ne'er a word on't.   10

Robin. That thou shalt see presently. Keep out of the circle, I say, lest I send you into the hostry with a vengeance.

Dick. That's like, 'faith. You had best leave your foolery, for an my master come, he'll conjure you, 'faith.

Robin. My master conjure me? I'll tell thee what: an my master   [15
come here, I'll clap as fair a pair of horns on's head as e'er thou sawest in thy life.

Dick. Thou needst not do that, for my mistress hath done it.

Robin. Ay, there be of us here that have waded as deep into matters as other men, if they were disposed to talk.   20

Dick. A plague take you! I thought you did not sneak up and down after her for nothing. But I prithee, tell me in good sadness, Robin, is that a conjuring book?

Robin. Do but speak what thou'lt have me to do, and I'll do't. If thou'lt dance naked, put off thy clothes, and I'll conjure thee   [25
about presently. Or if thou'lt go but to the tavern with me, I'll give thee white wine, red wine, claret wine, sack, muscadine, malmesey and whippincrust. Hold belly, hold, and we'll not pay one penny for it.

II,iii.

9 *'Snails* by God's nails.
16 *horns* the common sign of the cuckold.
22 *sadness* seriousness.

28 *whippincrust* possibly a corruption of 'hippocras,' a highly spiced and sugared wine.

Dick.   O brave! Prithee let's to it presently, for I am as dry as a dog.
Robin.   Come then, let's away.   30

Exeunt.

Enter the Chorus.   III,Prologue.
Chorus.   Learnèd Faustus,
To find the secrets of astronomy
Graven in the book of Jove's high firmament,
Did mount him up to scale Olympus' top,
Where, sitting in a chariot burning bright   5
Drawn by the strength of yokèd dragons' necks,
He views the clouds, the planets, and the stars,
The tropics, zones, and quarters of the sky,
From the bright circle of the hornèd moon
Even to the height of *Primum Mobile.*   10
And whirling round with this circumference,
Within the concave compass of the pole,
From east to west his dragons swiftly glide
And in eight days did bring him home again.
Not long he stayed within his quiet house   15
To rest his bones after his weary toil,
But new exploits do hale him out again,
And mounted then upon a dragon's back,
That with his wings did part the subtle air,
He now is gone to prove cosmography,   20
That measures coasts and kingdoms of the earth,
And, as I guess, will first arrive at Rome
To see the Pope and manner of his court
And take some part of holy Peter's feast,
The which this day is highly solemnized.   25

Exit.

Enter Faustus and Mephistophilis.   III,i.
Faustus.   Having now, my good Mephistophilis,
Passed with delight the stately town of Trier,

III, Prologue.

10 *Primum Mobile* in Ptolemaic astronomy the outermost sphere of creation
which moves the other nine spheres.

20 *prove cosmography* i.e., explore the
universe.

III,i.

2 *Trier* or Treves, a German city on
the Moselle river.

Environed round with airy mountain tops,
With walls of flint, and deep entrenchèd lakes,
Not to be won by any conquering prince;   5
From Paris next, coasting the realm of France,
We saw the river Main fall into Rhine,
Whose banks are set with groves of fruitful vines;
Then up to Naples, rich Campania,
Whose buildings fair and gorgeous to the eye,   10
The streets straight forth and paved with finest brick,
Quarters the town in four equivalents.
There saw we learnèd Maro's golden tomb,
The way he cut, an English mile in length,
Through a rock of stone in one night's space.   15
From thence to Venice, Padua, and the rest,
In midst of which a sumptuous temple stands,
That threats the stars with her aspiring top,
Whose frame is paved with sundry colored stones,
And roofed aloft with curious work in gold.   20
Thus hitherto hath Faustus spent his time.
But tell me now, what resting-place is this?
Hast thou, as erst I did command,
Conducted me within the walls of Rome?
Mephistophilis.   I have, my Faustus, and for proof thereof   25
This is the goodly palace of the Pope;
And 'cause we are no common guests,
I choose his privy chamber for our use.
Faustus.   I hope his holiness will bid us welcome.
Mephistophilis.   All's one, for we'll be bold with his venison.   30
But now, my Faustus, that thou may'st perceive
What Rome contains for to delight thine eyes,
Know that this city stands upon seven hills
That underprop the groundwork of the same.
Just through the midst runs flowing Tiber's stream,   35
With winding banks that cut it in two parts,
Over the which four stately bridges lean,
That make safe passage to each part of Rome.
Upon the bridge called Ponte Angelo
Erected is a castle passing strong,   40
Where thou shalt see such store of ordinance
As that the double cannons, forged of brass,
Do match the number of the days contained
Within the compass of one complete year;

---

4 *entrenchèd lakes* castle moats.
13 *Maro* Virgil.
14–15 *way . . . space* A tunnel between the bays of Naples and Baiae,
through Mt. Posilipo, was said to have

been cut by Virgil (regarded as a magician in the Middle Ages) by supernatural
art.
17–20 *In midst . . . gold* St. Mark's
cathedral in Venice.

Beside the gates and high pyramidès   45
That Julius Caesar brought from Africa
Faustus. Now, by the kingdoms of infernal rule,
Of Styx, of Acheron, and the fiery lake
Of ever-burning Phlegethon, I swear
That I do long to see the monuments   50
And situation of bright-splendent Rome.
Come, therefore, let's away.
Mephistophilis. Nay, stay my Faustus. I know you'd see the Pope
And take some part of holy Peter's feast,
The which, in state and high solemnity,
This day is held through Rome and Italy   55
In honor of the Pope's triumphant victory.
Faustus. Sweet Mephistophilis, thou pleasest me.
Whilst I am here on earth, let me be cloyed
With all things that delight the heart of man.   60
My four and twenty years of liberty
I'll spend in pleasure and in dalliance,
That Faustus' name, whilst this bright frame doth stand,
May be admirèd through the furthest land.
Mephistophilis. 'Tis well said, Faustus. Come then, stand by me   65
And thou shalt see them come immediately.
Faustus. Nay, stay, my gentle Mephistophilis,
And grant me my request, and then I go.
Thou know'st within the compass of eight days
We viewed the face of heaven, of earth, and hell.   70
So high our dragons soared into the air,
That looking down, the earth appeared to me
No bigger than my hand in quantity.
There did we view the kingdoms of the world,
And what might please mine eye I there beheld.   75
Then in this show let me an actor be,
That this proud Pope may Faustus' cunning see.
Mephistophilis. Let it be so, my Faustus. But, first stay
And view their triumphs as they pass this way,
And then devise what best contents thy mind   80
By cunning in thine art to cross the Pope
Or dash the pride of this solemnity,
To make his monks and abbots stand like apes
And point like antics at his triple crown,
To beat the beads about the friars' pates   85
Or clap huge horns upon the cardinals' heads,
Or any villainy thou canst devise,
And I'll perform it, Faustus. Hark, they come.
This day shall make thee be admired in Rome.

45–46 *gates . . . Africa* Before the gates of St. Peter's there still stands the obelisk which was brought to Rome from Heliopolis by the Emperor Caligula in the first century A.D.

79 *triumphs* spectacular displays.

Enter the Cardinals and Bishops, some bearing crosiers, some
the pillars; Monks and Friars singing their procession. Then
the Pope, and Raymond, King of Hungary, with Bruno, led
in chains.

Pope. Cast down our footstool.
Raymond.   Saxon Bruno, stoop,   90
  Whilst on thy back his holiness ascends
  Saint Peter's chair and state pontifical.
Bruno. Proud Lucifer, that state belongs to me,
  But thus I fall to Peter, not to thee.
Pope. To me and Peter shalt thou grovelling lie   95
  And crouch before the papal dignity.
  Sound trumpets then, for thus Saint Peter's heir
  From Bruno's back ascends Saint Peter's chair.
                           A flourish while he ascends.
  Thus, as the gods creep on with feet of wool
  Long ere with iron hands they punish men,   100
  So shall our sleeping vengeance now arise
  And smite with death thy hated enterprise.
  Lord Cardinals of France and Padua,
  Go forthwith to our holy consistory,
  And read amongst the Statutes Decretal   105
  What, by the holy council held at Trent,
  The sacred synod hath decreed for him
  That doth assume the papal government
  Without election and a true consent.
  Away, and bring us word with speed.   110
First Cardinal. We go my Lord.
                         Exeunt Cardinals.

Pope. Lord Raymond.   [*They talk apart.*]
Faustus. Go, haste thee, gentle Mephistophilis,
  Follow the cardinals to the consistory,
  And as they turn their superstitious books,   115
  Strike them with sloth and drowsy idleness,
  And make them sleep so sound that in their shapes
  Thyself and I may parley with this Pope,
  This proud confronter of the Emperor,
  And in despite of all his holiness   120
  Restore this Bruno to his liberty
  And bear him to the states of Germany.
Mephistophilis. Faustus, I go.
Faustus. Dispatch it soon.
  The Pope shall curse that Faustus came to Rome.   125
               Exeunt Faustus and Mephistophilis.

---

105 *Statutes Decretal* papal decrees   106 *council . . . Trent* held between
concerning religious doctrine or eccle-   1545 and 1563.
siastical law.

Bruno.   Pope Adrian, let me have some right of law.
I was elected by the Emperor.
Pope.   We will depose the Emperor for that deed
And curse the people that submit to him.
Both he and thou shalt stand excommunicate   130
And interdict from church's privilege
And all society of holy men.
He grows too proud in his authority,
Lifting his lofty head above the clouds,
And like a steeple over-peers the church.   135
But we'll pull down his haughty insolence,
And as Pope Alexander, our progenitor,
Trod on the neck of German Frederick,
Adding this golden sentence to our praise,
'That Peter's heirs should tread on emperors   140
And walk upon the dreadful adder's back,
Treading the lion and the dragon down
And fearless spurn the killing basilisk,'
So will we quell that haughty schismatic,
And by authority apostolical   145
Depose him from his regal government.
Bruno.   Pope Julius swore to princely Sigismond,
For him and the succeeding popes of Rome,
To hold the emperors their lawful lords.
Pope.   Pope Julius did abuse the church's rites,   150
And therefore none of his decrees can stand.
Is not all power on earth bestowed on us?
And therefore, though we would, we cannot err.
Behold this silver belt, whereto is fixed
Seven golden keys fast sealed with seven seals   155
In token of our sevenfold power from heaven,
To bind or loose, lock fast, condemn or judge,
Resign, or seal, or whatso pleaseth us.
Then he and thou and all the world shall stoop,
Or be assurèd of our dreadful curse   160
To light as heavy as the pains of hell.

126 *Pope Adrian* Marlowe is thinking probably of Pope Hadrian IV (1154–1159) who came into conflict with Frederick Barbarossa, the Holy Roman Emperor, whom he forced to submit to him. What historicity there may be in these scenes at the papal court is badly confused.

137–138 *Pope Alexander . . . Frederick* Pope Alexander III (1159–1181) successor to Hadrian IV, continued the struggle against Frederick Barbarossa and forced him to acknowledge the papal supremacy at Canossa.

143 *basilisk* a mythical monster with power to kill by its looks.

147 *Pope Julius . . . Sigismond* None of the three popes named Julius was contemporary with the Emperor Sigismund, who lived from 1368 to 1437. Sigismund did, however, in 1414 summon the Council of Constance which sought to end the Great Schism.

Enter Faustus and Mephistophilis, like the Cardinals.
Mephistophilis.   Now tell me, Faustus, are we not fitted well?
Faustus.   Yes, Mephistophilis, and two such cardinals
   Ne'er served a holy pope as we shall do.
   But whilst they sleep within the consistory,   165
   Let us salute his reverend fatherhood.
Raymond.   Behold, my lord, the cardinals are returned.
Pope.   Welcome, grave fathers. Answer presently:
   What have our holy council there decreed
   Concerning Bruno and the Emperor,   170
   In quittance of their late conspiracy
   Against our state and papal dignity?
Faustus.   Most sacred patron of the church of Rome,
   By full consent of all the synod
   Of priests and prelates it is thus decreed: 175
   That Bruno and the German Emperor
   Be held as Lollards and bold schismatics
   And proud disturbers of the church's peace.
   And if that Bruno by his own assent,
   Without enforcement of the German peers,   180
   Did seek to wear the triple diadem
   And by your death to climb Saint Peter's chair,
   The Statutes Decretal have thus decreed:
   He shall be straight condemned of heresy
   And on a pile of fagots burned to death.   185
Pope.   It is enough. Here, take him to your charge,
   And bear him straight to Ponte Angelo,
   And in the strongest tower enclose him fast.
   Tomorrow, sitting in our consistory
   With all our college of grave cardinals,   190
   We will determine of his life or death.
   Here, take his triple crown along with you,
   And leave it in the church's treasury.
   Make haste again, my good lord cardinals,
   And take our blessing apostolical.   195
Mephistophilis.   So, so. Was never devil thus blessed before.
Faustus.   Away, sweet Mephistophilis, be gone.
   The cardinals will be plagued for this anon.
         Exeunt Faustus and Mephistophilis [with Bruno].
Pope.   Go presently and bring a banquet forth,
   That we may solemnize Saint Peter's feast,   200
   And with Lord Raymond, King of Hungary,
   Drink to our late and happy victory.   *Exeunt.*

✱

177 *Lollards* followers of John Wyclif (1320?–1384), the English reformer.

III,ii.

A sennet [is sounded] while the banquet is brought in; and
then enter Faustus and Mephistophilis in their own shapes.

Mephistophilis.   Now, Faustus, come, prepare thyself for mirth.
  The sleepy cardinals are hard at hand
  To censure Bruno, that is posted hence,
  And on a proud-paced steed, as swift as thought,
  Flies o'er the Alps to fruitful Germany,   5
  There to salute the woeful Emperor.

Faustus.   The Pope will curse them for their sloth today,
  That slept both Bruno and his crown away.
  But now, that Faustus may delight his mind
  And by their folly make some merriment,   10
  Sweet Mephistophilis, so charm me here
  That I may walk invisible to all
  And do whate'er I please unseen of any.

Mephistophilis.   Faustus, thou shalt. Then kneel down presently:
          Whilst on thy head I lay my hand   15
          And charm thee with this magic wand.
          First wear this girdle; then appear
          Invisible to all are here.
          The planets seven, the gloomy air,
          Hell and the Furies' forkèd hair,   20
          Pluto's blue fire, and Hecate's tree,
          With magic spells so compass thee
          That no eye may thy body see.
  So Faustus.   Now, for all their holiness,
  Do what thou wilt, thou shalt not be discerned.   25

Faustus.   Thanks, Mephistophilis. Now friars take heed
  Lest Faustus make your shaven crowns to bleed.

Mephistophilis.   Faustus, no more. See where the cardinals come.
    Enter Pope and all the Lords. Enter the Cardinals with a book.

Pope.   Welcome, lord cardinals. Come, sit down.
  Lord Raymond, take your seat. Friars attend,   30
  And see that all things be in readiness,
  As best beseems this solemn festival.

First Cardinal.   First, may it please your sacred holiness
  To view the sentence of the reverend synod
  Concerning Bruno and the Emperor?   35

Pope.   What needs this question? Did I not tell you
  Tomorrow we would sit i' th' consistory
  And there determine of his punishment?
  You brought us word even now; it was decreed
  That Bruno and the cursèd Emperor   40
  Were by the holy council both condemned
  For loathèd Lollards and base schismatics.
  Then wherefore would you have me view that book?

First Cardinal.   Your grace mistakes. You gave us no such charge.
Raymond.   Deny it not. We all are witnesses   45
  That Bruno here was late delivered you,
  With his rich triple crown to be reserved
  And put into the church's treasury.
Both Cardinals.   By holy Paul, we saw them not.
Pope.   By Peter, you shall die   50.
  Unless you bring them forth immediately.
  Hale them to prison. Lade their limbs with gyves.
  False prelates, for this hateful treachery
  Cursed be your souls to hellish misery.
                    [*Exeunt the two Cardinals with Attendants.*]
Faustus.   So, they are safe. Now, Faustus, to the feast.   55.
  The Pope had never such a frolic guest.
Pope.   Lord Archbishop of Rheims, sit down with us.
Archbishop.   I thank your holiness.
Faustus.   Fall to. The devil choke you an you spare.
Pope.   Who's that spoke? Friars look about.   60.
Friar.   Here's nobody, if it like your holiness.
Pope.   Lord Raymond, pray fall to. I am beholding
  To the Bishop of Milan for this so rare a present.
Faustus.   I thank you, sir.   [*He snatches the dish.*]
Pope.   How now? Who snatched the meat from me?   65.
  Villains, why speak you not?
  My good Lord Archbishop, here's a most dainty dish
  Was sent me from a cardinal in France.
Faustus.   I'll have that too.   [*He snatches the dish.*]
Pope.   What Lollards do attend our holiness,   70.
  That we receive such great indignity?
  Fetch me some wine.
Faustus.   Ay, pray do, for Faustus is a-dry.
Pope.   Lord Raymond, I drink unto your grace.
Faustus.   I pledge your grace.   [*He snatches the cup.*]   75
Pope.   My wine gone too? Ye lubbers, look about
  And find the man that doth this villainy,
  Or by our sanctitude, you all shall die.
  I pray, my lords, have patience at this
  Troublesome banquet.   80
Archbishop.   Please it your holiness, I think it be some ghost crept out
  of purgatory, and now is come unto your holiness for his pardon.
Pope.   It may be so.
  Go then, command our priests to sing a dirge
  To lay the fury of this same troublesome ghost.   85.
                    [*Exit an attendant.*]
  Once again, my lord, fall to.
                    The Pope crosseth himself.
Faustus.   How now?

Must every bit be spicèd with a cross?
Nay then, take that.   [*He strikes the Pope.*]
Pope.   **O** I am slain. Help me, my lords.   90
O come and help to bear my body hence.
Damned be this soul for ever for this deed.
                    Exeunt the Pope and his train.
Mephistophilis.   Now, Faustus, what will you do now? For I can tell
you you'll be cursed with bell, book, and candle.
Faustus.   Bell, book, and candle; candle, book, and bell,   95
Forward and backward, to curse Faustus to hell.
          Enter the Friars with bell, book, and candle for the dirge.
First Friar.   Come, brethren, let's about our business with good devo-
          tion.   [*They chant.*]

          Cursed be he that stole his holiness' meat from the table.
                    Maledicat Dominus!   100
          Cursed be he that struck his holiness a blow on the face.
                    Maledicat Dominus!
          Cursed be he that struck Friar Sandelo a blow on the pate.
                    Maledicat Dominus!
          Cursed be he that disturbeth our holy dirge.   105
                    Maledicat Dominus!
          Cursed be he that took away his holiness' wine.
                    Maledicat Dominus! Et omnes sancti. Amen.

          [*Faustus and Mephistophilis*] beat the Friars, fling fireworks
                              among them, and exeunt.

          Enter [*Robin,*] *the clown, and Dick, with a cup.*   III,iii.
Dick.   Sirrah Robin, we were best look that your devil can answer the
          stealing of this same cup, for the vintner's boy follows us at the hard
          heels.
Robin.   'Tis no matter. Let him come. An he follow us, I'll so conjure
          him as he was never conjured in his life, I warrant him. Let me   [5
          see the cup.
                    Enter Vintner.
Dick.   Here 'tis. Yonder he comes. Now, Robin, now or never show thy
          cunning.
Vintner.   O, are you here? I am glad I have found you. You are a couple
          of fine companions. Pray, where's the cup you stole from the   [10
          tavern?

III,ii.
     95 *Bell, book, and candle* used traditionally in the office of excommunication.

Robin. How, how? We steal a cup? Take heed what you say. We look
not like cup stealers, I can tell you.

Vintner. Never deny't, for I know you have it, and I'll search you.

Robin. Search me? Ay, and spare not. Hold the cup, Dick.   [15
[*Aside to Dick.*] Come, come, search me, search me.

> [*The Vintner searches Robin.*]

Vintner. [*to Dick*]   Come on, sirrah, let me search you now.

Dick. Ay, ay, do, do. Hold the cup, Robin. [*Aside to Robin.*] I fear not
your searching. We scorn to steal your cups, I can tell you.

> [*The Vintner searches Dick.*]

Vintner. Never outface me for the matter, for sure the cup is be-   [20
tween you two.

Robin. Nay, there you lie. 'Tis beyond us both.

Vintner. A plague take you! I thought 'twas your knavery to take it
away. Come, give it me again.

Robin. Ay, much. When? Can you tell? Dick, make me a circle,   [25
and stand close at my back, and stir not for thy life. Vintner, you
shall have your cup anon. Say nothing, Dick, *O per se, O Demogorgon,
Belcher and Mephistophilis.*

> *Enter Mephistophilis.* [*Exit the Vintner, in fright.*]

Mephistophilis.   Monarch of hell, under whose black survey
Great potentates do kneel with awful fear,   30
Upon whose altars thousand souls do lie,
How am I vexèd by these villains' charms!
From Constantinople have they brought me now,
Only for pleasure of these damnèd slaves.

Robin. By Lady, sir, you have had a shrewd journey of it. Will it   [35
please you to take a shoulder of mutton to supper and a tester in
your purse, and go back again?

Dick. Ay, I pray you heartily, sir, for we called you but in jest, I promise you.

Mephistophilis.   To purge the rashness of this cursèd deed,   40
First be thou turnèd to this ugly shape,
For apish deeds transformèd to an ape.

Robin. O brave, an ape! I pray sir, let me have the carrying of him
about to show some tricks.

Mephistophilis. And so thou shalt. Be thou transformed to a dog,   [45
and carry him upon thy back. Away, be gone!

Robin. A dog? That's excellent. Let the maids look well to their porridge pots, for I'll into the kitchen presently. Come, Dick, come.

> *Exeunt* [*Robin and Dick,*] *the two clowns.*

Mephistophilis. Now with the flames of ever-burning fire,
I'll wing myself and forthwith fly amain   50
Unto my Faustus, to the great Turk's court.   *Exit.*

✱

III,iii.

36 *tester* sixpence.

Enter Chorus.   IV,Prologue.

Chorus.   When Faustus had with pleasure ta'en the view
    Of rarest things and royal courts of kings,
    He stayed his course and so returnèd home;
    Where such as bare his absence but with grief—
    I mean his friends and nearest companions—   5
    Did gratulate his safety with kind words,
    And in their conference of what befell,
    Touching his journey through the world and air,
    They put forth questions of astrology,
    Which Faustus answered with such learnèd skill   10
    As they admired and wondered at his wit.
    Now is his fame spread forth in every land.
    Amongst the rest, the Emperor is one—
    Carolus the fifth—at whose palace now
    Faustus is feasted 'mongst his noblemen.   15
    What there he did in trial of his art
    I leave untold, your eyes shall see performed.

                         Exit.

                 ✳

Enter Martino and Frederick, at several doors.   IV,i.

Martino.   What ho, officers, gentlemen,
    Hie to the presence to attend the Emperor.
    Good Frederick, see the rooms be voided straight;
    His majesty is coming to the hall.
    Go back, and see the state in readiness.   5
Frederick.   But where is Bruno, our elected Pope,
    That on a fury's back came post from Rome?
    Will not his grace consort the Emperor?
Martino.   O yes, and with him comes the German conjurer,
    The learnèd Faustus, fame of Wittenberg,   10
    The wonder of the world for magic art;
    And he intends to show great Carolus
    The race of all his stout progenitors,
    And bring in presence of his majesty
    The royal shapes and warlike semblances   15
    Of Alexander and his beauteous paramour.
Frederick.   Where is Benvolio?
Martino.   Fast asleep, I warrant you.

IV, Prologue.

   7 *conference* discussion.
   14 *Carolus* Charles V, King of Spain
(as Charles I from 1516 to 1556) and
Holy Roman Emperor from 1519 to 1556.

IV,i.

   2 *presence* presence chamber.
   5 *state* throne
   10 *fame* glory.
   16 *Alexander* Alexander the Great.

He took his rouse with stoups of Rhenish wine
So kindly yesternight to Bruno's health   20
That all this day the sluggard keeps his bed.
Frederick.   See, see, his window's ope. We'll call to him.
Martino.   What ho, Benvolio!
        Enter Benvolio above at a window, in his nightcap, buttoning.
Benvolio.   What a devil ail you two?
Martino.   Speak softly, sir, lest the devil hear you,   25
    For Faustus at the court is late arrived,
    And at his heels a thousand furies wait
    To accomplish whatsoever the doctor please.
Benvolio.   What of this?
Martino.   Come, leave thy chamber first, and thou shalt see   30
    This conjurer perform such rare exploits
    Before the Pope and royal Emperor
    As never yet was seen in Germany.
Benvolio.   Has not the Pope enough of conjuring yet?
    He was upon the devil's back late enough,   35
    And if he be so far in love with him,
    I would he would post with him to Rome again.
Frederick.   Speak, wilt thou come and see this sport?
Benvolio.   Not I.
Martino.   Wilt thou stand in thy window and see it then?
Benvolio.   Ay, and I fall not asleep i' th' meantime.   40
Martino.   The Emperor is at hand, who comes to see
    What wonders by black spells may compassed be.
Benvolio.   Well, go you attend the Emperor. I am content for this
    once to thrust my head out at a window, for they say if a man be drunk
    overnight the devil cannot hurt him in the morning. If that [45
    be true, I have a charm in my head shall control him as well as
    the conjurer, I warrant you.
                    *Exit [Frederick, with Martino. Benvolio remains
                                        at the window above].*

        *A sennet [is sounded. Enter] Charles, the German Emperor,
        Bruno, [the Duke of] Saxony, Faustus, Mephistophilis, Frede-
                        rick, Martino, and Attendants.*
Emperor.   Wonder of men, renowned magician,
    Thrice-learnèd Faustus, welcome to our court.
    This deed of thine, in setting Bruno free
    From his and our professèd enemy,

19 *took . . . stoups* i.e., had a drinking   32 *the Pope* i.e., Bruno.
bout with brimming goblets.

Shall add more excellence unto thine art   5
Than if by powerful necromantic spells
Thou couldst command the world's obedience.
Forever be beloved of Carolus,
And if this Bruno thou hast late redeemed
In peace possess the triple diadem   10
And sit in Peter's chair despite of chance,
Thou shalt be famous through all Italy
And honored of the German Emperor.

Faustus.   These gracious words, most royal Carolus,
Shall make poor Faustus to his utmost power   15
Both love and serve the German Emperor
And lay his life at holy Bruno's feet.
For proof whereof, if so your grace be pleased,
The doctor stands prepared by power of art
To cast his magic charms that shall pierce through   20
The ebon gates of ever-burning hell,
And hale the stubborn Furies from their caves
To compass whatsoe'er your grace commands.

Benvolio. [*above*]   Blood, he speaks terribly, but for all that, I do not
greatly believe him. He looks as like a conjurer as the Pope to a   [25
costermonger.

Emperor.   Then, Faustus, as thou late did'st promise us,
We would behold that famous conqueror,
Great Alexander, and his paramour
In their true shapes and state majestical,   30
That we may wonder at their excellence.

Faustus.   Your majesty shall see them presently.
Mephistophilis, away,
And with a solemn noise of trumpets' sound
Present before this royal Emperor,   35
Great Alexander and his beauteous paramour.

Mephistophilis.   Faustus, I will.

                                                        [*Exit.*]

Benvolio.   Well, master doctor, an your devils come not away quickly,
you shall have me asleep presently. Zounds, I could eat myself for
anger to think I have been such an ass all this while, to stand   [40
gaping after the devil's governor and can see nothing.

Faustus.   I'll make you feel something anon, if my art fail me not.
My lord, I must forewarn your majesty
That when my spirits present the royal shapes
Of Alexander and his paramour,   45
Your grace demand no questions of the king,
But in dumb silence let them come and go.

IV,ii.
    9 *redeemed* rescued.   25 *the Pope* i.e., Bruno.

Emperor.   Be it as Faustus please; we are content.
Benvolio.   Ay, ay, and I am content too. And thou bring Alexander
and his paramour before the Emperor, I'll be Actæon and turn   [50
myself to a stag.
Faustus.   And I'll play Diana and send you the horns presently.

[*A*] *sennet* [*is sounded*]. *Enter at one* [*door*] *the Emperor Alexander, at the other Darius. They meet* [*in combat*]. *Darius is
thrown down; Alexander kills him, takes off his crown, and,
offering to go out, his paramour meets him. He embraceth her
and sets Darius' crown upon her head; and coming back, both
salute the Emperor, who, leaving his state, offers to embrace
them, which Faustus seeing, suddenly stays him. Then trumpets
cease and music sounds.*

My gracious lord, you do forget yourself.
These are but shadows, not substantial.
Emperor.   O pardon me. My thoughts are so ravishèd   55
With sight of this renownèd emperor,
That in mine arms I would have compassed him.
But, Faustus, since I may not speak to them,
To satisfy my longing thoughts at full,
Let me this tell thee: I have heard it said   60
That this fair lady, whilst she lived on earth,
Had on her neck a little wart or mole;
How may I prove that saying to be true?
Faustus.   Your majesty may boldly go and see.
Emperor.   Faustus, I see it plain,   65
And in this sight thou better pleasest me
Than if I gained another monarchy.
Faustus.   Away! Be gone!

Exit show.

See, see, my gracious lord, what strange beast is yon, that thrusts his
head out at window?   70
Emperor.   O wondrous sight! See, Duke of Saxony,
Two spreading horns most strangely fastenèd
Upon the head of young Benvolio.
Saxony.   What? Is he asleep or dead?
Faustus.   He sleeps, my lord, but dreams not of his horns.   75
Emperor.   This sport is excellent. We'll call and wake him.
What ho, Benvolio!
Benvolio.   A plague upon you! Let me sleep a while.
Emperor.   I blame thee not to sleep much, having such a head of thine
own.   80
Saxony.   Look up, Benvolio; 'tis the Emperor calls.

50 *Actæon* See note to *Edward II*, I,i,
67.
52, SD *Darius* King Darius III of

Persia (336–330 B.C.) defeated at Granicus
in 334 B.C. by the Greeks under Alexander
the Great.

Benvolio.   The Emperor? Where? O zounds, my head!

Emperor.   Nay, and thy horns hold, 'tis no matter for thy head, for
that's armed sufficiently.

Faustus.   Why, how now, sir knight! What, hanged by the horns?   [85
This is most horrible. Fie, fie, pull in your head for shame. Let not all
the world wonder at you.

Benvolio.   Zounds, doctor, is this your villainy?

Faustus.   O say not so, sir. The doctor has no skill,
No art, no cunning, to present these lords   90
Or bring before this royal Emperor
The mighty monarch, warlike Alexander.
If Faustus do it, you are straight resolved
In bold Actæon's shape to turn a stag.
And therefore, my lord, so please your majesty,   95
I'll raise a kennel of hounds shall hunt him so
As all his footmanship shall scarce prevail
To keep his carcass from their bloody fangs.
Ho, Belimote, Argiron, Asterote!

Benvolio.   Hold, hold! Zounds, he'll raise up a kennel of devils,   [100
I think, anon. Good, my lord, entreat for me. 'Sblood, I am never able
to endure these torments.

Emperor.   Then, good master doctor,
Let me entreat you to remove his horns.
He has done penance now sufficiently.   105

Faustus.   My gracious lord, not so much for injury done to me, as to
delight your majesty with some mirth, hath Faustus justly requited
this injurious knight; which being all I desire, I am content to remove
his horns. Mephistophilis, transform him.

                    [*Mephistophilis removes the horns.*]
And hereafter, sir, look you speak well of scholars.   110

Benvolio. [aside]   Speak well of ye? 'Sblood, and scholars be such cuckold makers to clap horns of honest men's heads o' this order, I'll ne'er
trust smooth faces and small ruffs more. But an I be not revenged
for this, would I might be turned to a gaping oyster and drink nothing
but salt water.   115

                    [*Exit Benvolio above.*]

Emperor.   Come, Faustus. While the Emperor lives,
In recompense of this thy high desert,
Thou shalt command the state of Germany
And live beloved of mighty Carolus.

                                                        Exeunt.

---

108 *injurious* insulting.   113 *small ruffs* academic gowns.

Enter Benvolio, Martino, Frederick, and Soldiers.   IV,iii.

Martino.   Nay, sweet Benvolio, let us sway thy thoughts
  From this attempt against the conjurer.
Benvolio.   Away! You love me not to urge me thus.
  Shall I let slip so great an injury,
  When every servile groom jests at my wrongs   5
  And in their rustic gambols proudly say,
  'Benvolio's head was graced with horns today'?
  O, may these eyelids never close again
  Till with my sword I have that conjurer slain.
  If you will aid me in this enterprise,   10
  Then draw your weapons and be resolute.
  If not, depart. Here will Benvolio die,
  But Faustus' death shall quit my infamy.
Frederick.   Nay, we will stay with thee, betide what may,
  And kill that doctor if he come this way.   15
Benvolio.   Then, gentle Frederick, hie thee to the grove,
  And place our servants and our followers
  Close in an ambush there behind the trees.
  By this, I know, the conjurer is near.
  I saw him kneel and kiss the Emperor's hand   20
  And take his leave, laden with rich rewards.
  Then, soldiers, boldly fight. If Faustus die,
  Take you the wealth; leave us the victory.
Frederick.   Come, soldiers. Follow me unto the grove.
  Who kills him shall have gold and endless love.   25
                Exit Frederick with the Soldiers.
Benvolio.   My head is lighter than it was by th'horns,
  But yet my heart's more ponderous than my head
  And pants until I see that conjurer dead.
Martino.   Where shall we place ourselves, Benvolio?
Benvolio.   Here will we stay to bide the first assault.   30
  O, were that damnèd hell-hound but in place,
  Thou soon shouldst see me quit my foul disgrace.
                   Enter Frederick.
Frederick.   Close, close, the conjurer is at hand
  And all alone comes walking in his gown.
  Be ready then, and strike the peasant down.   35
Benvolio.   Mine be that honor then. Now, sword, strike home.
  For horns he gave I'll have his head anon.
          Enter Faustus with the false head.
Martino.   See, see, he comes.
Benvolio.   No words! This blow ends all.
  Hell take his soul; his body thus must fall.   [*He stabs Faustus.*]
Faustus. [*falling*]   Oh!   40

IV,iii.
 13 *quit* pay for.

Frederick.   Groan you, master doctor?

Benvolio.   Break may his heart with groans! Dear Frederick, see,
Thus will I end his griefs immediately.

Martino.   Strike with a willing hand. His head is off.

> [*Benvolio strikes off Faustus' false head.*]

Benvolio.   The devil's dead. The Furies now may laugh.   45

Frederick.   Was this that stern aspèct, that awful frown,
Made the grim monarch of infernal spirits
Tremble and quake at his commanding charms?

Martino.   Was this that damnèd head whose heart conspired
Benvolio's shame before the Emperor?   50

Benvolio.   Ay, that's the head, and here the body lies,
Justly rewarded for his villainies.

Frederick.   Come, let's devise how we may add more shame
To the black scandal of his hated name.

Benvolio.   First, on his head, in quittance of my wrongs,   55
I'll nail huge forkèd horns and let them hang
Within the window where he yoked me first,
That all the world may see my just revenge.

Martino.   What use shall we put his beard to?

Benvolio.   We'll sell it to a chimney-sweeper. It will wear out ten   [60
birchen brooms, I warrant you.

Frederick.   What shall eyes do?

Benvolio.   We'll put out his eyes, and they shall serve for buttons to
his lips to keep his tongue from catching cold.

Martino.   An excellent policy! And now, sirs, having divided him,   [65
what shall the body do?

> [*Faustus rises.*]

Benvolio.   Zounds, the devil's alive again.

Frederick.   Give him his head, for God's sake.

Faustus.   Nay, keep it. Faustus will have heads and hands,
Ay, all your hearts, to recompense this deed.   70
Knew you not, traitors, I was limited
For four-and-twenty years to breathe on earth?
And had you cut my body with your swords,
Or hewed this flesh and bones as small as sand,
Yet in a minute had my spirit returned,   75
And I had breathed a man made free from harm.
But wherefore do I dally my revenge?
Asteroth, Belimoth, Mephistophilis!

> *Enter Mephistophilis and other Devils.*

Go, horse these traitors on your fiery backs,
And mount aloft with them as high as heaven;   80
Thence pitch them headlong to the lowest hell.
Yet stay. The world shall see their misery,
And hell shall after plague their treachery.

71 *limited* given a specific term.

Go, Belimoth, and take this caitiff hence,
And hurl him in some lake of mud and dirt.   85
Take thou this other; drag him through the woods
Amongst the pricking thorns and sharpest briars,
Whilst with my gentle Mephistophilis
This traitor flies unto some steepy rock
That, rolling down, may break the villain's bones   90
As he intended to dismember me.
Fly hence. Dispatch my charge immediately.
Frederick.   Pity us, gentle Faustus. Save our lives.
Faustus.   Away!
Frederick.   He must needs go that the devil drives.
                              Exeunt Spirits with the Knights.

                    Enter the ambushed Soldiers.
First Soldier.   Come, sirs, prepare yourselves in readiness.   95
Make haste to help these noble gentlemen;
I heard them parley with the conjurer.
Second Soldier.   See where he comes. Dispatch and kill the slave.
Faustus.   What's here? An ambush to betray my life?
Then, Faustus, try thy skill. Base peasants, stand,   100
For lo, these trees remove at my command
And stand as bulwarks 'twixt yourselves and me,
To shield me from your hated treachery.
Yet to encounter this your weak attempt,
Behold an army comes incontinent.   105
            *Faustus strikes the door, and enter a Devil playing on a
            drum, after him another bearing an ensign, and divers
            with weapons, Mephistophilis with fireworks. They set
            upon the Soldiers and drive them out. [Exit Faustus.]*

    *Enter at several doors Benvolio, Frederick, and Martino, their
    heads and faces bloody and besmeared with mud and dirt, all
                  having horns on their heads.*
Martino.   What ho, Benvolio!
Benvolio.   Here! What, Frederick, ho!
Frederick.   O help me, gentle friend. Where is Martino?
Martino.   Dear Frederick, here,
Half smothered in a lake of mud and dirt,   5
Through which the Furies dragged me by the heels.
Frederick.   Martino, see! Benvolio's horns again.
Martino.   O misery! How now, Benvolio?

101 *remove* change their positions.   105 *incontinent* at once.

Benvolio.   Defend me, heaven. Shall I be haunted still?
Martino.   Nay, fear not man; we have not power to kill.   10
Benvolio.   My friends transformèd thus! O hellish spite!
　　Your heads are all set with horns.
Frederick.   You hit it right.
　　It is your own you mean. Feel on your head.
Benvolio.   Zounds, horns again!
Martino.   Nay, chafe not man. We all are sped.   15
Benvolio.   What devil attends this damned magician,
　　That, spite of spite, our wrongs are doublèd?
Frederick.   What may we do, that we may hide our shames?
Benvolio.   If we should follow him to work revenge,
　　He'd join long asses' ears to these huge horns,   20
　　And make us laughing-stocks to all the world.
Martino.   What shall we then do, dear Benvolio?
Benvolio.   I have a castle joining near these woods,
　　And thither we'll repair and live obscure
　　Till time shall alter these our brutish shapes.   25
　　Sith black disgrace hath thus eclipsed our fame,
　　We'll rather die with grief than live with shame.

　　　　　　　　　　　　　　　　　Exeunt omnes.

　　　　　　Enter Faustus and Mephistophilis.   IV,v.
Faustus.   Now, Mephistophilis, the restless course
　　That time doth run with calm and silent foot,
　　Shortening my days and thread of vital life,
　　Calls for the payment of my latest years.
　　Therefore, sweet Mephistophilis, let us   5
　　Make haste to Wittenberg.
Mephistophilis.   What, will you go on horseback, or on foot?
Faustus.   Nay, till I am past this fair and pleasant green,
　　I'll walk on foot.

　　　　　　　　　　　　　　　[Exit Mephistophilis.]

　　　　　　Enter a Horse-Courser.
Horse-Courser.   I have been all this day seeking one Master [10
　　Fustian. Mass, see where he is. God save you, master doctor.

IV,iv.
9 *haunted* (1) bewitched (2) hunted,
pursued (since he is a stag).
15 *sped* provided (with horns).

IV,v.
The first eleven lines of this scene,
omitted by Greg from his reconstruction
of the play, appear only in the 1604

quarto. While recognizing that they may
well be spurious, I have retained them
because they provide a transition to the
Horse-Courser episode and at the same
time remind the audience of the im-
pending tragedy of Faustus' death.
11 *Fustian* The perversion of Faustus'
name is a deliberate attempt at humor.

Faustus. What, horse-courser! You are well met.

Horse-Courser. I beseech your worship, accept of these forty dollars.

Faustus. Friend, thou canst not buy so good a horse for so small a price. I have no great need to sell him, but if thou likest him [15 for ten dollars more, take him, because I see thou hast a good mind to him.

Horse-Courser. I beseech you, sir, accept of this. I am a very poor man and have lost very much of late by horse-flesh, and this bargain will set me up again. 20

Faustus. Well, I will not stand with thee. Give me the money.

> [*The Horse-Courser gives Faustus money.*]

Now, sirrah, I must tell you that you may ride him o'er hedge and ditch, and spare him not. But, do you hear? In any case, ride him not into the water.

Horse-Courser. How sir? Not into the water? Why, will he not [25 drink of all waters?

Faustus. Yes, he will drink of all waters, but ride him not into the water—o'er hedge and ditch, or where thou wilt, but not into the water. Go, bid the hostler deliver him unto you, and remember what I say. 30

Horse-Courser. I warrant you, sir. O joyful day! Now am I a man made forever.

> *Exit.*

Faustus. What art thou, Faustus, but a man condemned to die?
Thy fatal time draws to a final end.
Despair doth drive distrust into my thoughts. 35
Confound these passions with a quiet sleep.
Tush! Christ did call the thief upon the cross;
Then rest thee, Faustus, quiet in conceit.

> *He sits to sleep* [*in his chair*].

Enter the Horse-Courser, wet.

Horse-Courser. O what a cozening doctor was this? I riding my horse into the water, thinking some hidden mystery had been in [40 the horse, I had nothing under me but a little straw and had much ado to escape drowning. Well, I'll go rouse him and make him give me my forty dollars again. Ho, sirrah doctor, you cozening scab! Master doctor, awake and rise, and give me my money again, for your horse is turned to a bottle of hay. Master doctor! 45

> *He* [*tries to wake Faustus, and in doing so*] *pulls off his leg.*

Alas, I am undone! What shall I do? I have pulled off his leg.

> [*Faustus awakes.*]

Faustus. O, help, help! The villain hath murdered me.

---

21 *stend . . . thee* bargain.
26 *drink . . . waters* be ready for anything (a common proverb of the time).

38 *conceit* thoughts.
40 *mystery* quality.
44 *scab* scurvy fellow.
45 *bottle* bundle.

Horse-Courser. Murder or not murder, now he has but one leg, I'll outrun him and cast this leg into some ditch or other.

Faustus. Stop him, stop him, stop him! Ha, ha, ha, Faustus hath [50 his leg again, and the horse-courser a bundle of hay for his forty dollars.

Enter Wagner.

How now, Wagner, what news with thee?

Wagner. If it please you, the Duke of Anholt doth earnestly entreat your company and hath sent some of his men to attend you with [55 provision fit for your journey.

Faustus. The Duke of Anholt's an honorable gentleman, and one to whom I must be no niggard of my cunning. Come away.

Exeunt.

IV,vi

Enter [Robin, the] Clown, Dick, [the] Horse-Courser, and a Carter.

Carter. Come, my masters, I'll bring you to the best beer in Europe. What ho, hostess! Where be these whores?

Enter Hostess.

Hostess. How now, what lack you? What, my old guests, welcome.

Robin. Sirrah, Dick, dost thou know why I stand so mute?

Dick. No, Robin; why is't?   5

Robin. I am eighteen pence on the score. But say nothing; see if she have forgotten me.

Hostess. Who's this that stands so solemnly by himself? What, my old guest?

Robin. O hostess, how do you? I hope my score stands still.   10

Hostess. Ay, there's no doubt of that, for methinks you make no haste to wipe it out.

Dick. Why, hostess, I say, fetch us some beer.

Hostess. You shall presently. Look up into th'hall there, ho!

Exit.

Dick. Come, sirs, what shall we do now till mine hostess come?   15

Carter. Marry, sir, I'll tell you the bravest tale how a conjurer served me. You know Doctor Fauster?

Horse-Courser. Ay, a plague take him. Here's some on's have cause to know him. Did he conjure thee too?

Carter. I'll tell you how he served me. As I was going to Witten- [20 berg t'other day with a load of hay, he met me and asked me what he should give me for as much hay as he could eat. Now, sir, I think-ing that a little would serve his turn, bade him take as much as he

IV,vi.

6 *on the score* in debt.   10 *stands still* does not go higher.

would for three farthings. So he presently gave me my money and
fell to eating; and as I am a cursen man, he never left eating till [25
he had eat up all my load of hay.

All. O monstrous! Eat a whole load of hay!

Robin. Yes, yes, that may be, for I have heard of one that has eat a
load of logs.

Horse-Courser. Now, sirs, you shall hear how villainously he [30
served me. I went to him yesterday to buy a horse of him, and he
would by no means sell him under forty dollars. So, sir, because I
knew him to be such a horse as would run over hedge and ditch and
never tire, I gave him his money. So when I had my horse, Doctor
Fauster bade me ride him night and day and spare him no time; [35
but, quoth he, in any case ride him not into the water. Now sir, I
thinking the horse had had some rare quality that he would not have
me know of, what did I but rid him into a great river, and when I
came just in the midst, my horse vanished away, and I sat straddling
upon a bottle of hay.   40

All. O brave doctor!

Horse-Courser. But you shall hear how bravely I served him for it. I
went me home to his house, and there I found him asleep. I kept a
hallooing and whooping in his ears, but all could not wake him.
I seeing that, took him by the leg and never rested pulling till [45
I had pulled me his leg quite off, and now 'tis at home in mine hostry.

Robin. And has the doctor but one leg then? That's excellent, for one
of his devils turned me into the likeness of an ape's face.

Carter. Some more drink, hostess.

Robin. Hark you, we'll into another room and drink a while, [50
and then we'll go seek out the doctor.

Exeunt.

Enter the Duke of Anholt, his Duchess, Faustus, and Mephis-
tophilis, [Servants and Attendants].

Duke. Thanks, master doctor, for these pleasant sights. Nor know I
how sufficiently to recompense your great deserts in erecting that enchanted castle in the air, the sight whereof so delighted me, as nothing in the world could please me more.

Faustus. I do think myself, my good lord, highly recompensed in [5
that it pleaseth your grace to think but well of that which Faustus
hath performed. But, gracious lady, it may be that you have taken
no pleasure in those sights. Therefore, I pray you, tell me what is
the thing you most desire to have; be it in the world, it shall be

25 *cursen* christened.

yours. I have heard that great-bellied women do long for things   [10
are rare and dainty.

Duchess.   True, master doctor, and since I find you so kind, I will
make known unto you what my heart desires to have. And were it
now summer, as it is January, a dead time of the winter, I would
request no better meat than a dish of ripe grapes.   15

Faustus.   This is but a small matter. Go, Mephistophilis, away!

                                           Exit Mephistophilis.

Madam I will do more than this for your content.

               Enter Mephistophilis again with the grapes.

Here; now taste ye these. They should be good, for they come from a
far country, I can tell you.

Duke.   This makes me wonder more than all the rest, that at this   [20
time of year, when every tree is barren of his fruit, from whence you
had these ripe grapes.

Faustus.   Please it, your grace, the year is divided into two circles over
the whole world, so that when it is winter with us, in the contrary
circle it is likewise summer with them, as in India, Saba, and   [25
such countries that lie far east, where they have fruit twice a year.
From whence, by means of a swift spirit that I have, I had these
grapes brought, as you see.

Duchess.   And trust me, they are the sweetest grapes that e'er I tasted.

          The Clown[s, Robin, Dick, the Carter, and the Horse-Courser,]
                                   bounce at the gate within.

Duke.   What rude disturbers have we at the gate?   30
Go, pacify their fury. Set it ope,
And then demand of them what they would have.

                                           [*Exit a Servant.*]

          They knock again and call out to talk with Faustus.

                    [*Enter Servant to them.*]

Servant.   Why, how now, masters, what a coil is there?
What is the reason you disturb the duke.

Dick.   We have no reason for it; therefore a fig for him.   35

Servant.   What, saucy varlets, dare you be so bold?

Horse-Courser.   I hope, sir, we have wit enough to be more bold than
welcome.

Servant.   It appears so. Pray be bold elsewhere,
And trouble not the duke.

Duke.   What would they have?   40

IV,vii.

25 *Saba* Sheba.

29, SD The staging of this scene presents considerable difficulty. It may be
that while Faustus, the Duke, and the
Duchess are on the inner stage the
clowns appear on the outer platform and
knock at the side door. They may have
approached the platform from the theater

pit. A servant moves from the inner to
the outer stage to address them. This
explanation, however, makes it difficult
to account for the stage direction 'within'
since this refers usually to action on the
inner stage. *bounce* bang.

33 *coil* disturbance.

Servant.   They all cry out to speak with Doctor Faustus.

Carter.   Ay, and we will speak with him.

Duke.   Will you, sir? Commit the rascals.

Dick.   Commit with us! He were as good commit with his father as commit with us.   45

Faustus.   I do beseech your grace, let them come in;
They are good subject for a merriment.

Duke.   Do as thou wilt, Faustus. I give thee leave.

Faustus.   I thank your grace.

> *Enter Robin, Dick, Carter, and Horse-Courser.*
>   Why, how now, my good friends?

'Faith you are too outrageous, but come near;   50
I have procured your pardons. Welcome all!

Robin.   Nay, sir, we will be welcome for our money, and we will pay for what we take. What ho! Give's half a dozen of beer here, and be hanged.

Faustus.   Nay, hark you; can you tell me where you are?   55

Carter.   Ay, marry can I: we are under heaven.

Servant.   Ay, but sir sauce-box, know you in what place?

Horse-Courser.   Ay, ay, the house is good enough to drink in. Zouns, fill us some beer, or we'll break all the barrels in the house and dash out all your brains with your bottles.   60

Faustus.   Be not so furious. Come, you shall have beer.
My lord, beseech you give me leave a while:
I'll gage my credit, 'twill content your grace.

Duke.   With all my heart, kind doctor. Please thyself;
Our servants and our court's at thy command.   65

Faustus.   I humbly thank your grace. Then fetch some beer.

Horse-Courser.   Ay, marry, there spake a doctor indeed, and 'faith,
I'll drink a health to thy wooden leg for that word.

Faustus.   My wooden leg? What dost thou mean by that?

Carter.   Ha, ha, ha! Dost hear him, Dick? He has forgot his leg.   70

Horse-Courser.   Ay, ay, he does not stand much upon that.

Faustus.   No, faith; not much upon a wooden leg.

Carter.   Good lord, that flesh and blood should be so frail with your worship! Do not you remember a horse-courser you sold a horse to?

Faustus.   Yes, I remember I sold one a horse.   75

Carter.   And do you remember you bid he should not ride into the water?

Faustus.   Yes, I do very well remember that.

Carter.   And do you remember nothing of your leg?

Faustus.   No, in good sooth.   80

Carter.   Then, I pray, remember your courtesy.

Faustus.   I thank you, sir.

---

50 *outrageous* violent.   81 *courtesy* curtsy, or leg.
71 *stand much* make much of (with a quibble).

Carter. 'Tis not so much worth. I pray you, tell me one thing.

Faustus. What's that?

Carter. Be both your legs bedfellows every night together? 85

Faustus. Wouldst thou make a Colossus of me, that thou askest me such questions?

Carter. No, truly, sir. I would make nothing of you, but I would fain know that.

Enter Hostess with drink.

Faustus. Then, I assure thee, certainly they are. 90

Carter. I thank you; I am fully satisfied.

Faustus. But wherefore dost thou ask?

Carter. For nothing, sir. But methinks you should have a wooden bedfellow of one of 'em.

Horse-Courser. Why, do you hear, sir; did not I pull off one of [95 your legs when you were asleep?

Faustus. But I have it again, now I am awake. Look you here, sir.

All. O horrible! Had the doctor three legs?

Carter. Do you remember, sir, how you cozened me and ate up my load of— 100

Faustus charms him dumb.

Dick. Do you remember how you made me wear an ape's—

[*Faustus charms him dumb.*]

Horse-Courser. You whoreson conjuring scab, do you remember how you cozened me with a ho—

[*Faustus charms him dumb.*]

Robin. Ha' you forgotten me? You think to carry it away with your *hey-pass* and *re-pass;* do you remember the dog's fa— 105

[*Faustus charms him dumb.*] *Exeunt Clowns.*

Hostess. Who pays for the ale? Hear you, master doctor, now you have sent away my guests, I pray who shall pay me for my a—

[*Faustus charms her dumb.*] *Exit Hostess.*

Duchess. My lord,
We are much beholding to this learnèd man.

Duke. So are we, madam, which we will recompense 110
With all the love and kindness that we may.
His artful sport drives all sad thoughts away.

Exeunt.

V,i.

Thunder and Lightning. Enter Devils with covered dishes. Mephistophilis leads them into Faustus' study. Then enter Wagner.

---

86 *Colossus* a giant statue said to have stood with its legs astride at the entrance to the ancient harbor of Rhodes.
104 *carry it away* come off best.

Wagner.   I think my master means to die shortly.
  He has made his will and given me his wealth,
  His house, his goods, and store of golden plate,
  Besides two thousand ducats ready coined.
  I wonder what he means. If death were nigh,   5
  He would not frolic thus. He's now at supper
  With the scholars, where there's such belly-cheer
  As Wagner in his life ne'er saw the like.
  And see where they come; belike the feast is done.
                                           Exit.

    Enter Faustus, Mephistophilis, and two or three Scholars.
First Scholar.   Master Doctor Faustus, since our conference about   [10
fair ladies, which was the beautifulest in all the world, we have determined with ourselves that Helen of Greece was the admirablest
lady that ever lived. Therefore, master doctor, if you will do us so
much favor as to let us see that peerless dame of Greece, whom all
the world admires for majesty, we should think ourselves much   [15
beholding unto you.
Faustus.   Gentlemen,
  For that I know your friendship is unfeigned,
  And Faustus' custom is not to deny
  The just requests of those that wish him well,   20
  You shall behold that peerless dame of Greece,
  No otherwise for pomp and majesty
  Than when Sir Paris crossed the seas with her
  And brought the spoils to rich Dardania.
  Be silent then, for danger is in words.   25
    Music sounds. Mephistophilis brings in Helen; she passeth
                       over the stage.
Second Scholar.   Was this fair Helen, whose admirèd worth
  Made Greece with ten years war afflict poor Troy?
  Too simple is my wit to tell her praise,
  Whom all the world admires for majesty.
Third Scholar.   No marvel though the angry Greeks pursued   30
  With ten years' war the rape of such a queen,
  Whose heavenly beauty passeth all compare.
First Scholar.   Since we have seen the pride of nature's works
  And only paragon of excellence,
  We'll take our leaves, and for this blessèd sight   35
  Happy and blest be Faustus evermore.
Faustus.   Gentlemen, farewell; the same wish I to you.
                              Exeunt Scholars.

            Enter an Old Man.
Old Man.   O gentle Faustus, leave this damnèd art,

V,i.
  9 *belike* no doubt.   24 *Dardania* Troy.

This magic that will charm thy soul to hell
And quite bereave thee of salvation.   40
Though thou hast now offended like a man,
Do not persevere in it like a devil.
Yet, yet, thou hast an amiable soul,
If sin by custom grow not into nature.
Then, Faustus, will repentance come too late;   45
Then thou art banished from the sight of heaven.
No mortal can express the pains of hell.
It may be this my exhortation
Seems harsh and all unpleasant; let it not,
For, gentle son, I speak it not in wrath   50
Or envy of thee, but in tender love
And pity of thy future misery.
And so have hope that this my kind rebuke,
Checking thy body, may amend thy soul.
Faustus.   Where art thou, Faustus? Wretch, what hast thou done?   55
Damned art thou, Faustus, damned; despair and die!
Hell claims his right, and with a roaring voice
Says, 'Faustus, come; thine hour is almost come';
And Faustus now will come to do thee right.
                              Mephistophilis gives him a dagger.
Old Man.   O stay, good Faustus, stay thy desperate steps.   60
I see an angel hovers o'er thy head,
And with a vial full of precious grace
Offers to pour the same into thy soul.
Then call for mercy and avoid despair.
Faustus.   Ah, my sweet friend, I feel thy words   65
To comfort my distressèd soul.
Leave me a while to ponder on my sins.
Old Man.   Faustus, I leave thee, but with grief of heart,
Fearing the enemy of thy hapless soul.
                                                          Exit.

Faustus.   Accursèd Faustus, where is mercy now?   70
I do repent, and yet I do despair.
Hell strives with grace for conquest in my breast.
What shall I do to shun the snares of death?
Mephistophilis.   Thou traitor, Faustus, I arrest thy soul
For disobedience to my sovereign lord.   75
Revolt, or I'll in piecemeal tear thy flesh.
Faustus.   I do repent I e'er offended him.
Sweet Mephistophilis, entreat thy lord
To pardon my unjust presumption,
And with my blood again I will confirm   80
The former vow I made to Lucifer.

43 *amiable* worthy of divine love or   51 *envy of* ill-will towards.
grace.   54 *Checking* admonishing.

Mephistophilis. Do it then, Faustus, with unfeignèd heart,
  Lest greater dangers do attend thy drift.

> [*Faustus stabs his arm and writes on a
> paper with his blood.*]

Faustus. Torment, sweet friend, that base and agèd man
  That durst dissuade me from thy Lucifer, 85
  With greatest torment that our hell affords.
Mephistophilis. His faith is great; I cannot touch his soul,
  But what I may afflict his body with
  I will attempt, which is but little worth.
Faustus. One thing, good servant, let me crave of thee 90
  To glut the longing of my heart's desire—
  That I may have unto my paramour
  That heavenly Helen which I saw of late,
  Whose sweet embracings may extinguish clear
  Those thoughts that do dissuade me from my vow, 95
  And keep mine oath I made to Lucifer.
Mephistophilis. This, or what else my Faustus shall desire,
  Shall be performed in twinkling of an eye.

> *Enter Helen again, passing over [the stage] between two Cupids.*

Faustus. Was this the face that launched a thousand ships
  And burnt the topless towers of Ilium?
  Sweet Helen, make me immortal with a kiss. 100

> [*She kisses him.*]

  Her lips suck forth my soul. See where it flies!
  Come, Helen, come, give me my soul again.
  Here will I dwell, for heaven is in these lips,
  And all is dross that is not Helena. 105

> [*Enter the Old Man.*]

  I will be Paris, and for love of thee
  Instead of Troy shall Wittenberg be sacked;
  And I will combat with weak Menelaus
  And wear thy colors on my plumèd crest.
  Yea, I will wound Achilles in the heel 110
  And then return to Helen for a kiss.
  O, thou art fairer than the evening's air,
  Clad in the beauty of a thousand stars.
  Brighter art thou than flaming Jupiter
  When he appeared to hapless Semele, 115
  More lovely than the monarch of the sky

---

82 *unfeignèd* honest
83 *drift* purpose.
108 *Menelaus* the husband of Helen of Troy.
110 *Achilles* the Greek hero of the Trojan war, wounded in the heel by Paris.

115 *Semele* the daughter of Cadmus and Harmonia who was beloved by Zeus to whom she bore the child, Dionysus.
116-117 *monarch . . . arms* No such episode is recorded in Greek mythology. Arethusa was a nymph, one of the Nereids, who governed a fountain on the isle of Ortygia near Syracuse.

In wanton Arethusa's azured arms,
And none but thou shalt be my paramour.

Exeunt [all but the Old Man].

Old Man.   Accursèd Faustus, miserable man,
That from thy soul exclud'st the grace of heaven   120
And fliest the throne of his tribunal seat!

Enter the Devils.

Satan begins to sift me with his pride.
As in this furnace God shall try my faith,
My faith, vile hell, shall triumph over thee.
Ambitious fiends, see how the heavens smiles   125
At your repulse and laughs your state to scorn.
Hence hell, for hence I fly unto my God.

Exeunt.

Thunder. Enter [above] Lucifer, Beëlzebub, and Mephistophilis.

Lucifer.   Thus from infernal Dis do we ascend
To view the subjects of our monarchy,
Those souls which sin seals the black sons of hell,
'Mong which as chief, Faustus, we come to thee,
Bringing with us lasting damnation   5
To wait upon thy soul. The time is come
Which makes it forfeit.

Mephistophilis.   And this gloomy night,
Here in this room will wretched Faustus be.

Beëlzebub.   And here we'll stay
To mark him how he doth demean himself.   10

Mephistophilis.   How should he, but in desperate lunacy?
Fond worldling, now his heart-blood dries with grief;
His conscience kills it, and his laboring brain
Begets a world of idle fantasies
To over-reach the devil. But all in vain;   15
His store of pleasures must be sauced with pain.
He and his servant, Wagner, are at hand.
Both come from drawing Faustus' latest will.
See where they come.

Enter Faustus and Wagner.

Faustus.   Say, Wagner, thou hast perused my will;   20
How dost thou like it?

Wagner.   Sir, so wondrous well

126 *state* royal power.   16 *sauced* paid for.

V,ii.
   1 *Dis* Hades, or hell

As in all humble duty I do yield
My life and lasting service for your love.

Enter the Scholars.

Faustus.   Gramercies, Wagner. Welcome, gentlemen.

[*Exit Wagner.*]

First Scholar.   Now, worthy Faustus, methinks your looks are changed. 25

Faustus.   Ah, gentlemen!

Second Scholar.   What ails Faustus?

Faustus.   Ah, my sweet chamber-fellow, had I lived with thee, then had I lived still, but now must die eternally. Look, sirs; comes he not? Comes he not?   30

First Scholar.   O my dear Faustus, what imports this fear?

Second Scholar.   Is all our pleasure turned to melancholy?

Third Scholar.   He is not well with being over-solitary.

Second Scholar.   If it be so, we'll have physicians, and Faustus shall be cured.   35

Third Scholar.   'Tis but a surfeit sir; fear nothing.

Faustus.   A surfeit of deadly sin that hath damned both body and soul.

Second Scholar.   Yet Faustus, look up to heaven, and remember mercy is infinite.   40

Faustus.   But Faustus' offence can ne'er be pardoned. The serpent that tempted Eve may be saved, but not Faustus. Ah gentlemen, hear me with patience and tremble not at my speeches. Though my heart pants and quivers to remember that I have been a student here these thirty years, O, would I had never seen Wittenberg, never read   [45 book. And what wonders I have done, all Germany can witness—yea, all the world—for which Faustus hath lost both Germany and the world, yea heaven itself, heaven the seat of God, the throne of the blessed, the kingdom of joy, and must remain in hell for ever. Hell, ah hell for ever! Sweet friends, what shall become of Faustus,   [50 being in hell for ever?

Second Scholar.   Yet Faustus, call on God.

Faustus.   On God, whom Faustus hath abjured? On God, whom Faustus hath blasphemed? Ah, my God, I would weep, but the devil draws in my tears. Gush forth blood instead of tears, yea life and   [55 soul. O, he stays my tongue! I would lift up my hands, but see, they hold 'em; they hold 'em.

All.   Who, Faustus?

Faustus.   Why, Lucifer and Mephistophilis. Ah, gentlemen, I gave them my soul for my cunning.   60

All.   God forbid!

Faustus.   God forbade it indeed, but Faustus hath done it. For the vain pleasure of four and twenty years hath Faustus lost eternal joy and felicity. I writ them a bill with mine own blood. The date is

---

24 *Gramercies* thanks.

expired. This is the time, and he will fetch me.   65

First Scholar.   Why did not Faustus tell us of this before, that divines
might have prayed for thee?

Faustus.   Oft have I thought to have done so, but the devil threatened
to tear me in pieces if I named God, to fetch me, body and soul, if
I once gave ear to divinity. And now 'tis too late. Gentlemen   [70
away, lest you perish with me.

Second Scholar.   O, what may we do to save Faustus?

Faustus.   Talk not of me, but save yourselves and depart.

Third Scholar.   God will strengthen me; I will stay with Faustus.

First Scholar.   Tempt not God, sweet friend, but let us into the   [75
next room and there pray for him.

Faustus.   Ay, pray for me, pray for me; and what noise soever you
hear, come not unto me, for nothing can rescue me.

Second Scholar.   Pray thou, and we will pray that God may have mercy
upon thee.   80

Faustus.   Gentlemen, farewell. If I live till morning, I'll visit you; if
not, Faustus is gone to hell.

All.   Faustus, farewell.

                                        Exeunt Scholars.

Mephistophilis.   [*above*] Ay, Faustus, now thou hast no hope of heaven;
Therefore despair. Think only upon hell,   85
For that must be thy mansion, there to dwell.

Faustus.   O thou bewitching fiend, 'twas thy temptation
Hath robbed me of eternal happiness.

Mephistophilis.   I do confess it, Faustus, and rejoice.
'Twas I, that when thou wert i' the way to heaven,   90
Damned up thy passage. When thou took'st the book
To view the Scriptures, then I turned the leaves
And led thine eye.
What, weep'st thou? 'Tis too late. Despair! Farewell!
Fools that will laugh on earth must weep in hell.   95

                                              Exit.

        Enter the Good Angel and the Bad Angel at several doors.

Good Angel.   Ah, Faustus, if thou hadst given ear to me,
Innumerable joys had followed thee;
But thou didst love the world.

Bad Angel.   Gave ear to me,
And now must taste hell's pains perpetually.

Good Angel.   O what will all thy riches, pleasures, pomps   100
Avail thee now?

Bad Angel.   Nothing but vex thee more,
To want in hell, that had on earth such store.

                        Music while the throne descends.

Good Angel.   O, thou hast lost celestial happiness,
Pleasures unspeakable, bliss without end.
Hadst thou affected sweet divinity,   105

Hell or the devil had had no power on thee.
Hadst thou kept on that way, Faustus, behold
In what resplendent glory thou hadst sat
In yonder throne, like those bright shining saints,
And triumphed over hell. That hast thou lost,   110
And now, poor soul, must thy good angel leave thee.
                              [*The throne ascends.*]
    The jaws of hell are open to receive thee.
                                                        Exit.

                              Hell is discovered.
Bad Angel.   Now, Faustus, let thine eyes with horror stare
    Into that vast perpetual torture-house.
    There are the Furies tossing damnèd souls   115
    On burning forks; their bodies boil in lead.
    There are live quarters broiling on the coals,
    That ne'er can die. This ever-burning chair
    Is for o'er-tortured souls to rest them in.
    These that are fed with sops of flaming fire   120
    Were gluttons and loved only delicates
    And laughed to see the poor starve at their gates.
    But yet all these are nothing; thou shalt see
    Ten thousand tortures that more horrid be.
Faustus.   O, I have seen enough to torture me.   125
Bad Angel.   Nay, thou must feel them, taste the smart of all.
    He that loves pleasure must for pleasure fall.
    And so I leave thee, Faustus, till anon;
    Then wilt thou tumble in confusion.
                                                        Exit.

                [*Hell disappears.*] *The clock strikes eleven.*
Faustus.   Ah Faustus,   130
    Now hast thou but one bare hour to live,
    And then thou must be damned perpetually.
    Stand still, you ever-moving spheres of heaven,
    That time may cease and midnight never come.
    Fair nature's eye, rise, rise again, and make   135
    Perpetual day; or let this hour be but
    A year, a month, a week, a natural day,
    That Faustus may repent and save his soul.
    O lente, lente currite noctis equi!
    The stars move still; time runs; the clock will strike;   140
    The devil will come, and Faustus must be damned.
    O, I'll leap up to my God! Who pulls me down?
    See, see, where Christ's blood streams in the firmament!
    One drop would save my soul, half a drop! Ah, my Christ!

139 *O . . . equi* O slowly, slowly, run   you horses of night (adapted from Ovid's
                                        Amores).

Rend not my heart for naming of my Christ!   145
Yet will I call on him. O, spare me, Lucifer!
Where is it now? 'Tis gone. And see where God
Stretcheth out his arm and bends his ireful brows.
Mountains and hills, come, come, and fall on me,
And hide me from the heavy wrath of God.   150
No, no!
Then will I headlong run into the earth.
Earth, gape! O no, it will not harbor me!
You stars that reigned at my nativity,
Whose influence hath allotted death and hell,   155
Now draw up Faustus like a foggy mist
Into the entrails of yon laboring cloud,
That when you vomit forth into the air,
My limbs may issue from your smoky mouths,
So that my soul may but ascend to heaven.   160

                             The watch strikes.

Ah, half the hour is past; 'twill all be past anon.
O God,
If thou wilt not have mercy on my soul,
Yet for Christ's sake, whose blood hath ransomed me,
Impose some end to my incessant pain.   165
Let Faustus live in hell a thousand years,
A hundred thousand, and at last be saved.
O, no end is limited to damnèd souls.
Why wert thou not a creature wanting soul?
Or why is this immortal that thou hast?   170
Ah, Pythagoras' *metempsychosis,* were that true,
This soul should fly from me and I be changed
Into some brutish beast. All beasts are happy,
For, when they die
Their souls are soon dissolved in elements,   175
But mine must live still to be plagued in hell.
Cursed be the parents that engendered me!
No, Faustus, curse thyself, curse Lucifer
That hath deprived thee of the joys of heaven.

                             The clock strikes twelve.

O, it strikes, it strikes! Now, body, turn to air,   180
Or Lucifer will bear thee quick to hell.
O soul, be changed to little water-drops,
And fall into the ocean, ne'er be found!

                     Thunder, and enter the Devils.

My God, my God, look not so fierce on me!
Adders and serpents, let me breathe a while!   185

---

171 *metempsychosis* belief in the trans-   Greek philosopher, Pythagoras of Samos.
migration of souls, associated with the   181 *quick* alive.

Ugly hell, gape not! Come not, Lucifer!
I'll burn my books! Ah, Mephistophilis!

Exeunt [Faustus and Devils].

Enter the Scholars.   **V,iii.**

First Scholar.   Come, gentlemen, let us go visit Faustus,
For such a dreadful night was never seen
Since first the world's creation did begin.
Such fearful shrieks and cries were never heard.
Pray heaven the doctor have escaped the danger.   5
Second Scholar.   O help us, heaven! See, here are Faustus' limbs,
All torn asunder by the hand of death.
Third Scholar.   The devils whom Faustus served have torn him thus;
For 'twixt the hours of twelve and one, methought
I heard him shriek and call aloud for help,   10
At which self time the house seemed all on fire
With dreadful horror of these damnèd fiends.
Second Scholar.   Well, gentlemen, though Faustus' end be such
As every Christian heart laments to think on,
Yet for he was a scholar, once admired   15
For wondrous knowledge in our German schools,
We'll give his mangled limbs due burial;
And all the students, clothed in mourning black,
Shall wait upon his heavy funeral.

Exeunt.

Epilogue.

Enter Chorus.

Chorus.   Cut is the branch that might have grown full straight,
And burnèd is Apollo's laurel bough
That sometime grew within this learnèd man.
Faustus is gone. Regard his hellish fall,
Whose fiendful fortune may exhort the wise   5
Only to wonder at unlawful things,
Whose deepness doth entice such forward wits
To practise more than heavenly power permits.

[Exit.]

Terminat hora diem; terminat author opus.

V,iii.

19 *wait upon* be present at. *heavy*
sorrowful.

Epilogue.

9 *Terminat . . . opus* The hour ends
the day; the author ends his work.

A Select Bibliography

I. PRINCIPAL EDITIONS

Alexander Dyce, ed. *The Works of Christopher Marlowe.* 3v. London, 1850.

Alexander Dyce, ed. *The Works of Christopher Marlowe.* London, 1858.

A. H. Bullen, ed. *The Works of Christopher Marlowe.* 3v. London, 1885.

C. F. Tucker Brooke, ed. *The Works of Christopher Marlowe.* London, 1910.

R. H. Case, gen. ed. *The Works and Life of Christopher Marlowe.* 6v. London, 1930–33.
1. *Life* and *Dido Queen of Carthage,* ed. C. F. Tucker Brooke.
2. *Tamburlaine the Great, I and II,* ed. U. M. Ellis-Fermor.
3. *The Jew of Malta* and *The Massacre at Paris,* ed. H. S. Bennett.
4. *Poems,* ed. L. C. Martin.
5. *Doctor Faustus,* ed. F. S. Boas.
6. *Edward II,* ed. H. B. Charlton and A. R. Waller, revised by F. N. Lees, 1955.

II. GENERAL STUDIES

John Bakeless, *The Tragicall History of Christopher Marlowe.* 2v. Cambridge, Mass., 1942.

David M. Bevington, *From Mankind to Marlowe.* Cambridge, Mass., 1962.

F. S. Boas, *Christopher Marlowe: A Biographical and Critical Study.* rev. ed. Oxford, 1953.

Douglas W. Cole, *Suffering and Evil in the Plays of Marlowe.* Princeton, 1962.

Mark Eccles, *Marlowe in London.* Cambridge, Mass., 1934.

T. S. Eliot, "Christopher Marlowe" in *Selected Essays.* New York, 1950.

U. M. Ellis-Fermor, *Christopher Marlowe.* London, 1926.

Philip Henderson, *Christopher Marlowe.* London, 1952.

Leslie Hotson, *The Death of Christopher Marlowe.* New York, 1925.

Paul H. Kocher, *Christopher Marlowe: A Study of his Thought, Learning, and Character*. Chapel Hill, N.C., 1946.

Harry Levin, *The Overreacher: A Study of Christopher Marlowe*. Cambridge, Mass., 1952.

Michel Poirier, *Christopher Marlowe*. London, 1951.

F. P. Wilson, *Marlowe and the Early Shakespeare*. Oxford, 1954.

III. TAMBURLAINE

R. W. Battenhouse, *Marlowe's Tamburlaine: A Study in Renaissance Moral Philosophy*. Nashville, Tenn., 1941.

H. G. Dick, "*Tamburlaine* Sources once more," *Studies in Philology*, XLVI (1949), 154–66.

G. I. Duthie, "The Dramatic Structure of Marlowe's *Tamburlaine the Great*," *Essays and Studies* (New Series) I (1948), 101–26.

Helen Gardner, "The Second Part of *Tamburlaine the Great*," *Modern Language Review*, XXXVII (1942), 18–24.

Irving Ribner, "The Idea of History in Marlowe's *Tamburlaine*," *ELH*, XX (1954), 251–66.

Ethel Seaton, "Marlowe's Map," *Essays and Studies*, X (1924), 13–35.

———, "Fresh Sources for Marlowe," *Review of English Studies*, V (1929), 385–401.

Hallett D. Smith, "Tamburlaine and the Renaissance," *Elizabethan Studies in Honor of George F. Reynolds*. Boulder, Col., 1945. Pp. 126–31.

Willard Thorp, "The Ethical Problem in Marlowe's *Tamburlaine*," *Journal of English and Germanic Philology*, XXIX (1930), 385–89.

Eugene M. Waith, *The Herculean Hero in Marlowe, Chapman, Shakespeare and Dryden* (New York, 1962).

IV. THE JEW OF MALTA

Howard S. Babb, "Policy in Marlowe's *The Jew of Malta*," *ELH*, XXIV (1957), 85–94.

Irving Ribner, "Marlowe and Machiavelli," *Comparative Literature*, VI (1954), 349–56.

V. EDWARD II

W. D. Briggs, ed. *Marlowe's Edward II*. London, 1914.

Robert Fricker, "The Dramatic Structure of *Edward II*," *English Studies*, XXXIV (1953), 204–17.

Clifford Leech, "Marlowe's *Edward II*: Power and Suffering," *Critical Quarterly*, I (1959), 181–96.

L. J. Mills, "The Meaning of *Edward II*," *Modern Philology*, XXXII (1934), 11–32.

Irving Ribner, *The English History Play in the Age of Shakespeare.* Princeton, 1957.

VI. DOCTOR FAUSTUS

Nicholas Brooke, "The Moral Tragedy of Doctor Faustus," *Cambridge Journal,* VII (1952), 662–87.

Lily B. Campbell, *"Doctor Faustus:* A Case of Conscience," *PMLA,* LXVII (1952), 219–39.

Helen Gardner, "Milton's Satan and the Theme of Damnation in Elizabethan Tragedy," *English Studies* (New Series) I (1948), 48–53.

W. W. Greg, "The Damnation of Faustus," *Modern Language Review,* XLI (1946), 97–107.

David Kaula, "Time and the Timeless in *Everyman* and *Doctor Faustus,"* *College English,* XXII (1960), 9–14.

Leo Kirschbaum, "Marlowe's *Faustus:* A Reconsideration," *Review of English Studies,* XIX (1943), 225–41.

M. M. Mahood, "Marlowe's Heroes," in *Poetry and Humanism.* London, 1950. Pp. 54–86.

Arthur Mizener, "The Tragedy of Marlowe's Doctor Faustus," *College English,* V (1943), 70–75.

Robert Ornstein, "The Comic Synthesis in *Doctor Faustus,"* *ELH,* XXII (1955), 165–72.

James Smith, "Marlowe's *Dr. Faustus,"* *Scrutiny,* VIII (1930), 36–55.

Textual Notes

In the following notes, preferred readings are in italics and rejected readings are in Roman type. I have generally listed Dyce as the authority for emendations which appear in his editions, even when he adapted these from earlier editors. The abbreviation "Eds." indicates readings on which all modern editors are in agreement.

DIDO QUEEN OF CARTHAGE

This play is extant in a single quarto, printed in 1594 by "the Widdowe Orwin, for Thomas Woodcocke," copies of which are in the Bodleian, the Folger Library, and the Huntington Library. The Huntington copy is the best of the three, and I have followed it closely, departing only in the following instances:

I,i.

10 *hair* (Dyce) aire (1594)
121, SD *and* cum (1594)
132 *Cymothoe* (Dyce) Cimodoæ (1594)
147 *Ceraunia's* (Dyce) Ceranias (1594)
154 *coming* (Dyce) cunning (1594)
159 *hair* (Dyce) air (1594)
248, SD *Exeunt* Exit (1594)

I,ii.

41 *Baucis'* (Eds.) Vausis (1594)

II,i.

47 *nobleman* (Eds.) Noble man (1594)
51 *names* (Eds.) meanes (1594)
72 *view* (Eds.) viewd (1594)
77–78 *Renownèd . . . Æneas* one line
in 1594. *Renownèd* Renowmed (1594)
153 *shepherds* (Eds.) shepherd (1594)
254 *wind* (Dyce) wound (1594)
275 *fane* (Dyce) Fawne (1594)
286 *swam* (Brooke) swomme (1594)

296 *swam* (Brooke) swomme (1594)
303, SD *all* omnes: manent (1594)
322 *Cytherea's* (Dyce) Citheidas (1594)

III,i.

SD *alone* solus (1594)
27 *learn'dst* (Dyce) learnst (1594)
57 *love* (Dyce) Iove (1594)
165 *now* (Dyce) how (1594)

III,ii.

3 *Fates* (Eds.) face (1594)
11 *let-out* (Eds.) left out (1594)
16 *mind* (Dyce) made (1594)
34 *from* fro (1594)
51 *changed* (Dyce) chaunge (1594)
70 *know'st* knowest (1594)
97 *have it* have (1594)

III,iii.

35 *Cupid* Asca. (1594)
40 *Cupid* Asca. (1594)

62, SD *all* omnes (1594)
64 *forfeit* far fet (1594)

III,iv.

36 *affect* effect (1594)
38 *fair in* (Dyce) faire (1594)

IV,i.

15 *Cupid* Asca. (1594)
35 *cares* (Eds.) eares (1594)

IV,ii.

SD *Enter* Enters (1594)

IV,iii.

18 *unrenownèd* unrenowmed (1594).
realms (Dyce) beames (1594)
28 *thy* (Dyce) my (1594)

IV,iv.

50 *fled'st* (Dyce) fleest (1594)
90 *lives* (Dyce) loues (1594)
119 *threaten* (Dyce) threatens (1594)
124 *Lord* omitted in 1594

V,i.

82, SD *Dido* Dido and Æneas (1594)
110 *Dido* (McKerrow) Speech prefix
begins line 111 in 1594
114 *chained* (Eds.) chaungd (1594)
117 *thy* (Eds.) my (1594)
138 *adhuc* (Eds.) adhaec (1594)
221 *kind* (Eds.) keend (1594)
248 *Arion's* (Dyce) Orions (1594)
268 *my* (Eds.) thy (1594)
274–275 *Not . . . arts* one line in 1594

TAMBURLAINE: PART ONE

The two parts of *Tamburlaine* were printed for the first time in a single black letter octavo by Richard Jones in 1590. Two copies are today extant, the one in the Bodleian and the other in the Huntington Library. Jones issued another edition in 1593, the unique copy of which is in the British Museum, and another in 1597, of which the only extant copy is in the Huntington Library. Part I was printed separately for Edward White in 1605 and Part II in 1606. The present text follows closely the Huntington Library copy of the 1590 octavo, which clearly formed the basis for the later texts. It has been departed from only in the following instances:

I,i.

15 *their* (Dyce) his (1590)
19 *through* (1605) thorough (1590)
82 *Theridamas* Therid. (1590)
83 *stay'st* stayest (1590)
84 *press* prease (1590)
87 *greater* [*task*] (Eds.) greater (1590)
106, SD *remain* Manent (1590)
108 *threaten* thraten (1590)
135, SD *Ceneus* Conerus (1590)
182 *lords* (1605) Lord (1590)

I,ii.

SD *laden* loden (1590)
67 *they* (Eds.) thee (1590)
88 *Rhodope* (Dyce) Rhodolfe (1590)
146 *lance* (Dyce) lanch (1590)
178 *raze* rase (1590)
187 *renownèd* renowmed (1590)
206 *Boötes* Botees (1590)

224 *Ah* (Brooke) Are (1590)
238 *renownèd* renowmed (1590)
243 *statues* (1605) statutes (1590)

II,i.

11 *burden* burthen (1590)
27 *sinewy* (Dyce) snowy (1590)
42 *strait* (Dyce) straight (1590)

II,ii.

15 *pitched* (1593, 1605) pitch (1590)
49 *lance* lanch (1590)

II,iii.

7 [*of*] *heaven* (Eds.) heauen (1590)
26 *top* (Dyce) stop (1590)
30 *renownèd* renowmed (1590)
33 *and* (1605) not (1590)
47 *burden* burthen (1590)
55 *curtle-axe* cutle-axe (1590)

II,v.

6 *renownèd* renowmed (1590)
20 *embassage* ambassage (1590)
32 *aimed* (1605) and (1590)
49, SD *all except* Manent (1590)
72 *Casane* Casanes (1590)

II,vi.

30 *ingratitude* ingratude (1590)

II,vii.

50 *harpy* (1593) harpyr (1590)
52, SD *Tamburlaine* He (1590)

III,i.

16 *Renownèd* Renowmed (1590)

III,ii.

1 *Agydas* speech prefix omitted in 1590

III,iii.

SD *Bashaw* Basso (1590)
60, SD *Bashaws* Bassoes (1590)
66 *Morocco* Moroccus (1590)
96 *renowned* renowmed (1590)
158 *air* (Dyce) lure (1590)
188, SD and stay (1590)
196 *murdering* murthering (1590)
211, SD Baiazeth flies, and he pursues

him. The battell short, and they enter (1590)
213 *foil* (Dyce) soil (1590)

IV,ii.

1, SD *Bajazeth* him (1590)
29 SD *Tamburlaine* He (1590)
45 *makes* (Dyce) make (1590)
49 *Clymene's* (Dyce) Clymeus (1590)

IV,iv.

SD *come* commeth (1590)
26–27 *My . . . yours* My . . . curses/ By . . . yours (1590)
41 SD *Bajazeth* He (1590). *the food* it (1590)
54, SD *Bajazeth* him (1590)
114 *Morocco* Morocus (1590)

V,i.

SD *Damascus* Damasco (1590)

V,ii.

56 *Virgins* Omnes (1590)
132, SD *Attendant* An (1590)
183–184 *Hover . . . Elysium* one line in 1590
340 *murdering* murthering (1590)
417 *Renownèd* Renowmed (1590)
453 *thee* the (1590)

TAMBURLAINE: PART TWO

Prologue.

8 *sad* (Eds.) said (1590)

I,i.

SD *Uribassa* Upibassa (1590) and at line 20
13 *Gazellus* Byr. (1590) and throughout scene
22 *Slavonians* Sclavonians (1590). *Almains* Almans (1590)
23 *murdering* murthering (1590)
25 *Orcanes* (Dyce) omitted in 1590
64 *Illyrians* (1606) Illicians (1590)

I,ii.

37 *Gazellus* Byr. (1590)
45 *Orcanes* Nat. (1590) and at lines 54, 60, 80

I,iii.

7 *renownèd* renowmed (1590)
15 *Cairo* Cario (1590)
19 *Cairo* Cario (1590)

I,iv.

18 *precious* procions (1590)
79 *superficies* (Eds.) superfluities (1590)
93 *murdered* murthered (1590)

I,vi.

1 *Morocco* Moroccus (1590). *Fez* Fesse (1590) and at lines 3, 13, 23
10 *Morocco* Morocus (1590)
17 *these* this (1590)
43 *Boötes'* Boetes (1590)
97 *orient* (Eds.) oriental (1590)

II,i.

2 *enflames* inflames (1590)
47 *consummate* (Dyce) consinuate (1590)

II,iv.

56 *author* (1606) anchor (1590)
123 *murdered* murthered (1590)
140 *statue* (1606) stature (1590)

III,i.

SD *Callapine* him (1590)

59 *Damascus* Damasco (1590)

III,ii.

39 *Those* (Dyce) Whose (1590)
82 *Murder* Murther (1590)

III,iii.

13 *friends* (Eds.) friend (1590)
33 *[any] issue* (Eds.) issue (1590)
56 *gabions* (Eds.) Galions (1590)

III,iv.

SD *Olympia* his wife (1590)
67–68 *And . . . Come* one line in 1590

III,v.

SD *with their train,* Almeda, with their traine (1590)
1 *Renownèd* Renowmed (1590)
126 *liv'st* liuest (1590)

IV,i.

6 *conquering* (Eds.) conquerings (1590)
29 *murderous* murtherous (1590)

IV,ii.

15, SD *Calyphas* him (1590)
54 *burden* burthen (1590)
82 *resist in* (Eds.) resisting (1590)
99 *Excel* (Dyce) Expel (1590)

IV,iii.

12 *murder* murther (1590)
71–72 *Why . . . precious* prose in 1590
83 *murderèd* murthered (1590)
87 *Elysium* Elisian (1590)

IV,iv.

SD *led by* led by with (1590)
81 *continent* (Eds.) content (1590)
83 *Concubines* Lad. (1590)
84, SD *The Soldiers* They (1590)

V,i.

24 *Citizen* omitted in 1590
38 *Second Citizen* Another (1590)
49 *Theridamas* omitted in 1590
62, SD *Orcanes . . . others* with others, the two spare kings (1590)
147, SD *They* bridle them (1590)

V,ii.

36 *Renownèd* Renowmed (1590)

V,iii.

1 *Theridamas* omitted in 1590
22 *burden* burthen (1590)
69 *murdering* murthering (1590)
82 *hypostasis* Hipostates (1590)
184, SD *Amyras* him (1590)
186 *burden* burthen (1590)
241 *cliffs* cliftes (1590)

THE JEW OF MALTA

The Jew of Malta has come down to us in a single quarto, printed by I. B. for Nicholas Vavasour in 1633. It is a poor text, full of typographical errors and with much confusion of prose and poetry. Not only was it carelessly printed, but the play seems to have suffered much alteration and degeneration between the times of its composition and its printing. A manuscript was prepared for the printer by Thomas Heywood, who wrote the prologues and epilogues for the Court and Cockpit performances. It is certain that Marlowe's play had undergone considerable revision before it achieved print, much of this probably by Heywood himself. The present edition is based on the Huntington Library copy of the 1633 quarto, which has been collated with a Xerox reproduction of the British Museum copy. The quarto has been departed from only in the following instances:

Prologue.

19 *empery* (Eds.) Empire (1633)

21 *Draco's* (Eds.) Drancus (1633)
26 *O' the* (Dyce) o'th (1633)

I,i.

1 *Barabas* Iew (1633) and throughout scene
4 *Samnites* (Dyce) Samintes (1633)
6 *silverlings* silverbings (1633)
23 *pebble* pibble (1633)
59 *'em* 'vm (1633)
69 *of* off (1633)
70–71 *And . . . Alexandria* (Eds.) one line in 1633
102 *every* enery (1633)
117 *Haply* Happily (1633)
160 *Haply* Happily (1633)
167 *Hum* Vmh (1633)
187 *proximus* proximas (1633)

I,ii.

SD *Governor* Gouernors (1633). *Bashaws* Bassoes (1633)
1 *Ferneze* Gouern. (1633) and throughout scene
2 *First Bashaw* Bass. (1633) and throughout scene
17 *governor* Gouernours (1633)
27 *governor* Gouernours (1633)
32 *governor* Gouernors (1633)
36 *First Officer* Officer (1633) and throughout scene
57 *First Jew* Iew (1633)
68 *Officer* Reader (1633) and in lines 73, 76
119–122 *Out . . . righteousness* (Dyce) Out . . . thus/ To . . . righteousness (1633)
129 *governor* Gouernors (1633)
137 *Ferneze* omitted in 1633
155 *i' the* i th' (1633)
165 *Primus* Primas (1633)
201–202 *You . . . want* one line in 1633
225 *Abigail* Abigall (1633)
276–277 *Why . . . house* one line in 1633
289–290 *Tush . . . mean'st* one line in 1633
303, SD Enter three Fryars and two Nuns (1633)
304 *Friar Jacomo* (Dyce) 1 Fry (1633) and throughout scene
304–305 *Sisters . . . nunnery* (Dyce) one line in 1633
306 *Abbess* (Dyce) 1 Nun (1633)
312 *Abbess* (Dyce) Nun (1633)
327 *Friar Barnardine* 2 Fry (1633)
337–338 *Why . . . Christians* Why . . . thou/ Amongst . . . Christians (1633)
353 *reck* wrecke (1633)

384 *countermured* (Collier) countermin'd (1633)

II,i.

39 *Bueno . . . era* (Eds.) Birn para todos, my ganada no er (1633)
64 *Hermoso . . . dineros* (Dyce) Hermoso Piarer, de les Denirch (1633)

II,ii.

SD *Ferneze* Governor (1633). *Knights* the Knights (1633)
1 *Ferneze* Gov. (1633) and throughout scene
11 *Turkish* (Eds.) Spanish (1633)
14 *luffed and tacked* (Dyce) left, and tooke (1633)
54 *thee* (Eds.) the (1633)

II,iii.

4 *sold* sold Ent. Bar. (1633)
53–54 *I . . . leprosy* I . . . the/ White leprosy (1633)
68–69 *Good . . . hands* (Dyce) one line in 1633
98 *First Officer* Officer (1633) and in lines 107, 159
112 *Slave* Itha. (1633) and in lines 114, 117, 121
136, SD Enter Mathias, Mater (1633)
143 *Katherine* Mater (1633) and throughout scene
162–163 *Faith . . . please* (Dyce) Faith . . . Ithamore/ My . . . please (1633)
199–200 *Faith . . . fire* (Bennett) one line in 1633
215–216 *O . . . diamond* One line in 1633
293 *yet* yer (1633)
317 *thou* (Dyce) thee (1633)
321 *o' the* (Dyce) a the (1633)
327 *rather* rathe (1633)
355–356 *You'll . . . Christian* (Brooke) You'll . . . Iewes/ Enow . . . Malta/ But . . . Christian (1633)
371–372 *I'll . . . him* I'll . . . he/ Shall . . . him (1633)

III,i.

1 *Bellamira* speech prefix omitted in 1633
13 *Bellamira* Curt. (1633) and throughout scene.

III,ii.

2, SD Enter Lodow. reading (1633)
9, SD Enter Gouernor, Mater (1633)
10 *Ferneze* Gov. (1633) and throughout scene

12 *Katherine* Mater (1633) and throughout scene

34 *they* [*reveal*] (Dyce) they (1633)

III,iii.

1-3 *Why . . . beguiled* (Eds.) Why . . . neatly/ Plotted . . . And/ Flatly . . . beguil'd (1633)

16 *Mathias'* Mathia (1633). *Lodowick's* Lodowick (1633)

19 *Mathias* Mathia (1633)

20 *met,* [*and*] (Eds.) met (1633)

28 *Jaques* (Eds.) Iaynes (1633)

40 *sire* (Dyce) sinne (1633)

43 *sire* (Brooke) Pryor (1633)

50 *Friar Jacomo* Fry. (1633) and throughout scene

68 *Jacomo* Iacomi (1633)

III,iv.

15 *self* (Dyce) life (1633)

34 *'less* (Dyce) least (1633)

36-38 *Who . . . sake* Who . . . and/ Throw . . . any/ Thing . . . sake (1633)

48-49 *I hold . . . sir* one line in 1633

52-53 *Well . . . too* Well . . . brought/ The . . . too (1633)

72 *Jaques* Jagues (1633)

82-83 *Pray . . . first* one line in 1633

III,v.

SD *Ferneze* Govern. (1633)

1 *Ferneze* Gov. (1633) and throughout scene. *Bashaw* Bashaws (1633)

26-27 *For . . . farewell* one line in 1633

III,vi.

SD Enter two Fryars and Abigall (1633)

1 *Friar Jacomo* 1 Fry. (1633) and throughout scene

3 *Friar Barnardine* 2 Fry. (1633) and throughout scene

42, SD Enter I Fryar. (1633)

IV,i.

11-13 *And . . . monks* And . . . hard/ By . . . Monks (1633)

17-19 *No . . . Diabolo* No . . . Hebrew/ Borne . . . Catho Diabola (1633)

18, SD Enter the two Fryars (1633)

24 *Friar Barnardine* 2 Fry. (1633) and throughout scene

25 *Friar Jacomo* 1 Fry. (1633) and throughout scene

41-43 *Fornication . . . dead* (Bullen) Fornication . . . country/ And dead (1633)

44-45 *Ay . . . Lodowick* (Dyce) one line in 1633

49 *intimates* (Brooke) inmates (1633)

55 *sold* so'd (1633)

92 *Friar Jacomo* (Dyce) 2. (1633)

97 *rogue* (Brooke) goe (1633)

102-103 *You . . . be gone* lines given to Ithamore in 1633

114 *convent* covent (1633)

IV,ii.

1 *Ithamore . . . asleep* in 1633 line continues Barabas' last speech without scene break.

13-15 *Come . . . awake* Come . . . noose/ Fryar awake. (1633)

20 *have* (Dyce) save (1633)

IV,iii.

7-8 *And . . . Barnardine* one line in 1633

13, SD Strike him, he falls (1633)

IV,iv.

SD *Bellamira* Curtezant (1633) and throughout scene

18 *Hodie* Hidie (1633)

52 *Bellamira* Allamira (1633)

61-62 *But . . . harm* But . . . were/ Reueal'd . . . harme (1633)

88 *overspread* (Dyce) ore-spread (1633)

100 *beard* (Eds.) sterd (1633)

IV,v.

63-64 *He . . . it* one line in 1633

IV,vi.

SD *Bellamira* Curtezane (1633) and throughout scene

4-5 *Of . . . thee* one line in 1633

5 *Bellamira* (Dyce) Pil. (1633)

27 *incony* incoomy (1633)

43 *Barabas* omitted in 1633

67 *nasty* (Dyce) masty (1633)

68 *Me* (Eds.) we (1633)

V,i.

SD *Ferneze* Gouernor (1633) and throughout scene

6 *First Knight* Kni. (1633) and throughout scene

6, SD *Bellamira* Curtezane (1633) and throughout scene

16-17 *Strong . . . all* Strong . . . my/ Lodging . . . all (1633)

18, SD *Barabas* Iew (1633)

29 [*He*] *forged* (Eds.) Forged (1633)

41, SD *Katherine* Mater (1633) and throughout scene

83 *report'st* (Eds.) reportest (1633)
84 *sluice* (Collier) Truce (1633)

V,ii.

SD *Ferneze* Gouernour (1633) and throughout scene
  10 *thee* the (1633)
  47, SD *Ferneze* Governor (1633)

V,iii.

  8 *countermured* (Deighton) counter-mined (1633)
  9–10 *And . . . reigned* (Eds.) lines transposed in 1633

V,iv.

SD *Ferneze* Gouernor (1633) and throughout scene ,

V,v.

  2 *First Carpenter* Serv. (1633)
  8 *First Carpenter* Carp. (1633)
  19, SD *Ferneze* Gouernour (1633) and throughout scene
  49 *sun* (Eds.) summe (1633)
  58–59 *Ay . . . attend* one line in 1633
  119 *all* (Eds.) call (1633)

THE MASSACRE AT PARIS

The Massacre at Paris, never entered in the Stationers' Register, has come down to us in an undated octavo, printed by Edward Allde for Edward White. It is a very bad text, derived probably by memorial reconstruction, and the version of the play it gives us is an entirely inadequate one. Greg has dated its printing in 1594. Copies are extant in the British Museum (2), the Dyce Collection, the Bodleian, the Pepys Collection at Magdalene College, Cambridge, the Chapin Collection in Williamstown, Mass., the Folger Library, and the Huntington Library. Greg reprinted it for the Malone Society in 1929. The present text is based on the Huntington Library copy of the octavo, which has been collated with a Xerox reproduction of one of the British Museum copies.

There is in the Folger Library a curious manuscript leaf containing thirty-three lines of the beginning of the eighteenth scene of the play. This leaf, originally in the hands of John Payne Collier and later in those of J. O. Halliwell, differs markedly from the octavo version of the scene in that it is much fuller. Collier believed that it came from a theater manuscript and that it might well be in Marlowe's own handwriting. Its authenticity has been persuasively argued by J. Q. Adams in "The *Massacre at Paris* Leaf," *The Library,* XIV (1933–1934), 447–469. Previous editors of *The Massacre at Paris* have had no opportunity to examine the leaf closely. Since I find no reason to doubt its authenticity, I have in scene xviii adopted its readings rather than those of the octavo. Otherwise I have departed from the octavo only in the following instances:

i.

13 *Catherine* Old Qu. (o) and throughout scene

19–21 *We . . . company* (Eds.) We . . . rest,/ With . . . think/ Yourself . . . company (o)

24–25 *Come . . . solemnity* one line in octavo

26, SD *Exeunt all except* Exit the King, Q Mother, and the Q of Nauar, and manet (o)

52 *the* (Eds.) ye (o)

ii.

19–20 *I . . . death* (Eds.) prose in octavo

88–90 *Then . . . thing* (Eds.) Then . . . Cardes,/ Within . . . thing (o)

92–93 *Ay . . . France* one line in octavo

iii.

1 *accept* (Eds.) except (o)

11 *Margaret* Q. Mar (o) and throughout scene

33–34 *We . . . this* (Dyce) prose in octavo

34–36 *These . . . all* (Dyce) prose in octavo.

iv.

1 *Catherine* Queene Mother (o) and throughout scene

5 *Charles* King (o) and throughout scene

9 *noblemen* noble men (o)

10–12 *Only . . . ends* (Eds.) Onely . . . honor,/ Knights . . . ends. (o)

32 *suspect* (Dyce) suspected (o)

33–35 *Shall . . . streets* (Dyce) Shall . . . Emperour,/ Then . . . tower/ At . . . streetes. (o)

36–37 *And . . . ring* one line in octavo

43 *humbly* (Eds.) humble (o)

57 *nobleman* noble man (o)

71, SD Exeunt omnes (o)

v.

1 *Anjou . . . swear* (Dyce) Anjou . . . Retes,/ Sweare (o)

11–12 *The . . . Lutherans* (Eds.) one line in octavo.

14–16 *Be . . . live* (Eds.) Be . . . thither/ And . . . liue (o)

24, SD Enter into the Admirals house, and he in his bed. (o)

39–40 *Ah . . . Lutherans* one line in octavo

vi.

1–2 *Tuez . . . Huguenots* one line in octavo

vii.

3 *Seroune's Wife* Wlfe (o)

6 *ha't* (Eds.) hate (o)

10–13 *Christ . . . him* prose in octavo

13 *he's* (Dyce) hee was (o)

viii.

1 *Seine* (Eds.) Rene (o)

7–9 *The . . . window* (Dyce) prose in octavo

15, SD Enter Ramus (o)

22–23 *O . . . offensious* (Dyce) prose in octavo

34 *Argumentum . . . inartificiale* (Dyce) Argumentum testimonis est in arte fetialis (o)

36–37 *How . . . him* (Eds.) prose in octavo

43 *Scheckius* Shekins (o)

50 *Sorbonnists* (Eds.) thorbonest (o)

55, SD *Ramus* him (o)

57 *Seine* Rene (o)

75, SD Enter Guise (o)

79, SD *the Schoolmasters* them (o)

86–87 *And . . . rings* one line in octavo

87 *the* ye (o)

ix.

29 *First Lord* Lord (o)

x.

14 *Catherine* Queene (o) and throughout scene

16–17 *But . . . sweet* one line in octavo

17 *The air's* thair's (o)

29–30 *Madam . . . storm* one line in octavo

46 *let* (Eds.) lets (o)

xi.

2 *First Protestant* Protestant (o)

7, SD kill them (o)

xii.

SD *Charles* of France (o)

1 *Charles* King (o) and throughout scene

4 *Catherine* Qu. (o) and throughout scene

10 *their* (Bullen) there (o)

xiii.

SD *Anjou* Henry (o). *Mugeroun* the

king's **Minions** (o). *a Cutpurse and others*
With others, and the Cutpurse (o)

2 *Catherine* Qu. (o) and throughout
scene.

31 **SD** *Mugeroun* He (o). *cutting the*
cutting of the (o)

38–39 *And . . . done* one line in
octavo

43, **SD** *Exeunt* Goe out (o)

56 *are* (Eds.) as (o)

68 *lord* (Eds.) lords (o)

xiv.

9, **SD** *The Duchess* She (o)

14–16 *To . . . array* prose in octavo

20, **SD** *seizes the paper* takes it (o)

26 *need* (Dyce) needs (o)

31 *Mort Dieu* Mor du (o)

xv.

39 *stead* steed (o)

xvi.

SD *Henry* of France (o)

1 *Henry* King (o) and throughout scene

10–14 *So . . . friend* (Eds.) prose in
octavo

18–19 *kings/ In Christendom* Kings in/
Christendom (o)

28 *mort de Dieu, il mourra* mor du
Il mora (o)

41–42 *But . . . him* prose in octavo

43–44 *I . . . friends* prose in octavo

xvii.

9 *noblemen* noble men (o)

xviii.

1–33 follow the Collier Ms. leaf. The
octavo reads as follows:

Enter a Souldier.

Soul. Sir, to you sir, that dares make
the Duke a cuckolde,

And vse a counterfeite key to his

priuie Chamber doore: And although you take out nothing but your
owne, yet you put in that which dis-
pleaseth him, and so forestall his market,
and set vp your standing where you
should not: and whereas hee is your
Landlord, you will take vpon you to be
his, and tyll the ground that he himself
should occupy, which is his own free
land. If it be not too free there's the
question: and though I come not to
take possession (as I would I might) yet
I meane to keepe you out, which I will
if this geare holde: what are ye come
so soone? haue at ye sir.

Enter Mugeroun.

He shootes at him and killes him.

Enter the Guise.

Guise. Holde thee tall Souldier, take
thee this and flye.   *Exit* Soul.

Lye there the Kings delight, and *Guises*
scorne.

Reuenge it *Henry* as thou list or dare,
I did it only in despite of thee.

Take him away.

14, SD Enter minion. He kills him
(Collier Leaf)

15 *Mugeroun* Minion (Collier Leaf)

31, SD *King* the King (o)

32 *Henry* King (o) and throughout
scene

32–35 *My . . . good* (Eds.) prose in
octavo

61 *factious* (Eds.) sexious (o)

85–86 *Did . . . command* one line in
octavo

92, SD *an Attendant* one (o)

97–98 *My . . . person* one line in
octavo

100 *quit* quite (o)

103, SD *Attendant* one (o)

xix.

SD *a letter* of a letter (o)

31, SD *Exit* Exeunt (o)

xx.

SD *Murderers* Murthers (o)

1 *Cossin* Captaine (o) and throughout
scene

7 *murder* murther (o)

16, SD *King* the King (o)

17 *Henry* King (o) and throughout
scene. *murderers* murtherers (o)

26 *Holà, varlet, hé!* (Eds.) Halla verlete
hey (o)

47–48 *So . . . Guise* one line in octavo

52 *o'er* (Eds.) over (o)

53 *o'er* (Eds.) over (o)

57–58 *Hold . . . hope* (Dyce) one line
in octavo

58, SD *Third Murderer* (Dyce) one of
the Murtherers (o)

60 *Third Murderer* Mur. (o) and
throughout scene

67–70 Yet . . . fear (Eds.) prose in
octavo

88–90 *What . . . comes* prose in octavo

119 *Guise's Son* Yong Guise (o) and
throughout scene

120–121 *Sirrah . . . traitor* prose in
octavo

123, SD *offers* offereth (o)

124–125 *Away . . . him* (Eds.) prose in octavo
125, SD *Guise's Son* Boy (o)
134–135 *My . . . news* (Eds.) prose in octavo
139 *Catherine* Queene (o) and throughout scene
152, SD *King* the King (o)

xxi.

13–15 *So . . . away* (Dyce) prose in octavo

xxii.

SD *a letter* of a letter (o)
1 *murdered* murthered (o)
14 *And all* (Eds.) His life, and all (o)

xxiii.

1 *Henry* King (o) and throughout scene

13 *Lutetia* (Dyce) Lucrecia (o)
29 *sends* (Dyce) send (o)
32 *Jacobe* (Dyce) Jacobus (o)
32 SD *reads* readeth (o). *gets* getteth (o)
45–47 *Sweet . . . sovereign* (Eds.) prose in octavo
53, SD *searches* searcheth (o)
57–58 *goes/ To wrack, and* (Dyce) goes to wrack./ And (o)
61 *enforce* (Dyce) incense (o)
69 *comfort* (Dyce) comforts (o)
72–73 *Alas . . . knife* prose in octavo
75–76 *O . . . again* (Dyce) one line in octavo
87–88 *die . . . Fight* (Eds.) dye./ My Lords, fight (o)

EDWARD THE SECOND

Our earliest extant text of *Edward II* is an octavo printed for William Jones in 1594, two copies of which today survive, the one in the Landesbibliothek in Cassel, Germany, and the other in the Zentralbibliothek in Zurich, Switzerland. Another printing, in quarto, was issued by Jones in 1598, and additional quartos followed by Roger Banes in 1612 and Henry Bell in 1622. Each of these editions was printed from the one previous to it.

There was in the possession of Alexander Dyce, and now in the Dyce Collection at South Kensington, an imperfect copy of the 1598 quarto, in which the title page and first seventy lines of the play have been supplied in a seventeenth-century handwriting, the manuscript title page bearing the date of 1593. That this could have been a mistake for 1598 is very unlikely because the manuscript lines bear a much closer resemblance to the 1594 text than they do to the 1598, and yet they diverge from the 1594 sufficiently to make it likely that they were, in fact, transcribed from a 1593 printing, no copy of which today is extant. The present text is based upon the Zurich copy of the 1594 octavo which has been departed from only in the following instances:

I,i.

22 *fawn* (Eds.) fanne (1594)
37 *Third Poor Man* Sold. (1594)
47 *Poor Men* Omnes (1594)
49 *Poor Men* Omnes (1594)

73, SD *and others* &c (1594). *King* the King (1594)
107 *Kent* Edm. (1594)
133, SD Exeunt Nobiles (1594)

142 *Why . . . am* Why . . . kneele,/
Knowest . . . am (1594)
176 *Coventry* Bish. (1594) and throughout scene

I,ii.

35 *Canterbury* Bish. (1594) and
throughout scene
45, SD *Queen* the Queene (1594)
77 *Canterbury* omitted in 1594

I,iv.

SD Enter Nobiles (1594)
3 *Canterbury* Bish. (1594) and throughout scene
7, SD *King* the King (1594)
93, SD Exeunt Nobiles (1594)
115 *ne'er* (Eds.) neare (1594)
143, SD *Enter* Enter Edmund and
(1594)
186, SD *Enter the Nobles to the*
Queene (1594)
267 *murderer* murtherer (1594)
346 *embroidery* imbrotherie (1594)
384, SD *all except the* Manent (1594)
392 *Hercules* (Eds.) Hector (1594)
415 *While others* whiles other (1594)

II,i.

1–2 *Spencer . . . dead* one line in
1594
56, SD *King's Niece* Ladie (1594) and
throughout scene

II,ii.

SD *Queen* the Queene (1594)
50–51 *My . . . friend* one line in
1594
69 *Kent* Edm. (1594) and throughout
scene
81–82 *Here . . . him* (Eds.) one line
in 1594. *Edward* omitted in 1594
99, SD *King* the King (1594)
110, SD *Messenger* Poast (1594)
197, SD Exeunt Nobiles (1594)
217–218 *Away . . . me* one line in
1594
222, SD *Queen* the Queene (1594). *two
Ladies* Ladies 3 (1594)
224 *'em* (Dyce) him (1594)
226 *Niece* La. (1594) and throughout
scene
246–247 *Ay . . . allied* one line in
1594
263, SD Exeunt omnes (1594)

II,iv.

SD *King* the king (1594)
11 *Niece* Lad. (1594)

15, SD *all but Queen* omnes, manent
(1594)
21, SD *Lancaster . . . Others* the Barons (1594)
69, SD *Exit* Exeunt (1594)

II,v.

7, SD Enter the Nobles (1594)
14–17 *Monster . . . death* Monster
. . . strumpet/ Traind . . . Warres,/ So
. . . knights,/ Looke . . . death (1594)
18 *King* (1598) Kind (1594)
20–22 *Go . . . cause* (Eds.) Go . . .
hence,/ For . . . off:/ Gaveston . . .
turne:/ It . . . cause (1594)
34–35 *His . . . Gaveston* one line in
1594
41 *Renownèd* Renowmed (1594)
49–50 *Shalt . . . him* Shalt . . .
graunt?/ Souldiers . . . him (1594)
69–70 *We . . . thief* (Eds.) We . . .
so,/ To . . . Theefe (1594)
72 *renown* renowm (1594)
98, SD Manent Penbrooke, Mat. Gauest.
& Penbrookes men, foure souldiers (1594)
104 *Arundel* Mat. (1594)
110, SD Exit cum seruis Pen. (1594)
111, SD Exeunt ambo. (1594)

III,i.

17, SD Manet Iames cum caeteris (1594)

III,ii.

10 *Spencer Junior* Spencer (1594) and
throughout scene.
31, SD *Spencer Senior* Hugh Spencer
an old man, father to the young Spencer
(1594)
32 *Spencer Senior* Spen. pa. (1594) and
throughout scene
58, SD *Queen* the Queene (1594)
88, SD *Arundel* Lord Matre (1594) and
throughout scene
125 *murder* murther (1594)
128 *He kneels* kneeles, and saith (1594)
148 *here's* (Eds.) heres is (1594)
179 *murdering* murthering (1594)

III,iii.

SD *King* the king (1594). *Senior . . .
Junior* the father . . . the sonne (1594)
10, SD *and others* cum caeteris (1594)
12–13 *And . . . company* one line in
1594
17 *Thou'd* Th'ad (1594). *them* (Brooke)
thee (1594)
41 *murder* murther (1594)
45 *Kent* Edm. (1594)
62–63 *I . . . Away* one line in 1594

70-71 *Do . . . gone* one line in 1594
77, SD *with all except* Manent (1594)
97, SD Exeunt omnes (1594)

IV,i.

SD *Kent* Edmund (1594) and throughout scene
10-11 *Thy . . . device* one line in
1594
11-12 *Holla . . . lord* one line in
1594
12-13 *Mortimer . . . happily* one line
in 1594

IV,ii.

SD *Queen* the Queene (1594)
20 *share of* (Brooke) shake off (1594)
34, SD *Kent* Edmund (1594) and
throughout scene

IV,iii.

SD *King* the king (1594). *Arundel*
Matr. (1594)
23, SD *Messenger* Post (1594) and in
line 25
28 *reads* reads the letter (1594). *premised* (1598) promised (1594)

IV,iv.

SD *Queen* the Queene (1594). *Kent*
Edmund (1594)
13-14 *Of . . . thou* one line in 1594

IV,v.

SD *King* the King (1594). *Junior* the
sonne (1594)
9 SD *Kent* Edmund (1594) and throughout scene
14 *Vile* vilde (1594)
27 SD *Queen* the Queene (1594)
36 *unfortunate* infortunate (1594)
54, SD *Senior* the father (1594)
71 *Unhappy* is Vnhappies (1594)
80 *Senior* pa. (1594)
88, SD Exeunt omnes (1594)

IV,vi.

26-27 *Your . . . abode* prose in 1594

V,i.

SD *King* the King. *the Bishop of Winchester* with a Bishop for the crowne
(1594)
13 *And highly* (Eds.) highly (1594)
38 *Winchester* Bish. (1594) and throughout scene
47 *vine* (Eds.) vines (1594)
55 *murdered* murthered (1594)
101 *murderer* murtherer (1594)

111, SD Enter Bartley (1594)
112 *Winchester* (Eds.) Bartley (1594)
113-114 *Call . . . lunatic* (Eds.) Call
. . . lorde,/ Away . . . me,/ Greefe . . .
lunatick (1594)
129 *Berkeley* Bartley (1594) and
throughout scene
155, SD Exeunt omnes (1594)

V,ii.

28 *Winchester* Bish. (1594)
30 *ere* (Charleton and Waller) or
(1594). *Berkeley* Bartley (1594) and
throughout scene
47 *Matrevis . . . presently* one line
in 1594
60 *Till* (Eds.) And (1594)
73, SD Manent Isabell and Mortimer
(1594)
81 *Kent* Edmun. (1594) and throughout scene
121, SD Exeunt omnes (1594)

V,iii.

SD *King* the king (1594)
29 *murder* murther (1594)
48, SD *Kent* Edmund (1594 and
throughout scene)
62, SD *King* the king (1594) Manent
Edmund and souldiers (1594)
67, SD Exeunt omnes (1594)

V,iv.

21-22 *Lightborn . . . wast* one line in
1594
45-46 *No . . . death* one line in 1594
54 *Aristarchus'* Aristorchus (1594)
59 *Puritan* (Eds.) paretaine (1594)
73 *Canterbury* Bish. (1594)
86 *Kent* Edm. (1594) and throughout
scene
106 *them* then (1594)
107, SD *Soldiers* They (1594)
109 *murdered* murthered (1594)
114, SD, Exeunt omnes (1594)

V,v.

37-38 *So . . . any* one line in 1594
44 *murder* murther (1594) and in lines
45, 86, 97
116, SD *Gurney* Then Gurney (1594)
118-119 *And . . . Away* one line in
1594
119, SD Exeunt omnes (1594)

V,vi.

1 *murderer* murtherer (1594)
14, SD *Queen* the Queene (1594)
23, SD *King* the king (1594)

24 *First Lord* Lords (1594)
38 *First Lord* Lords (1594)
46 *murder* murther (1594)
48 *murderer* murtherer (1594) and in
line 49

89 *Second Lord* Lords (1594) and in
line 91
93 *First Lord* Lords (1594)

DOCTOR FAUSTUS

Doctor Faustus was first printed for Thomas Bushell in 1604, in a black letter quarto of which one copy is today extant, in the Malone collection in the Bodleian. Sir Walter Greg has argued that this represents a memorial reconstruction of the original version of the play, shortened for performance in the provinces and subjected to a good deal of debasement and interpolation. This version was reprinted in 1609 and 1611. In 1616 appeared a new and enlarged edition of the play, printed for John Wright. This, Greg has held, was prepared from Marlowe's own drafts from which the theater prompt book had been transcribed. In the course of prompt book preparation the manuscript itself must have undergone a good deal of revision. It was, moreover, incomplete, perhaps damaged and illegible in parts. In preparing it for the press, an editor was obliged to reproduce many passages from the earlier text as reprinted in the 1611 quarto. He also made a number of cuts and alterations, some of them to remove what he regarded as profanity. This edition was reprinted with corrections, many of them having considerable authority, in 1619, and again in 1620, 1624, 1628, and 1631.

We thus have two widely divergent versions of the play, neither of which reproduces the text as Marlowe—and the collaborator with whom he must have worked—had left it. The present edition is based on the quarto of 1616, which, with Greg and F. S. Boas, I would regard as the more authoritative. Readings from the 1604 quarto have been adopted where this text was used as copy for the 1616 quarto and where there are obvious omissions and alterations in the 1616 quarto. Readings from the 1619 and later quartos have been adopted when they correct obvious misprints in the 1616 text. I have been guided in many of these matters by Sir Walter Greg's conjectural reconstruction of the play, published in 1950, and by his superb edition of the parallel texts, *Marlowe's Doctor Faustus 1604–1616*, of the same year. The 1616 quarto has been departed from in the following instances:

Prologue.

12 *Rhode* (Boas) Rhodes (1619)
16 *The . . . graced* (1604) omitted 1616
18 *whose . . . disputes* (1604) and sweetly can dispute (1616)

I,i.

12 *On cay mae on* (1604) Oeconomy (1616). *Galen* (1604) and Galen (1616)
13 *Seeing . . . medicus* (1604) omitted 1616
19 *Is . . . aphorisms* (1604) omitted 1616
22 *divers* (1619) thousand (1616)
44 *there's* (1604) there is (1616)
52 *signs* (Greg) scenes (1604) omitted 1616. *and* (1604) omitted 1616
55 *of* (1604) and (1616)
60 *Nor . . . clouds* (1604) omitted 1616
64 *try thy* (1604) tire my (1616)
70, SD *Enter . . . Angel* (1604) Enter the Angell and Spirit (1616)
76 *treasury* (1604) treasure (1616)
83 *India* (1619) Indian (1616)
91 *silk* (Dyce) skill (1616, 1604)
97 *Antwerp's* (1604) Anwerpe (1616)
104–106 *Yet . . . skill* (1604) omitted 1616
109–110 *Divinity . . . vile* (1604) omitted 1616
110 *vile* vilde (1604)
116 *Swarm* (1604) Sworn (1616)
119 *shadows* (1604) shadow (1616)
127 *Lapland* (1604) Lopland (1616)
130 *in* (1604) has (1616)
133 *stuffs* (1604) stuff'd (1616)
142 *renowned* renowm'd (1616)
152 *lusty* (1604) bushy (1616)
155 *Abanus'* (Greg) Albanus (1616)
167, SD Exeunt om. (1616)

I,iii.

SD *Enter . . . conjure* (1604) Faustus to them with this speech (1616)
12 *erring* (1604) euening (1616)
16 *Dei* (1604) dii (1616)
19 *Mephistophilis . . . moraris* (Boas) Mephistophilis, Dragon, quod tumeraris (1616)
22 *dicatus* (1619) dicatis (1604, 1616)
32–34 *Now . . . imagine* (1604) omitted 1616. *Now* (Bullen) No (1604)
34 *redis* (Boas) regis (1604)
44 *hither* (1619) now hither (1616)
45 *speeches* (1604) omitted 1616
46 *accidens* (1624) accident (1616)
53 *the Trinity* (1604) all godlinesse (1616)

55–56 *So . . . principle* one line in 1616
71 *fell* (1604) liue (1616)
77 *who* (1604) that (1616)
82 *strike* (1604) strikes (1616)
96 *aid* (1604) to aid (1616)
112 *desire* (1604) desir'd (1616)

I,iv.

2 *Robin* Clo. (1616) and throughout scene
3 *such pickedevants* (1604) beards (1616)
28 *again* (1619) omitted 1616

II,i.

2 *And canst* (1604) Canst (1616)
9 *Ay . . . again* (1604) omitted 1616
10 *To God* (1604) Why (1616)
10–11 *To . . . appetite* one line in 1616
15 *Bad Angel* Euill An (1616)
20 *men* (1604) them (1616)
31 *Mephistophilis* (1604) omitted 1616
38–39 *Stay . . . lord* (Boas) Stay . . . me,/ What . . . Lord (1616)
42 *others* (1604) other (1616)
52–54 *Lo . . . Lucifer's* (1604) prose in 1616. *I* (1604) Faustus hath (1616). *mine arm* (1604) his arme (1616). *my proper* (1604) his proper (1616). *my soul* (1604) his soule (1616)
66 *Ah* (1604) O (1616)
77 *God* (1604) heaven (1616)
92 *made* (1604) both (1616)
96–97 *at his command* (1604) by him commanded (1616)
102 *form or shape* (1604) shape and forme (1616)
106 *the . . . inviolate* (1604) these Articles aboue written being inviolate (1616)
108 *or goods* (1604) omitted 1616
113 *will I* (1604) I will (1616). *with* (1604) omitted 1616
138–141 *But . . . wife* prose in 1616 and 1604
138 *off* (1604) omitted 1616
142–143 *Mephistophilis . . . one* (1604) omitted 1616
145 *Sit . . . come* (1604) omitted 1616
145, SD *Enter . . . fireworks* (1604) He fetches in a woman deuill (1616)
147 *how dost thou like thy* (1604) wilt thou have a (1616)
157 *Hold* (1604) Here (1616). *thoroughly* (1604) well (1616)

II,ii.

6 *'tis* (1604) it is (1616)

7 *breathes* (1619) breathe (1616)

17 *Bad Angel* Evil Angil (1616). SD *Exeunt* Exit (1616)

20–21 *But . . . knives* (1604) omitted 1616. *thunder* (Greg) thunders (1604)

22 *Poison, guns* (1604) Swords, poyson (1616)

44 *erring* (1604) euening (1616)

44–45 *But . . . tempore* one line in 1616

55–56 *suppositions* (1604) questions (1616)

77–78 *'Tis . . . late* one line in 1616

88–89 *I . . . hell* one line in 1616

96 *I* (1604) Faustus (1616). *in* (1604) for (1616)

98–100 *Never . . . down* (1604) omitted 1616

116 *lips* (1604) omitted 1616

136 *this* (1604) these (1616)

146 *jolly* (1604) ancient (1616)

146–147 *and . . . city* (1604) omitted 1616

147 *Mistress* (1604) omitted 1616

153–156 *where . . . Lechery* (1604) omitted 1616

173, SD Exeunt omnes (1616)

II,iii.

1 *Robin* omitted 1616

III, Prologue.

1–2 *Learnèd . . . astronomy* one line in 1616

8 *tropics* (Greg) Tropick (1616)

III,i.

7 *Rhine* (1604) Rhines (1616)

12 *Quarters . . . equivalents* (1604) omitted 1616 *equivalents* equiuolence (1604)

16 *rest* (1604) East (1616)

17 *midst* (1604) one (1616)

37 *four* (1604) two (1616)

43 *match* (1604) watch (1616)

55 *in state and* (1619) this day with (1616)

77 *cunning* (1624) comming (1616) and in line 81

125, SD *Exeunt* Exit (1616)

155 *keys* (Boas) seales (1616)

III,ii.

58 *Archbishop* Bish. (1616) and in line 81

61 *Friar . . . holiness* (1604) omitted 1616

62 *Pope* (1604) omitted 1616

71–72 *That . . . wine* one line in 1616

74 *Raymond* (1619) Kaymond (1616)

86 *Once . . . to* (1604) omitted 1616

86, SD *The . . . himself* (1604) omitted 1616

87–88 *How . . . cross* one line in 1616

101 *blow on the* (1604) blow the (1616)

108 *Et . . . Amen* (1604) omitted 1616

III,iii.

29–31 *Monarch . . . lie* (1604) you Princely Legions of infernall rule (1616)

IV, Prologue.

1–17 *When . . . performed* (1604) omitted 1616

IV,ii.

25 *like a* (1619) a (1616)

IV,iii.

27 *heart's* (1619) heart (1616)

70 *Ay, all* (Dyce) I call (1616)

105, SD Exeunt omnes (1616)

IV,iv.

14 *Zounds* (1619) Zons (1616)

25 *these* (1619) this (1616)

IV,v.

SD Enter Faustus, and the Horse-Courser, and Mephistophilis (1616)

1–11 *Now . . . doctor* (1604) omitted 1616

1–2 *Now . . . foot* Now . . . time/ doth . . . foot (1604)

5–6 *Therefore . . . Wittenberg* one line in 1604

54 *Anholt* (Boas) Vanholt (1616) and in line 57

IV,vi.

3 *guests* (1619) Guesse (1616)

4 *Robin* Clow. (1616) and throughout scene

37 *rare quality* (1619) quality (1616)

51, SD Exeunt omnes (1616)

IV,vii.

SD *Anholt* (Boas) Vanholt (1616) and throughout scene

12 *Duchess* Lady (1616) and throughout scene

49, SD *Robin* Clowne (1616) and throughout scene

107 *guests* (1619) guesse (1616)

V,i.

1–9 *I . . . done* prose in 1616

17–18 *Gentlemen . . . unfeigned* one line in 1616

19 *And Faustus'* (1604) It is not Faustus (1616)

20 *requests* (1604) request (1616)

25, SD *sounds* (1604) sound (1616)

28 *Too . . . praise* speech given to Third Scholar in 1616

28 *praise* (1604) worth (1616)

30–32 *Third Scholar . . . compare* (1604) omitted in 1616

33 *Since* (1604) Now (1616). *works* (1604) worke (1616)

34 *And . . . excellence* (1604) omitted 1616

56 *Damned . . . die* (1604) omitted 1616

61 *hovers* (1604) hover (1616)

65 *Ah, my sweet* (1604) O (1616)

65–66 *Ah . . . soul* one line in 1616

70 *where . . . now* (1604) wretch, what hast thou done? (1616)

82 *Mephistophilis* (1604) omitted in 1616

84 *Faustus* (1604) omitted in 1616

94 *embracings* (1604) embraces (1616)

96 *mine oath* (1604) my vow (1616)

117 *azured* (1604) azure (1616)

119–127 *Old Man . . . God* (1604) omitted 1616

V,ii.

26 *Ah* (1604) O (1616)

28–30 *Ah . . . not* (1604) verse in 1616

42 *Ah* (1604) O (1616). *hear me* (1604) hear (1616)

44 *pants and quivers* (1604) pant & quiuer (1616)

50 *ah* (1604) O (1616)

54 *Ah* (1604) O (1616)

59 *Ah* (1604) O (1616)

61 *God* O God (1616)

76 *there pray* (1604) pray (1616)

96 *Ah* (Greg) O (1616)

108 *sat* set (1616)

116 *boil* (1620) broyle (1616)

130 *Ah* (1604) O (1616)

136–137 *be but/ A year* (Boas) be but a yeare/ A month (1604, 1616)

142 *my God* (1604) heauen (1616)

143 *See . . . firmament* (1604) omitted 1616

144 *would . . . Ah* (1604) of blood will save me; o (1616)

147–148 *'Tis . . . brows* (Dyce) tis gone:/ And see . . . arm,/ And . . . brows (1604). gone./ And see a threatning Arme, an angry Brow. (1616)

150 *God* (1604) heauen (1616)

151 *No, no!* (1604) No? (1616)

151–152 *No . . . earth* one line in 1604 and 1616

153 *Earth, gape* (1604) Gape earth (1616)

160 *So that* (1604) But let (1616). *may but* (1604) mount, and (1616)

161 *Ah* (1604) O (1616)

162–163 *O . . . soul* one line in 1604 O, if my soule must suffer for my sinne (1616)

164 *Yet . . . me* (1604) omitted 1616

168 *O, no* (1604) No (1616)

171 *Ah* (1604) Oh (1616)

173–174 *Into . . . die* (Eds.) Into . . . beast./ All die (1616)

180 *O, it* (1604) It (1616)

182 *to* (Greg) into (1604, 1616). *little* (1604) small (1616)

184 *My God, my God* (1604) O mercy heauen (1616)

187 *Ah* (1604) oh (1616)